Delving into the Issues of the Chinese Economy and the World by Marxist Economists

Editor-in-Chief
Cheng Enfu

translated by Zhu Jianting & Hu Yang

CANUT INTERNATIONAL PUBLISHERS

Istanbul - Berlin - London - Santiago

Academic Research on Contemporary China Book Series

Delving into the Issues of the Chinese Economy and
the World by Marxist Economists

Edited by Cheng Enfu (editor-in-chief)

Translated by Zhu Jianting, Hu Yang

The English version is published with financial support of the Innovation
Program of the Chinese Academy of Social Sciences

Original Title: 马克思主义经济学研究 (Makesi zhuyi jingjixue yanjiu)

Copyright © China Social Sciences Press, Beijing, 2016

Canut International Publishers

Canut Intl. Turkey, Teraziler Cad. No.29. Sancaktepe, Istanbul, Turkey

Canut Intl. Germany, Heerstr. 266, D-47053, Duisburg, Germany

Canut Intl. United Kingdom, 12a Guernsay Road, London E11 4BJ, England

Copyright © Canut International Publishers, 2020

Our website: www.canutbooks.com

ISBN: 978-605-9914-60-4

About the Editor

Cheng Enfu, former academic director of the Academy of Marxism attached to the Chinese Academy of Social Sciences (CASS) and chief editor of 2 international peer-reviewed journals, *World Review of Political Economy* (English) and *International Critical Thought* (English); He is one of the main founders of the Shanghai School of Economics. His works have won many national and Shanghai level academic awards. His many academic articles were published in national and international journals. His representative books include:

On Three Stages of Socialism (2001); Modern Political Economics (2003); Chinese and Russian Economists' Viewpoints on Chinese and Russian Economic Reform (2005); Exploration on Economic Theory in Contemporary China, Methodology of Economics (2013); Case Study for Modern Political Economics (2015), The Creation of Value by Living Labor. A Normative and Empirical Study (Canut Intl., 2019).

Publisher's Note

This book includes, 30 carefully selected articles, recently written by the renowned scholars, arranged and edited by Prof. Cheng Enfu. The book includes 4 parts as: basic principles of Marxist economics; contemporary socialist economy in China, contemporary capitalist economy and comparative studies on Marxist economics and Western economics, and the book includes a report article about the annual WAPE forum debates which gathered in Hanoi, Vietnam in 2014 May. Direction of the new round of reforms in China has been a hot debate in recently, which holds an important part of this book. Besides, the recent economic and financial crisis is an important research subject of the book, many articles have debated the short and long-term significance of the crisis, to understand and forecast the future trends of capitalism.

The 84,000 characters decision issued by the Third Plenary Session of the 18th CC of the CPC in November 2013, has given a new design to the new round of deepening reforms in China which has emphasized the reform direction as adhering to the basic economic system. The decision further defined the operation sphere of the market and government's role in regard to economy, as: "underlying issue is how to strike a balance between the role of the government and that of the market, and let the market play decisive role in allocating resources and let government play its functions better. It is a general rule of the market economy that the market decides the allocation of resources. We have to follow this rule when we improve the socialist market economy."

The authors have also critically discussed the current, fiscal and monetary policies of the government, debt-financing of local governments and the issues in regard to promoting technological innovation in the industrial sectors. One innovative aspect of the book includes recent research achievements on the basic principles of Marxist economics. The book with high academic value not only comprehensively reflects the debate in the Chinese academy but also provokes new debates in regard to Marxist economics, its relations with Western economics and displays the current academic levels in the main disciplines of economics in China. We hope the book can further promote the academic dialogue and exchange among the scholars of economics across the world.

Lastly, we present our cordial thanks to the leaders and editors of the China Social Science Press, also Xia Xia and Liu Kailin who have greatly contributed to the realization of the English version of the book.

Daivja Jindal,
February, 2018
London, UK

Editorial Board

Preface

Three generations of the collective leadership of the Communist Party of China (CPC), with Mao Zedong, Deng Xiaoping and Jiang Zemin, respectively holding the core position and the Central Committee of CPC, with Hu Jintao as the General Secretary, have constantly emphasized the vital importance of the theoretical work and study and researches of the Marxist theory. Since the 18th National Congress of CPC, the Central Committee of CPC, with Xi Jinping as the General Secretary, has regarded ideological work as an extremely significant task.

In January 2014, the document "Opinions of the Central Committee of the CPC for Further Prospering and Developing Philosophical Social Science" was issued, which underlined the task of implementing theoretical research and construction of Marxism. To carry out the demands of the Central Committee of CPC, to further develop the Chinese Academy of Social Sciences as the solid fortress of Marxism, think tank of CPC and the state and supreme palace of philosophy social science, Chinese Academy of Social Sciences has taken a series of important measures. In 2009, Chinese Academy of Social Sciences has issued the policy of strengthening Marxist theoretical subject construction and theoretical research as an important work and set up a leading group with the task of Marxist theoretical subject construction and Marxist theoretical research. After its establishment, the leading group has greatly increased the efforts for the construction of Marxist theoretical subject and built up a laboratory and center for Marxist theoretical studies, and simultaneously placed a greater emphasis on the research of basic theory of Marxism.

Since 2011, in order to push forward the research on basic theory of Marxism, Chinese Academy of Social Sciences has initiated to edit and publish Special Research Series on Marxism, which contains yearly collection of nationwide representative research articles so as to present excellent research findings in the relevant sphere.

Leading group of Marxist Theoretical Disciplines Construction and Theoretical Research, CASS

January, 2015

Contents

PART ONE: BASIC PRINCIPLES OF MARXIST ECONOMICS

PART TWO: CONTEMPORARY SOCIALIST ECONOMY IN CHINA

PART FOUR: COMPARATIVE STUDIES ON MARXIST ECONOMICS AND WESTERN ECONOMICS

Appendix

Part One

Basic Principles of Marxist Economics

On the Role of Government and Market in the Resource Allocation

Liu Guoguang

Abstract: Economic development creates material basis for ideological work. Ideological work can be supported solidly by the material basis, only if the economic development, our central work, is well done. The reverse is also correct. Ideological work can ensure the economic development and ensure constant, rapid and a healthy economic development. The idea of "right in economics and left in politics" should be analyzed in a dialectical manner and ambiguous understanding and careless interpretations of it should be avoided. The reform direction of socialist market economy essentially embodies the integration of economics and politics. Our reform aims to build up the socialist market economy, rather than a pure market economy. Market playing a critical role in resource allocation, does not mean the government will not adjust, control and plan in a macroscopic way, instead it implies that the key role of market in resource allocation in a microscopic way should be fully promoted. This is the general rule of market economy. To build up the socialist market economic system, the market value principle should be respected without abandoning the law of planned and proportional development under public economy.

Key words: economic development; ideology; socialist market economy; resource allocation

I will take the opportunity today to talk about my opinions on the roles of government and market in resource allocation. Any criticism and corrections are welcome.

I

The dialectical relation between economic construction and ideological work. On August 19, 2013, at the "National Ideological Work Conference", Xi Jinping pointed out: economic construction is the central work of the Party and the ideological work is our extremely important work."[1] This statement explains expressively the dialectical relation between the economic construction and the ideological work. Briefly speaking, economic construction creates the material basis for ideological work. Ideological work can be supported solidly by the material basis only if, the economic construction, our central work, is well done. It is the same the other way round. Ideological work can guarantee economic development and ensure constant, rapid and a healthy development of economic development.

According to the basic principle of historical materialism, the economic foundation determines superstructure. Superstructure refers to the social consciousness and superstructure also includes relevant political and legal systems based on certain social economy. In turn, superstructure also counteracts to effect the economic foundation. Of course, the ideological superstructure counteracts, to effect the economic foundation.

In the class society, including the primary stage of socialism, ideology has distinctive class nature. Capitalist economic foundation determines the ideology of capitalism and socialist economic foundation determines the ideology of socialism. The ideology representing the interests of the advanced class promotes the development of social economy and the ideology representing the interests of the reactionary class hinders the economic development of the society. Mao Zedong pointed out: "Whenever you want to overthrow a regime, you must first create public opinion, you must first do ideological work. This is the case with the revolutionary class, it is also the case with the counterrevolutionary class."[2] Gong Zizhen said: to overthrow a state, you should first abandon its history."[3] The collapse of the former Soviet Union has been a typical example. Nowadays, there are some remarks defaming revolutionary leaders, denying the 30 years of history before Reform and Opening-up and discrediting public ownership economy and state-owned property, which intends to overthrow the leadership of the Communist Party and dismantle the socialist economic system. Thus, we should increase our vigilance and be fully conscious of the importance, long term, complexity of ideological work and consolidate the leading position of Marxism in the ideological sphere.

---

1   Xi Jinping, Grasp the General Trend, Focus on Major Events and Strive to Improve Promotion and Ideological Work, *People's Daily*, August 21, 2013.
2   Mao Zedong, *Manuscript Since Founding of China* (Volume 10), Central Party Literature Press, 1996, p. 194.
3   *Collected Works of Gong Zizhen*, Shanghai People's Publishing House, 1975, p. 23.

Economic development and ideological work are not parallel, but certain ideological work and economic work are closely interwoven. Ideology penetrates the economic work and the economic work itself is imbued with ideological elements, for example, the guiding ideology of economic development belongs to the sphere of ideology.

At present, among the incorrect thoughts prevailing in the ideological sphere, Western constitutional democracy, universal values, historical nihilism and civil society belongs to political, cultural and social sectors, respectively, are not directly related with the economic sector. While the neo-liberalism thought trends belongs to the economic sphere and possesses an important position among various other thoughts. The core idea of neo-liberal economic theory, such as the hypothesis of "economic man", i.e. the theory of human nature which constantly pursuing private interests, pursues exclusivity of private ownership, also the market fundamentalism doctrine and minimum government intervention (night watchman), is broadly spread in the economic circles of our nation, and imposes huge influence on economic reform and economic development. It can be said that at present, in China, there exits the struggle between socialism with Chinese characteristics and neo-liberal thought trend, which is an ideological struggle in the economic sphere. The struggle is directly related to the success and failure of economic development, the future and destiny of socialism with Chinese characteristics and the direction of reform, i.e. between the path of market economy with full freedom or path of socialist market economy with Chinese characteristics.

In this respect, the Third Plenary Session of the 18th Central Committee of the CPC expressively stated: "Follow the path of socialism with Chinese characteristics unswervingly, neither take the rigid and closed old path nor taken the evil path of changing the flag."[4]

II

Both home and abroad, China's political and economic situation is described as "right in economics and left in politics", which means Chinese economy tends to be more and more freer and loosens control on several sectors by applying marketization, and meanwhile the politics tends to be more authoritative, holds high the banner of Marxism-Leninism and Mao Zedong Thought and tightens the control over the ideological sphere. It seems, in China, the economic sector tends to be "right" and political and ideological sectors tend to be "left". Both the right camp and left camp in the academy have different opinions and different perspectives, but if I speak simply, apart from their different opinions and different perspectives, such understanding of the question is theoretically, embodies a deep contradiction.

---

4 Hu Jintao, Unswervingly Advance along the Path of Socialism with Chinese Characteristics and Fight for Building a Moderately Prosperous Society in All Respects, *People's Daily*, November 18, 2012.

According to the basic theory of historical materialism, politics, ideology and superstructure is determined by the economic base. If the superstructure is in the same direction with economic base, the economic base can be consolidated; if the superstructure deviates from the economic base, then it will cause variations in the economic base, and the original superstructure may face the risk of collapse.

According to an analysis, the risks of "right in economics and left in politics" may cause division in society, and such a situation may not last long. If socialist economy was eroded by western neo-liberalism economic thought for a longer time, and follows increasing inclination of liberalization and privatization and decreasing inclination of planned economy and public economy, the economic base of socialism would finally erode and turn to something incompatible with socialist ideology and superstructure.

While with the development of private economy and enhancement of the power of capital, the influence of the liberal trend of thought may expanded as well, and its proponents will increase the demands of power separation even demand control of power. At that time, any endeavor to uphold the scientific socialism thought trend would be in vain. It is determined by the fact that the economic base determines superstructure and this is independent of man's will. We must be clearly be conscious of it and carelessness should be avoided.

Since the Reform and Opening-up, we have gradually built up a socialist market economy system. According to the decision at the Third Plenary Session of the 18th Central Committee of the Communist Party of China, in politics, we must "hold high the great banner of socialism with Chinese characteristics and follow the guidance of Marxism-Leninism, Mao Zedong Thought, Deng Xiaoping Theory, the important thought of the Three Represents and the Scientific Outlook on Development",[5] while in economy, we should "uphold the direction of reform towards the deepening of the socialist market economy".[6] That is to say, we should not only hold high Marxism-Leninism, Mao Zedong Thought, Deng Xiaoping Theory, the important thought of the Three Represents and the Scientific Outlook in politics but also follow "market economy" and "socialism" in the economic construction. Once the politics and economy is put in the right position, both will be distinguished from the so-called "right in economics and left in politics".

---

5   Resolution of the Central Committee of the Communist Party of China on Some Major Issues Concerning Comprehensively Deepening the Reform, *People's Daily*, November 16, 2013.
6   Ibid.

III

Here I would like to talk about the issue of "upholding the direction of reform towards the socialist market economy". The reform direction of socialist market economy is in itself includes the unity of economy and politics. The goal of our reform is to build up "socialist market economy". It is not simply market economy, but "socialism + or × market economy". "Socialist market economy" is a complete concept, it embodies an organic unity which cannot be separated. When the report of the 14th National Congress of CPC first proposed the reform goal of socialist market economy, it clearly added the adjective "socialist" before the term "market economy". In addition, there is a precondition: let market play an important role in resource allocation "under government's macroeconomic regulation". Resource allocation is divided into different levels such as macroeconomic level and microeconomic level and different sectors. At the microeconomic level of resource allocation, i.e. allocation of various resources in each market entity. Law of value can boost efficiency via change of supply and demand and competition system and play an extremely important role, or even a "corrective" role. On the other hand, at the macroeconomic level of resource allocation, the resource allocation at some aspects, such as comprehensive balance of overall supply and overall demand, proportional development of industrial sectors, natural resources and environmental protection, equal allocation of social resources, as well as the social security and welfare (housing, education and health care), may not be entirely allowed to depend on market regulation, let alone "decided" by it. Market mechanism may cause some defects and insufficiency at these macroeconomic sectors, which should be intervened by the government, regulated by the government and may need correction by plans, the government may need to restrain and supplement market actions and try to make up the defects of "invisible hand" by "visible hand".

In the past, when Deng Xiaoping suggested that socialism can also adopt market economy, he did not deny the plan economy and emphasized that plan economy and market economy can both be employed. When the report of the 14th National Congress of CPC mentioned that "market will play a basic role in resource allocation under government's macro-economic regulation", it expressly pointed out that "the national plan is an important means of macro-economic regulation". Before the 14th National Congress of CPC, General Secretary Jiang Zemin reminded us, when he stated to choose the reform goal of socialist market economy at advanced class of ministerial leaders in the Party School of the Central Committee of the CPC: "Commodity economy with plan is just the same as the market economy with plan. Socialist economy has been planned since its beginning, which is clear to everyone, and may not cause questions over cancellation of the nature of plan due to absence of 'plan' as wording in the discourse."[7] The above sentence expresses that socialist market economy is in essence a planned market economy and affirms the adoption of both plan and market means of resource allocation. But later, due to the

---

7 *Selected Works of Jiang Zemin*, Volume 1, People's Publishing House, 2006, p. 202.

influence of neo-liberalism economic thought trend, the tendency of highlighting market and weakening plan came into being. Some have voiced that we are dealing with market reform, thus the "plan" could be set aside. "The 11th five-year plan" was changed to "the 11th five-year projection", this mere difference in wording has aroused quite a fuss. Some one maintained that the planned economy faded away and the market economy is "in", thus "plan" became seemingly a restricted zone. However, the report of the 17th National Congress of CPC has mentioned that "play the guiding role of "national development project, plan and industrial policies in our macro-economic regulation". In *Decision of the Central Committee of the Communist Party of China on Some Major Issues Concerning Comprehensively Deepening the Reform* (hereinafter referred to as *Decision*) adopted by the Third Plenary Session of the 18th Central Committee of the CPC, said "better play the government's role" this wording follows closely "let market play its key role in resource allocation". Though there is no reference to "guidance of national plans", but the *Decision* maintains "improve the macro-economic regulation system guided by national development strategy and plan, with financial policy and currency policy as the major means". *Decision* also implies the meaning of "planned guidance", but avoids the word "plan". It is worth considering. The author holds that this will not make any difference as long as the "macro-economic regulation system" is "guided by the national development strategy and plan" as mentioned in *Decision*.

6

It's worth notice that General Secretary Xi Jinping pointed out in *Decision* that the "market will play a key role but not play entire role in resource allocation."[8] It is obvious that the "key role" of market is restrained. Thus, when *Decision* states the key role of market, it also lays emphasis on the role of government and the national plan. That is to say, government and national plan should both play a guiding role in resource allocation. In this way, "the dual regulatory roles" of market and government and the roles of market and plan stood out. The term, "dual regulatory roles" concerning market and government relations in *Decision* was proposed by economist Cheng Enfu[9] which makes much sense.

Next, in the regulation of resource allocation, what's the distinction between the market and government or plan? In the author's opinion, generally speaking, the function of market and government or plan can be distinguished according to two levels, i.e. microeconomic level and macroeconomic level of resource allocation. Market's key role in resource allocation will be restrained in the microeconomic level. And the government's role, such as reducing the number of administrative approvals for businesses, mainly involves the microeconomic level. As to the resource allocation in macro level, government should strengthen planned regulation and management, naturally which cannot

8   Resolution of the Central Committee of the Communist Party of China on Some Major Issues Concerning Comprehensively Deepening the Reform, *People's Daily*, November 16, 2013.
9   Cheng Enfu, *Ten Strategic Economic Thoughts of Xi Jinping*, People Forum, 2013(12).

be regulated by the market, the "invisible hand". Of course, it is still the government's responsibility to provide the needed services for the market, carry out regulation, and serve as the "night watchman".

IV

Such understanding on the relations between the "government" and the "market" or "plan" and "market" in socialist market economy complies with economic principles of Marxism and will benefit the reform direction of both the "market economy" and "socialism".

Decision adopted by the Third Plenary Session of the 18th Central Committee of the CPC pointed out: "It is the general principle of the market economy that market determines resource allocation", which is also the market value principle. But what socialist economy demands in regard to resource allocation is not the "market value" principle but the principle of "planned and proportional development." According to Marxism, in the social production of the "collective type", national economy should perform a planned development with certain proportionality criterion. Marx ever said: "The economizing of time, like the planned allocation of labor-time to various branches of production, remains the prime economic law, even on the basis of collective production. It still holds as a law even at a much higher stage."[10]

It implies that the allocation of labor time, proportionally in each production department and economizing of labor time in utility is the first economic principle of an advanced intensive economy. "Labor time" also includes both the live labor time and the materialized dead labor time, which means that human resources and material resources. It means allocating and saving resources with plan and with certain proportionality, which is the primary economic principle of collective social production. Observing, planned and proportional development is the steady, stable and coordinated development arranged by people orderly, which is not the same with the traditional administrative and command type of planned economy, let alone "semi-command economy" labeled scornfully by some liberal people. Here, "plan" mainly means a guiding type, strategic, and predictive plan, used to guide national level resource allocation and national economic development at macro level. Of course, it includes certain necessary directive indexes and contains certain accountability checks. During the reform period, we have gradually eliminated the disadvantages of the traditional planned economy and build up a socialist market economic system to adjust to national situation in primary stage of socialism by respecting the market value principle, but this doesn't mean that we should abandon the economic law of planned and proportional development under public economy.

7

---

10 *Collected Works of Marx and Engels*, Volume 8, People's Publishing House, 2009, p. 67.

In the primary stage of socialism, socialist economy includes market economy and becomes the market economy of socialism, but it is not the pure market economy or any market economy of another kind. Such socialist market economy should not be dominated by solely by the market value principle. It should be dominated by "the law of planned and proportional development" when market value principle comes into effect. Thus, if we specifically speak about the market economy, it is true to say that "It is a general rule of the market economy that the market decides the allocation of resources." , as mentioned in *Decision* adopted by the Third Plenary Session of the 18ᵗʰ Central Committee of the CPC. And the next sentence says: "We have to follow this rule when we improve the socialist market economy." Socialist market economy should not only comply with market value principle, which is not the sole principle of socialist market economy. Instead socialist market economy should also comply with the law of planned and proportional development. That is why, in socialist market economy, plan and market, government and market, automatic regulation and free regulation, "visible hand" and "invisible hand" should all pairs play important role in the resource allocation.

All in all, we must truly understand the relations between market and government, market and plan in socialist market economy through Marxist economic theories, and reject the liberal economic thoughts of Hayek and likewise. Only in this way, can we grasp the direction of Chinese reform and head for the future of China Dream.

Originally published in the journal
Contemporary Economic Research, 2014(3)

The Principles and Methods for an Accurate Reading of *Capital*

Wei Xinghua

Capital is a profound and famous work of Marxist theory, with both significant historical and practical meaning. When Xi Jinping investigated Renmin University of China in June 19, 2012, he firstly inspected the teaching and research center of *Capital* in the School of Economics. After the inspection, he gave an instructive speech. He stated, our Party is instructed by Marxism, thus, we should emphasize the study of basic Marxist theory. The Sinicization of Marxism has formed the Mao Zedong Thought and theoretical system of socialism with Chinese characteristics, the theoretical achievements of which are both obtained under the guidance of basic Marxist theory. *Capital* is one of the most famous classical Marxist works, which has gone through the tests of time and practice, shining with truth.

Capital is not a popular work, hence, its profound theoretical content can be grasped only by a careful reading. The beginner may find it difficult to read the original work, without any guidance. Thus, we have written *The Explanation of Specially Selected Parts of Capital* as a study guide book for the beginners, so as to explain the truth of this original work with an understandable language. Now, the author is to present some explanation to facilitate reading and understanding by readers.

I. Strive to explain accurately the content of *Capital* according to the original work

The author has found some flawed explanation of the original work during teaching and studies regarding *Capital*. For example:

(I) About employing "force of abstraction" when analyzing economic pattern

The preface of the second edition of Volume I of *Capital* states: "In the analysis of economic forms, moreover, neither microscopes nor chemical reagents are of use. The force of abstraction must replace both." The "force of abstraction" here is regarded as the same with "abstract method" and "scientific abstraction" in many works. For example, in early 1950s, as the general textbook of political economics in China, Object and Method of Political Economics, Volume I of the sixteen volumes states: "political economics is the same with all other social sciences, which can not employ experiment (under conditions created by man) as physics or chemistry, experiment should be replaced by abstraction method." As seen, the book separates abstract method with the experiment method of natural sciences. The same interpretation exists in some other Chinese works regarding *Capital*. It seems suggesting that the theories natural sciences can be proved by experiments without abstraction method and the abstraction method is only required in researches of economics and other social sciences. In fact, scientific abstraction method is needed in both natural sciences and economic researches. Abstraction method and scientific abstraction means proving the inherent laws through scientific analysis, inherent various phenomena. The experiments performed in natural science also need scientific abstraction. For example, heavy things always fall faster than light things. However, in vacuum, without air, wind and other resistance, the heavy things and light things may fall at the same speed thus such essence and the law can be abstracted. In economics, price is the phenomenon and value (labor) is the essence. Profit and interest is the phenomenon and surplus value is the essence. It does not result from the scientific abstraction in the laboratory, but from the scientific thought, i.e. "by the force of abstraction" used by Marx is also a scientific abstraction, but is different from the scientific abstraction used in natural science researches.

(II) About the peculiarities of the equivalent form

Three peculiarities of equivalent form was discussed in *Capital* when the issue of "value form or exchange value" was analyzed: firstly, "use value becomes the form of appearance of its opposite, of value"; secondly, "concrete labor becomes the form of appearance of its opposite, abstract human labor." thirdly, "real private labor takes the form of its opposite, i.e. labor in directly social form". Figuring out the peculiarities of equivalent is of great importance to understand the essence of currency. However, in some explanatory and reading guides, the essence is mistakenly explained. Some works just simply describe the three peculiarities above, without giving a scientific explanation; also some works tend to give out scientific explanation but deviate from the original meaning. For example, some works include such weird sentences as the following: in the value relation of 60 feet linen = 1 coat, coat is the equivalent form. Here the use value becomes the form of appearance of the value of linen. The specific labor that produces the coat becomes the appearance form of abstract labor that produces linen; the real private labor that produces coat becomes labor in directly social form that produces linen. In fact, here the attempted explanation of equivalent form does not give additional description of relation between equivalent form and relevant value form which was already clearly expressed by Marx, instead used to abstract the peculiarities of equivalent form from such relation. The purpose of explaining equivalent form is to express that in commodity exchange relation, the commodity, as an equivalent form, regards the use value as the appearance of value, i.e. the "image" of value or "value's mirror". Production is done with concrete labor, which "is only taken as the realization of labor", and becomes "the image of abstract human labor". The real private labor that produces the commodity "becomes the labor in directly social form", i.e. becomes the appearance or "image" of social labor. This is paving the way for explaining the essence and features of currency. In commodity exchange relation, metal currency is itself the appearance or image of value, and also the appearance or image of abstract labor and social labor.

(III) About understanding of "labor process in its (elementary) form"

In Chapter 7 of the Volume I of *Capital*, Marx discussed the labor process in its simple (elementary) form: "The elementary factors of the labour-process are 1) the personal activity of man, i.e. work itself, [as described above] 2) the subject of that work, and 3) its instruments." In relevant textbooks, the three elements are described as three elements of production, but they neglect the word "elementary (simple)". In some textbooks of political economics, "elementary" is recognized and has been included, but it deviates from the original meaning. The authors maintain that the so-called "elementary" is merely related to labor process but not to relation of production. In fact, Marx has also stated: "in the first place, have to consider the labour-process independently of the particular form it assumes under given social conditions." Therefore, it is the necessary "elementary factors" of the labor process without their relation with the relation of production. The so-called "elementary factors" refer to the factors with minimum limit necessary for any social production. This concept of Marx means that with the ever development of social production, the labor process may correspondingly need to have new elementary factors, such as management, divided coordination, science and so on. Marx has explained this and pointed out: "Merely speaking of the fact that labor process is the pure process between human and nature, the simple elements of labor process are common in all social development patterns. But each certain historical pattern will further develop the material basis and social pattern of the labor process."[1]

---

1 *Collected Works of Marx and Engels*, Vol. 7, People's Publishing House, 2009, p. 1000.

In fact, the development of "material basis" mentioned above is the development of the factors of labor process.

(IV) About the explanation on "Transition of the Laws of Property that Characterise Production of Commodities into Laws of Capitalist Appropriation"

In Chapter 24 of the Volume I of *Capital*, Marx discussed the this issue. Many works explain this as the transformation from simple commodity production to capitalist production, such as Remarks of *Capital* written by Lu Senbei ever popular in China. Such misunderstanding even exists in the *Anti-Dühring* written by Engels: "The commodity production will transform into capitalist production when it reaches certain development level." It has subsequently quoted *Capital*: "at this stage, the laws of appropriation or of private property, the laws which are based on the production and circulation of commodities, become by their own inner and inexorable dialectic changed into their very opposite." The explanation continues: "even if we assume that all private property was originally based on the owner's own labour, the progressive development of production and exchange nevertheless brings us of necessity to the present capitalist mode of production."[2] In fact, the transformation from simple commodity production to capitalist production was clearly expressed by Marx in his analysis on commodity and currency and in his debates statement on currency's transformation to capital. Here, we will discuss the essence of employee-employer relations in the process of capital accumulation and in the process capitalization of the surplus value. In the exchange relations between capital and wage worker, the respective ownership and equivalent exchange is recognized. But the production results are possessed by the capitalist. During capital accumulation, capitalists possess one part of surplus value of the laborer without pay as the additional capital to purchase additional labor power and then produce additional surplus value. Initially, equivalent exchange is conducted by respective ownership, but the corresponding production result is possessed by the capitalists. That is the essence of capital accumulation, which has no relation with the transformation of simple commodity production to capitalist commodity production and should be clarified.

(V) How does "the expansion of the difference between employed capital and the actually consumed capital" become the element of capital accumulation?

The question has been explained in various textbooks and study guides, but the explanations in some of them do not comply with the original meaning. Take the following statement as an example: consumed capital refers to the remaining value of fixed capital after deduction of the transferred value. For example, the fixed capital of capitalist is 10000 pounds, 8000 pounds of which is employed in the process of production and 2000 pounds of which has been left. The fixed capital works as before. The difference between 2 figures

2 *Collected Works of Marx and Engels*, Vol. 3, People's Publishing House, 1995, p. 506.

functions as "such natural power, which originally costs nothing, such natural power does not enter into the determination of price." In relevant textbooks of the Soviet Union, there is the same explanation. There is one specific chapter in Economic Doctrines of Marx, written by Kautsky, who was still Marxist at that time, describing the elements that influence capital accumulation level but he ignored describing the element of balanced expansion of employed capital and actually consumed capital. Obviously, Kautsky failed to figure out the original meaning. In fact, the consumed capital does not refer to the remaining value that has not yet been transferred into fixed capital, but refers to the value that has been transferred with consumption of fixed capital. The more the total fixed capital, the greater the value that has been transferred by consumption. Besides, the increase of balance between used capital and consumed capital does not only depend on the amount of fixed capital, but also depends on the turnover time of the fixed capital. The value transferred from fixed capital can serve as depreciation funds and can be used in accumulation. Marx had ever wrote to Engels about the issue, which can be seen from their communication. They had communicated for several times to discuss the issue.

(VI) About the use of "proportional" or "inversely proportional" in the general law of capitalist accumulation

Marx had ever pointed out in his discussion of capitalist accumulation: with the increase of capitalist accumulation, the reserve army of industrial workers will increase as well. "The greater this reserve army in proportion to the active labor-army, the greater is the mass of a consolidated surplus population, whose misery is in inverse ratio to the amount of torture it has to undergo in this form of labour. The more extensive, finally, the pauperized sections of the working class and the industrial reserve army, the greater is the official pauperism." The "inverse ratio" in this paragraph is "proportion" in French version. Therefore, in the Chinese version of *Capital*, a remark is added: "It is 'proportional' in the French version revised by Marx." Volume V of *Collected Works of Marx and Engels* published in 2009 also makes remark for "inverse ratio": "It is 'proportional' in the French version revised by Marx." Our *Dictionary of Political Economy* and some textbooks have also followed suit and added the remark of "inversely proportional" referring to the French version. The author holds that it is unreasonable to deal with this issue in this way as in the textbooks and study guides, which may cause confusion in the mind of students and other readers. In relevant textbooks and study guides of *Capital*, scientific judgment should be made to determine whether it is "proportional" or "inversely proportional." In *Political Economy* (*Capitalism Part*) (People's Publishing House, 1985 Edition) edited by Yu Guangyuan, Su Xing and Qiu Qihua, it is expressively changed to "proportional". The second edition of the Chinese version of *Capital* translated by Guo Dali and Wang Yanan and published in 1961 added the remark "inversely proportional" as follows: "In the recently published *Complete Works of Marx and Engels*, it has been changed to 'proportional' and remark has been added to express that the revision is made according to the French version revised by Marx." What we talk about here is the second edition of Russian version of *Complete Works of Marx and Engels*. Additionally, in the Soviet Union a commentary article was published on this issue titled as *A Few Amendments on Marx's Capital* (see Translated Works of Economics, Issue 4, 1963).

However, in the French version of *Capital* in 1980s, the "proportional" was changed to "inversely proportional" according to the German version. I hold that the "inverse ratio" in the German version is correct, while the "proportional" in French version is the mistake of the translator. Marx had not noticed such mistake when he revised the work. The foundation lies in the following: firstly, the first and second edition of Volume I of the German edition of *Capital* was edited by Marx himself and the following third and fourth editions of Volume I was revised and edited by Engels. It is "inverse ratio" in all editions, which is correct. The word "whose" in the above sentence "whose misery is in inverse ratio to the amount of torture it has to undergo in this form of labur." refer to the same laborers, which may refer to "active labor-army" and also to "industrial reserve army". As a part of active labor-army, they suffer and feel misery from laboring but are paid with salaries, which can reduce their poverty; as a part of "industrial reserve army" they have lost their job and got rid of the misery but now they are suffering from poverty. Therefore, the poverty is in "inversely proportional" to this form of labor. Secondly, Engels had found out a German version and French version in the remains of Marx. Some revision had been made in the German version and a remark was with reference to the French version. In the French version, the applicable revision had been labeled, and the revision belongs to the part of capitalist accumulation process. However, Marx had not requested a change to replace "inverse ratio" with "proportional" in the two remaining versions. Thirdly, if "inverse ratio" is corrected as "proportional", the word "whose" should also be changed accordingly, i.e. whose misery is in inverse ratio to the amount of torture, it has to undergo in this form of active labor-army. Because, if the amount of unemployed laborers become larger, the active laborers will feel more pressed and thus tolerate the sufferings in the process of laboring. Conversely, the larger the amount of active laborers, the greater their suffering, and the more difficult for unemployed laborers to hunt for jobs. Therefore, the two elements are proportional. The Russian version revised some content when it changed "inverse ratio" to "proportional" as follows: "their poverty is in inverse ratio to their suffering of laboring" to "their poverty is proportional to the suffering of active laborers". However, this change was made by the translator of Russian version, which does not exist in French version. Thus, it is correct to change "proportional" in the French version to "inverse ratio" according to the German version.

(VII) The issue about the wording that "commercial capital is the independent part separated from the industrial capital"

Within the economics books translated from the Soviet Union in the 1950s, there are many popular wordings such as "the commercial capital is the independent part separated from the industrial capital", the commercial capital "is separated from the industrial capital", and "is the transmuted form of industrial capital", and this has interpretation has influenced the relevant works in our country. Such wordings have been quite popular in the political economics textbooks and the relevant dictionaries of our country. For instance, Comrade Jiang Xuemo mentioned in the book "Political Economics": "commercial capital is nothing more than the commodity capital separated from the industrial capital." Some textbooks have also mentioned: the commercial capital of modern times is mainly separated from the industrial capital, and part of industrial capitalists separate themselves from the production field, and then specially engages in the sales of commodities, so part of industrial capitalists separate and then shift to commercial capital activity. In the capitalist society, part of industrial capitalists become independent and then differentiate and turn to the commercial capital, you cannot deny it, but this is not the common case. Moreover, you cannot say that the commercial capitalists are transformed from partial industrial capitalists through changing their professions to commodity sales management. The commercial capital is an independent department mainly and independently invested by the commercial capitalists. Actually, I think, the correct wording should be: the function of the commercial capital is the part separated from the commodity capital function of industrial capital. This is merely the independence of capital function, rather than the separation and independence of capital. Marx wrote: "take the total capital of society, one part of it—always exists in the form of commodities on the market, to be converted into money. Another part exists on the market in the form of money, to be converted into commodities. It is always in the process of this transition, of this formal metamorphosis. In as much as this function (process of circulation) acquires independent life as a special function of a special capital and is established by the division of labor as a function that falls to a particular group of capitalists, and then the commodity capital becomes the commodity-dealing (merchant capital) capital or commercial capital".

(VIII) The issue of the scientific analysis method employed by Marx

There is a statement by Marx about the analysis method in the first sentence of Part 1, Volume I of *Capital*: "scientific analysis of those forms, (Ed. of forms of social life) takes a course directly opposite to that of their (forms of social life) actual historical development. Man begins, (scientific analysis), post festum, (ed. namely) with the results of the process of development ready to hand before him." It is generally argued in the educational circles that, this is the very description of Marx about his scientific analysis method. M. Rosental, the famous scholar in the Soviet Union also explained this sentence in his book *The Issue of Dialectics in Marx's Capital* as follows: "this was the positive explanation of Marx for his own analysis method." In some relevant works of China, the same opinion is dominant. As a matter of fact, I think there is a misunderstanding. What Marx mentioned here is the non-scientific analysis method formerly adopted by scholars.

There are several points need to be figured out: firstly, the political economics method of Marx is different from the method of the predecessors. In the French version of preface for *Capital*, Marx clearly wrote: "the method of analysis which I have employed, and which had not formerly applied to economic subjects, makes the reading of the first chapters rather arduous, and it is to be feared that the French public, always impatient to come to a conclusion, eager to know the connexion between general principles and the immediate questions that have aroused their passions, may be disheartened because they will be unable to move on at once. That is a disadvantage I am powerless to overcome, unless it be by forewarning and forearming those readers who zealously seek the truth. There is no royal road to science, and only those who do not dread the fatiguing climb of its steep paths have a chance of gaining its luminous summits." The method used by Marx is the dialectical materialism and the historical materialism, which is the "abstract" method of science. No one has ever used it before. Secondly, the predecessors of Marx often adopted a course directly opposite to that of the actual historical development of forms of social life, in the analysis of forms of social life (economic formations), which began (scientific analysis), post festum, (ed. namely) with the results of the process of development we have ready to hand. For instance, the price and currency issue analysis is the discussion of price based on price, and the discussion of currency based on currency, so it is hard to reveal the law of value and figure out the essence of currency and its development laws. However, Marx firstly analyzed the substance of value and the quantity of value, revealed the law of value, and then further explained the movement of price. Firstly, he had analyzed the simple value form for the exchange of original object, and then discussed the expanded and general value form as well as the final currency form. The scientific analysis of Marx does not start from the result of the development process, and the theoretical analysis process is consistent with the actual development process, which is the unification of theoretical logic and historical logic. Thirdly, Marx pointed out that: when analyzing the economic life forms, "people try to understand their contents rather than their historical essence". They analyze from the price to export the decision on the quantity of value, and then analyze the currency form to export the decision on the characteristics of value. This is a "road in contrary to" the method adopted by Marx, i.e. he analyzed the amount of labor and value to export the price decision, and analyzed the value form and the development form to export the currency law. However, the non-scientificity of analyzing from completing the currency form relies on "the currency form, for which, the object form is adopted to cover the social nature of individual labor and the social relation of private worker, rather than revealing them". Marx pointed out in Chapter 2, Volume I of *Capital* that: "That money is a commodity is therefore a new discovery only for those who, when they analyse it, start from its (money) fully developed shape." Marx means those people who analyzed the commodity in an inverted order would hold that, 'currency was the commodity' and they made a new discovery. However, "the difficult thing is to understand how are the commodities as well as why and how to make it become currency, rather than regarding the currency as commodity". Marx wrote: Hence the riddle presented by money is but (instead) the riddle presented by commodities; only it now strikes us in its most glaring form." The analysis that started from the completed form of currency could not solve problems.

II. Focusing on the key theoretical opinions that may be easily neglected in the general economic textbooks and in the introduction type of texts

In *Capital*, some important theoretical opinions have guiding significance on the party construction and promotion of the socialist cause, but we see that they have been simply neglected, and in some relevant explanations and introduction type texts, their meanings have not been highlighted, either.

(I) The opinion of Marx to "exempt the capitalists and landlords under capitalist system from being personally responsible for the capitalist system."

In the first version of preface for Volume I of *Capital*, Marx specially stated that: "To prevent possible misunderstanding, a word. I paint the capitalist and the landlord in no sense couleur de rose [i.e., seen through rose-tinted glasses]. But here individuals are dealt with only in so far as they are the personifications of economic categories, embodiments of particular class-relations and class-interests. My standpoint, from which the evolution of the economic formation of society is viewed as a process of natural history, can less than any other make the individual responsible for relations whose creature he socially remains, however much he may subjectively raise himself above them." Thoroughly adopting the historical materialism, Marx analyzed the development process and class relations in social economy (ger. ökonomischen Gesellschaftsformen), which had not only revealed and criticized the essence of the class exploitative relations of capitalism, but also taken the capitalism as a kind of "natural history", i.e. a necessary process for the social historical development. Engels mentioned in his book review for Volume 1 of *Capital* that: "all the socialisms of Lasalle hurled abuse at the capitalists… and what we could see here was just the opposite. Mr. Marx clearly pointed out the historical necessity of the capitalist mode of production." The generation and development of capitalist system is a necessary phase in the historical development of humans, rather than the loss of someone in morality or justice or their false understanding, and its generation is an event which conforms to the laws of history. Therefore, the capitalists and the landlords are not personally responsible for the capitalist system. It can be seen that, the opinion of historical materialism is opposite to "the theory of the unique importance of class origin" that has been popular in our country for a long time. According to "the theory of the unique importance of class origin", the exploiters should not only be personally responsible for their practice of exploitation, but also argues that their offspring should take responsibility for their ancestors' exploitative relations, which is obviously unreasonable. If the Chinese Marxists, especially the decision-making groups can timely figure this out and grasp the important ideas of Marx, "the theory of the decisive importance of class origin of a person" will never gain popularity in our country, which had been prevalent in our country for more than ten years during the "cultural revolution" (The idea was reversed with the deepening of the Reform and Opening-up.).

(II) About the decisive role how to combine the factors of production with the labor power: in distinction between different economic systems

The ownership of means of production is the basis which decides the production relations system, and this is the basic principle of Marxism, but this is not enough. Think about it: generally, the non-workers occupy the means of production, while the workers are separated from them, so why can some non-workers occupying the means of production become the slave owners, or feudal lords, or capitalists? Why can the workers separated from the means of production become the slaves, serf, or salary earners? This should be defined as per the method of combining the means of production and the labor force. If the workers are taken as a "talking tool", and then combined with the means of production under the whipping and beating of the master, the workers are slaves, and the master is the slave owner, forming the slavery system. In case that the means of production are taken as the capital, and the workers sell their labor power to the capital owners as a commodity, together with the capital and hired labor combined production mode being adopted, the owner of the means of production is the capitalist, and the workers are the hired workers, forming the capitalist system.

In the study the economic system of socialism, the decisive role of public ownership of the production means should be focused. However, in case if we fail to focus on the proper mode of combing the factors of production with the labor force, for instance, failing to treat the workers as the master of the factors of production, or restricting the employees to have any production supervision right or speaking right; or letting the factory director and the manager handle affairs as per their own wills, and allow them ro seek private gains through their managerial power, which will damage the rights and interests of the employees. If so, can such public ownership bear the characteristics of socialism? In order to study *Capital*, this issue should be focused and studied in combination with the past socialism practices.

III. Bravely facing the difficult theoretical problems, and striving to grasp their true meaning

There are some difficult theoretical issues in *Capital*, and the educational circles have all expressed their own opinions, consequently today different interpretations exist. Some works have relatively systematic and correct interpretations of *Capital*. You can find important answers to some difficult theoretical opinions in *Capital*, but some interpretations have deviated from the real intention; some "readering guides" and "interpretation" books avoid the discussion on these controversial problems, which is a kind of loss; some of them hold their own opinions without solid arguments and evidences. The book *The Explanation* explains the different interpretations of the controversial issues in the academic circles, and strives to elaborate in accordance with the original intention.

(I) About the research object of *Capital*

It has been stated in the first version of preface for *Capital* that: "In this work I have to examine the capitalist mode of production and the conditions of production and exchange corresponding to that mode." Here, "the capitalist mode of production" is taken as the research object, so what is it? There are different opinions in the educational circles, and the discussion has been conducted for a long time. The book "Interpretation" has firstly explained the various interpretations, and then told us through its textual research that, it refers to the capitalist mode of production with the capital and the hired labor being combined. However, in the interpretations of the Preface, there is no need to discuss this, not only for its inconvenience, and more attention should be paid to the interpretations of the later chapters, and meanwhile, continuously obtaining and putting forward new arguments. For instance, when interpreting the Transformation of Money into Capital in Part 2 (Chapter 4), Volume I of *Capital*, the readers should be reminded that: in the three volumes of *Capital*, only this part explains its unique meaning with independent and single page (Page 2). In this Part 2, Chapter 4, there is no research on the capital production process of humans, the explanation of which starts from Chapter 7, The Labor Process and the Process of Producing Surplus. In Part 2, Chapter 4, it has been stated that the money is transformed into capital, and the labor power becomes a commodity, transforming labor to hired labor, forming the capitalist mode of production with the capital and hired labor being combined, and this decides the capitalist relation of production and exchange relations. In *The Explanation*, when elaborating the contents in the Circulation of Monetary Capital in Chapter 1, Volume II of *Capital*, one opinion of Marx is highlighted: "Whatever the social form of production, labourers and means of production always remain factors of it. But in a state of separation from each other either of these factors can be such only potentially. For production to go on at all they must unite. The specific manner in which this union is accomplished distinguishes the different economic epochs of the structure of society from one another. In the present case, the separation of the free worker from his means of production is the starting-point given, and we have seen how and under what conditions these two elements are united in the hands of the capitalist, namely, as the productive mode of existence of his capital." This indicates that: the special mode of combining the productive factors and the labor power forms different social-economic periods, i.e., different social-economy systems, and this has pointed out that: the separation of the workers from the production means and their concentration in the hands of the capitalists (the capital and hired labor combined mode) are the "established starting point" for the capitalist economic system. When explaining the contents of Distribution Relations and Production Relations in Chapter 51, Volume III of *Capital*, special attention should be paid to the argument of Marx, i.e. "the relation between the capital and the wage labor can determine all the characteristics of the production mode (refers to the capitalist mode of production. —my addition)." "Scientific analysis of the capitalist mode of production demonstrates the contrary, that it is a mode of production of a special kind, with specific historical features; that, like any other specific mode of production, it presupposes a given level of the social productive forces and their forms of development as its historical precondition: a precondition which is itself the historical result and product of a preceding process, and from which the new mode of production proceeds as its given basis; that the production relations corresponding to this specific, historically determined mode of production – relations which human beings enter into during the process of social life, in the creation of their social life-possess a specific, historical and transitory character; and, finally, that the distribution relations essentially coincident with these production relations are their opposite side, so that both share the same historically transitory character." From this argument, the capitalist social-economic system operating mode can be obtained: social productive forces—capitalist mode of production—capitalist production relations—capitalist distribution relation. It can be confirmed as per the contents of the formula that "the capitalist mode of production" is not a productive force, or the means of labor or labor organization in the meaning of productive force. It takes the established development phase of certain social productive force as the historical conditions, with "specific historical definition". The so-called "specific historical definition" refers to an event with historical temporality for a special social development phase only. It is exactly this capitalist mode of production with historical temporality that decides the suitable production relation "possessing a kind of specific, historical and temporary characteristics". Therefore, we have reasons to believe that, the "capitalist mode of production" mentioned here is the production mode which embodies the combination of the capitalist relation of production, the exchange relation and distribution relation with the "suitable" combination of capital and hired labor on this basis, and this is exactly the "capitalist mode of production" as the research object of *Capital*.

(II) About the essence of money

It has been further elaborated in the Exchange Process in Chapter 2, Volume I of *Capital* that, when the universal equivalent form "is fixed in certain special type of commodity", it will be crystallized into the money form. After that, it has also pointed out that: "Since all other commodities are merely particular equivalents of money, and money is their universal equivalent, they are related to money as particular commodities to the universal commodity." Here, money is defined as the "universal commodity" for general equivalent, and all the other commodities are taken as the "particular commodities" for the special equivalent of money. Such descriptions have been repeated for more than ten times in *Capital* and other works of Marx. However, for a long time, in the economic texts of our country, the essence of money has always been defined as "particular commodities" for the general equivalent, which reverses the real intention of Marx. Currently, there are still some people sticking to this opinion. In some works, when interpreting the contents of this chapter, some works even don't mention a single word about the above sentence of Marx, and in the book *The Explanation*, we have specially explained this sentence of Marx.

By the way, with respect to the key textbook for the theoretical research of Marxist theory *The Overview of Marxist Political Economy*, the wording of "particular commodities" considering the essence of money is abandoned in many of its revised manuscripts. But after it was published, this was changed into the statement saying that "the so-called money is a fixed and special commodity served as the universal equivalent", and this is abnormal and no one knows who has changes that, even Liu Shucheng, Zhang Yu and other final reviewers know nothing about it. So is this done by the editors of the press company? Comrade Liu Shucheng answered that the editors would never arbitrarily modify the contents without approval. We want to take this opportunity to explain that: the wording that the essence of currency is "particular commodities" is not the opinion of the academic editing group.

(III) About the socially necessary labor and its two meanings: determination of value and realization of value

For a long period, the educational circles have discussed what exactly decides the value, the socially necessary labor time (the first meaning of necessary labor time) mentioned in Volume I of *Capital*, or the socially necessary labor time of the other meaning mentioned in Volume III of *Capital*, or their joint effect? The essence of dispute is that: in case that the total volume of some commodities is more than or less than the market demand, what will be influenced, the value determination or the value realization? Actually, this has been clearly answered in *Capital*. The discussion on the relations between the two, i.e. the social labor time and the necessary labor time is mainly put forward in the Introduction about the land rent in Chapter 10 and Chapter 37, Volume III of *Capital*, stating that: "This quantitative limit to the quota of social labour time available for the various particular spheres of production is but a more developed expression of the law of value in general, although the necessary labour-time assumes a different meaning here." Meanwhile, it has also explained that, "such division of labor is in accordance with the proportion, so different types of products will be......sold as per their values". In case that the proportion for respectively using the total social labor time in each particular production field is damaged, "a violation of this proportion makes it impossible to realize the value of the commodity and thus the surplus-value contained in it." (Chapter 37, Volume III of *Capital*) I have highlighted the words "sold" and "realize" through marking, so as to emphasize the other meaning of socially necessary labor time. In fact socially necessary labor time is the issue about the "realization" of value and the surplus value, and on the other hand the issue about whether the total product can be "sold" as per the value, is the other meaning of socially necessary labor time which "determines" the value. In the book *The Explanation*, we have firstly explained the different interpretations about this issue among the educational circles, and then explained that, this issue is an issue about the realization of value, if we truly understand the real intention of *Capital*. In the key textbook for the theoretical research of Marxist theory and its construction *The Overview of Marxist Political Economy*, it has been clearly explained: the first meaning of socially necessary labor "involves the determination of value" and the second meaning "involves the realization of value". In the editing team, no one raised objections to this interpretation, thus the consulting team and the deliberation experts, and all of them have reached an agreement.

Originally published in the journal
Contemporary Economic Research, 2014(6)

Engels and the Early Debate on the "Transformation" Problem

— In Memory of the 120th Anniversary of the Publication of the Volume III of Capital

Gu Hailiang

Abstract: After over 10 years of the publishing of Volume II for *Capital* in 1885 to the publishing of Volume III of *Capital* in 1894, the early-phase discussion about the "transformation" problem had occurred. During this early phase debate, the main arguments included the argument of W. Lexis about the existing systematic deviation between price and value, the relation between this deviation and the organic composition of capital in different industries, besides the problem about the equivalence between the total surplus value and the total interest as well as other problems. Secondly, we see the argument of C. Schmidt on converting the "transformation" problem from a pure concept to a process, and putting forward the "cost + interest" pricing principle in the production price and other problems. Thirdly, we see the argument of Fireman on the deviation function of completion between the individual commodity price and value, the equivalence of total production price to the total value and other problems. Fourthly, we see the argument and efforts of Stiebling and J. Wolf to change the method of solving "transformation" problem to the cancelation of "transformation" problem. Against these arguments, Engels has played a special and important role in the early-phase discussions on the "transformation" problem, and his evaluation on various opinions can highlight his theoretical contribution in adhering to, inheriting and developing Marx economic thoughts. All of these have an important significance on the "transformation" problem upon which the debate continues for more than a century after the publication of Volume III of *Capital*.

Key words: the "transformation" problem; Engels; value; production price; surplus value; profit; average rate of profit

The so-called "transformation" problem in the research of Marxist economics refers to the problem of conversion of values of commodities into production price which is mentioned in Volume III, Chapter IX of Marx's *Capital*. In regard with the research on the history of Marxist economic thoughts, generally, the publishing of Volume III of *Capital* in 1894, or Böhm von Bawerk's *Karl Marx and the Close of His System* in 1896, or I. von Bortkiewicz' *Value and Price in Marxian System* in 1906 will be taken as the beginning of the century long debates on the "transformation" problem. In fact, after Volume II of *Capital* was published in 1885, the discussion on the "transformation" problem had already existed, and within 10 years after Volume III of *Capital* was published, the early-phase discussion on "transformation" problem was formed. In the early-phase discussion on the "transformation" problem, Engels has played an especially important role, which highlights his theoretical contribution in adhering to, inheriting and developing Marxist economic thoughts.

I. Engels' understanding of the "transformation" problem before editing *Capital*, Volume III

In the "Preface" of Volume II of *Capital* written in 1885, Engels elucidated the theoretical contribution of Marx regarding the "transformation" problem when criticizing the economic theory of Rodbertus. Engels held that, the primary cause or confusion for Ricardian School to be "rebuffed" in the "transformation" problem considering its theory and method was as follows: "According to the Ricardian law of value, two capitals employing the same and equally paid labor, all other conditions being equal, produce the same value and surplus value, or profit, in the same time. But if they employ unequal quantities of actual labor, they cannot produce equal surplus-values, or, as the Ricardians say, equal profits. Now in reality, the exact opposite takes place. As a matter of fact, equal capitals, regardless of the quantity of actual labor employed by them, produce equal average profits in equal times. Here we have, therefore, a clash with the law of value, which had been noticed by Ricardo himself, but which his school was unable to reconcile."[1]

Engels briefly summarized the theoretical contribution of Marx in solving this problem as a problem of "how to form equivalent average profit rate on the basis of law of value, without violating it."[2]

Engels pointed out that, before setting forth the "final conclusion" in Volume III of *Capital*, economists including Rodbertus still had the opportunity to put forward their own schemes for solving the problem. Some western scholars called it as the bulletin of "prize essay competition" about the "transformation" problem that was published before publishing Volume III of *Capital*.[3]

1   *Collected Works of Marx and Engels*, Vol. 6, People's Publishing House, 2009, p. 24.
2   Ibid., p. 25.
3   Howard, Michael C., John E. King, *The Political Economy of Marx*, London: Longman, 1985, p. 21.

Although Marx specifically interpreted the "transformation" problem, until he wrote the manuscripts of Volume III of *Capital*, his research on this problem could be traced back to *Economic Manuscripts of 1861-1863*. This Manuscript has firstly verified the transformation relation from value to production price, and carefully investigated the internal mechanism and basis process of the transformation. Especially in June, 1862, when writing in X notebook of the Manuscript, Marx systematically interpreted the overall "transformation" process, from value to production price for the first time, and revealed the formation and essence of "law of average price" (i.e., law of production price). Marx argued that, with respect to the economic reality of using equivalent capital to obtain equivalent profits, "If, however, it is to be explained directly from the law of value without any intermediate link, …this would become a problem much harder than squaring the circle, which can be solved algebraically."[4]

Marx had scientifically proved that, in the law of production price , the capitalists of each department could obtain the average profits in proportion to their respective advanced capital amount as per the average interest rate; the balance between the commodity value and the production price of each department were mainly incurred by the balance between the surplus value and average profits created by each department, and after all, it was incurred by the re-assignment of surplus value in each production department.

Before being engaged in editing the Volume III of *Capital* in 1885, especially before Marx passed away in 1883, Engels already had a relatively clear understanding and recognition on the "transformation" problem. G. Dostaler has argued that: "Marx had specifically and clearly explained the solution in the letter to Engels in 1862".[5]

The statement mentioned here refers to the statement of Marx in his letter to Engels on August 2, 1862. This letter was written after completing the production price argument in X note of the *Economic Manuscripts of 1861-63* and the letter had surely presented a "detailed and clear statement" of Marx expounding on the "transformation" problem.

Marx told Engels that: in the process of capitalist economy, "In these circumstances, given equal exploitation of the worker in different trades, different capitals in different spheres of production will, given equal size, yield very different amounts of surplus value and hence very different rates of profit, since profit is nothing but 'the proportion of the surplus value to the total capital advanced'. This will depend on the organic composition of the capital, i.e. on its division into constant and variable capital."[6]

---

4   *Collected Works of Marx and Engels*, Vol. 26, Book III, People's Publishing House, 1975, p. 90.

5   Gilles Dostaler, Marx's Theory of Value and the Transformation Problem: Some Lessons from a Debate, *Studies in Political Economics*, 1982, p. 80.

6   *Collected Works of Marx and Engels*, Vol. 10, People's Publishing House, 2009, p. 186.

In case of investigating of the total capital of the capitalist class, the competition for "transfer of capital or withdrawal of capital from one trade to the other), capitals of equal size in different trades, despite their different organic compositions, yield the same average rate of profit."[7] The "average profit" calculated as per the "average profit rate" is the "average profit". Through adjusting "the consumed capital + average profit", you can obtain the "average price" of the "cost price". Therefore, "It is the average price to which competition between different trades (by transfer of capital or withdrawal of capital) reduces the prices in different trades. Hence, competition reduces commodities not to their value, but to the cost price, which, depending on the organic composition of the respective capitals, is either above, below or = to their values."[8]

In this letter, Marx surely "made clear his complex statement with several sentences". Besides, Marx had also clearly hinted the complicity of the two types of capitals (variable capital and constant capital, fixed capital and circulating capital) during the transformation process from value to the production price: "In regard to the foregoing definition of cost price as distinct from value, it should further be noted that, besides the distinction between constant capital and variable capital, which arises out of the immediate production process of capital, there is the further distinction between fixed and circulating capital, which arises out of the circulation process of capital. However, the formula would become too involved if I were to seek to incorporate this in the above as well."[9]

This indicates that, Marx had briefly stated the problems, competition and transfer of capital into the capitalist production process and circulation process that must be involved in the "exploration" of "transformation" to Engels. Engels had probably understand the meaning of Marx. In the letter written back to Marx on August 8, 1862, Engels didn't raise questions considering Marx's statement about the "transformation" problem, and he just expressed his "confusion" in the letter about the absolute land rent problem, and suggested that Marx should "make further demonstration".[10] If Engels had no idea about the "transformation" problem, he wouldn't subtly express his "confusion" in the statement about the absolute land rent problem.

During the last ten-days of June, 1867, Engels read about the proof copy of "the chapter about the conversion of money into capital and the chapter about the generation of surplus value" in Volume I of Marx's *Capital*.[11] On June 24, Engels wrote a letter to Marx, and when talking about the proof copies of these two chapters, Engels wrote that: "with respect to the statement and the contents,

---

7   Ibid., p. 187.

8   Ibid., p. 188.

9   Ibid., p. 189.

10   *Collected Works of Marx and Engels*, Vol. 30, People's Publishing House, 1974, p. 275.

11   The chapters mentioned here refer to the chapters in the Volume I, first edition of the German version of *Capital*, relative to "Conversion of Money into Capital" in the Volume I, second edition of the German version of *Capital* as well as the various versions afterwards and the Sheet 3 "Absolute Surplus Value Production".

they were the most brilliant chapters so far."[12] After two days, Engels expressed his "disagreement" in his letter to Marx on June, 26 considering the problem that "the philistines and vulgar economists" might be "quite superficial" on the problems of value, cost, labor value, wage, etc. "I was surprised that you didn't notice this, therefore I would express you my disagreement immediately, so it was better to eliminate this in advance."[13]

Marx immediately replied to Engels considering his suggestion. In the letter written back to Engels on June 27, Marx mentioned that, the problem involved here amounts to the following: "in scientific terms, to the following question: How is the value of the commodity transformed into its price of production, in which 1. the whole of the labour appears paid for in the form of wages; 2. the surplus-labour, however, or the surplus-value, assumes the form of an addition to the price, and goes by the name of interest, profit, etc., over and above the cost-price (= price of the constant part of capital + wages).[14]

Marx added: "Answering this question presupposes: I. That the transformation of, for example, the value of a day's labour-power into wages or the price of a day's labour has been explained. This is done in Chapter V of this volume."[4]

Secondly, Marx wrote, "the transformation of surplus-value into profit, and of profit into average profit, etc., has been explained. This presupposes that the process of the circulation of capital has been previously explained, since the turnover of capital, etc., plays a part here. This matter cannot therefore be treated prior to the 3rd book (Volume II is to contain books 2 and 3)".[15] Marx's statement about "transformation" was more simple and accurate, and he had also elaborated the logical relationship of "transformation" of the value to the production price from the perspective of the overall logic and structure of *Capital*.

With respect to the understanding on this problem, Marx had also mentioned two important problems in respect to methodology: firstly, it is the statement about the "transformation". "Here it will be shown how the philistines' and vulgar economists' manner of conceiving things arises, namely, because the only thing that is ever reflected in their minds is the immediate form of appearance of relations, and not their inner connection. Incidentally, if the latter were the case, we would surely have no need of science at all."[16]

Secondly, as per the "dialectical ways of elaborating" Marx wrote: "if I wished to refute all such objections in advance, I should spoil the whole dialectical method of exposition. On the contrary, the good thing about this method is that it is constantly setting traps for those fellows which will provoke them into an untimely display of their idiocy."[17] Actually, just as the judgment of Marx,

27

---

12   *Collected Works of Marx and Engels*, Vol. 31, People's Publishing House, 1972, p. 316.
13   Ibid., p. 317.
14   *Collected Works of Marx and Engels*, Vol. 10, People's Publishing House, 2009, p. 265.
15   Ibid.
16   Ibid.
17   Ibid.

many later theoretical divisions about the "transformation" problem is caused by the inherent "internal connection" of the "transformation" problem itself considering the discussion on the "transformation" problem, and many people had been caught in the "trap" mentioned and predicted by Marx.

With respect to several correspondence between Engels and Marx, just as evaluated by M. Desai, this cannot only indicate "how sharp Engels was as a critical reader of Marx's work", but also indicates that Marx's "discovery of the problem was not an accident. It also gives us the clue as to why Engels was confident before he had looked at the notebooks that made up Volume III".[18]

In the first German version of Volume I of *Capital* published in 1867, although Marx didn't directly state the "transformation" problem would be later discussed in the Book (Volume) 3, he gave a hint (in two places) that the "transformation" problem would be discussed in Volume III of *Capital*. With respect to the two prompts, one of them pointed to the transformation relation between the surplus value and the profit, "in Volume III of the book, I would further explain that, the same surplus value rate could show extremely different profit rates, while different surplus value rates could also show the same profit rate under certain conditions".[19] The second note was the one mentioned before discussing the capital accumulation problem, "the surplus value could be divided into various different parts. These various parts were owned by different types of people, and then crystallized into different and mutually independent modes such as profit, interest, commercial profit, and land rent. These transformation forms of the surplus value will be studied in Volume III".[20] In the second and third German editions of *Capital*, although Marx had modified the discussions at the two places, the fundamental meaning was not changed.

Engels paid full attention to the discussions at the two places, and taken these discussions as the important opinions of Marx about the capital and surplus value theories. In the *Anti-Dühring* completed in 1878, while refuting the misinterpretation of Dühring about the surplus value theory of Marx, Engels also directly quoted the Marx's statements at these two places.[21] Engels mentioned in the preface of the second version of *Anti-Dühring* in 1885 that "the world view elaborated in this book were mostly confirmed and elaborated by Marx…before publishing, I used to read all the original manuscripts to him".[22] According to this fact, it can be regarded that Engels had fully understood the inherent meaning of these statements involving the "transformation" problem in the above two places.

---

18 Meghnad Desai, The Transformation Problem, *Journal of Economic Surveys,* 1988,2(4), p. 300.

19 Marx, *Capital* (according to the first German edition translation in Volume I), Economic Science Press, 1987, p. 497.

20 Ibid., p. 539.

21 *Collected Works of Marx and Engels*, Vol. 9, People's Publishing House, 2009, p. 220-221.

22 *Collected Works of Marx and Engels*, Vol. 9, People's Publishing House, 2009, p. 11.

II. Lexis and Schmidt's Exploration and Engels' Comments

The first responder to the "Prize Essay Competition" for the "transformation" problem put forward by Engels was the German statistician W. Lexis. In 1885, Lexis said in an article entitled "Marx's Theory of Capital" (Die Marx'sche Kapitaltheorie) that he had already solved the contradiction between the "Ricardo-Marx law of value and actual price formation'"[23] in an economy with equal profit rates. Lexis argued: "Whatever Volume III might bring, the only possible solution was one in which prices and labour values were allowed to diverge, in a manner that permitted the transfer of surplus value from capitalists using relatively large quantities of labour power to those using proportionally less." He added: "For us the decisive point is that, when two producers exchange a given quantity of different commodities, the one always gains as a result of the equalisation of profits [i.e. of the rate of profit] on capital as many labour units from the exchange as the other one loses . . . But since the losses and gains in surplus value within the capitalist class offset each other (sich gegenseitig aufheben), the total magnitude of surplus value is the same as if all prices were proportional to the true values (Idealwerten) of the commodities."[24]

Lexis specifically discussed the issue of systematic deviation between price and value, the issue of relationship between the deviation and the organic composition of capital in different industries, as well as the issue of equality between total surplus value and total profit. Lexis, thought the only way that the unequal surplus value could lead to the equal profit rate is that some capitalists sell their goods at a price higher than the conceptual value of what commodities they sell, while some others sell their goods at a price lower than the conceptual value of those commodities. He wrote: "But since the gains and losses of surplus value can offset each other within the capitalist class, therefore the total amount of surplus value together with all prices is the same as they are in proportion to the concept value of the commodities."[25]

Engels' comment on Lexis was as follows: "actually it is beyond our expectation that a man like the author with the complacency of a 'vulgar economist' can achieve this judgment", even Engels said: "who we meet is a vulgar economist in the cloak of a Marxist."[26] But Engels argued that "the issue is far from being settled here, albeit vaguely, superficially, but generally it was put forward rightly."[27] Desai thought that Engels' evaluations of "loose", "shallow", etc. made by Engels on Lexis are too harsh, because "Lexis gets two things correct; prices must deviate from values, and that total surplus value sets a limit to the total profits, since the transformation only redistributes total surplus value among the capitalists."[28] Similar with Desai, M. Howard and J. King have highly evaluated Lexis's comments, saying that "if only by

---

23   W. Lexis, *Die Marx'sche Kapitaltheorie*, Conrads Jahrbücher,1885(11), pp. 452-465
24   Ibid., p. 464.
25   Ibid., p. 465.
26   *Collected Works of Marx and Engels*, Vol. 7, People's Publishing House, 2009, p. 13, 14.
27   Ibid., p. 13.
28   See Meghnad Desai (1988), p. 301.

implication, the foundations of Marx's solution are present in Lexis's brief and early discussion of the transformation problem."[29]

In 1889, German economist Conrad Schmidt responded to the "Prize Essay Competition" for "transformation" problem. Engels called him "the first person who really tried to answer the question."[30] Schmidt thought in the article entitled "The Average Rate of Profit on the Basis of the Marxist Law of Value" (Die Durchschnittsprofitrate auf Grundlage des Marx' schen Werthgesetzes) that the workers produced surplus value reflected in the surplus products, but the capitalists must provide a certain amount of materialized labor in order to be able to appropriate the surplus products.

Thus, for a capitalist, the prepaid capital is the social necessary labor quantity of objectification that he has to pay for the purpose of appropriating the surplus products. Schmidt divided the total products into two parts: one part is the products required by production including constant capital and variable capital on their behalf, the other part is for the surplus products. Schmidt thought the "key" to solve the "transformation" problem lies in the determination of the sales prices of surplus products. In his view, the formation of average profit rate makes the price of each capitalist's surplus products proportional to the advanced capital, so that the price is certainly not equal to the quantity of materialized labor in the products. Therefore, only the socially necessary labor can create value, materialized labor in the surplus products is not the socially necessary labor, therefore it cannot determine the value of goods.[31]

Schmidt defined the average profit rate as:

$$\frac{\sum m}{\sum (c+v)}$$

(1)

$\sum m$ is the total surplus value, and $\sum (c + v)$ is the sum of constant capital and variable capital used.

Schmidt thought that the profit gained by individual capitalist, is determined by the arithmetic sum of general profit rate and total capital amount, namely:

$$\frac{\sum m}{\sum (c+v)} (c+v)$$

(2)

This determines both the exchange value of surplus product and its price that is exchange value expressed in the form of money. In Schmidt's view, the price of products consist of two parts: firstly, the price of part constant and variable

---

29   Howard, Michael C. and John E. King, *A History of Marxian Economics*, Vol, I, 1883-1929, London: Macmillan and Princeton: Princeton University Press, 1989, p. 26.
30   Collected Works of Marx and Engels, Volume 7, People's Publishing House, 2009, p. 15
31   C. Schmidt, *Die Durchschnittsprofitrate auf Grundlage des Marx'schen Werthgesetzes*, Stuttgart: Dietz,1889, pp. 11-16.

capital is determined by materialized labour in them,[32] the product's price and value in this part are same, they stand for the capitalist's expenditures for the constant and variable capitals; secondly, the price of surplus product is determined by the arithmetic sum of total capital amount and general profit rate, this part of products is equal in total capital amount and total surplus value. Finally, viewed from the total amount, the sum of all the prices of the goods is equal to the sum of their value.[33]

Thus, no matter whether total advanced capital that can observed in the money form of capital or in the commodity form of capital, profit rate level (1) will always remain the same.[34] Engels thought that Schmidt's analysis was incorrect. "If Schmidt uses this idea to make the price calculated on the base of average profit rate coordinated with the law of value, then he abandons the law of value itself, because he employs an idea which is completely contrary to the law of value, as a common decisive factor to be merged into this law."[35] It is clear that Schmidt had proposed the correct pricing principle of cost plus profit in production prices, but he erroneously separated the price determination of the surplus product from the price determination of constant capital and variable capital, which fundamentally misinterprets Marx's meaning of socially necessary labor, in fact, Schmidt's solution was equivalent to abandon Marx's theory of labor value.

In 1893, Schmidt published an article entitled The Average Rate of Profit on the Basis of the Marxist Law of Value" in *New Times* (ger. Neue Zeit) to discuss the "transformation" problem again, he focused on discussing the issue of competition which transfers the capital from the department with profit lower profit rate compared to the average profit to the department with profit rate higher than the average profit, thus Schmidt tried to prove that competition can make the ratio of the sales price of existing surplus-supplied goods to the value reduced to the level of "social capacity to pay" by this kind of capital transfer.[36] Engels' evaluation on this article was also critical, because "the view that competition is the major reason for equalization of profit is not a new thing" while using the price fluctuation of surplus-supplied goods to illustrate the average profit, in order to explain the "transformation" problem, also can't achieve the goal.[37]

Desai has argued that Schmidt proposed the pricing principle of cost plus profit in production price and used the calculation method of average profit rate same as Marx's, and actually what Schmidt here discussed is the extension of the "transformation" problem, making this issue change from a pure concept to a process, next Schmidt extends the issue from production price to market price". M. Desai's argument on the "transformation" problem being extended from the concept itself to the economic process is keenly pointed and creative. Desai also

---

32   Ibid., pp. 47, 48.
33   Ibid., p. 51.
34   See C. Schmidt (1889), pp. 52, 53.
35   *Collected Works of Marx and Engels*, Volume 7, People's Publishing House, 2009, p. 16.
36   C. Schmidt, Die Durchschnittsprofitrate und das Marx'sche Wertgesetz, *Die Neue Zeit*, 1892, 11/3.
37   *Collected Works of Marx and Engels*, Vol. 7, People's Publishing House, 2009, p. 167.

thought that Schmidt's mistake lies in that he sharply separated the value determination of surplus product and paid product, in Marx's view, all products are produced by labor and means of production, and surplus value is created by living labor.[38] But, Desai did not mention that Schmidt's debate was wrong at the outset, because Schmidt had chosen a solution plan to the "transformation" problem which abandoned the labor theory of value insisted on by Marx.

Howard and King have highly evaluated Schmidt's efforts, in their opinion as follows: Schmidt's solution consists of three core elements regarding the solution provided in Volume III of Marx's *Capital*. Firstly, Schmidt has argued that the profit of an individual capitalist was determined by both the arithmetic product of the capital advanced by him and the general (average) profit rate. Secondly, Schmidt has argued that total prices was equal to total values, and total profit was equal to total surplus value. Thirdly, Schmidt seemed to claim (albeit not very clearly) that the quantity of value has a logical priority in calculating the general profit (average) rate. Schmidt's main mistake is that he cannot transform the value of input into price like as transforming the value of output into price, at this point he and Marx are the same.[39]

Here, the evaluation of Howard and King on the so-called third "core element" is clearly biased. In fact Schmidt was very different from Marx at the outset, he had already made the "main mistake" of abandoning labor value theory before he wasn't exposed to the issue of the value for input products being transformed to production price, while Marx had never made the "same" mistake with Schmidt, in the discussion of the "transformation" problem Marx had clearly realized that and wrote: "the price of production price, which in this way deviates from the value of a commodity, entering into will be as the cost price of other commodities as one of its elements, so that the cost-price of a commodity may already contain a deviation from value within those means of production consumed by this means of production"[40]. This, is a brilliant answer by Marx to these two people, only missing here was a "supplementary explanation".

III. Exploration of Stiebeling, Wolf and Loria and Engels' Comments

From 1890 to 1894, the US statistician G.C. Stiebeling discussed the "transformation" problem in two booklets entitled *Law of Value and Profit Rate and Average Profit Rate Problem. The Critique on a Critique, With a Little Supplement*.[41] He argued that different capital amount of organic composition could not produce equivalent value and surplus value; the higher the organic composition, the higher the labor productivity, thus the higher the rate of exploitation. When the capital is equal, when the time is equal, but if the living

32

---

38   See Meghnad Desai (1988), p. p. 302.
39   See Howard, Michael C., John E. King (1989), p. 28.
40   *Collected Works of Marx and Engels*, Vol. 7, People's Publishing House, 2009, p. 229
41   G.C. Stiebeling, *Das Wertgesetz und die Profitrate*, New York: Heinrichs, 1890; *Das Problem der Durchschnittsprofitrate: Kritik einer Kritik mit Meinem Nachtrag*, New York: Labor News Co., 1893.

labor is not equal, different organic compositions will bring equivalent average profit rate through the change of surplus value rate."[42] At this point, Stiebeling brought the hypothesis that the production price of individual commodities was equal to their value, which demonstrated that he had a fundamental misunderstanding on the whole "transformation" problem. It can be considered that Stiebeling's solution to the "transformation" problem was to cancel the "transformation" problem itself.

Engels' evaluation on Stiebeling was: "from the beginning he took what he should prove as a premise" thus inevitably all of his debates and calculations has become "untenable" and "wrong".[43] But Engels did not deny the existence of some "exceptional" achievements in Stiebeling's exploration, for example, Stiebeling's demonstration on falling rate of profit by official statistics survey materials was fruitful. Stiebeling was an earlier scholar who attempted to systematically use survey statistics materials to study Marx's theory of value. He illustrated that the industries with higher organic composition had higher rate of exploitation in his analysis on survey materials of US conditions from 1870 to 1880; he argued the opposite was also true. He took two industries with the same profit rate (about 9%) as examples: one was coarse salt industry with 6.53 of organic composition and 0.58 of exploitation rate; another was the shipbuilding industry with 1.56 of organic composition and 0.14 of exploitation rate. Stiebeling sorted all 29 industries according to the high-low level of the organic composition, and divided them into two groups: the average organic composition of the top 14 industries was 5.50, their average exploitation rate was 1.38, and their average profit rate was 25.1%; the corresponding data of the bottom 15 industries was 2.58, 0.57 and profit rate of 22.1% consecutively.[44] Of course, even in this comparative, statistical study, Engels noticed that Stiebeling could not fight against the theory of "falling rate of profit is completely wrong".[45]

In 1891, German economist, Julius Wolf made an argument very similar to Stiebeling in his article *The Puzzle of Marx's Average Rate of Profit*.[46] Wolf argued: "in view of Marx, the improvement of labor productivity and the improvement of capital's organic composition are advancing side by side. Value of commodities (including labor power) and labor productivity are negatively correlated, and there is a direct link between surplus value and labor productivity. Therefore, according to Marx's theory, in regard with the increase of constant capital takes the assumption of increasing labor productivity as the premise, there is a direct link between the growth of surplus value and the expansion of constant capital share in total capital, due to the improvement of

33

---

42   G.C. Stiebeling, *Untersuchungen Über die Raten des Mehrwerths und Profits mit Bezug auf die Lösung des Problems der Durchschnitts-Profitrate*, New York: New York Labor News Co., 1894 (3), p. 3.
43   *Collected Works of Marx and Engels*, Vol. 7, People' Publishing House, 2009, p. 25.
44   See G.C. Stiebeling (1894), p. 23.
45   Collected Works of Marx and Engels, Volume 7, People's Publishing House, 2009, pp. 25, 26.
46   J. Wolf, Das Raetsel der Durchschnittsprofitrate bei Marx, *Jahrbücher für Nationalökonomie und Statistik*, 1891, pp. 57, 352-367.

labor productivity (by making workers' means of livelihood become cheaper) will cause the increase of surplus value".[47]

Wolf explained his viewpoints by numerical examples (see Table 1).

Table 1. Wolf's numerical examples

	Constant capital (c)	Variable capital (v)	Surplus value (s)	Total value (s+v+s)	Rate of exploitation (s/v)	Profit rate [s/(c+v)]
Capital I	5	5	1	11	20	10
Capital n	10	5	1,5	16,5	20	10

Source of data: J.Wolf, " Das Rätsel der Durchschnittsprofitrate bei Marx",
Jahrbucher fur Nationalökonomie und Statistik, 1891, p. 358.

In Table 1, organic composition of capital n is higher, the labor productivity is higher, so that surplus value is also more, the rate of exploitation is higher, and it has the same profit rate as Capital I mentioned in the table. For the above variables, the opposite is also the true. Wolf argued, here the value of commodity still depended on the labor amount materialized within the commodity, he said: "the law of value has not been destroyed," and there is no inconsistencies in Marx's view, and he added: "his theory provides a new evidence to prove how deep and visionary Marx's critical system on the capitalist economy is."[48] Engels wrote that in Volume I of *Capital*, there were at least hundreds of places where Marx wrote brilliant sentences opposing Wolf's "solutions", Engels wrote: "Marx thinks when variable capital decreases, the increase of relative surplus-value and the increase of constant capital will be proportional, while this assertion of Marx is very surprising enough, that dwarfs all the parliamentary rhetoric".[49] Engels added: "regardless of relatively speaking or absolutely speaking, Wolf didn't understand both absolute surplus value and relative surplus value at all", in fact, "it is him who stuck in the mistake".[50] Obviously, like Stiebeling, Wolf's solution to "transformation" problem was just to cancel the "transformation" problem itself.

Italian scholar Achille Loria once asserted in his article entitled *Karl Marx's Theory of Value* published in 1884, that equal profit rate and unequal organic composition was a contradiction not to be solved forever, and this was a significant defect in Marx's whole theoretical system.[51] In 1890, in the review fn

---

47 Ibid., p. 358.
48 Ibid., p. 360.
49 *Collected Works of Marx and Engels*, Vol. 7, People's Publishing House, 2009, p. 19.
50 Ibid., p. 19, 20.
51 A. Loria, La Théorie de la Valeur de Karl Marx, *Journal des Economistes*, 1884, pp. 137-139.

Schmidt's *Average Profit Rate on The Basis of Marx's Law of Value*, Loria proposed a solution to the issue of "transformation". Loria's solution to the issue of "transformation" can seen as follows (see Table 2).

Table 2: Loria's numerical examples

	Constant capital (c)	Variable capital (v)	Surplus value (s)	Total capital (c+v)	[s/(c+v)] (%)	Interest expenditure	Industry profit	Industry profit rate (%)	Profit rate of monetary capitalists (%)
Capital A	0	50	50	50	100	40	10	20	
Capital B	100	50	50	150	33 ⅓	20	30	20	
Capital C	200	50	50	250	20	0	50	20	
Total	300	150	150	450		60	90		
Capital D				300		60			20

Source of data: Loria, "Review of Schmidt, Die Durchschnittsprofitrate"
(The average profit rate), in Conrads Jahrbucher, 1890, 20, p. 274.

In Table 2, industrial capitalists A, B, and C have different organic composition of capital and same rate of exploitation. In case there is no non-industrial capital involved, their profit rates are different. In case capitalists who borrow loans is included, they use a part of surplus-value to pay the interest of money-capitalist D. The industrial profits left by industrial capitalists A, B, and C are proportional to the amount of capital used by them, thus forming an average industrial profit rate, which is the same as the profit rate of monetary capitalist D.[52] Loria did not make any reasonable account of his weird assumptions and reasoning. Engels pointed out in his comments to Loria: "But only a literary adventurer who in his heart sneezes at political economy, can venture the assertion that it has the magic power to absorb all surplus value in excess of the general rate of profit even before this general rate has taken shape, and to convert it into ground-rent for itself without, moreover, even having need to do with any real estate"[53] Engels also made a sharp attack against Loria: "What kind of a magician can imagine that Marx actually needed to play such a poor trick!"[54]

IV. Fireman and Lyle's Exploration and Engels' Comments

In 1892, the US chemist and a factory owner Peter Fireman tried to solve the "transformation" problem in his article entitled *Critique of Marx's Theory of Value*. Fireman distinguished two factors in the price of commodities: "component factor" of commodity value determined by materialized labor quantity in the commodity,

---

52   A. Loria, *Review of Schmidt, Die Durchschnittsprofitrate*, Conrads Jahrbucher, 1890, p. 20.
53   *Collected Works of Marx and Engels*, Vol. 7, People's Publishing House, 2009, p. 23.
54   Ibid.

and "distribution factor" representing the claims of product share of capitalists and landlords. Fireman thought due to social wealth was composed of total amount of human labor in the production of goods, therefore, as a whole, the value must be equal to the price: "when two commodities are exchanged, the price of one commodity is higher than its value, which is certainly equal to the price of another commodity lower than its value, and the reverse is also true",[55] the difference that occurs between price and value is caused by "distribution factor".

Fireman refuted Schmidt's solution, and he argued that Schmidt's solution was non-Marxist because Schmidt's solution refused to apply the law of value to the surplus products. Fireman also refuted Wolf's conclusion, Fireman argued: "since Wolf argued that the quantity of value would increase with the increase of labor productivity, which was contradictory to Marx's point of view."Fireman illustrated the relationship among price, value and organic composition of capital more clearly in each industrial sector. In Fireman's view, if profit is the form of surplus value, then, how should we understand the fact that the amount of surplus value depends on the number of workers, secondly, how should we understand, that in the meantime the amount of profit seems to be independent from the number of workers? Fireman's explanation is that, in the industrial sectors with the highest ratio of the capital invested on the means of production to the capital invested in wages (such as the ratio of constant capital to variable capital proposed by Marx, $c : v$), the sales price of their commodities will be higher than their value, which means that in the industrial sectors with the smallest ratio of constant capital to variable capital, the sales price of their commodities will be lower than their value, when the level of $c : v$ happens to be average, the commodities will be sold in accordance with their actual value.[56]

Fireman stressed that this was not contradictory with the law of value, because the total price is still equal to the total value. The difference between the price and the value of individual commodities is caused only due to the fluctuation in competition. Fireman added: "But in rigorous science, people can never interpret this fluctuation to be accurately calculated as a negation of the law."[57] Fireman used a simple numerical example to discuss the "transformation" problem, meanwhile he conducted general approach in his own solution, so that he could include the payment of land rent and profits, but Fireman did not make any analysis on this issue.[58] Engels argued that Fireman's exploration "has actually come into contact with the key point of the problem. But undue cold reception to his important paper proves that, Fireman even after this discovery, still needs to clear certain other intermediate links so as to completely and clearly solve the problem.[59]

---

55 P. Fireman, Kritik der Marx'schen Werttheorie, *Jahrbücher für Nationalöknomie und Statistik*, 1892, pp. 58, 798.

56 Ibid., pp. 58, 805, 806.

57 Ibid., p. 808.

58 Ibid., p. 805-807.

59 *Collected Works of Marx and Engels*, Vol. 7, People's Publishing House, 2009, p. 18.

In 1892, German scholar Lehr refuted Schmidt's analysis on the "transformation" problem in the article his article "Average Profit Rate on The Basis of Marx's Law of Value",[60] and also raised an objection to Wolf's point of view. Lehr made a unique algebraic expression of the "transformation" problem, and these algebraic expressions in fact he paved the way for the later numerous mathematical analyses on "transformation" problem made by V.K. Dmitriev and Bortkiewicz.[61]

Lehr used k_1, k_2, ... and v_1, v_2, ... to indicate the value of constant and variable capital used in industries 1, 2, ... respectively, and used m_1, m_2, ... to indicate the surplus value. For the whole economy, the corresponding sums are K, V and M respectively, and he used the same standpoint as Marx's, and used $M / (K + V)$ = r as the average profit rate. "Exchange value of each unit of commodities" is denoted with t_1, t_2, ...

Accordingly, Lehr obtained the following equations:

$$m_1 + m_2 + m_3 + ... = M \tag{1}$$

$$t_1 m_1 + t_2 m_2 + t_3 m_3 + ... = M \tag{2}$$

$$k_1 + v_1 + k_2 + v_2 + k_3 + v_3 + ... = K + V \tag{3}$$

$$(k_1 + v_1)\, r = t_1 m_1$$

$$(k_2 + v_2)\, r = t_2 m_2 \tag{4}$$

$$(k_1 + v_1 + m_1) = (k_1 + v_1)\,(1 + r)$$

$$(k_2 + v_2 + m_2) = (k_2 + v_2)\,(1 + r) \text{ etc.} \tag{5}$$

Equations (1) and (2) together indicate that total profit is equal to total surplus value. Equation (3) is purely definitive, while Equations (4) and (5) try to associate each sector's surplus value with profit as well as value with production price. Obviously Lehr's attempt was unsuccessful, since he assumed that within a single sector, the value quantity and price quantity are equal, and such an assumption was completely wrong. However, although Lehr did not explicitly wrote it, he actually set up a model with n + 1 equations and n + 1 unknowns (t_1, t_2, t_3, ..., r) by using equations (2) and (5), in this model, the number of constraint conditions and endogenous variables are the same. In fact, Lehr's only direct inference was as follows:

$$t_1 = t_2 = t_3 = ... = t_n = 1$$

This equation can be established if only organic compositions in all the industry for all capitalists is the same. Lehr was not able to explain Marx's theory, that is to say ti may be greater than or less than 1 unit value, the organic composition of capital in different industries may be higher or lower than the

---

60   J. Lehr, Die Durchschnittsprofitrate auf Grundlage des Marx'schen Wertgesetzes, *Vierteljahrschrift für Volkswirtschaft und Kulturgeschichte*, 1892, 29(1), pp. 145-174 and 1892, 29(2), pp. 68-92.
61   Ibid.

social average organic composition of capital. But Lehr still offered a mathematical example which vaguely expressed this point of view.[62]

Lehr did not continue to push his analysis deeper. If Lehr had tried to solve ti and r, he would find that his equation incorrectly set the relationship between value quantity and price—profit variables, which could push him to make a fundamental improvement in his analysis. If he had done so, he would be more close to the solution of Bortkiewicz. Lehr as a scholar who called himself "vulgar economist", did not agree with Marx's theory of value completely and could not give a further vibrant analytical answer to Marx's "transformation" problem.

V. Engels' Evaluation on the Early Debate of the "Transformation" Problem and Its Enlightenment

Engels made an evaluation on the main articles of the "Prize Essay Competition" for "transformation" problem with a larger length in the Preface of Volume III of *Capital*. On the whole, Engels praised Schmidt and Fireman's research, saying that "The outcome of the entire investigation shows again with reference to this question as well that it is the Marxian school alone which has accomplished something. If Fireman and Conrad Schmidt read this third book, each one, for his part, may well be satisfied with his own work."[63]

Engels rather had negative attitude regarding other researches. This "Prize Essay Competition" for "transformation" problem obviously left a deep memory to Engels. After the third volume of *Capital* was published in 1894, Engels wrote a letter to Schmidt on March 12, 1895, enthusiastically said: "with regard to Fireman, we should completely put him aside and don't talk about his work. Lexis just raised the question, and the same to you", and argued that "Fireman has only taken a step along the right path in his...."[64]

It is precisely because of having a profound understanding of Marx's "transformation" problem that Engels had confidently launched the "Prize Essay Competition" for the "transformation" problem before editing of Volume III of *Capital*. The publishing of Volume III of *Capital* was not as optimistic as what Engels had originally estimated, and it was published in the ninth year after Volume II of *Capital*. Obviously, in the process of editing Volume III of *Capital*, Engels had a clearer understanding of the "transformation" problem. In the "Preface" of the Volume III, Engels' various remarks and analyses on the "Prize Essay Competition" proves this point. Desai pointed out: if the "transformation" problem were merely a mathematical technical problem, "it should have been solved long ago and nothing left to discuss about it," which actually not the case; therefore, "Engels was wrong if he thought that the publication of volume III would settle all controversy. Indeed it made the transformation

---

62 Ibid.
63 *Collected Works of Marx and Engels*, Vol. 7, People's Publishing House, 2009, p. 26.
64 *Complete Works of Marx and Engels*, Vol. 39, People's Publishing House, 1974, p. 407

problem the main battleground between the Marxists and their opponents."[65]. Here, Desai had a misunderstanding of Engels, Engels did not think that Marx had "completely solved" the "transformation" problem in Volume III of *Capital*.

After Volume III of *Capital* was published in November, 1894, the paper entitled "Law of Value and Profit Rate" completed by Engels in May or June of the following year, was a supplementary explanation related to the "transformation" problem. Engels argued that Marx's view of "taking commodity value as a starting point to advance towards the production price both in theory and in history is perfectly appropriate" which was put forward in the debate related to value to be transformed into production price in Volume III of *Capital*, here Marx only made a "general outline", "If Marx had time to re-arrange and edit Volume III again, he without doubt would greatly give play to this paragraph."[66] Engels added: in the place where Marx did not have time to "play", where future generations need to "talk in some detail."[67]

Engels, in his article "Law of Value and Profit Rate", explained his view for further "playing": he pointed to d issues to be considered when exploring the transformations issue, "it is not only a purely logical process but also a historical process" as the third and fourth points Engels added: the thought reflection on illustrating the process, and the logical research of the internal relations of this process."[68] In Engels's view, Volume III of *Capital* had not "ended" the exploration on the "transformation" problem, on the contrary left a theoretical space which needed further development.

In order to clarify Desai's misunderstanding on Engels, we should also review Engels' discussions on the methodology of Marxist economics and on the "transformation" problem which he wrote after the publication of Volume III of *Capital*. In Engels' letter to Sombart on March 11, 1895, when he replied to the question of how the equalisation process of profit rate occurred, Engels wrote: But how has the equalisation been brought about in reality? This is a very interesting point, about which Marx himself does not say much. But his way of viewing things is not a doctrine but a method. It does not provide ready-made dogmas, but criteria for further research and the method for this research. Here therefore a certain amount of work has to be carried out, since Marx did not elaborate it himself in his first draft."[69] Perhaps few people knew Engels' famous discussion in this paragraph above which was later quoted numerously, he wrote it for the discussion of the "transformation" problem. Engels also argued: "This is a very interesting point, about which Marx himself does not say much." it certainly needed "serious study" he added: Marx's "unfinished work", and this will be a very valuable supplement to *Capital*".[70] Although the

65   See Meghnad Desai (1988), p. 296.
66   *Collected Works of Marx and Engels*, Vol. 7, People's Publishing House, 2009, p. 1015.
67   Ibid.
68   Ibid., p. 1013.
69   *Collected Works of Marx and Engels*, Vol. 10, People's Publishing House, 2009, p. 691.
70   Ibid., p. 691, 692.

"Prize Essay Competition" for "transformation" problem launched by Engels occurred before the publishing of the third volume of *Capital*, the "transformation" problem debate which lasts more than 100 years after the publishing of the third volume of *Capital*, still has an important impact. I think, in the exploration of "transformation" problem based on Marxist economics, the above early debates have the following more than three aspects:

Firstly, in Marx's economics thought system, the "transformation" problem involves the understanding of the mechanism and process of value-to-production price transformation, which is based on the theory of labor value. Without understanding value essence, value entity, value realization and its transformation mechanism, it will be impossible to make sense of the logical relationship of value in the abstract/general level transformed to production price in the concrete/specific level. The "transformation" problem also involves the understanding on the mechanism and process of the surplus value transformed to the average profit, which is based on the theory of surplus value. And without understanding the source and essence of surplus value, or without understanding the internal transformation mechanism of surplus value to profit as well as profit to average profit, it will be impossible to grasp the historical and theoretical logic in it. In fact, the debate of "transformation" problem over a hundred year is substantially about the debate of the scientific status and its theoretical significance to Marx's labor theory of value and his theory of surplus value. In this sense, Desai's viewpoint that "deriving prices from labour values and of showing that all profit arose from surplus value created by labourers" is "at the heart" of the "transformation" problem is the correct summary of the essence of the debate for more than hundred years.[71]

Secondly, the early debate on the "transformation" problem has in fact demonstrated the progressive nature and limitations of the later debates, for example: Lexis's discussion on the existing systematic deviation between prices and values, the relationship between this deviation and the differences of organic composition of capital in different industries, the equality between total surplus value and total profit and some other problems; Schmidt's discussion on transforming the "transformation" problem from a pure concept into a process, and putting forward the pricing principle of "cost and profit" in production price and some other problems; Fireman's discussion on the role of competition in regard to the deviation between individual commodity price and value according to the law of value, the total production value being equal to the total value. Stiebeling and Wolf's discussion on changing the solution to "transformation" problem into canceling "transformation" problem itself and their other contributions. But, all these discussions lack an overall grasp, and they often held their own point of view, therefore there occurred a fragmentation in the debate, drawbacks in the process of debate and some other problems inevitably appeared.

40

71　See Meghnad Desai (1988), p. 295.

If we look from the aspect of their methodology, they were not able to understand the method from abstract to concrete of the methodology of Marxian economics. Therefore, it was hard for them to avoid falling into the "trap" foreseen by Marx, because they did not grasp the method of "the abstract determinations lead towards a reproduction of the concrete by way of thought."[72]

Thirdly, the fact of the history of economic thought presenting in the early debate on "transformation" problem, is the different understandings on "transformation" problem and the different conclusions drawn, and all of these are directly related to the economics school which the debaters belong to. Engels' evaluation on various views of the "Prize Essay Competition" for "transformation" problem, has fully illustrated this point. Soon after the publishing of the third volume of *Capital*, Engels once mentioned three kinds of people with different attitudes to Marx's *Capital*: the first was "those who cannot read or do not want to read"; the second was "those who are not spending the necessary effort to understand it correctly, instead they spend more effort to distort it" and the third group was those "who really want to understand it."[73]

The debate on "transformation" problem in the twentieth century proves that almost every school of economics has its own interpretation of "transformation" problem and its own conclusions. Perhaps there will never be a "universally agreed" conclusion regarding the "transformation" problem, besides the unique conclusion based on Marx's economics.

41

Originally published in the journal
Contemporary Economic Research, 2014(3)

---

72   *Collected Works of Marx and Engels*, Vol. 8, People's Publishing House, 2009, p. 25
73   *Collected Works of Marx and Engels*, Vol. 7, People's publishing House, 2009, p. 1005.

On the Objectivity of
the Object of Research of the Political Economy

Ding Baojun, Gao Ling and Wang Jinqiu

Abstract: The object of research of political economy is the social production in a certain historical stage of human society, thus the object of research of political economy in the historical stage of capitalism is the capitalist social production, in this sense, objectively Marxist political economy and western bourgeois economics have the same objective object of research. The objectivity in regard to object of research political economy determines the truthfulness and the consistency of interpretation of political economy. Social production in a certain historical stage of human society is a specific particular social production, when compared to those in other social and historical stages. Social production, as the object of research of political economy in a certain stage of human society, and social production, in a certain stage of human society is the rational unity of natural attributes and social attributes of social mode of production. There is a hot debate on the object of research of political economy in the academic circle due to the unclear theoretical understanding of object of research or due to the inconsistent terminology. Clarifying the objectivity of the object of research political economy is of practical significance and vital for the consistency of its theoretical form and its benign construction as a discipline. It is also important to guarantee the guiding status of Marxist economics and Marxist materialist dialectics in the reform of state-owned enterprises led by Marxist materialist dialectics.

Key words: political economy; object of research; mode of production; production relations; ownership of the means of production

Marxist economists, from the classical writers Marx and Engels to the contemporary scholars, have some differences on the object of research of political economy; the same applies for the current academic circles. Western bourgeois economists also have different arguments on the object of research of political economy. There are not only divergent ideas between two ideological camps but also within the two camps itself. This paper discusses the object of research of political economy from the perspective of the objectivity and expression consistency of the object of research of political economy, so as to deepen the understanding of Marxist political economy.

I. Objectivity of the object of research of political economy

At present, many domestic scholars discuss the object of research of political economy starting from the understanding of some classic statements or starting from the cognition and understanding of classic statements made by representative figures. For example, among the Marxist economists, many people start from Marx's statement in the preface of the first edition of Volume I in *Capital*, and seek to establish a correct understanding on the object of research of Marxist political economy through their understanding of the connotations of production mode. On the other side some scholars approach to the issue by of starting from Stalin's statement in the book *Economic Problems of Socialism in the USSR*: "the object of research of political economy is social production relations". Western bourgeois economists often discuss the issue basing themselves on Robbins' classic statement so as to get their own conclusions. However, if analyzed carefully, the methodology of these discussions have certain drawbacks due to ignorance of a critical question—the logic behind the elucidatory statement made by classic Marxist writers.

(I) Material production as the object of research of political economy in a certain development stage of human society

Marx said in the preface to the first edition of the first volume of *Capital*: "In this work I have to examine the capitalist mode of production, and the conditions of production and exchange corresponding to that mode."[1] Here, Marx explicitly defined the object of research of political economy as the capitalist mode of production and the corresponding production and exchange relations corresponding to it. Marx also said in the *Introduction to the Critique of Political Economy (1857-1858)* "The object before us to begin with, is material production.[2] Here Marx defined the object of research of political economy as material production again. Some people deliberately differentiate the object of research in Marx's *Capital*, the object of research in the manuscript of *A Contribution to the Critique of Political Economy*, and the object of research in Marxist Political Economy. In our opinion this kind of differentiation is meaningless. Because *Capital* is merely a model of studying, the political economy of the

1   Karl Marx, *Capital*, Vol. 1, People's Publishing House, 2004, p. 8.
2   *Collected Works of Marx and Engels*, Vol. 8, People's Publishing House, 2009, pp. 5-7.

capitalist stage, the object of research of the political economy of the capitalist stage will not be changed due to completion or non-completion of writing program of *Capital* by Marx or even Marx has made some changes in his research program. Some people who study Marx's classic statements, have explored the meaning of the term "means of production" in the works of Marx. They have found that most often, Marx's use of this term "means of production" refers to production or production process.. However, if we only literally discuss the "production mode" and production, or production mode and production process, obviously it will be very different. We see that if we merely remain in the form of logical analysis, we will have to distinguish "production mode" and "production" by splitting the phrase "production mode" or further distinguish the difference between production mode and production. However, for Marx such differentiation was unnecessary in his work, since Marx based himself on historical materialism as his basic study methodology. Marx said: "What we call capitalist production is such a social production mode, under this production mode, production process is subordinated to capital, or to say, this kind of production mode is based on the relationship between capital and wage labor, and this relationship is decisive in this capitalist production mode."[3] Obviously, Marx here simply defined capitalist production as capitalist production mode again. Marx said: "When speaking of production, production always refers to the production in a certain stage of social development—production by social individuals. It might seem, therefore, that in order to talk about production at all we must either pursue the process of historic development through its different phases, or declare beforehand that we are dealing with a specific historic epoch such as e.g. modern bourgeois production."[4] Marx explicitly stated that the object of research of political economy was the material production on a certain development stage of human history. According to the basic principles of historical materialism, material production at a certain historical stage is a specific kind of material production (namely a specific kind of social production mode) compared to the material social production in the previous historical stage as well as the previous historical stage compared to the material production in the preceding social historical stage. Therefore, the capitalist production mode, is the material production of capitalist society analyzed from the angle of historical materialism and dialectics viewpoint.

(II) Objectivity of the object of research of political economy

Some people mystify the term "production mode", which seems to be unfathomable, an abstract category hard to understand. As a matter fact, it is a realistic objective existence. Marx made the following the classic statement in *Capital*, the First Version, Volume I, "so far, one of typical places for this production mode is Britain. Therefore, I mainly use Britain as the example to introduce it. But if the German readers shrug their shoulders hypocritically when seeing the situation of British industrial and agricultural workers or they

---

3   *Collected Works of Marx and Engels*, Vol. 47, People's Publishing House, 1979, p. 151.
4   *Collected Works of Marx and Engels*, Vol. 8, People's Publishing House, 2009, pp. 5-7.

thought German situation not as bad as Britain's, and optimistically comfort themselves, then I would've shouted them and said: this is talking about what are you experiencing!"[5]

Marx emphasizes two points here: Firstly, typical place of capitalist mode of production is the British capitalist production; secondly, the law of development of this British capitalist production applies to future development of Germany, and also to an underdeveloped capitalist nation. Marx's analysis of capitalist mode of production is the reflection of this objective reality of capitalist production.

One scientific conclusion can be made just when facing an objective fact, and only one scientific conclusion can be made, which is the theory of reflection as the component part of the epistemology of Marxist dialectical materialism and historical materialism.

In fact, modern western economics also point to the mode of production of the modern capitalist economy as the objective object of research. However, bourgeois economics deny historical attribute (temporality) of capitalist social production, they regard capitalist production as the most ideal economic formation that has always existed without any change. They cannot tolerate Marxist economists regarding the laws of capitalist mode of production as one specific historic stage of human society, i.e. the specific economic laws of the capitalist stage. Domestic scholars cannot ignore the fact that Western bourgeois economics consider modern capitalist production as an objective object of research. Starting from the agnosticism of Western bourgeois philosophies, they can argue that the same objective object of research can be a basis to arrive at two or more different paradigms of economic theory, reversely economic theories guided by different paradigms can be objective reflections of economic reality, denying that there is one common objective truth which still can be the source of different paradigms of economic theory. According to this flawed rationale, neither of the two different paradigms of economic theory is not necessarily embody scientific truth; consequently they argue that none of the two paradigms of economic theory can be used to criticize the other. According to the Western bourgeois economics, generally resource allocation is equaled to—specific—capitalized source allocation which strives to conceal the historical attribute and class attribute of the term.

We believe that the divergence between Marxist economics and bourgeois economics is not whether to study resource allocation, or not which noun is used to generalize resource allocation (Marx uses mode of production, while western economics uses resource allocation), but the difference between the two is what kind of world outlook and methodology will be used to study the issue of resource allocation. Western bourgeois economics use metaphysical methodology to study resource allocation, and generally, ignores or deliberately covers up the historical attribute and class attribute of resource allocation,

---

5   Karl Marx, *Capital*, Volume 1, People's Publishing House, 2004, p. 8.

and it denies capitalism possesses a particular mode of resource allocation. On the other hand, Marxist economics use the scientific methodological element of dialectical materialism and historical materialism to study resource allocation from its universal aspect, and further deepens study of resource allocation from a particular/ specific aspect, i.e. capitalist-specific mode of resource allocation. In fact, resource allocation has social attributes. It is thus clear that resource allocation and mode of production are not the concepts that have much in common. The issue of resource allocation is in essence how to combine laborers (producers) with means of production, which is exactly what the mode of product — which mode is used to produce is revealed and explained. The ideological and class nature of western bourgeoisie decides that western economics focuses on the general production instead of capitalist-specific production, thus it focuses and proposes statements in regard to the general theory of resource allocation, snipping out the specific social and historical attributes of resource allocation. The mode of production studied by Marxist economics is complete mode of resource allocation. Therefore, it doesn't mean that the essence of the mode of production studied by political economy will change when a wise man creates a new noun: the current resource allocation.

II. Consistency of the formulation of the object of research of the political economy

From the analysis above, we conclude that, there is some difference from the aspect of subjective level between western bourgeois economics and Marxist economics, former taking the resource allocation as the object of research and latter the social mode of production. But if we look from the aspect of objectivity level, western bourgeois economics and Marxist economics have the same object of research. This common objective object of research of both is the material mode of production in the modern and contemporary capitalist society.

(I) Problem of unity regarding the formulations made by classical writers of Marxism on the object of research of political economy

1. Consistency among different formulations related to object of research of political economy made by Marxist classical writers

Although there are many different statements related to the object of research of political economy made by Marxist classical writers, a careful study can reveal that the essence of these statements is essentially consistent. As mentioned, Marx stipulates the object of research in the preface of *Capital*, the first edition, the first volume is "capitalist mode of production". Before that, Marx stipulates the object of research of the political economy is "material production" in *Introduction to the Critique of Political Economy*, written by Marx during 1857-1858. We also can use historical materialism method to unify the two seemingly different statements. Now, we look to the discourses of other Marxist classical writers.

In *Anti-Dühring*, Engels creatively proposed the concept of political economy in broad terms, "political economy, from the broadest sense, is the science to study the law of production and exchange of material subsistence in human society".[6] We argue that the term "in human society" in this context suggests that generalized political economy studies the economic laws that apply to all or some historical stages of human society. "Production and exchange of material means of subsistence" means "mode of production", because a certain mode of production dominates the production and exchange of the corresponding material means of living, that is, as Marx said, "the production relations and exchange relations apply to the mode of production. Engels added the following, "Political economy, however, as the science of the conditions and forms under which the various human societies have produced and exchanged and on this basis have distributed their products—political economy in this wider sense has still to be brought into being. Such economic science as we possess up to the present is limited almost exclusively to the genesis and development of the capitalist mode of production."[7] From this passage, made by Engels, we can see that the currently available material available is not enough to study political economy in broad general sense, but the currently available material can basis for the study of a specific historical stage in human society–the mode of production of capitalist society. Here, Engels echoed the Marxist view of studying a particular historical stage–capitalist social production. Therefore, on the issue of the object of research of the political economy, their points of view are the same.

After Engels, Stalin wrote in *Economic Problems of Socialism in the USSR*: "Political economy investigates the laws of development of men's relations of production,. which include: It includes: a) the forms of ownership of the means of production; b) the status of the various social groups in production and their interrelations that follow from these forms, or what Marx calls: "they exchange their activities" c) the forms of distribution of products, which are entirely determined by them."[8]

On the basis of accepting Stalin's definition of production relations, Mao Zedong made some progress. In his view, "the object of research of political economy is mainly production relations, but to study the production relations, it must be linked to research on productive forces, on the other hand it must be linked to study of positive and negative effects of the superstructure on the production relations."[9]

From the development process of representation of the object of research of political economy by Marx, Engels, Stalin and Mao Zedong, the classic Marxist writers have consistency in their basic guiding ideology. The writers

6   *Collected Works of Marx and Engels*, Vol. 9, People's Publishing House, 2009, p. 153.
7   *Collected Works of Marx and Engels*, Vol. 8, People's Publishing House, 2009, p. 56.
8   Stalin, *Economic Problems of Socialism in the USSR*, People's Publishing House, 1961, p. 58.
9   Mao Zedong, The Talks of Reading Soviet Textbook's Political Economy (Excerpt), *Mao Zedong Collected Works*, Volume 8, People's Publishing House, 1999, p. 131.

after Marx have inherited Marx's basic viewpoints on historical materialism and regarded social production in the historical stage of human society as the object of research of political economy. Marx defined the object of research of *Capital* as the capitalist social mode of production. On the basis of Marx, Engels put forward the concept of general political economy, which has laid a methodological basis for the later study of social production of the socialist society by Stalin and Mao Zedong. In fact, both Stalin and Mao Zedong creatively carried out their research work on socialist social production on the basis of fully affirming Marx's *Capital*'s study achievements of capitalist mode of social production. Stalin, on the basis of inheriting the achievements of Marx and Engels of production research on the historical stage of capitalism, studied the production of the subsequent historical periods of socialism in human society. In this sense, Stalin's viewpoints are consistent with Marx's and Engels', that is, to study material production of a certain historical stage.

2. Problem regarding the differences and consistency of the formulations made by Marxist classical writers on the object of research of political economy

Above, we have analyzed the problems of consistency of ideas put forward by the Marxist classical writers on the object of research of political economy from the angle of the basic world outlook and methodology. Now let's look at their differences in their specific ideas and how should we handle these differences. The main reason behind the differences among the scholars in regard to the study of political economy is the definition of "production relations" given by Stalin. Sun Yefang's fierce criticism of Stalin's definition of production relations mainly concentrated on two aspects: Firstly, the definition of Stalin on production relations did not include the exchange or circulation categories. Sun Yefang believes that it was Stalin's "very mistake that led to the later socialist economic theory of "no circulation (exchange) in socialism theory". Stalin wrote: The province of political economy is the production, the economic, relations of men. It includes: a) the forms of ownership of the means of production; b) the status of the various social groups in production and their interrelations that follow from these forms, or what Marx calls: "they exchange their activities"; c) the forms of distribution of products, which are entirely determined by them. Secondly, the production relations defined by Stalin has separated the forms of ownership of the means of production from the relations of production. In the history of economic theory, the petty-bourgeois economist Proudhon had also defined ownership system as an independent economic category. Criticizing Proudhon's point of view, Marx once wrote: "To try to give a definition of property as an independent relation, a category apart, an abstract and eternal idea, can be nothing but an illusion of metaphysics or jurisprudence."[10] By using and appreciating Marx's comprehensive analysis regarding the relations of production Sun Yefang has criticized Stalin as follows: "In addition to the production, exchange and distribution being included and listed as the components of the relations of production, Stalin talked about another

49

---

10 *Collected Works of Marx and Engels*, Vol. 4, People's Publishing House, 1958, p. 180.

form of ownership, which means suggesting the study of ownership outside the relations of production, I think which is bound to fall into metaphysical or juridical illusion."[11]

In his Reading Notes on the Soviet Text Book on Political Economy prepared under leadership of Stalin, Mao Zedong pointed to one drawback of this text: "In posing questions, in researching problems, it always proceeds from general concepts or definitions. It gives definitions without making reasoned explanations. In fact, a definition should be the result, not the starting point, of an analysis." Another disadvantage of the book is making definition at first without reason. Definition is the result of analysis, not the starting point of analysis."[12] Stalin's definition of the relations of production has also the similar shortcoming, which was mentioned by Mao Zedong above. Accordingly, Sun Yefang's above critique of Stalin's definition—which highlights "the forms of ownership of the means of production"—has hit the nail on the head. In fact, although the form of ownership of the means of production looks simple, the issue is not so simple. In *Economic Manuscripts of 1857-1858*, Marx criticized bourgeois economists as follows: "they separate system of ownership by making deductions from general theory of their textbooks, and judge them from the angle of promoting or obstructing production.[13] In his letter to Annenkov, dated December 28, 1848, Marx wrote: "Finally, property constitutes the last category in Mr Proudhon's system. In the really existing world, on the other hand, the division of labor and all Mr Proudhon's other categories are social relations which together go to make up what is now known as property; outside these relations bourgeois property is nothing but a metaphysical or juridical illusion."[14] Here Marx clearly states that the category of the means of production cannot be independent of the property relations, such as division of labor, machinery, competition, monopoly. On the contrary, division of labor, machinery, competition, monopolies and other economic study fields come together to show a certain ownership form of the means of production of society. Therefore, in Stalin's definition of the relations of production, it is clear his emphasis on the ownership of the means of production demonstrates the misfortune of "metaphysics and juridical illusion."

Now let us discuss why there is no "exchange" in Stalin's definition of the relations of production. Stalin's explanation is based on such a thinking: since the "exchange" is understood as "commodity exchange" by most people, but the socialist society is not a commodity-producing society, in order to avoid misunderstanding, he wanted to write "the status of the various social groups

---

11   Sun Yefang, The Theory of Production Relation as the Object of Research of Political Economy, *Journal of Economic Research*, 1979(8). Sun Yefang paved the way to separately study the economics of the relations of production from the economics of the productive forces, criticized Stalin's excessive emphasis ownership factor in the production relations.
12   Mao Zedong, The Talks of Reading Soviet's the Textbook's Political Economy (Excerpt), *Mao Zedong Collected Works*, Vol. 8, People's Publishing House, 1999, p. 139.
13   *Collected Works of Marx and Engels*, Vol. 8, People's Publishing House, 2009, p. 11.
14   *Collected Works of Marx and Engels*, People's Publishing House, 1958, p. 48.

in production and their interrelations" as a substitute for "exchange" in the capitalist society.[15] Here, it is necessary to point out that the demise of commodity and currency relations in the non-capitalist society of the future is the fully agreed view of classical writers, including Marx and Engels. Although the current socialist practice has broken through this understanding, but this practice still needs further development and maturity, in this sense whether Stalin's this revision of definition is correct or not, will be tested by the historical development of human society.

(II) The problem of consistence among the formulations made by contemporary Marxist economists regarding the object of research of political economy

Sun Yefang's critique of Stalin's definition of production relations has aroused controversy in China's economic circles. On the issue of the object of research of political economy—affected by the views of Sun Yefang—some economists have returned to the original definitions of Marx and Engels. Many economists still adhere to Stalin's definition on the relations of production, but these economists do not seem to insist on the original statement of Stalin's definition of relations of production, instead they emphasize Mao's additions to Stalin's definition of production relations Consequently Mao Zedong's view on linking the productive forces with the superstructure when studying the relations of production is included in the conception and definition. At present, the following viewpoints are more influential in the academic circles: (1) The "mode of production approach". It is believed that the object of research of political economy is the mode of material production and production relations and the exchange relations corresponding to it. This is based on the preamble of Marx's *Capital*, first volume, first edition. (2) "The theory of intermediary production mode." It is believed that the object of research of political economy is the capitalist mode of production. Economists with this view put forward the principle of "productive forces-production-production relations" according to Marx's relevant representations. According to this principle, the mode of production is a intermediary range between the productive forces and the relations of production. Productive forces do not directly determine the relations of production, but it determines the mode of production and in turn the mode of production, further determines the relations of production. (3) "The mode of labor theory." It is believed the object of research of political economy is the social mode of capitalist labor process. The economists with this view have studied the use of the term "mode of production" in Marx's *Capital* and made the following conclusion: The mode of production as the object of research of political economy should refer to the mode of labor. (4) "Duality of mode of production." Starting from the duality of the production process, some economists has come to the conclusion that the mode of production has duality. The mode of production includes the natural form of production and the social form of production. (5) "Production relations". Some scholars argued that the object

51

---

15   Stalin, *Economic Problems of Socialism in the USSR*, People's Publishing House, 1961, p. 58.

of research of political economy is the production relations, but also based on their understanding of the connotation of the relations of production, these economists adhere to Stalin's definition of production relations.

In fact, the above-mentioned three kinds of viewpoints of (2), (3) and (4) are concrete explanations of the "mode of production" in the view of (1). So in this sense, the five academic viewpoints can be summed up in two major factions: the mode of production factions and the production relations factions. If we agree that Marx, Engels, Stalin and other classical writers study political economy under the guidance of historical materialism, we will advocate the point of view of political economy studying production relations should be understood as follows: we should focus on the social production of a certain historical period of human society. In this way we can unify the different theoretical perspectives advocated by contemporary Marxist economists in regard to the object of research of political economy. Of course, our view to focus "social production" unifies contemporary Marxist economists' different theoretical point of view from a certain social and historical point of view, but will not eliminate their differences in regard to their specific elaborations. The object of research of political economy is the social production mode of human society at a certain stage of development, which takes production from its 2 dual attributes, i.e. its natural attributes and social attributes. "Production relations" emphasizes the social attributes of production, while it ignores the natural attributes of production. Moreover, most scholars have inherited Stalin's definition of production relations without critique, because Stalin has metaphysically put the ownership of the means of production as prior compared to production relations, thus has great limitations.

The "mode of labor theory" emphasizes the natural attributes of production, while it ignores the social attributes of production. Of course, when we discuss the duality of the mode of production and its meanings we should also pay attention to the unity of different views. For example, in the classic Marxist works, the words used to express the same meaning as the mode of production include: the combination of certain social production, laborers and means of production, socio-economic form, and social production type, and so on. It does not make any sense to seek for gaps between these categories that have the same meaning with the mode of production. The expressions used to express the same meaning as "the mode of production is the unity of dual natures of production". And some say: mode of production is the unity of the natural attributes of production and the social attributes of production, and others say: the mode of production is unity of productive forces and production relations, and some say: mode of production is unification of mode of labor and capitalist exploitation, and there are many other statements. There is also no practical significance to find a gap between the false propositions, for example, modes\ of production is the unity of the dual natures of production. However, it should be pointed out that the consistency of these dual natures has an important realistic meaning to the unity of the Marxist economists.

In addition to the above-mentioned two camps of "relations of production" and "modes of production", there are also views that argue that the mode of production has multiple meanings. They argue that in Marx's writings the concept of Marx's mode of production has different meanings in different places. *The Mode of Production Has Different Meanings in Different Places* by Peng Xinzheng (1985), Xi Zhaoyong's (1998) *How to Understand Marx's Mode of Production–One of the Researches on Capital.*

Xi Zhaoyong argues that, "The way in which people reproduce themselves and produce their means of subsistence is one of the many meanings of the mode of production. And this is in fact means that the 'mode of production' is perceived in the sense of material production or productive forces."[16] In Marx's writings, the way in which people produce themselves and produce their means of subsistence is the mode of production. One can say that the mode of production emphasizes the importance of productive forces, but it cannot be said that the whole content of the mode of production is explained from the meaning of productive forces. It is obviously wrong to think that Marx's this statement means that he understands the mode of production from the aspect of productive forces. Can we say that that the way in which people reproduce themselves and their means of subsistence does not have any content of social relations of production? In fact, the way in which people reproduce themselves and their means of subsistence is the mode of production, encompasses both the mode of production in the sense of productive forces and the mode of production in the sense of production relations. As long as we are discussing production, whether people reproduce themselves or producing their means of subsistence, the subject and object of production cannot be separated, we cannot ignore the unity of the subject and object. In fact, within the unity of the producers and their object, their production not only has natural attributes, but also has social attributes.

Xi Zhaoyong wrote: "For Marx, production of relative surplus value, has revolutionized the technical properties of labor and social forms of organization of labor. Therefore, we can say the production of relative surplus value, is specific to capitalist mode of production and premise of this mode (my note: in the sense of productive forces) . In this way Marx gave another further meaning to the understanding of "mode of production" by analyzing labor from 2 aspects: material-technical properties of labor and social forms of organization of labor."[17]

In this statement of Marx quoted by Xi Zhaoyong, the "mode of production" corresponds to "material-technical properties of labor and social forms of organization of labor." If we look into the comment given by Xi Zhaoyong, we can clearly see that Xi Zhaoyong neglects that the "material-technical properties of

16　Xi Zhaoyong, How to Understand the "Mode of Production" said by Marx – About One of Research of the Object of research of "Capital", *Contemporary Economic Research*, 1998(4).

17　Ibid.

labor and social forms of organization of labor," which in fact means and embodies the duality of the production process: here I must say the material-technical properties of labor is the natural attribute (natural form) of labor, on the other hand the "social forms of organization of labor" is the social attribute, i.e. the social forms of labor.

I think that in this passage, Marx didn't abstract the social attributes of the mode of production, because he wanted to discuss the particular mode of production in the analysis of specific capitalism. There is no doubt that one socio-economic form or social production type is different from another socio-economic form, not only lies in the difference of the level of development of productive forces, but also the significant difference in social relations of production. Therefore, when we analyze specific mode of production under a specific socio-economic form, we should not abstract out the social attributes of production methods, because specific production mode is the specific nature of relations (combination) between workers and means of production under specific technical (natural) conditions and social integration methods determine this combination.

It is undoubtedly true, that the mode of production as one object of research of political economy refers to the research regarding combination of workers and means of production; moreover, it is the sole meaning of the mode of production which the dual nature of nature and society. But at the same time we must clear the relations between these 3 categories: productive forces, modes of production and relations of production However, Peng Xinzheng (1985) argues that "productive forces determine modes of production and the modes of production determines the relations of production."[18] Here the mode of production is understood as an independent category between productive forces and relations of production and then Peng Xinzheng thinks that productive forces determine mode of production, and then mode of production, determines the relations of production. We believe that this view is inappropriate. In fact, when we look into a certain mode of production, there must be a certain degree of social relations of production embodied in it, and in turn, a certain degree of social relations of production can only exist in a certain way of material production, and cannot be kept outside it. Marx said: "The hand-mill gives you society with the feudal lord; the steam-mill society with the industrial capitalist."19 In accordance with Marx's understanding, hand-mill mode of production, refers to feudal social productive forces, i.e. marks their level of development. At the same time feudal society, peasants have a certain personal dependence on feudal landlords which is a production relationship, which is embodied in the feudal production mode. Similarly, mode of production of the steam-mill is a sign of the level of development of the productive forces of the

18   Peng Xinzhen, Different Meaning of Mode of Production in Different Places, *Social Sciences in China*, 1985(4).
19   Karl Marx, *The Poverty of Philosophy*, Collected Works of Marx and Engels, People's Publishing House, 2009, p. 602.

capitalist society, and embodies the social relations wherein capitalists exploit the wage-laborers, thus the relation which embodies exploitative productive relations are also included in this mode of production. Correspondingly, the political economy (feudal stage), which aims at revealing the relations of production and exchange in the feudal society, its direct object of research should be the mode production in the form of hand-mill production. Similarly, political economy, in order to reveal the relations of production and exchange in the capitalist society, its direct object of research of research should be the mode production in the form of steam-mill production. Therefore, we advocate that in this way the object of research of political economy returns to classic representation given in the first volume of Marx's *Capital*.

In summary, the object of research of Marxist political economy is the social production in the certain historical stage of human society, and is a specific mode of social production from a historical materialist point of view. It refers to the combination mode of workers and means of production, as well as unity of natural and social attributes of production. In the classical works of Marx and Engels, the mode of production has only this specific and unique meaning. The so-called multiple meanings of the mode of production are just different manifestations of the duality of mode of production. Political economy is not technology, its research focus is to reveal the social attributes of a certain social production, which means to reveal certain production relations and exchange relations in a certain society. Marxist political economy adheres to the theory of reflection of materialist theory of epistemology. Therefore—social mode of production—as the object of research of political economy, is an objective historical existence, therefore, Marxist economists' representation on this objective historical existence should also be objective, and integral.

III. Clarification of realistic significance of objectivity as the object of research of political economy and discussing their relevance according to socialist economic theory with Chinese characteristics

(I) To clarify the consistency between the objectivity in research and the definition of object of research of political economy. This is conducive to our understanding of social mode of production within a certain stage of human society and a certain production relationship and the exchange relationship corresponding to it, and also it is conducive to adhering to the guiding position of Marxist economics in the field of economics

1. Strictly differentiate between the capitalist stage and the socialist stage of political economy and achieve new breakthroughs and new developments in the study of socialist economic theory with Chinese characteristics

In accordance with the view of historical materialism, Engels put forward the idea of broad connotations of the political economy, common law of historical stages of human society and also he defined the political economy in narrow sense as "the study of economic laws in a specific historical stage of human society. Engels also pointed out that only Marx had contributed to the study of economics in the various social and historical stages of the capitalist mode of production. For the political economy of the capitalist mode of production, Marx's *Capital* is the supreme achievement obtained based on inheriting outstanding achievements of bourgeois classical economics, and abandoning the dross part, i.e. the bourgeois vulgar economics in it. The socialist revolution gained victory in the Soviet Union and in Eastern European countries; "theory of disappearance of the political economy discipline" was once popular in Soviet Union and the Eastern European countries, which denied the existence of socialist political economy.

Stalin deeply studied the mode of production of socialist society, and criticized the "theory of disappearance of political economy" which was included in the *Economic Problems of Socialism in the USSR* and had an epoch-marking significance, and he personally presided over the preparation of this *Political Economy Textbook*, laying the foundation for the Political Economy of the Socialist Mode of Production. With the failure of the socialist countries, the Soviet Union and Eastern European countries in the late 1980s and early 1990s, the socialist political economy was excluded from the mainstream ideology in these countries. In our country, with deeper understanding of the basic national conditions of the primary stage of socialism, and as we continue to learn from the process of Reform and Opening-up the introduction and absorption of developed capitalist countries, economic management experience and economic management methods, some people mistakenly believe that China has abandoned socialism and taken the capitalist road, so they have advocated abolition of socialist political economy. In the field of economic theory and economics education, the research and propaganda work of socialist political economy has been diluted and negated unduly.

In the Marxist economic theory, advocating to cancel the boundary between the political economy of capitalism stage and socialism stage, and to combine them in a unified economics study, in our view, this is a false economic thought.

According to the Marxist view of historical materialism, human society through the leadership of the working class and its political party, through the socialist revolution, conquered the power and opened a new era of human history, a new socialist society is a new social form which is fundamentally different from that of capitalist society. Socialist political economy, which studies socialist social production, has emerged as a result. We know that new things, develop from weak to strong, and will finally assume dominant status in the field of economics. Of course, temporarily, since the current socialism is still in a difficult time, socialism with Chinese characteristics must also overcome difficulties to move forward, at this stage of socialist political economy also need to continue to boldly explore. But this cannot deny the existence of socialist political economy, we must get out of the wrong idea of copying Western bourgeois economics copy of the errors, and realize new breakthroughs and new developments in socialist economic theory with Chinese characteristics.

2. Adhering to the dominant position of Marxist economics and analysis of critical reference to Western bourgeois economics

In China's economics academy and economics education circles, there is such an erroneous view and erroneous practice which is prevalent: the Marxist political economy and Western economics are regarded as the two "independent" sciences regarding their object of research, research purposes and research methods, or they argue that we should not use Marxist political economy to criticize Western economics, and we cannot use Western economics to affirm our Marxist political economy. Some people have even suggested that the advantage of Marxist political economy is that it reveals the nature of the economic process, its shortcoming is that it does not reveal the operation of the economic process. On the contrary, they argue that the advantage of Western economics is that it reveals the economic process, while ignoring the study of the nature of the economic processes. And these people advocate the integration or combination of Marxist political economy and Western economics. We disagree with this view and proposition. Starting from the principle of the objectivity of the object of research of political economy we can see that the object of research of political economy is not a mysterious thing, but the objective existence of capitalist social production. Marx's *Capital* has taken the objective existence of the British capitalist production as the object of research, the object of this study in this book is Adam Smith and David Ricardo and the modern Western bourgeois economics developed by them. The objective law of the economic process is objective, according to the Marxist materialist epistemological theory of reflection, the theory of political economy is the only scientific political economy, and this is the Marxist political economy. Western economics is the economics of the Western bourgeois. The bourgeoisie was once an advanced class representing the progress of society in the history of mankind, but with the development of social history, after the anti-feudal task in the Anglo-French capitalist countries was completed, the bourgeoisie was transformed from a progressive class to a decaying class of the capitalist reactionary rule. In accordance with the change of class status of the bourgeoisie, accordingly, bourgeois economics also changed from bourgeois classical economics to bourgeois vulgar economics. Contemporary Western bourgeois economics is also a kind of vulgar economics. In dealing with the attitude of modern Western bourgeois economics, we should make concrete analysis on specific economic theory and take its essence to the dregs in the basic world outlook and methodology principle of dialectical materialism and historical materialism. The truth of Marxist political economy lies in its ability to reveal the natures hidden behind the economic phenomena, while the fatal weakness of modern western bourgeois economics is that it only focuses on the superficial appearance of the phenomena of economic operation. Here there is no so-called division of labor and cooperation between Marxist political economy and Western economics. In short, it is clear that there is consistency between definition of the object of research of political economy and the objectivity of political economy studies, this consistency helps for our grasp regarding a certain historical period of human society, its social mode of production and its production relations and the exchange relations corresponding to them. This approach is conducive to upholding Marxist economics, as the guide in the field of economics.

(II) Further clarifying the consistency between the objectivity and the definition of the object of research of political economy is conducive to guide China's cause of Reform and Opening-up with scientific theory

In accordance with the basic view of historical materialism, after the capitalist society is replaced by a socialist society, we must establish new socialist economic relations. The system of ownership as a core relationship must be studied within the entire socialist relations of production, otherwise the Proudhonist mistake is inevitable. In fact, the socialist countries of the Soviet Union and Eastern Europe established the public ownership of the means of production according to the definition of relations of production given by Stalin after the working class seized power, but the public ownership of the means of production of these countries have failed to be used in developing in social production. There are many reasons for this, however, economic reasons should not be overlooked. As mentioned above, Stalin separated the form of ownership of production means from other aspects of the relations of production, and Sun Yefang has rightly criticized Stalin for repeating Proudhon's mistakes. In our view, Sun Yefang's criticism is justified.

The famous Marxist economist of the Soviet Union, D.I. Rozenberg, has focused on the analysis of political economy sticking on ownership relations, in order to see the relations of production in distorting mirror. "Proudhon did not study the reality of production relations, instead 'studied' the issue as what he saw in the distorted mirror of bourgeois."[20] In fact, Marx attached great importance to the analysis of capitalist ownership system within capitalist production. But Marx did not directly write any chapter in *Capital* named as "capitalist ownership". According to Marx's critique of Proudhon, "in every historical era, ownership has developed differently and under a set of entirely different social relations.[21] If we say the capitalist system of private ownership of capitalism is operated in the 4 links of capitalist production, distribution, exchange and consumption, then why can socialist public ownership of the means of production cannot be able to produce socialist production, distribution, exchange and

20   D.I. Rozenberg, *History of Political Economy*, Volume 3, SDX Joint Publishing Company, 1960, p. 259.
21   Karl Marx, *The Poverty of Philosophy*, Collected Works of Marx and Engels, People's Publishing House, 2009, p 638

consumption and other specific aspects of development and expansion of them? Unfortunately, Sun Yefang's critique of Stalin's definition of production relations has not been well recognized by our economists. Many researchers either fall into the quagmire of property-rights analysis as advocated by the Western school of property rights, or have not yet separated themselves from metaphysics and jurisprudence. State-owned enterprises having "ambiguous or illusory property rights" or "the theory of absence of property rights" in the SOEs, in essence, argue that all levels of Chinese government does not represent the interests of people, or there is a chaos at the government level. These above theories of state-owned enterprises having "ambiguous or illusory property rights" or "the theory of absence of property rights" in the SOEs is actually advocating the death of our state-owned enterprises. So, we should ask a question: who can ensure that these other agents or institutions respected by these economists, such as the "investment companies" will be able to represent the interests of all the people, and that the "investment companies" will not cause? It should also be noted that, currently, people usually focus only on whether state-owned enterprises are privatized at a low price or only focus on the proportion of the state-owned economy in the whole national economy. However, nobody asks: is not the public ownership of the means of production the result of public ownership of the social production? Can the socialist public ownership really grow vigorously in the socialist relations of production? From the long-term perspective of socialist construction, why state-owned enterprises or publicly owned enterprises cannot be privatized for their full values? This is the key to the issue! Only if the public ownership of the means of production can play its effective role in social production, can we can talk about real socialist economic relation. Just as the territory of a country is the basic premise for the people of a country, the socialist public ownership of the means of production is also the premise for the survival and development of the vast working masses. Therefore, the public ownership of the means of production, should be treated as the territory of a sovereign state: "Even an inch of land has to be fought for!"

General Secretary Xi Jinping has stressed: "the state-owned enterprises should achieve self-improvement which means the deepening the reform, in the manner of the Phoenix Nirvana rebirth." Comrade Xi Jinping's thoughts on reforming state-owned enterprises has put forward the important task for our socialist political economy to study and design the social production mode of socialist production and the corresponding relations of production and exchange. Our socialist political economy should achieve have scientific revolution on the issue of object of research of political economy, on its research methods and other aspects in order to complete glorious and arduous historical missions we encounter in this great era!

Originally published in the journal
Taxation and Economy, 2014(4)

Did Marx Abandon the Theory of Tendency of the Rate of Profit To Fall?

*— The New Debate of the Law of the Rate of Profit to Fall
Triggered after the Publication of MEGA²II*

61

Xie Fusheng and Wang Jiateng

Abstract: Based on the study of the recent *MEGA²* text, M. Heinrich claimed that Marx not only abandoned the theory of the rate of profit to fall, but also failed to establish a complete crisis theory. Heinrich's article has sparked a heated debate at the international level. The relevant arguments seem to give an exaggerated emphasis on Engels revision of Marx, and even claim that Engels has deviated from Marx, which is quite doubtful and irresponsible. Marx never abandoned the theory of the rate of profit to fall, in short TRPF. Whether theoretically or empirically, the theory that the rate of profit tends to fall can be proved. Marx has fundamentally completed the construction of the general theory of crisis and developing a concrete crisis theory in combination with reality requires the continuous efforts of contemporary Marxists.

Key words: *MEGA²*; the theory of TRPF; theory of economic crisis

Introduction

The rate of profit is one of the most important concepts in Marxist economics. The rate of profit determines and influences the condition of capitalist accumulation. The rate of profit not only analyzes the macro-economic steady nature of capitalism, but also explains the staged nature of the development of capitalism.[1] Scholars of classical economics have paid attention to the empirical fact that along with the development of capitalism, the rate of profit tends to fall. Smith believed that the fall of the rate of profit is caused by the rise of wages and the fall of commodity prices caused by the intensification of competition caused by capital accumulation;[2] Ricardo believed that the population growth and the diminishing marginal returns on land causes an increase of wages, which in turn leads to the fall of the rate of profit;[3] John Stuart Mill believed that commercial revulsion, improvements in production, imports of cheap necessaries and tools and capital exports are the main factors hindering the fall of the rate of profit, but he also for the first time linked the fall of the rate of profit to the economic crisis ("commercial revulsion").[4] Marx pointed out that competition is the result of the role that capitalist economic laws are brought into play, not the cause, and that competition among different sectors of industry is the cause which sets off the equalization of the rate of profit and forms the general rate of profit, but competition does not lead to the fall of the general rate of profit.[5]

62In the Volume III of *Capital*, which was edited and completed by Engels, Marx pointed out: "The progressive tendency of the general rate of profit to fall is, therefore, just an expression peculiar to the capitalist mode of production of the progressive development of the social productivity of labour."[6] Marx put forward a well-known theory: Competition makes the capital through the increase of labor productivity to gain the value of proliferation, promote the organic composition of capital which leads to the tendency of falling rate of profits. In the long run, the tendency of decline in the rate of profits will undermine the basis for capital accumulation and will accelerate the demise of the capitalist system as a historical social formation. In the period after the publication of the third volume of *Capital*, many controversial studies were made regarding the fall of rate of profits and which discussed and evaluated Marx's theory. The controversy mainly revolves around two issues: tthe first thread concentrates on the logic, that is, whether the theory itself holds logically. One is the negation of the theory from the relationship between the organic

---

1   G. Duménil and D. Levy, *The Economics of the Rate of Profit*, Aldershot: Edward Elgar, 1993, pp. 4-12.

2   Smith, *An Inquiry into the Nature and Causes of the Wealth of Nations*, edited by Edwin Cannan (London: Methuen, 1904), p. 89.

3   Ricardo, *The Principles of Political Economy and Taxation*, London: John Murray, 1888, p. 76.

4   Mill, *Principles of Political Economy*, London: John W. Parker, West Strand, 1849, p. 90.

5   *Collected Works of Marx and Engels*, Vol. 46 (Lower Half), People's Publishing House, 1980, p. 271.

6   Karl Marx, *Capital*, Volume III, Penguin, 1981, p 319. .

composition of capital and the surplus value rate, and the second is based on the "salt theorem" , i.e. the mathematical model of the production price system proposed by Sraffa, that is, all the new technology aiming to reduce costs will lead to the increase in rate of profits. The second thread focuses on exploring the relationship between the decline in rate of profits and the capitalist economic crises. After the Great Depression of the 1930s, some Marxists began to consider the rise of organic composition of capital as the starting point of the crisis theory. In the 1970s, E. Mandel pointed out that the core issue of the long-term fluctuation of the world capitalist economic growth rate is the long-term trend of change in the rate of profit in the process of capital accumulation, his research has paved the way to a large number of empirical researches.[7]

In August 2012, with the efforts of many Marxist scholars from Germany, Japan and Russia, the second edition of the historical edition of *Complete Works of Marx and Engels*, Part II, *MEGA²* (Marx's *Capital* and its Preparatory Manuscripts) was completely published. *MEGA² II*'s publication has aroused strong interest in the international academic community, and, some scholars began to comment and make new interpretations after this new publication, which has caused a new round of debate. Michael Heinrich wrote in the journal of Monthly Review that the latest textual interpretation presented in the *MEGA²* publication indicates that Marx has not only "failed to prove" the falling tendency of rate of profits, but was always been skeptical of this assertion. The theory of crisis based on the decline of rate of profits presented in the third volume of *Capital* is only the result of Engels' intervention; Marx himself does not have complete crisis theory at all.[8] Heinrich's article immediately aroused a heated debate, Marxist economists from many countries have soon participated in this discussion. The publication of Heinrich's article brought about a wave of criticisms in the Internet written by Marxists such as Michael Roberts and A. Freeman who base their crisis theory precisely on Marx's law of the "tendency of the rate of profit to fall," or TRPF for short, the discussion was also echoed in China and domestic Marxist scholars have made more than 80 long comments on the issue. Secondly, we will first introduce Heinrich's basic ideas and logic, and then introduce the refutations made by the foreign Marxist economists refutations to his article, and finally, put forward our views by focusing on Marx's relevant discourse.[9]

---

7   Howard, *A History of Marxian Economics: 1929-1990*, Central Compilation & Translation Press, 2003, pp. 130-150, 317-322

8   M. Heinrich, Crisis Theory, the Law of the Tendency of the Rate of profit to Fall, and Marx's Studies in the 1870s, *Monthly Review* 2013(4), pp. 15-31.

9   Michael Roberts, Michael Heinrich, *Marx's Law and Crisis Theory*, http://thenextrecession.wordpress.com/2013/05/19/michael-heinrich-marxs-law-and-crisis-theory/

I. Heinrich's New Argument:
"Marx gave up the theory of TPRF"

Heinrich is a professor of economics at the School of Industrial and Economics, Berlin, Germany and is the managing editor of "PROKLA - Journal for Critical Social Sciences." His "new reading" of Marx apparently dominates the study of Marx in German universities. His main research interests are Marx's theory of economic theory and political economy, and the development of contemporary capitalism. His book "Guide to the Three Volumes of *Capital*" was published and translated by the Monthly Review Press (USA) in 2012.[10] As a German Marxist economics scholar, based on the *MEGA* text reading, his most basic view is that *Capital* should certainly be regarded as an unfinished work. So, in this latest article, how did Heinrich interpret Marx's theory of rate of profit tended to decline?

(I) Was the "Analysis Framework" changed by Marx

Heinrich had formerly suggested that Marx "did not make the final statement of his crisis theory"[11], Marx's theory of the crisis is not only unclear in its formulation, but also its theoretical building was incomplete, because Marx's "analytical framework" was always erratic. Heinrich basic assumptions are as follows: (1) Marx's attitude in regard to crisis theory has changed. In *The Communist Manifesto*, published in 1848, the economic crisis was seen as a direct threat to capitalist society. After the crisis which broke out in 1857-1858, Marx has paid close attention to the situation and made a lot of research, and wrote the manuscripts of *Foundations of the Critique of Political Economy (Rough Draft)* in short *Grundrisse*. However, this economic crisis soon passed, and the capitalist countries did not encounter social and political crises. "After 1857-1858, Marx no longer insisted in his theory that the capitalist economy will face a final total collapse, and gave up directly linking the crisis and revolution."[12] (2) Consequently, Marx changed his concepts and defined his new approach in his later manuscripts. For example, in *Grundrisse*, Marx had not made a distinction between "abstract labor" and "concrete labor", and stressed that the theory of duality of labor is "the key to understanding political economy." In another example, Marx originally intended to distinguish between "capital in general" and "competitive capital", but after 1863, he no longer referred to the concept of "capital in general". (3) Marx's writing plan has changed. In the *Preface to A Introduction to the Critique of Political Economy*, published in 1857-1858, Marx mentioned about his famous six-volume writing plan (capital, land tenure, wage labor, state, foreign trade, world markets). Between 1861-1863, he found that the six volumes were so complex that they could not be completed, and he announced that his study will be limited to the book of capital. As a result, Heinrich held that *Economic Manuscripts of*

64

10   M. Heinrich, *An Introduction to the Three Volumes of Karl Marx's Capital*, New York: Monthly Review Press, 2012.
11   M. Heinrich (2013), pp. 15-31.
12   Ibid.

1857-1858, *Economic Manuscripts of 1861-1863* and *Economic Manuscripts of 1863-1865* collectively assumed as the 3 manuscripts of *Capital*, are "problematic", because this assumption implies that Marx's research ideas have consistent continuity, thus such assumption obscures the transformation of Marx's theoretical framework.[13] With 1863 as the boundary, all manuscripts of Marx should be regarded as two separate sets of manuscripts: first set was, 1857-1863 the six volumes of *Critique of Political Economy*, and second set is the writings between 1863-1883, i.e. the four volumes of *Capital*.[14]

(II) The "failure" of the law of the TPRF

For Marx's law of declining rate of profit, Heinrich's interpretation is that, "according to Marx's theory, in the long run, the rate of profit will fall."[15] That is to say, Marx concluded that the law of rate of profit will always operate under any circumstances. Marx argued that in any case, the rate of profit will tend to fall. Based on such an absolute understanding, Heinrich began his criticism.

Firstly, the empirical research results cannot prove the declining trend of profits. He said: "starting from this law, Marx introduced a series of hypotheses, and these hypotheses cannot be proved theoretically, it is impossible to be certified. This 'Law' claimed that under the capitalist mode of production, with the development of productive forces a decline in rate of profits would be inevitable. Even if the rate of profits have fallen in the past years, it cannot be an evidence to support the theory. Because any law intends to describe the future, and from the facts of the past, we cannot get any conclusions about the future. Even if there are increases in the rate of profits in the past, this law of Marx cannot be refuted. Because Marx's law itself does not stipulate that the rates of profit will fall forever, only stipulates that a downward 'trend' will be there, and in the future may be possible."[16] Heinrich thus cancels a lot of positive or negative empirical research results.

Secondly, Heinrich questions Marx's formula regarding rate of profits tending to decline. According to Marx the rate of profit can be expressed as follows:

$$p = (s/v) / (1 + c/v)$$

In this formula the s denotes the surplus value, c denotes the constant capital, v denotes the variable capital, and p denotes the rate of profit. Obviously, the rate of profit and the surplus value rate s / v changes in the same direction, and the change of the organic composition shows a reverse direction. If we assume that the organic composition is rising and the surplus value remains constant, then the rate of profit will decline. This is what Marx called "the law itself," in which the rate of profit tends to decline. In spite of a series of "counter-measures" that would be taken by the capitalist class, Marx has argued that in the long run these

---

13   Ibid.
14   *Collected Works of Marx and Engels*, Vol. 31, People's Publishing House, 1972.
15   M. Heinrich (2013), pp. 15-31.
16   Ibid.

measures will not be sufficient to reverse the trend of declining rate of profits. Heinrich argued that the question was not whether the "law itself" would be able to overwhelm all "counter-measures" but that the "law itself" is not logically valid. In his view, the accumulation of capital on the one hand leads to the increase of organic composition, on the other hand leads to an increase in the rate of surplus value, which may offset the decline in rate of profits. Heinrich has stressed that Marx's conclusion is based on the assumption that the elements of the formula to be constant, but the rate of surplus value is not constant. Marx has elaborated the mechanism of relative surplus value production: the development of productive forces causes the technological progress, which is characterized by economizing of labor, thus wages become cheaper; in regard to real wages and working hours, the necessary labor time of workers is reduced. The surplus labor time lengthens. Thus, while technological progress leads to an increase in organic composition (an increase in denominator), it also leads to an increase in the rate of surplus-value since "we have no evidence which of the above changes faster", we cannot determine in which direction will the rate of profit will change. Heinrich has commented that Marx has always been unable to draw the final conclusion, so he repeatedly asserted that rate of profit will decline, and the more repetitive, Marx's own doubts have become more and more "obvious".

Thirdly, Marx has pointed out that the relative surplus value production leads to an increase in the rate of surplus value, although to some extent this is offset by the rise in organic composition caused by the decline in rate of profit, but this offsetting has a certain limit. "Two labourers, each working 12 hours daily, cannot produce the same mass of surplus-value as 24 who work only 2 hours, even if they could live on air and hence did not have to work for themselves at all. In this respect, then, the compensation of the reduced number of labourers by intensifying the degree of exploitation has certain insurmountable limits. It may, for this reason, well check the fall in the rate of profit, but cannot prevent it altogether."[17] Heinrich sees this proof as invalid: "Marx's conclusion is only correct if the capital (c + v) necessary to employ the two workers is of an amount at least as great as that required to employ twenty-four workers before."[18] Heinrich has argued that in the formula $p = s / (c + v)$, Marx only demonstrated that the surplus value s on the numerator may decline, but Marx did not take into account the devaluation of the advanced capital (c + v) on the denominator. With the development of productive forces, the value v of variable capital decreases, and this decline is not necessarily set off by the increase in the value of constant capital c, so the denominator does not necessarily increase; and once the denominator and numerator are reduced, the change of the rate of profit in the formula will be uncertain. In short, Heinrich has argued that the development of productive forces will make the means of production and worker's subsistence materials cheaper, consequently the advance capital to be invested will decrease, which may cause an increase in the rate of profits.

---

17   Karl Marx, *Capital*, Vol. 3, People's Publishing House, 2004, p. 356
18   M. Heinrich (2013), pp. 15-31.

(III) Theory of crisis: Was it Marx's or Engels'?

Heinrich claimed that the re-reading of *MEGA²* shows that, *Capital*, Volume III appears to present a more systematic and complete theory of the crisis, in fact, this is just an illusion due to random interventions made by Engels. Heinrich has argued that Marx's ideas regarding the theory of crisis is sporadically scattered throughout his many works, which lacks a complete system. In Marx's manuscript, this part of the manuscript on the falling trend in rate of profits was not divided into chapters, and had no subheadings; all the divisions in this chapter and the subheadings were added, by Engels. Heinrich wrote: "Engels has greatly modified the material left by Marx, he put together a chapter based on the 'law' worked on these materials, with additions, deletions, corrections, and divided it into four parts. This gives the reader the impression that Marx had already fundamentally completed his work on the crisis theory".[19]

Heinrich argued that Marx's emphasis on the lack of effective demand of workers in many places of his manuscripts does not imply that Marx favored the theory of under-consumption, but his emphasis at least suggests that he believed a complete theory of crisis must include an analysis of the interest-bearing capital and the credit system. Marx also did not intend to treat the "probable" decline in rate of profits as the basis of his crisis theory, to build a value does not involve the realization of the crisis theory. However, Marx could not complete his studies on the credit, and the central (National) bank and other issues due to his death. Engels, who had inherited his manuscripts, did not follow the research direction of Marx, instead, he, according to his approach "collaged" a theory of crises based on the increasing trend of organic composition and declining rate of rate of profits, thus caused a great delusion for Marx's followers. Therefore, the "systematic" crisis theory in the Volume III which was long studied and recognized by the people, is rather the product of Engels' ideas.

(IV) Marx's research in 1870s was trapped in self-doubt and self-negation

Further, Heinrich put forward a more shocking view: Marx has doubted on the decline of rate of profit, and in fact have admitted that he cannot complete *Capital*. Firstly, Heinrich claimed that Marx had doubts about the downward trend in rate of profits: "His doubts on the law of declining rate of profits must be a big headache for Marx."[20] He gives two evidences from Marx's text. (1) In his 1875 manuscript entitled *Mathematical Analysis of Surplus Value and Rate of profits* Marx gave some numerical examples of increasing rate of profits. Heinrich argued: Marx had "tried to clarify the relationship between the rate of surplus-value and the rate of profit mathematically by means of a large number of mathematical calculations and by assuming a variety of conditional analyzes, in order to prove "the law of profit". However, the results he reached demonstrate that various changes regarding the rate of profit may occur.[21] (2)

---

19   Ibid.
20   Ibid.
21   Ibid.

In his own use of *Capital*, Volume I (second edition), Marx added an endorsement, which was later retained by Engels as a footnote in *Capital*, the first volume, the third and fourth versions Engels wrote: "In Marx's copy there is here the marginal note: Here is note for working out later; if the extension is only quantitative, then for a greater and a smaller capital in the same branch of business the profits are as the magnitudes of the advanced capitals. If the quantitative extension induces qualitative change, then the rate of profit on the larger capital rises simultaneously." - F.E?.[22]

Secondly, Heinrich argued that Marx had already admitted that he could not complete the writing of *Capital*–not only in terms of editing it, but also theoretically. His only proof was Marx's letter to Danielson in 1879, in which Marx wrote that he "finally I could not complete the second volume (including the second and third volumes of *Capital*)."[23] Heinrich argued that this once again shows that Marx himself didn't have a complete theory of the crisis, "because Marx himself wanted to make a deeper study on the credit system, the capitalist state, the role of world market, and Marx was convinced that only after making these studies, and the crisis theory would be correct. This is why Marx in his later years began to study the credit issue and the United States, Russia, and even began to learn Russian language. The reason why Marx did not complete the third volume in his lifetime, *Capital*, because he felt that its theoretical construction was not yet complete; Heinrich means that Marx himself doubted this law and could not prove his hypotheses in the course of his life, then we can say that TPRF and the theory of crisis is built on the basis of such unfinished work, which is self-evident."

II. "Canceling Marx"?: Refutation of Heinrich

Heinrich's article aroused strong repercussions among Marxist scholars in the English-speaking world. Five Marxist economists, A. Kliman and Alan Freeman etc., respectively, from the United Kingdom, the United States and also from Russia, wrote an article jointly, to refute Heinrich. (Andrew Kliman, Alan Freeman, Nick Potts, Alexey Gusev, and Brendan Cooney) They pointed out that Heinrich's article was seriously wrong, because "a proper evaluation of an exegetical interpretation must still be based on the adequacy of its interpretive evidence and arguments. We intend to show that Heinrich's article is seriously wanting, and aims to "eliminate" Marx's theory."[24] So, how did these scholars refute it?

---

22   *Complete Works of Marx and Engels*, Vol. 1, People's Publishing House, 2004, p. 725
23   M. Heinrich (2013), pp. 15-31.
24   A. Kliman, A. Freeman, N. Potts, A. Gusev, B. Cooney, *The Unmaking of Marx's Capital: Heinrich's Attempt to Eliminate Marx's Crisis Theory*, MPRA Paper 48535, University Library of Munich, Germany, revised 22 July 2013.

(I) "Scarecrow target": What did Marx try to express?

A. Kliman and others have pointed out that Heinrich's critique of the premise that the rate of profit tends to decline in the understanding of the law from the outset is wrong. Heinrich did not give a direct citation from Marx when arguing that Marx's theory of the rate of profit "tend to" fall as a trend. They wrote "II. The LTFRP: Assertion of Inevitability or Explanation of Actual Phenomenon? A. Heinrich's primary interpretive confusion is introduced by attributing to Marx a claim that does not appear in Marx's text. "However," Heinrich states, "in the long term, according to Marx's thesis, the rate of profit must fall". He supplies no citation here, and Marx's text does not support his claim. In particular, the following statement directly contradicts it: "The law operates therefore simply as a tendency, whose effect is decisive only under particular circumstances and over long periods" (Marx 1991a, p. 346, emphasis added).

There are only two statements in the part of volume III devoted to the LTFRP that seem somewhat similar to what Heinrich has written. In one case, Marx (1991a, p. 337, emphasis added) writes, "In practice, however, the rate of profit will fall in the long run, as we have seen" (Aber in Wirklichkeit wird die Profitrate, wie bereits gesehn, auf die Dauer fallen). The statement that it "will fall" is not the same as the theoretical claim that it "must fall."This difference is crucial, because Heinrich's pronouncement that the LTFRP is a "failure" is based on Marx's "failure" to prove that the rate of profit must fall. But since Marx made no such claim, the absence of a proof does not consti- tute a failure. The other statement of Marx's (1991a, p. 319) that is somewhat similar to Heinrich's version is, "the rate of profit ... must therefore steadily fall." This statement includes the word "must," but it is contained in Marx's initial presentation of "the law itself," which holds the rate of surplus-value constant. Thus, Marx is simply saying that if constant capital increases faster than variable capital, while the rate of surplus-value is unchanged, then the rate of profit must steadily fall. This is a simple and unexceptionable mathematical deduction from his value theory, not a claim about what must actually occur in the long run."[25]

It can be seen that Marx's intention is that the rate of profit in the long run will play a decisive role, not ruling out the possibility of falls under certain conditions. Heinrich distorted Marx's theory, arguing: "what Marx wanted to prove is: no matter what happens, rate of profits are bound to decline. He first-ly changed Marx's "trend" secretly into an, inevitable "prophecy" that must happen in the future and then attempted to criticize it. The root of Heinrich's all errors, in fact, is that this absolute, mechanical misunderstanding. An anal-ogy in the article of Kliman et al. illustrates this very vividly. They wrote: "Simple as the law appears from the above arguments, not one of the previous writers on economics succeeded in discovering it, as we shall see later on. These economists perceived the phenomenon, but tortured themselves with

---

25 Ibid.

their contradictory attempts to explain it. And given the great importance that this law has for capitalist production, one might well say that it forms the mystery around whose solution the whole of political economy since Adam Smith revolves and that the difference between the various schools since Adam Smith consists in the different attempts made to solve it. ... Political economy has never found this puzzle's solution. [Marx 1991a, pp. 319–20, emphases added] Marx claims credit for having discovered the law, even though the economists "perceived the phenomenon," because he was the first to solve the mystery/puzzle, i.e. to successfully explain why the rate of profit tends to fall in the long run. He does not claim credit for discovering the phenomenon of a falling rate of profit. Nor does he claim (here or elsewhere) to have proved that the rate of profit must fall in the long run. Shortly after Contrasting the law to Marx's "explanation for this law," Heinrich briefly gets the law right, equating the law and the explanation: "The 'law' claims that a fall in the rate of profit results in the long-term from the capitalist mode of development of the forces of production." Notice that this statement does not say that the rate of profit must fall in the long run. It says that the capitalist mode of development of the forces of production—accumulation of capital accompanied by labour-saving technical change that increases productivity—is the dominant cause, in the long run, of the fall in the rate of profit. This is indeed Marx's explanation, Marx's law. The rate of profit falls only under particular circumstances, and it can fall for other reasons, such as rising wage rates (Marx 1991a, p. 346, p. 347), but if and when it does exhibit a long-term decline, the capitalist mode of development of the forces of production is the dominant cause of that decline. However, given Heinrich's preoccupation with Marx's "failure" to prove the proposition that the rate of profit must fall in the long run—with absolute certainty, come what may—it is clear that it is this proposition that he is referring to when he declares the law a failure. But this proposition is not Marx's law. It is not an explanation of an actual phenomenon. Thus, Heinrich simply does not understand what the LTFRP is or what Marx is trying to prove. As a result, he is in no position to evaluate the law's success or failure. Because he misconstrues the law as an assertion that the rate of profit must fall, he demands proof of this assertion and he triumphantly declares that the LTFRP is a failure since the assertion cannot be "proven." However, once one does understand what the LTFRP actually is and what Marx was actually trying to prove—the ability of his value theory, together with his theory of capitalist accumulation, to explain "an empirically confirmed fact"—it becomes clear that Heinrich's demand for proof and his declaration that the LTFRP is a failure are ludicrous. Consider another law that explains a phenomenon, the law of gravitation. It explains why and how bodies tend to move toward one another. But if Heinrich were a physicist, he would publish an article in the Monthly Physical Review, accompanied by an endorsement by the journal's editors, which tells us that the law of gravitation is instead an assertion that bodies must move toward one another, come what may. He would demand that this assertion be proven, after which he would point to the fact that the moon orbits the earth instead of crashing into it and thereby demonstrate that the assertion cannot be proven. And then he would triumphantly declare that the law of gravitation is a failure."[26] In fact, this is not the first time for Heinrich to use this technique. A typical example is the system reflects his thinking in the Guide of Marx's *Capital*, three volumes. Although looking from the title, it is declared as only an introduction to Marx's theory of capital, but what Heinrich has basically attempted is the criticism or "revision" of Marx's theory. He often constructs a "Marxist theory of capital" by himself to point out to its "defects" and then substitutes it with his own theory. The issue is that the "theory" he criticizes is, in fact, often not what Marx aimed to express or what Marx had indeed advocated. This is like manipulating a "scarecrow target" and then fighting against it, with the purpose of making his own theory look more convincing.

How to correctly understand the "trend" Marx has analyzed? Kliman et al. have argued that Marx, Smith, Ricardo and other classical political economists have just tried to explain the rate of profit to fall, which was considered as a commonly accepted fact. Marx said: "Simple as the law appears from the above arguments, not one of the previous writers on economics succeeded in discovering it, as we shall see later on. These economists perceived the phenomenon, but tortured themselves with their contradictory attempts to explain it. And given the great importance that this law has for capitalist production, one might well say that it forms the mystery around whose solution the whole of political economy since Adam Smith revolves and that the difference between the various schools since Adam Smith consists in the different attempts made to solve it. ... political economy has never found this puzzle's solution. [Marx 1991a, pp. 319–20, emphases added]".[27] What Marx meant was, "the capitalist mode of development of the forces of production—accumulation of capital accompanied by labour-saving technical change that increases productivity—is the dominant cause, in the long run, of the fall in the rate of profit. This is indeed Marx's explanation, Marx's law. The rate of profit falls only under particular circumstances, and it can fall for other reasons, such as rising wage rates (Marx 1991a, pp. 346-347)".[28]

(II) The increase of the rate of surplus-value and the limit of its compensation by the capitalists

How to treat Heinrich's critique based on Marx's formula (1) that capitalists can compensate the increase of the rate of surplus-value increase, how to understand Heinrich's proposition that "there is a limit" to this increase? How to prove that organic composition of capital in the long term must be higher than other variables, so that there will be indeed a downward trend in rate of profits? According to Kliman et al, to prove this point, we must return to Marx's basic assumptions regarding the capitalist mode of production and

---

26   Ibid.

27   Karl Marx, *Capital*, Volume 3, People's Publishing House, 2004, pp. 237-238

28   See A. Kliman, A. Freeman, N. Potts, A. Gusev, B. Cooney (2013).

capital accumulation. Marx, has argued that capital is the constant pursuit of the value of proliferation, and thus the accumulation of capital has become a spontaneous, original power, at the same time, the most important feature of capitalism labor-saving technological change. Assuming that the population, the workday and the labor intensity are constant, the living labor provided by the society in an economic cycle is constant, but the living labor is diluted day after day by the ever-increasing constant capital, causing decline in rate of profits. This is because the total amount of living labor is finite even if it is converted into surplus-value (which means that the productive forces are highly developed and the wages are so low that wages will be a negligible variable), under such a theoretical assumption capital accumulation will be infinite. Marx, therefore, analyzed this limit to prove his view that in the long run, the rate of profit will inevitably tend to decline, ultimately.

More importantly, Marx also expressed similar ideas in the Volume I of *Capital*, which was revised and corrected by himself. "It is impossible, for instance, to squeeze as much surplus-value out of 2 as out of 24 labourers. If each of these 24 men gives only one hour of surplus labour in 12, the 24 men give together 24 hours of surplus labour, while 24 hours is the total labour of the two men. Hence, the application of machinery to the production of surplus-value implies a contradiction which is immanent in it, since of the two factors of the surplus-value created by a given amount of capital, one, the rate of surplus-value, cannot be increased, except by diminishing the other, the number of workmen." ".... (Capitalist) he may compensate the decrease in the relative number of laborers exploited, by an increase not only of the relative, but of the absolute surplus labor."[29]

The problem with Heinrich's critique of Marx formula (1) is that: Heinrich here assumes fixed quantities of s and (c+v), under this assumption the reduction of (c+v) will cause the reduction of the total amount of advance capital. This implies the dis-accumulation of capital, which clearly contrasts Marx's ideas. Kliman et al, have pointed to this point as follows: "But if the advanced capital, c+v, needed to employ the two workers is not as great as the advanced capital that was formerly needed to employ twenty-four workers, accumulation has gone into reverse. In order to "prove" that falling employment of labour can always be offset by an increase in the rate of surplus-value, and that the rate of profit can therefore always rise, Heinrich presumes and has to presume the dis-accumulation of capital."[30] (2) When Heinrich argues that s/(c+v) is only a ratio, and even if the value of the constant capital approaches zero, so that all labor is converted into surplus value, then the rate of profit p = s/c will decline due to technological progress. But according to Marx's premises, in the capitalist mode of production, the productive forces development is demonstrated as using labor-saving technologies, thus amount of capital used for equal work constantly rises, constantly the ratio of surplus value to prepaid capital, i.e. s/c declines.

29   Karl Marx, *Capital*, Volume 1, People's Publishing House, 2004, p. 702
30   See A. Kliman, A. Freeman, N. Potts, A. Gusev, B. Cooney (2013).

(III) Did Marx Complete His Crisis Theory?

Heinrich has asserted: "Marx's letter to Danielson admits that he could not complete his *Capital*." But let's see what Marx actually wrote? "I should under no circumstances have published the volume II before the present English industrial crisis had reached its climax. This time the phenomena are unique, in many respects different from what they were in the past and this – quite apart from other modifying circumstances – is easily accounted for by the fact that never before was the English crisis preceded by tremendous crises now lasting already five years in the United States, South America, Germany, Austria, etc. It is therefore necessary to watch the present course of things until their maturity before you can 'consume' them 'productively', I mean 'theoretically'."[31] Obviously, this letter only shows that Marx hoped to wait for the latest materials, and data to test and enrich his *Capital*, which precisely reflected the rigorous attitude of Marx as a scientist and the spirit of seeking truth from facts, which cannot explain that Marx had "admitted that he could not complete the second volume".[32]

Kliman et al cited numerous facts to show that Marx was convinced that the theoretical construction of *Capital* was already there. As early as July 31, 1865, Marx wrote to Engels: "There are 3 more chapters to be written to complete the theoretical part (the first 3 books). Then there is still the 4th book, the historical-literary one, to be written, which will, comparatively speaking, be the easiest part for me, since all the problems have been resolved in the first 3 books, so that this last one is more by way of repetition in historical form. But I cannot bring myself to send anything off until I have the whole thing in front of me. Whatever shortcomings they may have, the advantage of my writings is that they are an artistic whole."[33] As you see, Marx argued that the theoretical problems were basically resolved. Marx's claim here is another proof of his desire to observe the latest developments in the crisis in 1879, reflecting his serious attitude towards his work. On February 13, 1866, Marx sent a letter to Engels: "The manuscript is completed, but it is too long, except for me, no one, even you cannot edit and make it ready for publishing, I happened to begin to transcribe and polish it on January 1, the work has progressed rapidly, because after such a long pain, I am naturally happy to lick the child."[34] Marx argued that the manuscript that contains the theoretical content has been completed, and all he needed was to arrange and "polish", make it easily readable. On April 30, 1867, Marx wrote to Meyer: "I hope that in a year from to-day the whole work will have been published. Volume II gives the continuation and conclusion of the theories. Volume III the history of political economy from the middle of the seventeenth century.[35] If Marx had doubts about his theory, or

73

---

31   https://www.marxists.org/archive/marx/works/1879/letters/79_04_10.htm

32   See A. Kliman, A. Freeman, N. Potts, A. Gusev, B. Cooney (2013).

33   *Complete Works of Marx and Engels*, Vol. 31, People's Publishing House, 1972, p. 135.

34   Ibid., p. 181.

35   Ibid., p. 543. Here Marx intended to publish the continuation of the first volume of *Capital* in one volume; this volume grew into two. Consequently the volume which had been planned as Volume III [Theories of Surplus Value] was numbered IV.

even did not complete the construction of the crisis theory, to Marx's consistent attitude, it was impossible to say these words for him. On November 3, 1877, Marx wrote to Schott, "began by writing Capital in a sequence (starting with the 3rd, historical section) quite the reverse of that in which it was presented to the public, saving only that the first volume—the last I tackled—was got ready for the press straight away, whereas the two others remained in the rough form which all research originally assumes."[36] Here, this suggests, yet again, that Marx regarded himself as having completed volume 3 of *Capital* before writing volume 1, although it was complete only in the theoretical sense, not in terms of form, which "remained ... rough draft stage."

(IV) Did Marx Abandon the Law of Rate of Profit to Fall?

Heinrich argued that, according to some of the increases in rate of profit enumerated in Marx's manuscripts suggest that Marx was perplexed to prove his theory. According to A. Kliman and et.al, this view is biased and a mistaken approach: Heinrich is simply misreading the texts in light of his incorrect belief that Marx tried to prove that the rate of profit must fall, under all circumstances. In light of that incorrect belief, every statement by Marx that the rate of profit does not necessarily fall appears to be an admission of failure, "suspicion" and uncertainty."[37]

In fact, if we read the third volume of the third volume of *Capital*, then we will immediately understand the methodology and approach in Marx's research: Firstly, he assume that most of the variables remain unchanged, and then began to release them one by one up or down. Therefore, contrary to Heinrich, the mathematical example cited by Marx is his natural research process only, and was not a "big headache" for Marx. . For how to understand Marx's words "Note here for working out later". Kliman et al. have pointed out that the "Note here for working out later" here is more likely to be a mere clerical error. Because of the context of this note, it is not difficult to see that here Marx has elaborated the "the TPRF itself", which means that the growth organic composition of capital will lead to a natural consequence of a decline in the rate of profit without the change in the rate of surplus value being taken into account, consequently the note ""here for working out later," is entirely contrary to the meaning of the context. If Heinrich's interpretation were correct, Marx's comment would be equivalent to Galileo writing "Note here for working out later: the earth is stationary" in the margin of his book."[38]

III. How to Understand this Controversy?

Whenever some new manuscripts of Marx and Engels were published, a series of debates occur in the academia. In 1932, the publication of *Economic and Philosophical Manuscripts of 1844* triggered the famous controversy of

---

36　*Complete Works of Marx and Engels*, Volume 34, People's Publishing House, 1972, p. 385.

37　See A. Kliman, A. Freeman, N. Potts, A. Gusev, B. Cooney (2013).

38　Ibid.

"young Marx" and the "old Marx". The concept of "alienation" and "humanistic Marx" has emerged in the Western Marxist academic circles. In 1939, the publication of *Economic Manuscripts of 1857-1858* had also triggered a round of heated discussion regarding Marxist theory of crisis and historical development tendency of capitalism. And, after the publication of *MEGA²*, the various versions of various manuscripts of *Capital* by Marx and Engels have been made public, Heinrich's articles have triggered controversy, in fact, can be regarded as the beginning of a new round of debates, with the recently available textual material. We can see, however, that Heinrich's so-called critique did not, in fact, offer any particularly novel idea (he has even completely avoided to talk about the controversy about the salt theorem), but repeated the ideas of Tugan-Baranovsky, et al. Researchers, as early as the end of the 19th Century have raised the idea of cross-examination of texts. Since most researchers are unfamiliar with German and have not yet studied *MEGA²* carefully, Heinrich's view seems to have some specific reliability as one of the few experts who is familiar with *MEGA²*'s original manuscript and who can write in English at the same time. For a time, the issue seems not to be whether the theory of declining profit is correct, but rather whether Marx intended to adhere to this theory, ultimately. Kliman et al. have made a brilliant refutation for each of his arguments. Below, we will combine the innovation *MEGA²II* version has brought with the discussions in Marx's manuscripts, and present our views around the following three questions.

(I) Did Engels "Betray" Marx?

Ever since Engels edited and published the Volume II of *Capital*, he has always been keen to avoid misinterpretation of Marx's meaning and cause a mediocre understanding of Marx's works. The incomplete parts of Marx's manuscripts and some incomplete statements regarding his ideas, have brought far more difficulties to Engels' editorial work than we can imagine today. In order to provide a readable book, Engels arranged all the available texts in a relatively systematic and complete structure, made re-arrangements regarding its contents in large scale, changed partial concepts and ideas, and added some new content.[39]

For example, a comparative study based on *MEGA²* texts shows that, regarding the chapter 3 of the third volume of *Capital*, Engels changed the third chapter of Marx's original manuscript into the third edited book, condensed more than 200 pages into 20-plus pages, divided three chapters and added the title to all in order to emphasize the content. In chapter 13, additional information was provided on profit and cost-price margins of prepaid capital. In chapter 15, replaced Marx's word "come off" (Klappen) ("this process will soon lead to the end of capitalist production", "Dieser Prozeß würde bald die kapitalistische Production zum Klappen bringen...") with the word "collapse"

---

39   Riccardo Bellofiore & Roberto Fineschi, *Re-reading Marx. New Perspectives after the Critical Edition*, Palgrave Macmillman, 2009, p. 43.

(Zusammenbruch) ("this process will soon make capitalist production collapse", and moved it to the end of this paragraph.[40]

As Klaus Müller, when criticizing Heinrich, pointed out with reference to the *MEGA²* II/4.3, wrote the following: "Engels made a careful and coherent compilation of the drafts written by Marx... Engels used the structure of Marx's original text and all its core content, with a clearer style ... The title to be drawn is precisely in conformity with the content of the original Marx's rough text. Heinrich accuses Engels of replacing Marx's expression "Klappen" ("This process would soon make the capitalist production "clap (or fold), ...", *MEGA²* 4.2, p. 315) by the term "collapse", thus intensively accentuated the wrong thought of automatic end (*MEGA²*/15, p. 243). But when people (systems or the like) clap (together)(or fold up), nothing is meant other than that they collapse. Moreover, this sentence of Marx does not prove the thesis of collapse either, because one has to read it to the end: "... if repugnant tendencies did not consistently have a decentralizing effect aside of the centripetal force" (identical in Marx and Engels). As a whole, this sentence can be read rather as a rejection rather than an affirmation of the thought of "collapse".[41]

If we follow the other manuscripts of Marx, we will find that Engels' changes are in line with Marx's intention. Marx wrote: "It reflected a reduction in the ratio of surplus-value of profits to pre-existing capital .... These contradictions lead to outbreaks, catastrophes, crises, at this time labor is temporarily interrupted and a large part of capital is destroyed, which makes the capital return back to the level in which it can continue to function, which, of course, can lead to an outbreak, a crisis ... These recurring disasters caused by crises can lead to a recurrence of catastrophes of greater magnitude and eventually this process will cause the capitalist production to a collapse."[42]

This above sentence cancelled by Engels is a qualifying sentence. "If there is no opposite trend, it always acts as a centrifugal force, besides the centripetal force." Marx and Engels did not say that the demise of capitalism would occur automatically due to the decline in rate of profits. Thus, Heinrich's accusation that Engels stressed that capitalism is automatically heading towards crisis, and collapse is untenable. Nor did he have any evidence that Engels had seriously altered or violated Marx's ideas, and Heinrich himself admitted that the editors in 19th Century enjoyed more freedom than contemporary ones. In fact, for the scattered manuscripts of Marx, these "enrichment, deletion, correction" type of interventions are exactly the works of a qualified editor should do." None of Marx's statements, in his drafts, about the crisis were discarded by Engels."[43] Engels could only do so by sorting out Marx's existing crisis theory to make

40   Klaus Müller, Das Gesetz des tendenziellen Falls der allgemeinen Profitrate-Engels versus Marx?, *Zeitschrift für marxistische Erneuerung*, 2011, Nr. 87(11).

41   Ibid.

42   *Complete Works of Marx and Engels*, Vol. 46 (II), People's Publishing House, Edition 1980, p. 269.

43   See Klaus Müller (2011).

it more legible. Too much exaggeration of Engels's modifications on Marx's available texts, and even declaring that Engels has deviated from Marx, is an irresponsible judgment.

(II) Did Marx Abandon the TRPF?

In the *Grundrisse* (Manuscripts of 1857-1858), Marx wrote: the falling trend of rate of profits is "the most important law of modern political economy".[44] In his 1861-1863 manuscript, he further pointed out that "the rate of profit in the capitalist production process has a downward trend".[45] Klaus Müller in his above article has pointed out that "there is no clue, even in present and later drafts, that Marx might have wavered on this issue."[46] In fact, Marx's analysis on the decline in rate of profit refers to the decline in the rate of profit of advanced capital, the intention of such judgment is that with the accumulation of capital, the capitalist production will encounter with its own limitations, this restriction itself will push the capitalists to further innovation to overcome this restriction. Marx wrote: This factor does not abolish the general law. But it causes that law to act rather as a tendency, i.e. as a law whose absolute action is checked, retarded, and weakened, by counteracting circumstances.....There must be some counteracting influences at work, which cross and annul the effect of the general law, and which give it merely the characteristic of a tendency, for which reason we have referred to the fall of the general rate of profit as a tendency to fall.....thus, the law acts only as a tendency. And it is only under certain circumstances and only after long periods that its effects become strikingly pronounced."[47]

In theory, even if there is a series of factors that make the rate of profit rise, Marx did not doubt this law. In *Economic Manuscripts of 1861-1863*, Marx abandoned the assumption that the rate of surplus-value remained constant, noting that "the rate of profit declines–although the rate of surplus-value remains constant or increases at this time–because, as labor productivity develops, variable capital reduces in comparison with constant capital. Therefore, the decline in rate of profits is not due to a decrease in labor productivity, instead caused by an increase in labor productivity."[48] In the *Outline*, Marx gave a subtle proof that "If the fraction (of the work day) was 1/1,000 and the productive force increases a thousand fold, then the value of capital does not grow a thousand fold, but rather by far less than 1/11; it grows by 1/1,000 − 1/1,000,000, i.e. by 1,000/1,000,000 − 1/1,000,000 = 999/1,000,000.)"[49]

---

44   Complete Works of Marx and Engels, Volume 46 (II), People's Publishing House, 1980, p. 267.

45   *Complete Works of Marx and Engels*, Vol. 4, People's Publishing House, 1985, p. 293.

46   Klaus Müller, *Anti-Engelsism, Declining Rate of Profit and Marx's Economic Manuscripts of 1867-1868, Marxism and Reality* will publish it.

47   Karl Marx, *Capital*, Vol. 3, People's Publishing House, Edition 2004, p. 266.

48   *Complete Works of Marx and Engels*, Volume 26, People's Publishing House, 1975, p. 498.

49   *Collected Works of Marx and Engels*, Vol. 46 (I), People's Publishing House, 1979, p. 304-305.

The constant technological innovation for capital-saving pointed out by any scholar so as to deny the law actually does not exist, because looking from the perspective of total social capital, the labor time required to reproduce the same capital is reduced, in fact, it is also an innovation for labor-saving innovation. If we look from the aspect of empirical studies, most of them also prove the correctness of Marx's theory of rate of profit decline. According to Heinrich, the laws of all natural sciences cannot be proved–because even if the results of the first ten thousand experiments coincide with the theory, there is no guarantee that the results of the next 1001th experiment will not violate the theory. Marx said that the rise of organic composition of capital will overwhelm other factors in the long run, so the rate of profit will demonstrate a downward trend, in the long-term. If the decline in rate of profit is observed in the long run, then Marx's theory is proven by empirical date. Basu and et.al studied the rate of profit changes in the US between 1869-1992, and discovered that the long-term trend of the rate of profit appears random walk of the "long wave" changes, once the retarding effects of the "counteracting circumstances" effect, the trend of the rate of profit does indeed show gradual decline over time.[50] Li Minqi et al., also studied the changes in the rate of profit and the rate of capital accumulation in the entire capitalist world since the mid-19th Century, looking into the four long-waves of capitalism, and affirmed the downward trend in profits rate.[51] W. Paul Cockshott et al. studied the rate of profits of different industries in the UK, and found that although the rate of surplus-value in the "aggregated industry groups" was significantly higher, there was still a significant negative correlation between rate of profits and organic composition rates.[52] This suggests that the increase in the surplus value rate is not sufficient to offset the declining trend in profits just due to the increase in organic composition of capitals.

(III) How to Treat Marx's Theory of Crisis

In contrast to Kliman et al, in Marx's writings, what we can see is a fragmentary account of the crisis from different perspectives. In fact, he did not come up with a logically consistent theory of crisis. In Marx's expositions regarding the crisis, his aim has been to point to the capitalist mode of production itself. However, as Marx himself pointed out, "real crisis can be explained only from the real movement of capitalistic production, competition, and credit."[53] Why did Marx focus mainly on capitalist production in the analysis of discussing the crises of capitalism? Marx himself pointed out the reason for doing so: "There are the formal possibilities of crisis ...... that is to say, crises are possible

50   Basu D. et.al., "Is There a Tendency for the Rate of Profit to Fall? Econometric Evidence for the U.S. Economy, 1948-2007", *Review of Radical Political Economics*, 2013, 45(1)

51   Li Mingqi, Zhu Andong, The World Rate of profit Increasing Wave and Historical Limitation of Capitalism, *Theory of Economics of Shanghai School* 2006(16).

52   Paul Cockshott, Allin F. Cottrell, Does Marx Need to Transform?, in: Bellofiore ed., *Marxian Economics: A Reappraisal*, NewYork: Macmillan and St. Martin's, 1998, 2, pp. 70-85.

53   *Collected Works of Marx and Engels*, Vol. 26, People's Publishing House, Edition 1975, p. 585

without credit, without money functioning as a means of payment. payments, But the second form is not possible without the first condition, that is to say without the separation of purchase and sale."[54] "The general possibility of crisis is… the separation, in time and place, of purchase and sale. But this is never the cause of the crisis."

"Thus, if the crisis occurs, therefore, because purchase and sale become separated, it becomes a money crisis as soon as money has developed as means of payment, and this second form of crisis follows as a matter of course, when the first occurs," "Therefore, in studying how and why the general possibility of the crisis will become a reality, excessive attention to the means of payment, as the cause is completely unnecessary."[55] Fluctuations in rate of profits manifest the tightness inherent in the process of capital accumulation, and the decline in rate of profits is a concentrated expression of the intensification of the multiple socio-economic contradictions inherent in capitalism. Contradictions associated with declining rate of profits has become the focus of Marx's writings. As the rate of profits tend to decline, the contradiction between the conditions and the realization of direct exploitation, the contradiction between the social productive forces and the social consumption power, the contradiction between capitalist value proliferation and the means for realizing this proliferation , the contradiction between overcapitalization and overpopulation; the contradiction between the development of productive forces and the limitations for the capital accumulation conditioned by the interests of capitalist class; these facts all demonstrate that the capitalist mode of production is a product of history. Therefore, we can say that Marx has basically completed the construction of his crisis theory. For contemporary Marxist scholars, how to analyze the contemporary facts of financialization and globalization and developing a more explanatory crisis theory and proving Marx's classic statements are still challenges that lay before us.

Originally publlished in the journal
Contemporary Economic Research, 2004(8)

---

54 Ibid., p. 587.
55 Ibid., pp. 587-588.

A Probe into the Origin of the Thought of Political Economy in Broad Sense

—Research Based on the Classical Texts by Marx and Engels during 1845-1867

Lu Jiang and Ge Yang

Abstract: Engels used the concept of "political economy in general" in *Anti-Dühring* and wrote that investigate the special laws of each individual stage in the evolution of production and exchange was not yet completed. Only when it has completed this investigation will it be able to establish the few quite general laws. Looking from the lifetime study of political economy by Marx and Engels, the nature of the researches of Marxist political economy has remained to be "in general". The first volume of *Das Kapital* by Marx himself personally proofread and published in 1867, although this work is a classical text of political economy in the narrow sense, it contains valuable thoughts from the aspect of general-in the broad sense- political economy. During 1845-1867, Marx and Engels completed the writing of *The Holy Family*, *German Ideology*, *The Communist Manifesto* and other important classical texts, and developed their research on political economics in broad sense which is in favor of the establishment and development of the text book system of general (broad system) Marxist political economy in colleges.

Keywords: 1845-1867; thought of political economics in broad sense; *Das Kapital*

The year of 2013 is the 130th anniversary of the death of Marx. The great thinker, revolutionist and economist who devoted himself to the liberation of the proletariat throughout the world studied the general law of the social and economic operation of capitalism all through his lifetime. His representative master work, *Das Kapital*, as a classic of political economy, cannot be belittled by the new characteristics of the capitalist society and the socialist economic operation of the present day, in no case can be declared as being outdated. On the other hand, the rich general political economy thoughts embodied in *Das Kapital* is a general Marxist scholar's study of providing invaluable advice and experience for how to inherit and develop Marxist political economy, how to reveal the general laws behind the complicated appearances and developments of the world economy, how to clarify and solve the social contradictions in the economic sphere.

Marx's systematic study of political economy began in late 1843, Marx wrote: "I studied the profession was the law, but I just put it in the philosophy and history as a secondary discipline to study. During 1842-1843, as the editor of *Rheinische Zeitung*, for the first time, I faced the difficulty to express a critique regarding the so-called material interests, the discussion of forest theft and real estate by the Rhine Provincial Council, the then governor of the Rhine province, conducted official debate on the condition Mosel farmers with *Rheinische Zeitung*, and finally, the debate about free trade and the protection of tariffs was the primary motivator for me to study the economic problems."[1] Marx began by writing a critique of the existing system and the bourgeoisie political economy, and before 1857 he completed important works, including the *Economic-Philosophic Manuscripts of 1844, The Holy Family, or Critique of Critical Criticism. Against Bruno Bauer and His Supporters, German Ideology, The Poverty of Philosophy, Wage Labor and Capital, The Communist Manifesto* in some of the above works with economics content he used political economy approach in narrow sense, laying some foundation for *Das Kapital*, but these works also contained a wealth of political economy thoughts in the general sense. This article focuses on extending analysis on the proposal, embodiment, role and influence of the book *The Holy Family*, with extended name or *The Holy Family or Critique of Critical Criticism. Against Bruno Bauer and Company, German Ideology, The Communist Manifesto* and the first volume of *Das Kapital*, I will also analyze several important book reviews written by Engels.[2]

82

---

1 *Complete Works of Marx and Engels*, Vol. 2, People's Publishing House, 2009, p. 588.

2 The argument and analysis of this article does not include *Economic and Philosophic Manuscripts of 1844* into the references, and the reasons is that this work and Engels' Umrisse zu einer Kritik der Nationalökonomie shall be specifically studied as the most important early period Marxist economic research, in particular, the general political economy thoughts in these two books should be separately studied in relation with other Marxist works.

I. During 1845-1848, from *The Holy Family or Critique of Critical Criticism. Against Bruno Bauer and Company* to *The Communist Manifesto*

In February 1845, Marx and Engels co-authored the critique of the young Hegelians' idealism and elaborated on the dialectical materialism and historical materialism in their book *The Holy Family, or Critique of Critical Criticism. Against Bruno Bauer and His Supporters*, which was published in Frankfurt-On-Main. This book contains a total of nine chapters, Chapters I, II and III were written by Engels, Chapters V, VIII and IX by Marx, Chapters IV, VI and VII by both, in which case, however, each has signed the particular chapter section or subsection, supplied with its own heading, that was written by him. Although the content and the main point of view of the book was to elaborate Marxist philosophy, but the economic analysis in it is very important, for example, Volume 55 of *Collected Works of Lenin* includes a "conspectus of the book *The Holy Family* which said: "Hitherto political economy proceeded from the wealth that the movement of private property supposedly creates for the nations to an apology of private property. Proudhon proceeds from the opposite side, which political economy sophistically conceals, from the poverty bred by the movement of private property, to his conclusions negating private property. The first criticism of private property proceeds, of course, from the fact in which its contradictory essence appears in the form that is most perceptible and most glaring and most directly arouses man's indignation—from the fact of poverty, of misery."[3] In the above book, the fourth and seventh chapter discusses economics, in the fourth chapter, Marx and Engels have put forward the concept of social relations of production by using the theory of historical materialism which was not yet fully developed. The seventh chapter has put forward the concept of "mode of production" and elaborated that the mode of material production is the most basic content of the development of social history. According to Engels's definition of general political economy in *Anti-Dühring* – "Political economy, in the widest sense, is the science of the laws governing the production and exchange of the material means of subsistence in human society." "Political economy, must first investigate the special laws of each individual stage in the evolution of production and exchange and only when it has completed this investigation will it be able to establish the few quite general laws which hold good for production and exchange in general.".... "Such an investigation and comparison has up to the present been undertaken, in general outline, only by Marx..." We can see that the view point that the "mode of production" and the "mode of material production" determining the social and historical development belongs to the category of generalized political economy. No matter how its social ideology changes, material production is the inevitable social phenomenon in every social stage of humankind, and since from the beginning of the human evolution to even the communist society, men must be in a position to live in order to be able to "make history." But

---

3 *Collected Works of Lenin*, Vol. 35, People's Publishing House, 1990, p. 9.

life involves before everything else eating and drinking, a habitation, clothing and many other things. The first historical act is thus the production of the means to satisfy these needs, the production of material life itself, will never disappear. *The Holy Family* put forward the concept of mode of production, thus has touched the core of political economy and its essential category. According to the materialist conception of history, the material content of the mode of production is the productive forces, and its social form is the production relations, the production mode is the dialectical unity of productive forces and the production relations in the process of material production.

Following the *The Holy Family*, Marx and Engels in 1845-1846 co-completed the most important milestone work in the formation of the Marxist concept of history—*German Ideology*, the book marked the formation of Marxist materialist conception of history, and it is also based on this scientific world view and methodology, Marx and Engels have made fundamental breakthrough in the analysis of political economy research. In *German Ideology*, Marx and Engels systematically demonstrated that the mode of production plays a decisive role in social life and that the relations of production must adapt to the development of productive forces. Marx and Engels wrote in their concluding remarks on the materialist conception of history: "This conception of history depends on our ability to expound the real process of production, starting out from the material production of life itself, and to comprehend the form of intercourse connected with this and created by this mode of production (i.e. civil society in its various stages), as the basis of all history."[4] "This view shows that: history does not end by being resolved into "self-consciousness" as "spirit of the spirit", but that in it at each stage there is found a material result: a sum of productive forces, a historically created relation of individuals to nature and to one another, which is handed down to each generation from its predecessor; a mass of productive forces, capital funds and conditions."[5] "These conditions of life, which different generations find in existence, decide also whether or not the periodically recurring revolutionary convulsion will be strong enough to overthrow the basis of the entire existing system. And if these material elements of a complete revolution are not present (namely, on the one hand the existing productive forces, on the other the formation of a revolutionary mass, which revolts not only against separate conditions of society up till then, but against the very "production of life" till then, the "total activity" on which it was based), then, as far as practical development is concerned, it is absolutely immaterial whether the idea of this revolution has been expressed a hundred times already, as the history of communism proves."[6] This paragraph is very rich in content, which contains several concepts as the embryonic form of broad political economy thinking, specifically there are several aspects: One is to formally put forward that the human material production is the starting point of the historical development; two, that the material production relations are

---

4 *Complete Works of Marx and Engels*, Vol. 1, People's Publishing House, 2009, p. 544.
5 Ibid.
6 Ibid., p. 545.

the basis of the whole social history; three, the production mode in regard to material products determines the nature of the society and history. Generalized political economy is the study of the production of material products within the various societal stages of mankind's development, it does not simply focus to a specific social formation as the object of its investigation, that is, it takes material production relations as the basis of the development of social history. Without such material production, human beings cannot survive, therefore, the study of general political economy, starting from the most primitive social formation of humankind, the starting point of the historical development is men's material production to satisfy his needs, i.e. the production of material life itself. Moreover, looking from the changes in social and historical forms, when the productive forces of a certain social stage develops to a certain level, and have already equipped with the capacity that will enable them achieve a comprehensive transformation of the material factors, then this social formation will inevitably be replaced with a new one, Marx and Engels used the term "periodic" to show that this is an objective law, but yet in *German Ideology*, Marx and Engels didn't specify in what form and how this objective law manifested itself.

In addition, in this book *German Ideology*, Marx and Engels for the first time expounded on the issue of social ideology and its changes and also discussed the issues of social development in the underdeveloped countries. They expressed: "in our view all historical collisions have their origin ...in the contradictions between productive forces and the form of intercourse (Ger. Verkehr), and incidentally, to lead to collisions in a country, this contradiction need not necessarily have reached its extreme limit in this particular country. The competition with industrially more advanced countries, brought about by the expansion of international intercourse, is sufficient to produce a similar contradiction in countries with a backward industry (e.g. the latent proletariat in Germany brought into view by view by the competition of English industry)."[7] This paragraph has already pointed out the internal dynamics of general political economy regarding the transition of social ideology in a country, here Germany, that is, the contradiction between the productive forces and the relation of production and productive forces in unity have the determinant position, whereas in this book Marx used, the term "form of intercourse" which he later changed to the term "the relations of production". This paragraph of Marx implies the idea that due to counter-action of productive relations upon the productive forces, a transformation in country can be achieved ahead of time. But, generally speaking, the duration of the transition, conditions and forms of this transition are determined by the condition and level of productive forces— irrespective of relations of production—thus we must develop the transition process basing ourselves on the development requirements of the productive forces and relations of production should fit to these requirements. But since, the relations of production counter-act upon the productive forces, therefore

85

---

7   Ibid., p. 567- 568.

it is not necessary to wait until the said contradiction between the productive forces and production relations develop to the extremely sharp point in a certain country, and will incidentally (in connection with), lead to collisions in this country. In addition, due to international exchanges, backward countries may embark on an abnormal development path. In the case of the example given by Marx in this book, industrial development in Germany was relatively backward, in regard to the stage of development of productive forces, Germany's conditions is not enough to produce the contradiction between the productive forces and production relations, but due international exchanges, due to industrial competition with the Britain will lead to collisions in Germany.

Marx and Engels have also analyzed the characteristics of the communist movement and expounded on the economic nature of communism in this book. They wrote: "Its (communism) organisation is, therefore, essentially economic, the material production of the conditions of this unity; it turns existing conditions into conditions of unity."[8] They added: "What appears accidental to the later age as opposed to the earlier—and this applies also to the elements handed down by an earlier age—is a form of intercourse (author's note production relations) which corresponded to a definite stage of development of the productive forces."[9] "These various conditions, which appear first as conditions of self-activity, later as fetters upon it, form in the whole evolution of history a coherent series of forms of intercourse.... Since these conditions correspond at every stage to the simultaneous development of the productive forces, their history is at the same time the history of the evolving productive forces taken over by each new generation, and is, therefore, the history of the development of the forces of the individuals themselves."[10] This paragraph clearly demonstrated that Marx and Engels studied the laws of economics from the whole process of the development of human social history, and pointed out that social and historical development is also the continuous development of human beings, and the basic element that runs through this process is the material conditions, which is consistent with the object of research of broad political economy as proposed by Engels.

In February 1848, *The Communist Manifesto* written between December 1847 January 1848 was published in London in the German language in a booklet form. This work has been a programmatic document of the scientific socialism component part of Marxism, which also touches to some contents of general political economy, with the greatest content of which is the related to transition issues. The beginning of *The Communist Manifesto* states: "The history of all societies has so far been a history of class struggle."[11] "The modern bourgeois society that has sprouted from the ruins of feudal society has not done away with class antagonisms. It has but established new classes, new conditions of oppression, new forms of struggle in place of the old ones."[12]

---

8   *Complete Works of Marx and Engels*, Vol. 1, People's Publishing House, 2009, p. 574.
9   Ibid., p. 575.
10   Ibid., p. 575-576.
11   *Complete Works of Marx and Engels*, Vol. 2, People's Publishing House, 2009, p. 31.
12   *Complete Works of Marx and Engels*, Vol. 2, People's Publishing House, 2009, p. 32.

"From the serfs of the Middle Ages sprang the chartered burghers of the earliest towns. From these burgesses the first elements of the bourgeoisie were developed."[13] This shows that the transition of social form is the result of class struggle, and class is the external manifestation of production relations, the classes demonstrated by different production relations are not the same, in the slavery period, the feudal period, the capitalist period, the class relations were respectively, the slave owners and slaves, landlords and serfs, capitalists and wage laborers and so on. Marx and Engels pointed out that the root causes of the transition: "the means of production and of exchange, on whose foundation the bourgeoisie built itself up, were generated in feudal society... in one word, the feudal relations of property became no longer compatible with the already developed productive forces; they became so many fetters. They had to be burst asunder; they were burst asunder."[14] "A similar movement is going on before our own eye.... The productive forces at the disposal of society no longer tend to further the development of the conditions of bourgeois property; on the contrary, they have become too powerful for these conditions, by which they are fettered,"[15] Obviously, the contradiction between productive forces and production relations is the fundamental reason for the transition of social ideology, which is also the main content of Marx's idea of "the decisive role of productive forces". In addition, the dialectical unity of productive forces and relations of production is the red line that runs through the system of general political economy.

The Communist Manifesto embodies the key thoughts regarding the general political economy in its contents, and certain thoughts of general political economy are also included in the preface of its German edition of 1872, in the preamble of its Russian edition of 1882; the preface of the German edition of 1883;and in the preface of its German edition of 1872. Marx and Engels has warned us that the practical application of the principles should be based on the certain historical conditions of time and place. They have studied the actual experience of the 1848 February Revolution, and they especially observed the Paris Commune experience—caused by large scale industrial development—from the aspect of proving the change of social ideology that occurred on the basis of the dialectical contradiction between the productive forces and the relations of production. In the preface of the, Marx and Engels put forward a very important question of the general political economy, that is, the issue of transition stage. They pointed out that "Now the question is: can the Russian obshchina (commune), though greatly undermined, yet a form of primeval common ownership of land, pass directly to the higher form of Communist common ownership? Or, on the contrary, must it first pass through the same process of dissolution such as constitutes the historical evolution of the West?"[16]

---

13   Ibid., p. 32.
14   Ibid., p. 36.
15   Ibid., p. 37.
16   Ibid., p. 8.

And Marx and Engels foresightedly added: "The only answer to that possible today is this: If the Russian Revolution becomes the signal for a proletarian revolution in the West, so that both complement each other, the present Russian common ownership of land may serve as the starting point for a communist development."[17] Studying this point of view that we should start from the actual historical development of country, Lenin led the Russian revolution and the first socialist country in the world was established, and the answer given by Marx and Engels became a reality. I think this issue has a very important guiding significance for the current backward countries to embark on the socialist road. The preamble of the German edition of 1883 was undersigned by Engels, who underlined the basic idea underlying the *The Communist Manifesto* was entirely put forward by Marxist, and Engels summarized it, in the preamble: "The basic thought running through the *Manifesto*—that economic production, and the structure of society of every historical epoch necessarily arising therefrom, constitute the foundation for the political and intellectual history of that epoch; that consequently (ever since the dissolution of the primeval communal ownership of land) all history has been a history of class struggles, of struggles between exploited and exploiting, between dominated and dominating classes at various stages of social evolution; that this struggle, however, has now reached a stage where the exploited and oppressed class (the proletariat) can no longer emancipate itself from the class which exploits and oppresses it (the bourgeoisie), without at the same time forever freeing the whole of society from exploitation, oppression, class struggles—this basic thought belongs solely and exclusively to Marx."[18] Obviously, this basic idea summarized by Engels and the material production as the basis of human history, proposed by Marx and Engels in *German Ideology* has been their starting point to understand the whole historical development. The material relations of production is the foundation of the whole social history, which is consistent with the idea that the mode of material production determines the nature of society and history are important concepts of the general political economy.

Therefore, in summary, Marx and Engels in their early works, *The Holy Family* to *German Ideology* and then to *The Communist Manifesto* have put forward the basic ideas of general political economy, and these ideas have been the core ideas of general political economy which were developed in their later periods.

II. 1857-1864: From *Critique of Political Economy* to the First International

Between August 1857 to January 1859, Marx completed his political economy study with two important essays, respectively, firstly, from late August to mid-September 1857, wrote *Introduction to Critique of Political Economy* (hereinafter referred to as the *Introduction*) and later between August 1858 to

---

17   *Complete Works of Marx and Engels*, Vol. 2, People's Publishing House, 2009, p. 8.
18   Ibid., p. 9.

January 1859 he wrote *A Contribution to the Critique of Political Economy*. In *Introduction* the last section titled as the "Method of Political Economy" emphasized: "The order obviously has to be (1) the general, abstract determinants which obtain in more or less all forms of society, but in the above-explained sense. (2) The categories which make up the inner structure of bourgeois society and on which the fundamental classes rest. Capital, wage labour, landed property. Their interrelation. Town and country. The three great social classes. Exchange between them. Circulation. Credit system (private). (3) Concentration of bourgeois society in the form of the state. Viewed in relation to itself. The 'unproductive' classes. Taxes. State debt. Public credit. The population. The colonies. Emigration. (4) The international relation of production. International division of labour. International exchange. Export and import. Rate of exchange. (5) The world market and crises."[19] In November 1857, Marx made a detailed revision of the writing program which was described in the "Preface" as 6 volumes: (1) capital, (2) landed property, (3) wage labour; (4) state, (5) foreign trade, (6) world market. The first volume "Capital" would be divided into 4 sub-parts (a) Capital (b) competition in capital; (c) credit; (d) capital in shares; and (c) capital. The first sub-part would include the general capital" under which there would be three chapters; (2) the flow of capital; (3) the unity of the two, or capital and profits, interest. Later, these three chapters under the "General capital" became the basis of the three volumes of *Das Kapital*.

In January 1859, Marx wrote the *"Preface" to Critique of Political Economy*, in which he said, "I examine the system of bourgeois economics in the following order: (1) capital, (2) landed property, (3) wage labour; (4) state, (5) foreign trade, (6) world market. Under the first three headings, I investigate the economic conditions of life of the three great classes into which modern bourgeois society is divided; the interconnection of the three other headings is obvious at a glance. The first section of the first book, which deals with capital, consists of the following chapters: 1. Commodities; 2. Money, or simple circulation; 3. Capital in general."[20]

Therefore, according to the writing plan, it is not difficult to see that the *A Contribution to the Critique of Political Economy* is the first complete work published in Marx's political economy writing plan, and that *Das Kapital*—his masterpiece—is a very small part of Marx's plan of political economy study and writing. In the preface of the first edition of the first volume of *Das Kapital* written by Marx, he wrote: "This work is a continuation of my *A Contribution to the Critique of Political Economy* published in 1859."[21]

Obviously, from the perspective of the political economy writing program, Marx's theory has obvious character and content of general political economy. *Das Kapital* is only the completed contents of the first item of first volume in

---

19   *Complete Works of Marx and Engels*, Vol. 8, People's Publishing House, 2009, pp. 32-33.
20   *Complete Works of Marx and Engels*, Vol. 2, People's Publishing House, 2009, p. 588.
21   *Complete Works of Marx and Engels*, Vol. 5, People's Publishing House, 2009, p. 7.

the planned six volumes, and for theoretical system and guiding ideology, and they will be integrated with other chapters and volumes, which inevitably puts *Das Kapital* in the category of general political economy, which studies the general law of the operation of the capitalist economy. Besides, if we carefully look into Marx's writings before the publication of *Das Kapital* and the book reviews written, after its the publication and its preamble, there is enough evidence that inferences—especially classifying *Das Kapital* in the category of general political economy—we have demonstrated in our article is correct.

With regard to *Introduction*, Lenin pointed out that in this preface Marx elaborated the basic principles of materialism as applied to the history of human society and human society. When Marx was alive, a second edition of this book was not published. The content of the *A Contribution to the Critique of Political Economy* consists of three parts: Preface, Chapter I - The Commodity and Chapter II - Money or Simple Circulation. In the Preface, Marx further explained and described the dialectical unity between the productive forces and the relations of production, the core idea of the general political economy. He pointed out: "In the social production of their existence, men inevitably enter into definite relations, which are independent of their will, namely relations of production appropriate to a given stage in the development of their material forces of production... The mode of production of material life conditions the general process of social, political and intellectual life..... At a certain stage of development, the material productive forces of society come into conflict with the existing relations of production or – this merely expresses the same thing in legal terms – with the property relations within the framework of which they have operated hitherto. From forms of development of the productive forces these relations turn into their fetters. Then begins an era of social revolution."[22] "No social order is ever destroyed before all the productive forces for which it is sufficient have been developed, and new superior relations of production never replace older ones before the material conditions for their existence have matured within the framework of the old society."[23] In fact, this paragraph also implies one basic principle general political economy regarding the transition issue, but this "two nevers" principle we gave quoted above were too absolute, according to this passage, the transition of social formations can only be strictly in accordance with the sequential order of social formations, and does not allow "leap-style" transition, which was discredited with the later practice. In 1867, Marx made an adjustment to this thesis in the preface to the first volume of *Das Kapital*.

With the development of the productive forces, the contradiction between the workers and the capitalists became more and more prominent. In 1864, the International Working Men's' Association was established. Marx wrote an *Inaugural Address of the International Working Men's Association* for the establishment of the Association. In the *Inaugural Address*, Marx talked about the

---

22 *Complete Works of Marx and Engels*, Vol. 2, People's Publishing House, 2009, pp. 591-592.
23 Ibid., p. 592.

cooperative factories and the prominent common problems of labor movement. He said: "We speak of the co-operative movement, especially the co-operative factories raised by the unassisted efforts of a few bold "hands".[24] "production on a large scale, and in accord with the behests of modern science, may be carried on without the existence of a class of masters employing a class of hands; that to bear fruit, the means of labor need not be monopolized as a means of dominion over, and of extortion against, the laboring man himself; and that, like slave labor, like serf labor, hired labor is but a transitory and inferior form, destined to disappear before associated labor plying its toil with a willing hand, a ready mind, and a joyous heart."[25] And Marx put forward in the Volume III of *Das Kapital*, argued that joint-stock companies and cooperative factories are the two main forms in the transition to a new mode of production, this new mode of production as the future communist mode of production, so Marx's *Inaugural Address* at the opening of the International Working Men's Association had already proposed a solution to the question of the modalities of the transition, but it was only elaborated and broadly explained in the Volume III of *Das Kapital*.

Based his exploration in this stage of exploration, in the course of writing his economic manuscripts, Marx had further cleared the principles of general political economy from the aspect of the issue of object of research, and he planned to write his masterpiece economics work with the attributes of general political economy. And besides with the development of the international labor movement, Marx realized that the mere study of the capitalist economic system alone could solve practical problems of the transition to a higher form of social formation, and the issue of free development of men.

III. Year 1867: *Das Kapital,* Volume I and Engels' Book Reviews

In 1867, *Das Kapital*, Volume I was published after repeated revisions by Marx. Marx stated in the preface of the first edition: "In this work I have to examine the capitalist mode of production, and the conditions of production and exchange corresponding to that mode. Up to the present time, their classic ground is England."[26] In other words, Marx's *Das Kapital* study had focused on revealing specific laws of capitalism and capitalist stage, but it also includes many thoughts of political economics in a broad sense. For example, in the preface of the first edition, Marx pointed out: "when a society has succeeded in discovering the path of the natural law which governs its moment, it can neither clear it at a leap nor abolish by decree the phases of its natural development. But it can shorten the period of gestation and lessen the pains of delivery."[27] This is of guiding importance to Engels' discussion on Russia when may develop into socialism without going through capitalism and to Lenin's discussion on the transition issue. Marx pointed out: "My standpoint, from which the evolution of the economic formation of society is viewed as a process of natural

---

24   *Complete Works of Marx and Engels*, Vol. 3, People's Publishing House, 2009, p. 12.
25   Ibid., pp. 12-13.
26   *Works of Marx and Engels*, Volume 5, People's Publishing House, 2009, p. 8.
27   Ibid., pp. 9-10.

history, can less than any other make the individual responsible for relations whose creature he socially remains, however much he may subjectively raise himself above them."[28] The so-called economic formation of society refers to the interpersonal relations in material production. It is a theory of general historical materialism and significant thought of political economics in a broad sense which evaluates the "development of production relations as a process of natural history". In Chapter 24 (Primitive Accumulation) in Volume I of *Das Kapital*, Marx talked about the historical trend of capitalist accumulation and stated: "Along with the constantly diminishing number of the magnates of capital... Centralisation of the means of production and socialisation of labour at last reach a point where they become incompatible with their capitalist integument. This integument is burst asunder. The knell of capitalist private property sounds. The expropriators are expropriated."[29] It fully expresses that the capitalism is not eternal as the bourgeois economists advocate. In the sense of historical materialism, it is merely a stage of development in human society and will be definitely replaced by more advanced economic formation of society (ger. ökonomische Gesellschaftsform). "The capitalist mode of production and appropriation, hence the capitalist private property, is the first negation of individual private property founded on the labour of the proprietor. Capitalist production begets, with the inexorability of a process of nature, its own negation. It is the negation of the negation. This does not re-establish private property for the producer, but gives him individual property based on the acquisition of the capitalist era: i.e. on cooperation and the possession in common of the land and of the means of production."[30] We understand that, the essence of "re-establishing private property for the producer" explores the distribution conditions and issues of ways and time to transit to future communist social formation, which has something in common with Engels' definition of political economics in a broad sense.

After publication of *Das Kapital*, Volume I, Engels wrote 9 book reviews and 1 outline. The 9 book reviews were written by Engels after consulting with Marx to break the silence after Marx's *A Contribution to the Critique of Political Economy* was published, Engels aimed to trigger a debate on it. In fact, upon the publication of *Das Kapital*, bourgeois scholars could not maintain their silence. We can see that in the 9 book reviews and 1 outline written by Engels, the political economics in the broad sense has been mentioned in this short review of political economics in the narrow sense. On October 12, 1867, Engels wrote in his book review of *Das Kapital*, Volume I published in the newspaper named *The Future*: "the sense of history which pervades the whole book and forbids the author (Marx) to take the laws of economics for eternal truths, for anything but the formulations of the conditions of existence of certain transitory states of society; we would, alas, look in vain among our official economists for that scholarship and acumen with which the various historical states of society and

---

28   Ibid., p. 10.
29   Ibid., p 874.
30   *Collected Works of Marx and Engels*, Vol. 5, People's Publishing House, 2009, p. 874

their conditions of existence are here presented."[31] In other words, Marx argued that the law of economy in a certain stage is merely the reflection of the "conditions of existence of certain transitory states of society. Different social state will have different law of economy. Obviously, "social state" here refers to social relations and the law of economy is the abstract expression of the development level of productive forces. Thus, the actual meaning of this sentence is productive forces determine the production relation and material basis determines superstructure, which is one of the basic principles of broad view of political economics. Likewise, Engels mentioned such idea in his book review published in *Dusseldorfer Zeitung*: "in this book the author's conception of the propositions of political economy not, as is usual, as eternally valid truths but as the results of certain historical developments."[32] "After the publication of this masterpiece, it will no longer be possible to treat slave labour, serf labour and free wage labour, for example, as economically alike, or to apply laws which are valid for modern large-scale industry, conditioned by free competition, without further ado to the conditions of antiquity or the guilds of the Middle Ages, or, when these modern laws do not fit ancient conditions, simply to declare the ancient conditions as heretical."[33] Thus, the law of economy is only the external manifestation of existing conditions of the specific social state. This conclusion is actually what broad political economics should continue to discuss and further analyze, and broad political economics should associate specific features of different social states. In 1867, Engels proposed his discussion on the transition issues in his book review published in *The Observer* (Der Beobachter). He stated: "Marx, represents money and very expertly traces in detail the various successive forms of industrial production: co-operation, the division of labour and with it manufacture in the narrower sense, and lastly machinery, large-scale industry and the corresponding social combinations and relations which naturally grow one from the other."[34] "We can here, too, see again a two-fold trend. In so far as he endeavors to show that present-day society, economically considered, is pregnant with another, higher form of society, he merely strives to present as law in the social sphere the same process which Darwin traced in natural history, a process of gradual evolution. Up to now such a gradual transformation has indeed taken place in social relations from antiquity through the Middle Ages to the present."[35] Engels answered the time and stage of Communism in his book review on *Democratic Weekly Paper* and said: "By no means. Marx sharply stresses the bad sides of capitalist production but with equal emphasis clearly proves that this social form was necessary to develop the productive forces of society to a level which will make possible an equal development worthy of human beings for all members of society.. All earlier forms of society were too poor for this. Capitalist production is the first to create the wealth and the productive forces necessary

---

31　*Complete Works of Marx and Engels*, Vol. 16, People's Publishing House, 1964, p. 234.

32　Ibid., p. 244, http://hiaw.org/defcon6/works/1867/reviews-capital/dzeitung.html.

33　Ibid., p. 245, http://hiaw.org/defcon6/works/1867/reviews-capital/dzeitung.html.

34　*Complete Works of Marx and Engels*, Vol. 16, People's Publishing House, 1964, p. 255.

35　Ibid.

for this."[36] Obviously, here, the transition stated by Engels is "gradual transformation " and "corresponding social combinations and relations which naturally grow one from the other" that is to say, the transition and change of a social state cannot be leap-style one and the future communism can only emerge and develop on the basis of capitalist system, which is opposite to Marx and Engels' later view which was mentioned in the Preface to the 1882 Russian Edition of the *The Communist Manifesto* where they proposed that Russian commune can directly transit to advanced communism without going through capitalist economic system. But it does not mean that Engels' discussion on transition issue in his book review in 1867 is incorrect. Because in 1867, the second industrial revolution had not reached its peak and the level of development of productive forces determined that the social relation could not achieve a "leap-style" development. In the end of the 19th Century, the second industrial revolution had achieved a vigorous development, with emerging worker movement, which aroused the attention of Marx and Engels, i.e. the ancient commune land ownership in Russia might possibly become the start of communist development, which means that the "leap-style" development could be possible.

IV. My brief comments and uncompleted tasks

To summarize, in the initial phase, Marx and Engels' research on political economy has begun from the aspect of broad sense. Besides, Marx was himself personally involved in the writing of *Anti-Dühring*, and the idea that "the system of political economics in broad sense has not yet been established" was also approved by Marx, thus it is not enough to merely pay attention to *Das Kapital* when studying the political economy of Marxism. Especially when the contemporary western neo-liberal economic thought keeps effecting our economics studies. According to Marx's research plan of political economics, combining with operating feature of our economy, we should strive to recover, establish and innovate the system of political economics from the aspect of broad sense, which constitutes the authentic development and adherence to Marxism and which can prove the validity and necessity of Chinese economics.[37] It should be noted that this article has only sorted out the political economics thoughts of Marxism in regard to the broad sense aspect, in the classical texts (between 1842-1845) written before the publication of *Das Kapital*, Volume I and book reviews written by Engels (1872-1883), Engels' supplement and perfection on broad political economics thoughts after death of Marx and Lenin's researches on broad political economics after death of Engels are all important parts of discussion on Marxist political economy, which will be studied by the author in subsequent works.

Originally published in the journal
Contemporary Economic Research, 2014(2)

---

36   Ibid., p. 271.

37   Please refer to the author's work Wang Yanan's Contribution to the Theory and Practice of Chinese Economics Research, *Economist* 2012(8).

Debate on the Two Views in the
Economic Field Continues

Xiang Qiyuan

There are two opposing views in the process of China's Reform and Opening-up, which was proposed by Jiang Zemin at the meeting to celebrate the seventieth anniversary of the founding of the CPC held in 1991. He said, "The field of ideology is an important arena where peaceful evolution and struggle to counter peaceful evolution fight against each other, and the confrontation between bourgeois liberalization and the Four Cardinal Principles is in essence a political struggle about whether to persist in the Communist Party's leadership and the socialist road, which usually turns to be a thought and theoretical struggle in the ideological field. The ideological propaganda front would be occupied by the capitalist ideology if not by the socialist ideology." "We must make a clear distinction between the two views on Reform and Opening-up, namely, we have to see clearly the fundamental boundary between the Reform and Opening-up based on the Four Cardinal Principles and the capitalized 'Reform and Opening-up' which is advocated by the supporters of bourgeois liberalization."[1]

The person who first revealed the essence of bourgeois liberalization is Mr. Deng Xiaoping. In the Sixth Plenary Session of the 12th Central Committee of the Chinese Communist Party in September 1986, he said, "I oppose bourgeois liberalization most. Why? Firstly, there appears a thought among the masses and the young people, that is, liberalization. Secondly, some people beat the drum on the side (support the view indirectly). For example, some people in Hong Kong and Taiwan oppose the Four Cardinal Principles and suggest that

---

1 *Selected Works of Jiang Zemin*, Vol. 1, Beijing: People's Publishing House, 2006, p. 160-163.

China should introduce the entire system of capitalism. And in their eyes that is the true modernization. What is liberalization indeed? In fact, it will lead China to the capitalist road." "Liberalization is confrontation, opposition or revision of our current policies and systems."[2] After the counterrevolutionary rebellion at some districts of Beijing was put down on June 9, 1989, Deng summarized the lessons from this event, "There is nothing wrong with the Four Cardinal Principles. If there is anything amiss, it is that these principles have not been thoroughly implemented: They have not been used as the basic concept to educate the people, educate the students, and educate all the cadres and Communist Party members. The nature of the current incident is basically the confrontation between the four cardinal principles and bourgeois liberalization.

On September 3, 1989, Deng said when meeting Professor Li Zhengdao, "the rebellion gives us a big lesson…Behind the reform there are two hands and we should not use only one hand. The reform is one and the struggle against bourgeois liberalization is the other. Sometimes, according to the real situation, one will outweigh the other."[3] He still stressed in the Southern Talks in 1992, "Throughout the process of Reform and Opening-up, we must also adhere to the Four Cardinal Principles. At the Sixth Plenary Session of the Twelfth Central Committee I said that the struggle against bourgeois liberalization must be conducted for twenty years. Now it seems it will take longer. The rampant spread of bourgeois liberalization may have grave consequences. It has taken the special economic zones more than ten years to reach the present stage. They can collapse overnight. Collapse is easy, but construction is difficult. If we don't nip bourgeois liberalization in the bud, we may find ourselves in trouble."[4]

After the Reform and Opening-up, economics circles in China have had heated debates on variety of economic issues. Of course, many of those ongoing debates are merely among those with different academic views, but partly they indeed embody a struggle between the two views on reform, which is worthy of our vigilance. Also, after the 18th CPC National Congress in 2012, there emerged different understandings and proposals about the direction of economic reforms. Some arguments after the 18th CPC National Congress are consistent with the past ones, which reflect the opposition between the two views.

Some people seem to support the policies concerning the Reform and Opening-up which were agreed in the 18th CPC National Congress, but in fact they have other suggestions or ideas which deny the fruits of economic reforms and changes since the 16th and 17th Congresses, asserting that China's reform has ceased and even went backwards over the past ten years.

---

2   *Selected Works of Deng Xiaoping*, Vol. 3, Beijing: People's Publishing House, 1993, p. 181-182.
3   *A Chronicle of Deng Xiaoping's Life*, Beijing: Central Party Literature Press, 2004, p. 1289.
4   *Selected Works of Deng Xiaoping*, Vol. 3, Beijing: People's Publishing House, 1993, p. 379.

On December 20, 2012, *The Financial Network* published the viewpoint put forward by Professor Zhang Weiying, the title of the article was "The Reform Progress Becomes Reversed and We Should Return to the Market-Oriented Reform". His article said, "Twenty years after the beginning of the reform, ideas defeated interests, but now interests defeat ideas. Almost all the policies are enacted to protect and increase self-interest of each sector." "After 30 years of reform, Keynesianism has not only become the guiding ideology of China's macroeconomic policies, but guides the formulation of China's '12th Five-Year Plan'. Now, a trend in which 'the state owned sector advances but the private sector retreats' has started in China, thus the reform is faced with a reverse progress." Soon after that, addressing many prestigious international economists at the sub-forum of the Boao Forum for Asia, Zhang Weiying clearly pointed out, "China hasn't carried out economic reform over the past ten years."

Renowned researcher Wu Jinglian basically holds the same view with Zhang Weiying when evaluating China's economic reform during the past ten years. He delivered a speech entitled "How Will China Restart the Reform" at the CEIBS Forum (China Europe International Business School) on March 17, 2013. He said, "In the past decade, Chinese people held different views about whether China continued the reform or changed its direction." In January 2012, the SDX Joint Publishing Company published a book written together by Wu Jinglian and Ma Guochuan and the title was *Restarting the Reform Agenda. Twenty Talks about China's Economic Reform* (hereafter referred to as *Wu's Book*). The book has described a lot of cases where the reform has ceased and even regressed, from the viewpoint of the two authors.

How to evaluate the reform in the past ten years is a serious issue, since each National Congress of the CPC serves as a link between past and future. Whether the 16th and 17th CPC national congresses have promoted advancement, pause or retreat is directly related to the starting point and direction of the reform advocated by the 18th CPC National Congress. Therefore, we should carefully read the summary statement given in the report of the 18th National Congress about the reform over the past decade.

The report of the 18th CPC National Congress under the headline of "Our Work in the Past Five Years and the Basic Experience We Have Gained in the Past Ten Years" stated the following: "Major progress has been registered in Reform and Opening-up. China's overall rural reform, the reform in tenure of collective forests and the reform of state-owned enterprises have been deepened, and the non-public sector of the economy has registered sound growth. The country's modern market system and macro-regulatory system have been steadily improved, and its reform of finance and taxation, banking, prices, science and technology, education, social security, medicine and public health, and public institutions has progressed steadily. China's open economy has reached a new level, and its import and export volume now ranks second in the world."

When referring to shortcomings at work and difficulties on the road ahead, the report pointed out that "Many systemic barriers stand in the way of promoting development in a scientific way. The tasks of deepening Reform and Opening-up and changing the growth model remain arduous."

The entire report has not mentioned reform pause or even regress at all. This fact may show that some people hold another standard in the evaluation of the reform. Those that meet their standard are evaluated as advancement and everything that fails to meet their standard is regarded as pause and regress.

Wu's Book sets the goal of the economic reform as "market-oriented reform". Gao Shangquan and Zhang Weiying have also repeatedly stressed the need to insist on the market orientation. I think this goal is unscientific. As we all know, the market economy is classified into the capitalist market economy and the socialist one. Both have something in common, but there are also obvious differences. The vague emphasis on the "market-oriented reform" without mentioning the reform of the socialist market economy is made for other aims.

The 14th CPC National Congress, held in 1992 had formally proposed the establishment of a socialist market economy. And a while later, the Third Plenary Session of the 14th Central Committee of the CPC and the Third Plenary Session of the 16th Central Committee of the CPC have issued special resolutions on how the socialist market economy would go forward. Over the two decades, the Party has continuously summed up experiences of the socialist market practice and gradually formed a comprehensive understanding of how China would establish and improve a socialist market economy. According to my knowledge, there are three key points in this understanding: Firstly, the socialist market economy is combined with the basic economic system of socialism. At the primary stage of socialism, the publicly owned economy, as the mainstay, should develop together with diverse forms of ownership (economies). Secondly, regulation by market and macroeconomic control and regulation by the government are complementary, inherently integrated and indispensable to each other. China's constant macroeconomic regulation and control is planned, which is significantly different from the occasional government adjustments in the capitalist market economy. Thirdly, the state-owned enterprises are the main force of the socialist market economy, thus their sound development is an important guarantee for the improvement of the socialist market economy.

The so-called "market-oriented reform" advocated by some people is completely different from the socialist market economy which was developed and established throughout the Party's two-decade exploration. In the first place, they oppose treating the public economy as the subject and the state-owned economy as the guidance for the market. By confronting the state-owned economy and state-owned enterprises against the "market-oriented reform", they seek to play down the role that the state-owned economy and state-owned enterprises play in the national economy. Furthermore, they strongly object to the government's macro-control over the market and argue that the government's role must be confined to providing public goods and confined to offer some complementary service for the market. Finally, they unrealistically exaggerate the status and role of the private economic sector in reform and state construction and advocate the privatization of state-owned economy. It is not hard for us to find that the theories of these views are inspired from market fundamentalism and neo-liberalism.

In the following part of the article, we will offer an evaluation about these people's attempts to attack and deny the state-owned economy and the state-owned enterprises under the mantle of "market-oriented reform".

On December 18, 2010, Prof. Zhang Weiying at the annual meeting of Finance, commented "We've always predicted that the proportion of contribution to GDP by the state-owned enterprises would reduce to one-third in thirty years and no one had believed it, now we predict this proportion will decline to less than 10% in the coming two and three decades. I'm very optimistic about that." "State-owned enterprises have nothing to do with the status of the CPC as a ruling party. If China's private enterprises rise, people's living standards will prosper. It's that simple. The ruling status of the CPC is fundamentally based on the improvement of people's life, which must be acknowledged." "Besides, the state-owned enterprises have nothing to do with the national security. In the countries with the weakest national security environment, state-owned enterprises always play a dominant role. By contrast, the countries where the private sector is dominant not only have domestic security, but also rule and lead other countries."

At the "2012 Annual Meeting of China Development Forum" held on March 17, 2012, Zhang Weiying stated: "I think the best macroeconomic policy is not the policy that the government spends money but the one that the government should spend as little money as possible, because it is rare that the governments spend money efficiently. In the next few years, it is significant for China to do three things well concerning the economic reform." "The first thing is to privatize state-owned enterprises. It is hard for us to imagine that China will truly enter the market economy under the situation that state-owned enterprises account for such a big proportion and occupy such a vital status. In fact, state-owned enterprises have become one of the obstacles on the road of China's further growth."

On January 21, 2013, Zhang Weiying pointed out at the press conference of *Wu's Book*, "The central government should do a few things to let us know China is indeed carrying out reform", and "What should it do specifically? Some SOEs have to retreat from the market and they shouldn't invest everywhere with the money they have earned by monopoly position. Or else, 30% or 50% of the shares of the four banks should be shared with the society or incorporated into the social security" (National Social Security Fund).

Not long ago, Zhang Weiying announced at the Boao Forum for Asia, "China hasn't implemented any economic reform during the past ten years. SOEs are getting more and more powerful and the government is intervening more and more frequently. This is a serious problem. If the government doesn't reverse the state-dominated economy, China will be unable to keep growing." "We must recognize the fact that economic development depends on entrepreneurship, especially on the spirit of private entrepreneurs. Thus, I hope the new session of government and the new leaders will continue with the market-oriented reforms and restart the interrupted privatization process of SOEs."

In the article Focuses in Market-Oriented Reform after the 18th CPC National Congress which was published in the 12th issue of Mayoral Reference in 2012, Mr. Gao Shangquan mentioned: "No consensus has been reached on how to define the state-owned economy. Some people claim that it is the political foundation of our Party. According to this view, it has to advance rather than retreat, since only 'advancement' can strengthen the rule of CPC and 'retreat' will undermine its ruling basis." "Practical experience both at home and abroad proves that the party's ruling basis is irrelevant to the proportion of the state-owned economy, but closely combined with three paired words, 'people's heart, people's life and people's opinion'."

Wu's Book talks much about the state-owned economy and enterprises. It basically holds the same view with Zhang and Gao. Its basic idea can be seen from summary words of Preface and in the Chapter Sixteen The Market-Oriented Reform Has Not Been Completed. In the Preface can be read: "China's reform is half done. The economic system set up in the late 20th Century is still a 'semi-regulated, semi-market' economy. The government and the state-owned economy no longer control everything, but still firmly grasp all the 'commanding heights' of the national economy and master and control the fate of the non-state economy." "The establishment of the market system has liberated the productive forces, which was suppressed by the backward system, consequently China's economy has grown rapidly. This is reflected mainly in following aspects: Firstly, the reform expands private business, promotes entrepreneurship and enthusiasm for business that had long been repressed has gushed forth in a sudden stream. By the end of the 20th Century, there appeared more than 30 million private companies in China, which function as the most fundamental driving force of China's unexpected and unprecedented development." "What is particularly serious is that stagnation and even retrogression of reform since the beginning of this century has strengthened the negative aspects of the 'semi-controlled (command) regulated and semi-market' economic system in China." "A conclusion is reached from the above analysis: China is now standing at the historic crossroads. To avoid any social crisis, we must make determined efforts to restart the reform, truly promote the market, law and democracy-oriented reform and establish an inclusive economic and political system."[5] There are some concluding thoughts in the Chapter Sixteen The

---

5 Wu Jinglian and Ma Guochuan, *The Restart of Reform Agenda—Twenty Points on China's Economic Reform*, Shanghai: SDX Joint Publishing Company, 2013, p. 1, 3-5.

Market-Oriented Reform Has Not Been Completed: "All in all, after 30 years, the market reform has achieved unprecedented achievements, laying a preliminary basis for the rapid rise of China's economy. However, China's reform hasn't obtained a complete success and hasn't overcome 'major setbacks'. For example, the initial market economic system established is not perfect. The current existing economic system has some important drawbacks. One major issue among them is that the government and state-owned enterprises are still playing a dominant role in resource allocation. This phenomenon is reflected in the following aspects: (1) Although the state-owned economy doesn't have superiority in contributing to the GDP, it still controls all the 'commanding heights' of the national economy… (2) Governments at all levels still maintain their power to interfere with our economy, maintain their power to distribute resources, govern the land, capital and other important economic resources; (3) The indispensable legal foundation for the modern market economy has not been established…"[6]

The leading figures above hold clear views. In their opinion, during the 30 years of Reform and Opening-up, the state-owned economic sector has not only failed to boost the national economy, but also played a negative role. The reason why China's economic system lies in the status of "semi-controlled (command) and semi-market" is that the state-owned economy still controls all the "commanding height" zones of the national economy. To promote what they call "market-oriented reform", China must further weaken its state-owned economy by making them quit from the "commanding heights" and give way to privatization. However, their proposal is clearly contrary to what is determined at the 18th CPC National Congress, and obviously contradicts the part Deepen economic structural reform across the board. "We should unwaveringly consolidate and develop the public sector of the economy; allow public ownership to take diverse forms; deepen reform of state-owned enterprises; improve the mechanisms for managing all types of state assets; and invest more of state capital in major industries and key fields that comprise the lifeline of the economy and are vital to national security. We should thus steadily enhance the vitality of the state-owned sector of the economy and its capacity to leverage and influence the economy. "Consolidating and developing" mentioned above is not promoting privatization; on the contrary, the document stipulates that we should allow more state-owned capital to flow into key industries and fields related to national security and economic lifelines rather than let it retreat; it stipulates that we should rather strengthen its control and not diminish.

Our Party has been always paying close attention to the state-owned economy. Some stipulations determined by the 18th CPC National Congress are also the extension of the stipulations determined by the national congresses of the Party since the 14th National Congress. Deng Xiaoping, Jiang Zemin and Hu Jintao have all delivered important instructions on how to consolidate and develop the public economy and state-owned economy. In an important speech delivered by Jiang Zemin in 2000, he made a profound analysis from a height of the economic basis of the socialist system. He said, "In our country, CPC is the ruling party which leads the people and exercises the state power. To operate effectively, the state power of our socialist country should be built on some economic and material forces. The state-owned economy which has developed and become stronger since the founding of the New China is an important foundation of our state power. The development of our state-owned economy is of great significance not only for ensuring steady economic development, and enhancing the comprehensive national strength and realizing fundamental interests of the overwhelming majority of the people, but also for consolidating and developing the socialist system, improving the great unity of various peoples across the country and guaranteeing the long-term security of the party and the country. Without the public economy, with the state-owned economy constituting its core, there would be no economic basis of socialism and there would be no economic basis and powerful material means for the CPC's ruling as well as the superstructure of the entire socialism." "Because of this, we've always emphasized the need to improve state-owned enterprises and economy. The 4th Plenary Session of the 15th Central Committee of the CPC specially made a decision about reform and strengthening of the state-owned enterprises. We stress the development of state-owned enterprises just to ensure the dominance of the state-owned economy over lifelines of the national economy and its guidance for the economic development and also to continuously consolidate and strengthen CPC's ruling as well as the economic basis of our socialist state power."[7]

I often ponder over one question: Why do the two reform views always debate on growth and decline of state-owned economy and state-owned enterprises over the two decades since the 1990s? It exactly indicates the fact that the state-owned economy is closely related to the survival of the socialist system. The dominant status of the public economy is the soul of the basic economic system at the primary stage of socialism, and the core of the pubic economy is the state-owned economy. If the state-owned economy is denied, the dominant status of the public economy will be lost. Without the dominant status of the public economy, the primary stage of socialism will not exist anymore, not to speak of realizing our pursuit to move forward along the road of socialism with Chinese characteristics.

Originally published in the journal Chinese Soul in September, 2013

------

7   *Selected Works of Jiang Zemin*, Vol. 3, Beijing: People's Publishing House, 2006, p. 71.

Part Two

Contemporary Socialist Economy in China

Perfect Our Dual Regulation System:
Market's Decisive Role and the Role of the Government

Cheng Enfu

103

Abstract: The Descision issued by the Third Plenary Session of the 18th Central Committee of the CPC has pointed out that we should make market play a decisive role in resource allocation and make government better play its role. Our knowledge on the roles of the market and government has gradually deepened. Having different features as economic regulation mechanisms, market regulation and government regulation both have functional weaknesses. Therefore, we should fully play market's decisive role in resource allocation, optimize the factor market system, establish the principles of equal, open and transparent markets and perfect the mechanism that the prices are mainly determined by market; we should better give play to the government's role, improve macroeconomic and microeconomic regulating system, comprehensively implement government functions, optimize government's organizational structure and endeavor to perfect using the "two hands" adjusting system of both market and government.

Key words: market regulation; government regulation; market's role; government's role

Economic regulation system is the core of economic operating mechanism and plays a decisive role in optimizing resource allocation. General Secretary Xi Jinping emphasized in his speech in 2013: we should integrate the goals of letting the market play a decisive role in allocating resources and letting the government play a better role. In the Third Plenary Session of the 18th Central Committee of the CPC, he further emphasized: "What we implement is socialist market economic system, we should still play the superiority of our socialist system and active role of CPC and government. Market should play a decisive role, but not entire role, in resource allocation."[1]

Letting "two roles" is not only related with the shaping of "economic new normal" such as boosting reform, stabilizing growth, transforming the growth mode, adjusting economic structure, increasing efficiency and preventing risks, but also relates to whether complete competitive market mechanism can truly resolve the high housing prices, high drug price, disordered price increases, low welfare, polarization between the rich and the poor, difficulties in employment, food and drug safety, serious bribery issues, frequent labor conflicts, low-quality urbanization and other urgent livelihood problems. The issue of relation between market and government is one of the basic theories of political economics and also the key to speed up and better develop national economy and deepen economic system reform. Therefore, research on this issue is of great and practical significance.

104 I. On gradually deepening the cognition of market and government functions

Practice is the sole criterion for testing the truth. Marxist scientific theories develop during practice. So does the socialist market economy theory. Our exploration on economic adjusting method has also deepened gradually. Commodity, currency and market have been taken as gathering of evil since utopian Socialism. Winstanley stated: "Humans will lose their innocence and purity after they begin buying and selling" and "mutual oppression and fooling".[2]

The founders of scientific socialism held that: certain degree of commodity-currency relations and cooperative economy of the old society, can exist when it transits to communist society. But with the development and practice of capitalist market economy, there will exist corruption, polarization between the rich and the poor and periodic economic crises. Thus, they have concluded that after stepping into the future communist society, "the seizure of the means of production by society puts an end to commodity production and therewith to the domination of the product over the producer. Anarchy in social production is replaced by conscious organization on a planned basis."[3]

---

1 Xi Jinping: Explanation about Decision of the Central Committee of the Communist Party of China on Some Major Issues Concerning Comprehensively Deepening the Reform, *People's Daily*, November 16, 2013.
2 Winstanley, *Works of Winstanley*, translated by Ren Guodong, Commercial Press, 1965, p. 100.
3 *Selected Works of Marx and Engels*, Vol. 3, People's Publishing House, 2012, p. 815.

After the October Revolution in Russia, faced with the economic difficulties caused by the "wartime communism policy", Lenin timely proposed to regard "market and trade" as the basis of social economy, even asserted that "we have to admit that our opinion on socialism has totally changed".[4]

Lenin's practice on "new economic policy" had primarily demonstrated the fact that productive forces had lagged behind considerably and the complicated situation of the social economy determines that the socialist economic construction cannot surpass the stages of commodity production and commodity exchange. After death of Lenin, the Soviet Union established a rigorous planned economy under the leadership of Stalin.

In the early period of the founding of new China, our country has copied the steps of the Soviet Union to build a planned economy system. Later on, although the Communist Party of China represented by Mao Zedong had conducted various creative exploration,[5] what implemented was a system centered around the planned economy. Since the capitalist market economy and the planned economy in primary stage of socialism both include insurmountable defects, the objective goal of reform is to combine basic economic system of socialism with the socialist market economy.

Since Reform and Opening-up in 1978, Deng Xiaoping has led CPC to explore the market economy issues. He himself had discussed this issue for many times (10 times before 1992 Southern Talks and 2 times after that—refer to *Chronological Biography of Deng Xiaoping*, 12 times in total). In 1992, the 14th National Congress of CPC finally proposed that the economic system reform for our nation as building a socialist market economic system. Practice has fully demonstrated that market is one effective means for resource allocation and economic adjustment, which can be adopted by both capitalism and socialism. However, the superiority of socialist market economy is that it can better give play to the government's role through the basic economic system of socialism centering at public ownership and resolve polarization between the rich and the poor and periodic economic crises which are fully exposed in capitalist market economy. Since 1992, the average annual economic growth rate has exceeded 9% and China has rapidly become an economic power with great global influence.

After our practice for over 20 years, our socialist market economic system has been established preliminarily and improved in certain way, but it still has many defects that restrain market's potential and hinder the market and the law of value from fully playing their roles. These mainly show as the following: firstly, market order is not regulated, there is still much phenomenon in which the economic interests are obtained inappropriately; secondly, the development of production factors market is lagging behind, some production factors

---

4   *Complete Works of Lenin*, Vol. 42, People's Publishing House, 1987, p. 367.
5   Cheng Enfu et al., *Research on Socialist Economic System with Chinese Characteristics*, Economic Science Press 2013, p. 140.

are waiting unused, resources are consumed excessively and a large number of utilizable potential resources are missed; thirdly, market principle is not unitary , there are many departmental protectionism and local protectionism; fourthly, market competition is insufficient, which hinders survival of the fittest and weakens structural adjustment. Meanwhile, the deficiencies of market adjustment (spontaneity, blindness, egoism, unreason) are also exposed, such as illegal business, speculative transactions, and ecological crisis, polarization between the rich and the poor, regional disparities, high housing prices, high drug price and so on. This all show that we still face shortage, off-side and misplaced government adjustment. President Xi Jinping pointed out that "these issues are hard to tackle, perfect socialist market economic system is hard to form, transformation of our growth mode and economic structure adjustment is hard to push forward".[6] Under such a backdrop, it is crucial whether "the market plays a decisive role in allocating resources and letting the government play a better role, and it is the key in resolving every contradiction in our current economic social development.

II. About issues regarding market adjustment and the strengths and weaknesses in its functioning

The law of value is the inherent link of commodity production and commodity exchange. Market economy is the economic system and economic operation method which is automatically governed by the law of value. With increases in the level of socialization of production domestically and in the level of economic opening, the function of market adjustment will keep strengthening. Objectively, attention should be paid to the law of value and its way of manifestation, i.e. the role of market adjustment in larger scale and higher level.

The so-called market adjustment is to adjust the supply and demand of commodities, services and resources through associated functions of price, competition, supply and demand and other systems, in order to guide the flow of economic resources to every aspect of the society and enable that economic interests are allocated respectively between different stakeholders, leading to the growth and sound development of national economy. Specifically, the strength or positive effects of market adjustment function are shown in five aspects: firstly, micro-economic balancing function, in other words, the market instructs the operating individuals who make independent decisions to follow strictly the changes in the factual demand, which accordingly will adjust the relation between supply and demand and balance the two in micro level; secondly, short-term resource allocating function, if put another way, the market can rapidly instruct that the economic resources should flow into the high-return sector in a short term, directly affecting the short-term resource allocation of economic subject; thirdly, market's signal transmitting function, that is to say, market can

---

6 Xi Jinping, Properly Give Play to the Roles of the Market and Government, Promote China's Economy and Society to Maintain a Healthy Development, *People's Daily*, May 28, 2014.

reflect the market demand and supply and competition situation through price signals and instructs the producers and operators to rapidly and independently make decisions; fourthly, scientific and technological innovative function, in other words, the market can instruct the producers and operators to improve production materials, improve production technologies and commodity quality and develop social productive forces; fifthly, it has the function of stimulating the partial interests, that is to say, the market can stimulate the producers to strengthen their operating management and internal and external cooperation based on their partial interest to boost economic development.

However, market adjustment also has insurmountable weaknesses in its function. Firstly, it tends to deviate from the macroeconomic goals. Because the market adjustment has features such as spontaneity, blindness, partial interests and irregularity, the subject of market behavior can hardly focus on the general goal of macro economy and long-term interest of the whole society due to its self-indulgent for own interests. Secondly, the sectors of economy which can be adjusted tends to be limited. In fact, not all sectors are appropriate for market adjustment. Unlike the general commodity production and exchange sectors, some sectors which suffer from natural monopoly due to scale of economies rule, such as infrastructures like transportation, water supply and power supply sectors, it is not possible to completely adopt market adjustment. In public welfare and non-profit sectors, such as education, health, environmental protection, cultural protection, basic research and national defense economy, the attempts to put the market adjustment at dominating place may even cause adverse consequence. Thirdly, it tends to trigger polarization between the rich and the poor. If the distribution of social wealth and income is totally dominated by market, then distribution will actually be dominated by capital, especially private capital, which will definitely cause "Matthew Effect". Fourthly, the adjustment and coordination of industries is relatively difficult. Market adjustment tends to cause the producers to focus more on short-term resource allocation and short-term income and return increases, while those basic industries having longer recovering time of capital and long-term profitability may be neglected and thus investments to some industries may be excessive. Fifthly, the real transaction prices are costly. In the contemporary market economy with its increasing scale, the supply and demand and transaction prices are interrelated and change frequently, which will definitely cause the market subject to spend great investigating cost, decision making cost, adaptation cost and even correcting cost. Accordingly, the microeconomic subject and the entire society will both undertake higher costs.

It should be pointed out that the theories by western economics regarding market adjusting function has also changed in different times. Classic economist J. Say had started from the commodity economy of barter and claimed that "supply can create its demand" and proposed omnipotence of market adjustment. A. Smith proposed "invisible hand" allocating resources, in order to curb the real effects of laisser-faire capitalism. Inherent harmony of individual interests and social interest is the premise of laisser-faire thought, which aims to consolidate capital interest and can hardly provide effective solution for the realization of the universal social interest. Faced with the disordered state of social production caused by the monopoly capitalism, new and classic Keynesianism has proposed that the government should intervene and make up for the malfunctioning aspects of the market and have affirmed various kinds of defects in the functioning of the market. However, in order to adapt to the demand of expansion by the international monopoly capital under the condition of economic globalization, neo-liberalism has abandoned government intervention and praised the "omnipotence of market" and "market fundamentalism" and "sole market-oriented reform"(if we use critical terms used by the representatives of contemporary Keynesianism, such as Stiglitz and Krugman). In general, faced with the functioning defects of resource allocation by market, the western scholars have proposed views such as the market structure theory, public goods theory, spillover effect or external effect, asymmetric information, imperfect market and unfair allocation, which are insightful. In practice, from laisser-faire capitalism to private or state monopoly capitalism, even to international monopoly capital system, the working scope and scale of resource allocation by market is not the same and the consequences are also different. In real economic life, neither does the function of resource allocation by market have no constraint nor is it realized independently. Since 19th Century, various economic crises, financial crises and fiscal crises, as well as contradiction between the rich and the poor in the western capitalist market economies all prove the objectivity of above analysis and verify that the advantages of market should be developed and the disadvantages of market should be abandoned.

III. About government's regulation: Strengths and weaknesses in its functioning

Government intervention or regulation is the important part of modern economic activities. What is government adjustment? Government adjustment in a broad sense covers the adjustments by the national legislative authority and administrative authority, as two aspects of national adjustment. After the great crisis in 1930s in the West, government's intervention and adjustment on economic life has become a normal phenomenon of economic operation globally. The so-called government adjustment means the government adopts economy, law, administration, persuasion and other means to adjust the economic acts of all kinds of economic subjects to realize the general and long-term targets of economic and social development. Government adjustment is not randomly or disorderly conducted, on the contrary it has an internal law, instead, it contains the law of proportional and planned development. In order to achieve steady and sound development of economy and society, the decisive role of market in resource allocation should be given play and the society should consciously perform macro and short term direct adjustment and micro regulation according to the general goals of economic development. It is objective and necessary for the government to undertake such functions. Then, what are the weaknesses of government adjustment?

In the macroeconomic level, the scientific adjustment function of government lies in preparing and realizing of the general goals of economic and social development. The primary target of government adjustment is to enable the stable macro economic situation. "Scientific macroeconomic adjustment is the internal requirement of playing the full advantages of socialist market economy system and it is the very function of government. The solution of such problem is not the advantage of market."[7] Employment is a social issue, but the ordinary market subject does not pay attention to the general situation of employment. Stability of prices determines the accuracy of signals given by the market prices. While on the other side the market operators, as individuals, tend to demand transparent or opaque signals to increase their benefits; the overall balance between supply and demand and also equilibrium of international payments are determined by the overall actions of millions of producers and operators. While the ordinary individual operators have no ability or motivation to maintain the balance of the two above. The imbalance of international payments makes huge impact on the economies of countries, especially in the developing countries and causes serious negative effects. Non-public sector of economy focuses on profits in the microeconomic level and it can hardly resolve the extreme disparity between the rich and the poor within the enterprise and in the whole society through market adjustments and individual market subject focuses on profits in the microeconomic level and it can hardly increase the macro-economic profits, social profits and ecological profits of the whole society. Some scholars have pointed out: "Government function and the other kind of macroeconomic adjustments are the functions aiming the whole economy, whole society, culture, ecological civilization and other construction aspects. It far exceeds the scope of resource allocation by market and its function cannot be completely realized by the market."[8] Practice proves that in order to the realize social development goal of macro-economy, government can detach from the economic decision process of single enterprises, also detach from short-term and partial interest decisions, and it can focus adjusting resource allocation and economic operation from an overall and comprehensive perspective, which can maintain the stability of macro-economy and ensure the realization of goals such as full employment, stable prices, balance between demand and supply, balance of international payments, common prosperity and sustainable and coordinated development of human, environment and resources.

---

7   Zhou Xincheng, How to Interpret "Let Market Play a Decisive Role in Resource Allocation", *Leading Journal of Ideological & Theoretical Education* 2014(1).
8   Wei Xinghua, Grasp A New Round of Theoretical Instruction and Strategic Deployment of Deepened Economic System Reform, *Journal for Party and Administrative Cadres*, 2014(1).

Looking from an intermediate level, the advantages of government's scientific adjustment lie in their solutions to imbalanced development of industries structure and imbalanced regional economic development. Because government adjustment has certain foresight, general vision and strategy, it can pay more attention to coordinated development and comprehensive balance among industries and regions. Unlike market which excessively focuses on short-term benefits of allocation of resources, government adjustment can focus on repairing the "disadvantages" of economic and social development, and focus on investing into newly emerging industries which have long term and great strategic importance, and focus to basic industries that involves the livelihood and regional development. For example, government can boost the large-scale application of new technologies through means like financial policies, speed up the elimination of consuming the outdated production capacity and accelerating the transformation and upgrading of the industrial structure. The planned and proportional development of regional economies and the "belt and road economy" (Yangtze belt, One Belt, One Road) in the Pearl River Delta, Yangtze River Delta, Beijing, Tianjin and Hebei, middle China and regions of western China and northeast China regions are closely related with the active adjustment by the central and provincial governments.

In the microeconomic level, the advantages of government's scientific adjustment lie in its necessary regulation or supervision. The order and high efficiency of modern market economy cannot be purely built on self-consciousness and self-discipline basis of the ordinary market subject. Instead, government adjustment has fairness and authority, can better regulate the honest operation of economic subject legally and able to safeguard the normal order of market with economic and administrative means such as admission, punishment and black list systems. Pre-supervision, supervision in process and post-supervision has different functions as cases may be and all 3 of them are indispensable. For example, in aspects such as lowest salary system, laborer's rights and interests and evaluations on environmental protection, government adopts policies and laws to regulate them, which can effectively ensure laborer's interests and maintain the interests of society and public which cannot be done well by the market adjustment.

Government adjustment also has drawbacks. In terms of the deficiency and disadvantages of government adjustment, they are mainly related to subjectivity of government choices, subjective changes in adjustment policies, lack of coordination between departments and lack of motivation mechanisms for the undertakers of adjustments (officers). Specifically, firstly, the choices of government adjustment may be harmful, which means governments tend to deviate from the demands of the whole society. For example, "GDP First" preference will lead to blind investments, excessive investment subsidies and ignorance of people's livelihood and ecological construction. Secondly, government adjustment has inappropriate procedures, which is inclined to fall into non-democratic procedures, too late measures and higher costs of adjustment, and it can hardly respond to market changes timely and flexibly. Thirdly, government adjustment is poorly compatible, tends to obey interest demands by specific groups or by an enacting department or by local interest, and causes internal frictions in policies. Fourthly, government adjustment has insufficient motivation, which is inclined to decrease the initiative of government adjustment, which is not strong enough to solve the already exposed conflicts and problems, and arouses bureaucracy in the government and decreases the efficiency of government adjustment. Practice has proved that currently, over-staffing in medium and small departments of the government, excessive reviews, passing its own responsibility to other departments and local protectionism, to a degree lead to "improper order", "difficultly enacted order" and low efficiency in scientific government adjustment.

IV. On the different features of market adjustment and government adjustment

The Third Plenary Session of the 18th Central Committee of the CPC has proposed: we should integrate the goals of letting the market play a decisive role in allocating resources and letting the government play a better role," But it is partially understood by some public figures and even interpreted as certain kind neo-liberal view. For example, some articles have argued that, the proposal for the decisive role of the market is a "breakthrough idea and shows us true route map for reform", in fact which should be based on reform of China's basic economic system, reform of the market system, government functioning and macro regulation and accordingly the reform strategy of "crossing the river by feeling the stones" which emphasizes testing our economic policy and practice.

Thus, we must accurately understand the meaning of "market's decisive role" under socialist market economy with Chinese characteristics proposed by the Third Plenary Session of the 18th Central Committee of the CPC and President Xi Jinping. Generally speaking, it places emphasis on the dual adjustment of market and government, but the functions and roles of market and government are different being in a dialectical relation. Then, what are the different features of the dual adjustment of market and government?

Firstly, in different macro and microeconomic levels, "the theory of market's decisive role" emphasizes that the government's macroeconomic adjustment and microeconomic regulation should be adopted jointly to correct some negative consequences of "market's decisive role". President Xi Jinping has pointed out that in China's socialist market economy, market plays a decisive role, but not the entire role in resource allocation. We should "improve the macroeconomic adjusting system orienting at national development strategy and plan with major means of fiscal policy and monetary policy".[9] The independent autonomous role of the law of value may still bring about negative consequences.

---

9   Decision of the Central Committee of the Communist Party of China on Some Major Issues Concerning Comprehensively Deepening the Reform, *People's Daily*, November 16, 2013.

Government's macro adjustment and microeconomic regulation must be adopted to avoid or decrease such negative consequences. Macroeconomic adjustment mainly includes pre-regulation, regulation in process and post-regulation of investments, consumption and other market activities through fiscal and monetary economic means and policies as well as the proper administrative means to realize macroeconomic targets such as full employment, stable prices, reasonable growth mode and balanced international payments. Microeconomic regulation or adjustment by government mainly adopts economic, legal and administrative means to lead behaviors of microeconomic subjects so as to maintain the normal competitive market order, to boost scientific and technological innovation, develop independent intellectual property, improve social harmony and keep decent ecology to realize comprehensive, coordinated and sustainable development of economy, politics, society, culture and ecology.

Secondly, if we look into the "market's decisive role regarding production materials and resources allocation ", its accurate meaning includes the short-term allocation of general resources by market, which is combined with government's long-term allocation of numerous general resources and government's direct allocation of special resources such as natural resources and infrastructure. The efficiency of "market's decisive role" is mainly shown in the short-term allocation of general resources driven by short-term interests and driven by the law of value; while the efficiency of government's allocation on resources is mainly shown in the long-term allocation of numerous general resources and regulation of allocation of special resources such as natural resources, infrastructure and transportation. Therefore, market plays fully decisive role in short-term allocation of general resources. Government conducts planned and long-term allocation of numerous general resources through balancing the short-term and long-term interests. Due to the non-renewable nature of special resources such as natural resources, government will strengthen the regulation and allocation of these resources through planning and balancing the short-term and long-term interests, and balancing of partial and overall interests. The market's operation or effect in regard to specific production projects does not equal to determination by market's effect. Because the essence of market's effect means micro economic subject's autonomous decision regarding resources in specific production projects. In fact, major projects involving livelihood of people tend to be decided firstly by the government and then operated and ran by the market. Since the Reform and Opening-up, China has implemented "market's decisive role" in resources such as rare earth and coal, which has led to destructive and non-efficient exploitation of resources and exporting of them at low prices and led to the phenomena of "coal bosses" who became rich overnight and to frequent labor accidents, giving an impressive lesson. At present, the large scale production capacity in steel, iron, coal and other industries is excessive, residential houses prices are high and there exists a real estate "bubble", all of which are related to excessive market function and lacking of government function.

Apart from the two points above, we should analyze the features of dual adjustment of market and government from another three aspects.

Firstly, it is about market and government's function in allocating resources in non-material production sectors such as education, culture and health care services. Market's decisive role can also be utilized in the allocation of general cultural resources and health care resources, but when we discuss the resource allocation regarding the non-material production sectors such as education, culture and health care, government's leading role should be coordinated with market's main role. Vigorous development of education and culture is an important part of economic and social development, and an important carrier of socialist core value system. The social benefit should be seen as the first priority and combined with economic benefit, in this way market's function in the allocation of these resources will be diminished. Many of such educational and cultural projects have such functions as universality, long-term spiritual-intellectual support for the socialist system, protecting cultural heritage, promote cultural cohesion and cultural guidance, which should only be allocated in a highly efficient manner through government's leading role. Just as President Xi Jinping put it, cultural sector has both industrial and ideological properties, regardless of reform, the guidance of this sector cannot be cancelled and we cannot give up our leading position.

Secondly, the issue is about the relation between market and government involved in resources allocation. Is resource allocation only engaged with the relation between market and government roles? Comprehensively evaluating, resource allocation has two levels. The first level is market's allocation and government's allocation; the second level is private allocation and public allocation. "Market's decisive role" in socialism with Chinese characteristics relates with the mixed economy with public economy sectors as the mainstay. The public economy sector's dominant status qualitatively and quantitatively is the internal requirement and natural property of socialist market economy with Chinese characteristics. "In socialist economy, unlike capitalism, the function of public economy sector is not to engage in the industries that the private enterprises are unwilling to operate in order to supplement the drawbacks of the private enterprises and the market system, instead, it aims to realize the stable and coordinated development of national economy and consolidation and improvement of socialism."[10]

The Third Plenary Session of the 18th Central Committee of the CPC also expressively pointed out: "We must unswervingly consolidate and develop the public economy, persist in the dominant position of public ownership, give full play to the leading role of the state-owned sector, and continuously increase its vitality, controlling force and influence."[11]

---

10 Liu Guoguang, Two Fundamental Differences between Socialist Market Economy and the Capitalist Market Economy, *Red Flag*, 2010(21).
11 Communiqué of the Third Plenary Session of the 18th Central Committee of the CPC, *People's Daily*, November 13, 2013.

If the public economy is not treated as dominant in the socialist economy, government's adjustment function will be weakened greatly, which will greatly hinder the implementation of economic and social development strategy of the country and the country will lack the economic basis that will guarantee the fundamental interest of the masses and common prosperity. Thus propositions to privatize state enterprises and public schools and hospitals is typically for neo-liberalism.

At the current stage, China adopts the basic economic system with public ownership as mainstay and development of various other ownership sectors in tandem, which is more suitable to the internal requirements of contemporary market economy implemented in China than contemporary capitalist economic system with private ownership as the mainstay, the former is of course more efficient and fair. Therefore, we should strengthen our support for state-owned enterprises especially the key enterprises. The state-owned enterprises are of great importance and life-line for the destiny of our national economy, and they are guarantees for the nation at critical times. What western countries such as the US's fear is just the mightiness of the CPC. One of the reasons behind the CPC's strength is the financial, material and manpower support given by the state-owned enterprises which lead the destiny of national economy, which is the most crucial point. Thus the operation of state-owned enterprises is not completely determined by market, but by political decisions, which means it is wrong to believe that state-owned enterprise is definitely a bad system and the only solution is to "abandon the state-owned enterprises." Practice at home and abroad have proved that the nation will not suffer from financial crises, economic crises and fiscal crisis as well as polarization between the rich and the poor like in capitalism when as it does not maintain public economy as the mainstay and state ownership as the dominant relation. Fundamental difference between socialism and capitalism is their basic economic systems, which lies in the social ownership of production materials, that is to say, whether which one is dominant element in mixed ownership: public capital or private capital.

Therefore, we should not only focus develop mixed ownership and non-public economy, and in turn neglect the role of public economy in reforms, at the same time we should not only focus on market's decisive role in resources allocation, and in turn neglect the effective role of government. Those views and measures that misinterpret the spirit of the Third Plenary Session of the 18th Central Committee of the CPC and the speech of President Xi Jinping are wrong. Speaking from the aspect of economics, the faith in socialism is firstly presented as faith in public ownership and common prosperity which is the result of it. Besides, economy determines politics and economic basis determines superstructure. Public ownership is the socialist economic basis of the socialist superstructure and the basis of the rule and leadership by the CPC and it is also main subject which leads various main pillars of the Chinese economy during the primary stage of socialism.

Thirdly, there is the issue of distribution, what are features of market's role and government's role in the distribution sphere?. This involves the fifth perspective in the analysis. In the distribution sphere, market and government play great adjusting roles respectively both in wealth and income distribution. Firstly, at the primary distribution level, market plays great adjusting role in distributing wealth and income through the spontaneous effect of the law of value, while the government also plays certain adjusting roles in distribution of wealth and income through preparing and enactment of relevant laws and regulations. In this way, with the government's this role, the reasonable increase of labor incomes can be realized in primary distribution, labor rights can be truly maintained and we can realize our policy of "limit the high incomes, improve the low incomes and expand the middle incomes". Secondly, in the secondary distribution or redistribution, government should play a greater role to correct and adjust the issues such as polarization between the rich and the poor caused by primary distribution, boost the actual increase in residents' wealth and income, proportionally in line with economic development. In the past, market's decisive role was emphasized in the housing issues of urban residents, which has led to sharp rises of housing prices, real estate developers have become rich overnight and complaints have been abundant. Government has not play its regulatory role actively until recent years, since government becomes active, the housing issue, an important livelihood issue has turned to be more easily tackled.

V. On the Necessity of Improving Market System during the Deepening of Reforms

As the market plays its roles through its inherent market mechanisms, so how to perfect this system, so that the reform is deepened? As pointed out explicitly by President Xi Jinping: "Establishing a unified, open, competitive and orderly market system is the basis for the market to play a decisive role in the allocation of resources. We must accelerate the formation of a modern market system with business autonomy, fair competition, consumer's free choice and consumption, and free exchange of goods and elements, exert great efforts to clear market barriers, and improve the efficiency of resource allocation and fairness."[12] It is thus clear that the establishment of a sound market system will be put in a foundational status. To sum up, to build a sound market system, we should do the following:

Firstly, improve the system of factor markets. The market system is an objective and organic system that consists of several components. It is an organic whole which includes interconnected and interrelated markets such as the commodity markets like the consumer products and means of production, the factor markets like the capital market, labor, technology, information and real estate markets, and includes the special trading markets like the futures, auctions and

---

12 Decision of the Central Committee of the Communist Party of China on Some Major Issues Concerning Comprehensively Deepening the Reform, *People's Daily*, November 16, 2013.

property rights markets. Since the Reform and Opening-up, China's commodity markets have seen a rapid development, but its factor markets such as land, capital and technology products, i.e. the factors markets had a lagging growth, and as a result, the price of factors in the market can not reflect the scarcity and supply-demand situation, well. After the Third Plenary Session of the 18th Central Committee of the CPC, China mainly worked on three aspects: building up an integrated "construction lands" market for the rural and the urban regions, improving the financial products markets system, and establishing a sound market-oriented technological innovation mechanism. It should be said that, these are all measures with very strong realistic pertinence. Land, capital and technology are all important production factors and improving these factor markets will produce profound influence on the transformation of the economic growth mode of China, improve the optimization of resource allocation, promote competition and push forward the building of an innovative country.

Secondly, establishing fair, open and transparent market rules. The fair, open and transparent market rules are the primary premise for fair market competition. Only by striving to remove market barriers could we improve the resource allocation efficiency. This requires us to continue to explore the negative list approach, set unified market access criteria, continue to explore the market access management mode for incoming foreign investments, boost the facilitation of industrial and commercial registration rules, reform the market monitoring system, and set up a sound market exit mechanism, etc. These measures will have important effects on the fight against regional and departmental protection, fight against monopoly and unfair competition and help to buildan honest society.

Thirdly, improve the mechanisms where the prices are mainly determined by the market. Formation of prices through a sound market system is the main mechanism for the market to promote the optimal allocation of resources. Whether the price can flexibly reflect the changes in the magnitude of values, the resource scarcity and the supply and demand is the main sign of whether the market system is perfect or not. Therefore, in order to promote the perfection of the market system, the range of government led pricing must be limited. On the one hand, we should clearly declare the range of government pricing, limit them within the key utility services, public services, and network-based natural monopoly links, and stress that the government led pricing should increase transparency and accept public supervision. On the other hand, we should restore the commodity attribute of some special resources (goods), advance the price reform in goods such as water, petroleum, natural gas, electricity, transport and telecom fields, and promote the marketization and standardization of prices with them. However, that the phrase "government should not exert improper intervention" does not mean that the government must not intervene at all. The key lies in whether the government's intervention is appropriate and beneficial to social welfare and good for people's livelihood, which is a question not to be viewed from one single side.

VI. On How to Better Play the Government's Role

Since the Third Plenary Session of the 18th Central Committee of the CPC, the theorists and the economists presented the idea of "the government must act" or else "the government's role will be determined by the market", based on the one-sided understanding of "market determinism", they believe that the government is the main barrier to the realization of "market determinism" and have argued that the "focus" or "center" of deepening the reform should be the "government reform", which can be briefly defined as "simplifying the administration and transferring the powers to lower levels."At the 15th group study session of the Political Bureau of the CPC Central Committee, President Xi Jinping stated, "China should make good use of the roles of the market—the 'invisible' hand, and the role of the government—the 'visible' hand", he added: "we cannot use the decisive role of the market in the allocation of resources to replace or even negate the role of the government, nor the vice versa."[13] How could we square the basic issue, such as "improving the government's role" and sticking to the basic economic system, with the idea of "market determinism"? Neither is it right to simply emphasize "the simplification of administration and delegation of administrative powers to lower levels". It should be a systematic project to build up a sound macro-control system, comprehensively and properly perform the government's functions and streamline the government's organizational structure, the core of which is to build a democratic and efficient government ruled by law and a service-oriented government. For the time being, great attention should be paid to the following reforms and improvements:

Firstly, build up a sound macro-control and micro-regulatory system.

According to the Decision made in the Third Plenary Session of the 18th Central Committee of the CPC, three changes will take place in China's macro-control architecture: firstly, for the ordinary economic subjects, the stress on national development strategy and national plan's guiding role will be highlighted more predominantly. And among the macro-economic tools one of the "primary means", the "financial policy" will be replaced by "monetary policy". Secondly, to solve the difficulties concerning leading the local government's policies by the central government's regulation and control policies, new approach will bring more effective leadership to local governments which will emphasizing the need to improve the assessment system, an new approach will correct the biased understanding of purely judging the local administration's performance by the economic growth rate, that means the weight of other indexes will be increased, i.e. resource consumption, environmental damage, ecological benefits, and excess production capacity, which will all strengthen the restraints on the local provincial governments. Thirdly, the issue of coordinated development of the international economy, to solve the issue more efficiently close attention should be paid to form a more efficient mechanism for

---

13   Xi Jinping, Properly Give Play to the Roles of the Market and Government, Promote China's Economy and Society to Maintain a Healthy Development, *People's Daily*, May 28, 2014.

participating in the coordination of international macroeconomic policies, thus China will play its role in the improvement of international economic governance structure. At present, the attention should be given to regulate the issues of drug, medicine and food safety and high housing price issues.

Secondly, comprehensively and properly perform the government's functions.

The scientific and efficient regulation by the government should be based on the government's proper application of its functions, and adapt to the new requirements of new changes in the macro-control system. In order to better release the potential of the market, limiting part of the government's powers is indeed a very important orientation. Necessity or regulations for government approvals for those economic activities that can be effectively regulated by the market should be cancelled, which will hinder the government from "overstepping" its functions. At the same time, the government should focus and strengthen the formulation and implementation of development strategies, plans, policies and criteria, and enhance the supervision of market activities. And it should enhance its capacity of offering various types of public services without any "omission". In principle, all logistic operations and services sold to government should be subject to competition mechanism. Non-public sector should acquire business through their past performance of business contracts, a system of "entrustment agreement"[14], or by other regulatory means." The government should be kept away from the problem of "dislocation".

118

The shifting of the role of the state requires further optimization of the government organizations. President Xi Jinping has proposed the concepts of "improving and optimizing the structure of government organizations, function composition and working procedures", and added we should "deepen the reform of the system concerning the matters subject to government examination and approval, continue to streamline administration", "we should steadily advance the reform to establish larger government departments and improve division of functions among them", "government organizations which undertake executive powers and supervision oversight should check each other and they should function concertedly", "we should strictly control the size of government bodies, cut the number of their leading officials, reduce their administrative costs."

I fully agree that China should steadily advance the reform to establish larger government departments, as soon as possible, keep no more than 20 organs under the state council, and at the same time, cut down the number of the existing administrations directly under the State Council. Besides, China should follow the practice of other countries with high administrative efficiency, reduce the number of deputies and the size of government departments at all levels, and in

14 "Entrustment agreement" is necessary in order to set out the public service obligations of the undertaking and must have been committed to the organization through an official act having legal force under the national law of the state. Thirdly, optimizing the structure of government organizations.

principle we should the practice of the manning from subordinate government organs in the form of external "secondment", we should form and implement strict working procedures, timetable, rewarding and demotion and punishment measures, we should highlight the fight against bureaucracy and departmentalism, and let the governmental departments at all levels deepen the education of implementing the mass line.

The ideas of renowned western economists are also worth noting. Several years ago, Samuelson suggested that China should take the middle course, neither get too skewed toward either side in terms of the relationship between the market and the government. Stiglitz, in his speech in Tsinghua University, in the first half of this year said that China's market plays too big a role, while the government plays too small a role, China levies nearly no tax on the returns of private capital, which causes a large the distribution gap.

VII. On the Complementary Roles of Market and Government

Are the roles and functions of the market and the government constitute a relation of counter-acting or counter-balance relationship? No. They are economic regulation modes and mechanisms which do not exactly work within the same level and field. All in all, in the future, we should see that market plays its decisive role and the government will play its role better, and these two supplement each other as an organic whole, rather than having a diametrically opposed relation. It is necessary to use the market's outstanding regulatory role to suppress the failures of "government's regulation", and we should also use the government's outstanding regulatory role to correct the failures of the "market regulation", Thus we should form a larger, stronger and efficient market and a stronger and effective government, wherein both will undertake greater roles. This will not only help the socialist state to bring into play its benign regulatory role, but at the same time, will avoid stepping into the self-trap of neo-liberalism by top-level design and avoid encountering the risks of financial and economic crises. What we advocate here is fundamentally different from what our domestic neo-liberalism proponents advocate, i.e. their so-called "China being semi-command economy" argument and also different from their "market determinism" theory. Also different from the so-called "modern market economic system" that advocates a competitive market mechanism without government regulation, different from the reform proposition based on market fundamentalism which praises the "omnipotence of the market" which rejects the necessary macro-control and micro-regulation by the government, which is also strongly criticized by various Keynesians.

Originally published in the journal Social Sciences in Chinese Higher Education Institutions, 2014(6)

Constructing the Socialist Economic System with Chinese Characteristics with the Thinking of Totality

Hu Leming

In order to accomplish the strategic objectives and work arrangements set by the 18th Central Committee of the CPC, and form a comprehensive, scientifically standardized, and effective economic system, *Decision of the Central Committee of the Communist Party of China on Some Major Issues Concerning Comprehensively Deepening the Reform* adopted at the Third Plenary Session of the 18th CPC Central Committee (hereinafter referred to as *Decision*), highlighted the vital role of economic system reform and reflected the action logic of building the socialist economic system with Chinese characteristics based on the holistic thinking.

Building the socialist economic system with Chinese characteristics is a holistic undertaking

Holistic thinking or totality is the basic methodology used by Karl Marx to examine the human society and its development history. Marx defined totality as the indivisible function of interdependence, interrelation, mutual influence, and interactions among aspects of relevance; holistic thinking is an approach that analyzes objects by placing them in multiple structures and complex relations. While examining the human society and its development history by applying the holistic thinking, we must see the human society as a historical totality, a structural totality, a spatial totality, and thus, scientifically understand the development history of human society and fully consider the interaction and interrelation between its economy, politics, society and culture and other aspects in perspective, and grasp the unity nature in the law of human's social development and the diversity of the human's social development with its specific development path at different times and in different countries. Obviously, the socialist economic system with Chinese characteristics is a total existence, and building the socialist economic system with Chinese characteristics is an overall comprehensive undertaking. Therefore, we should understand the socialist economic system with Chinese characteristics and its building based on such holistic thinking.

Theory is a reflection of the reality. The building of socialist economic system with Chinese characteristics is a brand-new practice. As there is no existing complete experience for us to learn from, we have to make explorations and innovations and go through a gradual accumulation of knowledge, and a gradual deepening of cognition from partial to the whole. The Third Plenary Session of the 11th Central Committee of the CPC in 1978, sounded the trumpet for Reform and Opening-up, starting a new path of building socialist economic system with Chinese Characteristics with the focus on the reform of economic system in rural areas. The Third Plenary Session of the 12th central Committee of the CPC marked the beginning of city-centered reform of economic system; the Third Plenary Session of the 14th and 16th Central Committee of the CPC stressed the establishment and improvement of socialist market economic system; the Third Plenary Session of the 18th Central Committee of the CPC highlighted the guiding role of the economic system reform, and at the same time, clearly advocated the idea of further deepening the comprehensive reform in the political, cultural, social, and ecological civilization fields, pointed out the general goal of the deepening reform is "to improve and develop the socialist system with Chinese characteristics, and advance the social governance system and modernization of the governance ability", which all vividly embodied the action logic of building socialist economic system with Chinese characteristics based on the holistic thinking.

When advancing the deepening of the reform comprehensively on the basis of the holistic thinking, embodies the idea of adapting to the requirements of the era. The emerging systematicness and complexity of social practice in the contemporary development stage of socialist reform with Chinese characteristics and the trend of coexistence of emerging high "discretization" and "totalisation" of contemporary human society's development require us to observe the socialist economic system with Chinese characteristics and its building in accordance with the Marxist principle of totality. The economic system is the rules and constraints that regulate the behaviors of subjects in their economic activities that are based on real social and economic relations, and also reflect the development and changes in the real social and economic relations. Obviously, none of the countries have a single, isolated economic system, but a system that consists of many sub-specific systems and arrangements (plural, not single). We believe that, as a structural totality, the socialist economic system with Chinese characteristics has meaning at least three levels: firstly, the basic economic system of socialism with Chinese characteristics; secondly, the economic operation system with Chinese characteristics; thirdly, the socialist economic security system with Chinese characteristics. All the three systems depend on, support each other, and form an organic whole. The basic economic system decides the fundamental nature and development direction of the economic system and lays the foundation for economic development; the economic operation system decides the quality and rate of economic growth and influences the efficiency of economic development; the economic security system provides supports and guarantees for the basic economic system and the economic operation system, and frames and underlines the value of economic development. In the primary stage of socialism, to build the socialist system with Chinese characteristics, we must persist in and improve the basic economic system, establish and improve the economic operation system, and establish and improve the economic security system.

Adhere to and improve the basic economic system

Decision states that, "the basic economic system with the public ownership at the core, jointly developing with many kinds of ownership systems, is the main pillar of the socialism with Chinese characteristics, and is the basis for the socialist market economy system". The practice over the 30 years since the Reform and Opening-up proves that the basic economic system adapts to China's economic and social development requirements at the present stage, is conductive to the stable and healthy development of the economy and society. To realize the scientific development of the Chinese economy and society and the Chinese people's great national rejuvenation, we must always persist in and improve the basic economic system of socialism with Chinese characteristics.

We must continuously consolidate and develop the leading position of public ownership. The public ownership of means of production is the basis of socialist economic system, the essential characteristic that makes the socialism different from the capitalism, it is this economic basis that makes the working people master the country, and the fundamental requirements of releasing and developing the productive forces, and it is the underlying premise for achieving the common prosperity. Firstly, we must always ensure the advantageous position of public-owned assets. "The property rights of the public economy are inviolable". Therefore, we must protect the property rights of public economy just as how we protect the personal private property, and always ensure the unswerving advantageous position of public-owned assets. We must reasonably adjust the layout and structure of public-owned assets, improve the operation supervision and the supervision of publicly-owned assets, and continuously enhance the overall quality and allocation efficiency of such assets, and thus make better use of the public-owned assets to keep the macro-economy stable and realize the scientific development. Secondly, we must consolidate and strengthen the leading position of state economy. "Owned by the whole people, the state-owned enterprises are an important force for advancing national modernization and protecting the common interests of the people." Thence, we must always maintain the dominant position of state economy in the major industries and key fields that comprise the lifeline of the economy and are vital to economic security, including the financial industry, modernize the enterprise governance structure and management system that adapts to the laws of market economy and the actual conditions of China, enhance the vitality of the state-owned economy, and bring into full play its influence and driving force in the economic and social fields. Thirdly, we must continuously consolidate and develop the collective economy, especially the rural collective economy. "We must maintain the collective ownership of the rural land, protect farmers' contracted land-use rights by law, and boost the collective economy," encourage the rural areas to develop the cooperative economy, and support large-scale, specialized and modernized farming enterprises. Besides, "we must actively develop a diversified ownership economy", and explore diversified forms of effectively realizing public ownership. "Developing a mixed economy in which state capital, collective capital, and private capital can hold shares in one another and become mutually integrated is an important way to realize the basic economic system of China. It is conducive to improving the amplification functions of state-owned capital, preserving and increasing the value, and improving its competitiveness. It is also conducive to enabling capitals with all kinds of ownership to draw on one another's strong points to offset weaknesses, stimulate one another and develop together." "This is an effective channel and inevitable choice for us to adhere to the dominant role of the public economy and improve its vitality, its dominant status and influence in the new circumstances." Developing such a mixed economy is conducive both to use the institutional advantages of the state-owned economy, realizing the driving role of the stated-owned economy with exogenous forces, and is conducive to enhancing the competitiveness of Chinese enterprises in the international arena.

We must support the sound development of non-public economy. The existence and development of non-public economy is the objective requirement of the hierarchical and unevenly scattered characteristics of productive forces in the primary stage of Chinese socialism. It is conducive to full mobilization of all human resources and positive factors in all different fields of the society, and conductive to increase the employment rate and better meeting the demand, and revitalizing the economic development. Firstly, we must intensify institutional innovation, and improve our policy systems for the development of non-public economy. We should relax controls over market access, put the principle of fair competition into practice, further increase the fiscal and financial support for non-public economy, and improve the social services targeting the non-public economy. Secondly, support the non-public economy to accelerate the transformation of its economic development mode, strengthen non-public enterprises' independent innovation capability, enhance the development quality and overall quality of non-public economy, and drive non-public enterprises to improve their competitiveness in the international arena. Thirdly, we must lead the non-public economy to increase its sense of social responsibility, request them to conduct their production and operation following the market rules and establish and improve modern enterprise systems.

We must handle the relation between the leading position of the public economy and the joint development of different ownership economies in a dialectic way. We must unswervingly consolidate and develop public economy, maintain the leading position of the public ownership; we must unswervingly encourage, support and guide the development of non-public economy, and stimulate its vitality and creativity. To do this, firstly, we must properly handle the relation between socialism and capitalism. In no way, should we simply put socialism and capitalism into absolute opposition and seek to establish a "pure" socialist economy. We must admit the historical role of different non-public economies and judge the merits of various forms of ownership by the "three favorables"[1] criteria (whether it is favorable for promoting the growth of the productive forces in a socialist society, whether it is favorable for increasing the overall strength of the socialist state, whether it is favorable for raising the people's living standards).

In the primary stage of socialism, the public economy and the non-public economies are all an integral part of socialist market economy. Secondly, that we must unswervingly encourage, support and guide the development of non-public economies does not mean that we should fully push the private ownership system of capitalism. The public ownership of means of production is a fundamental principle of socialism. Without the leading position of public economy, there will be no solid economic basis and powerful material means and basis for the governance by the communist party and basis for the whole socialist superstructure, and we will have no means to prevent growing income disparity and will not be able to realize the common prosperity. Thirdly, that we shall unswervingly consolidate and develop the public economy does not mean to implement a single public ownership system. In the primary stage of socialism, consolidating and developing the public economy and at the same time allowing the space for the non-public economy can fully mobilize the underlying economic resources of the society, and adapt to the needs of consolidating and developing the public economy sector itself.

Establish and improve the economic operation system

The success of "China mode" and the great achievements made in the development of socialist economy with Chinese characteristics are based on not only the basic economic system of the socialism with Chinese characteristics, but also the socialist economic operation system with Chinese characteristics. To better boost the economic development in the primary stage of socialism, we must establish and improve the socialist economic operation sphere with Chinese characteristics, while maintaining and improving the basic economic system of socialism with Chinese characteristics.

---

1   The criteria of "Three Favorables" were firstly proposed by Deng Xiaoping in 1992.

Decision clearly stated that, "The economic system reform is the focus of comprehensively deepening the reform. The core task is to properly balance the relationship between the government and the market, so that the market can play its decisive role in the allocation of resources and the government can exert its role more effectively." It is beyond all questions that it is the general law of the market economy that the market should play the decisive role in resource allocation. Otherwise, it will not be a market economy if the resource allocation is not determined by the market, but regulated by the government or the society. Therefore, we must develop a unified, open, competitive and orderly market system, which includes building up fair, open and transparent market rules, reforming the market supervision system, and building up an integrated construction land markets in the rural and urban areas and a modern financial market system. At the same time, we should improve the mechanism where the prices are mainly determined by the market. "Any price that can be determined by the market should be left to the market, and the government should not attempt improper interventions." "Of course, our market economy possesses socialist nature. We need to give leverage to the superiority of our socialist system, and let the Party and the government perform their positive regulatory functions. The market plays a decisive role in allocating resources, but it does not mean that market is not the sole regulator." Besides, the decisive role of the market is only limited to resource allocation in the economic sphere, but as to the resource allocation in the social fields and eco-fields such as healthcare, education and environmental protection, the government and social organizations must still play their important regulatory roles.

Due to the inevitability of market failures, the modern market economy needs the government to effectively play its role. "Scientific macro-control and effective governance are the intrinsic requirements for giving more leverage to the advantages of the socialist market economy. For this purpose, we must continuously improve the macro-control system, comprehensively and properly perform government duties and streamline government structure, so as to enable the government exercise its duties and functions effectively. Besides, we should strengthen and streamline public services, ensure fair competition, intensify the market supervision, keep the macro-economy stable, safeguard the market order, push for sustainable development, boost common prosperity and remedy all kinds of market failures. Therefore, that the government, in general, does not directly intervene in the micro-economic operation in the modern market economy does not mean that the government simply does nothing. On the contrary, facing the challenges brought by globalization, in order to promote the competitive advantages of a nation, the governments have become even more important, and the government's roles have become more detailed and complex. Without proper and effective performance of government roles, there will be no way for the market to play its decisive role. To allow the market play its decisive role in resource allocation and letting government to play its due role are an organic and unified whole.

Obviously, in the modern market economy, simply relying on market regulation and government control cannot effectively achieve the goal of healthy economic operation. Besides these two regulation mechanisms, we still need a third regulation mechanism, i.e. the social regulation. Different from the former two mechanisms, the social regulation is mainly based on socialist values or social justice. Apart from playing its important role in the narrow-sense of social field, social regulation also works where the regulation by market and government fails and makes up for the shortages and leaks of the former two regulations. Our experience in developing the modern market economy proves that, "the most successful society is the one that combines the market forces with the sense of moral responsibility." *Decision* clearly states that we must "correctly handle the relationship between the government and society, intensify efforts to separate government administration and social organizations, encourage the social organizations to clarify their rights and obligations, and enforce self-management and play their role in accordance with the law. Social organizations should be commissioned to provide public services that they are apt to supply and tackle matters that they are able to tackle."[2] It can been expected that with the continuous development and improvement of the socialist market economy with Chinese characteristics, the social regulation and related institutional arrangements will grow increasingly rich, and thus form a socialist economic operation system that consists of sound regulation by the three: market, government and the society.

Establish and develop the system of economic security

The economic system is a structural totality, and the benign operation of its basic economic system and economic operation system needs the effective supports from institutional arrangements in the political and culture fields, which provide the important guarantee for the effective enforcement and value target of basic economic system and economic operation system, constituting the economic security system of socialism with Chinese characteristics. To build up a socialist economic system with Chinese characteristics that is structurally complete, scientifically standardized and effective in operation, we must gradually establish and improve an effective system of economic security.

In politics, *Decision* re-asserted that, "we should uphold the central position of the people and promote the innovations in the people's congress system in theory and practice." This is the inevitable requirement of maintaining the leading position of public ownership and effective functioning of regulation by the government and society, and the important guarantee for the two. *Decision* reasserted that, "we will, under the Party's leadership, carry out extensive consultations on major issues related to economic and social development as well as specific problems involving the people's immediate interests, and conduct consultations before and during the implementation of policy decisions." This is the inevitable choice we have made to adapt to and allow diversified interests of economic players in the market economy, and it is conducive to the effective

---

2   See Third Plenum of the 18th Central Committee of the CPC.

expression of interest appeals by all players and the realization and implementation of scientific long-term strategy for economic and social development. *Decision* reaffirmed that, "We will establish and improve supervision by urban residents and villagers, encouraging them to conduct self-management, self-service, self-education and self-oversight in exercising urban and rural community governance, in managing community-level public affairs and in running public service programs. We will improve the democratic management system in enterprises and public institutions with workers and employees' congress as its basic form, strengthen the building of the democratic mechanism in social organizations, and ensure employees' democratic rights in participating in management and supervision. This is the realization mechanism of the value pursuit of the basic economic system of socialism with Chinese characteristics, and also the micro basis for the effective operation of the economic operation system of socialism with Chinese characteristics"

In the culture, *Decision* reaffirms that, "we must adhere to the orientation of advanced socialist culture and the socialist path of making cultural advances with Chinese characteristics, cultivate and practice core socialist values, consolidate the guiding role of Marxism in the area of ideology, and consolidate the common ideological foundation for the concerted endeavor for the entire Party and the people of all ethnic groups throughout the country. We will put people at the center of our work and give priority to social benefits, while integrating them with economic returns, so as to deepen the cultural reform by way of arousing the cultural creativity of the entire nation as the central task." It is obvious that without a creative ideological build up, there will be no maintenance or innovation of any social system. Facing the impacts caused by foreign culture and ideology brought by globalization, and to ensure the good operation of basic socialist economic system and economic operation system with Chinese characteristics, we must break away from the market value pursuit that puts the personal interests as the first priority, and guide people's economic behaviors with socialist core value system, build up a good interaction framework between the interest pursuit and ethic culture, mould and consolidate the common ideological basis for the variety of economic behaviors.

In the law enforcement field, *Decision* states that, "To build a China under the rule of law, we must uphold the unity of the rule of law, law-based government and law-based administration, and the integral development of a law-based country, law-based government and law-based society as a whole." Obviously, without an authoritative socialist judicial system, legal authority of the Constitution and the independent, fair and efficient legal enforcement system, the basic socialist economic system and the economic operation system with Chinese characteristics will lose the basic conditions for its effective operation.

Originally published in the journal Marxism Studies, 2014(1)

Reflection on the Idea That Comprehensive Reform Must Adhere to and Advance on the Correct Track

Xiang Qiyuan

Abstract: *Decision of the Central Committee of the Communist Party of China on Some Major Issues Concerning Comprehensively Deepening the Reform* passed by the Third Plenary Session of the 18th Central Committee of the CPC has reflected, from the very start to the end, the dialectic thinking about inheritance and development, change and continuity we have practiced in the different spheres of deepening reform. How to grasp such dialectical relation should start from the theory of basic social contradictions of historical materialism as its theoretical basis. This is of great importance to distinguish the basic socialist systems from their specific links and specific systems, and achieving such a clear distinction will provide us the theoretical basis for judging which parts of them should be changed, and which part should not be changed, in the course of Reform and Opening-up. During the 30-plus years since China's Reform and Opening-up, the struggle between two views of reform have never ceased, and the debate has always been inseparable from the different opinions on the state-owned economy. This shows that the state-owned economy concerns the life and death of the socialist system. If the state-owned economy is denied, the public economy will lose its leading position. If the leading position of the public economy is lost, the socialist system will cease to exist, let alone its advance along the path of socialism with Chinese characteristics.

Key words: Historical materialism; reform direction; state-owned economy, two views regarding Reform and Opening-up; path of socialism with Chinese characteristics

I

After the 18th CPC National Congress, President Xi Jinping has made numerous important speeches on comprehensive reform. In his visit to Shenzhen, he stated: Our reform has always been a thorough reform. I don't agree with the idea that China's reform has been falling behind in some regard. It might be quicker or slower in some ways and at some points….. The key is what to reform and what not. There are things we have not changed, cannot change, and will not change no matter in how long a time. Therefore this cannot be characterized as failure to reform." The essence of the question is what to change and what not to change. Certain things that aren't being changed and can't be changed will never be changed, but this does not mean we are not reforming. "Some people define reform as changes towards the "universal" values of the west, the western political system, otherwise it will not constitute reform. This is a stealthy tampering of the concept and a misunderstanding of our reform. Of course we must uphold the banner of reform, but our reform is reform that keeps us moving forward on the path of socialism with Chinese characters. We will walk neither the closed and rigid old path, nor the evil path of changing the flag."

At the 2013 APEC summit, Xi Jinping has remarked: China is a big country. It cannot afford to make drastic mistakes on fundamental issues, for such mistakes cannot be rectified or reversed If it does, they may be irreversible and irreparable. Our position is that we must be both bold enough to explore and make advances, and be prudent enough when planning our actions. We must stick to the right direction of the Reform and Opening-up, address the deep-seated problems that have accumulated over the years, and must not stop, even for a minute, in our pursuit of Reform and Opening-up.[1] We should fully grasp President Xi's profound dialectical approach on continuation and development, change and continuity.

Decision of the Central Committee of the Communist Party of China on Some Major Issues Concerning Comprehensively Deepening the Reform (hereinafter referred to as *Decision*) passed by the Third Plenary Session of the 18th Central Committee of the CPC reflected, from the very start to the end, the dialectic thinking about inheritance and development, changes and continuities in different fields of deepening reform. In Part I of the *Decision*, "The major significance of and guiding ideology for comprehensively deepening reform", the fourth point clearly states that: the success of Reform and Opening-up has provided us with important experience for deepening the reform comprehensively. We have to adhere to it in the long term. What is the most important is to uphold the leadership of the Party, adhere to the Party's basic line, reject both the old and rigid closed-door policy and any attempt to abandon socialism and take an erroneous path, firmly take the socialist road and ensure that our reform

---

1   Xi Jinping, *China cannot Make Any Drastic Mistake on Issues of Fundamental Importance*, http://new.china.com/zh_cn/domestic/945/20131008/18076592.html, 2013-10-08.

is in the right direction. We should emancipate the mind, seek truth from facts, keep up with the times, be realistic and pragmatic, base ourselves on reality in everything we do, summarize successful domestic experience, learn useful experience from other countries, and boldly promote innovation both in theory and practice."[2] This remark intensively embodies the dialectical thinking about continuation and development, changes and continuities, and helps us to accurately understand the essence of deepening reform and modernization strategies in various fields.

Part II of the *Decision*, "Persist in and improve the basic economic system", starts out clearly as the following: "The basic economic system with public ownership playing a dominant role and different economic sectors developing side by side is an important pillar of the socialist system with Chinese characteristics and is the foundation of the socialist market economy. Both the public and non-public sectors are key components of the socialist market economy, and are important bases for the economic and social development of China. We must unswervingly consolidate and develop the public economy, persist in the dominant position of public ownership, give full play to the leading role of the state-owned sector, and continuously increase its vitality, controlling force and influence. We must unwaveringly encourage, support and guide the development of the non-public sector, and stimulate its dynamism and creativity. It also points out that it is necessary to improve the property rights protection system, vigorously develop a mixed economy, promote establishment of the modern corporate system in state-owned enterprises, and support the healthy development of the non-public sectors."[3] In this important brief remark, to achieve the common development of public economy and non-public economy and adhere to the two unswerving pursuits are the basic principles that have been emphasized since the 14th CPC National Congress. Especially, the leading position of public economy and the dominant position of state economy should not be weakened but strengthened during the gradual deepening reform. Otherwise, the Chinese society cannot be a socialist society at the primary stage, and the Chinese market economy cannot be a socialist market economy. Some contents of the reform specified in this passage, such as "improving the property rights protection system, actively developing mixed ownership economy, boosting the state-owned enterprises to improve modern enterprise system, supporting the healthy development of non-public economy," have long been advocated and implemented to different degrees, and the new contents and new requirements are an embodiment of the dialectical thinking about changes and continuities. For example, "The property rights of the public economy are inviolable, the same as are those of the non-public economy", "We will allow more state-owned enterprises (SOEs) and enterprises of other types of ownership to develop into mixed enterprises. We will allow non-state-owned capital to hold

---

2   CPC Central Committee Decision Concerning Some Major Issues in Comprehensive Deepening Reform, *People's Daily*, November 16, 2013.
3   Ibid.

shares in projects invested by state-owned capital. We will allow mixed enterprises to implement employee stock ownership plans (ESOP) to form communities of capital owners and laborers." The ideas in the above passage are all new contents worth noting.

Part III of *Decision*, "Speeding up the improvement of modern market system", it states clearly, at the very start, that "Establishing a unified, open, competitive and orderly market system is the basis for the market to play a decisive role in the allocation of resources. We must put in place a modern market system in which enterprises enjoy independent management and fair competition, consumers have free choice and make autonomous consumption decisions, products and factors of production flow freely and are exchanged on an equal basis, strive to remove market barriers, and raise the efficiency and fairness of resource allocation."[4] The market's role in resource allocation which was clearly expressed in this part is changed from "the basic role", as mentioned in the past plenary sessions of the 18th Central Committee of the CPC, to the "decisive" role. This is a new highlight which has aroused public concern when discussing the content of comprehensive reform, and also a new major theoretic breakthrough made by the CPC. Since after the 14th National Congress, the CPC came up with the idea that the market should play a basic role in resource allocation under the government's macro-control. During the twenty years since the 14th National Congress in 1992 to the 18th National Party Congress, China has at the initial level established the socialist market economic system. The positive and negative experience we accumulated in this process is no doubt the indispensable reference for the theoretical point of view was outlined in the *Decision* that market should play a decisive role in the resource allocation. Besides, the crux of the market's decisive role in the resource allocation is to further handle the relation between government and market, and solve and make up the defects and failures of market system, and aims to avoid both the improper government intervention and also inefficiency in regard to the supervision of the market. It should also be noted that there is a dialectical relation in the shift of government duties. In *Explanatory Notes* for *Decision of the Central Committee of the Communist Party of China on Some Major Issues Concerning Comprehensively Deepening the Reform*, Xi Jinping commented: "Our market economy is socialist, of course. We need to give leverage to the superiority of our socialist system, and let the Party and government perform their positive functions. The market plays a decisive role in allocating resources, but is not the sole actor in this regard." We should understand the view of point of this connotation fully.

In Reform and Opening-up, we must seriously consider which should be changed and which cannot be changed. Attempt to change those things we should keep unchangeable and continuing our efforts to change what should not be changed will bring about negative or even far more serious consequences.

---

4   CPC Central Committee Decision Concerning Some Major Issues in Comprehensive Deepening Reform, *People's Daily*, November 16, 2013.

Therefore, as to how to scientifically handle the dialectical relation between the change and continuity, the author believes that we should use the historical materialist view point in regard to the law of motion of basic social contradictions in the social formation as our theoretical basis.

Marx said: "In the social production of their life, men inevitably enter into definite relations that are independent of their will, namely relations of production appropriate to a given stage in the development of their material forces of production. The totality of these relations of production constitutes the economic structure of society, the real foundation, on which arises a legal and political superstructure and to which correspond definite forms of social consciousness. The mode of production of material life conditions the general process of social, political and intellectual life. It is not the consciousness of men that determines their existence, but their social existence that determines their consciousness. At a certain stage of development, the material productive forces of society come into conflict with the existing relations of production or – this merely expresses the same thing in legal terms – with the property relations within the framework of which they have operated hitherto. From forms of development of the productive forces these relations turn into their fetters. Then begins an era of social revolution. The changes in the economic foundation lead sooner or later to the transformation of the whole immense superstructure."

As the basis of historical materialism, Marx's classic presentation of social basic contradictions reveals the common and general law of human social development, and this has different degree of particularity in different social formations. When Karl Marx and Friedrich Engels were alive, yet there was no socialist practice in the world. Therefore, they could not make a concrete analysis of the specific forms in regard to the law of motion of basic social contradictions in the future society.

The first person who has applied the basic social contradiction theory of Marxist historical materialism into socialist practice and revealed the specific law of the motion of socialist society, was Mao Zedong. After long-time practice and thinking, Mao Zedong made a comprehensive, systematic and in-depth discussion regarding the basic social contradictions in socialist society, in the essay published in 1957 titled *On the Correct Handling of Contradictions among the People*. He pointed out that: "Many people dare not openly admit that contradictions still exist among the people, it is precisely these contradictions that push our society forward." "Contradictions in the socialist society are fundamentally different from those in the old society, such as in the capitalist society. In capitalist society, contradictions find expression in acute antagonisms and conflicts, in sharp class struggles; they cannot be resolved by the capitalist system itself and can only be resolved by socialist revolution. The case is quite different with contradictions in socialist society; on the contrary, they are not antagonistic and can be ceaselessly resolved by the socialist system itself." "In socialist society the basic contradictions are still those between the relations of production and the productive forces and between the superstructure and the economic base. However, they are fundamentally different in character and have different features from the contradictions between the relations of production and the productive forces and between the superstructure and the economic base in the old societies."

"To sum up, socialist relations of production have been established and are suited to the development of the productive forces, but these relations are still far from perfect, and their imperfect aspects stand in contradiction to the development of the productive forces. There is conformity as well as contradiction between the relations of production and the development of the productive forces; similarly, there is conformity as well as contradiction between the superstructure and the economic base." "We must continue to resolve such contradictions in the light of specific conditions. Of course, new problems will emerge as these contradictions are resolved. And further efforts will be required to resolve them."[5]

Mao Zedong's above statements have great innovative significance in the development history of Marxism.

Firstly, he does not only point out that basic contradictions in the socialist society are the contradictions between the relations of production and the productive forces and between the superstructure and the economic base, which exist in the whole course, since the establishment of socialist society to its full maturity, but he has also emphasized that the basic contradictions of the socialist society are different from those in the old societies, such as the capitalist society. The contradictions in the socialist society are contradictions among the people. These are not antagonist contradictions and can be resolved by the socialist society itself.

Secondly, the basic system of the socialist society, i.e. the contents that can reflect the fundamental nature of socialism in relations of production and the superstructure should be distinguished from the specific links and systems of the relations of production and superstructure. The basic socialist system is in correspondence with the growth of productive forces, and therefore, should be maintained and consolidated. However, with the continuous development of productive forces, some specific links and systems in the relations of production and superstructure may become in contradiction with the productive forces, and new reforms will be required. Therefore, the basic contradictions of the socialist society are always moving forward in a motion mode of changes and continuities.

Making the differentiation between the basic socialist system and its specific links and systems is an innovation of great significance we have made in our new practice. It provides the Marxist theoretical basis for us when we need to make reforms in the specific links and systems that have become contradictory with the growth of productive forces in China's Reform and Opening-up.

---

5   *Collected Works of Mao Zedong*, Vol. 7, People's Publishing House, 1999, pp. 213-215.

Deng Xiaoping inherited and developed Mao's theory of basic contradictions in the socialist society. He pointed out that: Concerning the basic contradictions, I think that the wording of Comrade Mao Zedong from *On the Correct Handling of Contradictions Among the People* is relatively good. Comrade Mao Zedong said: "In socialist society, the basic contradictions are still those between production relationships and productive forces, and between the superstructure and the economic base."…. "Here, comrade Mao Zedong wrote a long paragraph, which I will not repeat now. Naturally, pointing out to these basic contradictions is not completely resolving the problem, deeper concrete research on this issue is needed. However, seen from more than 20 years of the practice, this wording is more appropriate than some other wordings."[6] Through our exploration throughout the Reform and Opening-up, under the guidance of Deng Xiaoping Theory, the basic line of "one central task, two basic points" was formed, which contained the idea of correctly handling the basic contradictions in the socialist society. Upholding the Four Cardinal Principles[7] is to uphold and improve the contents of the relations of production and superstructure that reflect the fundamental nature of socialism. China's Reform and Opening-up is a great revolution with unprecedented breadth and depth in its content of scope, but essentially, it has still been the reform of the specific systems and links in the relations of production and superstructure that were not in correspondence with the growth of productive forces. Upholding the Four Cardinal Principles and persisting in the Reform and Opening-up supplement each other, and jointly drive the socialist society forward. This is why Deng Xiaoping repeatedly stresses that the Party's basic line should be upheld for a long time in the future. He stressed in his "Southern Inspection Tour" speech in 1992 that: we should adhere to the basic line for a hundred years, with no vacillation.[8]

135

II

Jiang Zemin remarked in an important speech in 1991 that there were two opposite views on Reform and Opening-up. He said that: the field of ideology is an important field of struggles between peaceful evolution and counter struggle against peaceful evolution. The collisions and struggles between the bourgeois liberalism and Four Cardinal principles are, in essence, a political struggle on whether to persist in the leadership by the CPC and the socialist path", "we should draw a distinction between the Reform and Opening-up upholding the Four Cardinal Principles and the 'Reform and Opening-up' based on capitalism promoted by the bourgeois liberalization".[9]

---

6   *Selected Works of Deng Xiaoping*, Vol. 2, People's Publishing House, 1994, p. 181.

7   The idea of Upholding the Four Cardinal Principles, was first proposed by Deng Xiaoping in 1979, which includes: the principle of upholding the socialist path; the principle of upholding the people's democratic dictatorship; the principle of upholding the leadership of the Communist Party of China (CPC), and the principle of upholding Mao Zedong Thought and Marxism-Leninism.

8   *Selected Works of Deng Xiaoping*, Vol. 3, People's Publishing House, 1993, p. 371.

9   *Selected Works of Jiang Zemin*, Vol. 1, People's Publishing House, 2006, p. 160, p. 163.

In China, Deng Xiaoping is the first leader who paid attention to the breeding of bourgeois liberalism trend of thought and its hazards. In September 1986, Deng Xiaoping said in the Sixth Plenary Session of the 12th Central Committee of the CPC that: with regard to the question of opposing bourgeois liberalization, I am the one who talks about it most often and most determinedly." "What is liberalism? It is an attempt to turn China's present policies in the direction of capitalism." "Liberalization by itself means antagonism to our current policies and systems and a wish to revise them."[10] In 1989, not long after quelling the political disturbance, when meeting Professor T.D. Lee in September, Deng Xiaoping said: "Reform and Opening-up needs to push both for the reform and fight against liberalism. Which can further strengthened depending on the actual situations".[11]

In 1992, Deng Xiaoping reminded us in his Southern Tour speech: "in the whole process of Reform and Opening-up, we should always adhere to the Four Cardinal Principles. In the Sixth Plenary Session of the 12th Central Committee, I said that the struggle against bourgeois liberalization shall be carried out for the next twenty years. It seems today that the struggle should be carried out for even more than twenty years. If bourgeois liberalization is allowed to spread unchecked, the consequences will be extremely serious. We have spent 20 years or so building the special zones to be as they are now. To make them collapse would be a matter of only one night, just as the case of the Soviet Union. Collapse is easy, but construction is difficult. If we don't nip the bourgeois liberalization in the bud, we may find ourselves in trouble."[12]

Just as Deng Xiaoping foresaw, during the 30-plus years since the Reform and Opening-up, the debate between the two views on reform has never ceased. It covers a broad range, including the spheres of economy, politics, culture, society, and ideology, etc. The debate continues even after the Party national congress and the Third Plenary Session of the 18th Central Committee of the CPC. The advocates of capitalist liberalization have worn the mantle of Reform and Opening-up proponents, yet essentially they oppose the Four Cardinal Principles, and attack those contents that reflect the fundamental nature of socialism in the relations of production and superstructure, which should not and cannot be changed.

In the next section, I will focus on analyzing fallacy of those using the excuse of "marketization reforms" to attack the path of socialism with Chinese characteristics, especially the leading position of public economy and the dominant position of state economy.

---

10   *Selected Works of Deng Xiaoping*, Vol. 2, People's Publishing House, 1994, pp. 181-182.
11   CC of the CPC, Party Literature Research Office, *Chronicles of Deng Xiaoping (1975-1997)*, Vol. 2, Central Party Literature Press, 2004, pp. 1289.
12   *Selected Works of Deng Xiaoping*, Vol. 3, People's Publishing House, 1993, p. 379.

In 2013, some scholars have published the book titled *Twenty Lectures on China's Economic Reform: Re-launching the Reform Project* (hereinafter referred to as *Re-launching*). In the preface to the book, it was stated that, "China is only halfway down the path of reform. The economic system that was initially established at the end of the 20th Century was still a mixed system that was controlled half by the government and half by the market. Although the government and the state economy no longer encompass everything, they still take the high ground in the national economy and dictate the fate of non-state economy." "The establishment of the market system releases the productive forces that have been depressed by the backward system for so long, bringing about high growth rates in the Chinese economy. This is manifested in that: firstly, the reform has provided space for private startup businesses, and releases the long-depressed entrepreneurship and entrepreneurial enthusiasm of the Chinese people. By the end of the 20th Century, over 30 million private enterprises have popped up in China, turning an unexpected fundamental driving force of economic development." "What is particularly serious is that, as there is a stagnancy or backsliding trend at the start of the 21st Century, the negative side of the current mixed economic system of China is defined as: "China's economic system, which was initially established at the start of the 21st Century, is still a 'mixed system' of 'semi-control and semi-market, and this 'mixed system' ' is further strengthened." "China is standing at the crossroads of history. In order to avoid social crisis, it must decisively and resolutely re-launch the reform project, veritably, not vocally, push for the reform towards market-oriented economy, governance by law and democratic politics, and establish a tolerant economic system and political system."

The 16th lecture of the book, "Market-oriented reform is not yet completed", contains a summarizing remark: to sum up, after 30 plus years, the market-oriented reform has made great achievements and laid the preliminary system foundation for rapid rise of the Chinese economy. However, China's reform has not yet achieved full success, still has a lot of problems to conquer. Among them, the most prominent one is that the government and state-owned enterprises still dominate the allocation of resources. More specifically, (i) although the state economy does not have the lion's share in the GDP, it still controls the commanding heights of the national economy, (ii) the government organs at all levels have the huge power of controlling the flow direction of important economic resources, such as land and funds; (iii) the rule of law, the indispensable cornerstone of modern market economy, is not yet established..."[13]

Several economic analyses in regard to some specific issues of the current market economy in *Re-launching* is not entirely useless, but fundamentally those wrote the *Re-launching* are pursuing a capitalist market economy rather than a socialist market economy. This is visibly manifested in their comment on China's state-owned economy. From their point of view, after over 30-year

---

13   See Wu Jinglian & Ma Guochuan's *Twenty Lectures on China's Economic Reform: Re-launching the Reform Project*, SDX Joint Publishing Company, 2013, p. 241.

Reform and Opening-up, the state-owned economy does not only help in boosting the economy, instead it is a barrier to economic progress. Their proposals to break down the barriers is to further weaken the state-owned economy and promote privatization. This not only contradict the realities of our practice in building socialism in China, also goes against the consistent position put forward by all the party congresses before the 18th Congress of the CPC.

On October 28, 2013, the main author of *Re-launching* further expounded his view on whether the socialism has anything to do with state economy, in an interview claimed to be "foresight into the Third Plenary Session of the 18th Central Committee of the CPC", he said: the question is how to define socialism. My definition of socialism is to realize the social justice and common prosperity, a social ideal." "This includes the view that state ownership is an advanced form of public ownership and a goal that socialism must pursue.' I could say that this definition is the definition from the Soviet Union's textbook which is wrong. I agreed with Deng Xiaoping that the essence, and the superiority of socialism are to gradually realize common prosperity. Socialism has nothing to do with the ratio of public ownership in the whole economy. However, now the scale of state-owned system is too large, in order to carry out strategic restructuring, state-owned enterprises need to withdraw from some sectors." "I stick to the view expressed in my letter to the Central Committee of the CPC in 1997, i.e. the socialism has nothing to do with the ratio of state ownership. For this purpose, I carefully checked with *Deng Xiaoping's Selected Works*, which contained no such speech."

The distorted socialism long advocated by the main author of *Re-launching* has nothing in common with the scientific socialism that Marx and Engels devoted their life to. The basic contents of scientific socialism, such as the establishment of dictatorship of proletariat, common ownership of means of production by the whole people, implementation of the system of distribution according to work in the first phase of communism, have been further expounded in the well-known works like *The Principles of Communism, The Communist Manifesto, Class Struggles in France, 1848 to 1850, Critique of the Gotha Program, Anti-Dühring*, etc. To prattle about social justice and common prosperity, without taking into account the proletariat's class struggle against the bourgeois and the fundamental reform that substitutes the public ownership of means of production for private ownership is to oppose the reality of socialism in the name of "socialism". It is not hard to find this kind of fallacy in the speeches for presidential election or congressional elections of the capitalist countries.

The rhetoric that the state ownership is an advanced form of public ownership is not from the political economy textbooks of the Soviet Union, instead Marx and Engels wrote in *The Communist Manifesto*: "The proletariat will use its political supremacy to wrest, by degree, all capital from the bourgeoisie, to centralize all instruments of production in the hands of the state, i.e., of the proletariat organized as the ruling class; and to increase the total productive forces as rapidly as possible."[14] Engels said in *Anti-Dühring*: "The proletariat will obtain the state power and first of all, turn the means of production into state assets."[15]

Here it shall be seriously pointed out that it is inadvisable for any scholar to interpret the state leader's important comments out of its context, or willfully twist them for his own purpose. The main author of *Re-launching* said that he agrees with Deng Xiaoping's definition of socialism that the essence and the superiority of socialism are to gradually realize common prosperity. Socialism has nothing to do with the ratio of public ownership in the whole economy. However, these words do not match with Deng's original intention. Deng Xiaoping's original words were: "essence, socialism is about liberating and developing the productive forces, eliminating exploitation and polarization, and ultimately, it is about achieving prosperity for all.".[16] The elimination of exploitation means to substitute the capitalist private ownership with socialist public ownership of means of production, which is a major revolutionary change in the relations of production. Only with such a precondition could we realize the elimination of polarization and achieve prosperity for all. By deliberate omission of the "elimination of exploitation" in the quotation of Deng Xiaoping's remark, the main author of *Re-launching* extremely twisted the original meaning. Deng Xiaoping also said: "Sticking to the socialist direction in the reform is an amply important issue." "The policies of invigorating our domestic economy and opening to the outside world are being carried out in accordance with the principles of socialism. Socialism has two major requirements. Firstly, its economy must be dominated by public ownership and secondly, there must be no polarization. Public ownership may consist of both ownership by the entire people and ownership by the collective."[17] As is well known, the ownership by the entire people is the state-owned ownership. Therefore, saying that the socialism has nothing to do with the ratio of state economy totally runs contrary to Deng Xiaoping's original meaning.

There is also another professor who echoed the ideas mentioned by the author of the book *Re-launching*. On March 17, 2013, at the 2012 annual conference of China Development Forum, he said, "The most important is to do three things in the economic reform fields." "The first is to privatize the state-owned enterprises. It is hard to imagine that China can enter the real market economy, with the state-owned enterprises accounting for such a large share and taking such an important status. In fact, the state-owned enterprises have become one of the main barriers for further growth in future China."

On January 21, 2013, at the book launch meeting of the book *Re-launching*, the professor put forward that, "The central government should do something to let the people know that the country is indeed reforming." "What specific

---

14   *Collected Works of Marx and Engels*, Vol. 2, People's Press, 2009, p. 52.
15   *Collected Works of Marx and Engels*, Vol. 9, People's Press, 2009, p. 297.
16   *Collected Works of Deng Xiaoping*, Vol. 3, People's Press, 1993, p. 373.
17   Ibid., p. 138.

things could the central government do? Maybe, firstly, it should reform the state-owned enterprises, restrict them from making further investments with the money earned from the monopolized industries."

Not long ago, on the sub-forum of Boao Forum for Asia, the professor also commented: in the past decade, China did not proceed any economic reform. State-owned enterprises becoming increasingly stronger and more intervention from the government are the major issues. If the government does not reverse the economy led by the state-owned sector and dominated by state-owned enterprises, China would not be able to continue its growth." "We must realize that it is a fact that the economic development rests with entrepreneurship, especially the enterprising spirit of private entrepreneurs."

After the *Decision* of the Third Plenary Session of the 18th Central Committee of the CPC was published, the professor said in an interview: "In a market where the state-owned enterprises play the dominant role, there is no way to establish a market environment with fair competition." "The ratio (of state-owned enterprises in Britain) before Prime Minister Thatcher conducted the reform was 10%. I used this number according to the international practice." "Eventually, the state economy will exist, but not such a big share as it is now. More should be released to the market."

There is also a former high-ranking official who holds approximately similar views with the two above-mentioned scholars. After the 18th CPC National Congress, he wrote in the essay *Focus of Market-oriented Reform* which was published in *Mayor's Reference*, Issue 12, 2012, "there is not yet a consensus on how to position the state-owned economy. Some people believe that the state-owned economy is the ruling basis of the CPC. According to this idea, the state-owned economy should only grow stronger, cannot be weakened. That means only state-owned economy growing stronger could strengthen the CPC's ruling basis, and if the state economy grows weaker, the ruling base of the CPC will be weakened." "The practice both at home and abroad shows that: the Party's ruling basis lies not in the ratio of state economy, but in the support given by the people, the people's livelihood and the will of people." I wrote an article to criticize this wrong idea.[18] Before the Third Plenary Session of the 18th Central Committee of the CPC, apart from repeating the view that the state-owned economy is not the ruling basis of the CPC, he also proposed to change the principle of "keeping public ownership as the mainstay of the economy" which is stipulated in the current Constitution of the PRC. Marxist economist He Ganqiang specially wrote an article to criticize this proposal, pointing out that advocating the dominant position of public ownership is to support the public ownership being the mainstay of the economy and oppose its substitution by the private ownership as the mainstay of the economy. Thus, the state economy will lose its dominant position, since there is no economy in

---

18 Xiang Qiyuan, How to Correctly Understand the Socialist Market Economy with Chinese Characteristics –Discussion with Mr. Gao Shang, *Studies on Marxism* 2013(5).

which the private ownership is the mainstay and the state economy enjoys the dominant position.[19]

The national congresses of the CPC since the 14th Central Committee has always attached great importance to the state-owned economy's status and its role in the socialist market economy and also its position in the overall socialist construction. The *Decision* of the Third Plenary Session of the 18th Central Committee of the CPC stated: "Adhering to and improving the basic economic with public ownership playing a dominant role and different economic sectors developing side by side is an important pillar of the socialist system with Chinese characteristics and is the foundation of the socialist market economy. Adhering to and …. We must unswervingly consolidate and develop the public economy, persist in the dominant position of public ownership, give full play to the leading role of the state-owned sector, and continuously increase its vitality, controlling force and influence."[20] These remarks embody the CPC's consistent stand.

In order to more determinedly respond to the above-stated erroneous ideological attack against the socialist state-owned economy, next I will quote two remarks from Jiang Zemin to underline the consistency of above ideas. Firstly, in 1993, Jiang Zemin said in his speech "Well-run State Economy Is of Vital Importance to Build the Socialist Market Economy": "implementing the reform to achieve well-run big and medium state-owned enterprises is the main contents and important guarantee for building the socialist market economic system, and the main force in developing the socialist market economy. Only by allowing the big and medium state-owned enterprises to access the market, participate in market competition and become the mainstay of the market, could we build a complete, sound and developed market system, and ensure the market's unified, open, orderly and competitive nature."[21]

Secondly, in 2000, Jiang Zemin further analyzed the historical status of state-owned economy in China, from the height of consolidating the socialist economic foundation. He said, "In China, the CPC is the ruling party that leads the people to exercise the state power. In the socialist country, for effective operation, the state power must control certain economic and material force. The state-owned economy that has been continuously developing since the establishment of new China is an important basis of the state power of the socialist state. The development of state-owned economy in China is not only of great significance to ensure the stable development of national economy, increase the country's comprehensive strength, and realize the fundamental interests of the broadest masses of people, but also to consolidate and develop the socialist system, enhance the unity of all ethnic groups, and guarantee the lasting

---

19   He Ganqiang, Analysis of the Essence of "Keeping the Dominant Position of Public Ownership – On an Insider's "Suggestions for Reform", *Political Economics* 2013(4).

20   CPC Central Committee *Decision* Concerning Some Major Issues in Comprehensive Deepening Reform, *People's Daily*, November 16, 2013.

21   Jiang Zemin, *On Socialist Market Economy*, Central Party Literature Press, 2006, p .106.

stability of the Party and the state. Without the state economy-led public economy, there would remain no economic basis for socialism, and no economic
base and strong material means for the CPC's ruling status and no economic
basis for the whole socialist superstructure."[22]

The above statements of Jiang Zemin has led me to a deeper evaluation on
the fundamental nature of the state economy and its historical status. For a long
time, I've been thinking about a question: why, in the two decades from the
1990s to now, does the debate between the two views on reform always focus
on conflicting cognition of the state-owned economy? It implies that the state-
owned economy concerns the existence of socialist system. Maintaining the
public ownership as the mainstay of economy is the soul of the basic economic
system of socialism with Chinese characteristics, and the core of the public
ownership is the state economy. If the state economy is denied, the public economy will lose its leading position, and the socialism system will cease to exist,
let alone moving on along the path of socialism with Chinese characteristics.

Originally published in the journal
Studies on Mao Zedong and Deng Xiaoping Theories, 2014(2)

---

22 *Selected Works of Jiang Zemin*, Vol. 3, People's Press, 2006, p. 71.

Analysis of the Changes in the Circumstances of China's Economic Growth

Lin Gang

Abstract: The analysis of the changes in the circumstances of China's economic growth can be made from the two dimensions of supply and demand which embody favorable and adverse circumstances. Adverse conditions of China's economic growth mainly include that: in the supply side, labor supply is reducing, saving rate declines, restraint of the natural resources is strong, environmental constraints are aggravating and technological innovation is stagnant. In the demand side, the expansion of domestic consumption market is restricted by unfair income distribution, the foreign markets are becoming smaller, and government investment is reduced. Favorable conditions of China's economic growth mainly include: in the supply side, high-quality labor supply is increasing, part of the saving rate downtrend is offset by the emergence of education dividends, the state's investments in science and technology and education is increasing, vigorously promoting the new energy sources in China makes energy supply situations eased; in the demand side, urbanization has not been completed, regional disparity is narrowing, the reform with keynote of common prosperity and fairly sharing economic growth achievements will also have a huge role in promoting domestic demand. To seek advantages and avoid disadvantages requires us to further deepen reform and take common prosperity and fairly sharing the benefits of the economic growth as the reform keynote.

Key words: economic growth; conditional change; supply; demand; favorable conditions; adverse conditions

China's economy has grown at a rapid pace for more than 30 years. From the perspective of the development process of other countries in the world, such as Japan and South Korea in Asia, the economic growth rate began to decrease in the third decade, while their economic growth rate was very fast in the first two decades, and the third decade, it reached the slow inflection point of growth rate. In contrast to China's economic growth, in the big background of world economic development, whether economic growth rate can be maintained, after such a long period of sustained 20-year double-digit growth, how about the next situation? These questions deserve our deep examination.

In 2010, the World Bank published a report of the "Middle-Income Trap", which argued that a country would easily fall into the middle-income trap after entering the middle income level, and would be in a state of economic stagnation and the economic growth rate would fall, mainly referring to Latin American countries, also known as the Latin American trap. Discussing whether such a Latin American trap will also emerge in China needs our careful analysis of how the basic conditions for China's economic growth will change over the next five years, 10 years, or more years. Many experts and scholars pay more attention to the current changes, and concern about each quarter's quarterly report of National Bureau of Statistics. All comrades who study macro economy are doing so. The record of each quarter's quarterly report has had some fluctuations till now; under not so good circumstances, enterprise business is difficult, and the profits decline. Of course, there was some good news, for example, electricity consumption began to increase from March on. Short-term fluctuations often cause people to make the simple judgment on long-term trends according to trend extrapolation method, for example, China has passed the third decade, like South Korea and Japan, as the economic growth rate declined and fell into the Latin America Trap. Now China's per capita GDP has more than 6,000 US dollars, which belongs to above average according to the United Nations standards. Although the per capita income ranking is lower, China has been already a middle-income country. So what about our future economic growth? Will the growth rate also begin to slow? This is an issue of national strength, so we need to study this issue, too.

The analysis of economic growth conditions can be carried out from two sides, the first analysis is from the supply side of economic growth, and the second can be analyzed from the demand side. It can draw a comprehensive judgment when combining the analysis of two sides. Our research is carried out according to this idea, but in the analysis, it is divided into favorable conditions and adverse conditions. Using this simple method is also a more reliable method study, which may be more reliable than those complex models. Since it is not possible like physical model to grasp a change as complex and uncertain as economy, so far, economics does not have a model to accurately predict economic development. For example, almost no Western mainstream economists made the right prediction on the 2008 world financial crisis, someone once asked an economist at the Royal Academy of Sciences: "why haven't you predicted out such a big matter, the financial crisis? Have you showed this aspect of materials to the experts?" The economist immediately wrote back a Letter to the Queen to report the reason. Non-mainstream economists also took the opportunity to write a letter to the Queen to attack the mainstream economics. I am surprised to read this. We should use a simple model, and should not simply focus on those complex data models. It can be called a good study as long as to sort out those influence factors clearly and find out a solution with target.

The first issue, first of all to consider the challenges we face, that is, what are the disadvantages in the changes of economic growth conditions. This issue should be discussed in terms of both supply and demand.

The first adverse condition in supply is a reduction in the supply of labor. Especially the neo-classical economic growth theory, or the non-classical Keynesian theory economic growth, one of the most basic variables is labor, the other is the capital, and the technical factors are added. The first factor is labor; economic growth is controlled by the labor force. What about the supply of labor in our country? The economist of Chinese Academy of Social Sciences Cai Hang proposed that China has reached the Lewis Turning-Point, after industrialization reaching a certain extent, the rural labor supply will reduce, the changes of labor marginal product will lead to the Lewis Turning-Point, and demographic dividend is about to disappear. Everyone is more familiar with this, what he said is not unfounded. An important reason for China's economic growth over the past 30 years was very abundant labor supply, young people occupy very big proportion in the age structure of the entire population, and there is abundant labor supply. This abundant supply of labor in China can be linked to the three times of population peaks in history. The first peak was from 1954 to 1957, engaged in land reform, production resumed, and the population had great growth, though it included part of the compensatory growth after the war. The second peak was from 1962 to 1969, followed by the peak from 1984 to 1987, the three times of population peaks made China's labor supply very abundant. During the first two peaks, the birth rate was higher than 30%; during the latter peak, the birth rate was 20%. According to the estimation of United Nations, our total population would peak in 2013, with 1462 million of population. The working-age population (referring to the working population aged from 15 to 65) would peak by 2015, with peak value of 998 million. Some people think that from 1978 to 2010 the growth rate of labor force is very high, the opposite will happen later. At present, the proportion of young migrant workers has begun to decline, and in accordance with United Nations standards, China is now an aging country. In 2009, there were 167 million people over the age of 60, 110 million people over the age of 65, it is estimated that in 2020 population of over 60-year old and 65-year old people will reach 234 million and 164 million. The average age of labor population is changing, in which the proportion of young adults is declining, and the supply of labor is less abundant than that in the past. This is the most basic condition which affects economic growth.

The second is the savings rate, or the decline in the supply of capital. Firstly, another important factor supporting high growth rates is the saving rate, which is ultimately related to the age structure. Because the labor people are more, so the saving people are more. How about China's current specific situations? The saving rate in 2008 was very high, reaching 51.4%, 13.5 percentage points higher than that in 1978, with an average annual increase of 0.44 percentage points. But compared with the increase in aging of the population, namely dependency ratio, specifically the ratio of non-working-age population (the population under 4 years old plus the population over 65 years old) and the working-age population (15-65 years old) was also higher. Thus the saving rate was accordingly reduced. From 1982 to 2009, the total dependency ratio fell from 38.5% in 1982 to 27 % in 2009, while the saving rate increased from 33.5% to 54.1% in the same period. When the dependency ratio falls, the savings rate will increase, but in turn, when the dependency ratio increases, the saving rate will decrease. Secondly, with the establishment and improvement of the social security system, People's savings in pension, medical and education will also be reduced. Part of our savings is due to the lack of social security system in the past, we didn't spend this batch of money, now we focus on people's livelihood and construct social security system, and this batch of money will be consumed as investment and will not form savings. Thirdly, the proportion of the initial income distribution regarding laborers and low income group has increased, and the proportion of consumption increased, so the saving rate also declined. The proportion of laborers' income in the GDP declined from 53% in 1991 to 48% in 2005, after the Reform and Opening-up to the outside world, this ratio saw a downward trend, therefore the saving rate of China was in a rising trend.

According to the data provided by the National Development and Reform Commission and the National Economic Research Institute, the savings rate at the end of the 12th Five-Year Plan period decreased slightly compared to 2009, and it has decreased rapidly by 2015. Since the income proportion to GDP of laborers in the past was low, currently the situation that the government and enterprises take away most part of GDP will change, the proportion of workers' income in GDP is increasing, as well as a series of policies have launched, for example raising the minimum wage, etc, thus many people's income standard will be increased, the proportion of labor income in GDP will increase, so that the saving rate will decline. This is an adverse change factor. However, specific to the increase in workers' income, it is unfavorable from the supply point of view, but is advantageous from the demand point of view. This is a fundamental condition of the change, that is, the support by savings in building investment capital.

The third is a strong constraint on natural resources. On the one hand, China's past resource consumption is very high, on the other hand, the difficulty level of resource exploration at home and aboard will become bigger and bigger. China's gross domestic product (GDP) accounted for 8.5% of the world's total in 2009, but steel was 46%, coal was 45%, cement was 48%, oil was 10% and natural gas was 10% in the proportion of manufacturing resource consumption, so that energy consumption per unit product in main industries was 40% higher than the world's advanced level. In 2004, China's medium and long-term plan put forward to control the total energy consumption in the 3 billion tons standard, and this indicator had broken through by 2009, over twice as much as 1.45 billion tons in 2001, the increase of our energy consumption was faster than that of the economic growth rate. Annual newly-increased consumption from 2000 to 2009 was 170 million tons; in case of according to this standard, it will have reached more than 5 billion tons of standard coal by 2020. In case of at this rate of consumption, the Chinese people will question the sustainability of development, and it will also be a disaster for the people of the whole world. Because our massive consumption will raise the world's energy prices, which is unsustainable, China has chosen to purchase resources from foreign countries, but such an option is less feasible, we cannot expect a ceaseless energy supply from abroad.. This is a very serious factor, this factor will lead to unsustainable economy, while energy prices will be elevated, the cost will promote price rising and the situation of stagflation will appear. This kind of situation once appeared in some countries, for example, US oil crisis in the 1970s was caused by oil price rising. For our economic growth, resources are a serious factor, and the variation trend is unfavorable.

The fourth is that environmental constraints are aggravated. Our environment has been polluted to a degree that is not suitable for human survival and habitation. China has committed internationally to reduce carbon emissions by 40% to 50% by 2020 compared with 2005, which also limits our energy consumption. We can no longer take a high energy consumption approach to obtain high economic growth rate. For us, it has been impracticable in accordance with the past development mode.

The fifth is the lack of technological innovation. Lack of technological innovation is reflected in the change of the total factor productivity in the whole country. The technological inventions of the original manufacturing industry are very few, and the improvement of the total factor productivity in the past is also slowing down. Since 2009, the contribution rate of total factor productivity growth rate to economic growth has decreased significantly; the contribution rate of total factor productivity to economic growth has been 10.8% from 1979 to 1989, 30.8% from 1990 to 1999, 23.5% from 2000 to 2007; the corresponding capital contribution rates in these years were 43.6%, 54.8% and 60%, and the contribution rates became higher and higher, however, the contribution rates of total factor productivity have been decreasing since 2009. Investing more money but achieving a smaller economic growth rate, the reason is lack of R & D investment no matter in governments or in enterprises. Since 1990, there has been a rapid growth, R & D strength (proportion of research and development investment in GDP) reached 1.54% in 2009, which was the highest level of history, but compared with the level of developed countries it was very low. For example, in manufacturing industry in 2009, the R & D strength was 3.3% in US, 3.7% in Japan, and 2.0% in South Korea. In terms of R & D, their investment was higher than China's. We have to change this situation by improving China's R & D investment, strengthening technological innovation and increasing the contribution of economic growth.

It is hard to support us to keep the past growth due to the reduction in labor supply, decline in the rate of savings, strong constraints on natural resources, increasing constraints on environmental protection and lack of technological innovation, which are five supply factors of adverse conditions.

Demand factors of adverse conditions include the following aspects. Firstly, the expansion of the domestic consumer market is constrained by unfair distribution of income. Back in 2000, some researcher from the Chinese Academy of Social Sciences proposed that China's Gini coefficient has ascended to the first rank in the world. Everyone thought that this view was messed up and was dissatisfied with the Reform and Opening-up. But what this researcher calculated was a fact. Now China's Gini coefficient may have reached 0.5, and the income gap is too large. The gap between different regions is widening, and the gap between different social strata is also widening. In different regions, the city's income was 1.82 times of that in rural areas in 1983, and it was 3.33 times in 2009. In different social strata, the income of 20% of the highest income households was 2.1 times of the income of 20% of the lowest income households in urban areas, it expended to 5.7 times in 2009, while it was expanded from 6.5 times to 7.5 times in rural areas. After 1986, the proportion of labor income in the gross national product (GDP) continued to decline. The working people haven't shared the fruits of economic labor correspondingly, and they have no ability to consume the goods that they produce.

Market economy is a kind of economy with both buying and selling, however, the situation that there is only selling but without buying appears. Some people argue that the unfair income was due to monopolistic behavior of state-owned enterprises, which does not hold water. The proportion of state-owned enterprises in the total output value is only 30%, so how could the unfair distribution be caused due to the problems of state-owned enterprises with output value of 30%? Some monopoly industries are due to technological reasons, for example, the power industry is a natural monopoly, and this kind of government monopoly enterprises is better than the private ones. In fact, since Reform and Opening-up our non-public economy has seen a rapid development.

It is caused by such a phenomenon linked together, and we should not ignore this problem. In the early stage of socialism, the existence of high supply of labor plays a favorable effect, which we should continue to encourage, but the condition of income distribution unfavorable for the workers will restrain the supply of labor. Therefore, we should adopt a series of policies, to curb this effect such as paying more attention to the interests of the workers, enabling the workers share the benefits of economic growth, plus pay more attention to people's livelihood and build a more solid social security system, so as to solve this problem.

Currently, we see that the problem has not been fundamentally resolved, and the whole situation remains unchanged, thus the Gini coefficient is still relatively high, the existence of this factor will hinder the expansion of our domestic market, because economic growth should promote the expansion of domestic market, but our country's market expansion rate and production capacity growth rate are quite incompatible, which will limit China's economic growth in the long term, which is an adverse factor in the demand side.

Another adverse factor in the demand is that foreign markets diminishing. This is related to the world economic crisis, when such crises occur in foreign economies problems are inevitable, and foreign markets become smaller. Unfair distribution of domestic income leads to that domestic market growth and GDP growth are disproportionate. But why is our economy growing so fast? Because our economy relies on exports, to export the goods which are not sold out in the domestic market, makes China's great dependence on exports, and the exports account for the largest proportion of GDP. In the international economic relations, China's economic growth depends on export, and export is as the main driving force of China's economic growth.

China with its huge population and a continental country, has a high degree of dependence on foreign trade which is even higher than Japan. The highest point of dependence to foreign trade in our country trade reached 65.3% in 2005, and the highest degree of dependence to export was 35.9%, that is to say China's 1/3 of the produced goods have to rely on foreign consumption. The foreign trade surplus in the GDP accounted for 7.6% in 2007. In 2011, the dependence to foreign trade was 48%, the dependence to export was 25%, and the foreign trade surplus in GDP accounted for 2.7%. Although this data has declined over the years, why the data reduced in 2011 can be attributed to the sovereign debt crisis in the West, therefore China's dependence degree of foreign trade has decreased, and the foreign trade surplus was reduced, and even for the first time, a negative growth situation has occurred. For such an excessive dependence on export revenues leads to great risks due to its side effects.

The huge level foreign exchange reserves leads to a strong pressure of inflation which is imported from the external world. I think we should not export for the sake of exporting. Exports must be for the sake of increasing the welfare of the Chinese people, not for the sake of increasing the welfare of other nations, but the current export strategy of our country leads to increase in the welfare of other nations. Due to China's production overcapacity, unfair distribution of income, and lack of purchasing power by people, consequently a large number of goods have to be exported.

Since China still holds lower ranking goods, in catching up the industrial upgrading, others which hold higher ranks in the industrial upgrading produce high-technology goods, but our country just exports those goods with lower prices. Similarly, if we compare the prices in the US markets, of those same goods produced in China, we see that they are sold cheaper than in China. Thus in fact, China favors the United States, increases exports, earns US dollar as foreign exchange, then purchases US treasury bonds, which means the treasury bonds issued by the United States and held by the Chinese treasury become a capital transfer to US which favors the US in another way. Besides these bonds held by the Chinese treasury is used funding the US Navy and Army so as to suppress China's national security. China does not pay enough attention to the regulation of income distribution, which results in excess production capacity and leads to its dependence on foreign markets.

In a certain period, China's foreign trade led economic growth, was seemingly driven by external demand, in fact, it was not a favorable situation. This situation can no longer be sustained, because many factors are changing. Many foreign nations only consume without production, leading to the economic crises thus a decline of purchasing power occurs in those nations, so we can no longer rely on exports to maintain a high degree of economic growth. Changes in the domestic market and foreign market are two basic change trends effecting the demand status. In the current state, if you make trend extrapolation analysis and this situation continues, it will certainly be unfavorable for our economic growth quality.

The above mentioned cases demonstrate the unfavorable changes in the two aspects of supply conditions and demand conditions that we may also face in China's future economic development. China also possesses favorable factors in regard to both aspects demand and supply, and they will play their roles in the future.

The second issue is favorable conditions for economic growth. The first favorable condition in the supply side is the increase in high-quality labor supply. The number of college graduates has surpassed 7 million while it was less than 1 million people in the recent past, a significant increase in the number, which of course, will cause an urgent employment problem, but with the supply of high-quality labor force increasing, and the improvement of the education level of the population will lead to great advantages for the economic growth, namely the education dividend. Thus while China's demographic dividend is disappears its education dividend is developing rapidly. It is difficult to calculate the advantages of this education dividend, but certainly it is a positive factor.

The second factor is linked to the first factor, this factor may offset a part of the downward trend in the saving rate. With the increase in the level of education among the working class, their demands will increase which in turn will raise their wages, and that will trigger the saving rate to a higher level. This is what I mean when I say education will offset a part of the savings rate decline brought about by decline in the number of workers. I will not enter concrete numerical estimations here which is quite complex.

The third factor is the recent significant increase in science and technology and education by the state. In 2012, the proportion of China's education expenditures was over 4% of the total GDP, the Ministry of Education has raised 9 years of compulsory education to 12 years, state investment and its supports to scientific research units and R & D enterprises have also increased remarkably, thus the innovation abilities of our country will soon improve to higher levels. This investment will be a favorable factor.

The fourth factor is that our country attaches due importance to the development of new energy sources than any country. For example, China's new-energy battery panels are appreciated all over the world markets and are heavily exported, related technologies have gradually matured, and their extensive application into utilization will further ease tension regarding China's energy supply.

In short, the supply of highly-qualified and educated labor force increases, part of the downtrend in the saving rate might be set off by the emergence of education dividends, increase of investments in science and technology and education and China's strong promotion of new energy sources makes will ease the energy supply situation. These are the 4 favorable conditions in the supply side.

Favorable conditions in demand side: the first is that urbanization has not yet been completed. China is still a country in the process of increasing urbanization, the proportion of urban population will increase greatly in the future decades, and which will release the great potential demand, which will promote a more qualified growth. For example, if a family moves to the city demanding a living area of 50 square meters, and if there will at least 100,000 families to migrate in a year, we can just imagine the enormous increase for the housing and home furniture and others. China's urbanization will take a long time to complete, which can offset all of the negative factors which we have listed above.

The second is the narrowing of regional development disparities. Along with the narrowing of regional development disparities the inequalities of social distribution among the regions can be greatly improved. Since 2012, a lot of data released by the National Bureau of Statistics shows that the economic growth rate in China's central regions is the fastest, followed by the western regions; the economic growth rate of the eastern regions is slowest. The enterprises in the central regions work in an environment which are relatively backward in regard to development and these regions also lag behind in the urbanization rate, these enterprises use the advantage of high labor supply and since development space is larger than other developed regions, I think this can also offset a large part of the adverse factors in regard to demand aspect.

The third is the reform measure with the keynote emphasizing common prosperity and fair distribution of the benefits of economic growth, which will also have a huge effect in promoting the domestic demand. The establishment of the social security system, the implementation of 12 years of compulsory education, full coverage in the health care support system and the improved pension system, will produce a huge demand. At the same time, due to great improvements in regard to basic security, people will easily increase their consumption level and reduce their social security savings, it can also increase the total demand.

All in all, when considering the adverse conditions, we should also notice the existing favorable conditions. Even if the favorable factors would indeed prove to be effective and can become a positive driving force for economic growth, we still need to deepen the reform further and promote common prosperity and make laboring people share the fruits of economic growth and realize the reform goals.

In general, the first task should be to overcome the adverse changes in supply factors by changing the mode of production; the second is to mitigate the adverse changes in the demand structure by narrowing the income gaps.

By fully allowing favorable factors to play their roles we can promote a steady economic growth. The reform keynote should no longer emphasize marketization, since market-oriented reforms have been basically completed. It is remarkable that recently, in some forums, some radical advocates of marketization and on the other side some of those comrades who oppose all kind of government regulations, seem to have some unspoken understandings in their minds, for example some believe that anti-monopoly regulations would lead to the privatization of all publicly owned enterprises, thus the public monopoly will transform to private monopoly.

Also the their views in regard to the political system reform are quite different. The reform should solve the issue of social unfair distribution and change the mode of economic growth as two main tasks, instead of continuing to develop marketization, especially the western marketization aims to cancel all of the public ownership. Reform should not allow a direction as proposed by western extreme conservatism, instead just opt for the opposite direction. We know that, the market can not eliminate the unfair distribution of income, when the distribution of means of production is unfair, instead the marketization will enlarge the unfair social distribution and also enlarge the unfair distribution of production costs, now it is time to find ways how to limit them. In the primary stage of socialism, China should unswervingly promote the economic development by making pro-labor adjustments in the distribution relation, and strive for a relatively fair social income distribution, and meanwhile avoid hurting the interests of the entrepreneurs too heavily. In order, to achieve an optimum adjustment, we should on the one hand, ensure that the proportion of working people's income in GDP increases, on the other hand let our entrepreneurs understand that the increase in working people's income will be beneficial to their own interests in the long run, and that they will be able to promote their product and service sales. Therefore, reform should push forward the improvements in education and health care unswervingly, rather than deepening marketization. Some people argue that China's financial systems are not deep and diversified enough, for example we do not have the financial derivatives market. Why do some people always think that the moon in United States is more round? Why do some people always think that the United States should be our role model?

Our economic growth is faster than the US, and we don't have economic crisis like in the United States either, why should we establish the derivatives market to deal with our economic problems? We should develop our own judgments, not blindly worship the economic policies of the US, on the contrary, we should look into the unfavorable factors which hinder our economic development, reveal the problems in the economic growth, consequently explore the ways to solve these problems. Obviously these problems cannot be resolved by marketization, we should avoid prejudices and explore other feasible ways. Of course, we cannot depart from the premise of taking the market as the decisive mechanism for the resources allocation. Through such a reform direction, we should achieve the transformation of the economic growth mode, meanwhile alleviate the huge deviation between production capacity and demand caused by our unfair domestic demand which is among top ranks in the international arena. And enable that our economy growth both possesses optimum supply and demand conditions, so that we can continue to have a steady economic development.

153

References

Zhu Fuen, Liu Na, The Development of Cultural Industries Is the Focus to Accelerate the Transformation of Economic Development Mode, *Theoretical Exploration*, 2012(3).

Wang Tao, The Focus of Transformation of Economic Development Mode – Taking the Suzhou City as an Example, *Theoretical Exploration*, 2011(2).

Zhang Ping, Thinking for Cracking the Plight of Economic Growth Slowing Down in Developed Regions, *Journal of Guangdong University of Business Studies*, 2012(5).

Zhang Enbi, "Public Consumption, Consumer Equity and Domestic Demand-driven Economic Growth", *Journal of Guangdong University of Business Studies*, 2011(3).

Zhou Decai, Lu Xiaoyong, Yang Yi, Li Yanqi: The Empirical Evidences on the Relationship between China's Financial Development and Economic Growth Cycle, *Journal of Shanxi University of Finance and Economics*, 2013(12).

Yang Zhifeng, The Analysis of Industrialization Impact on the Economic Growth: 1981-2008, *Journal of Shanxi University of Finance and Economics*, 2011(3).

Yan Chunying, The New Problems Faced by China's Economic Growth and the Counter-measures, *Modern Economic Research*, 2013(6).

Zhang Ping, Fu Minjie: China's Economic Growth Prospects and Policy Options Under Global Re-balancing, *Modern Economic Research*, 2012(1).

Zhang Ping, Dai Lei: "China's Economic Growth and Post-Crisis Era Equilibrium Adjustment", *Modern Economic Research*, 2011(1).

Originally published in the journal
Theoretical Exploration, 2014(3)

154

An Analysis on the Problems of the Current Income Distribution in China and Countermeasures

Rong Shengxian, Hong Yuanpeng and Tao Youzhi

155

Abstract: Currently, there exists the issue of increasing income distribution gap differences among the people of our country, and this was gradually formed along with the rapid economic development of the past decades. The source of the distribution issue can be made clear, and the solutions can also be found through analyzing the issue by the fundamental principles of Marxist distribution theory. It is necessary to normalize the distribution situation, perfect the collective salary consultation system in the enterprises, and form an olive-type social structure and distribution pattern.

Key words: income distribution; fairness and efficiency; common prosperity

Since Reform and Opening-up, the Chinese economy has encountered a rapid growth seen, and people's living standards have also increased comprehensively. Meanwhile, the income gaps have also constantly enlarged, and the distribution issue has become more and more grave. It is time for us to properly solve the currently existing problems in the income distribution of our country, otherwise, the social contradictions will be intensified, and the social stability will be negatively influenced. Below I will discuss my suggestions to solve the income distribution issues.

I. Correctly handling the relationship between fairness and efficiency

The relationship between fairness and efficiency is an old problem, but it still needs to be carefully studied and solved. Firstly, we need to figure out what is fairness? We believe that, fairness is the judgment of social individuals regarding the treatment towards themselves and others' based on mainstream values., which is to say that, whether the judgment is fair or not is based on mainstream values, and the judgment whether it is fair depends on whether its own judgment on the treatment is rational.

In our country, the mainstream value is the socialist value, and this is the value recognized and practiced by the overwhelming majority of the Chinese people, therefore only a specific fairness concept based on socialist values can have practical significance. In case most people do feel fairness, the society tends to be fair; in case that most people do not feel fairness, the society tends to be unfair. Obviously, most of us feel the unfair conditions in the current society. Since the fairness issue has become the main contradiction, currently, we need to carefully handle it.

The 14th National Congress of the CPC, in 1992, put forward the principle of "taking efficiency first, while paying due consideration to fairness", which was correct under the condition that the fairness issue hadn't become the main contradiction in the society. The Report of the 17th National Congress of CPC put forward the concept: "the relationship between fairness and efficiency must be properly handled for both the primary distribution and the re-distribution, and most stress should be given on fairness in regard to re-distribution", and this concept was proposed when the fairness issue was becoming more and more serious. Although the fairness issue was not the main contradiction at that time, it had become an important contradiction that should be paid attention, so the concept proposed in the 17th National Congress of CPC could meet the objective requirements of the then social development, which was correct.

To sum up the theories about fairness and efficiency, we can list the following :"the theory of efficiency first", "the theory of paying equal stress to efficiency and fairness", "theory of combining fairness and efficiency", and "the theory of efficiency first, and fairness secondary". We cannot abstractly decide which theory is correct, and which one is wrong, since we need to analyze the issue in combination with the social reality of an epoch. When the fairness issue is no longer the main contradiction, "the theory of efficiency first", "the theory of efficiency firstly, and justice secondary" are proper and feasible; when the fairness issue has become an important problem, "the theory of paying equal stress to efficiency and fairness", and "theory of combining fairness and efficiency" are proper and feasible. When the fairness issue has become the main social contradiction of the society, "the theory of fairness first, and efficiency secondary" should be followed, to thoroughly solve the fairness problem.

No matter under what circumstances, the fairness and efficiency issue and their relation is always an important theoretical issue in the social income distribution of socialism, and meanwhile, an important practical issue and a complex problem, which should be subject to overall consideration. Therefore, we need to handle the fairness and efficiency issue as per the following principle:

Firstly, the relevant countermeasures should be considered as per the principle that distribution is decided by production. Under general normal conditions, the income distribution should be subject to "efficiency first" principle, which includes two meanings: firstly, the contribution size or magnitude made by the distributed to production size should be considered. Distributed people having higher efficiency and bigger contribution should enjoy more; and the distributed people having lower efficiency and smaller contribution should enjoy fewer. Secondly, we should also consider, the size or magnitude of people's contribution to the future production efficiency. Those people exerting bigger contribution to the future production efficiency should enjoy more, or those contributing less should enjoy fewer. Secondly, in the sphere of primary distribution and re-distribution, the relationship between efficiency and fairness should also be well and correctly handled. The primary distribution should pay attention to efficiency, and hard working, so as to realize the synchronous increase of labor remuneration and the rate of labor productivity. Redistribution plays more attention to fairness, and hard working, so as to diminish the income distribution gaps among towns and countries, regions, and industries. Thirdly, the relationship between efficiency and fairness should be handled differently during different times. Efficiency should be focused during the flourishing period of equalitarianism and equalization of incomes, and we should focus on fairness, in the periods of big income gaps, and extremely big inequality between the rich and the poor. To sum up, regarding income distribution, the relationship between efficiency and fairness must be well handled, and needs comprehensive and appropriate arrangements.

II. Narrowing income gaps, and striving to achieve common prosperity

As can be seen in the data published by the State Statistics Bureau, the current income distribution of our country is unfair, with huge gaps, which is intensively reflected in the income gap between urban and rural residents, workers and peasants, and among the industries, especially between the workers laboring in the monopoly industries and the competitive industries. And this seriously influences the reasonable distribution and circulation and preferential configuration of the allocation of labor resources among the industries, and even negatively influences the harmony in the society.

Firstly, when we consider the income gap between urban and rural areas, in 1985, the urban residents' disposable income per capita was 1.89 times of the disposable income of rural residences, and after that, there occurred a year-by-year increasing trend[1] in 2007, the ratio had increased to 3.33 times, the maximum ratio of income gap between urban and rural areas.

Thereafter, the ratio has always fluctuated around the peak ratio reached in 2007, and then in 2010, the ratio has slightly decreased for the better, but it still remained to be high.

Secondly, when considering the income differences among industries, as per the 98 kinds of industry in the society, the income distribution between the highest and lowest industry has increased to 13.2 times in 2009 from 7.8 times in 2005. And especially the income distribution between the monopoly industries and the competitive industries, causes great dissatisfaction among the concerned people.

Monopoly industries, have priority in the resource allocation, and they can decide their prices independently, "everything can go very smoothly", and they earn high profits, without facing risks similar to those faced by the competitive industries. While in the competitive industries, the resource allocation is competitive, and their product sales are also competitive, their operations are harder, they undertake great risks, besides, their profit rates are far lower than that of the monopoly industries. The relevant researches have pointed out that, the actual income difference between the monopolized industries and other industries can be 5-10 times.[2]

Finally, as can be seen from the comparison of five respective income groups between the urban and rural residents, the income difference between the highest income group and the lowest income group of the urban and rural areas has been 3.6 times, 3.7 times, 5.5 times, and 5.7 times in 2000, 2005, 2007, and 2008, respectively. In the aforementioned four years, the income difference between the highest income group and the lowest income group in the agriculture-forestry sector has been 6.5 times, 7.3 times, 7.3 times and 7.5 times, respectively.

With respect to the income difference between the highest income group (about 120 million people) of the cities and towns and the lowest income group of villages (about 140 million people), which was 14.1 times in 2000 has rapidly increased to 21.5 times in 2005, 21.9 times in 2007, and 23.1 times in 2008,[3] and in the recent years, this ratio has further increased.

---

1   Data source: please refer to http://www.stas.gov.cn for the National Annual Statistical Bulletin from 1985 to 2015 published by the National Bureau of Statistics of the People's Republic of China. Unless otherwise specified in the article, all the data referred in the article are originated from this source, and no further indications will be made thereafter.

2   Chen Chengming et al., *China Characteristic Socialism Economic Theory Course*, Shanghai University of Finance and Economics Press, 2013, p. 83.

3   Hu Angang et al., *China Marching Towards 2015*, Zhejiang People's Publishing House, 2010, pp. 96-97.

With respect to the national level, the fact that Gini coefficient is too big, will not only influence the production efficiency of workers, but also concerns the harmony in the entire society. As can be seen in Table 1, the Gini coefficient for the incomes of residents nationwide has remained at a high level of 0.47-0.50 between 2003 to 2012, which has been far higher than the internationally recognized warning line of 0.4.

Table 1: 2003-2012 National Resident Income Gini Coefficient Figures

Year	2003	2004	2005	2006	2007	2008	2009	2010	2011	2012
Gini Coefficient	0.479	0.473	0.485	0.487	0.484	0.491	0.490	0.481	0.477	0.474

Data source: New Opportunity, New Risk and New Selection written by Zhou Zhenhua et al. Gezhi Press, 2013, p. 146.

So how to treat the sensitive fact of increasing income gap ? Comrade Deng Xiaoping used to point out that, the objective for enlarging the regional income gaps was to "stimulate and drive some regions to realize prosperity earlier", and meanwhile, let the regions which achieved prosperity earlier help the less developed regions achieve prosperity , and for the same reason, he said: "let some people get rich first".[4] With respect to the specific phenomenon of increasing income gap, he also pointed out that, we were still in the primary stage of socialism, consequently our essential task is to develop productive forces, rather than restricting them in many ways. "Our primary goal in adhering to the socialist road, is realization of common prosperity, but egalitarianism is not permissible."[5] He firmly argued that, no polarization would occur as long as we adhered to the socialist path. The current income distribution problems in our country have become highly prominent, indicating the importance and urgency of fairness.

Common prosperity is the ideal that the Chinese people have assiduously sought for a thousand years, and meanwhile, a fundamental characteristic of socialism. In the speech made by Deng Xiaoping during the southern tour in 1992, he clearly pointed out that "the essence of socialism is to liberate and develop productive forces, eliminate exploitation, remove polarization, and finally achieve common prosperity".[6]

Analyzing this significant theoretical problem, he placed common prosperity at such a height: it was not only the essential characteristic of socialism, but also the final goal of the socialist society. Common prosperity is the essential characteristic of the socialist society which distinguishes it from all the other exploitative societies, "predominance of public ownership and common

---

4   *Selected Works of Deng Xiaoping*, Volume 3, People's Press, 1993, p. 111.

5   Ibid, p. 155.

6   Ibid., p. 373.

prosperity are the two fundamental socialist principles that we must adhere to."[7] The theory and core values of socialism let us know that polarization is not socialism, and ultimately, socialism aims to realize fairness, eliminate polarization, and realize common prosperity.

Deng Xiaoping's idea about common prosperity was initially proposed in 1978, and at that time, his specific thoughts were as follows: "in economic policy, I believe that, to let some people and some regions, enterprises, workers and farmers obtain more and live a better life due to their hard work and bigger contributions. Since part of people could live a better life, this would certainly demonstrate big example power, to influence the neighbors, and drive other regions, and let the people of other units learn from them. Through doing this, the entire national economy could be constantly developed forward as per a wave mode, and people of all nationalities could become prosperous sooner."[8]

Deng Xiaoping not only emphasized the goal of common prosperity, but also clearly point out the specific modes, methods and steps for realizing this goal. The concept of common prosperity contains an essential theoretical value and realistic meaning. Firstly, as the brand new stage for the human's historical development, socialism cannot be built on the basis of poverty. We need to use all means to develop productive forces, accumulate rich social wealth, provide more economic benefits for people as much as possible, and enlarge the range of products that can be provided to people for distribution and consumption. Secondly, the common prosperity is the essential objective of socialism, and meanwhile, the essential characteristic and the goal of socialist society. The concept of common prosperity does not only points to the goal, but also provides a methodology to realize this goal; it does not only point to the contents, but also points to their forms, with strict scientificalness. Thirdly, it points to the specific steps to realize common prosperity. It is a process wherein we can provide more economic benefits for the people, and the first step for realizing common prosperity is to let some regions and some people get rich first, and the goal is to more rapidly realize common prosperity. Besides, those regions and individuals who become rich first, should be obligated to help the less developed areas and individuals, and this is the essential methodology for avoiding social polarization.

The concept of socialist distribution by Deng Xiaoping as letting some regions, enterprises and people get rich first, and then push all the people to realize common prosperity, has largely enriched and developed Marxism.

However, how to correctly recognize and handle the issue of narrowing the differences and realizing common prosperity can still be a relatively complex problem. Currently, in order to solve the fairness problem, and eliminate the symptoms of polarization, we need to follow the following principles, to gradually solve the fairness problem:

---

7   Ibid., p. 111.
8   *Selected Works of Deng Xiaoping*, Volume 3, People's Press, 1993, p. 152.

Firstly, the narrowing of the gaps and difference, we mention here is not the full elimination of differences. During the primary stage of socialism, most differences can be narrowed, but elimination is impossible, and even during the more advanced stages of socialism, differences might still exist.

Secondly, the narrowing of differences is not only a process, but also a gradual process. Some narrowing can be achieved earlier and faster such as the difference between the urban workers and migrant workers in the cities; but some of them cannot be realized in a short time, which need to be gradually realized such as the differences between urban and rural areas.

Thirdly, many of differences can be hard to be fully eliminated during the socialism stage. Without contradictions, conflicts, competitions, or without people pursuing for various, different interests, the human society cannot realize progress, and the socialism will never move forward, either.

Fourthly, common prosperity is not the equal wealth and prosperity for all the people. The prosperity level of people in a country should have a standard, and once reaching this certain standard, it can be considered as prosperity is achieved, in a relative sense. But yet there will be differences of level of wealth among different groups, so no absolute equalitarianism can be achieved.

Fifthly, achieving common prosperity does not mean we achieve it altogether at the same time in a synchronized manner, and it refers to letting some regions and people become rich first and then promote, trigger and push others to realize common prosperity.

Sixthly, the common prosperity cannot be based on gifting or favoring people, and it requires a top-level design, also requires the support of the society, there is no "god" or "emperor" who will gifts to people, therefore, people have to save themselves with their own efforts, rely on their own hard work to become prosperous.

Comrade Mao Zedong used to say: "We must help all our young people to understand that ours is still a very poor country, that we cannot change this situation radically in a short time, and that only through the united efforts of our younger generation and all our people, working with their own hands, can China be made strong and prosperous within a period of several decades. The establishment of our socialist system has opened the road leading to the ideal society of the future, but to translate this ideal into reality needs hard work."[9]

III. Distributing the "cake", while making the "cake" bigger

The distribution in our country is unreasonable, with massive income gaps, and the opinions of people regarding this issue are relatively consistent. But when it comes to solving this problem? The divergence is big. If we compare the distribution to a "cake", some people hold that it is necessary to firstly divide the "cake", to demonstrate fairness; others hold that it is necessary to

---

9   *Selected Works of Mao Zedong*, Volume 5, People's Press, 1977, p. 386.

make bigger "cake", since only a bigger "cake" can allow people to have a bigger portion. Some people disagree with the latter opinion, arguing that unfair distribution of the "cake" will negatively influence people's enthusiasm for producing "cakes", which will greatly hinder people making a bigger cake. Both proponents have their own reasoning, so what should be the solution?

"Making cake" and "dividing cake" (distribution) cannot be regarded as two different and opposite things; on the contrary, they can mutually promote each other. They are in a dialectical relationship which mutually promote one another rather than being incompatible as fire and water.

"Making cake" can directly reflect whether the labor provided by the workers can be paid, and in case that the corresponding "cake" can be obtained as per the labor amount and quality provided by all people, the workers can feel that this is fair and reasonable; meanwhile, this will also stimulate the enthusiasm for working again, and further making better "cakes". This is the issue mentioned in the Third Plenary Session of the 18th CPC Central Committee (2013) as follows: "place emphasis on protecting labor income, strive to synchronize the increase of remuneration for labor with the growth of labor productivity, and raise the proportion of labor remuneration in primary distribution." In case that the labor provided by the workers (including the quality and quantity) cannot obtain the corresponding "cake" they deserve, the enthusiasm of the workers will be damaged, and meanwhile, the production of the "cake" will also be effected, and this effect will display itself especially within the primary distribution, it can exert great effect on each worker's enthusiasm. In case that the primary distribution is unreasonable, the degree of correction within the re-distribution will be quite limited and will not satisfy them fully. Since the primary distribution is the major part of the entire distribution process, the re-distribution in the posterior (afterwards) can be merely deemed as the subordinate part. From this point of view, "distributing cake" is very important, and we need to realize fairness, justice, reasonability and order.

"Dividing the cake" is very important, but this involves certain restrictions. A wise distribution can be able to solve the issue of how to realize a fair distribution under certain quantity of "cake", but distribution cannot solve the issue of enlarging the whole amount to be distributed. Therefore, to solve the latter issue we need to make the second level of efforts, i.e., make the "cake" bigger. To make the "cake" bigger can have more significant meaning, for instance, in case of dividing 500g "cake" for 10 people, provided that each person's labor quantity and labor quality are the same, so that we can strictly implement equitable distribution, each person can only get 50 gm. piece of the "cake". If we can be able to make the "cake" bigger today, although the labor quantity and quality of individuals are still the same, the cake earned by each person will no longer be 50 gm./piece, but may be 250g or 500g for each person. So, where does this 250g or 500g come from? This is due to the increase in productive forces, rather than coming from the sky. Therefore, the remuneration of the workers should be constantly increased, and the synchronized increase of both the labor remuneration and labor productivity can only be realized on the basis of increasing labor productivity. There are many ways to increase the labor productivity, and the most essential aspects are as follows:

1. Greatly increasing the laboring enthusiasm of workers. This is the most basic method and minimum premise to increase the labor productivity. The so-called "high enthusiasm for labor" among the workers means both to work and make qualified contribution as end product, and also means trying their best during every minute of the working day. And such working demonstrates a sharp contrast with working without making qualified contribution, i.e. unskilled work. Some workers are slow and inefficient in work, therefore it is not easy to increase the labor productivity, and even in some cases we cannot ensure the basic level of labor productivity.

2. Improving the technical-technological proficiency of the workers. Due to different technical proficiency levels among the workers, their labor efficiency cannot be the same and this we can observe within production as the common sense. Therefore, in order to increase the labor productivity, each worker should work hard to learn culture, technology, and improve their personal technical or operating level, as soon as possible.

3. Reasonableness of the production process. When we examine the whole production of an enterprise, the more products it produces, the more complex will be the production process, and it will have many sub-production units, there will be sub-departments under every department. Thus, it will be very important to arrange such complex production and arrange and coordinate the relations between every different production departments. If the arrangement and coordination is not smooth, and remains poor, then inevitably the production efficiency will be low.

4. Upgrading of the machinery and equipment. The labor productivity is directly related with advanced machinery and equipment. The advanced equipment can create higher labor productivity, and it is impossible to obtain the efficiency of the 21st Century with "the equipment of the Li Hongzhang period". Therefore, in order to improve the labor productivity, it is very important to correctly use the optimum machinery, and not act blindly in this regard. Even if we do not have or cannot buy advanced machinery, to replace the ones in our hand, we can still make some wise arrangements to improve the productivity.

5. Scientific-technological innovation. Promoting innovation driven production and reforms in production processes are not only designed by countries but also by individual enterprises. If an enterprise wants to continuously improve labor productivity, it must be good at technological innovations. And in regard to enterprises there are two important aspects of such innovations: firstly, the enterprise can innovate the process or innovate the arrangement of production, i.e. product processing or such arrangements which directly improve labor productivity. And, the second innovation method is, making innovation by employing upgraded and more efficient machinery, which will in turn increase

labor productivity, we can say this is the indirect way. If an enterprise can improve its equipment and technical process, shorten manufacturing time and simplify manufacturing procedures without reducing the product quality, productivity will be improved.

6. Innovation in management. Enterprises improve efficiency through innovation in management, give full play to talents, making best use of everything through management innovations, improve marketing strategies by management innovation, accelerate their capital turnover, thus they can greatly improve the efficiency of production.

Currently, in China we need to introduce the most advanced information management system, and utilize advanced computer technology to improve the efficiency in management. Through the use and mining of big data, actively adopting the cloud technology, we should improve information management and knowledge innovation and other means so that our country's management level can be at the forefront in the global arena.

IV. Regulating the distribution order, so as to form a reasonable and an orderly distribution pattern

(I) Achieve reasonableness: the current unreasonable distribution pattern should be changed

In the current distribution system of our country, an unreasonable situation exists, which needs to be gradually resolved through re-adjusting the distribution processes. Firstly, we should improve the proportion of labor remuneration in the primary distribution. The essence of primary distribution requires that the market plays decisive role in the pricing mechanism of various production factors being used and each factor of production (including labor), should get their share of distribution according to their "contribution in magnitude and value" as determined by the market mechanism, i.e. this is the principle of functional income distribution. Looking from the aspect of market's decisive role, if we are sure that the share of consumption in the primary distribution is too low, it will lead to a situation wherein the distribution among various factors (specifically the labor factor, is discriminated) will be unreasonable.

This is the situation mentioned in the Third Plenum of the 18th Central Committee: "place emphasis on protecting labor income,..... and raise the proportion of labor remuneration in primary distribution." In such situation "the protection of labor incomes" needs to be adjusted upward.

Secondly, it is necessary to perfect the decision making in regard to wages and attain a normal growth mechanism. With respect to the relationship between wages and production, there used to be an old saying: "the more the production is, the more you will earn", which indicated that there should be a reasonable proportional relation between production increase and remuneration of labor. When the production increases, the wages should also be increased accordingly.

However, our country has failed to define a scientific and reasonable proportional relation for a long time, so in the future, we need to correct this situation.

Thirdly, it is necessary to narrow the income distribution differences among the urban and rural areas, among different regions and among different industries. The gaps in such aspects are quite big, and this is a prominent issue which exists in the current distribution system of our country. With respect to the solutions, we need to make specific analysis, find the right remedies, and meanwhile, conduct comprehensive consideration, and try to achieve overall progress. Such when narrowing the gap between urban and rural areas, specifically we need to start from resolving the dual structure of the urban and rural areas, improve the agricultural labor productivity, and solve the income problem of peasants. Besides, we also need to change the current unreasonable income distribution status, and meanwhile, adjust the excessively high incomes downwards, clean up and standardize hidden incomes, and restrict and punish illegal incomes.

(II) Standardization: the establishment of a standardized distribution pattern

There is another issue in the current distribution of our country, i.e. the huge imbalances and arbitrariness regarding distribution among some departments, regions, industries and wage earners. Those who control money, can increase wages and bonuses on the other hand who control power are able to arbitrarily adjust and increase salaries, openly, without needing to hide their acts. if they are not able to increase salaries, they arbitrarily increase bonus and allowance pays. We must adopt decisive measures to eliminate, forbid and standardize such practices and conditions behind them. In order to establish a standardized distribution pattern, firstly, we need to establish the mechanism of letting the market decide the prices of the following factors such as: labor, capital, knowledge, technology, management and others. The distribution among these factors should be fair, and equalitarianism should be strictly avoided. Currently, in regard to all above production factors, without exception, there is the issue of equalitarianism, as the biggest problem to be solved. Their contributions are not fairly evaluated. It is reasonable and fair to give different remunerations to each production factor, according to their contribution in regard to production or economic development, and we must insist on this policy. Besides, we need to formulate a set of salary mechanism which considers the proportional contribution of all the factors, such as the eight-level salary system implemented in the enterprises, and the post salary system implemented for the civil servants in the past. Secondly, we need to perfect the minimum wages and the security system for wage payments. Especially care for those workers, we know that they have different talents, and physical conditions, and some of them earn so little and can hardly maintain their lives. For such workers, the relevant departments of the state should adjust the minimum wages and provide wage payment security system, to help them maintain their lives. Thirdly, we should improve the collective wage negotiation system. The contradictions exist between the workers and the employers which is an objective reality.

The workers ask for fair remuneration for their labor contribution, and the employers always pursue to pay as less as possible, so as to increase the surplus value, so this will be conflicts between the two parties, even confrontations can occur. How to solve such problems? Either, employers having the final say, or workers having the final say, cannot be accepted, the best method would be to solve the conflicts through negotiations among the two parties. This requires the relevant departments of the state to provide active guidance, and necessary supervision, the departments should promote enterprises to establish negotiation teams and labor union organizations should also be encouraged as soon as possible, to improve wage negotiation system in the enterprises.

(III) The goal should be the gradual formation of an olive-shaped distribution pattern

For any country, the distribution pattern includes three types: the first one is pagoda tower type: there are few rich people, and most people are situated at different degrees of poverty. The old China before the establishment of new China belonged to such category. The second one is the inverted pagoda tower type: most people are rich, only a gradual decrease in prosperity can be observed, and there are few poor, which is the situation in some developed countries. The third one is the olive type. There are few extremely rich and poor people, and most people are situated at the middle income level, they are affluent, but not extremely rich. Among these three types, our country is now pursuing for the third one, as mentioned in the Third Plenary Session of the 18th Central Committee of the CPC: "We will strive to narrow the income gap between urban and rural areas, different regions and different sectors, thus gradually forming an olive-shaped distribution structure in the country."[10]

To realize this goal, in addition to our above mentioned "reasonableness", and "standardization" propositions, we offer the following measures:

Firstly, we should perfect the income redistribution system. Due to "market failures" and due to scarcity of production factors, there occurs rich and poor in the distribution. With respect to this situation, the visible hand—i.e. the government should play its role to make due adjustments. In fact, under the market economy conditions, essentially, re-distribution function should be implemented by the government, which is government's counter-measure against the "market failures". How to surpass such "market failures"? This requires "the utilization of redistribution and regulatory mechanisms to improve the issue of income gaps among different groups, for example expanding social security payment for the disadvantaged groups and effecting transfer payments to them as the main measure, and reinforce the regulatory effect of taxing system".[11] Transferring of incomes from the rich, and subsidizing the low-income labor group, through redistribution, the income gap between the rich and the poor can be narrowed.

---

10   *Compilation of Documents of the Third Plenary Session of the 18th Central Committee of the Communist Party of China*, People's Press, 2013, p. 66.

11   Ibid.

Secondly, we should accelerate the promotion of new-type urbanization. Sizable development gap between urban and rural regions and sizable difference of income between workers and peasants are the two prominent distribution problems in China at present. How to solve this? This requires to "promote people-oriented urbanization and coordinated development of urbanization and new rural construction".[12] The core of new-type urbanization is people, and the goal is to solve the "three rural issues", i.e. the hardships faced by the peasants, the poor status of rural areas, and the backward agriculture, and this requires that we should insist on the policy of industry sector paying back to the agricultural sector (once the agricultural sector had supported the industry sector), urban regions supporting the rural areas, and continue the policy of more giving and less taking from the agricultural sector, so as to accelerate the realization of the integration between urban and rural development. Thirdly, we should increase the residents' property income through multiple ways. The first way, as we have mentioned above is "to adjust the extremely high income of the rich", the second measure is "to support the poor" by the visible hand, and the third measure is how to make the majority of the people become "moderately prosperous" as in the olive type distribution. All these should be done according to the policy mentioned in the Third Plenary Session of the 18th Central Committee of the CPC: "increase the residents' property income through multiple ways."[13]

For instance, some people can increase their incomes through "expanding their investments and promote farmers' joint-stock partnerships, grant farmers the rights to possess, profit from, pull out with compensation, mortgage, guarantee and inherit shares of collective assets." and some people can increase their incomes by their investments into the shares of listed companies by "optimizing the profit distribution of the listed companies", and some people can stabilize and enlarge their incomes through protecting "the legal interests of medium and small sized investors", etc.

167

To sum up, both the government regulation and market mechanisms should be effectively utilized. The essential path to solve the income distribution issue is to effectively integrate the government regulation and the market mechanisms. In other words, the governmental regulation and market mechanism should be organically combined, plus we should develop relevant industrial policies, income policies. Along with the establishment of scientific, and reasonable government role to make up for the market mechanisms. Under such market mechanism, the income distribution will gradually become reasonable, and social fairness can be achieved.

Originally published in
Journal of Fudan University (Social Sciences Edition) 2014(5)

---

12   Ibid., p. 42.
13   Ibid., p. 66.

Is the State-owned Economy Irrelevant to Socialism?

Zhang Yu and Wang Ting

Abstract: The state-owned economy possesses the dual attributes of public and class natures. The characteristic of state-owned economy is mainly determined by the characteristic of production relations that constitutes the dominant position. The essential difference between the socialist and capitalist state is their different positions and roles, which are naturally determined by different production relations. The socialist economy is based on public ownership, and led by the state-owned economy, which reflects the new type of economic relations such as regulation by the society, distribution according to labor contribution, democratic management and sharing of the residual. However, the capitalist economy is based on the wage labor relationship, and the state-owned economy is merely the supplementary form of private capital. The essence of deepening the reform of state-owned economic sector is to establish an "effective realization form" of public ownership in practice, make the state-owned economy better reflect the inherent characteristics of socialism, so that socialism can display its inherent systemic superiority.

Key words: socialism; public ownership; state-owned economy; economic system reform

The state-owned economy plays an important role in the socialist economic system with Chinese characteristics, and this has been clearly stated in the Constitution of our state. As pointed out in Article 6 of the Constitution, the basis of the socialist economic system of the People's Republic of China is the socialist public ownership of the means of production, i.e., the ownership by the whole people and the collective ownership by the working people. As pointed out in Article 7, "the state economy is the sector of socialist economy under ownership by the whole people; it is the leading force in the national economy. The state ensures the consolidation and growth of the state economy."

The statement in the Constitution has not only explained the important position of state-owned economy during the current stage of economic system in our country, but also affirmed the socialist nature of state-owned economy. However, for the socialist nature of state-owned economy, in the recent years, some people question that the state ownership is not equivalent to public ownership and argue that it cannot be evaluated as socialist. They argue that the state-owned economy also existed in the slave society, feudal society and capitalist society, and that it is a traditional concept to regard the state ownership as the foundation of socialist system, which should be abandoned. Some people have therefore held that the state ownership has nothing to do with socialism, demand the privatization of state-owned economy, and meanwhile, try hard to create a favorable public opinion for this goal. Is the state-owned economy irrelevant to socialism? What is the relationship between the state-owned economy and socialism? This is an important issue related to the fate of socialism, which we will comprehensively analyze and examine below.

I. The duality of state-owned economy

Historically, the state-owned economy does not exclusively belong to socialist society, in fact the state-owned economy can be found in the slave society, feudal society, capitalist society and other various pre-capitalist social formations. For instance, from the Western Zhou Dynasty to Ming and Qing Dynasty, lots of state-owned farms, state-run businesses and handicraft industries existed in the ancient Chinese society. In the capitalist society, the existence of state-owned economy has been much more common. Therefore, we cannot simply say that the state-owned economy is equivalent to the socialism.

So, what is the essential attribute of state-owned economy? What determines its unique nature? The state-owned economy always possesses dual characteristics: the public and social characteristics, which means that it possesses a public character so as to discharge certain social functions.

Just as said by Engels: "the core characteristic of the state is public power that is separated from the populace", "...the exercise of a social function was everywhere the basis of political supremacy; and further that political supremacy has existed for any length of time only when it discharged its social functions."[1] With respect to the public functions of the state, especially some

---

1   Selected Works of Marx and Engels, Vol. 4, People's Press, 1995, p. 116.

economic functions it undertakes, such as leading public administration, collecting financial revenues and taxes, controlling key economic resources, and regulating productive relations, and all these functions cannot be borne by the privately owned sector of the economy, which means that the state-owned economy should be consolidated.

From this aspect, the state-owned economy is a kind of mode and method of the state, which undertakes public and social functions, and this has been the same in various different social formations of the past, for instance, in the autocratic feudal society of China, agricultural land was the most important production means and economic resource, so the governors of past dynasties paid great attention to the regulation and control of land assets, and the central feudal authority directly controlled vast land resources, so throughout the history, various land ownership (control) modes had existed, i.e. the system of land equalization policy in Tang Dynasty, the public farming in Song Dynasty, and others. After entering into the capitalist society, along with the development of socialized mass production, the state-owned economy was also extensively promoted.

Especially after the World War II, the developed capitalist countries have experienced several waves of nationalization, thus the state-owned economy widely existed in the banking sector, space and nuclear industry, petroleum, coal, electric power, railways, roads, ports, civil aviation, aircraft manufacturing, shipbuilding industry and some other industries, and meanwhile, they have exerted important effects to the economic life. Under the capitalist system, in some periods state-owned economy has become inevitable. Engels pointed out that: "the reactive force for the sharp increase of productive forces in its capitalist attribute required us to admit the increasingly increased pressure on the social nature of productive forces, and this had forced the possible restrictions of capitalist class itself in the capital relation, and the productive forces had been increasingly regarded as the social productive forces."[2]

Within a certain development period, the official representative of the capitalist society—the state will have to undertake the guidance of production, and meanwhile, implement nationalization to respond to the requirements of continuous socialization of productive forces. Although such changes and the development of the state-owned economy cannot fundamentally change essential characteristics of the capitalist economic system, this causes partial qualitative changes in the capitalist production relations, which means the sublation of the private capitalist property structures, in this way capitalist production relations are adapted to the development requirements of continuous socialization of production to a certain extent, and which also reflects the interest of the society to a certain extent, imbued with direct social characteristics. Thus with such adjustments reforms capitalism can open even a greater room for the development of social productive forces, which in turn creates conditions for alleviating the

---

2 Ibid., p. 628.

economic and social contradictions in the capitalist society, and meanwhile further transforms capitalism towards socialism, as predicted by Marx.

However, it is also held by Marxism that, the public and social functions of a state are merely a superficial event, and ultimately, the state is nothing but the tool of the ruling class, which represents the interests of the ruling class concealed behind the public character of the state, i.e. its class character. From this aspect, the state-owned economy is merely a tool and production mode for realizing the interest of the ruling class, with distinct class characteristics. Engels' descriptions about the character of capitalist state brightly clarifies this point: "And the modern State, again, is only the organization that bourgeois society takes on in order to support the external conditions of the capitalist mode of production against the encroachments as well of the workers as of individual capitalists. The modern state, no matter what its form, is essentially a capitalist machine, the state of the capitalists, the ideal personification of the total national capital. The more it proceeds to the taking over of the productive forces, the more does it actually become the national (total, general) capitalist, the more citizens does it exploit. The workers remain wage workers – proletarians. The capitalist relationship is not done away with. It is rather brought to a head."[3] Along with the replacement of the private ownership of the production means, by the public ownership, the state will lose its capitalist class attribute, "The proletariat seizes the public power, and by means of this transforms the socialized means of production, slipping from the hands of the bourgeoisie, into public property. By this act, the proletariat frees the means of production from the character of capital they have thus far borne, and gives their socialized character complete freedom to work itself out."[4]

Due to the aforementioned reasons, Marx and Engels clearly criticized the mistaken opinion of regarding all kinds of state ownership as socialism. Engels pointed out that: "Since Bismarck went in for State-ownership of industrial establishments, a kind of spurious socialism has arisen, degenerating, now and again, into something of flunkyism, that without more ado declares all State-ownership, even of the Bismarkian sort, to be socialistic. Certainly, if the taking over by the State of the tobacco industry is socialistic, then Napoleon and Metternich must be numbered among the founders of Socialism."[5]

In a word, the state possesses duality, and it is not only a public power, with certain properties of publicity or sociality, but also a tool of class rule with obvious class and historical characteristics. Just as pointed out by Marx, the functions of a state "not only includes executing of various public affairs and the general interest of all citizens its social character, but also includes various special functions (for example, 'police', the 'judiciary', and the 'administration') …which are the representatives of the state and their task is to administer the state against the civil society".[6]

3   Selected Works of Marx and Engels, Volume 3, People's Press, 1995, p. 629.
4   Ibid., p. 759.
5   Ibid., p. 752.
6   Collected Works of Marx and Engels, Vol. 25, People's Publishing House, 1974, p. 432.

Consequently the characteristics of the state-owned economy can only be correctly grasped when the duality of the state is understood. The characteristics of the state-owned economy are not abstract, or unchangeable, and its characteristics is determined by characteristics of production relations which is dominant leading position in the society and also determined by the class characteristics of the state. This is the starting point for us to correctly understand the state-owned economy.

II. Nature and role of state-owned economy under socialism

The socialist economy and capitalist economy are both based on the large-scale social production, and the development of capitalist state-owned economy has provided some useful enlightenment for socialism, Marx wrote: "State ownership of the productive forces is not the solution of the conflict, but concealed within it are the technical conditions which form the elements of that solution. This solution can only consist in the practical recognition of the social nature of the modern forces of production…."[7]

Here Marx emphasizes the recognition of the social nature of modern productive forces, implement social ownership of the means of production, and regulate social production on such a basis. However, we must see not only recognize commonality but also the fundamental differences between socialism and capitalism. In a capitalist society, the dominant production relationship is the capitalist wage-labor relationship. The establishment of the state-owned economy is to ease the basic contradictions of capitalism, create conditions for capital accumulation under capitalism, and serve the demands of capital's proliferation. However, in the socialist society, the dominant production relationship is the socialist public ownership of the means of production, while the state-owned economy is the main form of socialist public ownership. Marx and Engels once made it clear that, "the theory of the Communists may be summed up in the single sentence: Abolition of private property."[8] The decisive difference between capitalist system and socialist system of course is that socialism organizes production on the basis of implementing the public ownership of all means of production (firstly in individual countries).[9] Although China is in the primary stage of socialism at present and has shifted from highly centralized planned economy to the socialist market economy, the public ownership is still the basis of the socialist economic system. China's basic economic system during the primary stage of socialism includes the dominant position of public ownership and diverse forms of ownership developing in tandem. It is preciously because of such an economic basis and basic system that China's state-owned economy has socialist nature. At the present stage, why does the socialist public ownership mainly appear as the state ownership, rather than the collective ownership or other ownership forms? The reason is that the socialist

7   Collected Works of Marx and Engels, Vol. 3, People's Publishing House, 1995, p. 629.
8   Collected Works of Marx and Engels, Vol. 1, People's Publishing House, 1995, p. 286.
9   Collected Works of Marx and Engels, Vol. 4, People's Publishing House, 1995, p. 693.

public ownership is based on large-scale social production, and high degree of socialization in production which enables the working people to unite and conduct unified and planned regulation of the means of production on the basis of their common interests. In order to ensure that such possession by the whole society will not remain just a formal measure, and that this measure will not be frustrated by the conflicts among partial interests, or will not become a "illusionary theoretical fiction" we need to establish a tangible organization to represent the common interests of the society. Under the conditions that the state exists, the state will be the official representative of the whole society and public ownership can only be represented by the state. Therefore, it is inevitable that in the real socialist society, the public ownership should appear in the form of state ownership. As long as the public ownership and the state as a social organization exist, the state ownership will be inevitable. In fact, Marx and Engels have explicitly affirmed that under the existence of state, the public ownership will certainly take the form of state ownership. In *The Communist Manifesto*, they wrote, "The proletariat will use its political supremacy to seize all the capitals from the bourgeoisie step by step, concentrate all the means of production in the hands of the proletariat of the state as the ruling class; and try to increase the total productive forces as rapidly as possible."[10] In the *Anti-Dühring*, Engels explicitly pointed out that, "The proletariat will seize the state power and turn the means of production into state property."[11] In the basic socialist economic system, the public economy not only includes the economic sector which is under the ownership by the whole people or state-owned economy, but also includes the collective ownership sector. However, we should make clear how the collectively owned economic sector attains the socialist nature. It is under the precondition that the state-owned economy plays a leading role in the whole economic system. Otherwise, the collective economy is just a small boat in the vast ocean that may be overthrown at any time. The reason is that the collective economy is an intermediate form of ownership, with dual natures as public and private contents. Internally, the collective economy is of public nature, which includes equal ownership of means of the production by all the members of the collective and externally, it has private ownership character because the ownership only belongs to the members of the enterprise. Therefore, the collective ownership has and inherent natural instability, thus it cannot become the leading form of ownership in any society. On the contrary, its nature and roles depend on the nature of the ownership that takes the leading position. When expounding on the nature of cooperative factories in the capitalist society, Marx pointed out: "The co-operative factories of the labourers themselves represent within the old form the first sprouts of the new, although they naturally reproduce, and must reproduce, everywhere in their actual organisation all the shortcomings of the prevailing system"[12]

---

10 Collected Works of Marx and Engels, Vol. 1, People's Publishing House, 1995, p. 293.
11 Collected Works of Marx and Engels, Vol. 3, People's Publishing House, 1995, p. 630.
12 Collected Works of Marx and Engels, Vol. 7, People's Publishing House, 1995, p. 499.

In the socialist market economy, like the non-public economy sectors such as the enterprises owned by individuals, private and foreign enterprises sector of economy, the collective economy is also engaged in business activities which pursues private and group interest, therefore it has contradictions with the society's overall and long-term interests. Therefore, this reality requires the coordination and guidance of the state-owned economy in order to ensure that this sector would serve the overall interests of the socialist society. Marx was aware of this point in those years. When talking about the conditions of maintaining the cooperative system in the future society, Marx said, "Things must be dealt with in such a manner. Society (i.e. the state at first) is made to hold the ownership of the means of production and so that the particular interests of the cooperatives will not outweigh the overall interests of the whole society."[13]

In this sense, we can say that there will be no socialism without the state-owned economy, and the socialist system is inseparable from the state-owned economy at the current stage. As the main form of public ownership and an important part of the basic socialist economic system, there is significant difference between the socialist state-owned economy and the capitalist state-owned economy. The latter is only a supplement form of the private capital. Capitalist state-owned economy, mainly produces the products that the private capital is not willing to or unable to produce, and makes up the deficiencies for the private capital, and offers the general conditions for the proliferation of capital, which are not vital functions for the capitalist system, in some countries it covers a larger sphere, in others lesser. As some scholars have pointed out, capitalism is based on private ownership, and if the SOE's do not perform well, in such a situation, capitalism will not be damaged, even slightly.

The establishment of state-owned enterprises in the capitalist countries, this sector does not belong to the intrinsic elements of the capitalist system.[14]

However, in socialist economy, the state-owned economy is the leading element of the national economy, contrary to the capitalist economy, the state-owned economy mainly exists in the fields that private enterprises are not willing to, or cannot effectively operate. This point was not given due attention in the traditional socialist economies, which is also true for China before Reform and Opening-up, this new perspective is repeatedly affirmed in the relevant documents of the CPC issued since Reform and Opening-up. For example, the report of the 12th National Congress of the Communist Party of China pointed out, "the socialist state economy dominates the whole national economy. Consolidating and developing the state owned economy is the decisive condition for ensuring that the economy under collective ownership by the working people will move along the socialist path and that the individual economy will serve the socialist path."[15]

175

---

13   Collected Works of Marx and Engels, Vol. 4, People's Publishing House, 1995, p. 675.

14   Wei Xinghua, Insist on and Improve the Economic System of Socialism with Chinese Characteristics. China Review of Political Economy, 2012(1).

15   Selected Important Documents since the 12th Congress, Vol. 1, People's Publishing House, 1986, p. 20.

The CPC Central Committee Resolution on Some Major Issues in State-owned Enterprises Reform and Development passed by the Fourth Plenary Session of the 15th Central Committee of the CPC pointed out: "the public economy, which includes the state-owned economy, is the economic base of China's socialist system. It is the basic force for the country to guide, promote and regulate the economic and social development, and is an important guarantee for realizing the fundamental interests and common prosperity of the broad masses of the people." "State-owned enterprises are pillars of China's national economy. China must always rely on and bring into full play the important role of the state-owned enterprises in developing the productive forces of the socialist society and in realizing the country's industrialization and modernization."[16]

The CC report to the 16th National Congress emphasized that: "Expansion of the state economy and its control of the lifeline of the national economy is of crucial importance in displaying the superiority of the socialist system and reinforcing the economic strength, national defense capabilities and national cohesion."[17] The Resolution concerning the comprehensive deepening of reform passed at the Third Plenary Session of the 18th Central Committee of the CPC pointed out that: "Owned by the whole people, state-owned enterprises are an important force for advancing national modernization and protecting the common interests of the people."[18] The above statements clearly show the position and role of the state-owned economy in the socialist market economy of China.

At present, the society still has several ambiguous, prejudiced or confused ideas about the dominant position of public ownership and the leading role of the state-owned economy, which needs to be clarified. For example, some people label the economic sector under ownership by the whole people, i.e. the state-owned economy as the "bureaucratic monopoly capital", while they appreciate the private economy that belongs to private ownership category as "public" enterprises, and evaluate the market competition between the state-owned enterprises and private enterprises as "fight for profits among the people".

And some people argue that the state-owned enterprises should can only operate in the non-competitive sectors, and should not participate in the market competition and seek more profits, the state-owned enterprises should retreat from the competitive sectors of the economy" otherwise, "the economic reform path will face a regression". Some scholars believe that state-owned enterprises should only offer public goods or services and operate in those sectors which the private enterprises are not willing to engage. Some people attempt to advertise their views behind the proposition contained in the Resolution of the Third Plenary Session of the 18th CPC Central Committee: the public and non-public

---

16   Selected Important Documents since the 15th Congress, Vol.2, People's Publishing House, 2001, p. 1004.
17   Selected Important Documents since the 16th Congress, Vol.1, People's Publishing House, 2005, p. 21.
18   CPC Central Committee Resolution Concerning Some Major Issues in Comprehensive Deepening of reform, People's Publishing People's Congress, 2013, p. 8.

sectors are key components of the socialist market economy and are important bases for China's social and economic development" basing themselves on this phrase they deny the basic economic system of socialism dominated by public ownership and led by state-owned economy. The basic flaw of the above arguments is that they misinterpret China's basic economic system, and confuse the socialist state-owned economy with the capitalist state-owned economy, and the socialist market economy based on public ownership with the capitalist market economy based on private ownership. These arguments not only lack solid theoretical basis, but can cause lasting damages in practice.

III. Basic characteristics of production relations in the socialist state-owned economy

The above statements explain the socialist nature of state-owned economy from the perspective of its status and roles. However, it is to be stressed that the socialist nature of the state-owned system has its specific contents and requirements. According to the Marxist political economy, the ownership is, in essence, a relation of production, an economic process, rather than an abstract legal provision. Marx stressed: "The relations of production in their totality constitute what are called the social relations, society." ... "The ownership assumes different forms under completely different social relations in each historic era. Therefore, society is……such totalities of production relations and capitalist is the personification of production relation, personification of one production relation of bourgeois society."[19]

Similarly, the state-owned economy of each era is also developed in different ways under completely different social relations. Only when the state ownership becomes the expression forms of the socialist public ownership, and manifests the specific contents and requirements of the relations of production in the socialist public ownership can the state ownership be equated with the public ownership. Otherwise, the public ownership and state ownership will become an empty legal provision without any contents just like a dead letter. Thence, in what aspects do the relation of production of the state-owned economy and its socialist nature manifest itself?

Firstly, social regulation. Social regulation and planning is not only the historical nature of public ownership but also the inevitable result of public ownership wherein the members of the whole society can control and regulate the means of production, owned by them according to their collective will. Just as the spontaneousness nature is the typical characteristics of the capitalist economic operation, the socialist public ownership must seek to realize the common interests of the society in a planned way as the historical basis for its existence. Under the condition of socialist market economy, although a state-owned enterprises is a relatively independent commodity producer, they have to pursue their own interests and engage in production according to market demands.

---

19   Collected Works of Marx and Engels, Vol. 1, People's Press, 1995, p. 177.

But, the state-owned enterprises can only enjoy a relative independence. While pursuing their own interests, the state-owned enterprises should also meet the common interests of the society, assume certain social responsibilities, and accept the supervision and administration by the people's representatives, namely the State-owned Assets Supervision and Administration Department (SASAC). Otherwise, the state-owned economy will become the tool of purely pursuing individual interests or interests of small groups thus degenerating into a de facto private ownership and lose its public ownership nature.

Secondly, economic democracy. The public ownership of means of production embodies an equal relationship among the working people in regard to their position towards ownership of the means of production, and thus they form a community of common interests, and the state is the representative of such common interest. This requires, above all, a fully democratic administrative system to ensure the effective realization of this common interest. The lack of such a democratic administrative system will lead to the breeding of all kinds of bureaucracy and corruption, thus the administrators (civil servants) of the public ownership economy that should represent the common interest will degenerate, consequently the requirements and basic principles of the public ownership cannot be realized; the common interests cannot be guaranteed and the whole socialist system will be endangered. As stressed by Mao Zedong, "the rights of the working people to manage the state, the army, all kinds of enterprises, and the cultural and educational affairs are in fact among the most prominent rights enjoyed by the working people under the socialist system."[20]

Thirdly, distribution according to work. The distribution according to work is an essential requirement of the socialist public ownership and embodies implementation of public ownership of means of production in its distribution link. In the market economy, as the labor contribution cannot be calculated directly, consequently in reality distribution according to work is just the distribution of "operating income" of enterprises, which is affected by many factors, such as the supply and demand relation, the situation of competition and price fluctuations. Therefore, the realization of distribution according to work greatly differs from the ideal distribution. However, In the case of the state owned economy sector, the basic principle of distribution according to work must be adhered to, which means we should oppose both exploitation and petty bourgeois egalitarianism and due to historical limitations we can tolerate the differences among the workers in regard to their capabilities and in regard to their contribution to production and we can also tolerate these factors on the income distribution, but we cannot allow inequality and difference among workers in regard to their status towards public ownership of the means of production and we cannot allow these factors affecting the income distribution.

Fourthly, sharing of the surplus. Ownership of economic surplus by people is the basic demonstration of the ownership of the means of production. The

---

20 Collected Works of Mao Zedong, Vol. 8, People's Publishing House, 1999, p. 129.

fundamental difference between the private ownership and public ownership is that in private ownership, the economic surplus belongs to private productive asset owners; however, in public ownership, the economic surplus belongs to all members of the society. To be specific, in the state-owned economy, the revenues of SOEs that is transferred to the state consists of two parts. One part is the income taxes that both the state-owned enterprises and other enterprises must pay and all the enterprises are treated equally. Another part is the state-owned capital gains (dividends) by, which are the dividend incomes obtained by the state as the owner of such state enterprises, which indicates the economic realization of state ownership. The latter part of revenues are used to satisfy and serve the common interests of the society, such as improving the public welfare, guaranteeing and improving the people's livelihood, etc. Therefore, the state-owned economy, as a form of socialist public ownership, has its conditions and contents, and it is by no means just a slogan or an empty discourse. Deepening the reform of state-owned economy is to seek for effective realization forms of the public ownership in practice so that the state-owned economy can better reflect its socialist nature and can give full play to its systematic (socialist) institutional advantages.

VI. Deepening the state-owned economy reform so we can give full play to the superiority of socialist system

After over 30 years of exploration and practice, China's state-owned economy reform has made great progress, we have greatly enhanced the economic efficiency, remarkably improved the layout of the economic structure, and our administrative systems have become more reasonable, and in general we have basically achieved to establish the market economy system. On the other side, the state-owned economy has also accumulated some problems and drawbacks, such as the lack of supervision on their powers, abuse of powers by the managers for personal private gains, too high unfair income by monopoly enterprises, and irregularities in their major decision making, which have all prompted discontent among the people. The CPC Central Committee's *Resolution On Some Major Issues Concerning Comprehensively Deepening Reform* passed in the Third Plenary Session, has drawn a grand blueprint for comprehensively deepening of reform in the economic system in the new period, and the Resolution has made an overall plan for further deepening the reform of state-owned economy. Thus, the state-owned economy is ushering in a new round of reform process. Essentially, the deepening of reform of state-owned economy in the new historical period fundamentally aims to better realize the organic integration of socialism with market economy, give full play to the decisive role of the market, so that they can better display the superiority of the socialist system and aims to fully reflect the socialist nature of the state-owned economy.

Firstly, we must unswervingly consolidate and develop the public economy, uphold the leading position of the public ownership, fully play the leading role of the state-owned economy, incessantly strengthen the vitality, control power and the influence of the state-owned economy. We should note that, deepening the reform of public economy is not to carry out the privatization, but to form a perfect system and mechanism to further develop the public economy so that it can better serve the interest of the whole people. Privatization does not meet the requirements of the production development, nor does it meet the interests of the broad masses of the people and conform with the tide of history. If the dominant position of public ownership is undermined, the socialist nature of the state-owned economy cannot be guaranteed.

Secondly, we must actively develop the mixed ownership. The "Resolution" has pointed out: "Vigorously developing a mixed economy with cross holding by and mutual fusion between state-owned capital, collective capital and non-public capital is an important way to materialize the basic economic system of China." It is conducive to improve the amplification function of the state-owned economy, can maintain and increase its asset value and improve its competitiveness. It is conducive to enable all kinds of capital ownership forms to draw on one another's strong points to offset their weaknesses, stimulate one another and can develop together. This is an effective way and inevitable choice for adhering to the dominant role of the public economy and improving its vitality, and enhancing its control capacity and influence in the new circumstances. However, we should be noted that promoting the joint and coordinated development of the economy with diverse forms of ownership is based on the precondition of maintaining the dominant position of public ownership and maintaining the leading role of the state-owned economy, and the mixed ownership reform in regard to state-owned economy should not be misconstrued as privatization of the state-owned economy.

Thirdly, we must improve the unified supervisory system upon the state-owned assets. At present, the state-owned economy exists in different fields, industries and in enterprisers of different types, and is subject to administration by different departments of the state. Those administrated by the State-owned Assets Supervision and Administration Commission (SASAC) is just one part of the state-owned assets; there are many inconsistent and irregular policies on the state-owned assets administration management, insufficient coordination and cooperation, and the state-owned assets of the financial industries, culture industries and other sectors have no definite and well established administrative centers and a complete administrative system like in the SASAC (The State-owned Assets Supervision and Administration Commission of the State Council which leads in the industrial sector. Therefore, we should innovate the state-owned assets management system, establish an integrated organizational system for the state-owned assets management that will be responsible for making unified plans and supervise all kind of state-owned assets as a whole, including those in agriculture, industry, finance, culture and other different sectors, including competitive and monopoly types.

Fourthly, we should strengthen the economic democracy. If we look into the content of economic democracy, it includes both the macro aspects and the micro aspects. At the macro level, the essence of economic democracy is to practice the principle of ensuring that the people are the masters of the state in all the fields and aspects of administrating the national economy, especially in administrating process of the state-owned assets, strengthen supervision over reform efforts and administrative process of state-owned assets by the People's Congresses at all levels and all walks of life, thus reflect the interest of the over-whelming majority of people in the economic decisions. At the micro level, we should establish and improve the democratic enterprise management system and its democratic mechanisms, and enable full play of the working people's enthusiasm and creativity. At the same time, we should further enhance the social responsibility of the state-owned enterprises, and increase the openness and transparency in regard to major issues in their operation and management.

Fifthly, we must effectively carry out the distribution principle of accord-ing to work contribution. At present, the principle of distribution according to work is not yet fully carried out in the internal distribution of the state-owned economy. Firstly due to that, the state-owned enterprises are not yet free from the egalitarianism or "eating from the big pot" practice, and fail to fully embody the principle of "more work, more earning" for the works. Secondly, due to that, there is no effective regulation for the income gap caused by the inequality in regard to the control type of ownership of the state-owned assets, and the issue of abnormal high income (profit in West) of some monopolized or special industries is still to be resolved. At the same time, some state-owned enterprises do not have a sound profit distribution and a dividend distribution system for capital gains, and how to better distribute the profits of the state-owned enterprises among the whole people has not been well resolved.

Sixthly, we must guarantee the common interests of the people. In regard to this matter, the "Resolution" has come up with clear proposals and requirements: Owned by the whole people, the state-owned enterprises are an important force for advancing national modernization and protecting the common interests of the people. State-owned capital investment operations must serve the strategic goals of the state, invest more in key industries and areas that are vital for national economic security and national economic lifeline. State-owned enterprises should focus on providing public services, improve the state-owned capital operating financial bud-get system, and increase the proportion of the state-owned capital gains (profits) that are handed to the central public finance. Resolution said: We will transfer part of the state-owned capital to social security funds. We will improve the budget-ing system for the operation of state-owned capital, and increase the proportion of state-owned capital gains that are turned over to the public finance to 30 percent by 2020, to be used to ensure and improve the people's livelihood. These instructions comprehensively reflect the socialist nature of the state-owned economy.

All in all, the deepening of reform of state-owned enterprises should ful-ly observe the laws of the market economy, fully reflect the requirements of socialism, and organically combine the advantages of socialism with the strong aspects of the market economy. Only in this way could we sublate and transcend the logic of private ownership and fully play the strengths of the state-owned economy.

References

Decision of the Central Committee of the Communist Party of China on Some Major Issues Concerning Comprehensively Deepening the Reform, People's Publishing House, 2013.

Zhang Shigu, Shang Guiyu, *Form and Development of Marx and Engels's Theory of Communist Society*, Jiangsu People's Publishing House, 1983.

Zhang Tongyu, *Studies on the Contemporary Capitalist Ownership Structure*, Economic Science Press, 2009.

Guo Xianglin, *Chinese Ancient Macroeconomic Management*, Shanghai University of Finance & Economics Press, 2001.

Wei Xinghua and Zhang Yu, *The Economic Theory of Socialism*, Higher Education Press, 2013.

Originally published in the journal Marxism Studies, 2014(6)

On Promoting the Scientization of Reform Theories

He Ganqiang

Abstract: The CPC has put forward the basic theory of economic reform guided by Marxism, but the "westernization" reform theory plays a negative which undermines the reform; "westernization" reform theory aims to frustrate the socialist economic base, poses a great danger which can lead to the demise of the nation and the CPC. The key to promote scientization of economic reform theory requires that the leading cadres at all levels should discard the misunderstandings of "westernization" reform theory under the guidance of historical materialism. Currently, in the process of solving the practical economic problems, we should promote the implementation of the CPC's the basic theory of economic reform, grasp the main contradictions behind the real economic problems when promoting the reform, and rely on the broad masses of people while promoting the scientization of economic reform theories.

Key words: economic reform theories, theory of "westernization" reform, misunderstanding; scientization of theories

The Resolution On Some Major Issues Concerning Comprehensively Deepening Reform passed at the Third Plenary Session of the 18th Central Committee of the CPC stresses that, as regards the guiding ideology of reform, "The most important matter is persisting in the leadership of the Party, implementing the Party's basic line, not marching the old path of feudalism and closedness, nor marching the evil path of changing banners, persisting in marching the path of Socialism with Chinese characteristics, and guarantee the correct direction of reform from beginning to end…"[1] In no way can we do this if we don't have the confidence in the path, guiding theories and political line brought forward in the CPC's 18th National Congress. As for the reform of the economic system, the writer believes, the most important is that we should establish the confidence in observing the basic theories of Marxism, and adhere to the basic reform theories we have formed in the past economic system reform process. The good and bad lessons we have learned from the reforms of Soviet Union and the Eastern European countries and the problems in Chinese reform have proved that we will never achieve the reform goals in regard to socialist economy with Chinese characteristics if we guide the economic reform in China with the theories of modern western bourgeois economics, i.e. "westernization" reform, other than the above-stated theories. Therefore, at present, to thoroughly implement the guidelines of the Third Plenary Session of the 18th Central Committee of the CPC, it is imperative to study how to promote the scientization of economic reform theories in the economic system reform field. This essay intends to offer some related suggestions for further discussion in the academia.

I. The economic reform theories must be scientized

1. It is imperative to promote the scientization of economic reform theories. The economic reform theories consist the following components: the nature, contents, goals and means and other basic aspects of the economic system reform. Like all theories, the result of social practice is the only criterion for testing the truth of such theories.

After more than 30 years' practice of reform, on the one hand, China's economic aggregate was elevated to the second place in the world, and its comprehensive national strength, the people's overall living standards, its international competitiveness and influence have all been pushed to a new level. However, on the other hand, there is no lack of bad phenomena like the income polarization tendency, excess production capacity, and imbalanced economic structure, serious environmental pollution, increasing inflationary pressures, foreign exchange reserve depreciation, and housing problems for the common people. The co-existing upward and downward economic situations are the basis for us to judge whether the specific theories and policies guiding the reform are scientific or not.

There are some people who believe that the economic reform is absolutely correct and that the people are supporting all the specific reform measures. This appears as a supportive attitude towards reform, but in fact, it totally ignores the fact that like any other social practice, the reform may be right, and may be wrong. It denies that the social practice is the only criterion for testing the truth, and refuses to face the objective results of specific practices and rejects to reflect on specific reform measures and even deems the correction of errors in reforming the process as opposing the reform. This view dogmatically treats the "reform" concept with formal logic, thus violates the Marxist epistemology.

The guided and organized unfolding of economic reform in China is a conscientious practice under the guidance of Marxism. The co-existence of upward and downward economic phenomena actually reflects that the specific theories applied in the economic reform practice contain some unscientific elements. Therefore, it is an imperative for us to reflect on the reform steps, affirm the scientific elements, sublate the unscientific elements and promote the scientization of economic reform theories, with Marxist historical materialism as the guide; this is conducive to further deepen the reform and promote scientific development and common prosperity.

2. The CPC has put forward the basic theories for scientific economic reform. Basis of the reform: China is in the stage of commodity economy, a stage that human society cannot overstep, and in the primary stage of socialism with the characteristics of transitional economic pattern; the object of the reform: the highly centralized planned commodity economy mechanism established under the influence of socialist natural economy theory, which no longer corresponded to the economic pattern, and all the improper regulations and rules formulated on such a basis. What is the direction of the reform: to promote the organic fusion of public ownership and market economy, establish and improve the socialist market economy system, and achieve the unity of planned control by the state and regulation by the market. The nature of the reform: self improvement and development of socialist system with Chinese characteristics. The goal of the reform: release and develop the social productive forces, fully motivate all positive elements, boost scientific development, and promote common prosperity for the people. These basic theories are permeated by the historical materialism, and they aim to unite the superiority of socialist public ownership superiority with corresponding socialized production and also unite the advantages of the labor division system to promote the development of social productive forces. No doubt, it is due to the effect of basic theories that the economic reform in China has taken an overall positive nature and that China is an exception in the big picture of global economic crisis, and stands firm against the "turmoils" plotted by foreign and domestic hostile forces.

3. We must fully recognize the negative effect of the "westernization" theory of reform. The currently emerging negative economic phenomena show that the CPC's basic theories of economic reform still need to be enriched, improved and concretized. But first of all, let's consider why indeed such negative economic phenomena occur? Apart from that the reform is an unprecedented new practice with high complexity and that the concretization of the basic theories cannot keep pace with the requirements of practice, the main reason is that such basic theories and principles are often shelved or "marginalized" during the specific practices. What is more serious is that some government officials and think tanks apply the "westernization" reform theories in the economic system reform practice and come up with such ideas of reform that are divorced from the people's interests in practice.

As long as we persist in seeking truth from facts, it is not difficult to see that it is these people's mechanical use of the neo-liberal economics and their suggestions for "MBOs" (management buy-out) in regard to enterprises reform which aims to privatize the public capital and equity that has caused the serious decrease in the proportion of the state-owned economy, and the urban collective economy has nearly disappeared, and 80% of laborers in the secondary and tertiary industries have become wage laborers in the private and foreign-owned sectors of the economy;[2] it is this mechanical use of the so-called the "factor value" theory of the western mainstream economics and the idea of granting the "right of surplus claim" incentives to the "entrepreneurs", that have introduced the exploitative relations in China's primary distribution and have caused the income polarization trend; it is this mechanical use of the "liberalization of trade and liberalization of capital flow" theory of the neo-liberalism, and the policy of "trading domestic market for gettng technology" has increased unchecked, and another idea is to "seek foreign investment from whatever source".[3] Thus China has given up the necessary control of foreign investment entry, and ignored national intellectual property rights and brands that try to develop advanced technologies. All these policies have enabled the foreign businesses to control many industries in China. And "thanks" to the excessive foreign investment generated therefrom and foreign exchange reserve brought by high trade surplus, China is exposed to the losses brought by the

2   Quoted from the speech made by Chairman of the National Federation of Industry and Commerce Chairman, Wang Qinmin in the 2012-2013 China Private Economy Development Situation Workshop (February 1, 2013) Speech title: "Thoroughly Apply the Guideline of the 18th National Congress of the CPC to Create an Enabling Environment for Healthy Development of Private Economy." Wang Qinmin stated that in 2012, the employment of private sector accounts for 80% of all jobs. See, http://www.gycc.org.cn/Article/ShowArticle.asp?ArticleID=1401.

3   Meaning that no one cares about the nature of the ownership of the capital, as long as it is invested in China, this is a slogan put forward by quite a few government officials under the capital flow liberalization suggestions. The objective reason behind this slogan is that whether the foreign or private capital, it will bring tax revenue for the local government, as long as it is invested in China and the subjective reason is that the tax increase has become one of the major criterion to measure the achievement of local officials.

devaluation of currencies in developed countries like the US. Also the blindly introduction of foreign investment has caused China's ecological environment to deteriorate;[4] We can say that: it is the mechanical use of Keynesianism, implementing the macroeconomic control in light of the so-called "troika" of—investment, consumption, and foreign trade,[5] ignoring the maintenance of the basic economic system of socialism, and neglecting to observe the law of value and social reproduction theory revealed by Marx to implement the planned control on the basis of improving the ownership of means of production. And this neglect causes the long term structural economic imbalance in China and increases inflationary pressures. All the above shows that the present negative economic phenomena are all related to the "westernization" reform theory.

The guiding ideology of the western bourgeois economics is the historical idealism, which sees the capitalist economy as the only reasonable economic pattern and advocates that the private ownership and market can do anything. As it observes and analyzes the economic issues from the perspective of private owners, it does not have an impartial attitude, with such ideas, it cannot delve into the essence of the economic pattern to expound the economic phenomena and cannot solve the economic conflicts from the root; as it analyzes the economy on the precondition of "self-interest man" and maintenance of bourgeois class interest, it will hinder the unity of socialist public ownership and market economy, will undermine public ownership sector of the economy and dispel the accountability and authority of the state's planned regulation. Therefore, the westernization reform theories will undermine, not construct, the economy of a country which is under the people's democratic dictatorship based on the alliance of workers and peasants. To address both the symptoms and cause and correctly understand the negative economic phenomena, we must promote the scientization of economic reform theories, and resolutely get rid of "westernization" reform theories.

---

4   Guo Shanghua, The Revelation of Ecological Socialism's Proposition on Ecological Colonization for China's Adjustment of Foreign Capital Policy, *Contemporary World & Socialism*, 2008(3).

5   For example, some economic reform think tanks have recently proposed in general that China must boost demand to stimulate domestic needs. However, the theories behind the proposition are the so-called "under-consumption" of bourgeois economics, which has long been criticized by Marx, because the under consumption, just another expression of overproduction, cannot solve the crisis at all. The crisis could only be really overcome by the elimination of capitalist private ownership. Nowadays in China, only by maintaining the dominant position of public ownership, could we increase the income of the majority, eliminate income polarization, and promote the basic balance between the market demand and supply.

II. Intelligibly grasp the essence and the danger of "westernization" reform theories

1. Boundaries must be set between the scientific economic reform theory and "westernization" reform theories. We must fully recognize that the theory of "westernization" reform theory aims to destroy the socialist economic base and has the great hazards of wrecking the country and the CPC. Therefore, to promote the scientization of economic reform theories, we must get rid of erroneous propositions of "westernization" reform theory. This is not a pure theoretical struggle, but the manifestation of the bitter class struggle of vital importance to the existence of the Party and the state in the economics field. An analysis of the new characteristics of contemporary imperialism and summarizing the harsh lessons from the Soviet Union and Eastern European countries' perish could prove that our this judgment is definitely not an alarmist on.

2. "Westernization" reform theories are the instruments of imperialist powers aiming "peaceful evolution" of China. The emergence of "westernization" reform theories is not accidental. Internally, its emergence is directly related to some Chinese scholars' giving up the guiding position of Marxism and mechanically using the western bourgeois economics; externally, we should fully recognize that it is, in essence, the instrument of contemporary imperial powers for ideological and cultural infiltration targeting the developing countries and advancing peaceful evolution strategy targeting socialist countries.

The veteran proletarian revolutionist, Chen Yun, in 1989, commented: "if we look in the light of historical facts, in the past imperialist aggression and permeation used to resort to violence, in the later phase they have combined violence and ideological infiltration, and now imperialism has shifted to ideological struggle (including struggles in political, cultural and economic spheres), especially the so-called 'peaceful evolution' of socialist countries." "The view that argues Lenin's imperialism theory is outdated is totally wrong and proves very dangerous."[6] Since the 1980s, the state monopoly capitalism of imperialist countries represented by the US has given way to a new phase of global monopoly-finance capital which dominates economic globalization process. It is out of historical necessity that they have shifted to "ideological" "peaceful evolution" means targeting the socialist countries. The capital originated in industrial capital, and later, came into co-existence with trade capital and bank capital. Once the bank capital emerges, along with the extension of circulation, increases the power of money as the universal equivalent, "increases the power of money, that absolutely social form of wealth ever ready for use."[7]

As the capitalist commodity production requires the capital in monetary form or the money capital becomes the first cause of the capital movement process,[8] it decides that among various forms of capitals, the bank capital must

---

6   Chen Yun, *Selected Works*, People's Press, 1995, p. 370.

7   Karl Marx, *Capital*, Vol. 1, People's Press, 2004, p. 154

8   Ibid., p. 393.

take control of the whole society's capital movement; it is even more so for the contemporary finance-monopoly capital that combined the bank capital with the industrial and commercial capitals that applies advanced technologies. Limitless pursuit of abstract wealth is the only goal of the capital movement. In order to dictate the global economy, under the historical conditions that the violent aggressive means they have used was met resistance from the nationalist liberation movements and socialist movement and they could not achieve their intended goals, the international finance-monopoly capital that uses the capitalist state as its governing tool shifted to "ideological infiltration" means and tries its best to find a way out, for the financial-monopoly capital. Among which, the political and cultural means are for realizing the economic control upon other countries and seeking higher monopoly profits and excess profits. The main goal of its aggression targeting socialist countries is to destroy the economic basis of public ownership. Though the imperialists do not recognize the scientific theory of historical materialism that economic base decides the superstructure, as personification of finance-monopoly capital, they are aware that only the economic fragmentation of the target countries would lead to the political and military decentralization and that they would be able to eliminate the opposing forces. Therefore, they are bound to promote the so-called "Washington Consensus" of the neo-liberalism, and take the promotion of privatization as the basic goal of implementing "peaceful evolution" strategy to socialist countries. Hence, our economic system reform provides an opportunity for them, and the western bourgeois economics, especially the neo-liberal economics that advocates the superiority of capitalist private ownership economy are used as tools for infiltrating the neoliberal economic theory. This proves that the "westernization" reform theories are, in essence, those theories that serve international finance-monopoly capital's subversion of socialist economic system. Seen in this way, to oppose the "westernization" economic reform theories, in no doubt, has the attribute of maintaining the national economic safety.

3. Allowing the "westernization" reform theory spread unchecked will lead to the destruction of the state and the Party.

Failure to recognize the "westernization" reform theory's danger to our country and Party will lead to extremely serious consequences. The historic lessons from the destruction of the Soviet Union and Eastern European countries constitute very good examples. In the 1960s and 1970s, the economists in Soviet Union and Eastern European countries guided their studies of economic system reform with Marxism and have paid great attention to maintain the economic base of public ownership. On such a basis, they have studies on how the socialist economic management can overcome subjectivism, how could a socialist economy observe the law of value, they have emphasized the currency/commodity relation and material/interest relation, and the working class's democratic participation in enterprise administration; some of these economists came up with the correct thinking that "the nature of relations of production itself decides several basic elements of economic operation mechanism" and that the economic pattern is the concrete form of the basic relations of production.[9]

However, in the 1980s, the imperialist countries sped up their "peaceful evolution" strategy, diligently fostered their agents in the Soviet Union and Eastern European countries, and vigorously implemented ideological infiltration and induction, which have changed the mainstream reform opinions of the Marxist economists in these countries. Looking back at their economic discourse, it is not difficult to see that: the internal relation between the economic system (relations of ownership of means of production) and economic structure was weakened; the studies on market mechanism focused on the demand/supply relations and were cut apart from the ownership relation; great importance was attached to the studies on the planning/market relation, which ignored the combination between public ownership and market; they have emphasized the market competition mechanism, without analyzing its difference with market competition in capitalist economy; they have put the concept of buyer's market (in favor of buyers) and seller's market, without looking at differences between buyer's market and the capitalist market. They have begun to distinguish the economic system with economic mechanisms, and begun to evaluate the socialist system as the cause of the "shortage economy"; and dogmatically proposed that the administrative market regulation mode was a characteristic of socialist market economy, these ideas confused capitalist market economy with macro control in the developed capitalist countries, with the reform goal of socialist countries. They have proposed to regulate the distribution relations with macro distribution plan, without studying on how to improve the ownership relations in order to enhance the primary distribution relations; believed that the state ownership was a form of public ownership, but not the basic form, proposed to replace the state ownership with individual enterprise ownership. They have believed that independent operation of businesses was incompatible with state ownership, stressing completely cutting off the relation between enterprises and the state. To sum up, these ideas were more or less influenced by the views of western neo-liberal economics. They gradually came to understand the reform as removing the basic socialist system based on public ownership of means of production; in the end, many of them began to openly advocate "privatization".[10]

---

9   Wu Yifeng et al., *Formation and Development of Marxist Economics Theory*, China Renmin University Press, 1998, p 541

10   A typical example is the change of Prof. Kornai, an academician of the Hungarian Academy of Sciences. In 1980, he published the book *Economics of Shortage* (translated into Chinese in 1986), claiming that the "shortage economy" is one mark of the successful system reform; in 1985, he came to China to attend the International Economic System Reform Seminar of "Bashan Steamship", claimed that the goal of economic system reform is the mode (market regulation mode with macro control), saying nothing about the relation between public ownership and economic system; in 1990, when leaders of the Soviet Union, following the so-called "the expert opinions" of the US, enacted the "500 days program" to conduct the privatization "reform", Kornai's new book *The Road to a Free Economy* was

The Soviet Union and Eastern European countries' perish in the chaos of so called "reform" could not be attributed to anything other than that the "westernization reform theory" which led the guiding ideology of reform go astray. Thus it can be seen that drawing the boundary with "westernization" reform theories and sticking to Marxism as the guiding ideology for economic reform concerns the existence of China and the CPC.

III. Discard the misunderstandings in regard to "Westernization" reform theories

1. We should comprehensively recognize that the "westernization" reform theories are still spreading unchecked. Since the western bourgeois economics is not a scientific theory but an ideological instrument with which the imperialism carries out "the peaceful evolution" against socialist countries. As we examine the economic reform practice both at home and abroad we can see that the mechanical use of western bourgeois economics guiding our reform will lead to serious consequences. Thus, to uphold the great banner of socialism with Chinese characteristics, we should not allow the "westernization" reform theories dominating the reform.

However, the reality is not optimistic. Even after the 18th National Congress of the CPC, there are some people in the economics academic community who analyze the reform experience with their capital fetishism-permeated "bonus theory". And some journals are still using the "Kuznets Inverted U curve", "Lewis Turning Point", "Middle Income Trap" and other trendy concepts of western economics to analyze the economic development of China. And some government think tanks are even enacting the "westernization" reform program similar to the Soviet Union's "500 days program". A top think tank and the World Bank co-published the report "China 2030: Building a Modern, Harmonious, and Creative High-income Society", which openly promoted neo-liberalism. The report proposes that: "the share of SOEs in industrial output should decline from the current 27% in 2010 to around 10% in 2030", that China should "deepen the financial sector reforms through the participation of foreign financial institutions" and other such propositions that seriously violate

191

---

translated into Russian language and published in Moscow. He said in the book's preface –To Soviet Union readers—that "the human society turned to *market economy based on private ownership* at the end of 15th Century. *This is the primary road*." Soviet Union, followed by other countries, took the "*second road, bureaucratic control of a command-economy nature based on public ownership*"; and now the *reform is following* "*the third road*, which deviates from the Stalin System and is in essence different from the economic system of present western developed countries", "This book will continue my previous analysis. I believe now more than ever that the experiment cannot succeed. There is no third road." The people that have been following the second road for dozens of years will agree that, "only *the first road* that they had stepped on after a long-time and their helpful exploration *is the normal economy*". (refer to Jonas Kornai's *The Road to a Free Economy* (in Russian language), China Economy Publishing House, 1990:pp 2-3. [Italics added])

the "top-level design" specified by the PRC Constitution.[11] These propositions are still advertised by quite a few people.

2. The key to the solution is that the key leading officials at all levels should avoid the misunderstandings on "westernization" reform theories. As the "westernization" reform theories continues to spread, we could not rule out the possibility that there are some people in China cooperating with the international hostile forces to subvert our economy. Looking from this perspective, it is very important that the Third Plenary Session of the 18th Central Committee of the CPC has decided to reinforce the Party's leadership over reform and has decided to establish a "central reform leading team for comprehensively deepening the reform".[12] However, it should be noted that there are many people that have blind faith in "Westernization" reform theory. To enable people to surpass the misunderstanding, the key is that the leading officials at all levels must take the lead to develop a staunch attitude in regard to Marxist theories in both economic theories and practice area and they should draw a clear boundary between the CPC's basic reform theory and the "westernization" reform theories, I propose the following ideas:

Don't make the mistake to think that the "modern economics" is scientific. Generally speaking, the humankind's cognition in regard to nature has developed in tandem of with the development of social productive forces, so the modern natural sciences are more scientific than those past alchemy sciences. However, as the research subject of economics is in essence the material interest relations of people in a society under certain historical conditions, which, in a class society, represent the material interest of certain class, so, the scientificalness degree of economics theories should not be judged by the time sequence. We should fully understand that just as in the recent history, the class nature of the western economics, known as the "modern economics" that it represents the interests of the bourgeois, never changes. And although it belongs to the modern economics, it is in no way an impartial economic science. It is constantly boosted as "modern" and its class and non-scientific nature is concealed for personal gains. In fact, the only correct scientific modern economics that could guide China to lead a proper reform is the one that sticks to and makes innovation in regard to basic principles of Marxist economics in leading our reform and construction practice under the guidance of historical materialism and proves to be correct by practice.

<hr>

11   The World Bank, Development Research Center of the State Council, the People's Republic of China, *China 2030: Building a Modern, Harmonious and Creative High-Income Society*, p. 110: "The share of SOEs in industrial output will decline from the current 27% in 2010 to around 10% in 2030." (http://www.wds.worldbank.org/external/default/WDSContentServer/WDSP/IB/2012/02/28/000356161_20120228001303/Rendered/PDF/671790WP0P127500China020300complete.pdf) and the Chinese version Report: Special Section V: Chapter III: China's integration into global market, http://www.shihang.org/zh/news/2012/02/27/china-2030-executive-summary.

12   *CPC Central Committee Resolution On Some Major Issues Concerning Comprehensively Deepening of Reform* passed at the Third Plenary Session of the 18th Central Committee of the CPC on November 12, 2013, People's Daily, Front Page, November 16, 2013.

Don't make the mistake to think that the economics of developed countries is more advanced or scientific. Historically, the bourgeois economics has indeed conducted honest exploration of economic relationships, to better serve interest of the bourgeois, and played a positive role in criticizing the feudal system at the early days of capitalism. However, even back then, as it served the exploiting class and followed historical idealism, the scientific elements in its theories were often mixed with vulgar ideas and principles. And as the capitalist society developed and the class struggles continued to expand and intensify, its selfless and scientific study manner "gave way to the evil will of advocacy of narrow bourgeois interests,[13] and its scientific elements have gradually diminished. The pseudo scientific nature of the modern bourgeois economics as a whole can be seen from that it cannot satisfy the monopoly bourgeois' demands to dominate the world. We know that after the WWII, the capitalist countries started to implement Keynesianism to ease the economic contradictions. However, still, soon later in the first half of 1970s, the "stagflation" crisis broke out and Keynesianism was discarded. The neo-liberalism became fashionable from then on. But, by 2008, with the global finance and economic crisis which spread in the capitalist countries, the neo-liberalism could not save capitalism. It is in the recent crisis that Marx's *Das Kapital* became one of the biggest hit in the capitalist countries once again. We believe, just as the outer shell of the capitalist relations of production is being be broken by the continuous deepening of socialization of production, the modern bourgeois economics that advocates the capitalist relations of production will eventually be discarded by the development of modern society.

Don't make the mistake to think that the empirical approach of the western economics is scientific. The empirical methodology is an approach that starts from observation of objective facts. The western bourgeois economics stresses the empirical approach, thus some scholars believe that the western bourgeois economics is scientific and belittle the Marxist economics. However, starting from facts require us to distinguish between the truth and the illusion in facts, thus reveal the difference and relation between phenomena and essence. The most important weakness of the empirical approach of "westernization" reform theories is that it halts at the level of economic phenomena or even start its analysis from illusions. Its analysis in regard to most fundamental economic interest relations skips over the ownership of means of production, thus ignores this essential relation. Its analysis of income distribution focuses on data, but ignores the causes and effects, thus fails to reveal the internal relations behind the data, therefore, cannot propose any reliable solution to actual problems. This empirical approach often attempts to display its "scientificity" with abundant statistical data and mathematical models, thus conceals its weak economic logics, and advertises its digital logic. According to historical materialism, the scientific mathematical analysis must stick to the dialectical relationship between unity and opposition of quantity and quality, and bases its analysis of

---

13   Karl Marx, *Capital*, Vol. 1, People's Press, 2004, p. 17.

economic essence with the analysis of economic quantities. The quantitative model of modern western bourgeois economics which lacks the analysis of economic essence is no more than vague and general formalism (in fact these models are quite simple in the eye of mathematicians).

Don't make the mistake to think that the modern western macro-economic analysis method can be mechanically utilized. The capitalist countries have derived this approach from Keynesianism, and based on Keynesianism built a set of macroeconomic control methods, in fact some people believe this approach is scientific and can be copied in China. In fact, the macroeconomic control aims for safeguarding the capitalist profits or the capitalist exploitation relations; its theories understand the demand-supply relations just at the market level, and ignores that the essence of demand-supply relations are the relations of classes and stratums which are determined by the ownership of means of production.[14] Modern western macro-economics does not distinguish between the currency and monetary capital, confuses the loan of capital in the form of currency with the loan of currency, and never aims to understand the root cause for the macroeconomic imbalance of capitalism is the conflict between the socialization of production and private ownership of capitalism, therefore, it can only cure the symptoms, but not the disease. And in practice, while it temporarily tries to ease the contradiction between supply/demand structure through financial and monetary policies, it further expands and deepens the structural imbalances, and eventually lead to the so-called "stagnation" problem in which the production stagnation and currency inflation occurs at the same time. How could we blindly believe such a macro-economics that even the western countries themselves are casting away?

Don't make the mistake to think that the western development economics can guide China's scientific development. The western development economics studies developing countries' industrialization and modernization process. As a developing country, China has much to learn from the western development economics. However, it should be noted that as regards to its mode of thinking and theoretical base, this western development economics is an important part of the bourgeois economics and it uses the same empirical approach and the principles of western macro and microeconomics; its studies on the historical process of capitalist industrialization and urbanization, on the international economic relations between developing countries and developed countries and the income distribution of developing countries never focuses on the important roles of ownership relations of means of production that objectively exist in certain historical form. The mechanical utilization of the western

---

14 Marx pointed out: In further analysis supply and demand presuppose the existence of different classes and sections of classes which divide the total revenue of a society and consume it among themselves as revenue, and, therefore, make up the demand created by revenue. While on the other hand it requires an insight into the overall structure of the capitalist production process for an understanding of the supply and demand created among themselves by producers as such. (*Capital*, Vol.3, People's Press, 2004, p. 217)

development economics will inevitably ignore the characteristics of China's actual conditions and the important role of socialist relations of production in industrialization, informatization, modernization and urbanization. Copying the theories and views that describe the general phenomena of the capitalist economic development to China which is in the primary stage of socialism will suffocate the enthusiasm and creativity of China's working people during the socialist modernization process.

3. Encourage leading officials to study and apply Marxist philosophy and economics. Some of the above-listed misunderstandings are produced when people see the modern and booming scenes of developed capitalist countries in their short-term overseas trips, and some are formed when they were using the western bourgeois economics for reference in the studies of the general laws of market economy. The lack of understanding of basic theories of Marxist philosophy and economics lead to the lack of dialectical thinking, and the ignorance that they have already sublated the theories of modern bourgeois economics, thus they intend to blindly copy them to China. In order to discard their misunderstanding of "westernization" reform theories, the leading officials at all levels should, firstly, seriously study and comprehend the historical materialism and dialectics so as to have a firm faith in socialism, and learn to scientifically analyze the relations and differences between economic phenomena and the essence, and cognize the similarities and differences between socialist market economy and developed capitalist market economy, and figure out the nature and tasks of the reform in China. Secondly, they should study the basic theories of Marxist economics, comprehend the basic internal relations between the ownership of means of production, distribution, circulation and consumption, grasp the essence and forms of the basic categories such as commodity, currency, capital, land ownership and total revenue of the society; so as to figure out the correctness and profundity of the leading position of public ownership in the basic economic system of socialism stipulated in China's constitution, the extreme significance of insisting on independence of national economy, under the background of economic globalization led by the current imperialist countries, and figure out that promoting the combination of public ownership and market economy is an important theoretical innovation that truly embodies the economic system reform. Thus, it can be seen that arranging the leading officials' education pointedly is the precondition for them to be confident in sticking to Marxist theories and in promoting scientization of reform theories.

IV. Important links in the promotion of the scientization of economic reform theories

1. Promote the scientization of reform theories in finding solutions for the realistic economic problems. The materialist dialectics tells us that "the problem and the solution to it often emerge simultaneously".[15] The scientific approach to reform is contained in the problems we have encountered in the reform practice, and as long as we can figure out the internal relations of the realistic problem under the guidance of historical materialism, we will get on the right track to properly deepening the reform and promoting the scientization of reform theories. For this purpose, we must have faith in Marxist theories, in path and system, correct the erroneous inclination to mislead the reform with "westernization" reform theories, and promote the concretization and actualization of the CPC's basic reform theories and the scientization of reform theories while guiding the solution of realistic economic problems such as the widening income gaps problem, economic structure adjustment, currency inflation, with the basic theories of historical materialism and Marxist economics.[16]

2. Set right the guidelines of government's reform think tanks and continue reforming those government organs governing the reform. If we remember the failures in implementing, or see the marginalization of the CPC's basic reform theories in concrete reform practices, it will be easy to see that some administrative organs and reform think tanks have impure guidelines, i.e. they fail to insist on Marxism as the guiding ideology. Some officials at the top government bodies never consider that CPC Central Committee's basic guideline that the reform is the self-improvement and development of the socialist system in the actual reform practice.[17] They oppose the reform of economic management system in tandem with the improvement of socialist relations of production. We can say that they see the "socialism" in the socialist market economic system as a void label, and aim to design our market economy by learning from the market economy of developed capitalism and try to put such abstract ideas into the reform practice. This greatly confuses people and harms the image of the CPC and the government prestige among the masses, leads to such a situation: "as if the CPC preaches the socialism of Chinese characteristics, but practices capitalism with Chinese characteristics in the economic practice". The facts show that if we don't take ideological and organizational actions to make the reform think tanks and the leading reform organs stick to the CPC's basic reform theories and pool the grassroots' reform wisdom; we would not be able to realize the scientization of economic reform theories.

15　Karl Marx, *Capital*, Vol. 1, People's Press, 2004, p. 107.
16　See He Ganqiang, We must Persist in Marxism and Do Not Practice Privatization, *Modern Economic Research* 2007(7).
17　*CPC Central Committee Resolution Concerning Economic System Reform*, People's Press, 1984, p. 10.

3. We must grasp the main conflicts behind the realistic economic problems in order to promote reform. The scientific reform requires observing the dialectical materialist theory of unity of cognition and practice which emphasizes "practice, cognition, further practice and further cognition".[18] Therefore, we should find solutions to problems and innovate our system while solving the concrete economic problems such as the widening of income gap, excess production capacity, long-term imbalance we face in regard to industrial structure, ecological environmental pollution, and immigration of young adults from rural areas to cities. Some may say that these problems are caused by the incomplete reform of old system, and therefore, advocate continuing the reform practice guided by the "westernization" reform theories. This advocate is not convincing, and will only accumulate the malpractices. It should be noted that some malpractices, to a great extent, are formed in the reform process over the past three decades of reform. Therefore, it is imperative to reflect on whether the reform steps and newly formed systems in practice correspond to the actual situations of China, and if they are conducive to the development of social productive forces, or conducive to the interests of the masses, and carefully correct or improve such steps. This is what we call seeking truth from facts.

When making an in-depth analysis based on historical materialism, it is easy to find that the promotion of privatization "reform" will harm the core of the basic economic system of socialism—and the dominant position of public ownership economy will be seriously weakened, which is the root cause of many problems. If we can resolve this basic contradiction and implement new reform measures, the economic operation will soon take on a new look. This is because by restoring, consolidating and gradually reinforcing the dominant position of the public ownership economy, the weight of distribution according to work will be increased as regards to distribution of national income, and this certainly will narrow the income gaps in the primary distribution and create the basic conditions for balancing the aggregate demand/supply in the markets, greatly reduce the fiscal burden that the government undertakes in the secondary re-distribution to narrow the income gap, and thus create the basic conditions for local governments being dependent on fiscal deficits and debts when implementing their investments and designing their expenditure budgets; advance the effective combination of public ownership economy and social division of labor in the market and give play to their advantages which will push the reform of social relations of production so as to satisfy the needs of socialization of production to a great extent, objectively organize the social division of labor following the law of value and constrain the market mechanism's blind spontaneity and promote balanced industrial structure; reforming the housing market system from the present "private construction and private ownership" mechanism (houses are built by private real estate development companies and owned by private owners) into the public construction and rental mechanism will thoroughly eliminate the inequity caused by the flow

---

18 *Selected Works of Mao Zedong*, Vol. 1, People's Press, 1995, p. 296.

of rent of urban state-owned land into private hands, and with the organizing efforts of the people's government, possibly change the structure of housing industry that mainly offers high-end luxury type of houses and helps the private real estate development companies to grab high profits, as well as creating numerous bad phenomena such as the real estate development companies speculating on house building—by using the bank loans and state-owned lands in order to seek personal gains. Under such conditions the common people cannot afford to buy a house, but the rich people can easily speculate by house purchases, and breed corruptions; sticking to the dominant position of public ownership, and working on the majority's income level and interests, and stimulating the industry development with more subways, buses and taxies, other than sedan cars, will definitely change the excess production capacity, traffic congestions, excessive carbon dioxide emission and other problems; giving play to the inherent advantages and traditions of the collaboration within the economy dominated by public ownership, developing advanced technologies to stimulate the non-public economy will improve the international competitiveness of the Chinese economy, change the unfavorable situation wherein the foreign capital controls many industries of China; boosting the collective ownership of rural lands to realize the second leap, and vigorously developing the collective industrial and commercial economy in rural areas will ensure that the farmers in the collectives can enjoy the benefits brought by rural industrialization and urbanization, change the irrational situation that the private and foreign trade companies controlling the leading manufacturing companies in commercial and industrial fields and take the surplus value created by farmers' agricultural labor, and stop the immigration of young adults from rural areas to cities, training talents for the building of new socialist countryside and change the situation that great number of elderly people and children are left behind in the countryside; the public ownership economy and people's government have common fundamental interests, and by insisting on the dominant position of public ownership economy and the regulation of market by the people's government, a majority of the market players will consciously respond and give effective play to the government's economic administrative functions of regulating the market. These analyses show that insisting on reinvigorating the seriously weakened public ownership economy, consolidating and improving the basic economic system of socialism dominated by public ownership is the key link that must be grasped at present, and proposing a series of scientific reform measures on such a basis will cure both the symptoms and the disease and monitor the reform stepping into a scientific path.

4. We must rely on the masses when boosting the innovation of reform theories. Mao Zedong pointed out: "the masses are the real heroes, while we are often childish and ignorant"[19]. Currently, the promotion of scientization of economic reform theories should firmly stick to the basic historical-materialist view. Since the reform of socialism with Chinese characteristics is a great

---

19 *Selected Works of Mao Zedong*, Vol. 3, People's Press, 1995, p. 790.

undertaking which needs the participation of millions of people, the positive energy of the reform is already contained in the people's practice. Therefore, the leading officials at all levels should highly value the people's creativity in the reform practice, and fully recognize that over the years, the Marxist scholars have made a lot of proposals for system innovation to promote the combination of public ownership and market economy, and it is urgently needed to organize the people to study these proposals and put them into practice at the government level. We know that many successful SOEs and urban collective enterprises have accumulated a wealth of experience in adapting to the market economy and achieved successes in the spheres of enterprise system innovation, and therefore, it is also urgently needed to find out the general law of the micro-level fusion between the public ownership economy and the market economy from these experiences and spread these experiences to the whole country. Also many successful rural collective enterprises and cooperative enterprises which stick to the unified business practice inherent in the collective economy during the development process of market economy; we should spread their valuable experiences to promote the collective agricultural economy, based on the household responsibility system and in this way step forward to realize the second leap of the rural collective economy advocated by Deng Xiaoping. To sum up, as long as the leading officials at all levels can stick to the historical materialism as the ideological guide and give full play to the CPC's fine tradition of maintaining close contacts with the masses, they will be able to promote the scientization of reform theories and lead the reform to serve the great cause of socialism with Chinese characteristics.

Originally published in the Journal of Social Sciences Research, 2014(3)

On the Combination of the Socialist State-owned Economy and Market Economy

Xu Chuanchen and Zhai Xuquan

Abstract: The combination of socialist mode of production and market economy is based on large scale social production. Basing ourselves on this combination, firstly provides a more reliable material foundation and guarantee for the implementation of long-term development strategy of China, secondly provides a more reliable material foundation and guarantee for us to effectively surmount the market failures and to establish and improve the social security system. However, with currently prevalent neo-liberal trend, the dominant position of the public ownership economy is disgraced. Therefore restoring and consolidating the dominant position of the public ownership economy led by state-owned enterprises (SOEs) and enhancing the international competitiveness of Chinese state-owned enterprises (SOEs) is the only correct reform direction that will lead to a better combination of the socialist state-owned economy and market economy.

Key words: socialism, capitalism, market economy, state-owned economy, common prosperity

I. The capitalist market economy does not exclude the state-owned enterprises as the subject of market competition

(I) Main characteristics of the subjects of market competition

(1) The decisive condition for the emergence of market economy is the existence of different independent material interests, and consequently its subjects

Commodity economy and market economy are both, in essence, exchange economy. The emergence of surplus products determined by the social division of labor is the fundamental condition for the commodity economy, as pointed out by Marx, "The social division of labor causes his labor to be as one-sided as his wants are many-sided", "commodities cannot go to the market and make exchange of their own,"[1] objectively speaking, this makes the different separate material interests, which are represented by different separate commodity owners in the exchange, the decisive condition for the emergence of commodity economy. Therefore, when expounding on the exchange process, Marx emphasizes the different separate commodity owners – "one use value is not exchanged for another of the same kind", "we must, therefore, have recourse to their guardians, who are also their owners…In order that these objects may enter into relation with each other as commodities, their guardians must place themselves in relation to one another, as persons whose will resides in those objects, and must behave in such a way that each does not appropriate the commodity of the other, and part with his own, except by means of an act done by mutual consent. They must therefore, mutually recognize in each other the rights of private proprietors."[2] After all, "Only such products can become commodities with regard to each other, as result from different kinds of labor, each kind being carried on independently for the account of private individuals."[3]

(2) Subjectivity is the primary characteristic of market competition

Roughly speaking, market competition in the market economy, is the competitive relations which reflect different material interests in the economic life. The subjectivity is the primary characteristic of market competition. There would not be market competition without such interests in the economic life, and the market competition determines that the different competing actors in the market have autonomy and spontaneity, which further determines that the different actors have exclusive statuses in this competition. Therefore, to be specific, the market competition is the universal exclusive relationship formed between different separate commodity owners based on the contract that the separate material interests that spontaneously pursue the expansion of their own interests, and recognize each other's ownership upon the commodities. Therefore, becoming separated commodity owner is an essential condition for the subject of market interests to participate in the market competition, because

---

1 Karl Marx, *Capital*, Volume 1, People's Press, 1963, p. 5-928.

2 Ibid.

3 Ibid.

the "difference" embodies widely "different use values", "commodity owner" reflects the distinct property rights, and here the term "separate" reflects the autonomy of the interest. Seen in this way, in the market economy, as long as the subject of the interest attempting to participate in the market competition has distinct property rights, it will make its own management decisions, assumes sole responsibility for its own profits and losses, and spontaneously receives and transmits market signals, thus they can become the real players of market competition. Thence, theoretically, the market economy does not rule out that the state-owned enterprises can become player of the market competition.

(II) Superiority and limitations of capitalist market economy

(1) Superiority of capitalist market economy

The emergence of capitalist mode of production is based on certain historical conditions. Marx argued that, "the dissolution of feudal society set free the elements of the capitalist society… the starting point of the development that gave rise to the wage-laborer and the capitalist, was the servitude of the laborer", "Capital... the historical conditions of its existence.... There, the owner of the means of production and subsistence meets in the market with the free laborer, who sells his own labor force… And this one historical condition comprises a world's history. Capital, therefore, announces from its first appearance a new epoch in the process of social production".[4] It is in such historical context that the separation of laborer and the means of production has robbed the laborers from all means of production except their own freedom, and the capitalist's actual consumption of the laborers is the materialization process of labor, or the value production process. Forcedly driven by capital, the commercialization of labor begins and this gradually expands its scope, on which the wage-labor system has emerged.

The founders of Marxism have held that we should treat capital from a dialectical point. Marx argued that "it is one of the civilising aspects of capital that it enforces this surplus-labour in a manner and under conditions which are more advantageous to the development of the productive forces, social relations, and the creation of the elements for a new and higher form than under the preceding forms of slavery, serfdom, etc.".[5] Although Marx lashes out that: "capital comes dripping from head to foot, from every pore with blood and dirt",[6] the process that the ownership of commodity transforms the law of capitalist occupation, i.e. the separation of laborers and means of production, has greatly enhanced the utilization rate of laborers to the greatest extent, making capitalist mode of production the most powerful practitioner of the truth that "only the living labor is the only source of value created". Aristotle argued that "money maker seeks wealth without limit", which shows that the fundamental reason that the capitalist mode of production promotes the social productive

---

4   Ibid.
5   Ibid..
6   Ibid.

forces is that the capitalist seeks capital appreciation, also known as the surplus value, without limit. This is why the capitalist mode of production can remain stable for a rather long period of time, and has created great wealth that is unprecedented in the human history.

(2) Limitations of the capitalist market economy

Marx pointed out, "no social form vanishes before all the productive forces that it can accommodate are fully exhausted, and new superior relations of production will never replace older ones before the material conditions for their existence have matured within the framework of the old society".[7]

The full development of capital is a stage which cannot be bypassed in the historical forward progress of the productive forces. However, due to the progress of productive forces and excessive concentration of the means of production in the hands of a small minority, the contradiction between the socialized production and private ownership of means of production in the capitalist mode of production becomes irreconcilable. A time will come when "the propertied will become the propertiless", and the mode of allocating resources by the market will precisely play a catalyzer role in triggering the internal contradictions of capitalism.

The founders of Marxism have argued that the emergence of wage laborers marks the universal commodification of the products of labor as a commodity (the commodity form), and inevitably commodifies the other factors of production. From then on, the development of commodity economy has entered a higher advanced stage, and the capitalist market economy was gradually formed. The generalization of commodity form of the product of labor and the commodification of other factors of production reinforces the law of value's function of automatically adjusting the distribution of laborers and other factors of production among different sectors of the social production on a pro rata basis in the resource-allocating market mechanism, so as to adapt to the development degree of the socialized production. However, under the capitalist private ownership of means of production, the capitalists' limitless pursuit of surplus value leads to excessive concentration of means of production in the hands of a minority, thus causes ever increasing separation between the laborers and the means of production and wealth polarization between the rich and the poor, which objectively sharpen the internal contradictions of capitalism.

(III) The basic contradictions of capitalism lead to the situation in which the state leads the direction of production

Engels has pointed out: "This rebellion of the productive forces, as they grow more and more powerful, against their quality as capital, this stronger and stronger command that their social character shall be recognized, forces the capitalist class itself to treat them more and more as social productive forces, so far as this is possible under capitalist conditions... the official representative

---

7　*Selected Works of Marx and Engels*, Vol. 2, People's Press, 1995, p. 33.

of capitalist society—the state—will ultimately have to undertake the direction of production."[8]

After the industrial revolution, economic crises started to occur frequently in capitalist countries, and facts demonstrated that "nationalization" (state ownership), here and there, was used by the capitalist countries as the antidote to deal with economic crises. IMF's surveys have demonstrated that in the 1980s, in the western European countries, known as the most advantageous countries of the world, the industrial output of the state-owned enterprises accounted for above 20% of the total value of industrial output of the whole country. In 1984 to 1993, the government investment in the US, Japan, Germany, the UK, France, and Italy accounted for, respectively, 15.6%, 23.8%, 11.6%, 17.2%, 16.2% and 16.7% of each country's total investment on average. However, during outbreak of the financial crisis in the US in 2008, the average share of the state-owned economy to national economy in Euro zone countries was 10.8%. The state's leading the direction of production is determined by the social nature of productive forces. The development of state-owned economy is an inevitable requirement and response to further development of ever socializing production.

If the state-owned enterprises, as the main form of the state-owned economy, have distinct property rights, make their own management decisions, assume sole responsibility for their own profits and losses, and spontaneously receive and transmit market signals, they can become the real market competition players, and further become the state's most straightforward and effective instrument for directing the production. Thus it can be seen that the capitalist market economy does not rule out state-owned enterprises as the player in the market competition. Instead, it needs the state-owned enterprises to promote the development of productive forces as the players in the market competition. This is why it is a time-tested fact in regard to the capitalist countries which use the nationalization means to cope with periodical economic crises to a certain degree. Capitalist state-owned enterprises, theoretically or in practice, become real market players. Thus, the development of capitalist market economy has provided sufficient theoretical base and reform courage for building the socialist market economy system in China, wherein SOEs become market players.

II. The path and necessity of the combination of the socialist state-owned economy with the market economy

(I) The fundamental difference between the socialist market economy and capitalist market economy

The fundamental difference between the socialist market economy and capitalist market economy should be explained firstly from the formation conditions of the market economy and secondly on the basis of how the capitalist mode of production is combined with market economy or how socialist mode

---

8 *Selected Works of Marx and Engels*, Vol.3, People's Press, 1995, pp. 751-752.

of production is combined with market economy. Market economy can only exist on the conditions of social division of labor and existence of different independent material benefits, therefore whether capitalist mode of production is combined with market economy or socialist mode of production is combined with market economy, both should give consideration to above two aspects: advanced social division of labor and different independent material benefits, without such a consideration, a policy will lose its scientific and advanced character.

In the capitalist market economy, the contradiction between the capitalist's private ownership of means of production and socialized production is irreconcilable, this is because the capitalist market economy takes the private ownership as the main pillar. While combining with the market economy, the capitalist mode of production naturally, one-sidedly, narrowly, concentrates and builds large-scale capitalist private ownership of means of production, which will inevitably lead to the basic contradiction of capitalism and its irreconcilability, thus inevitably leading to the serious polarization of wealth and the periodic occurrence of economic crises, so Wang Jiafei[9] has argued that, capitalist countries alternately use statist and private means in their pursuit of easing the prominent economic contradictions of capitalism, but various contradictions showing different forms are in essence connected to each other and co-deepen like the drill effect. In the socialist market economy, the public ownership of the means of production and the social division of labor have natural adaptability, the combination between the socialist mode of production and market economy is the condition of social division of labor, at the same time, the economic agents of the public sector and the economic agents of the non-public sector objectively become different independent material interest subjects, which just makes socialist mode of production and market economy combine theoretically, comprehensively and fully. This shows, that the fundamental difference between the socialist market economy and the capitalist market economy lies in the different nature of the ownership's structural body, and compared with the capitalist market economy system, the socialist market economy system has scientific and superiority, that is, the socialist market economy is more advanced market economy than the capitalist market economy.

(II) The fundamental difference between the socialist state-owned economy and the state-owned economy of capitalism

The fundamental difference between the socialist state-owned economy and the state-owned economy of capitalism is the difference between the existence scope and the existence purpose, which manifests intuitively whether the two can provide profits in the interests of the whole people. Indeed, the existence scope and the existence purpose of the socialist state-owned economy and the

---

9   Wang Jiafei, The Recognition of The Historical Mission of Our Country's State-Owned Economy Under The Condition of Modern Market Economy, *Journal of Marxism Studies* 2011(9).

state-owned economy of capitalism is determined by the foothold of the combination between the socialist mode of production or the capitalist mode of production and the market economy respectively – such different nature of the structural layout of the ownership of means of production means the basic difference between the socialist countries and capitalist countries.

The existence scope of the socialist state-owned economy and the state-owned economy of capitalism are different in the market operation. Although the capitalist market economy does not exclude taking state-owned enterprises as the main players of the market competition, the system of capitalist private ownership of means of production determines that the state economy of the capitalism can only widely exists in such a range that, it can help and make up for market failures and guarantee national security. In terms of the state-owned economy itself, whether in the socialist countries and capitalist countries, they all have the common theoretical basis for its existence, as proposed by Xu Chuanzhan and Zhang Wancheng,[10] firstly, to provide public goods. Secondly, to exist in naturally monopolized industries. Thirdly, to benefit and help the realization of macro-control. Fourthly, to benefit national economic security and the realization of national strategic goals. But in capitalist countries, this is the insurmountable "Leichi limit"[11] of the existence scope of state-owned economy. But in our country with public ownership as the main pillar, and a variety of forms of ownership co-exist, the existence scope of socialist state-owned economy adapts to the development degree of the socialized production and can be further promoted only on this basis. The adaptability between the existence scope of socialist state-owned economy and the development degree of socialized production provides a fundamental guarantee for us to solve issue of developing and freeing the productive forces, which constitutes the principal contradiction at the present stage in China.

207

The fundamental existence purpose of the state-owned economy of capitalism and the socialist state-owned economy is different. The existence of the state-owned economy of capitalism takes the maintenance of the fundamental interests of the bourgeois class through guaranteeing the relative economic and political stability of the country in the capitalist countries as the ultimate goal; the existence of the socialist state-owned economy takes the maintenance of the fundamental interests of the overwhelming majority of people and follows concept of "people-oriented" ultimately under the leadership of the CPC as the superior goal. Therefore, this also determines the difference between the distribution system, the macroeconomic regulation power and the relationship of the market competition subjects in economic activities which is different in socialist and capitalist countries.

---

10   Xu Chuanzhan, Zhang Wancheng, The Theoretical Basis for the Existence of the State-owned Economy, *Journal of Social Science of Jilin University* 2002(5).

11   As the ancient Chinese had such a saying "Don't get yourself one step beyond Leichi" (a lake in the Anhui Province), people use "leichi" to refer to the unsurpassable limit.

(III) The necessity behind the combination of socialist state–owned economy and the market economy

As the stage of full development of capital cannot be by-passed in the historical forward development process of the productive forces, in the same way the market economy is also a resource allocation mode which cannot be by-passed.

The author believes that the market economy is a resource allocation mode which has its most developed basis (before socialism) in the capitalist mode of production, it is also a resource allocation mode that is going to die in the communist mode of production, but in the stage within which the capital has not fully developed and the material wealth is not yet abundant enough, the socialist market economic system, which is more advanced than the capitalist market economy system has a room to develop. It is the best economic system when we are in the long run passing from market resource allocation mode to the higher one, i.e. the "consciously, planned" resource allocation mode, as we are constantly exploring and aiming to consolidate and develop China's current basic socialist economic system. Marx said in the preface of *Das Kapital*: "The wealth of those societies in which the capitalist mode of production prevails, presents itself as "an immense accumulation of commodities."[12] The author thinks that the wealth of society wherein the socialist mode of production dominates should be characterized by fair distribution of the immensely massive commodity production. The socialist market economic system reform increases the productivity and utilization ratio of labor across the national scale and promotes the development of productive forces, which means that the very policy of "state-owned enterprises retreating and private-owned enterprises advancing" is a process of creating wealth for people, and return of wealth to people.

However "state-owned enterprises retreating and the private-owned enterprises advancing" is not an irreversible and inevitable trend, because the retreating of the state-owned economy today, will bring more favorable results for their future progress. The state-owned economy retreating from some industries and fields of economy—to a certain extent—can improve the economic structure of the state-owned economy and also optimize the layout of state-owned economy and upgrade the structure of the leading state-owned industries. In this way state-owned capital will have a more rational distribution. We think this approach will be positive achievement in our efforts to combine socialized production with the market economy on a higher level.

(IV) The correct path to combine the socialist state-owned economy and market economy

(1) Promoting the reform of the shareholding system

The share-holding system is the product of the combination of socialized production and market economy, which properly fits the current development level of productive forces in the primary stage of socialism and the socialist

---

12   Karl Marx, *Capital*, Volume 1, People's Publishing House, 1963, pp. 5-92.

market economy system. The diversified ownership structure of our country can not only widely exist in the socialist market economy on the macro level, but also exists in the market competition on the micro-level, therefore the share-holding system is the key to realize the combination between the socialist state-owned economy and market economy.

In *The Decision of the CPC Central Committee on the Major Issues of Reform and Development of State-owned Enterprises*, promulgated in 1999 the following policies were proposed: "the leading role of the State-owned economy in the national economy mainly relies on its capability to control. The role of State-owned economy should be materialized by solely State-owned enterprises, and by energetic development of the shareholding system through the establishment of State holding and joint-stock enterprises."

Deepening the reform of the state-owned enterprises' by the share-holding system has the following three advantages: firstly, the reform of the state-owned enterprises' share-holding system is the specific way to complete the transformation of the state-owned equity, enables the flow of state-owned capital, enables that the state-owned capital can flexibly exits or enable it to enter into some other fields or industries to a certain extent, which is conducive to the optimal allocation of state-owned capital. Secondly, the reform of state-owned enterprises' shareholding system can improve the control and supervision upon the state-owned capital. In general, the state-owned capital needs to hold greater than 50% or equal to 51% of the shares to control the total stock of a company, but in special circumstances that the stock equity is highly dispersed among other subjects, the state-owned capital just needs to hold 20%-30% of the shares to effectively hold the control of the whole stock of the company. Thirdly, the reform of state-owned enterprises' shareholding system can form a diversified stock equity relationship, which is not only good for the regulation and preservation and increase of the value of the state-owned assets, but it is also beneficial to establish a corporate governance structure, thus providing a guarantee for that our country's state-owned enterprises become standard subjects of the market competition through introducing the modern enterprise system. The reform of state-owned enterprises' shareholding system makes state-owned enterprises gain a steady stream of vitality in the process of developing and growing, which not only effectively expands the scope of the control power of the state-owned economy sector, but also avoids the outflow of domestic private capital to other countries. At the same time, in regard to the subjects of the other sectors of the economy whose development may face bottlenecks, by depending upon its market competitiveness, the state-owned economy can support its further development by means of buying shares, making the state-owned capital achieve the goals of combining concentration and dispersal natures in the domestic asset market.

(2) Promote the building of the modern enterprise system in the state-owned sector

The modern enterprise system, and further modernization of them in this respect, offers systematic guarantee to the state-owned enterprises—they being the main competing actors in the market—in the following three aspects: firstly, the establishment of legal corporate property right system makes the enterprise's property rights more clear, namely the state-owned capital invested by the state is the enterprise's legal corporate property, the enterprise as a legal person has an independent right to dispose regarding the enterprise's legal corporate property, and the state maintains and possesses the ownership as the investor. Secondly, the establishment of limited liability system makes the state no longer having infinite responsibility to guard the state-owned enterprises, which has made the state-owned enterprises truly assume sole responsibility for one's own profits or losses. Thirdly, by establishing a corporate governance structure, and by transforming the enterprise to legal person which can use independent rights of management, the state still has the approval right in regard to major corporate events in the meeting of shareholders as a stock holder, thus the board of directors has the decision-making authority on the enterprise's production and management, only in accordance with the law.

We should be clear that the establishment of modern enterprise system is to seek an effective path to combine the socialist state-owned economy and market economy to make our country's state-owned enterprises obtain stronger vitality and higher efficiency, and it is definitely contrary to the strategy of privatization. Clarifying the borders of property rights mainly refers to handling the right relation between the ownership with our country as the investor and the independent control right for property of the enterprise legal person under the condition of market economy, namely the establishment of the modern enterprise system. Clarifying the borders of property rights definitely does not mean to weaken and waver the state's status and its role as the investor, and also the independent control right—by the legal person—upon the property of the enterprise, does not mean assigning or giving the state property to individuals, in the final analysis, we can't change the nature of public ownership status of the socialist state-owned enterprise.

III. The combination of large-scale state-owned economy and market economy is the advantage of the socialist system with Chinese characteristics

(I) The combination of large-scale state-owned economy and market economy has the ability to effectively make up for market failure

In Western economics, market failure is defined as the inefficiency of the allocation of resources by the market, due to the public goods supply, natural monopoly, transaction costs, externalities and information asymmetric information and information drawbacks. Marx also has pointed out: "These forms contain the formal possibilities of crises... the development of this possibility into actuality also needs to have entire range of relationships and ways."[13]

---

13   Karl Marx, *Capital*, Vol. 1, People's Publishing House, 1963, p. 5-928.

Under the condition of resources being allocated by the market, since this quality is one aspect or condition among the "entire range of relationships and ways" as mentioned above by Marx, the market failure may likely become a cause triggering an actuality of a crisis, and with the deepening of the wave of economic globalization, both a capitalist market economies and socialist market economies will be faced by the challenges of market failures. But in comparison, socialist market economy which relies upon the combination of large-scale state-owned economy and market economy, possesses a better and more effective re-agency or response ability and enjoys more effective tools to make up for the market failures compared to the capitalist market economy.

The consequences of market failures mainly manifest themselves as the issues of unfair distribution of income and wealth, besides as negative externalities, competition failures, monopoly in the market, unemployment, imbalanced regional development, the shortage of supply in public goods products and irrational and excessive use of resources owned by the whole society including nature and ecology.[14]

In general, from the point of view of the current general theoretical basis of state-owned economy, the existence range and purpose and mode of capitalist state-owned economy determine that the capitalist countries can only give relative effective remedies to the problems of negative externalities, such as the shortage in public goods supply and irrational and excessive use of public resources, and can only give temporary relief to the problems of unemployment and imbalanced regional development, as for the unfair income and wealth distribution, competition failure and market monopoly are problems that capitalist countries are unable to eradicate. In particular, if we look from the point of view of the current specific theoretical basis of our country's state-owned economy, with its existence range and purpose (mode) determines that our country by combining large-scale state-owned economy and market economy can effectively make up for market failures.

(II) The combination of large-scale state-owned economy and market economy can effectively enable the implementation of long-term national development strategies

The long-term development strategy formulated and introduced by the government affects the development direction and the quality of the national economy in regard to macro level, and also affects the adjustment of industrial structure and the enterprises' survival conditions at the medium level, and also affects the overwhelming majority of people's fundamental interests at micro level. One of the main superiority of the socialist system with Chinese characteristics is to undertake great projects by concentrating human, material and financial resources at a certain target, this is because our country possesses

---

14　Negative externalities occur when production and/or consumption impose external costs on third parties outside of the market for which no appropriate compensation is paid. This causes social costs to exceed private costs.

a large-scale state-owned economy in unity with the market economy which makes Chinese government's macroeconomic regulation and control far more effective than that of the capitalist countries in speed and strength, thus can effectively lead and implement the country's long-term development strategy, and this is what the capitalist countries cannot easily do. Along with the deepening of socialized production, if we aim to improve the effectiveness of macroeconomic regulation and control of the government, we must control the fundamental spheres which are the lifeline of the economy, enable that government can lead the production in the more fields, consequently this objectively requires that the state-owned economy must possess a considerable proportion in the national economy.

(III) The combination of large-scale state-owned economy and market economy can provide a more reliable material basis for the establishment of and a more solid material basis for perfecting the social security system

Economic base determines the superstructure, thus the nature of the built of the social security system's economic basis fundamentally determines the protection of the social security system. Social security system of the capitalist countries, has certain drawbacks compared with the socialist countries: firstly, under the same condition of market economy, the capitalist countries take the fiscal revenues of the state as the main pillar of the national social security system, while the socialist countries, do not only have the fiscal revenue as the main pillar, instead they also have the profit of large-scale state-owned economic as a reliable support. Secondly, in the eyes of capitalist states, the establishment and perfection of the social security system not only aims to pacify and palsy the less earning segments of the laborers and they are also designed as the means to maintain the exploitation environment of capitalists exploitation environment, while in the socialist countries, they are the basic measures and means to realize the fair distribution of wealth and the people's common prosperity.

It is precisely because the economic basis of and purpose of establishing and improving of the social security system in a capitalist country and socialist country are different, this objectively causes that social security system of a capitalist country cannot enjoy a stable development. Since Reform and Opening-up in our country, along with the development of productive forces and the deepening of the reform of market economy system, we have successfully established a stable social security system, constantly increased its coverage spheres, the diversified the social groups benefiting from it and have made other achievements on the basis of government's increasing fiscal revenues and powerful guarantee provided by the large-scale state-owned economy sector.

IV. The direction of the deepening reform of state-owned enterprises in China

(I) The privatization of state-owned enterprises shakes the dominant position of the public sector of the economy

The dominant position of the public sector of the economy in our country is directly related to our country's socialist nature and directly related with foundation of our party's rule, without such a material foundation the Party cannot lead and rule. And the public sector of the economy having a dominant position in the national economy means that the state-owned economy can be able to play its leading role in the national economy. This further warns that as the major players of state-owned economy, the state-owned enterprises should enjoy the dominant position in China's socialist market economy.

During our efforts to establish and deepen the socialist market economy, some "western mainstream discourses" have wantonly advocated and worshipped the neo-liberalism, advertised the privatization as the eternal "panacea" to promote the economic growth. Historically, the so-called neo-liberalism has puzzled the world in the 1990s with the mask of "Washington consensus", which led Latin American countries' economies to the verge of collapse. More directly, it has led to the collapse of the US's biggest political rival, the Soviet union. The GDP of the Soviet Union declined by 55%, causing a more devastating economic loss than that in the World War II. Even more astonishingly that GDPs of most developed capitalist countries could only achieve a growth rate of 2%-3%, specifically, a major economic power Japan, unexpectedly experienced the condition of nearly negative growth, as was Horizontally, today the "western mainstream discourse " still continues to advertise the neo-liberalism to other countries, but they have changed the concept of "nationalization" with several shifts, as follows: from "a medicine" to "a specific medicine" then to "a common medicine" when capitalist countries should use in order to alleviate their economic crisis, which all make the people all over the world, realize the essence of this neo-liberalism. The painful historical lessons of Latin American countries and the Soviet Union during the 1990s warns us that we should correctly handle the "privatization" issue brought forward by the neo-liberal economic policies while implementing further reforms in regard to state-owned enterprises in the current stage of our country.

(II) Restoring and strengthening the leading position of public ownership with state-owned enterprises as the principle agents, is the correct reform direction to stick to and improve the socialist basic economic system

This judgment accords with the following basic principle of Marx's historical materialism: "the nature of a social formation is determined by the dominant (among others) relations of production in its socio-economic formation." We can also know the principle that the quantitative change causes to a qualitative change, consequently we should keep in mind that, in order to ensure the control of the state-owned economy upon the national economy, it must have a certain quantitative magnitude, otherwise we know that "even a wisest woman cannot cook a meal without rice". The proportion that the public sector of the economy should occupy must be equal to or greater than 51%, as the fundamental expression of the socialist nature of our country. And it has been proved thus far, we should while vigorously supporting and fully developing the non-public sector of the economy, we should simultaneously take a diversified approach when consolidating the dominant position of public ownership by giving priority to the state-owned enterprises and implement the following: firstly, we should adhere to the direction when deepening the reform of state-owned enterprises, secondly, continue the reform of shareholding system in SOEs; thirdly, continue the reform of establishing the modern enterprise system in the SOEs and thus improve their control force, energy and efficiency of the state-owned sector of the economy, which completely meets the requirement of the dynamic changes in regard to developing the control power of the state-owned economy.

After 30-plus years of our unremitting exploration during the Reform and Opening-up period, as the main subjects of the socialist market economy in our country, the socialist state-owned enterprises' powerful control power is fully reflected in the following three aspects: Firstly, they control the country's economic lifeline, thus ensure the national economic security. Facts have proven that faced by the regional and even global economic shocks caused by the Asian financial crisis in 1997 and U.S. financial crisis in 2008, the socialist state owned economy sector offers a risk prevention ability which is incomparable to other ownership economies. With the powerful support of the state-owned enterprises, rather than suffering a catastrophe in the economic crisis, our country has seized the opportunity to develop rapidly. Secondly, they have been advantageous when are promoting the upgrading of the industrial structure and improve the quality of economic mode. The blind pursuit of profit maximization of privately owned enterprises makes the economic development mode way difficult to change, while our state-owned enterprises have dared to innovate, bravely reformed, themselves which objectively made them take the lead in entering into the production mode of resource intensification, capital centralization and human talent concentration, consequently they have become the pioneers of all other enterprises in China with such an enterprise modernization leap, thus promoted the upgrading of the industrial structure in China. Thirdly, they have set examples and offered guidance to various other existing forms of ownership economies. State-owned enterprises are the most direct tools for the party and government, in conducting macro-economic regulation and control on the national economy, they are also the "hard core" and "backbone" we rely when fully implementing the concept of "people-oriented" in the socialist market economy. The solid strength of state-owned enterprises enable them to enter into such industries which require high investment, and where there high barriers to hinder newcomers, so whether in domestic or international market, the state-owned enterprises have played the role of bulldozer cutting the road for others and expanded growth soil for other ownership sectors of the economy.

However, since 2003, the dominant position of the public sector of the economy in our country had already started to shake. According to Zhao Huaquan's statistics[15], in 2003, the public sector of the economy accounted for only 57.0% of the national economy in our country, while the non-public economy accounted for the 42.8% of the national economy. In 2006, the public sector of the economy accounted for 48.6% of the national economy in our country, while the non-public economy accounted for 51.2%. In 2008, the public sector of the economy accounted for 35.2% of the national economy in our country, while the non-public economy accounted for 64.2% of the national economy; In 2010, the public sector of the economy accounted for 26.9% of the national economy (the state-owned economy accounted for 22.2%, the collective economy accounted for 4.7%), while the non-public sector of the economy accounted for 73% of the national economy (the individual economy accounted for 2.2%, the private economy accounted for 45.7%, the foreign economy accounted for 25.1%). But in Norway, which is regarded as a socialist country in the Western media, in 2008, the proportion of shares or other equity possessed by the government in GDP has been close to 70%, and in Finland and Sweden shares or other equity possessed by these government, respectively was also close to 30% of the GDP.[16]

Deng Xiaoping has pointed out: "the public ownership should maintain its dominant position" and "achieving common prosperity" is the basic principle the socialism which we should adhere to. But with the shake and even loss of the dominant position of the public sector of the economy, whether the state-owned enterprises can give full play to their advantages I have mentioned above, is difficult to judge. Therefore, with above figures in mind, restoration and consolidation of the dominant position of public ownership, the state-owned enterprises as the core of it should be the reform direction to stick to and improve the socialist's basic economic system in future. Economist Gu Hongmei has argued that the efficiency of the socialist state-owned economy is higher than that of the capitalist state-owned economy, which is why the restoration and consolidation of the dominant position of public ownership, state-owned enterprises as its core is the our most effective tool mean to narrow polarization and realize the common prosperity.[17]

15 See article by Zhao Huaquan, The Quantitative Analysis and Evaluation of The Dominant Position of Public Ownership, in: *Journal of Studies On Contemporary Economics* 2012(3).
16 Forfás, *The Role of State Owned Enterprises: Providing Infrastructure and Supporting the Economic Recovery*, http ://www.forfas.ie.2010-07.
17 Gu Hongmei, The Comparative Study of Socialist State-owned Economy and State-owned Economy of Capitalism-and the Evaluation of Indiscrimination of the State-owned Corporate Ownership System, *Jianghan BBS* 2012(12).

(III) The participation of China's state-owned enterprises in the international competition is the inherent requirement and historical mission for their further development and expansion

Only in the field of capital management can the state-owned economy fully realize its function and value, and can more effectively reflect the superiority of the socialist system of our country, this not only requires that the state-owned economy should do everything to increase its own value in the international market, but also requires that they should actively participate in international competition so as to improve their international competitiveness. An important cause behind the Latin American countries' economies falling to the verge of collapse in the 1990s and the reason behind collapse of the Soviet Union was the total privatization of its state-owned economy and their significantly weakened competitiveness in the world market. As a result, continuing to improve the concentration of state-owned enterprises in China is an important way to enhance the international competitiveness of the Chinese state-owned enterprises. consequently by only developing and expanding the state-owned enterprises will enable them gain foothold in the international competition by their own native trade-marks. Thus, if the public ownership economy with state-owned enterprises at its core are excluded from the competitive fields, not only the dominant position of public ownership in the domestic market will be endangered, but also their ability to cope with the more intense and brutal international competition, in the international market will be impossible, due to lack of sufficient capital. We should note that deepening the "Opening-up" does not only means "bringing in foreign capital", but also means "going global". After China's state-owned enterprises have achieved full development in the domestic market with the support of state's finance and favorable government policies, their participation in the international competition does not only derive from their inherent requirement of further development and strengthening but this participation is also the historical mission entrusted to them by the country and the people.

There are two main ways that the state-owned enterprises of China can participate the international competition in the international market: firstly, they can actively participate in the international competition of commodity markets. Secondly, they can actively participate in the international competition of the capital markets. The main purpose behind China's state-owned enterprises participating in the international competition of commodity markets is to surpass their internal problems in regard, to adapting to the established rules international markets and aims to improve their corporate governance structures. Our state-owned flagship enterprises, China National Petroleum Corporation (CNPC), State Grid Corporation (SGC), China's No. 1 automobile manufacturer, and several other "Chinese trump card" companies have simultaneously started the "going out" wave and soon their achievements echoed in the world markets. Meanwhile, they have discovered their weaknesses and gaps in comparison with the multinationals of the developed countries, for them this gap meant that there was room for improvement, and they were determined to face the challenges. The state-owned enterprises in our country should be encouraged to utilize opportunities offered by the current situation, and we should undertake the heavy task of further expanding the size of the state-owned economy, encourage them to constantly improve themselves through competition with other large multinational companies in the world market. Our country has always aimed to strengthen the "south-south cooperation" by exporting state-owned capital, state-owned enterprises acting as carriers. The third world countries demand reliable, strong and sustainable capital to develop their social productive forces and improve people's living standards. The solid strength of China's state-owned capital and its favorable credits can exactly meet the fundamental demands of the third world countries. Capital can only realize value proliferation in the circulation process, as the representatives of both our country and people, the state-owned enterprise have the responsibility and obligation to make scientific risk assessment in regard to the international investment environment, heavily enter in the international capital markets in a stable and secure manner.

The state-owned enterprises in China are the flagships of China in the international economic competition, because in the fierce international competition, the state-owned enterprises do not only improve their international competitiveness, but also can promote the further development of the host countries or economies where they invest. Moreover, they are the main means in realizing the goal of maintaining of or help to increase the asset quality and asset value of the state-owned economy of China. Therefore, our country's state-owned enterprises are the main legions for the great rejuvenation of the Chinese nation, which undertake the great mission that the history and the people have rendered to them. Only by consolidating the dominant position of the public sector of the economy, with state-owned enterprises as its core, and with better combination of large-scale state-owned economy and market economy, and by deepening the reform of state-owned enterprises and improving the international competitive power of state-owned enterprises can we better develop socialism and achieve common prosperity.

Originally published in the journal
Research on Financial and Economic Issues, 2014(7)

Watch out for the Independent Innovation Strategy to Avoid the Repetition of the Mistake of Westernization Movement

Jia Genliang

Abstract: At present, the institutional environment for China's independent innovation has not improved, compared to that when the policy was proposed in the beginning of 2006. Instead of independent innovation we observe a new kind of "Westernization" similar to the Westernization movement in late Qing dynasty, which manifests itself as four aspects: foreign exchange purchases continue to be the basic source for the issuance of paper money, result of which is the excessively high investment costs for the domestic scientific and technological innovation and which causes diminishing of funds to be allocated in favor of domestic private enterprises, weakening them in the competition against the foreign funded capital. Free trade system causes indigenous scientific and technological innovation lose its dependency, under this background domestic industries are faced by harder competition of the high-end products in the domestic value chain. And, high dependency on foreign direct investment is the new and distinctive feature of the new "Westernization movement"; Chinese enterprises are not supported through procurement or purchases by the government for their independent innovative products. The policy of "innovation driven development" put forward in the 18th Congress should be based on a kind of brand-new development pattern, which should at least include the following elements: protection of the domestic industry and the domestic market, implement sovereign credit policies, repurchase of the foreign funded enterprises, and strict implementation of "the government measures decree" of the "procurement of independent innovative products" issued in 2007.

Keywords: Strategy of "innovation driven development"; independent innovation; "Westernization movement"; the "new westernization movement"

The year 2014 is the 120th anniversary of the bankruptcy of Westernization Movement and also the defeat of China in the Sino-Japanese War (1894-1895). The Westernization Movement sought to achieve the goal of self-strengthening and seeking prosperity by purchasing and introducing the foreign advanced technology and equipment under the "free trade" system imposed by the imperialist powers to the late Qing Dynasty government. But this modernization path which could not favor the economic development of a backward country, and which contradicted the law of history went bankrupt with the defeat of China in the Sino-Japanese war of 1894-95.

The policy of "offering market for technology" that started in 1992 is the resumption of the development path of past Westernization Movement or the beginning of the New Westernization Movement. But, in January 2006, the Chinese government explicitly put forward the strategy of independent innovation, of which the purpose was to try to reverse this trend. However, in the past 8 years, although China has made some achievements in independent innovation, its traditional development model of incorporating free trade, free investment and financial liberalization into the global value chain division and its dependence on foreign direct investment, when aiming economic growth has not changed.

Instead this traditional development model is further pushed to the extreme under the name of "using the Opening-up to promote the reform". At present, the institutional environment for independent innovation is more worrying than that in 2005. "The independent innovation strategy" faces the threat of falling back to a New Westernization. If this situation cannot be fundamentally changed, the author doubts whether the independent innovation strategy can achieve final success. Currently, the institutional environment for independent innovation shows similar "westernization" characteristics China has practiced in the 19th Century. The following are the four prominent aspects observed by the author.

I. The defects in the currency issuance mechanism by the Central bank, lead to excessively high investment costs for indigenous scientific and technological innovation and causes extreme lack of funds for domestic private enterprises

In the past ten years, RMB is fundamentally issued on the basis of the foreign trade surplus, especially the trade surplus of foreign funded companies operating in China, i.e. on the basis of incoming or highly welcomed foreign direct investments, incoming hot money and other foreign currency inflows. By the end of December 2012, China's funds outstanding for foreign exchange accounted for 23.667 trillion Yuan and the base currency for 25.2345 trillion Yuan.[1]

---

1   Refer to the monetary authorities' balance sheet of the People's Bank of China in 2012.

The ratio between the funds outstanding for foreign exchange and the base currency was as high as 93.8%. The ratio between foreign exchange reserve figure and the monetary base was 93.8%, the foreign exchange inflows continued to be basic determinant for the issuance of RMB, which has been the root cause of the "subprime mortgage" (underground private lending) crisis in Wenzhou in 2011 and the "shortage of liquidity" in June, 2013.[2]

In the contemporary world economy, the monetary sovereignty is even more important than a nation's territorial rights, in this paper the author will argue the traditional export-led development model and the current monetary policy of the Central bank (The People's Bank of China) which determines that the country's foreign exchange reserves, be the basic scale for the issuance of M1, and will ponder on the five major grave consequences of these policies, which will not be repeated here. In terms of independent innovation, because the cost of innovation investment capital is excessively high and due to extreme lack of money by domestic enterprises, they are unable to compete with multinational corporations operating in China. Most of the foreign exchange inflows are possessed by multinational companies. Only when they are converted to RMB by the central bank of China, can they circulate domestically,

Due to this policy , such US dollar inflows and consequent additional monetary base (M1), i.e. the RMB issuance by the Central Bank, in the last 10 years is much more than the quantity issued in the 54 years from 1949 to 2003, thus today's so-called "excess liquidity" phenomenon has occurred.

221

In order to avoid excess liquidity triggering high inflation rates, the central bank does not implement the policy of blocking the U.S. dollar inflows from the source as suggested by the author.[3] It chooses another way: the central bank adopts the credit tightening measures such as increasing the Bank deposit reserve ratio rates of the commercial banks, and central bank also issues Treasury bills to suck the excess liquidity in the market.

I have analyzed in my articles as early as 2011 that this credit crunch policy hits the domestic private enterprises, whereas it means following an "economic concession" policy, the monetary policy of China is not regulated by its central bank but foreign funded companies take the lead.

And I wrote that, due to the increase of the deposit reserve ratio of the commercial banks, lending rates of banks increase. And since the domestic private enterprises are not able to get loans from the banking system because of the reason I have explained above which causes higher lending rates, they are forced to appeal to shadow banks, i.e. usury, as the lifesaver, which looks like quench a thirst with poison, as a result, numerous domestic private enterprises

---

2   Wenzhou crisis of 2011, in the Wenzhou city a great number of cases related to illegal private lending activities, involving up to billions of yuan was revealed by the police and 39 suspects arrested.

3   Jia Genliang, The Fundamental Cause of Foreign Exchange Reserve Lies in the Foreign Capital and Debt, *China Economic Weekly* 2011(38).

go bankrupt or struggle on the edge of survival. Whereas, the foreign-funded enterprises indirectly possess the right to issue money (enjoy high liquidity) thus can grant credits through shadow banking, since they bring US dollars into China. The foreign-funded enterprises do not only use their funds as credits through shadow banking, but also use this opportunity to acquire domestic private enterprises, which leads to rapid expansion and reinforcement of the foreign capital's control over China's real economy, of course this is not what some hope: "state retreats and civil sector advances", in fact just the reverse is occurring.

The dollar hegemony and the monetary policy of China's central bank is the main reason for the above difficult situation of the domestic private enterprises in our country. By allowing the influence of dollar hegemony on China's economy, the domestic private enterprises are faced with survival problems, severely lack funds, cannot even dream of investing for any innovation.

So, how are state-owned enterprises effected by the above polices? Some argue that it is not very difficult for the state-owned enterprises to borrow bank loans. If even so, the state-owned enterprises cannot compete with the foreign capital, because the costs of borrowing capital funds for state-owned enterprises are far higher than that of foreign multinationals operating in China. As the US Fed's benchmark interest rates remain at the level of 0-0.5% for a long period of time the US multinationals companies can borrow at very low interest rates, such as 1.5% averagely, from the US banking system, plus they convert these borrowed funds into RMB, without any high costs in China, whereas one-year deposit rate of Chinese banks in China is 3.2%, and state-owned enterprises' borrowing cost is at least more than 4.5% annually, which means their cost of borrowing by the state-owned enterprises is at least more than double compared to multinational companies.[4]

Therefore, while US companies can finance their technological innovation with lower interest rates, Chinese companies lack funds for technological innovation or they can only carry out technological innovation under the conditions of higher financial costs compared to US companies. Then, how will they be able to compete with them, in international markets, with the multinational companies operating in China?

Besides, the impact of foreign exchange reserves on China's currency issuance has also led to a serious shortage of funds for education, science and technological investments, and government subsidies for medical care, social security and agriculture, etc. Since the decisions on the issuance of RMB and the credit volume are affected by the inflow of U.S. dollars, available financial funds for China's non-profitable domestic public expenditures or public services are squeezed.

---

4   The inflation caused by the inflow of US dollar, the deposit rate as high as 3.2% also can't hold the value of deposits.

And this policy only serves to create a kind of foreign capital led and export-oriented economy, under the yoke of U.S. dollar. For example, as early as in 1993, when the central government formulated the educational reform and development plan of the 1990-2000, it was stated that by the year 2000, the state budget for education should account for 4% of GDP.

However, this inspiring ambitious goal has not been achieved till now. In 2007, the highest figure we have reached in recent years was only 3.32%. The serious shortage of social public expenditures and long-term government debts have seriously damaged the incentive system for industrial innovations, which has greatly increased the innovation costs for domestic enterprises. In the past three years, the author and some other scholars have put forward many pertinent suggestions on how to get rid of the influence of US dollar hegemony, implement a sovereign credit system, provide reasonable financing for science and technology and industrial innovation, etc., but were not adopted by the monetary authorities.[5]

II. Free trade makes the scientific and technological innovation in our country increasingly lose its competitive edge, hinders its aim move towards the higher end of the value chain

Independent scientific and technological innovation, especially the breakthrough in core technologies is the foundation for industries to move towards the higher end of the value chain.

However, as our country follows the principle of comparative advantage and energetically develops the export of labor-intensive products, it continues to remain disadvantaged in the international division of labor and trapped at the lower end of the global industrial value chain, resulting in the serious imbalance of the foreign trade structure and thus excessive trade surplus. Consequently, an unfavorable situation is formed, in which a large number of low-end products are exported and high-end products are imported, and breakthroughs in core technology has long been severely suppressed in our country, due to lack of proper financial and other incentives. Currently, for China it has formed the unfavorable situations export surplus based on a large number of low-end products and import of plenty of high-end products, and the core technology breakthrough has long been severely suppressed in our country due to lack of market induction and the stimulation of huge profits for foreign multinationals.

The large number of low-end products export causes a vicious competition and price-cutting wars among domestic enterprises, resulting a serious deterioration of the terms of trade in the export of industrial goods in the past ten years, thus our country has fallen into the trap of "impoverishing growth".

---

5   Jia Genliang, The World Economic Depression and China's Economic Development Strategy, *The Dynamics of Foreign Theoretical Trends* 2011(12).

In order to solve this problem of excessive trade surplus, especially the imbalance of Sino-US trade, in 2010, our government adopted the strategy of "expanding imports" This strategy firstly aimed to expand the import of advanced technology and equipment, and consideration for import substitution policy has been neglected. Consequently, such a strategy will undoubtedly make our country's import and export structure further stuck in the "bad trade" structure of "exporting of low-end products and importing high-end products", thus further strengthen the long existing dilemma of "introduction-backward-re-introduction-re-backward" in our country which is very unfavorable for the transformation of the mode of economic development and independent innovation. If we do not terminate the strategy of "expanding imports" and implement the strategy of balanced growth of national economy suggested by the author, our country will be trapped in this "bad trade" structure deeper and deeper, consequently our control over the domestic market will diminish, and scientific and technological innovation for producing high-end products and elevating our status in the global industrial value chain will be largely hindered.[6]

The author's case study of the photovoltaic industry in China and the robot industry shows that, because the domestic enterprises general lack core technologies, the multinationals hold the leading status in the global value chain and in a state of complete competition in the domestic market, consequently China's strategic emerging industries have generally fallen into the trap of "low-end processing in high-end industry".

"Low-end processing in high-end industry" refers to reliance on the low-end production factors, such as cheap labor and ignorance of the ecological-environmental costs, etc. when enterprises participate in the international division of labor, which make the strategic emerging industries of China completely unable, to compete with those in the developed countries.

The current development mode of the domestic strategic emerging industries in fact still belongs to the mode of Westernization Movement that believes in free trade and relies on the core technology of the developed countries. Without revolutionizing this development mode, it will hinder the historic opportunity of "the third industrial revolution".[7]

Seen from the successful historical experience of the rise of the developed countries, if our country wants to get rid of from the plight of "low-end of high-end industry", we must refuse to join in the global value chain with the high-end value chain of the developed countries' multinational companies remaining at the core of it. We should refuse to accept the industrial transfer into our soil by the developed countries, instead develop our capacity of leading

6   Jia Genliang, The Concern of Import expansion Strategy and the New Debate on Balanced Growth of the National Economy, Contemporary Economics Studies, 2012.

7   Jia Genliang, The Key To Welcoming The Third Industrial Revolution Is The Revolution Of The Development Mode: Case Study And Reflection Of The Photovoltaic And Robot Industry In China, *Economic Theory and Economic Management* 2013(5).

markets by using our huge domestic market scale as a leverage for the independent innovation to ascend the ladders of value chains, and thus set this policy as the core of establishing an independent national value chain. These are the basic conditions for our country to implement "innovation-driven development strategy". However, since China's economists and policy-makers generally accept the theory of free trade and comparative advantages, and never realize the decisive role of the high-end links in the value chain that effect "the wealth or poverty of nations", this approach becomes the root cause why China gives the high-end ladders of value chain in the domestic market to the multinational companies of the developed countries and falls into "low-end of high-end industry". Thus China's huge domestic market becomes the tool of serving as the "hope chest " for other countries' high-end products.

South Korea and Finland, for example, due to their small domestic markets, in the era of rapid change of information technology in the 1980s, had to mainly relied on the international market to supply power for their technological innovation. However, it was also successful under the condition of the protection of domestic market (Finland banned foreign electronic products from entering into the domestic market before 1987) so as to achieve entering into the global value chain through strictly restricting the foreign direct investment, thus they promoted independent innovation of the core technology and ascended the ladders of value chain. However, attaching themselves to the idea of global free trade, especially China and many other developing countries have opened up their domestic market are missing the unprecedented historical opportunity for ascending in the ladder of value chain. According to the Smith's theorem that "technological innovation is restricted by the size of the market", since every country will prefer to implement trade protectionism, China's industrial products which are in the low-end field of the value chain will not be able to create market for its few high-end products.

According to the Smith's theorem, because of their small domestic market, South Korea and Finland's high-end information technology innovation would not have any chance to achieve success at all.

It is just because of the global free trade policy, especially due to China's vast open domestic market provides a fundamental guarantee and vast market for these two countries' to develop their independent innovation of their core technologies and ascend higher ladders of value chain. But with a mistaken approach China's vast domestic market scale has become a stepping stone for other countries' high-end industrial products.

China's neoliberals have always been promoting the government to establish the "China, Japan and South Korea Free Trade Zone" as a modern version of "Greater East Asian Co-prosperity Sphere". Now, they are strongly advocating joining the "Trans-pacific partnership agreement (TPP)" which is in fact used to blockade China by the United States. If the Chinese government is misled by them, then the TPP will lead to the influx of a large number of high-end products from the US, Japan and Korea into our country, our country's industrial value chain will be more comprehensively controlled by multinational companies of the developed countries, the space for indigenous science and technological innovation will be compressed, and we will lose the possibility for the transformation of the pattern of economic development in our country.[8] "Import of high-end products and export of low-end products" pattern formed since the mid 1990s and "expansion of imports strategy" implemented since 2010 in essence still follow the ideological path of the Westernization Movement to achieve the purpose of "learning from foreigners for self-improvement" which means purchasing foreign advanced technology and equipment. However, the heavy lesson of failure learned from the Westernization Movement and the successful experience of Japanese Meiji Restoration indicate that modernization can't be bought with money, and the more core technology and the more key equipment a developing country purchases from abroad, the bigger will be the technological gap between it and developed countries.

III. High dependence on foreign direct investment is a new and distinctive feature of the New Westernization Movement

The above discussion has shown that under the free trade conditions without tariff protection in the developing countries, the developed countries' enterprises will certainly destroy the high-end industry of value chain in the developing countries by virtue of the absolute advantage of technology, productivity, brand and management superiority and other aspects. This is the reason why the Western developed countries adopted trade protectionism in the process of their industrialization in their history. Under the circumstance that the developed countries use foreign direct investment to get concessions, if they don't put strict restrictions against their foreign investment, the multinational companies of the developed countries will more easily destroy the high-end industrial value chain in the developing countries. This is because, under the free trade conditions but without direct investment, companies of the developed countries will save from their high costs of production, by using lower labor costs in the developing countries, which means they will be able to compete easily with domestic companies.

To some extent, this weakens the competitiveness of the products of the developed countries. However, in the case of direct foreign investment, the multinational companies of the developed countries can directly use the developing countries' cheap labor, and conduct direct competition with local companies in the developing countries. The only advantage of the developing countries' national enterprises, i.e. the low-cost labor will lose its value, and the vast majority of high-end industry of value chain will be directly destroyed by the developed countries, and will hinder domestic companies going abroad for new

---

8 Jia Genliang, Why China away from the TPP, *Journal of Exploration and Contend* 2013(9).

markets. The above situation is what occurs in China during 20-plus years. The Chinese government has not only failed to take proper industrial policies to protect the local high-end industry which is still at "infant" stage, but also has adopted a series of extremely disadvantageous policies for Chinese enterprises, such as tax preference, cheap land sales, lowering the labor costs, reducing the environmental protection requirements, and exempting the import tariffs on products which is used for science and technological development, and has vigorously introduced foreign investments, thus forming the export-oriented development mode that relies on the foreign direct investment to promote China's economic growth. Thence, let us discuss whether Chinese companies cannot naturally compete with the foreign-funded enterprises, if therefore China's economic development should rely on foreign direct investment?

Lu Feng and Mr Yu's research shows that the reason why foreign-funded companies in China have shown higher competitiveness than Chinese enterprises mainly lies in two aspects: crowding-out effect and policy distortion. Crowding-out effect refers to that the foreign investment occupying the technology, productivity and many other absolute advantages thus can lead investment projects with high returns, since most Chinese companies are unable to compete with the foreign investment in leading such projects, they have to use their investments for promoting the export of labor-intensive products and need try to increase most of their investment in this direction, which is the reason why China can't sublate the extensive growth mode.

On the other hand, the competitiveness of foreign companies in China (characterized by higher profit rates) is to a great extent caused by a series of policy-distorting environment, which embodies concessive state policies of China to attract foreign investment.[9] The two reasons indicate that the reason why most of the Chinese enterprises cannot compete with the foreign-funded enterprise in the domestic market is directly related with the government policy.

Therefore, how was Chinese economy's high reliance on foreign direct investment formed? Lu Feng and Yu Yongding, illustrate this by citing the research results of Yue Jianyong, Huang Yasheng and Zhou Lian: in the early 1990s, China's economy was in the dual change of transition and development; lots of bottlenecks had led to the change of the state-owned enterprises and their management systems were changed; China's economy was unable to develop rapidly as expected by those policies to accelerate the economic growth. Thence, accelerating the economic growth through the use of foreign investment and getting rid of the difficulties in overcoming the institutional reform in a short term became an important motivation for the introduction of the foreign capital. When maintaining a high growth rate became the overriding political goal, taking the GDP growth performance as the measure "attracting business and foreign investment" to various regions became a major impetus

9   Lu Feng, Yu Yongding, Double Surplus Capability Gap and Independent Innovation-Macroscopic and Microscopic View of the Transformation of the Mode of Economic Development, *Journal of Chinese Academy of Social Sciences* 2012(6).

to introduce the foreign direct investment regardless of all costs. However, these studies fail to notice that the mechanism of China central bank's currency issuance is another important reason for the introduction of foreign direct investment at any cost by the local governments at all levels: when the foreign exchange inflows have become the criterion for the RMB issuance and credit issuance, only after the local governments get the US dollars can they have the funds for development; without the US dollar investment inflow, the regions will be unable to develop due to lack of funds. Central government's above currency issuance mechanism drives the provincial governments to crazily introduce foreign direct investment that increasingly control China's economy.

It is obvious that both theoretical logic and the empirical evidence prove that the foreign-funded enterprises does not belong to China's independent innovation capacity. Lu Feng and Yu Yongding came to the conclusion that the real reason behind China's economic growth to rely on foreign capital is that the Chinese government takes relying on foreign capital as a way to realize the development. This conclusion may make shock some people, but in my opinion, this is beyond dispute. In January 2006, China's independent innovation strategy decision not only failed to curb this trend, but was also resolutely resisted by the following argument that was popular in the society: "foreign-funded enterprises in China are in fact Chinese enterprises, the innovation in the foreign-funded companies in China should be evaluated as is China's independent innovation." Under the guidance of such kind of ideology, highly dependence on foreign direct investment inevitably becomes the new and distinctive feature of the present new Westernization Movement, because during the period of Westernization Movement in 1861-1894, the late Qing dynasty government also treated the foreign-funded enterprises as native businesses. The prevalence of this "comprador" ideology in current China is unprecedented; it startlingly makes government departments at all levels become the proponents of foreign capital.

Different attitudes towards foreign investment has been an important factor which has determined the failure of "Westernization movement" in the late Qing dynasty era and conversely explain the success of the Meiji Restoration in Japan. In modern history (especially in the 19th Century), under the pressure of gunboat policy of the western imperialist powers, both Japan and China had lost their tariff barriers. As a result, different attitudes towards foreign investment became one of the decisive factors for the significant difference between these two countries. During the Meiji Restoration period in Japan, since the Japanese people strongly opposed to the natives handling affairs in service of the foreigners, in Japan at that time, essentially there did not exist the soil for the survival of a comprador class with "Chinese characteristics." For the Meiji government, the basic policy, whether the development of the military industry or the civilian industry, whether state-owned enterprises or private enterprises, was as follows: "The Japanese leaders have been selective when introducing foreign capital for fear that Japan's economy would be controlled by foreign capital."[10] For the foreign direct investment that was allowed to Japan, the goal of the Meiji government was very clear: support the Japanese-owned enterprises, and squeeze the foreign-funded enterprises. For example, by funding and fostering the Mitsubishi Steamboat Zaibatsu in the 1870s, the Japanese government defeated the powerful Pacific Mail Company and the magnate British "P&O" Shipping and Logistics Company, and completely expelled the foreign powers from Japan's sea routes. An independent industrial system was not only the economic basis for the Japanese to defeat the China's Qing government in the Sino-Japanese war, but also was the premise for the abolition of unequal treaties imposed by the foreign powers against Japan in 1911.

However, unlike Japan's attitude toward foreign investment, the Qing government's goals were to "share a little part of the benefits of the foreign traders", and give super privileges to foreign traders and foreign goods. Under the guidance of such thought, the foreign capital had not only controlled the export of commodities during the Westernization Movement period in late Qing dynasty, but also obtained generous privileges just as pointed out by Zheng Guanying in the book Warnings in the Flourishing Age: "With the 22th year of Daoguang" 22th year the ban on maritime trade was freed[11]... , also foreigners could trade freely ... In Xianfeng 8th year, in November, the treaty between China and the West was refreshed..., a levy of 2.5 lian silver per 100 lian was agreed ... This shows the "care" given to foreign businesses and how they were favored. They have grabbed a thick share compared with the Chinese bit... Therefore, that was the foreign businesses which have grabbed the profits, while the Chinese businesses found it difficult to advance forward, for the same foreign goods flowing into the Chinese soil, the foreigners did not need pay, while the Chinese had to donate for them."[12] Just under the guidance of such idea, the "contract for common benefits" was signed between the China Merchants Steamship Bureau attached to Qing government and the British Butterfield & Swire Co., Ltd. and also with Jordine, Matheson & Co., Ltd., which not only enabled the strength of the two foreign-funded enterprises considerably exceed that of the China Merchants Steamship Bureau, but also hindered the possibility of other national capitalists to develop modern native shipping industry due to the monopolistic nature of the contract.[13] The failure of the Sino-Japanese war marked the complete bankrupt of Westernization Movement that relied on the western powers, in current China its lessons deserve profound reflection against the background of the new "westernization movement".

10   Hong Zhi, *Vanishing of the Blooming Dynasty: 110th Anniversary of the Sino-Japanese war*, The Chinese press, 2004, p. 24.
11   In the 22th year of Daoguang (1842), the Qing government signed the humiliating Nanking treaty.
12   Quote from Hong Zhi, *Vanishing of the Blooming Dynasty: 110th Anniversary of the Sino-Japanese war*, The Chinese press, 2004, pp. 112-113.
13   Jiang Xiuping, The Comparison between Modern Enterprises Founded during Westernization Movement in China and Japan Meiji Restoration, *Journal of Research on China's Social Economic History* 1992.

IV. Our country has lost its sovereign rights of procurement regarding independent innovative products

On June 28th, 2011, under the high influence of multinational companies, and coached by the office of the US Chamber of Commerce in China, the office of the European Union Chamber of Commerce in China and the United States government, the Chinese Ministry of Finance has announced that, since July 1st, 2011, it would stop implementing the three documents: "The Management Method of Government Procurement Budget for Independent Innovative Products", "The Evaluation Method of Government Procurement for Independent Innovative Products" and "The Management Method of Government Procurement Contract System for Independent Innovative Products" issued by the Ministry of Finance in 2007. Before this announcement, it was reported that on May 11th, 2011, after the US's Washington Post newspaper learned about the achieved results of the 3rd Round of Sino-US Strategic and Economic Dialogue meeting, it excitedly wrote: "(This) is a landmark." However, for those who truly advocate Chinese independent innovation strategy, this was undoubtedly a bad news, a mark of a new period. Since then, government support for the independent innovation by domestic enterprises, i.e. government procurements, became was almost impossible.

Supporting the independent innovation of domestic enterprises by using public procurements is a major means, across the world among the policy makers and "considered by many people as the most promising current policy tool for innovation and industrial upgrading." It has played a key role in pushing United States to a leading position in the high-tech industry internationally. In the developing countries, although free trade severely suppresses independent innovation by domestic enterprises, the government procurements for independent innovative products, still gives an opportunity for the developing countries to catch up technologically to a degree, which is also allowed by the world free trade system and the WTO.

As pointed out by Rainer Kattel and Veiko Lember, many development economists have argued that WTO rules limit the implementation of classical industrialization policies which have been successful in the developing countries of the East Asia. Their research has demonstrated that: although WTO rules which govern investment, trade, intellectual property rights (IPR), services and also public procurement, impose serious restrictions on the developing countries, nevertheless, if the developing countries do not ratify the WTO's Government Procurement Agreement, the WTO still allows some policy space that can be used by the developing countries; but if the developing countries ratify the government procurement agreement of the WTO, it would be very difficult to implement the government procurement policy for independent innovative products in those fields, that play a key role in national competitiveness and economic growth." therefore, the two scholars have suggested that the developing countries should join the said agreement of WTO.[14] China did not join in the procurement

---

14   Rainer Kattel and Velko Lember, Why Developing Countries Do Not Join in the WTO Government Procurement Agreement?, *Journal of Foreign Theoretical Trends* 2012(2).

agreement of the WTO and thence could freely implement the three documents about the government procurement of independent innovative products that were promulgated by the Ministry of Finance in 2007, which includes China's specific policy measures for independent innovation adopted by Chinese government in the face of the technological monopoly enjoyed by multinational companies in China. However, after the issuance of these three documents in 2007, the Chamber of Commerce offices of the United States and European Union in China have made a lot of defamation and sharp attacks against the government policy and have greatly interfered in China's internal affairs. They have spread the rumors that the overall administrative environment for foreign capital has deteriorated in China and slandered the possible procurement policy that would benefit Chinese enterprises, as trade protectionism and abetted the various media outlets of the developed countries to attack Chinese government, en masse. In May 2010, the US's International Trade Committee issued its annual China report titled, "China the Impact of Intellectual Property Infringement and Independent Innovation Policy on the U.S. Economy" which said: "China's independent innovation policy puts the US enterprises and other foreign companies at a competitive disadvantage in the Chinese market, has formed a new barrier, harms the US's and other countries' direct investment and export to China." In 2010, between May 3 to 6, before the opening of the second round of the "Sino-US Strategic and Economic Dialogue" the leaders of the office of US Chamber of Commerce in China have made a lobbying trip to think-tanks in Washington, paid visit to the Obama administration and the US Congress. Multinational corporations of the developed countries in China have feared: "if the Chinese government supports technological innovation by native enterprises via government procurements, then how to maintain our technological monopoly position and control the Chinese economy?" Although, WTO rules allow those developed countries who have ratified the WTO Government Procurement Agreement to support their technological innovation, they by no means allow China to implement such policy; would never like to see even the slightest threat to the dominant position of the multinationals in China.

This is why the US government and multinationals have relentlessly tried to hinder China's government procurement policy for independent innovation. Finally, the US and European multinationals have achieved their goals in the third round of Sino-US Strategic and Economic Dialogue in May 2011. Consequently, our country is not able to practice the government procurement policy to support the technological innovation of the native enterprises, and the technological monopoly position of the developed countries' multinationals in China has been further consolidated and strengthened.

Originally published in the journal Tianjin University of Commerce, 2014(1)

Part Three

Contemporary Capitalist Economy

Why the US Declines

Hu Angang

Abstract: Since Reform and Opening-up, China's economy has created miracles unprecedented in the development of human history one after another. As the second largest economy after the US, all sectors of China's national economy has been surpassing US level constantly, meanwhile we should also clearly see that the development path of socialism with Chinese characteristics enjoys unique advantages of its political system. Through the life-cycle theory of the states, the author reveals the process of gradual decline of the US in terms of five indexes, such as the GDP, volume of exports, manufacturing output, human resources and comprehensive national strength, and analyzes the causes of this phenomenon in detail. He concludes that the contest among the states is essentially the contest of systems. The decline of the US will become an inevitable fate due to cultural causes, military issues, plundering by its financial groups and carving up of the whole continents for greedy interests and several other flaws in its systems, while our new socialist path will further demonstrate its superiority and vitality.

Key words: life-cycle theory of the states; national innovation theory; competition of systems; contemporary socialist system

I. The Law of Uneven World Development

What is the law of the modern world development? Nearly 100 years ago, Lenin pointed out: "The uneven economic and political development is an absolute law of capitalism."[1] At that time, it was just during the First World War (June 1914-November 1918),[2] after that, the Great Depression Crisis of Capitalist (1929-1933), the World War II (September 1, 1939-September 2, 1945)[3] and the Cold War (1945-1991)[4] broke out. The world paid a huge cost for these; only the US was the biggest beneficiary as well as the only victor, and it has become the world's most powerful country.

According to Angus Madison's summary, since 1820, the world's modern economic history has the following three characteristics: (1) the world's economic growth is particularly rapid. An important characteristic of modern economic growth is that the population growth rate is relatively high, the economic growth rate is higher than the population growth rate, the per capita income level continues to grow, and trade growth rate is higher than the economic growth rate. (2) There is imbalance in economic growth among different regions and countries in the world. The mode of economic growth is very different. The per capita income gap between countries and regions is wide. (3) The world economic growth is not stable, both experienced economic prosperity, also experienced a recession, showing a phased characteristic.[5] Angus Maddison described more about the world's uneven development since 1820, especially the "Big Divergence" between the south and north countries.

According to the World Economic Database (1820-2008) provided by Angus Maddison,[6] we have made a long-term forecast and prospect for the world and major countries in 2030, the main conclusion is that the growth rate of the South countries is higher, while the growth rate of the North countries is lower, the unprecedented great convergence between the South and North countries happens in the whole world, the North-South pattern sees a reversal, the main development indicators will change from a thirty-seventy ratio (for the North

---

1   Lenin pointed out: "The uneven economic and political development is an absolute law of capitalism." Lenin: On the Slogan of the European Union, August 1915, *Selected Works of Lenin*, Vol. 2, People's Publishing House, 1995, p. 709.

2   During the First World War, about 65 million were involved in the war, about 10 million people were killed, and about 20 million injured. The war caused serious economic losses, the estimated economic losses were about USD. 170 billion (at the currency value of the year)

3   Most researches have suggested that, during the World War II, there were about 60 million people killed in this war, including about 20 million soldiers and 40 million civilians, and many of these civilians died of infectious diseases, hunger, massacres, bombings and deliberate genocide crimes.

4   The Cold War which started in the 1950s after the World War II, has ended along with the Gorbachev's political and democratic reforms in the Soviet Union during 1980s, which contributed to the collapse of the socialist regimes of the Soviet Union and Eastern European countries, the Cold War formally lasted until the early 1990s.

5   Angus Maddison, *Review of the World Economy for Two Hundred Years*, Chinese version, The Reform Press, 1997, pp. 1-11.

6   Angus Maddion, *Historical Statistics of the World Economy: 1-2008 AD.*

to the South) to current 50-50 ratio, then to a seventy-thirty ratio (for the South to the North) in a 20-30 years time.[7]

This shows that the imbalanced economic and political development of various countries is still the universal law of the world in the 21st Century, but it has been entirely different from that in the 19th Century and 20th Century, there has occurred big change regarding the status of the North-South countries, a new World War is impossible to break out any more, but in our era the "world is not still peaceful".

At present, there are not only 239 countries and regions[8] in the world, G8 mechanism is replaced by G20 countries, which represent about 80% of the world's population and 85% of World's GDP, which has becoming a new progressive mechanism of global governance.[9] Today, we observe two major global trends which are unprecedented in the history of mankind, which coexist at the same time and interact with each other: the first is the economic globalization and regional integration, the interests of all countries in the world are increasingly linked together and their fates are interrelated; the second is the increasingly fierce international competition, that is commercial wars replacing the military wars and technological innovation replacing nuclear deterrence, which has become the main mode of international competition. Against such a background, any country or region cannot be "alone" or "stand aloof", closing to the outside will bring outdatedness, but even Opening-up to the outside world may not cure falling behind. As said in CC Report of the 16th National Party Congress (2002): "The situation is pressing, not to advance will mean retrogressing."[10]

After entering the 21st Century, this prediction began to be verified. More obvious and more prominent is that China is rapidly rising and US faces an accelerated decline. Of course there isn't much controversy on the former fact, even President Obama also publicly stated that "US welcomes a strong, successful, prosperous China in the world to play an important role."[11] But the latter- accelerated decline- is quite controversial, since the US scholars, are divided into different voices.[12] As Chinese scholars, we have our own long-term follow-up specialized research, which gives a clear rather than vague answer and a pragmatic rather than taken-for-granted view on this.

235

---

7   Hu Angang, Yan Yilong, Wei Xing, *2030 China: Towards Common Prosperity*, Renmin University of China Press, 2011, pp. 23-25.

8   Among them 193 are UN members.

9   Atlantic Council, *Envisioning the 2030: US Strategy for a Post-Western World*, 2012, p. 4.

10   Jiang Zemin, "Building a Well-off Society in an All-round Way and Creating a New Situation in the Cause of Socialism with Chinese Characteristics–A Report at the 16th National Congress of the Communist Party of China", Nov. 8, 2002.

11   Welcome Speech by U.S. President Barack Obama at the banquet held at the White House for the Chinese President Hu Jintao. Xinhuanet Washington wire on January 19, 2011.

12   There are many people holding "US Decline Theory", For example, in 1987 professor of history from US Yale University Paul Kennedy put forward" the US Decline Theory" in the book titled as *The Rise and Fall of the Great Powers: Economic Changes and Military Conflicts in 1500-2000*; Handel Jones: *China and US: The Uneasy Partnership That Will Change the World*, Mc-Graw-Hill Co.,Inc,2010; Dr Marvin Folkertsma (a professor of political science and fellow for American studies with The Center for Vision & Values at Grove City College).

Here we need to answer several relevant critical questions: Has the US really entered the declining stage? If yes, what are its important signs? Is it a short-term decline or long-term decline? What causes the US decline? Is it because of the rise of the China, or because of its internal causes such as US's own problems? What are the consequences, if US continues to decline? For China, how should we grasp the strategic opportunities, enhance China's strategic capacity and take the opportunity to build a new type of major-country relations?

II. The accelerated decline of US and the accelerated rise of China

The author uses the life-cycle theory of the states to describe, recognize and understand the rise and fall of the states, and has selected five quantitative indexes (GDP, amount of exports, manufacturing output, human resources and comprehensive national strength) and compares them with the world's total figures to calculate, measure and examine the life-cycle of a country or different countries.[13]

This can both verify the rising period of US in history (such as 1870-1913) and verify its peak era (1945-1955), mighty era (1955-1990), exclusively-dominant era (1990-2000) and decline era (after 2000) of the US after the two world wars.

20 years ago, along with the collapse of the Soviet Union and the end of the Cold War, US became the world's sole super-hegemon, and the so-called "one superpower and several major powers" world pattern was formed. The US maintained a relatively high growth rate in the 1990s, its main economic indicators compared with the world total was basically in a stable level, even in the late 1990s, it was still rising due to the ICT revolution, the proportion of US's GDP in the world rose from 26.1% in 1990 to 30.8% in 2000. This might be the last short-term economic boom since the World War II, accompanied by a cumulative economic bubble, followed by the bursting of the dot-com bubble.[14] All these have also led to the emergence of US's real estate bubble in 2008.

When the US became an arrogant superpower, it was unconsciously falling into the "US Syndrome", and there has been an unforeseen acceleration of decline. After more than 10-plus years in the 21st Century has passed, the proportion of US GDP in the world's total has dropped to 22.0% until 2012, which had decreased by 8.8% compared to that in 2000, encountering an average annual decline of 0.73%.

---

13   Hu Angang, Life Cycle of Nations and the Rise of China, *Teaching and Research* 2006(1).

14   Internet bubble (also known as Technet bubble or dot-com bubble) refers to the speculative bubble between 1995-2001, and the event that the share price of technology and emerging Internet-related businesses rose rapidly in the stock markets of Europe and American continent and those in Asian countries, Nasdaq index reached its highest point of 5132.52 on March 10, 2000. Then the burst of the Internet network economic bubbles made the IT industry lose about 5 trillion US dollars from market capitalization between March 2000 to October 2002.

At the same time, the proportion of the export trade value of US goods and services in the world's total also decreased from 11.8% in 2000 to 8.7% in 2012. From the perspective of comprehensive national strength criterion, the proportion of US in the world's total has decreased from 19.9% in 2000 to 17.5% in 2010. From a microeconomic perspective, the number of US enterprises among The World Top 500 Enterprises published in the Fortune magazine was viewed to decrease from the peak of 177 in 2007 to 132 in 2012, with a decrease of 45 enterprises (see Table 1). This is an important stage of continuous decline in US, and the extremely arrogant superpower in the world will be a thing of the past very soon. But the US intellectual elites do not agree.[15]

Reversely, the first decade in the 21st Century has been an important stage for China's rapid rise. China's proportion of GDP in the world's total rose from 3.7% in 2000 to 11.6% in 2012. The proportion of China's goods and services in the world's total rose from 4.3% in 2000 to 11.5% in 2012. At the same time, the relative gap between total economic aggregate and export trade volumes in China and US have rapidly narrowed from 8.3 times and 2.7 times in 2000, to 1.9 times and 0.75 times in 2012 respectively. Looking from the perspective of comprehensive national strength, China's proportion in the world's total rose from 8.0% in 2000 to 14.0% in 2010.

Table 1. The proportion of US's major economic indicators in the world (1990-2012)

	1990	2000	2005	2010	2012	2000-2012 variation
GDP (exchange rate method) (%)	26.1	30.8	27.7	22.9	22	-8.8
Exports of goods and services (%)	11.3	11.8	8.6	8.4	8.7	-3.1
Federal Government Expenditure (%)	18.7	16.1	16.7	18.8	18.6	2.5
Military Expenditure (%)	37.4	41.5	44.9	42.6	39.1	-2.4
Comprehensive national strength (%)	22.0	19.9	18.7	17.5		
The world's top 500 enterprises (pcs)	164	174	177	140	132	42

Note: The military expenditure in this table is calculated according to the purchasing power parity (PPP) in current US dollars, other data is calculated according to the exchange rate method, and in US dollars; data of the world's top 500 enterprises in the "Fortune" magazine.

---

15   Like Joseph Nye, Professor of Kennedy School of Government, Harvard University, USA, The Decline and Collapse of the US Decline Demise Theory (CNN International, Inc. Website, October 7, 2011) Richard Haas, President of the US Diplomatic Association: How to Build a Second American Century (US Washington Post website, April 23, 2013)

The China's (Mainland) number of The World Top 500 Enterprises published in US's Fortune magazine has increased from 9 in 2000 to 70 in 2012, with an increase of 61 (see Table 2). It has surpassed Japan, ranking the second in the world.

**Table 2. The proportion of China's major
economic indicators in the world (1990-2012)**

	1990	2000	2005	2010	2012	2000-2012 variation
GDP (exchange rate method) (%)	1.8	3.7	4.9	9.4	11.6	7.9
Exports of goods and services (%)	1.8	4.3	7.3	10.4	11.5	7.2
Central government expenditure (%)	1.2	2.6	3.8	6	6.4	3.8
Military expenditure (%)	1.2	3	4.1	7.4	9.5	6.5
Comprehensive national strength (%)	6	8	9.7	14		
The world's top 500 enterprises (pcs)	1	9	15	43	70	61

Note: The military expenditure in this table is calculated according to the purchasing power parity (PPP) in current US dollars, other data is calculated according to the exchange rate method in US dollars; data of the world's top 500 enterprises is in the "Fortune" magazine.

In the course of China's rapid rise, the proportion of China's military expenditures in 2012 accounted only 9.5% of the world total, which is more modest and slightly lower compared to China's GDP and export trade in proportion in the world total figures (see Table 2).

From the perspective of the future trends, with the constant improvement of proportion of China's above indicators in the world's total, in 2020 it will be about one-fifth in the world's total, the due rise in the proportion of China's military expenditures in the world's total is also a must. China has greater economic strength so as to support the modernization construction of military and national defense. The modernization construction of its military and national defense, especially the Navy's modernization and ocean-going military vessel construction will ensure China's expanding overseas interests. Reversely, the US has to "cut" its military expenditures, as long as China keeps "increasing" its military expenditures, it will significantly narrow the relative gap with the US defense strength.

III. Root Causes of the US Decline

Looking from the perspective of modern world history of economic development, what determines the prosperity or decline of a country? There may be multiple interpretations. The author uses the "national innovation theory" to explore this question. Innovation is a fundamental motivation for a rapid development of a country, for its rapid rise and strengthening. A country's rise may be due to competition between countries, from passive response to active response, from imitative innovation to pro-active innovation; on the contrary, a country's decline may also be due to competition among countries, innovation being weakened or even disappearing. At that time, I have mainly concentrated on the analysis of China, and used the "life-cycle of the states" theory to explain why modern China of the 19th Century moved towards a decline from being strong country and also explain why contemporary China is moving from decline towards being strong,[16] I did not have time to analyze the issue whether US declines and why it declines, but I have always taken the US as China's pursuant object, continued my research about the US's development trend in order to truly know "both ourselves and our adversaries".

Why is US declining from its peak? This is not the fault of China, the rise of China is a natural thing, identically, and the decline of US is also a very normal historical phenomenon. Why do we say so? We can make comparison by using the proportions of a country's major economic indicators and population indicators in proportion to the world's total. The modernization has occurred early or late in different countries, the change of their statuses will show different historical development tracks, from an abnormal to a normal one.

The proportion of an economic indicator (for example the GDP) in the world's total is higher than the proportion of population indicator in the world's total will appear in the countries that have started developing earlier, conversely the late developing countries appeared a trend of divergence to the earlier developing countries, obviously this is unfair and abnormal; when the late developing countries also start an economic take-off, there has occurred the trend of convergence between the two groups, the early and late coming ones. Consequently, the situations like the decline of proportion of US GDP in the world's total and the rise of proportion of China's GDP in the world's total will appear, which means a turn from abnormal to normal. Even so, the proportion of US GDP is still higher compared than the proportion of its population in the world, and the proportion of China's GDP is still lower than its proportion in the world population. This shows that the proportion of US's GDP will decline further, and the proportion of China's GDP still has a further rising space, so when China has started to economic take-off stage with the Reform and Opening-up, the rise of China and the decline of US has become a normal phenomenon, rather than being an abnormal phenomenon. In addition to these objective reasons, the decline of US also derives from several subjective reasons.

However, US lacks grave "self-recognition", always defines its own problems as "China's offenses". For example, as US' unemployment rate soars, the number of employment vacancies reduces, especially the number of manufacturing vacancies reduce, the media blames China for "grabbing US jobs", for

---

16   Hu Angang, The Life-Cycle of the States Theory, and the Rise of China, *Teaching and Research* 2006(1).

another example, as the US export values face a relatively decline, it desperately increases imports, which causes a constant and irreversible trade deficit, then the US media blames the Chinese side for manipulating the RMB exchange rates. Although I am not a "healer" for US "doctor" (referring to Americanist), but for China (referring to China expert), my research shows that the root causes of US decline is internal. The US can be compared to a "Western giant", figuratively speaking, it has been suffering from "American Disease" or "American Syndrome" or "American Chronic Disease" for a long time, and it is just like the chronic "obesity" disease which is very common among the US people.[17] Here, I will briefly summarize as follows:

First, US's two diseases as "conceit" and "arrogance"

In 1956, Mao Zedong said: "Modesty helps one goes forward, whereas conceit makes one lag behind; we should always remember this truth."[18] It applies to both a person and a country. Looking from the perspective of the development stage, China's development level is low, we are not qualified to be proud, but rather choose to be only modest and prudent; US's development level is the highest, they are always qualified to be proud and arrogant, and they despise China's progress; looking from the perspective of cultural background, China regards modesty as virtue, while US regards pride as virtue; looking from the perspective of the bilateral exchanges, China is willing to learn from US and make foreign things serve China. US never wants to learn from China or allow Chinese things serve US. This proves Mao Zedong's saying that China will change with each passing day,[19] and US will lag behind and decline.[20] This is the cultural root of US decline. Even if they realize that, it will be very difficult for them to change it.

Secondly, US's "war addiction " and "military intervention" disease

Historically, whenever US launched a war, the proportion of its GDP compared to the world's total has declined. If calculating according to the data of international US dollar prices in 1990 provided by Angus Madison, after the Korean War (1950-1955) initiated by the US, the proportion of US's GDP in

---

17   The obesity rate among the US population has grown from 13% in 1962 to 19.4% in 1997, 24.5% in 2004 and 26.6% in 2007. In 2010, 35.7% of adults and 17% of children had obesity problem.

18   Mao Zedong pointed out that we must not have the arrogant attitude of great-nation chauvinism and never be arrogant due to several revolutionary victories or some achievements in the socialist construction. All countries, big or small, should be equal, they all have their own strengths and weaknesses. There is no reason to be arrogant, even if we have achieved great successes in our work. Mao Zedong: "Opening Speech at The Eighth National Congress of the Communist Party of China ", September 15, 1956, Collected Works of Mao Zedong, Volume 7, People's Publishing House, 1999, p. 117.

19   From *The Book of Rites - The Great Learning*: "If you can make things better for one day, you should make them better every day and never stop doing so!".

20   On August 8, 2008, the author and John Thornton (Chairman of the Board of Directors of the Brookings Institution, of USA) gave a briefing on Mao's views and gave a frank statement, which was met with astonishment.

the world has declined by 0.8%, after the Vietnam War (1965-1975) it declined by 3.1%,[21] being the longest period and the highest falling range. But US has never learned a lesson, let alone "repenting and making a fresh start". In the 21st Century, the US has launched two wars during the first administration term of George W. Bush only due to the 9/11 terrorist attack, the first was the War in Afghanistan (October 2001-December 2014), the second is the Iraq War (March 20, 2003- December 18, 2011). The US scholars have labeled Bush's decision-making as the "rape of the democratic system."[22] If we calculate according to the data of international dollar prices in 1990, the proportion of US GDP compared to the world total has declined by 3.3%.[23] The cost of these two wars were much higher than that of the Vietnam War; the relative cost is roughly the same, and this has obviously accelerated the decline of the US.

Thirdly, US's "crisis is caused by capitalism"

The US capitalism has its inherent disadvantage for the outbreak of economic crises, thus it embodies inevitable concomitants of these crises. The "Great Depression" once occurred in history, and the US Crisis had evolved into a world crisis. The subprime mortgage crisis of the 21st Century,[24] its roots were in the 1990s, the US mortgage credits bubble burst in 2005 -2006, and the mortgage credits default rate rapidly surfaced, and Mortgage-Backed Security (MBS) possessed by the financial companies lost most of its value universally. It was marked by the bankruptcy of New Century Financial Company, the second largest subprime mortgage company in US, an event in April 2007, the crisis spread from the real estate market to the credit market,[25] and then evolved into a global financial crisis. Despite the current slight recovery in the US economy, the US GDP has only reached to 105% of the 2007's GDP figure, calculated at constant price, but total employment ratio was only 97% of the 2007 figure (146.1 million employees).[26]

---

21   Angus Maddison, *Historical Statistics of the World Economy: 1-2008 AD.*

22   Robert Kuttner, founder of The American Prospect magazine, pointed out in 2007: "Our democratic system itself has been damaged to a terrible degree. The Bush administration is arrogant, wrongly launching the war in Iraq, while the US economy is in recession." Robert Kuttner, "The Squandering of America: How the Failure of Our Politics Undermines Our Prosperity, the English Version. The Fall of Great Powers–The End of US Political Decline and Economic Prosperity", Chinese edition, CITIC Publishing House 2009, pp. 242-243.

23   Angus Maddison, *Historical Statistics of the World Economy: 1-2008 AD.*

24   Subprime crisis, fully to say Subprime Mortgage Crisis, is a financial crisis triggered by a sharp increase in domestic mortgage loan defaults and foreclosure property in the United States.

25   Between January 1 to October 11, 2008 US stock holders have suffered a loss of about USD. 8 trillion since the total market capitalization of USD. 20 trillion has fallen to USD. 12 trillion. The average rate of loss was around 40% in the other countries.

26   The lowest figure of the US employment was 139.1 million in 2010. Data Source: International Monetary Fund database.

The US is still under the threat of financial crisis. The US federal government can be called as "contemporary Jia's mansion" who lives beyond its income and survives by borrowing, the proportion of budget deficit of the federal government to the GDP continues to expand, the relative proportion of general government debt in GDP, has raised from 54.7% in 2001 to 76.1% in 2008 in Bush's term, with an increase of 21.4 percentage points; it was raised to 103.0% in Obama's first term, with an increase of 26.9 percentage points compared with that of 2008. This is a typical "After me the Deluge!", and every administration leaves a heavy debt to future generations.

Fourth, US' "excessive military expenditure disease"

The proportion of US military expenditures accounted for more than 40% in the world from 2000 to 2010, and it reached a peak of 44.9% in 2005, equivalent to 1.6 times of the proportion of US GDP in the world's total, and equivalent to 5.2 times of the proportion of US exports in the world's total, still equivalent to 1.78 times of the proportion of US GDP in the world's total (22.0%) even though it fell to 39.1% in 2012, and equivalent to 4.49 times of the proportion of (goods and services) export volume in the world's total (8.7%). This is a typical demonstration of over-expansion and "losses outweigh the gains". Paul Kennedy believed: "if a country allocates a significant portion of its resources not for creating (productive) wealth, but for (non-productive) military purposes, in the long run, it will probably face a decline of national power."

242   Likewise, if a country is strategically overstretched (such as encroaching vast territories and engaging in costly wars), it will take a risk that the potential benefits gained from the outward expansion are likely to be offset by the enormous costs it undertakes. Plus, if such a country is in a period of relative economic recession, this difficulty will become more grave. I also believe that there is a striking "time lag" between a country's economic-strength curve and the military-impact curve.[27] Obviously, the decline curve regarding the proportion of US economy and its export trade volume compared to the world total respectively and the continuous rise of the proportion of US military expenditure in the world's total began to decline, and a "time lag" has emerged.

Why has US always maintained excessive military expenditure? This is because US has an army that is the most powerful and most expensive in the world and deploys a huge number of military bases globally[28] also possesses

---

27   Paul Kennedy, *The Rise and Fall of the Great Powers: Economic Changes and Military Conflicts in 1500-2000*, Chinese edition, International Cultural Publishing House, p. 36, p. 39, p. 42.

28   The distribution of US' overseas military bases can be divided into three strategic areas and 14 base groups. Three strategic areas refer to Europe, Middle East and North Africa; Asia, the Pacific and the Indian Ocean; North and South America. There are 203 overseas military facilities which is located in more than 32 countries and regions in the world, including 102 facilities for its Army, 32 facilities for Navy, 9 facilities for Marine Corps, 50 facilities for Air Force, and the rest belongs to the Ministry of Defense and joint service. US Navy has 331,600 people (not including the Marine Corps), which makes up 6 fleets, namely the 2nd Fleet (Atlantic), the 3rd Fleet (East, South, North Pacific), the 4th Fleet (Central

a huge complex of military industry, which forms two specific interest groups above and independent of US society. They act as each other's "community of interest partner", just as Olsen's definition of "distributional coalition."[29]

On the one hand, the United States Department of Defense and the Army always deliberately exaggerate the global threats, behind which are the strong political needs of increasing military expenditure. This is the so-called the law of military costs increasing day by day. On the other hand, the US military industry needs to get a large number of orders from the Ministry of Defense, in order to survive. This is the so-called law of survival needs increasing day by day. The Pentagon and the Wall Street, both constitute the most powerful specific interest groups in the US which pursue to maximize the national defense budget.

They co-operate in lobbying the US presidential office and Congress, and they are best qualified to speak on the United States Federal Government budget. Although the current Obama administration was forced to cut military expenditures faced by the financial crisis,[30] this has not changed the basic pattern of excessive military expenditures of the US. The United States think tanks do not realize that this is a fatal injury causing the decline of the US, on the contrary they regard this as the advantage for a strong US.[31]

They two major crises of contemporary capitalism: jointly created by wars and military interventions with the pretext of restricting the weapons of mass destruction; secondly the world economic crisis triggered by financial speculation. Neither the generals in the Pentagon nor the financial magnates in the

243

---

and South American Sea), 5th Fleet (Indian Ocean, Persian Gulf, the Red Sea), the 6th Fleet, (Mediterranean, Black Sea), and the 7th Fleet (Western Pacific, Indian Ocean).

29   This quietly accords with "the interest group theory" in the Rise and Decline of Nations: Economic Growth, Stagflation and Social Rigidities (By Mancur Olson, University of Maryland, 1982). It is an important root cause for a country's decline that an interest groups follows the pursuit of maximizing its special interests. The monopoly, conservatism, inefficiency and special interest groups controlling the government are the root causes for the decline of a country.

30   US defense expenditure in the 2013-2021 fiscal year will be forced to diminish to about 500 billion US dollars. It will be reduced by 46 billion in the 2013 fiscal year (October 2012-September 2013), equivalent to about 9% of the defense budget of that year, and it must be completed within the next seven months. The United States had already decided to cut its defense expenditures by about 487 billion US dollars in 10 years. Plus the mandatory reductions, the total reduction will reach about 1 trillion US dollars. China News Service, March 5, 2013.

31   The United States has the most powerful military might in the world, argued by Richard Haas, President of the Council on Foreign Relations Despite the implementation of the automatic reduction plan, the United States core defense expenditure is still as high as 500 billion US dollars, which is higher than the sum of defense expenditure of 10 countries that are close behind it. Its superiority will remain for a long time to come. (US "Washington Post" Website, April 23, 2013) US Economic Strategy Institute, Clyde Prestowitz thinks that US clearly has the most powerful military power in the world, and in any case no country can challenge its status. (US Foreign Policy website, April 29, 2013)

Wall Street can create material wealth, the former destroys material wealth, the latter creates only a virtual wealth, nor both can do any good for the people, the former is engaged in killing innocent people, the latter loots large number of investors and vast number of share holders. Exactly speaking, they are the "initiators" of US's accelerating decline.

IV. Conclusion: the competition among nations is essentially the competition of systems

The competition among the nations is essentially the competition of systems, different systems arise in different times, different countries embody different epochal characters and national characters, they have strengths and weaknesses, rivaling nations coexist while competing. Those vital systems have learning ability, creativity and thus competitiveness; even once being in a weaker and bad position they will also enter into a growth stage and acceleration stage and then reach a strong stage along with the historical course of life cycle of a country. Faced with the international competition, those countries who can't keep up with the times, even the most powerful country will inevitably enter the phase of aging gradually, move towards degradation, and then decline.

Modern US capitalist system which originated more than two hundred years ago has proved its superiority over the traditional feudal system which had lasted for thousands of years, and the United States that emerged in the barren new continent became the world's most developed and most powerful country, and in 1990s it declared "the end of history " after the collapse of the Soviet Union and the end of the Cold War. But the development of history cannot be so simple, but beyond the predictions of the US think tanks, it has entered into a decline period, to a large extent due to the structural problems of "three transformations" (aging, rigidity, degradation) of its system, The US think tanks do not realize this point, and they are still pretentious and arrogant.

The PRC which was founded in the 1940s has created a modern socialist system. In 1956, Mao Zedong wrote: "if we rely on the superiority of the socialist system and work hard for 50 (referring to 2006) or 60 years (referring to by 2016), China can catch up or surpass the most developed capitalist country." namely the US. At that time, Mao Zedong did not know how big the GDP gap between China and US was; he selected the steel output as the criterion. In fact, in 1950, US and China's GDP were 5.94 times apart; it reduced to 4.63 times by 1957, and demonstrated the characteristics of an accelerated catch-up. The author calls this period as the first "golden development period" of new China.[32]

After 1978, Deng Xiaoping not only designed and led the Reform and Opening-up, but also reshaped and improved the party and state leadership and the government system, and the superiority of the socialist system was

32   Hu Angang, *History of Chinese Political Economy (1949-1976)*, Tsinghua University Press, 2011, pp, 45-49.

demonstrated once again, consequently by 1992, the GDP gap between China and US has narrowed to 2.41 times.[33]

Deng Xiaoping initiated the second "golden development period" of the new China, which has been lasting, up until now and greatly shows that China's socialist system is superior to the capitalist system of the US. The author calls it as the "three transformations" of the Chinese system (rejuvenation, advancing with the times, evolution). In other words, China, as a new socialist country, can innovate without being trapped into rigidity and stagnation, can persistently innovate without interruption or premature ending, and can be more innovative without being arrogant or outdated than other rival countries (such as the United States, the European Union and Japan, etc.)[34]

Originally published in the journal Academia, 2014(5)

---

33   Angus Maddison, *Historical Statistics of the World Economy: 1-2008 AD*.
34   Hu Angang, *Chinese Path and Chinese Dream*, Zhejiang People's Publishing House, 2013, p. 81.

From the "US-European Model" to the "Competitive Market System"

— A Debate with Mr. Wu Jinglian

Fang Xingqi

Abstract: Wu Jinglian's "competitive market system" originates from the logical "US-European Model", rather than the actually existing "US-European Model" in the US and European society. It advocates the establishment of a modern "competitive market system" based on the privatization of state-owned and collective economy and the consolidation and development of the monopoly position of Western transnational corporations in China. Such a capitalist modern "market economic system" under the strong controlling force of the western multinationals can objectively only form a kind of dependent state monopoly capitalism. We reject both the old and rigid closed-door policy of the past and any attempt to abandon socialism and follow an erroneous path, instead we should take the path of socialist market economy with public ownership as the mainstay and state regulation.

Key words: privatization; state-owned enterprises; private enterprises; foreign-funded enterprises; US-European Model

Wu Jinglian argues that "China's economic system, which was initially established before the end of the 20th Century, is still a 'mixed system' of 'semi-control and semi-market', and this system is still far short of the meeting the requirement of 'market playing the fundamental role in resource allocation', therefore, "in the economic system aspect, the core issue of further deepening of the reform is still to establish and improve towards a perfect competitive market system, as well as allow the market fully play a fundamental role in the allocation of resources."[1] However, can the "competitive market system" be capable of letting the market fully play a fundamental role in the allocation of resources? This is a question which needs to be discussed with Wu Jinglian.

I. Two Kinds of "US-European Model" in Reality

Wu Jinglian argues that "free-market economic model" refers to the "US-European-Model" which is commonly practiced by those countries with "mature market economy countries." The modern economics science which reflects the motion laws of this economic model teaches that the basic function of the government is to provide public goods, rather than provide private products to the market. An excessive government intervention will hinder the effective operation of the market and breed corruption." "The market economy has much more advantages than the planned economy regarding the effective allocation of resources and regarding the establishment of an effective incentive mechanism. The core mechanism of the market economy system is its market pricing system. The relative prices of various resources formed by the market competition signal the possible best information regarding the scarcity degree of various resources, when there are millions of various resources in the society. The individual members of the society can grasp the competitive trend situations through observing the relative prices of commodities and thus can make the right decisions for resource allocation so as to achieve an efficient allocation of social resources at a relatively low information cost. Meanwhile, each actor who participates the market activities is restrained both by competition and by property right, which can greatly reduce the incentive costs. The combination of the two aspects embodied within, enables the market economy to become a kind of economic system efficient in resource allocation and efficient in operations. Without establishing such an economic system, the resource allocation will lack reliable guidance, consequently the economic resources cannot be allocated effectively, and people's hard work cannot be motivated."[2]

However, the "US-European Model" that Wu Jinglian describes only exists in the textbooks of neo-liberal economics. In the US and European society, the true realistic practice of the "US-European Model" is completely different from the teaching of it in the textbooks.

---

1   Wu Jinglian, Ma Guochuan, *Twenty Issues on China Economy*, SDX Joint Publishing Company, 2012 version, p. 1, p. 254.
2   Ibid., p. 209, pp. 25-26.

Take US as an example, a small number of large enterprises occupy the monopoly positions not only in the domestic economic activities but also occupy such monopoly positions in their global economic activities, thus the "market-determined-prices" are manipulated by such monopoly enterprises to a large extent.

In addition, giant enterprises and governments generally have an "innocent" or "legitimate" money trading and power exchange or power sharing relationship, which points to a legal corruption. Because of the convergence and fusion of interests between the US government and big enterprises (the government uses the economic strength of big enterprises to maintain its dominant status in the global level; these enterprises benefit and use the powers of government to restrict their foreign rivals at home and expand their foreign markets) which constitutes the current state monopoly capitalism in the West. Moreover, under the normal state of economic activity, the government injects large sums of money into big enterprises in the form of incentives or subsidies, R & D support, by purchasing of military equipment. While under the abnormal state of economic activities, the government offers life buoy to those monopoly enterprises which are deemed "too big to fail" in the form of tax reductions, interest reduction, debt guarantee, or buying commercial paper directly and injects equity capital, trusteeship and so on. This is the reality behind the "US-European Model". The situation of "each participant in the market activities is restrained both by completion and by property right" as mentioned above by Wu Jinglian, is inexistent and at least does not apply to those big enterprises which are dominant in the US. The actual economic operation in the US points to a situation where "profits are privatized, and risks are socialized." Therefore, the so-called "social individual members of the society can grasp the trend of competitive situation through the relative prices of commodities and consequently can make right decisions for resource allocation accordingly so as to achieve the efficient allocation of social resources at a relatively low information cost", is nothing but "a myth from ancient Greece."

Even the most determined neo-liberal figure Greenspan has also observed this. In 1996, Greenspan, as the chairman of the Federal Reserve, realized that the US stock market had formed a very dangerous bubble, and has suggested strict measures to cope with this situation.

For this purpose, when he addressed with the topic of Confronting Challenge of Central Banking in a Democratic Society at the US Enterprise Association's annual dinner on December 5, 1996, he stated that the stock market was in an "irrationally prosperous" state, and Greenspan has raised some self-evident questions in his unique way of expression: "But where do we draw the line on what prices matter? Certainly prices of goods and services now being produced—our basic measure of inflation—matter. But what about futures prices or more importantly prices of claims on future goods and services, like equities, real estate, or other earning assets? Is the stability of these prices essential to the stability of the economy? Clearly, sustained low inflation implies less uncertainty about the future, and lower risk premiums imply higher prices of stocks and other earning assets. We can see that in the inverse relationship exhibited by price/earnings ratios and the rate of inflation in the past. But how do we know when irrational exuberance has unduly escalated asset values, which then become subject to unexpected and prolonged contractions as they have in Japan over the past decade? And how do we factor that assessment into monetary policy? We as central bankers need not be concerned if a collapsing financial asset bubble does not threaten to impair the real economy, its production, jobs, and price stability. Indeed, the sharp stock market break of 1987 had few negative consequences for the economy. But we should not underestimate or become complacent about the complexity of the interactions of asset markets and the economy. Thus, evaluating shifts in balance sheets generally, and in asset prices particularly, must be an integral part of the development of monetary policy.[3]

Objectively speaking, Greenspan notices that a laissez-faire stock market leading to economic risk has changed from the traditional inflation to asset price inflation. Regrettably, Greenspan, who is said to be acting as an independent chairman of the Federal Reserve, succumbed to political pressure from the US government and the US Congress, and became "an accommodator during biggest speculative frenzy" in 1997.

In a word, in reality, the mature market economy in US and Europe is only an economic system with imperfect competition, incomplete information and interaction between government and big enterprise. If I quote in a western scholar's words, "US-European Model" is an incomplete market economy, as well as a mixed economic system both under the influence of government and market functions." Particularly worth mentioning is that US's industrial innovation in the 1990s was not the product of "market pricing system" but achieved by the guiding role of government. In the 1980s, the international market share of many Japan's industrial products was far more than that of the US's industrial products, thus accelerating the decline of US economic hegemony. "Japan's interests first" era as exclaimed by the US media, was not far off. In those days also, the western public opinion generally agreed that US era has ended, and the 21st Century would be a Japanese century. In order to reverse this situation, Reagan-administration which had run out of resources due to the arms race could only use non-economic means to curb the rapid development momentum of the Japanese economy. Against the background of the collapse of the Soviet Union, the Clinton administration used the strategic principle of "resources to be invested in the human resources" to replace the strategic principle of "resources to be invested in the military build-up" implemented by the Reagan and Senior Bush administrations. The reason for such a big change was because "the Cold War had ended and the competition between countries had transferred from the military sphere to the economic sphere", and in this

---

3 *Bubble Man*, authored by Peter Hatch: translated by Fan Lifu, Sun Bingjie and Sun Yue, Northeast University of Finance and Economics Press, 2008, pp. 104, 107-108.

sense, it was considered that "US's rival was Japan." Under this strategic policy, the Clinton administration proposed the National Information Infrastructure (Nil) concept similar to the Kennedy Administration's Apollo program, which combined the current computer network with information networks that will be created in the future so as to develop a large-scale US information base. This policy reflected the ambition of the United States to make its artificial intelligence industry become dominant in the world. In order to realize the "Nil" policy, the Clinton administration, on the one hand, promoted military and nuclear science and technology transfer to the civil sectors so as to accelerate innovation in the field of artificial intelligence industry; on the other hand, put the government into a leading status, which would lead the industries, and which would promote universities and scientific research units to form joint research bodies with university-industry-government combination so as to accelerate the development of cutting-edge technologies. Due to the clear target of industrial innovation and government leadership the US became "leader of the worldwide technological innovation and of the artificial intelligence".[4]

Here is not difficult to see that the "US-European Model" adopted by Wu Jinglian from the neo-liberal economics and the true "US-European Style that actually exists in the US and European societies, are two different economic modes. The former is the "US-European Model" imbued by market fundamentalism presented with a pleasant logic, the latter is the realistic pragmatic implementation of the "US-European Model". But it is difficult to understand why Wu Jinglian insists on advocating the hypothetical "US-European Model" as the goal for China's market-oriented reform.

II. The "competitive market system" does not go beyond the logic of the "US-European model"

Zhou Shulian, a CASS researcher has once argued: "the most prominent characteristics of Wu Jinglian's work can be summarized as: the one word—persistence. His persistence is obviously reflected in his work, study and life. Marching to science of market competition operations, learning English, studying western market economics, writing articles, are what he is always engaged in."[5] Through his "persistence" in studying the Western market economics, Wu Jinglian considers himself as a scholar having the "most up to date knowledge of modern economics" (in fact, neo-liberal economics), and fond of being the follower of the "logic of the US-European model".

When he mentions his beloved term as China's goal for him, i.e. the so-called "market-oriented reforms", he surely calls it as the "the US- European Model logic". Wu Jinglian believes that the "free market economic model" which he advocates is the US-European Model logic, which is "commonly

---

4 *US President's Economic Report: 2001*, China Financial and Economic Publishing House, 2003, p. 20.

5 Cited the book by Wu Xiaolian, *My Father and I, Wu Jinglian*, Contemporary China Publishing House, 2007, p. 159.

shared by mature market economy countries." Therefore, it goes without saying that China should become a "mature market economy country" whose "market economy status", would be recognized by the US and European countries, which means that the US-European Model logic should be adopted as the goal of Reform and Opening-up, other models than this model, non-American and European models (including Chinese model) must be completely denied. To this end, he has Sinicized the "US-European Model logic" as the "competitive market system."

Based on the neo-liberal economics of the West, Wu Jinglian has argued that China's market-oriented reform has to establish the "competitive market system" as its core. To this end, an important component of transformation from China's "planned economy to market economy, should be the thorough transformation of property rights system of the planned economy", for a "new property right system." What Wu Jinglian disappointed much is that "during the Chinese reform process, the establishment of new property right system was realized gradually, underwent a long process, differing from that of Russia, Eastern Europe and etc., which have chosen the way of rapid large-scale privatization of old state-owned enterprises and collective farms" Obviously, in the opinion of Wu Jinglian, the large-scale privatization of state-owned economy and collective economy is an important content for establishing the "competitive market system".[6]

Wu Jinglian said, "with respect to the property right system, land property rights have the most far reaching influence because this issue involves most of the population." … In this respect, "the rural reform in China is incomplete." For him the current land contract system is a go-round which maintains the old collective land ownership. What the farmers get is only the land use rights on contractual terms, rather than permanent land use rights with the authority at their disposal, and extending the land contract durations for farmers does not mean returning of the 'land to the tiller' as was practiced in the early 1950s.

Since the farmers haven't got permanent use rights for the contracted land, they lack enthusiasm for cultivating the arable land and do not invest for soil improvements. The implication is clear: the land contract system—in anyway—does not shake the collective ownership. To achieve a thorough rural reform, it is necessary to realize the principle of "tillers gaining the ownership of their farmlands", that is, the privatization of rural lands.

However, Wu Jinglian has made an interpretation on the private nature of rural household contract responsibility system: "From 1980 to the end of 1982, China's rural areas generally implemented 'the household contract system', thus the old people's commune system was eliminated. Due to this household contract system, although the government documents tend to call it as the co-operative economy under the collective ownership category', in fact it has been

6   Wu Jinglian, Ma Guochuan, *Restarting the Reform Agenda - Twenty Talks about China's Economic Reform*, Sanlian Bookstore, 2012, p. 132.

a owner system enterprise established on the land collectively contracted (according to Chinese law, it is called as 'individually-owned enterprises'). Thus, Wu Jinglian has emphasized the private nature of contract economy, the new "rural household based contract system has played the main force to break the dominant status of the old pattern of the state-owned and quasi-state-owned economy."[7]

In Wu Jinglian's view, compared with the incomplete reform of the collective land ownership economy, the ownership reform of state-owned enterprises has to a certain extent, touched the state-owned property system. He wrote: "by the turn of the century, including the township enterprises, most local small and medium sized enterprises had changed their ownership structure, and were no longer subordinated to county and township governments and were turned to independent private enterprises. Also, the vast majority of state-controlled smaller scale secondary enterprises become as multi-shareholder companies, their shares are being traded in domestic and foreign stock markets, consequently with them the power of the market was greatly enhanced."

Until the early 21st Century, "comprehensive restructuring was implemented regarding the small and medium-sized state-owned enterprises, most of which have become individually-owned or corporate enterprises", and on the other side the non-financial enterprises, "the vast majority of state-owned enterprises have been reorganized in two forms as relatively state-controlled companies or the majority shareholding companies."

253

Looking into the financial enterprises, "four major state-owned commercial banks were listed in the overseas stock-markets which has provided the necessary micro-foundation for the establishment of the Chinese financial market." "In addition, "foreign-invested enterprises have formed a new economic sector, their operation have rapidly changed old the market structure and have brought more competition in the market which we have lacked., Besides, they have also helped to break the domestic market segmentation, and accelerated the reform of administrative-led resource allocation system towards the market-led resource allocation system. Therefore, foreign direct investments not only bring the capital we need, and the technology and management needed by China's economic development, but also strengthen the market competition and promote the reform of domestic marketization in the economic system."[8]

In short, "whether the establishment of the rural household based contract responsibility system, or the rise of township enterprises, or the promotion of the individual economy, these reforms have allowed the development of individual owners and allowed them to hire labor, besides opening the door to allow foreign enterprise investments, which all means that the national economy has gradually added a new non-state economic component." Therefore,

---

7   Ibid., p. 201, p. 79, p. 88.
8   Wu Jinglian, Ma Guochuan, *Twenty Issues on China Economy*, SDX Joint Publishing Company 2012, p. 211, p. 142-143, p. 102-103.

"after the household based contract system was put into full implementation, the Chinese agricultural production has showed great development for many consecutive years", and the private enterprises have become "China's major driving force of unprecedented development" On the other hand Sino-foreign joint ventures and wholly foreign-owned enterprises have also become "another major basic driving force promoting China's economic development." In Wu Jinglian's view, thanks to the joint effect of these above elements, in over 30 years "China's economy, has achieved a high-speed growth."[9]

However, Wu Jinglian believes that the reform task of the privatization of state-owned economy is not yet been completed, "many competitive industries are still under the administrative monopoly of state-owned enterprises. Among the industrial and commercial enterprises those listed in the stock market (multi-shared) are mostly the second level- middle size independent private ones, but the big size first level enterprises are still solely state-owned." Therefore, "in the economic system, the core issue of further reform is still to establish and perfect the competitive market system, so that the market can play its fundamental role in the allocation of resources." According to Wu Jinglian: "in the current China, the threat to the equal competitive market conditions mainly comes from two aspects: first, the state-owned economy has monopolized some of the important industries, secondly, the government overly intervenes in the market, therefore further reform should address these two issues."[10]

To be specific, Wu Jinglian advocates targeting argues the economic monopoly of the big state-owned companies: "we must vigorously promote the adjustment of the current layout of state-owned sector of the economy, so that the state-owned capital would withdraw from those competitive industries, where they have not retreated yet," he has added: "we should also promote non state-owned capital as entering into these industries, and promote the diversification of shares of the SOEs, and based on these measures, we should promote the establishment of effective corporate governance mechanism in the SOEs" the long-standing issue of China. Next, he has advocated "the shares (equity capital) of state-owned enterprises should be transferred to the National Council for Social Security Fund[11], thus the individual social security accounts of the old-age workers should be enriched by state owned equity and profits of state owned assets.

Under relevant provisions of the Interim Management Measures on the Investments of the National Social Security Fund, the Interim Management Measures on the Overseas Investments of the National Social Security Fund, the NSSF are permitted to invest in the following products:

---

9   Ibid., pp. 91/3, 90/3.
10   Ibid., p. 143, p. 254.
11   On 1 August 2000, the Central Committee of CPC and the State Council decided to establish National Social Security Fund (NSSF), and set up the National Council for Social Security Fund (SSF) for managing and operating the NSSF's assets. NSSF aims to be a solution to the issue of aging and serves as a strategic reserve fund accumulated by the central government to support future social security expenditures and other social security needs.

1. Domestic investments: bank deposits, treasury bonds, financial bonds, corporate bonds, securitized products, securities investment funds, stocks, industrial investments, industrial investment funds and trust investments.

2. Overseas investments: bank deposits, foreign treasury bonds, bonds of international financial organizations, bonds of foreign entities, foreign corporate bonds, overseas bonds issued by the Chinese government or Chinese enterprises, money market products such as banking drafts and large CDs, stocks, funds, derivative instruments such as swaps and futures, and such other investment products or instruments jointly approved by the Ministry of Treasury and the Ministry of Labor and Social Security.

In parallel to Wu Jinglian, Chen Qingtai, a former government official, has suggested: "we should carry out the capitalization of state owned assets, and transfer currently held shares of state-owned capital in the general industries[12] (currently SOEs control 30% to 50% these industries) to social security funds and other public funds, which means that ownership by the whole people is realized by making them real shareholders."[13]

Finally, Wu Jinglian has further suggested that the state-owned capital should retreat from the vital industrial sectors and key industries which are the lifeblood of the Chinese national economy. Because, in Wu Jinglian's view, "in the current world, it can be said that no country excludes the state-owned sector of the economy, but in most of the other countries, the reason why state-owned enterprises exist, is that they can provide those goods and services which the private enterprises cannot provide or not willing to provide , that is, they are there to provide non-competitive and non-exclusive public goods, SOEs in the other countries are more inclined to act anti-competitively than private enterprises, therefore state-owned enterprises are completely excluded from the "competitive market system."[14] As Wu Jinglian expresses: the completion of the state-owned economic reform, does not mean that he advocates "the abolition of all state-owned enterprises," on the contrary, he suggests "a variety of other forms of public ownership (such as enterprises owned by various forms of funds and foundations, various forms of cooperative organizations, community ownership type of enterprises). He has argued: "exploration and innovation regarding the forms of public ownership should not be limited to Soviet-style state ownership and Soviet-style 'collective ownership' and state ownership should not be evaluated as 'the highest form of public ownership, which should be the inevitable goal of socialist endeavor...", "whether China

255

---

12 General industries are less prone to government intervention, such as agriculture and semi-finished and finished manufacturers. It is exactly the same as what Professor Zhang Weiying said: "the listing of shares of large state-owned enterprises takes long procedures and tiring operations, something must be done to smoothly decrease the shares held by SOEs."

13 Wu Jinglian, Ma Guochuan, *Twenty Issues on China Economy*, SDX Joint Publishing Company 2012, p. 205, p. 255.

14 Ibid., p. 138.

has a socialist nature or not, should not be decided whether it promotes the state ownership or collective ownership. If this view of Wu Jinglian is correct, then, Gates and Buffett's charity funds, and Soros' "open society" funds, all would be the forms of realization of public ownership. This means that feudal socialism, petty-bourgeois socialism, "true" socialism and the bourgeois socialisms, which Marx and Engels criticized in *The Communist Manifesto*, all belong to Wu Jinglian's "more explicit definition of socialism"[15]. Although we appreciate Wu Jinglian's style lacking Marxist theory in the T shape stage, we are aware that Wu Jinglian's ideas repeat the old concepts in a new framework.

At this point, Wu Jinglian has commented: "China should build an inclusive economic system", … "the main features of this system should be: protection of private property (private ownership), creating a fair competition environment (ensure the enthusiasm of individuals and further promote rule by law), encourage investments in the field of scientific and technological innovation." "Otherwise, government intervention into the economy, monopoly and control of state-owned economy" will be further strengthened, the trend of state capitalism will become quite obvious." Wu Jinglian warns: "the so-called state capitalism, is the national capital which takes political power as its fundamental force so as to compete with other form of capital categories, and will inevitably establish a set of political and economic mechanisms that controls the markets", and if we consider "China's historical background and remember that it lacks democracy and rule of law, consequently state capitalism in China will probably convert to crony capitalism, to the "bureaucratic capitalism" as defined by Mao Zedong "comprodor, feudal, and state monopoly capitalism"[16].

At this point, we finally grasp Wu Jinglian's "competitive market system", as the "unique feasible path for China," which embodies such a true intention: China's market-oriented reform should establish a competitive market system, and the main threat to equal competitive market comes from the state-owned economy, which embodies economic and administrative monopoly. Therefore, in order to build a fully competitive market system, the state-owned economy must "retreat from the general competitive industrial sector" and open a free room for the development of non-public economy. Actually, this means, combining the subject, i.e. private ownership group with the market economy, similar to what we know: "empty the cage and let the right birds out", so that Mises and Hayek's capitalist market economy theory will turn to reality in China. Should the dogmatic market economy theory, which will only lead to capitalist market economy, become a reality, will it be able to establish an efficient "competitive market system"? Our answer is no.

Because till today, the biggest monopolist enterprises in China's domestic market is either the magnates which are solely foreign owned US-European based transnational monopolies or Sino-Chinese big corporations. The father

---

15   Ibid., p. 137.
16   Wu Jinglian, Ma Guochuan, *Twenty Issues on China Economy*, SDX Joint Publishing Company 2012, pp. 257-258, p. 211, p. 222.

of hybrid rice, esteemed scholar Yuan Longping, said: "with the further opening of China's markets, transnational corporations have rushed in, and invested in every link of agricultural industry chain, including research of seeds, cultivation, agricultural production, processing, logistics, sales, marketing and etc. and some relevant industries are totally under the control of foreign capital. Except the two principal grains – wheat and rice, whose domestic production is relatively abundant, with regard to soybean and corn, China has turned to one of the biggest importers of soybean, which was the biggest soybean exporter in the recent past, and has also become a corn importer. That means the development of our national seed industry is faced with a grave situation.[17] Besides, 21 most important industries of the national economy: the light industry, chemical industry, pharmaceutical, machinery, electronics and others, etc., in these industries the subsidiaries of multinational companies control 1/3 of their the domestic market shares, regarding a part of the 21 industries, the subsidiaries of multinational companies control 50% of the market shares, which nearly means absolute market control." The control of foreign capital in the domestic circulation/trade industry has reached 80%, and regarding the products such as the mobile phones, computers, the IA server industry, network equipment, computer processors and other industries, foreign capital possesses an absolute monopoly. "The degree of foreign control in the automotive industry is more than 95%, daily chemicals industry is almost completely controlled by foreign funded companies."[18] A more severe situation is that, the multinational companies originating from which possess core technologies, strong brands, global production and sales networks, backed by their governments which enjoy strong positions in the international institutions and international world order, squeeze Chinese industries within the low end ladder of the global industrial chain.

If we completely give up the role of government, strive solely on market rules of competition, whether the state-owned enterprises or domestic Chinese enterprises would not be able survive faced by the competiton of Western monopolies, that means either state-owned enterprises or the domestic private enterprises, their common long term vested interests are threatened by big foreign-funded monopoly enterprises.

We think the main task of the new round of reform is to change this grave situation, rather than the privatization of state-owned enterprises. Because, besieged economically by foreign funded enterprises, both the state-owned enterprises and private enterprises, if faced by the reality of Wu Jinglian's proposition of "SOEs retreating from general industries" should be disaster, just paving the way for the absolute domination of foreign-funded enterprises,

257

---

17   Zang Yunpeng, *The Truth of Chinese Agriculture*, Peking University Press, 2013, p. 1.
18   Cheng Enfu, Fang Xingqi: State-owned Enterprises and Private Enterprises Should Implement Mutually Help, Guangming Daily June 10, 2012; Xu Xuhong: Reform of State-owned Enterprises Shouldn't Be Unilaterally Comprehended as Privatization, published in "Journal of People's Political Consultative Conference" April 17, 2012.

which naturally means that domestic Chinese enterprises will also be the losers in most of the cases. The analysis above does not mean that we advocate "buy goods produced by the Chinese" just as what is advertised by the Americans, or repel foreign-funded enterprises under the pretext of economic security (of course we oppose privileged status enjoyed by the foreign-funded enterprises in China). Instead, we want to emphasize that the new round of reform should consider cultivating a generation of domestic enterprises which can develop their own core technologies, brands and which are able to set up their own global production and sales network, rather than one-sidedly favoring foreign-funded enterprises when entering the domestic markets and render them with advantages in dominating the domestic markets.

The above-mentioned fact "could not be concealed with superficial false appearance" even though so-called "competitive market system" is established by adopting the way proposed by Wu Jinglian, that privatization of state-owned economy and collective economy, it is actually a kind of "state monopoly capitalism maintaining feudal and comprador natures." This is perhaps what Wu Jinglian longing for. he has made it clear that "over 30 years of Reform and Opening-up has brought us remarkable achievements, we've overcome shortage economy, becoming the world's second largest economy. We are not gray outsiders under planning system, but the beneficiaries of civilization at almost same pace with the international community. Such experience is only a tiny case of civilized communication between China and the world, but it eloquently illustrates the possibility of successful open relations, but on the other hand, hostility, tension and other aspects corrupt this civilized relation."Actually, the Westernization Movement period, Northern times, golden decade led by national the government… any rapid development period for China was when it was open to outside world". "What is our goal after our country become prosperous and strong? What are our values after our country become prosperous" where is the key for us to serve the world and human civilization? It is regretful that, these problems haven't been settled, our society has been caught in the successive rounds of the emotions of weakness syndrome. We don't recognize that people in the outside world, treat each other equally, consequently once again to take it for granted that they are conspiring against us."[19] This above comment by Wu Jinglian is enough to show that Wu Jinglian "persistently" defends the monopoly status of thewestern transnational corporations in China, labels those people who oppose foreign monopolies in China as "populists and nationalists", and he argues: "foreign direct investment not only brings in the required capital, technology and management that favor the development of Chinese economy but also promote reform of the domestic market-oriented economic system by strengthening market competition" and "persistently" help us to gets rid of the two barriers of government and state-owned economy, facilitates US and European transnational monopolies marching into our market."

258

---

19   From Zhang Yunpeng, *Agricultural Truth in China*, Peking University Press, 2013, p. 7.

To sum up, what Wu Jinglian advocates is "competitive market system" based on the privatization of the state-owned economy and the collective economy, and the consolidation and development of the monopoly position of Western multinationals in China. Wu Jinglian disagrees to construct modern free "competitive market system", wherein public ownership is the mainstay and the government's macroeconomic regulation is improved and perfected. Is his opinion in line with the socialist economic system with Chinese characteristics, which our Party repeatedly stresses? Doesn't the "unique and possible way" put forward by him belong to "the only possible way out", we should ask, if it does not mean changing our socialist path, and shifting to the erroneous path, which will lead to raising the evil flag , then what is it?

Conclusions

It has been over 170 years since after the 1840, China has gone through such an evolution as follows: China has undergone a great change from the heyday splendid time of the British Empire to its decline and we have seen the decline of the US's hegemony's splendid time, after its peak in 1950s to its decline in 1970s against the background of change of the world's economic and political pattern. During the 19th Century all above developments, has led China to experience the forced opening and then a forced isolation imposed by the western powers, and later China has experienced the historical process of self-opening up. But, Wu Jinglian has turned a blind eye to these world historical changes, and ignores China's national conditions, and responses, therefore he inevitably confuses the old China, New China's first 30 years and the next 30 years preceding the former, besides in these 3 periods the issues of China has changed correspondingly which is ignored by him which reverses the black and white, confuse right and wrong; which also means that he possesses a deep-rooted world view of a petty farmer, for him things are either good or bad, either this or that. Wu Jinglian – a man, who had "yesterday" argued the transition from collective ownership to ownership by the whole people, and transition from socialism to communism people. However, "today", he argues a "modern market economic system" in which the state-owned economy owned by the whole people and the collective economy should be privatized. However, such a "capitalist transition to modern market economic system" implies a kind of "bourgeois socialism" under the conditions that western transnational corporation's strong control on markets and major world powers' strong control on international economy order, will objectively only lead to a dependent state monopoly capitalism.

Marx had put forward a path of socialist development in a largely agricultural country which would the public ownership as the starting point and is as the starting point, and advocated inheriting "all the positive achievements" of the capitalism. Lenin proposed a path of building socialism with Russian characteristics through state capitalism to socialism, he made certain important contributions to Marxism and made an exploration to establish a path of socialism with Russian characteristics. Stalin put forward a single ownership system, i.e. the public ownership, and an economic system which rejects market orientation and the closed rigid path of socialist development. In the 1980s the Soviet Union and Eastern European countries have tried to abandon the rigid path of socialist development, however, they have taken the erroneous path and inevitably changed the leading banner.

Path of socialism with Chinese Characteristics sticks to and develops Marxism—Leninism and Mao Zedong Thought. The scientific socialism practice of more than 30 years of Reform and Opening-up has fully proved, and the future of socialist practice will also further prove: the path of socialism with Chinese characteristics is the fundamental direction of contemporary China's development and progress, only socialism with Chinese characteristics can develop China. We must unswervingly hold high the great banner of socialism with Chinese characteristics, and neither take the old closed and rigid path, nor change our flag and take the errenous, evil path. China can only choose the principle of socialist market economy in tandem with government regulation based on the public ownership as the main pillar. Wu Jinglian has argued: "if the current social trends of China, can be fully, debated argued on a rational platform, this debate will be helpful to promote China's smooth social transformation."[20]

We agree with this point, but the debate argument must be conducted as per the way put forward by Sun Yefang that "we should spare no efforts to advocate, at the same time be eagerly seeking", that is "academic circles could only form a healthy rational debate situation wherein truth is in the first place, and wherein we do not look for the wind direction".[21] We have exactly written this article to respond Wu Jinglian's call for a rational debate, but at the same time we insist in Sun Yefang's above principle, to discuss with Wu Jinglian, if there is any mistake any inappropriate wording in it, and we expect correction of it, but also very welcome Wu Jinglian's counter-debate and counter-criticism.

---

20   Wu Jinglian, Ma Guochuan, *Twenty Lectures on Chinese Economy*, Sanlian Bookstore, 2012, p. 254.
21   Deng Jiarong, *The Scholar Boarded the Millennium Monument: Sun Yefang*, China Financial Publishing House, 2006, p. 315.

References

Ding Xiaoqin, Current Situation, Basic Contradiction and Trend of Contemporary Capitalism Development, *Journal of Economics Study of Shanghai School*, 2007(19), Shanghai University of Finance and Economics Press.

Yang Chengxun, Answers to Some Issues on "Socialist Market Economy, *Journal of Economics Study of Shanghai School*, 2006(14), Shanghai University of Finance and Economics Press.

Cheng Enfu, The Development and Reform Target of the Chinese Macro-economy, *Journal of Economics of Shanghai School*, 2007(17), Shanghai University of Finance and Economics Press.

Fang Xingqi, Mises' Fallacy: Socialism Is Infeasible and Capitalism Is the Unique Way, *Journal of Studies on Marxism*, 2012(12).

Cheng Enfu, Fang Xingqi, State-owned Enterprises and Private Enterprises Should Mutually Help, *Guangming Daily*, June 10, 2012.

(Originally publlished in the journal
Marxism Studies, 2014(1))

Critique of Sustainable Development of Capitalism

Yu Kaihong and Zhao Lei

263

Abstract: In the background of global ecological problems, people began to reflect on the relationship between the capitalist system and the ecological environment. Is sustainable capitalism feasible? As soon as this issue was put forward, it triggered a widespread debate in the academia. Many western mainstream economists have analyzed the ecological problems under the capitalist system from the aspects of economy, politics, science and technology, and finally agreed that under the capitalist system, the ecological problems can be solved, and capitalism can entirely achieve sustainable development. This paper criticizes the view that the technological progress and capitalist system can bring sustainable capitalism, and holds that the capitalist system cannot escape the dilemma of development and escape the economic crisis and ecological crisis. This is also strongly supported by classical Marxism and ecological Marxism.

Key words: sustainable capitalism; classical Marxism; ecological Marxism; ecological socialism

I. The Prescription of capitalist type of sustainable development

Capitalism has been closely associated with economic crises and ecological crises since its inception. Marx once pointed out that in capitalist society "the conflict becomes inevitable, and because it cannot be destroyed before the capitalist mode of production itself is destroyed, so that the conflict is resolved, so it becomes cyclical.[1] At the same time, Marx also predicted that under the capitalist system "capitalist production collects the population together in great centres, and causes the urban population to achieve an ever-greater preponderance. This has two results. On the one hand it concentrates the historical motive force of society; on the other hand, it disturbs the metabolic interaction between man and the earth, i.e. it prevents the return to the soil of its constituent elements consumed by man in the form of food and clothing; hence it hinders the operation of the eternal natural condition for the lasting fertility of the soil…"[2]

The famous US economist John Bellamy Foster has argued that it is this "material exchange crack" which leads to alienation of nature and at the same time alienation of human society: "because what is causing the ecological damage and what is causing the social damage is the same thing: it's the rift in the production system; it's the alienation of nature, which is one with the alienation of human society. In Marx's perspective these things are actually a whole—it's an alienated whole, and we have to restore the integrity of it."[3]

264

Although Marx and his followers thought that the development of capitalism was unsustainable, many Western economists also acknowledged that there are various constraints in the development of capitalism, but also argued that scientific and technological progress in the capitalist world and the corresponding developments in the market system, and with other positive developments, capitalism can fully achieve the sustainable development of capitalism.

(I) The Progress of Science and Technology and the Sustainable Development of Capitalism

The development of capitalism was inseparable from the advancement of science and technology. The first industrial revolution marked by the invention of the steam engine by Watt had rapidly liberated the productive forces and promoted the vigorous development of capitalism. With the establishment of the capitalist system in the world and the rapid development of science and technology, the extensive use of electricity technology as the symbol of the second industrial revolution developed and pushed capitalism from the "steam technology age" to promote the "electrical technology age." The third wave of scientific and technological revolution, which has begun in the 1940s, has greatly promoted the development of capitalist economy, politics and culture and contributed to the emergence and development of state monopoly capitalism.

---

1 *Collected Works of Marx and Engels*, Vol. 3, People's Publishing House, 1995, p. 626.
2 *Collected Works of Marx and Engels*, Vol. 23, People's Publishing House, 1972, p. 551.
3 https://mronline.org/2013/08/07/foster070813-html.

From the three scientific and technological revolutions brought about by the development of capitalism, many Western scholars believe that the further development and application of science and technology will help the capitalist world to overcome the ecological crisis and save the developed capitalist countries, and simultaneously this will also promote sustainable development in Third World countries.

For example, along with the development and innovation of energy sources and new energy production ways, many Western scholars, hold the view that although currently the human beings face the situation that non-renewable resources (such as oil, natural gas, etc.) are limited, but new energy sources and production ways will be gradually discovered, which can better meet human needs for further development, such as the nuclear energy (or atomic energy). Claude Mandil, Executive Director, International Energy Agency (IEA) stressed: "Nuclear energy must be part of our energy mix, firstly, because the non-renewable resources are, so far 20% of the world population doesn't use electricity: secondly, burning fossil energy sources, coal, fuels, etc, produces carbon dioxide but nuclear energy is "carbon-free" source, thirdly, the International Energy Agency has estimated, with the current technological level, the cost of nuclear power production is cheaper than producing electricity energy by using natural gas and coal." Yukiya Amano, Director General of the International Atomic Energy Agency (IAEA), declared in June 2012: "nuclear energy power will play an increasingly important role in sustainable development in the next few decades."[4] Therefore, the International Energy Agency has issued a warning that, if governments do not take immediate actions to save energy, invest in nuclear power facilities and biofuels, the world will "move from one crisis to another." In other words, in order to face the shortage of renewable resources, and to face the possible consecutive crises due to this shortage, we have no alternative than nuclear energy.[5]

Yet, there are some experts who have argued that although the non-renewable resources are in shortage, along with the continuous progress of human science and technology, some renewable resources will replace those non-renewable resources, which will suffice to support the continuous development of human beings, solar and wind energy are such representative energy sources. Hermann Scheer, President of EUROSOLAR–The European Association for Renewable Energy, General Chairman World Council for Renewable Energy (WCRE) a prominent advocate of the "solar energy based world economy," has commented: "For an unimaginable length of time the sun will be bestowing its energy on humans, animals, and plants. And that in such a prodigal quantity that it would be able to meet the most sumptuous energy needs of even drastically growing populations of humans, animals, and plants. Thousands of solar energy enthusiasts derive this hope from the fact that every day the sun supplies the

---

4   Recovery and Decline of The World's Nuclear Energy, http://www.clinaelc.cn/ch—jxzl/2013092581958.htm1.

5   Nuclear Power, The Economist, Nov. 9, 2006.

earth with 15,000 times as much energy as the total daily commercial energy consumption of the human population at present. Under the term "solar energy "they nowadays subsume all sources of energy except the fossil, nuclear, and geothermic ones: the energy of sunshine, wind energy, energy of flowing water, energy from biomass etc."[6]

So, the famous eco-naturalist Barry Commoner boldly predicted that "solar energy cannot only replace a large number of traditional fuels, and traditional sources, but also can eliminate environmental pollution greatly, but also can reverse the rising trend in energy costs, this trend will significantly effect the economic system."[7]

Biomass energy is also a renewable energy source which many experts and scholars are passionate about. The research and development of biomass energy has become an important energy sphere and many governments around the world, have made new investment projects, in this regard: such as the US's biomass energy farms, Japan's Sunshine Project, Brazil Alcohol Energy projects and India's green energy projects. In some capitalist countries, the production and operation of the biomass energy industry has been realized in large scale, such as the United States, Sweden, Austria and other countries, biomass energy into high-grade energy accounts for 4% of its primary energy consumption, 6% and 10% respectively. Brazil, the developing capitalist country, has implemented the world's largest ethanol development technology, with ethanol accounting for more than half of its national fuel consumption. In some less developed countries (e.g. Sudan), biomass energy use accounts for 87% of the country's total energy consumption. Experts estimate that by the middle of the 21st Century, biomass will be able to provide 60% of the world's electricity and 40% of the direct fuel. These data are all that the development and utilization of biomass energy has been a number of global experts and scholars and governments respected, they all agreed that as a clean energy, biomass energy can not only alleviate the global shortage of energy, but also to protect ecological environment from pollution and destruction. Thomas Koberger, former Swedish Energy Director for Renewable Energy and chairman of the Swedish Renewable Energy Council, commented: "We can actually generate significant thermal energy from several waste products, rather than creating environmental problems when seeking more energy sources."

P. Hawken and A. Lovins have pointed to the future of capitalism in regard to innovations and new progress in the capitalist technology. "Imagine for a moment a world where cities have become peaceful and serene because cars and buses are whisper quiet, vehicles exhaust only water vapor, and parks and greenways have replaced unneeded urban freeways. OPEC has ceased to function because the price of oil has fallen to five dollars a barrel, but there

266

---

6   Hermann Scheer, *Solare Weltwirtschaft: Strategie für die Ökologische Moderne*, Berlin, 1999, p. 66.
7   Barry Commoner, *The Poverty of Power, Energy and Economic Crisis*, New York, 1976, p. 122.

are few buyers for it because cheaper and better ways now exist to get the services people once turned to oil to provide. Living standards for all people have dramatically improved, particularly for the poor and those in developing countries. Involuntary unemployment no longer exists, and income taxes have been largely eliminated. Houses, even low-income housing units, can pay part of their mortgage costs by the energy they produce."[8]

(II) The perfection of market system and the sustainable development of capitalism

Many Western economists believe that under the capitalist system, the main cause of ecological problems lies in the market failures, as long as we can find solutions for these "ecological problems caused by market failures", capitalism can achieve sustainable development. Such as green tax, also known as environmental tax, ecological tax, establishment of such new tax forms aims to protect the environment and ecology, to achieve rational and humanly development and rational utilization of the environment and ecology in order to ensure the sustainable development of mankind. A.C. Pigou, father of welfare economics, was the first figure who proposed the green tax idea—the famous "Pigovian tax"—he defined it as: this is a tax on any market activity that generates negative externalities (costs not included in the market price). The tax is intended to correct an inefficient market outcome, and does so by being set equal to the social cost of the negative externalities. In the presence of negative externalities, the social cost of a market activity is not covered by the private cost of the activity. In such a case, the market outcome is not efficient and may lead to over-consumption of the product. Often-cited examples of such externalities are environmental pollution, and increased public healthcare costs associated with tobacco and sugary drink consumption. On the basis of the Pigovian tax, Paul Hawken, Amory Lovins, and I. Hunter Lovins in "Natural Capitalism: Creating the Next Industrial Revolution" have proposed a green tax model which suggests reducing the personal income tax while increasing the gasoline tax (environmental tax) and this suggestion was well received by (conservative) economist, Gregory Mankiw (former head of George W. Bush's Council of Economic Advisors), who argued that: "Instead of the government involving itself directly in employing people to restore the environment, suppose it simply cut income taxes by precisely the amount that it would garner from the gasoline tax. Here is Mankiw's assessment: Cutting income taxes while increasing gasoline taxes would lead to more rapid economic growth, less traffic congestion, safer roads and reduced risk of global warming—all without jeopardizing long-term fiscal solvency. This may be the closest thing to a free lunch that economics has to offer."[9]

---

8   Paul Hawken, Amory Lovins and L. Hunter Lovins, *Natural capitalism: creating the next Industrial Revolution*, Boston: Little, Brown, 1999, p. 5.
9   Article by David Schweickart, Is it possible for sustainable capitalism? International Political Studies, 2009(2).

On the contrary, with such an innovative tax the government can increase the consumption of other commodities caused by the increase of personal disposable income, this will lead to the expansion of many industries, create more new jobs and increase employment figures thus create more financial funds for the budgets.

II. A palliative cure cannot alter the fate of capitalist development

(I) The progress of science and technology cannot fundamentally change the fate of capitalist development

The extensive application of science and technology has promoted the rapid economic development in the capitalist society and the world economy and led to great improvements in the quality of human life. As Marx put it, "The bourgeoisie, during its rule of scarce one hundred years, has created more massive and more colossal productive forces than have all preceding generations together. Subjection of Nature's forces to man, machinery, application of chemistry to industry and agriculture, steam-navigation, railways, electric telegraphs, clearing of whole continents for cultivation, canalisation of rivers, whole populations conjured out of the ground—what earlier century had even a presentiment that such productive forces slumbered in the lap of social labour?"[10] Marx added: "But far-reaching consequences of those (above) effects and changes which are only manifested at a later stage, by gradual repetition and accumulation, are completely ignored"[11], this "far-reaching results" refer to ecological environmental problems of capitalism and the ecological crises caused by these environmental problems, which have occurred in the most developed countries in the 20th Century, has shocked the world, these "eight public nuisance" events[12] have demonstrated that the development of science and technology, cannot directly and spontaneously lead to the mitigation of ecological problems of capitalism, but display a tendency of worsening.

Since then, both the ruling and opposition political parties of Western developed countries have put ecological issues into their policy agenda, and this is one of the important chips for them to win more voter support. But, as O'Connor has argued, the use of capitalist science and technology is based on cost and sales revenues or profits in the first place, and capitalist production cannot be based on ecological principles unless each capitalist or firm believes it to be profitable or unless radical ecological campaigns or new environmental

---

10   Selected Works of Marx and Engels, Volume 1, People's Publishing House, 1995, p. 277.

11   Selected Works of Marx and Engels, Volume 4, People's Publishing House, 1995, p. 385.

12   "Eight Public Nuisance" incidents, refer to the December 1930, the Belgian Mas River smoke incident; May 1943 May-October photochemical smog event in Los Angeles; October 1948, United States of Dornora, Pennsylvania smoke incident; October 1952 Britain London's smoke incident; 1953 Kumamoto County, Japan Minamata incident; 1955-1972 March Itai disease in Toyama Perfecture, County, Japan,; 1961 Japan's Yokkaichi asthma incident; 1968 Japan's Aichi Prefecture and 23 county rice bran event.

laws are not imposed on them. These political parties do not recognize that the mode of capitalist use of science and technology is one of the important causes of the capitalist ecological crisis, but constantly develop and use new science and technology to confront the ecological crisis, such as clean energy is called "nuclear power."

Andre Gorz, a famous ecologist thinker commented: "The nuclear program is not a purely technical choice, but a political and ideological choice,"[13] The idea that nuclear programs can reduce pollution" is a deceptive and dangerous point of view. Because the environmental problems caused by nuclear power production are also very serious, including nuclear radiation, nuclear accidents, nuclear waste, nuclear pollution which can also effect the food chain, etc., will have a huge threat to the natural environment and human itself. In addition, the nuclear waste transport, stacking, handling issues are quite difficult issues, in contemporary capitalist society, there are lots of different types of radiation–photons, electrons, alpha particles, neutrons, and more exotic types. A "shield" blocks radiation by interacting with it. The rate of interaction depends on many things–the energy of the radiation, the composition of the shield, atomic number, etc. But it also depends on the amount of atoms it has to cross, and it is quite hard to completely eliminate such nuclear radiation risks, and it also takes hundreds of years to treat nuclear waste using the cooling method and needs governments' long-term supervision efforts. Shortly after Gorz pointed to the risks of nuclear programs, Chernobyl nuclear accident event shocked the world. According to the Belarusian National Academy of Sciences report: a total of 2 billion people in the world were affected by the accident, Chernobyl nuclear power plant explosion, caused great financial losses for the Soviet Union which amounted to to hundreds of billions of dollars.

Thus, we cannot say nuclear technology is indeed a "clean technology". On the contrary, as Gorz commented: due to political and ideological reasons, high-tech technologies, including nuclear technology, are being advertised by politicians as "clean technologies", promoted and sold all around the world. J.B. Foster also made a profound analysis: precisely that fundamental feature of capitalism is capital accumulation, in order to achieve this goal, it will continue to expand, as long as the technological development is conducive to capital expansion, it will be vigorously developed, and those technologies which are not conducive to capital appreciation will be excluded. Is hydro-electricity a clean energy technology? The answer to this question can be deduced from the current trend that Western developed countries are one after the other demolishing numerous dams. In 1994 the US Government has declared: "The US's era of big dams has ended", strict restrictions on new dams construction was imposed, and the US government ordered to dismantle the 578 dams—andonly in the first 4 years of the 21st Century (2000-2003) 149 dams were demolished, among which 39% percent of the dams were criticized for their destruction of coastal migratory species, causing habitat alteration of the coastal wildlife, and

269

---

13   André Gorz, *Ecology as Politics*, London, Pluto Press.1980 , p. 103.

destruction of watershed ecology.[14] The problem of Reservoir sedimentation problems of the dams has also been an important reason for the dismantling of the dams.

Some experts estimate that the cost of dredging (dredging) is about 20 times as much as constructing a dam with the same capacity. Therefore, whether in the United States or in Canada, Europe and Japan and other developed countries and regions, the Government have dismantled a large number of dams to restore the rivers and the entire basin of the ecological environment. This is not only unique to developed countries. In some developing countries, dams that have been demolished due to ecological and environmental problems, such as in South Korea, Thailand, Africa, Ghana, Uganda and other countries. As Fred Pearce, a British environmental and development expert, has commented: "Today many of the world's largest hydropower dams occupy the best sites for energy production, but their service life will be far shorter than normal coal mines."[15] Fred Pearce added: when these dams will be stopped, their magnificent throats of rivers will be as useless due to global warming just as the pumped-out wells." … "The truth is that if you indeed want to design hydroelectric power as a renewable source, it is almost impossible to be cheap, and if it is cheap, it will be non- renewable."[16] Thus, we can see that hydroelectricity energy source is also not a low-cost clean energy technology, on the contrary, it does not only have a short period of service life, but also requires high maintenance costs, and more importantly this technology is prone to cause a series of ecological and environmental problems, thus can become an important source of ecological crisis.

Since the 1990s, along with the increase of awareness for the environmental protection issues which have continued to spread across the world, the electric motor vehicles as an important invention environmental protection, has been commercialized, the governments have introduced relevant policies to encourage and support the electric and hybrid vehicles production. This new innovation was advertised as the electric vehicles with "zero emission", "high power"; can they really be effective in the protection of the environment, thus enable "green growth"?

The answer is a clear "no" first, the most important and most obvious reason is that the pollution by vehicles of the environment is not only from its combustion of gasoline delivered via the exhaust mechanism. Experiments made by scientists at the Heidelberg Institute for Environment and Forecasting (1993) have demonstrated that only 40% of the pollution by vehicles comes from the "driving" stage, while the other 60% comes from the other stages of utilization, the 54% come from the "pre-driving" stage, 6% came from the scrap stage.

14   Peng Hui, Liu Defu, Tian Bin, "Analysis of International Dam Removal Trend", *Journal of China Rural Water and Hydropower*. 2009(5).
15   Fred Pearce, *The Dammed: Rivers, Dams and the Coming Water Crisis*, London, 1992, p. 226.
16   Ibid.

Before the "driving" stage, the most important is the stage of production, which includes the production of the car itself and the production of its raw materials. Secondly, most of the electricity required for the electric vehicles comes from the coal, on the other side compared to the combustive gasoline-powered and gas powered vehicles, pollution by electric vehicles, are much more serious

Thirdly, the required battery production for the electric cars constitutes a great threat for the ecology. Since the production of lithium-ion batteries or nickel batteries for electric vehicles consumes plenty of iron, copper, rare earth and other mineral resources, the mining, processing of these minerals will bring more ecological damage and environmental pollution. These facts demonstrate that electric vehicles or hybrid electric vehicles which are promoted by R&D and car manufacturing enterprises under slogans of "zero emission" and "high power", and they are heavily lobbying the governments to guarantee their continued support for the expansion of production, they try every means to attract and seduce the consumers, certainly, it gives serious pollution to the environment instead of being pollution free, contrary to what they guarantee to the governments.

Obviously, although the advancement in science and technology can alleviate some aspects of ecological damage caused by capitalism, but from another point of view capitalism brings new ecological and environmental problems, just as hydropower energy, on the other hand although industrial technologies develop and ease some past damages, human population grows geometrically which greatly triggers energy consumption, thus the current energy demand which further reveals the drawbacks in the development dynamics of the capitalist society, as the ecological issues such as climate change, basin climate and river basin problems in many regions of the world, silt deposition, extinction of plant and animal species and many others. In addition, even if the rapid development of science and technology proves to be favorable for the global environment and ecology with the new energy sources and energy-saving products, since the initial investment costs for such achievements are too heavy, and the duration of return on investment is too long, embody high risks, consequently capitalists readily reject such projects. Therefore, the capitalists always do everything possible to defend the oil way of oil which has brought us to this point, and refuse to invest in solar energy and other new energy sources. As David Pepper said, "In the free market system, resource conservation, recycling and pollution control are hampered by the drive to increase productivity and pursuit for maximum surplus value."[17] Thus we can observe that the relationship between science & technology and environment has become a hot issue of academic debate. The shallow ecology, which held the view of technological optimism, and which entrusts its hopes to the development of the technology in resolving the environmental problems. On the other side fully disappointed by the merits of technology in solving the problem there occurred the

271

17   David Pepper, *Ecological Socialism: From Deep Ecology to Social Justice*, Liu Yingyi, Shandong University Press, 2007, p. 107.

technological pessimism. Here, intervenes the deep ecological theory, which has dialectically surpassed the two ideas and combined itself with the Western Marxism studies and established the ecological-socialist theory, which aims to revolutionize the social system by the socialist revolution.

(II) The pursuit of "perfecting" the capitalist economic system is not a panacea to cure the insurmountable maladies of capitalism

On the one hand, the capitalist economic system is based on the private ownership of capital, consequently in order to seek the maximization of personal interests, competition has become and inevitable and "perfect" means. Thus, under the command of the "invisible hand" of competition, such individuals, in order to constantly maximize their interests and their domination over the market, always pursue to find ways in occupying more and more resources and continuously expand the scale of production, so that they can achieve maximum level of output from these resources. This kind of "productionist" capitalist economic system is the drive behind the continuous depletion of natural resources and geometrical increase of market products, which accelerates and deepens the relations between man and nature.

On the other hand, the continuous increase of the production inevitably requires increased demand in the markets in order to guarantee the realization of product value. Thus, the capitalists continuously promote endless consumption and the consumerism culture and consumerist way of life, marketing agents agitate and drive consumers to transfer their value needs to the advertised goods, marketers often capitalize on consumer culture by emphasizing the way a particular good will alter someone's life, thus strive to achieve the purpose of controlling people's inner world. At the same time, consumers also regard consumption as a way of releasing and compensating the oppression and suffering caused by "productionist alienation". "Human beings become weaker and emotionally dependent on the alienated consumption of commodities, attempting to escape the authoritarian organization (coordination) and boredom of alienated labor, thus they become dependent on consumer behavior".[18]

Therefore, in essence, this consumption is not the true consumption, but a "manipulated consumption" and "false consumption"[19], is the alienated consumption. "Alienated consumption is a phenomenon in which people feel imposed to acquire commodities in order to compensate their monotonous, non-creative and often under-paid labor"[20], is the numbness of the consumer spirit and man's self-destruction. As Fromm has commented: "In the nineteenth Century the problem was that God is dead; in the twentieth Century the

---

18   Ben Agger, *Introduction to Western Marxism*, Shen Zhiyi, Chinese People's University Press, 1991, p. 493.

19   H. Marcuse, *One-dimensional Man*, Shanghai Translation Publishing House, 1989, p. 6.

20   Ben Agger, *Introduction to Western Marxism*, trans. by Shen Shen Zhi, Renmin University of China Press, 1991, p. 494-495.

problem is that man is dead."[21] In contrast to above "productionism", it goes without saying that the amount and carrying capacity of natural resources and ecological environment of our planet available for men are limited, production alienation of capitalism and alienation of consumption brought about by ceaseless possession and destruction of natural resources and ecological environment inevitably leads to the outbreak and deepening of ecological crisis of capitalism.

Therefore, as long as the capitalist system is not eliminated, wherein the pursuit of profit maximization as the goal of productionism and consumerism dominates, it is impossible to achieve any fundamental changes in regard to depletion and degradation of natural resources and ecological environment.

III. The Globalization and Burdening of Ecological Crisis by the Developed Capitalist Countries

Marx said, "Capital came into the world, from head to toe, dripping from every pore with blood and dirt."[22] This sentence not only describes the primitive accumulation of capitalism in its early period, wherein capitalist states invaded the weak countries by the gunboat policy, the evil slave trade and full exploitation of the proletariat, and but also describes the exhaustion and plunder of natural resources and ecological environment of other countries.

Therefore, just from the outset, imperialism did not only embody economic and political hegemony by the capitalist countries, but also included the ecological hegemony, which degraded many countries and regions of the world under the colonial yoke of major capitalist powers. They have grabbed raw materials of colonies and exported goods were flooded to them. In this way natural resources of colonies were wantonly exploited and their ecological environment was arbitrarily depleted; all these were the burdening of ecological crisis by the capitalist countries in the early stage of capitalism, i.e. the naked imperialism.

The capitalist system based on free competition cannot eliminate the contradiction between its unlimited desire for profits and limited resources. The ecological crisis is inevitably accompanied by the economic crisis becoming the "magic spell" in the development of capitalism. However, the reality appears to deviate from the theory, so many Western scholars have advocated that the emergence of ecological problems does not lie in the "capitalist system itself", but rather due to "unhealthy business behavior."[23] Therefore, they through a series of political and economic means, Western countries can better solve the domestic environmental problems. There are also many Chinese scholars who

---

21   E. Fromm, *The Sane Society*, The Chinese Literature and Art Publishing Company, 1988, p. 366.

22   Marx, *Das Kapital*, Volume 1, People's Publishing House, 1975, p. 829.

23   Paul Hawken, *The Ecology of Commerce: A Declaration of Sustainable Development*, Shanghai Translation Publishing House, 2007.

believe that "in these countries a kind of ecological civilization has begun to take shape."[24]

At the end of the World War II, a heavy blow was hit to the old colonial system which gradually led to its collapse consequently the blatant colonial plunder of their resources, and ecology has become history, and former possession and destruction was greatly limited.

But due to shortage of domestic resources and their unlimited profit desire, the developed capitalist countries did not abandon the plundering of resources and ecological destruction of backward countries, but shifted their means from direct to indirect, from blatant into subtle ways, thus many people believe that the developed capitalist countries of the North owe a serious "ecological debt" to the newly independent countries. J.B. Foster commented: "the debt accumulated by Northern, industrial countries toward Third World countries on account of resource plundering, environmental damages, and the free occupation of environmental space to deposit wastes, (such as greenhouse gases) from the industrial countries."[25]

Specifically, on the one hand, the developed capitalist developed countries through international trade, transnational corporations and with other means frenziedly looting the natural resources and raw materials products of the Third World countries, but they leave waste, pollution and ecological destruction as a burden to these countries. On the other hand, through the unequal possession and unequal utilization of world's large portion of public goods (such as public waters, air, climate, etc.) they pass the ecological burden—which in fact should be borne by them—to backward countries. Thus, it can be seen that developed capitalist countries—to a certain extent—have eased their seriously growing ecological crisis, by shifting their resource consumption, environmental pollution and ecological damage, through unfair means to the developing countries. Therefore, we can say that the "magnificent prosperity" of the developed capitalist countries "is closely related to the poverty and exploitation of human and natural resources of the whole world".[26]

The "Kyoto Treaty" of 1997, has aimed to save the mankind from the threats of climate warming, however, the US government "declared its unilateral retreat from the Kyoto Treaty" by the excuse that the "Treaty would posit a direct threat to US interests"[27] but in fact the US government aimed to quit "the ecological debt" and continue to transfer ecological crisis to the developing country, as long as possible.[28] Canada government also declared its retreat from the Kyoto Treaty in 2011. The above indicates that the so-called "green

---

24 Wang Hongbin, Western Developed Countries, The Construction of Ecological Civilization Practice, Achievement and its Plight, Marxist Studies. 2011/3.
25 John Bellamy Foster, Brett Clark, *Ecological Imperialism: The Curse of Capitalism*, London: Merlin Press, 2003, p. 193.
26 Ibid., p. 196.
27 John Bellamy Foster, *Ecology Against Capitalism*, Shanghai Translation Publishing House, 2006, p. 60.
28 Ibid., p. 5.

capitalism" and "sustainable capitalism" propagated by the developed capitalist countries are completely deceptive, in fact they are also aware that the so-called "green" and "sustainable" economy they advertise will be realized on the basis of exploiting and pillaging the ecological resources of the developing countries. As J.B. Forster wrote: "as long as capitalism exists, the danger will always be there: 'its destructive impulses' may ... as the primary goal and pursues economic growth at all costs, including the exploitation and sacrifice of the interests of the majority of human beings in the world."[29] At the same time, the developed capitalist countries do not only shift the ecological crisis to the developing countries, but also to the next generations. David Pepper, the British Ecological Marxist wrote: "in fact, in the capitalist economy it is an irresistible trend to 'exploit' resources, just to grab their current value, by discarding their future yields, thus the cost of externalization is transferred to the future generations."[30] That is to say, the next generations will have to shoulder the "ecological debt" caused by the wanton expansion of capitalism. However, the question is, whether the developed countries can really achieve "sustainable capitalism" by their cunning strategy of shifting the ecological crisis? Certainly not. The interconnection view of Marxist dialectical materialism stipulates that each level of matter exists as a type of organization, in which the elements that make up a whole, or system, are marked by a specific type of interconnection, which is objective and can't be changed by the will of men. The developed countries take every possible measure to realize their strategy of transferring ecological crisis on the shoulders of developing country, in their attempt to establish a "sustainable" and "green" capitalism, which obviously denies the interconnection view of Marxist dialectical materialism. Therefore, this "utopia" is eventually destined to collapse, "it brings about disasters to the entire, and digs the grave for itself, as well."[31] The developed capitalist countries, ignoring that the human race and the planet are in unity, interconnected and mutually effect each other, with a short-sighted view of transferring the ecological crisis to the developing countries, which will lead to ecological disasters in some countries or regions; we know that looking from a comprehensive and long term aspect, these ecological disasters will certainly bring about severe "self-defeating" negative consequences the developed capitalist countries, which means digging their own graves. El Nino and the La Nina environmental phenomenon and the greenhouse effect etc., have demonstrated that many environmental problems and ecological disasters, not only affect a certain region, but the entire earth, thus contemporary capitalism is "an uncontrollable force that threatens the whole mankind with ecological crisis"[32], and

275

29   Ibid., p. 3.
30   David Pepper, *Eco-socialism: From Deep Ecology to Social Justice*, Translated by Liu Ying, Shandong University environment and ecology, which is obviously not sustainable, Publishing House, 2007, p. 105.
31   Chen Yongseng, Foster's Criticism of Ecological Imperialism and Its Enlightenment, *Journal of Scientific Socialism*, 2009(1).
32   Joel Kovel, *The Enemy of Nature: The End of Capitalism or the End of the World?*, New York: Zed Books, 2007, p. XI.

"unsustainable in terms of human development".[33] When criticizing the capitalist agriculture (certainly including the exploitation and utilization of other natural resources – Note by the author), Marx wrote: "Capitalist production… disturbs the metabolic interaction between man and the earth… All progress in capitalist agriculture is a progress in the art, not only of robbing the worker, but of robbing the soil; all progress in increasing the fertility of the soil for a given time is progress towards ruining the more long-lasting sources of that fertility… Capitalist production, therefore, only develops the technique and the degree of combination of the social process of production by simultaneously undermining the original sources of all wealth—the soil and the worker."[34]

In other words, any development of capitalism, in fact depends on the price paid—i.e. the destruction of humankind's survival environment and ecology, it is obvious that such development is unsustainable.

IV. As Affirmed by Marxism: Capitalism Will Extinguish

Although Marx and Engels did not exclusively study the issue of relations between human and nature, the relationship between human and ecology and the contradiction between them under the capitalist system, they have profoundly disclosed and criticized the greed and the anti-ecological nature of the capitalism in their several works, with numerous statements. Marx pointed out: Accumulation for accumulation's sake, production for production's sake: by this formula classical economy expressed the historical mission... of capitalism,[35] which leads to the situation that "capitalist production… disturbs the metabolic interaction between man and the earth, i.e. prevents the return to the soil of its constituent elements consumed by man in the form of food and clothing; it therefore violates the conditions necessary to lasting fertility of the land".[36]

Thus, "capitalism only develops the techniques and the degree of combining of the social process of production by simultaneously undermining the source of all wealth—soil and the worker."[37] Finally, with the continuous development of the capitalist industry and business, "the industry and commerce has provided various means of using land, which has given rise to increasingly barren land".[38] Hence, Marx warned capitalists to respect the laws of nature: "if the human progress plan which is not made according to the natural law, it will bring about the disaster".[39]

33   Paul Hawken, Amory Lovins and L. Hunter Lovins, *Natural Capitalism: Creating the Next Industrial Revolution*, Boston: Little, Brown, 1999, p. 1.

34   Marx, *Das Kapital*, Vol. 3, People's Publishing House, 1975, pp. 552-553.

35   Marx, *Das Kapital*, Vol. 1, People's Publishing House, 2004, p. 652.

36   Ibid., p. 579.

37   Ibid., p. 580.

38   Marx, *Das Kapital*, Vol. 3, People's Publishing House, 2004, p. 916-917.

39   *Selected Works of Marx and Engels*, Vol. 4, People's Publishing House, 1995, p. 383.

Meanwhile, Engels also warned that "Let us not, however, flatter ourselves overmuch on account of our human victories over nature. For each such victory nature takes its revenge on us. Each victory, it is true, in the first place brings about the results we expected, but in the second and third places it has quite different, unforeseen effects which will exceed our achievements."[40] Therefore, it can be seen that "the productive forces developing in the womb of bourgeois society create the material condition for solving this contradiction", and "the material condition for solving such contradiction" is displayed as unavoidable ecological problems under the capitalist system.

Following the footsteps of Marx and Engels, many western scholars have continued to analyze, have further summarized and deepen the thoughts in regard to relationships between human and nature, between human and ecology under the mode of capitalist production. The Western Marxist scholars represented by Frankfurt School have proposed that the ecological Marxism constitutes an important branch of current study of the Western Marxism thought trend. The ecological Marxism concentrates on analyzing the contradiction between human and nature, between human and ecology under the capitalist system, they generally agree that the alienation of relationship between human and human, between human and nature will inevitably lead to the degradation of ecology and ecological crises and unsustainable capitalism. The source of ecological crises is the capitalist system itself, therefore, the ecological socialism thought trend actively advocates the numerous ideas of Marxism in regard to nature and ecology Marxists. Just as Saral Sarkar wrote: "Only if we wipe out the capitalist system and establish a real socialist society successfully, our earth can be saved. Therefore, it is desirable and necessary to establish a new eco-socialist society. This inherent contradiction between private economic rationality and common weal including that of the children and future generations is the strongest argument for socialism. The alternative policy proposal of eco-socialists should be based on this fact."[41] This new type of socialist society should aim at establishing a green and fair ecological socialism. According to the propositions of ecological Marxists and ecological-socialism, most of them envisage that imagined that under the eco-socialist social system human and nature will be in equal footing and will interact harmoniously.

The ecological-Marxists have highlighted that the relationship between human and nature deteriorates due to alienation of both in production and consumption spheres, which inevitably lead to ecological crises. Hence, the development and utilization of the natural resource and ecological environment must be properly planned so as to coordinate with the human interest and ecology benefits under the ecological socialism. Meanwhile, eco-Marxists define ecological socialism as the principle of unifying the economic development with the ecological criteria. They believe that in the ecological socialism

---

40   Ibid.

41   Saral Sarkar, *Eco-Socialism or Ecological Capitalism*, translated by Zhang Shulan, Shandong University Publishing House, 2008.

the relationship between the economic development and ecology must be so handled that the capitalist production principle should be abandoned—which means surpassing the capitalist production principle which follows the law of maximizing economic benefits should be completely transformed and enable that the economic development of human society should meet the requirements of ecological development, accordingly ecological criteria should be used in restraining and restricting the production (as well as consumption).

Therefore, the ecological Marxists have appealed: humankind should all to the principle of "development reduction", which means reducing the scale of the production and consumption, and strictly reject profit-driven and excessive production and excessive consumption, in this way we should enable that the human's economic rationality pursuit will be consistent with the ecological rationality, all of which are contents of ecological socialism. Furthermore, ecological Marxists have also created some important ideas in regard to social and political spheres, they adhere to the grass-roots democracy and participative democracy system, and oppose hegemonism and power politics.

V. Conclusion

Western economists have been the apologists of the capitalist system since its emergence, and have always attempted to prove that capitalist system will survive forever. However, it can be seen that the economic crises erupting from time to time, since 1848 have demonstrated that the eternal capitalism was just an illusion not true, and Marx has conducted a comprehensive scientific analysis in *Das Kapital* that the capitalism would be finally replaced by socialism. Although, Marx and Engels have criticized the economic crisis of capitalism, it continues to move forward with some self-adjustments, however it cannot avoid severe ecological crises, thus ecological crises has become another cancerous tumor which will determine the fate of capitalism, second after the economic crises. Many bourgeois economists have racked their brains to prove that the ecological issues could be solved through technological innovation, institutional innovations and other kind of reforms in the framework of capitalist system, but they have not only employed a selective approach which neglected the profit-seeking nature of the capitalist system, but also concealed hegemonism and power politics of capitalism which are closely related with the global ecological issue, plus the ecological imperialism which is most often conducted by developed capitalist countries.

On the basis of adhering to the analysis paradigm of Marxism, ecological Marxism has proposed the charming idea of ecological socialism, the views of ecological socialism do not only deny the contemporary capitalist system, but at the same time provides important references and advices for China and other socialist countries that can be utilized in their process of building socialism.

References

Selected Works of Marx and Engels, Vol. 1, People's Publishing House, 1995.

Selected Works of Marx and Engels, Vol. 3, People's Publishing House, 1995.

Selected Works of Marx and Engels, Vol. 4, People's Publishing House, 1995.

Selected Works of Marx and Engels, Vol. 23, People's Publishing House, 1972.

Karl Marx, *Das Kapital*, Vol. 1, People's Publishing House, 1975.

Karl Marx, *Das Kapital*, Vol. 3, People's Publishing House, 1975.

Paul Hawken, Amory Lovins and L.Hunter Lovins: *Natural Capitalism: Creating the Nest Industrial Revolution*, Boston: Little, Brown, 1999.

Fred Pearce, *The Dammed: Rivers, Dams and the Coming World Water Crisis*, London, 1992.

"Nuclear Power", *The Economist*, Nov. 9, 2006.

Barry Commoner, *The Poverty of Power, Energy and Economic Crisis*, New York, 1976.

André Gorz, *Ecology as Politics*, London. Pluto, 1980.

Hermann Scheer, *Solare Weltwirtschaft: Strategie für die Ökologische Moderne*, Berlin, 1999.

Paul Hawken, Amiory Lovins and L. Hunter Lovins, *Natural Capitalism: Creating the Nest Industrial Revolution*, Boston: Little Brown, 1999.

Joel Kovel, *The Enemy of Nature: The End of Capitalism or the End of the World?*, New York: Zed Books, 2007.

Ben Agger, *Introduction to Western Marxism*, translated by Shen Zhi, Chinese Renmin University Press, 1991.

Herbert Marcuse, *One-Dimensional Man*, Shanghai Translation Publishing House, 1989.

David Pepper, *Eco-socialism: From Deep Ecology to Social Justice*, Translated by Liu Ying, Shandong University Publishing House, 2007.

Erich Fromm, *The Sane Society*, Chinese Literature and Art Publishing Company, 1988.

Saral Sarkar, *Eco-Socialism or Ecological Capitalism*, translated by Zhang Shulan, Shandong University Publishing House, 2008.

Paul Hawken, *Business Ecology: Declaration of Sustainable Development*, Shanghai Translation Publishing House, 2007.

David Schweickart, Is Sustainable Capitalism Possible?, *Journal of International Political Studies*, 2009(2).

John Bellamy Foster, Brett Clark, *Ecological Imperialism: The Curse of Capitalism*, London: Merlin Press, 2003.

John Bellamy Forster, *Ecological Crisis and Capitalism*, Shanghai Translation Publishing House, 2006.

Chen Yongsen, Foster's Criticism of Ecological Imperialism and Its Enlightenment, *Journal of Scientific Socialism*, 2009(1).

Peng Hui, Liu Defu and Tian Bin, Current Status Analysis of Dam Demolitions across the Global, *Journal of China Countryside Water Conservancy and Hydropower*, 2009(5).

Wang Hongbin, "Practices, Achievements and Difficulties of Western Developed Countries in Building Ecological Civilization", *Journal of Marxism*, 2011(3).

(Originally published in the Journal of
New Theoretical Trends, 2014(6))

Trend of International Economic Crisis and Capitalism: From the Angle of Class Analysis

Zhu Andong and Cai Wanhuan

Abstract: The class analysis is an important methodology of Marxism Economics as well as an essential viewpoint for correctly understanding the problems of the capitalist society. Using this methodology we can analyze the new changes in the class structure of the capitalist countries before and after the 2007 crisis, thus we can grasp the development trend of the capitalist system, in the post-crisis era to broaden our understanding with a new perspective. The class structure before crisis was as follows: the capitalist class, particularly the financial capitalists, had expanded, and the laborer class had weakened, and the middle class was quite squeezed. And the class structure after the crisis displays the following characteristics: the financial capitalist class wasn't weakened in real terms instead its class power continues to swell, the middle class continues to weaken, the public is awakening, and the class power of the laborers force growing, but we can say that there is no power which can challenge capitalism. On the basis of above class analysis, we can say that the western capitalist countries will not take the path of social democracy road in the short term as in the period of post-World War II, instead big capitalist class will turn right. However, the proceeding beyond capitalism is a historical trend and eventually the socialist movement will gain its strength.

Key words: International financial and economic crisis; class analysis; class structure; middle-class

As the most serious economic crisis since the Great Depression of the 1930s, the international financial and economic crisis continues since 2008, and has not yet completely got out of the quagmire. Well, can the financial and economic crisis be solved? When will it be resolved? In which direction will the capitalism evolve? This article will attempt to use Marxist class analysis method to analyze the new changes in the class structures of the capitalist countries before and after crisis so as to grasp the development trend of the capitalist system, in the post-crisis era to broaden our understanding with a new perspective.

I. Introduction: Importance of Class Analysis

From the perspective of Marxism economics, the source of international financial and economic crisis is the basic contradiction of capitalist system. Neoliberalism has been carried out since 1970, which has led to the suppression of the laboring class, enlarged the gap between the rich and the poor, promoted the financialization of the economies, and sharpened the major structural contradictions of the world economy, caused over-capacity in the global level and a series of other problems. The impact, duration and influence scope caused by this crisis is such grave that the theme of the first workshop in the Davos Forum of 2012 was the "Capitalist Crisis—Social and Environmental Justice." Great Debate for Capitalism", and nearly half of the figures which took the speaker stage have argued that capitalism can't deal with the challenges of 21st Century.[1] Francis Fukuyama, who had advocated that "capitalism was the end of human history", evaluated the current capitalism which has fallen into a quagmire had to admit that: growing inequality is the phenomenon which poses an important challenge to capitalism.[2] Whether this crisis indicates the end of the capitalist system, and how it will affect economic and social development in the western countries, and on the question of what trends will this crisis trigger in the capitalist system, there are mainly two viewpoints and theories among the scholars: one argues that capitalism will not perish, instead capitalism will make certain adjustments within the framework of capitalist system.

While the second view argues that capitalism will be replaced by a new society. Richard Pomfret, who holds the former viewpoint, wrote: many previous crises were relieved through adjustments in the financial market and by strictly adopting certain macroeconomic policies, this crisis is no exception and will be solved by similar ways, such policy adjustments are conventional in the evolution of the capitalist system, thus it will not lead to the decay of capitalism.[3] Gerard Duménil and Dominique Levy held that: after the failure of neoliberal mode of capitalism, there are three possible directions in the future

---

1   Doubt the Centralized Outbreak of Capitalism in Western Country, and Discuss about Which Mode can be Selected from, uploaded on Xinhua Net on January 30th 2012, refers to http://new.xinhuanet.com/world/2012—01/30/c_122629711.htm.

2   Sick Western, All Walks of Life Begins to Introspect the Capitalism, uploaded on Xinhuanet on February 11 2012, refers to http://news.xinhuanet.com/2012—02/11/c_111512355.htm.

3   Richard Pomfret, "The Financial Sector and the Future of Capitalism", in: *Economic Systems*, Vol.34, No.1, 2010.

development of capitalism. The possibility of the "middle-left" route or solution and extreme-right militaristic route is lesser, the most possible route would be the so-called "new corporate capitalism" (Managerial Capitalism). Those who have originally advocated neo-liberal mode and the "small government" model, are now shifting to support the "Managerial Capitalism" mode. That is the entire economy will be regulated and managed by the major bankers and big capitalists in such a way that, the interests of big capitalists will be maintained, and they call it the "middle-right" route.[4]

Among those who hold the latter viewpoint, David M. Kotz, argues that in several years to come this crisis can provide opportunities for us to organize the left route, and find a realistic alternative to replace current capitalism.[5] Giovanni Arrighi has argued that China's development path which is independent from the US and Europe and quite different from theirs can provide a kind of alternative to the capitalist system.[6] Ximena de la Barra has argued global power center is passing through a severe structural contradictions and crisis which particularly destructs the environment and human development which can promote a coalition between the two movements, and which can lead to a post-capitalist alternative to the current capitalism, i.e. an "emancipatory agenda" based on grass-root social movements which aim a harmonious development between man and nature such an allied movement has emerged in Latin America, which is called as the "Socialism of the 21st Century" by Ximena de la Barra.[7] Li Minqi has argued that there is a close relation with the degree of development of global class struggle and the prospects of current crisis of capitalism. Three results may occur in the course of development of the global class struggles: firstly, the world capitalist system may be adjusted successfully, and the global economy will continue to follow the mode of endless profits in production and accumulation; secondly, the world capitalist may be overthrown; the global class struggle may aim at establishing a new global system, which will be built on the basis of the sustainable production and for basic needs of all humankind.[8] The analysis of the international financial and economic crisis by western theorists has gone deep into the analysis of the capitalist system itself. As a result, a great deal of fruitful discussions and propositions were put forward on the root causes, mechanism, characteristics and development trend of the current crisis; however, there are relatively a few literature which study the current capitalism from the perspective of class analysis. This article aims to provide a new perspective in the analysis of capitalist development trend by

283

---

4 See Gerard Duménil, Dominique Levy, *The Crisis of Neo-liberalism*, Massachusetts: Harvard University Press, 2011

5 David M. Kotz: "The Final Conflict: What Can Cause a System-Threatening Crisis of Capitalism?" in: *Science & Society*, Vol.74, No.3, July, 2010, pp. 362-379.

6 Giovanni Arrighi, Adam Smith in Beijing, *Social Sciences Academic Press*, 2009.

7 Ximena de la Barra, "Sacrificing Neoliberalism to Save Capitalism: Latin America Resists and Offers", in: *Critical Sociology*, Vol.36, No.5, 2010.

8 Minqi Li, "The End of the 'End of History': The Structural Crisis of Capitalism and the Fate of Humanity", in: *Science & Society*, Vol.74, No.3, 2010.

comparing the new changes in the class structure of capitalist countries before and after the crisis by using the class analysis method of Marxism. The class analysis method is an important analytical method of Marxist economics. The scientific conclusion reached by Marx in his three volumes of *Das Kapital* was summarized in the last Chapter of Volume III as follows: whether the class is divided on the basis of occupying the fruits of others by possessing the means of production. In capitalist economy, the capitalist and working classes are corresponding products adapting for the capitalist mode of production; the class struggle is inevitable; this internal contradiction of the capitalist economic relationship must be solved by the class struggle, which is inevitable, so as to promote the progress of human society. Therefore, in this sense all social histories are involved into the class struggle.[9]

The class analysis methodology is also an important perspective for correctly understanding the social problem of capitalism. The root cause source of this international financial and economic crisis is the basic contradiction between the relative low consumption capacity of the working class and the constant expansion of production and the wealth increasingly concentrating in the hands of the capitalist class, and the huge amount of consumption credits offered by the banks, certainly can't solve this contradiction. I think, without the class analysis, it is impossible to find the root cause of the crisis, thus the way out and solutions to the crisis cannot be found. Western governments—according to prescriptions proposed by mainstream (bourgeois) economics, are applying a series of economic stimulation plans, including fresh capital injection to those companies and banks which are in severe crisis in order to rescue them, and apply tax reductions to them, they reduce public expenditures reduction etc., which are not only generally ineffective, but which further intensify the class contradictions. The "Occupy Wall Street" movement in the USA which has lasted for several months in 2011 and the protests and strikes throughout 2012 in the European continent, once again demonstrate that many economic and social problems will not be solved by class ignoring class differences and class contradictions; thus many economic and social policies to counter the crisis will not bring effective solutions, on the contrary more likely to be counterproductive.

II. Changes in the Class Structure of Capitalist Countries from 1970s to the Period before the 2007 Crisis

In the period after the World War II, major developed capitalist countries have rapidly recovered their economies and achieved a fast growth for a certain period, and the class contradictions were relatively relieved, which is known as the so-called "golden age" of the world capitalism. This is closely related to a series of social democratic policies adopted by capitalist countries since they have felt the ideological threat posed by the socialist camp led by the Soviet Union; at the same time such "golden age" was related to infamy of

---

9   Refer to *Collected Works of Marx and Engels*, Vol. 2, People's Publishing House, 2009, p. 43.

liberal capitalism and the defeat of Fascism and rise of democratic demands by the people for active democratic participation, more political and economic rights.[10]

In the "golden age", the policies of western governments were guided by Keynesian economics, tone of the purposes of which was to maintain the unemployment rate at a low level for a long period in the future; and the developed countries have basically achieved this goal. Under these circumstances, expectation and ability of workers to struggle for higher wages were strengthened; the real level of workers' wages have also risen rapidly, even higher than increase in the labor productivity, all have which has caused squeezing of capitalist profits, consequently an economic crisis occurred due to squeeze of capitalist profits. On one hand, the decline in profit rates made the capitalist class unwilling to invest, which led to economic stagnation. On the other hand, the ability and expectations of workers struggling for higher salaries, and their real wages have risen, in turn individual capitalists have resorted to increase the prices of products in order to guarantee their profit shares and profit rates. If every capitalist act in this manner, the general price level will certainly increase. Due to strong collective negotiation ability of the workers, the rises in the product prices could be compensated by the wage increases, which has formed a vicious circle of alternately increases: once wages and once commodity prices.

Under such a background of "stagflation" as we have defined above, Mrs. Thatcher ascended to power in 1979, and in the US, Reagan ascended to power in 1980, the two events paved the way for the large scale practices of Neo-liberal economic policies. Neo-liberalism, is the economic doctrine which maintains the interests of monopoly capital class, particularly the financial capital stratum, which uses various means to exploit and re-exploit the workers both within and outside the production process. Neo-liberalism has attacked the right of the labor class, and reduced the real wages of workers, expanded the gap between the rich and the poor, and sharpened the state of insufficient consumption by the lower classes, promoted the global overcapacity in the production facilities, simultaneously it has led vicious, cut-throat competition among the capitalists and further financialization, all of which have intensified the basic contradiction of capitalism and led to the eruption of a new crisis.

(I) Expansion of the class power of capitalists, especifically the financial capitalists

Since the state machinery serves as a tool for class rule, the policies made by the western governments aimed at safeguarding the interests of the capitalist class, which we can obviously observe in the period before the 2007 crisis. For example, US government has always sold the mining licenses to big companies with lower fees. There is one clause in the bill issued by US government which aims to provide medicare benefits to public, but this special clause

10 Li Minqi and Zhu Andong, Brief History of World Capitalism Development: 1870-1973 and *Theory Front of Chinese Higher Education Institution*, Vol. 6, 2005.

stipulated that the government should not bargain with the drug manufacturer for the medicine prices, which is an obvious favor to pharmacy manufacturers; it is estimated that such favors has reached to 500 billion USD in 10 years.[11] Furthermore, US is quite keen in designing its foreign policies with many warring situations as a means of foreign policy, the purpose behind such foreign policies is to serve the interests of the monopoly-capitalist class, but this causes a severe contradiction between the monopoly-capitalist interest group and those who pay the costs of militarization. For example, US has initiated a war against Iraq in the name national security, and used the money paid by tax payers for buying weaponry from the arms dealers and manufacturers. After the Iraq war, the monopoly-capitalist groups such as the giant petroleum companies gained massive profits by obtaining oil drilling privileges, but the whole war costs were borne by the ordinary US people.

Since the 1970s, the rapid development of the information technology has given the capital high degree of mobility and liquidity, which has provided the technological basis and material conditions for the globalization and financialization of the capital. At the same time, the neo-liberal policies have promoted various restrictions to eliminate and reduce the interest-seeking activities conducted by the government and people, and promoted certain institutional basis and policy guarantee to push forward globalization and financialization of capital. Although the financial sector of the economy doesn't create value, but it can allow to make lucrative profits by attracting more capital investors and by crating financial bubbles, consequently financial sector is the beloved sector among the rent-seeking capitalists. Because only in the financial capital form, can the capital be free from the shackles of its material form, and can achieve maximum mobility and liquidity. In this way financial capital can fully display its nature of pursuit for maximum value appreciation. When the capital form transforms to financial capital form, there appears a differentiation in the capitalist class, and the "predator class" is formed, i.e. the financial capitalist class. This class basing itself on the financial capital can control and lead the capitalist production and can use its great advantage to regulate and distribute the profits of the whole capitalist class, and compared with the industrial capitalist class, the financial capital possesses greater advantages.

In this period, not only the internal class structure of the capitalist countries is changed, but the wealth polarization among the countries of the world has become increasingly grave, the 8% as the richest group in the total world population possesses 50% of the whole revenues in the globe, while 1% richest in the total world population possesses the 15% of the whole revenues.[12] The strong wave of economic globalization has incorporated all the countries of the world into the capitalist system; thus the capitalist classes of the world with common interests have formed a global capitalist class, but contrarily economic globalization has not led

11   Joseph Stiglitz, *Inequality Cost*, China Machine Press. 2013. pp. 191, 65, 9, 196.
12   Joseph E. Stiglitz, "Inequality is a Choice", in: *New York Times*, October13, 2013, see http://opinionator.blogs,nytirnes.corn/2013/10/13/inequality-is-a-choice.

to global mobility and movement of the labor force has not occurred, consequently the pattern of strong capital class and weak labor class has been consolidated.

(II) Squeeze of middle class between 1970s to 2007

The term "middle class" in the strict sense doesn't belong to the Marxist Economics. In line with the classic elucidations of class concept made by Marx, Lenin has commented that income of a person does not determine his/her class status, instead the scientific basis to determine a person's class status should be based on the possession of the means of production or possession of the fruits of others' labor.

The generation of so-called "middle class" concept cannot refute Marx's arguments on the general laws capitalist. Let's take the professional company managers as an example, judging their dual status, we can say that, their wages also include the exploitation, i.e. surplus-value grabbed from workers. Moreover, the middle class in the western capitalist countries is different from those in the developing countries, especially different from China.

As the core countries of the world capitalist system, they use their advantages in the spheres of economy, politics and military in order to constantly acquire surplus-value from the other countries of the world, which makes it possible for some part of the working class in these countries to share the surplus-value acquired by their capitalists. Judging this reality, Lenin has vividly described these workers in the highly developed countries as the "labor aristocracy", i.e. the so-called "middle class" in the contemporary western society.

At the beginning of the 20th Century, Lenin has pointed out that the capitalist development entered into the imperialism stage, and that most of the territories of the world has been basically partitioned among the great powers, and the monopoly bourgeoisie of these great powers cultivate the labor aristocracy class by buying the upper-strata of workers by using a part of excess profits obtained by domestic and external exploitation. Consequently, Lenin pointed out: "This "stratum of workers-turned-bourgeois, or the labour aristocracy, who are quite philistine in their mode of life, in the size of their earnings and in their entire outlook ... are the real agents of the bourgeoisie in the working-class movement, the labour lieutenants of the capitalist class; which make them close their eyes to the poverty and bankruptcy of the poor masses."[13]

Therefore, this article doesn't agree with the term "middle class", and for the sake of simplicity for the reader, this article borrows this term to refer to the stratum of the working class that "enjoys" relatively higher income. In the contemporary western countries, the term "middle class" is frequently mentioned. Generally, there are two criteria when defining the middle class: firstly, the group which earns income through high degree professional knowledge such as attorneys, scholars-teachers and doctors, etc,; secondly, they define it by the annual revenue earned by a single person, e.g. a person earning annual income of USD

---

13   *Collected Works of Lenin*, Vol. 21, People's Publishing House, 1990, pp. 259-260.

40,000 to 250,000 is considered as a member of the middle class. Before the 2007 crisis, the financial capitalist class further transfers the revenue to capitalist class during consumption through using several means such as consumption credits to workers, and made some worker groups become their victims by implementing of greedy credit receiving conditions (with high interest rates) and by over issuance of credit cards for everybody. In this way the real disposable income of a worker for her/his personal consumption has stagnated or decreased, which has further intensifies the contradiction between the capital and labor.

Furthermore, in the pre-crisis period, the bubble status in the stock market has encouraged the residents to borrow more and more from the financial institutions with the slogan of "fortune effect". With the rapid rise of housing and stock prices, those who have borrowed from financial institutions have felt that they have become prosperous people, and have decided to borrow more and more. Consequently, the debts borrowed by each US household have increased violently, which accounted the 130% of their disposable incomes. Only between 2004 to 2006 alone, each US household borrowed US 840 billion of home credits, from financial institutions through mortgaging houses. Once the housing prices fell dramatically, the middle class members which have borrowed for buying houses will be likely forced to insolvency and thus lose their houses.

(III) The class force of the laborers has weakened

Since 1970s, under the guidance of neo-liberal doctrine, the western countries have taken a series of measures (e.g. direct attacks against the labor unions, and they have relieved controls upon the labor market, etc.) to fight against the laboring class and to ensure maintaining profit rates for the capitalist class. All have which have caused decreases in the member numbers of the labor unions, to the increase of unemployment rate, and the decline in their real wages, consequently the income gaps among the population of the developed capitalist countries have enlarged, which has aggravated class contradictions.

Since the labor organizations were strongly attacked and weakened, consequently there occurred the decrease in the number of labor union members. Over the past 30 years or so, most countries have experienced a drop in the membership rate of trade unions. The membership rates of US labor unions had seen a sharp rise before and during the World War II, and had increased from 10% to nearly 35%. However, with the prevalence of McCarthyist anti-communism policy after the World War II, the effect of labor unions were weakened and has decreased to 25.3% in 1975, and declined to 11.4% in 2010 they were frustrated by a more serious attack by Neo-liberalism. The union membership rate in the private sector of the economy is lower, was less than 7% in 2010. According to OECD statistics, from 1978 to 2008, the average membership rate of national labor union has decreased from 34% to 17.9%.[14]

---

14 Data source: Economic Cooperation Organization website (http://statsistics.oecd.org/index.aspx):

Alongside with the weakening of labor unions, the wages of workers were pushed down in order to establish a competitive labor market, a consequent of which was the reduction of wages. Many governments have consciously increased the unemployment rates in order to reduce the inflation rates and to stabilize their economies. Compared with the past periods, the unemployment rates in the US have drastically increased in the Neo-liberal period, and the unemployment rate has exceeded 10% after financial and economic crisis. The unemployment rate in Europe has also been high since 1990s in a long period.

Due to high level of unemployment rates and the decline of labor union forces, the fighting capacity and fighting will of workers in many countries have diminished greatly, thus real wages of workers also showed a downward trend. Influenced by financial crisis, the real hourly wages of US workers are still under the 1973 levels. During the neo-liberal period, in the other western countries, the real worker wages ceased to gain increases, or even declined. The conditions in the developing countries is even more tragic. In short, the neo-liberalism aims to safeguard the interests of capitalist class, especially the financial capitalist class, resulting in the expansion of financial capitalist class, the squeeze of "middle class" and the increasingly deterioration of life condition of worker class; the fortune is further collected by the capitalist class, and the status of working class including the middle class is lower than the "golden age" after Second World War. Paul Krugman, has summed this situation as follows: "there is no purely economic reason why we cannot reduce inequality in America, we should put time back, and reverse those policies which trigger inequality." "we can put time back to the era of Great Depression (1929) where tiny numbers of tycoons ruled."[15]

III. Class Structure Changes that Occurred in Capitalist Countries since the Outbreak of the 2007 Crisis

After the crisis, the western countries have neither realized the drawbacks of neo-liberalism nor implemented any measures to adjust the unreasonable class structure caused by the neo-liberal policies, on the contrary, the policies and measures taken by western national government have continued to exacerbate this unreasonableness.

(I) The financial capitalists group were not hit in real terms, besides the right-wing forces have expanded

After the crisis has erupted in the initial phase, all governments took measures to "rescue markets" successively, and made rescue plans to save a batch of companies mainly including the large-scale financial enterprises, in fact the content of this policy was using public funds to save the international monopoly capital which is led by financial capital, i.e. the perpetrators of this crisis.

15　Paul Krugman, *What Happened to America?*, CITIC Publishing House, 2008, p. 7.

In the short term, these measures have indeed avoided the collapse of international financial system and prevented serious decline in their economies, but these measures has increased the public debt of major western countries to an unprecedented and unsustainable level, resulting in the crisis of sovereign debt.

Although the crisis counter-measures taken by western governments can be described as short-sightedness, but such counter-measures have greatly favored the capitalist class and big companies.

In order to stimulate the economic growth, most of the governments carried out the tax reduction plans for businesses, beneficiaries of which were the rich. Take the US for example, the maximum business tax rates was decreased from 70% in the Carter administration period to 35%, later in the Bush administration period, the tax rate for capital gains was considerably reduced. By 2007, once again, the tax rate for capital gains was decreased from 35% to 15%, because as we know the common people, which account for the 90% of the population, only obtained less than 10% of the capital gains.

Such the decrease for the rich only brought very little positive effect for the common people, but on the other side such measures have made 400 most richest man in the US increase their average annual incomes by USD 45 million in 2007, and USD 30 million in the 2008.[16]

In the third quarter of 2010, all US enterprises gained a profit of USD 1,660 billion, which has been the world record, unprecedented for decades. Since after carrying out the "rescue markets" counter-measure, the rich people have encountered a comeback, the income concentration towards the minority rich was elevated to a higher level, 95% of the incomes were grabbed by the richest 1% of the total population, while those who make the 0.1% of population grabs 60% of the whole income, and their annual incomes exceeded US 1.9 million.[17]

Instead of facing frustration, the financial capitalists were favored by the crisis, they have further expanded their interests by the virtue of the above government measures, including the tax reduction policies. Just as what Warren Buffett-the investor—has commented: "There's class warfare, all right, but it's my class, the rich class, that's making war, and we're winning."[18]

When various economic and social crises occur, ruling classes need to make concessions, but today many western ruling classes are unwilling to compromise, which causes disputes between the ruling parties, and a political impasse has occurred in many countries. For example, in the US the Republicans and Democratic Party didn't compromise with each other so as to safeguard the interest of capital groups they represent, consequently, the annual budget wasn't approved in 2014, and the none-core department of the US Federal Government

---

16 Joseph Stiglitz, *Inequality Cost*, China Machine Press, 2013. p. 191, p 65, p. 9 and p. 196.
17 Paul Krugman, "Rich Man's Recovery", in: *New York Times*, September 12, 2013, see http://www.nytimes.com/2013/09/13/opinion/krugman-rich-mans-recovery.html?ref=paulkrugman&_r=0.
18 See http://www.nytimes.com/2006/11/26/business/youmioney/26every.html.

was closed for 16 days due to this situation from October 1th 2013. This situation was repeated for 2 days in June 2018.

Under the background of depressed economic situation, the right-wing forces have expanded, i.e. US's newly established Tea Party which promotes conservative economic policies has conducted several protests, advocating that the government should reduce the scale, expenditures, tax and weaken the regulations and supervision. With regard to Japan being trapped in recession for a long period, extreme right-wing forces have continuously expanded, and Japan's military expenditures has increased in order to divert the domestic crisis. On September 25 2013, Shinzo Abe, the Japanese Prime Minister even described himself as a "far-right militarist" in a speech he gave in the US.[19]

(II) The middle class continues to be squeezed

Although, in absolute levels, the worker wages of the developed capitalist countries are much higher than the age of Marx and Engels, although especially the living conditions of the middle class are greatly improved, but the status of workers, as the instruments of labor has not changed. Normally, improvement in workers' wages is brought about by the development of times, but the very increases in worker wages is related with the value of labor-power. However, the essence of worker's "relative poverty" is that the worker wage can only be equal to the value (price) labor-power. In this sense, we can say that, the workers of the contemporary developed capitalist countries, i.e. the so-called middle class is still in "poverty" since they don't have the means of production.

The US has always regarded itself as a middle-class country, but currently the members of middle-class has decreased greatly, and currently when we compare the group in the bottom which do the jobs which require less skills and the upper group which do the jobs which require higher skills, the difference between the two groups is disappearing, consequently the "good prestigious jobs" which only belonged to the middle class in the past is bygone. This phenomenon is called as the "polarization" of the labor force, or the "polarization" of the labor market.[20]

With the disappearance of this kind of former middle-class "good jobs", the general wages level has declined, and the wage/income gap between the capitalist class and the middle class has enlarged. The "polarization" in the labor market means that on the one hand the capitalist class earns more, and on the other hand those who belong to the middle-class have slipped to the bottom.

The 2007 crisis has led to the reduction of profit channels for the capitalist class, thus in order to safeguard their own interests, part of the profits which they shared with the middle class, in the past is decreased, which has put the middle-class into a difficult situation. Generally, they are faced with

19   Shinzo Abe, You Can Call Me As A Far-right Militarist, from Sohu Net on September 27th 2013, see http://news.sohu.com/20130927/n387327318.shtml.
20   According to the data from US commercial investigation bureau, the rate of poverty in the US was 15% in 2011, and the poor people has reached 46.2 million.

unemployment, reduction of wages, depreciation of housing prices and lack of social security, etc. The status of middle-class has become vulnerable, and a failure to pay a single installment of a mortgage loan may cause them lose their homes. Such homeless state may result an unemployment for them and lead to the breakdown of their families. Currently, the homes of about 2 million residents have lost their homes due to non-performed loans. And, the mortgage loans value, borne by 23% of the US families is higher than the real market value of these homes, also about 50 million US citizens don't have health insurances, and a single person who is faced with serious illness, may negatively affect the living condition of the whole family and push them into an under-class.

(III) The people are awakening, and the power of labor class is growing, but still far from forming a real challenge against the capital

After making huge capital injection to "rescue the market" as a counter-crisis measure, the western countries have generally adopted expansionist monetary policies and tight fiscal policies. The expansionist monetary policies when implemented in tandem with "loose monetary" policies and injecting excess liquidity into the markets has not brought the expected effect on the real economy. If we can call such "loose monetary policy" as an "ineffective short-term remedy", we can say that the tight fiscal policy is equivalent to "thirst-quenching drink" which just makes you feel good.

Since, the western countries attribute the outbreak of the sovereign debt crisis to the fiscal deficits caused by high social welfare expenditures by the government, they have designed counter-measures to reduce government expenditures, wherein the main part of the reduction is related with social welfare expenditures. This inevitably deteriorates the difficult life conditions of the middle and low income groups. If the people's tax payments are used by the governments for "rescuing markets" and rescue the "failed big companies", when a crisis occurs, and people face social welfare reductions, this situation can only be described as "robbing the poor to benefit the rich". This will inevitably further intensify the polarization between the rich and the poor in these countries, gradually and increase the number of poor population,[21] and cause the stagnation of consumption, and further deepen the crisis. Currently, the unemployment rates in these countries reflect the performance of the real economy to a certain degree. According to the data provided by the website of the EU Bureau of Labor Statistics, the unemployment rate of entire EU has reached 11.3% which is a historical record, an increase of 1.3 percent points compared to 2011, the average unemployment rate of 17 Eurozone countries has reached 12.5%, an increase of 1.8 percent points than a year ago. The worst condition has occurred Spain, and the unemployment rate in this country has reached 26.6% by January 2013, and the unemployment rate of the youth under the age of 25 has reached 55.5%.[22]

---

21   Joseph Stiglitz, *Inequality Cost*, China Machine Press, 2013. p. 191, p 65, p. 9 and p. 196.
22   See   http://epp.eurostat.ec.europa.eu/tgm/table,do?tab=table&-language=en&pcode=teilm020&tableSelection=1&plugin=1.

In fact, none of the crisis measures taken by the US government has aimed to improve income distribution between the workers and capitalists, among the four fiscal policy bills after the crisis, there is only one bill which aimed to promote employment conditions but even this reform was financed by government funds and didn't hurt the capitalist class. Although the fiscal policies of western governments directly addresses the insufficient effective demand, they attempt to increase the effective demand through reducing taxes; however, compared with investment increase, the multiplier effect of the tax reduction policy is much smaller, and this measure of increasing effective demand through improving the revenues of big companies and improving the incomes of individuals will hardly solve the difficulties of the US economy due to excessive indebted situation of the US government; because the newly added revenues are often used for relieving the debt pressure of the government instead of promoting new consumption and new investment.

With the deterioration of life conditions, the class contradictions have also intensified, thus various protests, parades, demonstrations and strike events are taking place one after the other and the financial and economic crisis is gradually evolving to a social and political crisis. In 2011, the movements such as "Occupy Wall Street" and "Occupy London" has been occurring in an endless stream in Europe and in the US, the protestors are shouting the slogans of "you saved the banks, while we are betrayed" and "levy tax to Wall Street instead of targeting the poor", which express the feelings of common people in the US.

On November 14, 2012, the members of labor unions from 23 European countries have taken the streets, and protested the austerity policies, the number of protestors has reached many millions which has become the largest one in the history of Europe.[23] However, the negative image of failed socialism in the last decade of the 20th Century is not repaired, and the true path of transcending capitalism hasn't established yet, consequently these protest movements can't form a force which can shake the capitalism order, as we have seen in the first half of the 20th Century, therefore the general trend of strong capital and weak labor has not changed.

IV. Trend of Adjustments in the Capitalist System after the 2007 Crisis from the Perspective of Comparison of Class Forces

Before the outbreak of the recent international financial and economic crisis, the western countries have self-proclaimed that they were aiming an "olive form" of inclusive society, wherein the rich class and poor class were much lesser than the middle- class. They have advertised their polices as pro-middle-class, and middle-class as the pillar of social stability, and they have advertised that forming the "olive form" of inclusive society is an important basis for whether a country or region can achieve a sustainable development as well as a major precondition for achieving a high-quality democracy.

23   Joint Strike by 23 European Countries, uploaded on Observer Network on November 15, see http://www.guancha.cn/europe/2012_11_15_109588.shtml.

However, a series of counter-crisis measures taken by western countries before and after crisis has brought about the following influences: the "olive form" inclusive society of middle class was transformed to the "sand clock form" wherein capitalist class has constantly strengthened its class power, the power of the middle-class was squeezed and has slipped to the bottom, towards the working class at the bottom of the society. And a bi-polar class structure formation is gradually strengthening. This kind of "sand clock" class structure have caused the following three development trends in the western world.

(I) The western world will not follow the social democratic path in a short-term as occurred in era of post-World War II

Except those special monetary crises which solely occur on the basis of money credit irregularities, most often, the essence of capitalist economic crises occur due to the contradiction between infinite expansion of the production and relative poor purchasing power of the working class. And these crises generally results in sharpening and intensifying the class contradictions in the capitalist countries.

Therefore, when such crisis occurs, the capitalist countries always takes ameliorative measures to adjust the labor-capital relations within the framework of capitalist system in the process of solving the crisis such as: promoting collective bargaining between capitalists and labor unions, launch moderate wage increases for workers, establish a relatively perfect social welfare system, etc.

One of the most typical example, is the social democratic policy implemented by north European countries such as Sweden and Norway. In fact, the social democratic policy includes some adjustments in private ownership plus adjustments in the secondary distribution , i.e. in regard with the private ownership of the means of production, the social democratic policy insists on the capitalist system of private ownership and in the secondary distribution, the government adjusts the excessive high incomes by virtue of tax increases for businesses and launching transfer payments to the needy groups, in order to narrow the gap between the high-income and low-income groups, consequently aims to establish horizontal coverage of all social classes and vertical social welfare system "from cradle to grave", in this way superficially a seemingly a harmonious situation occurs between labor and capital, plus , and a relative stable social structure is aimed formulated as "two smalls and one big in the middle." After the outbreak of the recent international financial and economic crisis, many western people and scholars have cherished the memories of the "golden period" of capitalist development in the period after the World War II, and demanded that the governments should take measures resuming the social democratic policies in that era.

When the international financial and economic crisis first occurred in the US as a subprime crisis in 2007, US and European governments attempted to adopt some reforms to limit high incomes of big company executives, and attempted to increase the incomes of the poor classes, and tried to improve the level of social expenditures, so as to overcome the crisis. When the US government provided huge rescue funds to the Wall Street's big finance companies, to rescue the market, Obama has publicly criticized the greed and irresponsibility of the Wall Street company executives and decided to limit their annual wages, and urged the US congress to issue a new payroll tax system and unemployment relief payment acts, and intensively promoted the Medicare and insurance reform in favor of the lower classes, and advocated to improve the social welfare level of US's common people, etc. However, the social democratic path just aims to relieve class contradictions, maintain economic stability and thus maintain the capitalist class rule, consequently such measures as above may only temporarily ease the problems, but cannot solve basic contradictions. And also such relief measures can only work on the premise that the economic development is in a good shape, therefore such transfer payments as secondary distribution will not endanger the overall interests of capitalists. Once the crisis occurs, and the profit rates decline, since the means of production is still in the hands of capitalists, they will easily give up sharing a part of their profits by others, and will discard the social democratic system.

In the process of solving the recent international financial and economic crisis, we observe that in general US has carried out some limited social democratic measures, but in the main the government has adopted pro-big capital policies whose results were not satisfactory as follows: on one hand, the economic depression continues, and the level of employment has not resumed the pre-crisis level ; on the other hand, as the government is ongoing the policy of capital injections and tax reduction policies, these have caused the sovereign debt crisis. Therefore, US right-wing forces represented by the Tea Party began to propose some limited social democratic policies, they have urged the government to reduce budget deficits, cut the size of government debt and substantially reduce social security and welfare expenditures, which will negatively impact the living standards of the low income groups. Also in Europe, similar measures and reasons have led to the outbreak of the sovereign debt crisis; the right-wing forces of Europe also target the welfare state system of Europe, and argue that the excessive welfare expenditures lead to lack of motivation for economic development and cause heavy debt pressure to be borne by the government, thus they constantly attack the welfare policies. Faced with the offensive and attacks of the right-wing forces, the governments of the developed countries (both in the USA and EU)—given the current background of strong capital and weak labor—may possibly opt the path of "robbing the poor in favor of the rich", which lays the foundation for the further intensification of the basic contradiction of capitalism, in the near future. From the facts above, it can be seen that the capitalist countries will not opt for the social democratic path in the short-term.

(II) Big capitalists class is turning further to right

After the outbreak of this international financial and economic crisis, right-wing forces in some of the capitalist countries have not only failed to analyze the root causes of the crisis, instead they advocated a strange combination of relations between supply and demand situation, i.e, reduce deficits and tax reductions. They have argued that the deficit reduction can increase the confidence among the people towards the governments and towards the economy, and the tax reductions can improve the economic efficiency, and put the money in the hands of those who are good at spending it.[24] According to these right-wing elements, the reduction of deficits and tax cuts will mean significant reduction of government expenditures and shrinkage in the scale of government scale (small government fetish), the current facts indicate that such policies have been included to the agenda of European and US governments.

Currently, the capitalist governments display such trends in their policies as follows: in the aspect of domestic affairs, the right-wing elements not only demand the shrinkage of the government sizes, but also demand and reducing public expenditures and tax cuts. In the foreign policies, on the one hand they promote unilateralism, and create certain threat theories, i.e. terrorism threat from the failed states, to promote war-like situation and expand the domestic armament, thus aim to shift people's focus to foreign issues and curtail the domestic conflicts. The above two policies are led by the big capital class, and serve their interests. During the Cold War, the US used the "Soviet threat theory" as an excuse, to allocate large sums of funds to equip its military forces.

After Cold War, the former hostile powers can no longer pose a military threat to US, but still the US has been to increase its military expenditures, developing its military equipment and continues to establish new military bases all over the world. After the "9/11" event, US promoted the pre-emptive attack strategy and launched the Iraq and Afghanistan Wars, etc. and frequently militarily intervened the internal affairs of other countries with pretext of "human rights", which resulted the Libya chaos and the so-called "Arab spring" turmoil. These indicate that the reinforcement of US hegemonism and militarism is not related with its ambitions to strengthen and consolidate its military hegemony status, globally, but also closely related with the domestic big military industry interest groups. Particularly, after the recent international financial and economic crisis, the economic hegemonic status of the US has been challenged, the new newly emerging economies have shown a good performance, and the world economic pattern is gradually changing, therefore US feels it must rely on its arms to maintain its status of economic hegemony. That is to say, US has opted for the path of "military Keynesianism".

The "military Keynesianism" pursued by the US inevitably causes impulse for wars and collisions. The war policies stimulate the growth of US economy, increases its military expenditures and expands the demand to its military

---

24　Joseph Stiglitz, *Inequality Cost*, China Machine Press, 2013. p. 191, p 65, p. 9 and p. 196.

equipment, and promotes the production in its military industry which in turn stimulates its economic growth. According to US official government data, the contribution of the military expenditures to the real GDP growth of the US since the 21ˢᵗ Century is much higher than the 1990s, and has constantly increased. The contribution rate was 0.14 percent points, when the US launched the Afghanistan War in 2001, increased to 0.28 points in 2002, and to 0.36 points in 2003 when it launched the Iraq War, but has fallen to 0.07 percent points in 2005 and 2006. However, after the crisis, contribution rate was realized as increases in 2008, 2009 and 2010, respectively as 0.36, 0.27 and 0.22 percent points.[25]

Before the recent crisis, class forces of the capitalist class was even more swollen than post-World War II era, it has occupied an absolute dominant position in the fields of economy, politics, military and culture in the western capitalist countries. After crisis, the capitalist class reinforced its activities of exploiting surplus-value, and mobilized government public fiscal funds to save itself, and in order to further attack the working class forces, and in order to squeeze the middle class. However, this has been a short-sighted behavior which can't be continued in the long- term.

The source of the current crisis is the excessive gap and contradiction between the working class and the capitalist class, alongside with crisis, the behaviors of capitalist class and the demands of the right-wing elements have further exacerbated this contradiction, the consequences of which will inevitably lead to class collisions and cause economic stagnation and social unrest situation.

V. Transcendence of capitalism is a historical trend

Capitalism, which is a particular stage of the development in human society, has historically contributed to the great development of productive forces. But, when all the productive forces that the capitalist system can develop and embody are fully released,the capitalist system has become an obstacle to the further development of the productive forces. Marx wrote: "The development of Modern Industry, therefore, cuts from under its feet the very foundation on which the bourgeoisie produces and appropriates products. What the bourgeoisie therefore produces, above all, are its own grave-diggers. Its fall and the victory of the proletariat are equally inevitable."[26]

This historical law has proven itself, since the early 20ᵗʰ Century, thus the decline of capitalism and the rise of socialism have become an irreversible historical trend.

It can be seen by a horizontal comparison that socialism has shown and will further demonstrate its superiority in solving the various contradictions brought by the development of capitalism for several hundreds of years. The October Revolution and the rise of socialism after World War II, many countries have

25 Economic Report of the President, 2011.
26 *Works of Marx and Engels*, Vol. 2, People's Publishing House, 2009, p. 31, p. 43.

embarked the path of socialism and have made great economic and social achievements. After suffering from huge income polarization, frequent outbreaks of economic stagnation, economic crises and social unrest economic stagnation, caused by neo-liberalism, Venezuela began to implement the 21st Century socialism; Bolivia began to implement the communitarian socialism; and the Latin American countries such as Brazil and Argentina adopted a kind of socialist reforms to a certain degree, which have achieved important changes in their economic and social development and bettered the people's living conditions in these countries. After the outbreak of the recent crisis, the demonstrators of the "Occupy Wall Street" movement and the Great Strike movement by the workers of 23 European countries have also demanded change towards socialism.

The demise of the capitalist system is inevitable. Marx wrote: "It is one of the civilizing aspects of capital that it enforces this surplus-labour in a manner and under conditions which are more advantageous to the development of the productive forces, social relations, and the creation of the elements for a new and higher form than under the preceding forms of slavery, serfdom, etc."[27]

The development of capitalism economy objectively creates the conditions for the birth of socialism. At the same time, however, we should realize that capitalism will never perish automatically. The capitalist class, in order to maintain system of private ownership of the means of production and appropriate the surplus-value will need to use several tools of state and state violence to relentlessly suppress the movement working class movement. Therefore, it is necessary to develop the struggle of labor class and sharpen its class consciousness.

After observing the change in working class's power before and after crisis we can say that, on the one hand, the revolution of the information technology has significantly improved the productive forces but on the other hand, causes the "de-skilling" of the workers, thus the subordination degree of labor to capital further deepens, and the exploitation degree of the labor deepens, and the trend of workers' "relative poverty" becomes more obviously. After the crisis the middle-class is squeezed and many of its members have slipped to the working class ranks, which has further strengthened the class power of the workers. The transformation from "olive form" to "sand clock" distribution structure means that the constant expansion of two poles in class structure of western countries continues and the class contradictions are constantly the sharpening. Only if the consciousness of the working class encounters awakening from class-in-itself to the class-for-itself, the change from capitalism to socialism will be a reality.

Originally published in the journal
Contemporary World and Socialism, 2014(1)

---

27 *Collected Works of Marx and Engels*, Vol. 7, People's Publishing House, 2009, pp. 927-928.

How to Understand the "Large Market and Small Government" Mode of Western Market Economy

He Zili

The "large market and small government" mode of western market economy is a common policy hailed by the western developed countries. This article analyzes the basic features, institutional causation and limitation of this market economy mode, and seeks favorable inspiration for correctly understanding the relationship between the government and market, thus aims to propose several ideas for perfecting and improving the socialist market economy system on the basis of summarizing and absorbing its experiences.

I. The Features of the "Large Market and Small Government" Mode

The "large market and small government" mode of the western market economy, embodies the private ownership and wage labor system as its basic economic systems as well as the foundation for the entire market economy system, wherein the market plays a leading role in allocating resources, and the only function of government is to provide public goods and services: such as the establishment of the social welfare system, the maintenance of the market order, and limited macroeconomic intervention. And the government doesn't directly intervene in the social and economic activities. Specifically, this system is characterized by the following most notable features:

Firstly, the private ownership and the wage labor system have had dominant position. At all of the different development stages of western capitalist market economy, the private ownership as the foundation of market economy has never changed, and only the realization form of private ownership has seen several changes in phasal development. Beginning from the early capitalism period to contemporary capitalism, the small scale individual private business organizations integrated their ownership with the management right, the stock company system has separated the ownership from the management right, and the global multinational corporations has mostly become the properties of the private ownership economic organizations. The impetus for this model is to pursue the maximum interest and profit of private capital, which is decided by this model; all systems under this model are arranged for the interest and will of the private capital.

Secondly, the role played by the private enterprises in the decision-making is more influential than those played by the governments. The economic decision-making power is highly centralized by the private enterprise considered as the core for making decision; the decision for the new products, purpose, quantity, and means of production is taken by the private enterprises; and the allocation of production factors and distribution of final yield are realized through independently signing agreements by themselves. The status of government decision-making can be different in some periods, but in general doesn't exceed the leading role of the private enterprises.

Thirdly, the market plays a decisive regulatory role in the process of resource allocation. The private capital plays as a dominant force in the implementation of the "large market and small government" mode of the western market economy.

The decision for private capital was made according to the price mechanism, supply and demand mechanism and competitive mechanisms such as market regulation so as to decide what will be produced and the purpose, the quantity, and the means of production. The western countries advocate the self-regulating function of market, and hold that the market can effectively allocate the resources through the price signal mechanism plus the supply and demand mechanism. In case of the economy fluctuates or even falls into a depression, which is generally considered as a temporary phenomenon, the market would bring the economy to equilibrium, recovery and prosperity. Therefore, the government intervention should be extremely limited. When the economic fluctuation or crisis becomes excessively fierce, and the economy is trapped into a recession status, the western countries always use the fiscal and monetary policies to intervene, however, the intervention degree is so limited that they cannot achieve the expected results.

II. Reasons behind the Formation of the Western Market Economy Mode of "Large Market and Small Government"

The "large market and small government" mode of the western market economy was formed with the objective necessity through the economic system, political environment and bourgeoisie ideology rather than being accidental.

Firstly, the capitalist economic system is based on private ownership and the wage labor system. The economic order allowing laissez-faire and free competition is supported by the private capital, which instinctively resists and opposes to any institutional arrangement that restricts the maximization of the private interests under the condition of private ownership and the wage labor system. Therefore, as long as the private ownership and the wage labor system are implemented, the economic system mostly preferred by the private capital is the free market economy; only with the implementation of the free market economy, it can be possible for the private capital to lead and govern the resource allocation.

Secondly, the political and legal system is characterized by balance of three powers. The western political philosophy and system distrusts and restricts the governments radically. With regard to the arrangement of western "separation of the three powers", the supreme decision-making organ is the legislative body. And, as the executive power, the basic function of government is to carry out various policies, laws and regulations approved by the legislative body.

During the political practice, in form, the legislative organ (the parliament) is the space wherein the representatives of all classes express and realize their interests. In fact, the legislative body is controlled by minority of private capital interest group which utilizes huge amount of money to bribe the legislative organization, and which controls the public power, and manipulate the legislative body to approve the bill in favor of the private capital interest group.

The function of government is to serve the private capital interest group. Under the multi-party system, different party representatives represent the interest demands and volition of different interest groups, thus different parties fiercely struggle to realize the interests of the groups they represent and mutually constraint each other which makes it quite difficult for them to reach an agreement on major economic and social problems. The struggles are so fierce that, the US has begun a government shutdown for the first time since 2013 due to severe conflict between Democrats and Republicans.

Consequently, the government which serves as the executive body faces severe difficulties in timely responding to the problems and handling major problems and contradictions occurring in regards to economic and social development.

Under the condition that the parliaments find it hard to make due decisions timely and effectively, and since the status and role of government are strictly limited and weakened by the parliaments, and since the status and role of market are greatly reinforced; the market almost plays the decisive action in all aspects of social and economic life. Obviously, the major political reason behind the formation of the "large market and small government" mode is the current prevalent political system, aiming at restraining and restricting the government.

· Thirdly, this mode takes the neo-liberal ideology as its pillar. The mainstream ideology of the contemporary western capitalist countries has been the neo-liberalism. Hayek and Nozick, the two representatives of the contemporary neo-liberalism, have pushed neo-liberalism to the extreme.

These two scholars have considered the government's role as an inherently "evil" in itself, they have put individual rights and freedoms against social equality. Whether it violates or not the individual rights is regarded as the supreme criterion to judge the legitimacy of a government.

They have adopted a nearly anarchist attitude in regard to the governments' role in economic life, and have advocated that the government doing nothing would be the best option. This quite radical neo-liberal political and economic philosophy has been prevalent in the western countries since the 1970s. Having been influenced by such a biased approach, the western countries have weakened the functions of the government domestically, and promoted liberalism, and strongly advocated the so-called "universal values" internationally for the whole world.

At the same time the western countries aim that the neo-classical economics—which advocates the policies of overall privatization and marketization—should become mainstream economics doctrine all across the world, plus promotes the resurgence of the Austrian School which had once advocated that the government with small scale and doing nothing.

Consequently, the western countries have carried out a series of policy measures aiming at strengthening the role of market regulation and weakening the government intervention, consequently the western market economic system has become more biased towards any market regulation by the governments, thus in this course "large market and small government" mode, has become the typical feature of the western market economy system.

III. Limitations of the "Large Market and Small Government" Mode of the Western Market Economy

"Large market and small government" mode of the Western market economy is established on private ownership and the wage labor which emphasizes the self-regulating role of the market and demonizes the positive status and role of government, which intensifies its limitations, i.e., and intensifies the contradiction between high degree of socialized production ever increasing and private ownership of production means sharpens.

Firstly, we see increasingly serious de-industrialization and industrial hollowing, and that the competitiveness of industry is greatly decreasing. The western countries have basically given up the guidance of government for economic development under the background of the prevalent neo-liberalism policies since the 1970s, and have heavily relied on market's self-regulating role.

"Large market and small government" mode has become the common policy means for all the western countries in adjusting their economic structures.

The governments have basically given up their due duties and guiding role for the transformation and upgrading of industrial structures, resulting in that the dominant position of the industrial structure was replaced by the service industry from the early manufacturing industry. Since the 1970s, the spinning, garment, ship building, steel making, appliance and auto industries have been in decline in the western countries and the above industries have been transferred to the newly emerging market economy countries, and the financial service industry consisting of trade, finance, insurance, consultancy, advertisement, travel and restaurant sectors have constantly become the backbone of their economies. Currently, the proportion of three sectors' industrial output in comparison to their GDPs in the western developed countries is as follows: about 10% of the GDP is produced by the primary industry, 15% by the secondary industry, and 75% by the tertiary industry.

Secondly, the financial liberalization frequently causes crises, and the global economy is affected negatively. The western countries have basically carried out financial deregulation and financial liberalization under the influence of neoliberal policies since the 1970s. Having begun breaking through the boundaries of the domestic division of labor, the multi-national companies have comprehensively undertaken various financial businesses. And, in the financial sector many new financial instruments have been discovered, the traditional credit businesses of banks have gradually decreased, the bond issuance business has rapidly increased, the securitization trend in the financial business has rapidly developed. In order to solve the economic "stagflation" of the 1970s, and aiming to recover the past prosperity (golden-era), the western countries have promoted financial liberalization, but the underlying reason behind such moves is to create more opportunities for the financial oligarchy group to make lucrative profits, through appropriation of huge surplus based on financial capital. As a result, this huge surplus pursuit of the financial oligarchy group, causes serious fluctuations in the international finance markets, even frequent eruption of financial crises. Thus the global financial crisis caused by US subprime mortgage crisis in 2008 has deeply influenced the global economy.

Thirdly, the economies have been highly fiscalized (financialized), and the virtual fictive economy sector is seriously detached from the real economy sector, financialization of economy causes severe disconnection between virtual economy and real economy. Under the mode of "large market and small government", western governments have not only facilitated and supported the financial liberalization, but also cleared the way for financial capital gaining dominant position in national economy and also in globalization, which inevitably accelerated detachment between the virtual economy and real economy. As we know, initially, at the beginning, financial capital became the financial oligarchy groups relying on their control over capital supply to dominate real economy. Then, greedy financial oligarchy groups have further detached from the real economy, and expanded itself in an unprecedented speed, it grabbed huge wealth from stock market operations, securities and fund markets at home and abroad by various new financial tools such as the derivatives and hedge funds and others, thus the wealth of financial oligarchy has expanded unprecedentedly, while the real economy sectors have constantly declined.

Fourthly, the fiscal debts are increasing, and the outbreak of debt crises have become more frequent. With the de-industrialization of the economies and with the development of financial services industry, the incomes of the overwhelming majority of middle-class people have gradually declined, while a handful of financial capitalist group have grabbed huge profits which has led to serious polarization of social wealth. In order to avoid the intensification of social contradictions, the governments in the west were forced to increase the social welfare expenditures, but the phenomenon that the public revenue is less than the public expenditure has become more obvious under the condition of constant decline of fiscal revenue sources which is caused by the de-industrialization and financialization; the governments were forced to maintain the level of public expenditures by issuing bonds, which has resulted in heavy government debts. Currently, the governments of the western developed countries bear considerable debt.

Fifthly, the status of middle-class has declined, and the polarization in the society and social contradictions are constantly intensifying. Nowadays, the 1% richest among the US families have grabbed approximately 40% of the whole social wealth, while 80% of the families in the bottom of society only possess 16% of the wealth. With the decline of middle class and vanishing of its stabilizing role in the social and political life, a new structure of the western society consisting of 1% richest group and the 99% group with low incomes have formed, which seems returning back to the period of early capitalism wherein the wealth distribution was extremely unequal, thus again the social class structure mainly consists of the poor and rich with two poles.

Sixthly, economic recovery has become a hopeless wish and the stagnant economic situation has become a norm. After the outbreak of global financial crisis, the western governments have actively tried to reverse the crisis and recession situation, aimed at achieving economic recovery. The counter-crisis measures taken by all western governments are almost identical: firstly, the large-scale financial institutions are supported by the governments through injecting capital to them, so as to prevent a possible graver crisis that may cause by the complete collapse of the financial system; secondly, the large-scale enterprises which seem going bankrupt are supported by the government, with rescue funds; thirdly, the fiscal expenditures, fiscal deficits and debt pressures upon the governments are reduced; fourthly, a loose monetary policy is adopted, and the interest rates are decreased to nearly zero in order to stimulate the consumption and investments; fifthly, the "re-industrialization" policy is implemented to encourage overseas investments by domestic companies and limited measures are taken to improve the employment rates; sixthly, the investments for infrastructure, environment protection and clean energy have been increased, so as to create new economic growth spheres; seventhly, strict trade protectionism policies are implemented to hinder import of products and services from foreign countries that try to enter into their domestic markets, under the cloak of "fighting against the dumping prices" and under the cloak of safeguarding the national security. These measures and policies have made a certain positive effect in resisting the deepening of the financial crisis, and the economy seems to be recovering. However, the above policies haven't solved the underlying deep problem that has triggered the financial crisis, and did not improve the figures reflecting the health of economic life such as the employment, budget revenues, investment, consumption and technological innovation, instead these data have been constantly deteriorating.

The problems such as the de-industrialization, virtualization of economy, polarization of income and wealth, fiscal debts and stagnant process of economic normalization are closely related to the mode of "large market and small government" of the western market economy, which advocates that the government shouldn't intervene the economy, and result from the excessively emphasizing on the private ownership and market, and defaming the state-owned sector and neglects the status and role of government intervention.

Andrew Liveris, the CEO of the US company the Dow Chemical has commented: "Many wise men have suggested that, the pure free market principles won't solely balance an economy—at least the healthy ones—find the right balance. But as we have seen increasingly over the past decade an economy will not simply balance itself. Doing so requires action; it requires intervention." He warned anxiously: "it's time to recognize that if we don't act soon, if we continue to let markets rule in every instance, we will become the global economy's biggest bystander, its biggest drain. Our consumers will find themselves with more debt and less money to spend; our future generations will lack opportunities. It is time for us to recognize the cost of inaction—not just for the US, but also for the entire global economy ... in certain key areas, we actually need more government, not less." The above critique is quite sharp and meaningful.

IV. Several Enlightenments and Propositions

China has started new round of economic reforms, which aims to reinforce and perfect socialism with Chinese characteristics, and perfecting and improving the socialist market economic system. In the process of deepening the reform, we should also summarize the experiences and lessons of and draw from the strong elements of the "large market and small government" mode of the west, and most fundamentally opt for starting from the general laws of China's national conditions and economic development, so as to innovate and perfect our socialist market economy model.

Firstly, we should unswervingly stick to the dominant position of socialist public ownership. The primary task of China's economic reform should be to enhance the dominant position of the public ownership, and avoid overall privatization. Sticking to and reinforcing the dominant position of public ownership means to insist in the socialist orientation of the reform; if the direction of reform is wrong, the reform will end in failure, and the path of socialism and the cause of China's national rejuvenation will be ruined. And, in the new round of reforms, we should maintain the dominant position of socialist public ownership and the socialist orientation of reform.

Secondly, we should correctly understand the decisive role of market in allocating resources. As we have analyzed above the "large market and small government" mode of the western free market economy model, the market cannot solve everything, nevertheless we should objectively understand the decisive role of the market. Recognizing that the market mechanism playing a decisive role in allocating resources is an important step for improving the socialist market economic system. Since it has been only a short period when we have started to develop the socialist market economy in China, this market economy cannot be perfect within such a short period, consequently needs to be enriched in practice and needs improvements.

Market mechanisms playing decisive role in the allocation of resources means: further extending the autonomous management rights of the enterprise, and enhance the independent decision-making level of the market actors, perfecting the market system, and avoid the market entrance barriers so as to enable that various production factors can freely and orderly flow to different regions and industrial sectors, thus realize the optimal combination of production factors; improve the operation rules of the market, and encourage and stimulate the market actors that they can develop independent innovation and that they can enjoy the dividends of their innovations in the aspect of technology, product innovation, management, organization and system by sticking to the principle of survival of the fittest.

At the same time, it should be pointed out that emphasizing the decisive role of market does not mean neglecting the inherent defects and drawbacks of the market mechanism or fully relying on or indulging ourselves in the role of market allocating resources. Consequently, the resource allocation performed by the market should be closely watched with scientific tools, so that its negative effects, i.e. the failures of market in its self-regulating can be reduced to a great degree.

Thirdly, we should correctly grasp the role of government and allow it better play its role in the socio-economic system. As the most important defect of the western market economy doctrine and practice, i.e, the "large market and small government" mode, which demonizes the positive role of government causes grave problems in the development of western economies. In the process of perfecting and improving the socialist market economic system, we should better play the government's role. Emphasizing that government should play its role better, neither means to weaken the role of market playing its role, nor does it mean the government should replace the market, but it means that the government should help the market play its decisive role better. And that the government should handle those issues which can't be solved by the market. Hereby, we propose that, the following three issues should be handled by the government:

Firstly, government should assume the role of leading and guiding the resource allocation. When we evaluate the regulation by the market, we can see that the resources are allocated through market price signals which exert their influence on the decision-making act of the market players. However, the market price signals, information situation in regard to developments in the markets, is characterized by short-term instant information, such information embodies time lag, incompleteness and certain ambiguity, consequently, with such information it is quite difficult for the market players to make the scientific decisions. Countless cases in regard to western market economies can prove that markets are unable to lead and guide rapid, coordinated and sustainable development of economies. But the government can lead and guides the decision-making act of the market players through its comprehensive ability of collecting and disseminating economic information and data, based on which it can design economic development strategies and programs more efficiently, thus the governments can more efficiently conduct macroeconomic regulations, so that the decisions made by the market players will be consistent with the goals and orientation of economic development. All these capabilities of the government enables the optimum arrangement of major economic structures and optimization of the productivity layout of the whole economy, and can mitigate the negative effects of the business cycle fluctuations, and can avoid partial and systematic risks, and can avoid turbulences in regard to market expectations, all in all, can promote sustainable and healthy development of the economy.

Secondly, government should also participate in the resource allocation process. In the socialist market economy, it is quite necessary for government to participate in the resource allocation through investing in and developing the state-owned economy which is an important force to promote national modernization and safeguarding the common interest of the overwhelming majority of people. And developing the state-owned economy will facilitate the elimination of social polarization in the society and achieving common prosperity for all, and promoting the unity between individual interests and social interest, unity between fairness and efficiency, and unity between regulation by the government and the market. Therefore, strengthening and expanding of the state-owned economy is the premise for government to better play its role, which is the major task of perfecting and improving the socialist market economic system. In order to enable the state-owned economy better serve the strategic goals of the country, it is necessary that the state-owned economy should take the lead in key industries and key sectors that have a bearing on national economic security, and the lifeline of the national economy, and should play a leading role in the aspects of providing public services, promoting newly emerging promising strategic industries, in protecting the ecological environment, in supporting the scientific and technological research and progress, and safeguarding national security and certain other spheres.

Thirdly, government should provide stronger institutional support which will help better allocation of resources. The resource allocation by the markets needs proper institutional support. There are two forms of institutional support for the markets: one is related to habits and customs of a specific cultural tradition; second is legal and regulatory institutions which should be consciously and scientifically established and should be provided by the government. In China, it is a top priority to establish a market economy which operates according to law and which is governed by law, and the key issue to achieve this goal is the improvement of our social governance.

Currently, in the sphere of governance we should underline the following: firstly, the government departments should reinforce their capability of developing and implementing, development strategies, programming them, designing policies and standards; secondly strengthen the governments at all levels to better perform public service, market regulation functions, social governance, environmental protection and their other duties; thirdly, strengthening the central government's macro-control mechanism and institutional innovation capability and establishing corresponding systems to implement them.

The status and role of the government in the market economy is indispensable. And it will be completely wrong to despise, weaken or even belittle the status and role of government in the allocation of resources; only by insisting on the organic unity between the market regulation and government intervention, can we establish an effective and scientific market economic system.

Fourthly, the fruits of the reform should be shared by the whole people and we should strive to achieve common prosperity. The "big market small market" mode of the Western market economy is based on private ownership, which emphasizes that in the society people enjoy equality for opportunities, but on the other side neglects equity in process and results but neglects the increasing polarization of wealth and income in the two poles of the society. The minority grabs great majority of the social wealth, while the income levels of the majority do not improve, even continue to decline, this causes them heavily borrow consumption credits and use credit cards which gives the feeling of illusory prosperity, based on indebtedness, which greatly harms the internal impetus for the sustained growth of economy.

When perfecting and improving the socialist market economy, it is necessary to attach due importance to fairness, but also we have to pay attention to efficiency and to the results of the work done, in order to achieve the proper unity between fairness and efficiency, the unity between economic development and improvement of people's livelihood improvement. To this end, we must strive to perfect the socialist relations of production and relations of distribution, promote economic democracy, safeguard the rights and interests of workers, establish harmonious labor relations, explore effective forms in realizing the principle of "distribution according to work" without neglecting the principle of distribution according to the contribution of other productive factors, narrow the income gaps, reverse the increasing trend of polarization; and enable that the fruits of reform is shared by the whole society. Only by adhering to our goal of common prosperity, can we display the superiority of the socialist system, can we enhance the cohesion among all the strata of people, and only in this way, can we persist in and make socialism with Chinese characteristics become common ideal and pursuit of all the people.

Originally published in the journal Red Flag Manuscripts, 2014(22)

The Manifestation of the Economic Globalization of the Developed Countries since the 1970s and Its Influence on the Hired Workers

Sun Shoutao   <u>311</u>

Abstract: On the basis of the economic integration of the world in the past few centuries, qualitative changes have taken place in the internationalized development of capitalist economy since 1970s, generating the globalization tendency and presenting new characteristics. In the process of economic globalization, the capital of the developed countries has launched a new round of class struggle against labor, and reorganized the social class relations, particularly the labor-capital relations: on the one hand, the realization of capital through the globalized layout of the production process led to the "de-industrialization" in the industrial structure; on the other hand, in the enterprise operation, capital implemented business "out-sourcing" with the aid of information technology. "De-industrialization" has greatly affected the blue-collar workers in the developed countries and weakened the organization and power of the traditional industrial workers with the "blue-collar workers" as the mainstay, while business "out-sourcing" had a great impact on the white-collar employees and worsened their living conditions.

Key words: de-industrialization; business out-sourcing; blue-collar workers; white-collar employees

Research on the social class structure changes and research on the employment conditions of laborers in the contemporary developed capitalist countries needs a global perspective.[1] With the rapid and in-depth development of the economic globalization, the configuration of social and economic resources have been extended from nation-state to global level.

In regard with the developed countries, the economic globalization that has developed since 1970s has shown the following characteristics: on the one side, in the aspect of industrial sectors level, the social division of labor has been extended, and the industrial structure of the developed country have assumed the features of "de-industrialization"; on the other hand, in the aspect of enterprises level, the division of labor has been improved especially among the multinational corporations, demonstrating itself as the increase of "out-sourcing" business, which has led to the formation of a global division of work structure. The economic globalization dominated by the big capital has seriously impacted the laborers in the developed country: i.e. the "de-industrialization" process has weakened the organization status and class force of the blue-collar workers of the developed countries, on the other side, the increased "out-sourcing" business is mainly affecting the white-collar employees, deteriorates their living and working conditions.

I. The Nature and the Historical Orientation of the Economic Globalization

312

The economic globalization has been the hot spot issue drawing the attention of the academia both at home and abroad. Since the 1990s, relevant discussions and controversies have emerged in an endless stream. There has occurred sharp differences in regard to the definition, motive force, impetus and historical orientation of the economic globalization.

The neo-liberalism school argues that the economic globalization mainly refers to the free flow of production factors across the world, in order to achieve the optimum solution in regard to the allocation of resources. While, the left-wing economists and Marxist economics schools have emphasized the aspect of institutional relations, and have defined the economic globalization as the globalization of capitalism, have argued that globalization equals capitalism and its economic form and development is similar to capitalism, in fact capitalism has been a global system, just from the beginning.[2] Although some scholars have talked about the "new stage of the globalization", the said stage is the part of a long history. Some scholars have even linked the economic globalization with imperialism, and have argued that the globalization is "the contemporary form of expression of imperialism".[3]

---

1   Tao Wenzhao, "New Changes in the Class Structure of the Western Developed Countries" *Journal of Thoughts and Theories Education*, 2005(9).

2   John. B. Foster, *Monopoly Capital and New Globalization*, translated by Chen Xigui, Journal of New Foreign Theoretical Trends. 2003(6).

3   François Chesnais, *Financial Globalization*, translated by Qi Jianhua and Hu Zhenliang, Central Compilation & Translation Press, 2011, Preface , p. 5.

During the discussions, people have paid attention to some new common phenomenon such as the increase in the degree of economic internationalization, the rapid expansion of international trade, increasingly remarkable status and role of multi-national corporations, and constantly increasing degree of financial liberalization, etc.

A consensus has been reached in the discussions made by the leaders of the International Monetary Fund (IMF)[4]: "the growing economic interdependence of countries worldwide through increasing volume and variety of cross-border transactions in goods and services, freer international capital flows, and more rapid and widespread diffusion of technology."

However, understandings for the historical position of the above given new phenomenon is quite different. In summary, there are two trends among the scholars, in regard to the historical status and orientation of globalization:[5] some scholars emphasize the qualitative changes and historical discontinuities and argue that the economic globalization is a brand new phenomenon as well as the new stage in the process of world's economic development. But the other group of scholars rather emphasize the historical continuity in the process, and argue that the current economic globalization is only a continuation of the pre-existing internationalization trend.

Firstly, the quantitative change theory of economic globalization emphasizes that the current globalization is not a new phenomenon, but it is the deepening and extension in the degree of economic internationalization. First of all, the so-called highly internationalized economy is not without a precedent, since the 1960s there has been a trend of internationalization of economy.

Looking from certain aspect, we can say that currently, the degree of internationalization of economy is not as deep as than the period between 1870-1914. Secondly, the true multinational companies are still rare. Most of the multinational companies still make their operations based on their home country their main assets, production and sales activities are still within the nation-state. Thirdly, the free flow of capital hasn't led to a large-scale investment and employment transfer from the developed countries to the developing ones.

On the contrary, foreign direct investments are mainly concentrated in advanced industrialized countries, the Third World still remains marginalized in both investment and trade. Some left wing scholars, Paul Q. Hirst and Grahame Thompson, have argued that, the current facts doesn't indicate the emergence of globalization, at best, we can say that there is only a high level of internationalization, the current level of economic integration hasn't surpassed that of the late 19th Century.[6]

---

4   Quoted from article by Zhang Tongyu and Ding Guojie: Economic Globalization: Various Theoretical Debates and Its Evolution, *Journal of Contemporary Economic Research*. 2005/1.
5   Liu Xianfqi, Neo-liberal Globalization of World Capitalism, *Journal of New Foreign Theoretical Trends*. 2005(3).
6   Quoted from Zhou Huiming's article Globalization, Capitalism and Socialist Thoughts of the Foreign Left-Wing, *Journal of Theory and Vision*, 2003(2).

Some scholars even held that the globalization is a myth, its extent has been exaggerated, and the so-called globalization is the global operation of the multinational enterprises from three giants and led by far the most powerful countries such as United States, Western Europe and Japan—"Three Pole Group".

In its report, the Investment Department of the UNCTAD Transnational Corporations defined globalization as: "international economic integration" and indicated that there occurred two peaks in the history of economic globalization: the first peak occurred in 1870-1913, which was led by Britain, the factory of the world at that time.[7]

These 43 years were called by the West as the "Golden Age" of international economic integration. In these years, the production factors including capital, commodities and labor have flowed freely among the industrial countries and among their dependent countries under the financial system of gold standard which was more freely than now. This golden age was interrupted by two world wars. Rodrik held that the information revolution since the 1970s has really accelerated the reaction speed of markets to the changes in the world change, but current the proportion of the international flow of commodities, services and capital hasn't hugely increased compared to the gold standard period. The commodities and capital markets of various countries are still separated from each other.[8]

The price of tradable commodities among different countries are slowly arriving, the same price level of those days. Although the proportion between domestic investment and saving in the developed countries is almost 1:1 proportion; if look at the trends, portfolio assets of individuals and institutional investors are not yet international in their scope.

Therefore, Rodrik has argued that the current level of world's economic integration hasn't even reached the level of integration that occurred in the gold standard period.

Immanuel Wallerstein, who represents the world system theory, held that capitalism has not been a process within the nation-state from the very beginning, and always saw the world as a stage, we have always lived in the modern world system based on the capitalist mode of production which lives on the accumulation of capital as the driving force and as its goal.

Giovanni Arrighi proposed the theory of four "long centuries" in the history of capitalism: the accumulation period of Genoa, accumulation period of Netherland, the accumulation period of Britain and lastly the US' accumulation;

7　United Nations World Investment Report 1994, pp. 117-156; according to the opinion of Prof. Chen Baosen the above term should be translated as "international economic combination"; refer to Analysis of the US "New Economy", published by the China Financial Economic Publishing House. 2002, p. 120.

8　Quoted from Bi Rong, Marketing Tendency of Corporate Finance in Developed Countries during the Era of Financial Globalization, Doctoral Dissertation, Nankai University. 2004, pp. 6-7.

Giovanni Arrighi elucidated that in these four periods, physical capital expansion and financial capital expansion has occurred alternately.[9]

Samir Amin held that the current economic globalization is the third stage of the expansion of imperialism; although its scope has somehow deepened, its goals are not changed, still needs to control market expansion, plunder world's natural resources and exploit the countries of the periphery.[10]

Secondly, the qualitative theory of globalism has argued that the current globalization is new and unprecedented. The prominent scholars that hold this view have highlighted that the many phenomena that have emerged in the current economic globalization show that the world economy has undergone qualitative changes, which marks a whole new historical stage. Paul Krugman has pointed out[11]: before the 1970s the development of world economic integration has never exceeded the level achieved in the early period of 20th Century, which can be evidenced by the new level of trade's proportion in the GDP. After the 1970s, the proportion of trade in the total world output has increased to an unprecedented level, wherein such change not only means a quantitative increase but also marks a qualitative change. Frederic Pryor, has examined a series of statistical indexes meticulously,[12] and found out that, after the 1970s, such as the proportion of the import and export of goods and services in the GDPs has risen rapidly, professionalization and specialization of labor division has enhanced, the labor, capital and information flows have increased radically.

Therefore, he has argued that there is an obvious qualitative difference between the US's current globalization and the past internationalization: firstly, the internationalization embodies the trade of products and services, besides the international flow of labor and capital, secondly, the globalization is much more directly related to the international movement of money and information, as well as decision-making mechanisms by the governments, decision-making mechanisms of the productive departments and individuals; the first and second aspect are linked, there are qualitative differences between the two.

Some western left-wing scholars have argued that[13]: the essence of economic globalization is that capitalism has entered the era of transnational capitalism, in the past space was subordinated to time, but on the contrary currently the

9   Sun Shoutao, Discussion about the Accumulation Cycle Theory of G. Arrighi, *Journal of Productivity Research*. 2006(2). *Long 20 Century – Money, Power and Source of Our Society*, Jiangsu People's Publishing House, 2001; G. Arrighi, et al. Chaos and Governance in the Modern World System, translated by Wang Yujie, SDX Joint Publishing. 2003.
10   Wang Yizhou, Third World under the Background of Globalization – Interview Records with Samir Amin, *Journal of World Economy and Politics*. 2001(2).
11   Krugman, Paul, "Growing World Trade: Causes and Consequences", in: *Europe: Much Ado About Nothing?*, edited by Mathias Dewatripont, Andre Sapir, Khalid Sekkat, New York: Oxford University Press. 1999.
12   Pryor, Frederic, "Internationalization and Globalization of the US Economy", in: *Globalizing America: The USA In World Integration*, edited by T. L. Brewer, Gavin Boyd, Northampton MA: Edward Elgar, 2000.
13   Yang Haifeng, Spatial Exhibition of Capital and Globalization, *Journal of Beijing University*, 2015(4).

time has become subordinated to space. What is prominent in this new era is the operation of global capitalism, which combines the space production, planning and the power of capital. So, the so-called globalization is the exhibition of capital in space.

As a whole, their ideas sum up to: globalization has developed on the basis of the internationalization of capitalist economy. In the past few centuries, the process of world economic integration has created the foundation for the development of economic globalization. Finally, I can add the following: qualitative changes have occurred in the 1970s, creating a trend toward globalization. Compared with the past internationalization, the current globalization has made even greater progress, but not limited with that it has gained new characteristics: such as the huge expansion of international trade, increase of short-term speculative capital flows and establishment of the global layout for the economic activities of the multi-national enterprises. This economic globalization has greatly affected the labor forces employed in the developed countries.

II. Features and Performance of Economic Globalization

Since the 1970s, in the process of economic globalization, during the establishment of global layout of the production process, developed countries have relocated their capital and factories, which has caused that their manufacturing industries have seen relative decline in the aspect of industrial sectors which can be called as the "de-industrialization". Meanwhile, by virtue of the increasingly strengthening information technology, they have further promoted "outsourcing" business and at the same time, they have attempted to realize, both the de-centralized global allocation of resources (including qualified human sources) and the centralized control of information and finance.

(I) "De-industrialization" of the Industrial Structure

De-industrialization (or "non-industrialization") refers to the decrease in the proportion of industry in the economy and the increase in the proportion of service sector caused by the economic development.[14] This phenomenon is also called as the "economic servitization" or "hollowing of the industry". The information revolution and economic globalization has greatly enhanced the "de-industrialization" trend in the industrial structure of developed countries. The technical basis of rapid development of "de-industrialization" is due to wide application of information technologies. This is also the key technological condition for economic globalization.

Nitin Nohria, a professor of Harvard University, commented: "the cheaper and stronger the information technologies and transportation costs became, relatively, it has become possible that the similar phenomenon of the past century has re-appeared—with a larger scale—in the regions and across the nation-states. Which has linked once- isolated markets into a sole and huge market. ...since the

---

14   Yang Chenglin and Qiao Xiaonan, De-industrialization Process in Developed Countries, *Journal of Literature Review, and Reform,* 2012(9).

1970s, 1930s, new information technologies and jet aircraft usage has caused a similar effect, in the US (super state) and across the globe."[15]

Nitin Nohria, has summarized the adjustments and upgrading of the US industrial structure after Second World War: "Firstly, the relative decline of the industrial manufacturing sector was generally constant from 1955 to 1998. The share of industrial manufacturing had decreased by 25% from 1955 to 1974, and had decreased by 33% from 1974 to 1998. Although these manufacturing companies have taken various measures, they were unable to reverse this trend of relative decline. Secondly, it is important to note that the government services, transportation and communications sectors, wholesale and retail trade have remained stable in this period… Thirdly, the service industry has been the biggest winner, the traditional service industries (services by specialized professionals, real estate and transportation, etc.) financial services, health and media services and information technology services have risen sharply in the 1980s and 1990s. In 1998, government and services industry has accounted for more than 3/4 of GDP."[16]

The development of information technologies have promoted as the industrial upgrading in US and also helped the US to realize a global industrial production layout and helped it to achieve structural adjustment of its industry.

Prof. Chen Baosen has classified the industrial structure of the US into 4 levels, after this structural adjustment: firstly, backed by the information technology revolution, bio-engineering, new material and new energy industries and other high-tech industries, have developed rapidly which were led and driven by the information industry, and the output value and employment of these sectors have increased significantly.

Secondly, the traditional capital-intensive and technology-intensive manufacturing industries were upgraded by using information technology their industries, their output value has continued to grow but encountered a slow speed, but employment in these industries has decreased. Compared with the high-tech industries, their share in the total output and in total employment had decreased (except the quantity of products they have produced).

Thirdly, as a whole, the manufacturing industry using intensive labor encountered an outward-oriented shift and globalized its production, but generally the production of this sector had decreased and its product supply has become dependent on imports; some industries were transformed by the use of high-technology, thus their technological level and competitiveness were improved.

Fourthly, newly emerging service industries and traditional service industries have developed vigorously, their output value and employment magnitude have continually increased and greatly surpassed both the agriculture and manufacturing sectors of the economy.[17]

---

15 Quoted from Chen Baosen, *Analysis of US's "New Economy"*, China Financial Economic Publishing House, 2002, p. 55.
16 Ibid., pp. 57-58.
17 Ibid.

"De-industrialization" doesn't mean overall contraction of the industrial sector, rather it means the shrinkage of the traditional manufacturing industry sector which was faced by a fierce competition. In 1970s, the traditional manufacturing industries of the developed countries were trapped by a serious crisis and fell into a difficult situation.

Firstly, the increase in raw material costs and increase in labor costs, combined by excess production capacity have made the traditional manufacture industries more and more less profitable.

Secondly, after World War II, some newly emerging developing countries have greatly increased their competitiveness in regard to traditional industrial products, having used their advantages of labor and resources costs, they have gradually captured the international markets of the developed country or even strongly entered into their own markets.

Thirdly, through long-term period of development after Second World War, the gaps among the economically developed countries were narrowed. And, there an increasingly fierce competition among them in certain production sectors—those having certain technological content (e.g. auto manufacturing and household appliance, etc). Under these circumstances, the capitals of the developed countries were forced to adjust the industrial structures faced by the fierce competition and decrease of profit rate, consequently decided to transfer those labor-intensive labor and capital-intensive enterprises to certain developing countries which have offered relatively better investment conditions, so as to fully use the cheaper labor costs, rich resources and large markets of these countries.

The developed countries have greatly increased their investments in the developing countries, and the pace of industrial transfer has significantly accelerated while the manufacturing industry in the developed countries was rapidly reduced. If we take the US as example. The employment ratio of the US manufacturing industry had decreased by 16.2% points from 25.1% to 8.9% between 1970 and 2010. The number of employed workers was reduced by 35.4% from 17.848 million to 11.528 million. The absolute number of employees in the manufacturing industry had arrived at reached a peak, 19.426 million (nearly about 20 million people) in 1979, but descended to 11.528 million in 2010. The absolute number of employees in the mining industry had reached to 1.18 million in 1981, but it fell to 572,000 in 2003, and further fell to 70,500 in 2010.[18]

Both, the absolute number and relative number of employees have continually declined since 1970s. Several major manufacturing industries such as steel, household appliance, auto manufacturing, textile and cloth were heavily affected, and many people have lost their jobs. Under these conditions, large number of laborers have shifted to service industries, therefore the absolute number and relative number of employees in most service industries have increased greatly.

---

18 Economic Report of the US President 2013, Table B-46. p. 378.

"Nearly 2 million people were laid off in the US manufacturing industry from 1979 to 1996, while employment in the service sector with low productivity has increased by nearly 30 million."[19]

And, in 1990, the number of employees hired by the US's Beverly service company and a chain home-nursing company home, was similar to the staff employed by Chrysler Auto Manufacturing Company (respectively 115,174 and 116,250). But, in 1980s, there were only 3 million newly-added service workers in fast food restaurants, bars and restaurants, and this figure was more than total number of workers engaged in the automobile, steel and textile industries of the US.[20]

(II) The recent trend of business "out-sourcing" by the multinationals

Since the 1980s, the out-sourcing type of business has become a strategic option for multinational enterprises, especially the development of the out-sourcing business and out-sourcing market have greatly increased since the 1990s. Some large companies by using their information technology advantages have began to transfer some service production work to an external service provider, thus the out-sourcing service business has drawn the attention of people from all walks of life, the impacts and advantages and disadvantages of this kind of business sparked heated debates all around the world.[21] Outsourcing business refers to transferring of some internal businesses or functions of an enterprise to the external service provider through an outsourcing contract. Through such a transfer, the production activity or a function which originally belonged to the labor division system of the enterprise is being converted to market relationship (domestically or internationally) by social labor division system. The essence of out-sourcing is the transformation of labor division within an enterprise to a labor division in society. Such business out-sourcing, in this broad sense has long existed in the construction-building, manufacturing industries and by government departments. The history of out-sourcing business in regard to information technology services can be traced back to World War II; many of the companies which had provided the United States Federal Government with information technology services have become international giant international enterprises.

Outsourcing across borders, called as "off-sourcing", is the product of economic globalization. What we want talk about in this article is mainly this form of outsourcing that transcends borders. This kind of out-sourcing has rapidly developed because of the technical support of IT technology revolution. In the 1990s, the United States was the first country to make breakthrough advances

---

19 David Coates, *Models of Capitalism: Growth and Stagnation in the Modern Era*, trans. by Geng Xiulin and Zong Zhaochang, Jiangsu People's Publishing House. 2001, p. 288.
20 Robert Reich, *The Work of Nations. Preparing Ourselves for 21st Century Capitalism*, translated by Shanghai Municipal CPPCC translation group and oriental compilation, Shanghai Translation Publishing House, 1998, p. 179.
21 Jing Linbo, Hypothesis for Doubting the Decrease of Out-sourcing Service Cost – Take Information Technology Out-sourcing for Example, *Economic Research*, 2005(1).

in information technology and communication, enabling the establishment of an information network. By this advance, the multinational corporations could expand their business globally at a low cost and with a strong coordination and centralized control. This new exchange of information within the companies and between the companies and the consumer created completely new conditions. Meanwhile, under the of the development of the Internet, US was the first country to make an experiment in the production process towards separating the production and management processes such as financial accounting, strategic management, research and development, design and marketing, manufacturing and other functions by allocating all these to different countries so as to take advantage of their geographical advantages to reduce the costs. Modern information technology enabled the effective global application of this new management system, and promoted the layout of US multinational companies in the process of global production and operation. With the advances in the information technology and high-speed data networks, the scope of the cross-border outsourcing has expanded to a series of business operations and management matters, including finance, insurance, health care, human resources, mortgage, credit card, asset management, consumer service, sales and research & development. According to the degree of its complexity, the Business Process Outsourcing (BPO) is divided into following five levels:[22] first, back office business such as input and conversion of data, and file management, etc.; second, customer services such as call centers, on-line customer services and remote marketing; third, ordinary business such as finance, accounting, human resources, procurement and information technology service, etc.; fourth, information services and decision analysis such as research and consultancy, customer analysis, insurance claim and risk management, etc.; and fifth, research development such as engineering design, architectural design, new product and new technology design. In order to achieve the business out-sourcing, U.S. companies use the high-speed data lines to transmit the documents and images to some countries with low wage levels such as India and Mexico.

According to the Turner data search company[23], the demand of developed countries for overseas information technology is now growing at double-digit rates, and the market for Business Process Out-sourcing (BPO) is growing more rapidly through processing bills and information cards for managing human resources, etc. As of now (2006), India has undertaken most of this work. Some low-end BPO businesses (such as the data input, form processing and software test) have been increasingly outsourced to Chinese enterprises, while India continues to lead the high-end function of this field (such as research and design). According to another report[24]: from 2008 to 2012, the offshore service outsourcing undertaken by Chinese service out-sourcing enterprises was increased from

---

22   Zhen Bingxi, International Service Out-sourcing under the Background of Economic Globalization, *Journal of Seeking Truth*, 2005(9).

23   China and India Competition for the Global Out-sourcing Service Market, *Reference News*. May 10 2006(4).

24   China Seems More Professional in Out-sourcing, *People's Daily*. May 30, 2013(1).

4.69 billion U.S. dollars to 33.64 billion U.S. dollars, with an average annual increase over 60%; China has become the second largest service out-sourcing country in the world (India ranks the first position). The global off-sourcing share of China has increased from 7.7% in 2008 to 27.7% in 2012.

The use of outsourcing to separate some of the regional functions of enterprise management and production is an important means for the developed countries to strengthen their capital management. The combination of the capital uses outsourcing and non-standard forms of employment, divides the labor force and increases the control and exploitation of teh wage labor.[25]

"Currently, the corporations adopt the following means: such as flexible employment systems, simplifying production process and establishment of working teams, which seems to be methods for enhancing the labor intensity, accelerating the speed of assembly lines, reducing the number of workers and outsourcing some component parts of the production process."[26] It is also interesting to note that some companies outsourced their original employees to independent contractors for taking on the original jobs or changed their jobs as expatriates (contract labor) to employment service centers (human resources provider). Through converting the employment relationship to the market relationship in this way, the employers can take advantage of reducing the wages and benefits of their workers through depriving them of their job security and avoiding various statutory obligations related to the employment relationship. According to the survey conducted by US Department of Labor 1995, nearly 17% of 5 million contract labor worked for their original corporation, including Xerox, Hoffman-La-Roche, Delta Air Lines, Digital Equipment and Chevron. A survey conducted by the American Management Association has also pointed out that 30% out of 720 newly downsized corporations hired their former employees but no longer gave medical insurance and pensions.[27]

III. Influence of Economic Globalization on the Laborers

Economic globalization has greatly affected the laboring classes: the "deindustrialization" of industrial structure in the process of globalization has greatly affected the blue-collar workers in the developed countries, resulting in weakening the organization and class force of the workers which worked in the traditional industries and mainly the "blue-collar workers" were affected from this new situation. Plus the "out-sourcing" business promoted by the big corporations has mainly frustrated the white-collar employees in the developed countries, thus their living conditions have gradually deteriorated.

---

25 Sun Shoutao and Gu Zili, Hierarchical Characteristics of Working Class in the Developed Countries since 1970s, *Journal of Education and Research*, 2012(10).
26 Phillip Anthony O'Hara, Controversy over Whether the World Capitalism Enters into an Ascending Stage for a Long Time, translated by Liu Ying, *Journal of Foreign Theoretical Trends*. 2005(1).
27 Quote from Edward Luttwak, *Turbo Capitalism – Winners and Losers in the Process of Global Economy*, translated by Chu Lvyuan, Guangming Daily Press. 2000, p. 77.

(I) "De-industrialization" weakens the blue-collar workers

Since the 1970s, the "de-industrialization" trend in the developed countries has greatly weakened the organization and the class force of the "blue-collar workers" which worked in the traditional industries. After World War II, the economic prosperity brought by Fordist chain production model which was used in the large-scale manufacturing industries such as auto, steel, building, textile, civil aircraft and durable consumer goods. In these industries, the labor force mainly consisting of blue-collar employees have better defended their interests through collective bargaining supported by the labor unions. This advantage of workers mainly reflects the effect of "tripartite system" (labor-capital-state) used by the Western countries in regard to the labor-capital relationship-conflicts which was formed in this so called "golden period". However, later this "tripartite system" was significantly weakened in the process of economic globalization.

Alongside with the process of the information technology (IT) revolution and economic globalization, the traditional manufacturing sectors were constantly re-constructed due to capital exit from these sectors, external relocation of the factories and introduction of new technologies which can save labor because of facing many direct attacks from the organized labor, i.e., labor unions.

This industrial reconstruction either refers to that new industrial layout re-structuring is designed considering the factor of labor union organization level, the operation of a company is moved to a region or to a sub-sector wherein the organization level of labor unions are lower, secondly for an industrial branch an advanced production technology is enforced, or it means, as a first step, moving a certain industry to a new region in the same country, such as to the undeveloped regions of a country (such as from northern to southern regions of the US) and secondly, later the industry may be transferred to developing countries. For a long period, "US capitalists have always systematically used the black population to reduce the wage costs in the national level and reinforce the exploitation of southern workers (including white people and black people). Governments have promulgated some anti-labor laws, which promote various types of freelance employment tricks that give free hand to employer enterprises, besides these anti-labor laws include some articles which makes it hard for the workers to join the trade unions. With such indirect support, capitalists do their best to use this advantage labor-union free zones as an exploitation haven, and also use this method, to gradually increase their attacks against the working class".[28] The manufacturing corporations were continually transferred to overseas by the developed countries for the purpose of exploiting foreign labor with low cost and other cheaper resources in these countries, and also to attack against labor class forces and social movements in their home countries.

---

28 Wayne Jan, Southward Shift of Auto Giants To Exploit Cheaper Labor, *Selection of Economic Translation* (9th edition), Commercial Press. 1979, pp. 102-108.

"The move by multinational corporations to the South, can be compared to big US companies moving from the north of US to the Southern states"[29], and the labor force has gradually lost their control on labor markets and conditions of employment. As Robert Johnson, a New York financier, put it, "Now, the capital is flexible by gaining wings, and the employers are free to choose from at one and the same time the labor markets from 20 different countries. However, the labor force cannot move out of one region. The power has been transferred to the employers".[30]

During the de-industrialization process, the factory migration has heavily affected the workers in the developed countries. For example[31], Radio Corporation of US had two large-scale television factories in Tennessee and Ohio in the past. As the workers at the Tennessee branch organized the labor union and went on a strike for 11 weeks to improve their working conditions, the Radio Corporation of America (RCA) closed two of its factories in 1971, and transferred the production of all black-white television to Taiwan, and 6000 workers of these two factories lost their jobs.

In 1970s, US corporations of the electronic industry one after the other closed the original factories in the US, and transferred them to Taiwan, Korea, Singapore, Hong Kong and Mexico where wages were lower.

This trend was further promoted in the 1990s. US's General Electric Company transferred its factory to some countries with lower wages such as Mexico so as to reduce its costs. In 1999, the department of aircraft engines in General Electric Company designed a global project, and increased its engineers employed in the other countries—10 fold, 300 in total—located them in the countries such as Brazil, Mexico and Turkey. When 425 workers of the Auto Compressor Company, a US-Japan joint venture in Michigan, got organized to demand a wage increase from 12-14 dollars per hour to 16-18 dollars per hour, the Japan executive who was dispatched for solving the dispute told them: if you opt to vote for a wage increase, we will not hesitate to relocate the factory."

According to the survey conducted by the industry-labor relations Institute in the Neil Wilson University, 62% of manufacturers threatened to shut down their factories when the workers organize in trade unions.[32] Today, most industrial sectors with low-technology and low-skilled workers such as cloth, shoes, toy and simple electrical devices have disappeared from the developed countries.

323

---

29   Quoted from David W. Ewing, Multinational Corporation is Tested, in: *Selected Translations*. 1975(7).

30   William Greider, *One World, Ready or Not: Manic Logic of Global Capitalism*, Simon & Schuster. 1997, p. 24.

31   Mitchell Zimmermann, Profit Pursuit and Factory Relocation Abroad, in: *Selected Translations*. 1975(7).

32   Chen Baosen, *Analysis of the US's "New Economy"*, China Financial Economic Publishing House. 2002, p. 326.

The original manufacturers in the developed countries either moved their factories abroad or became importers of the commodities they had previously produced. The world's leading enterprises such as Nike Corporation producing sneakers or Mattel Inc. producing children toys do not produce these products themselves. They have just signed off-sourcing production contracts with factories in the developing countries which frequently changed, mainly with some companies located in Indonesia, Poland and Mexico or also in the United States.

That is to say, the production will be shifted to a country where costs are cheaper.

When the companies of the developed countries transferred or reduced the scale of production in the traditional manufacturing industries, millions of blue-collar workers were laid off. Three large-scale auto manufacturing companies in the US laid off 130,000 workers in the 1980s. From 1973 to early 1990s, the workers working in the US steel industry had decreased from 509,000 to 196,000, wherein the number of the workers in six largest steel companies has been reduced by 179,000 to 92,000. Nippon Steel Corporation's workforce was reduced by 10% since the mid-1980s. From 1976 to 1989, the number of workers in the EEC steel industry was reduced from 760,000 to 400,000.[33] Although many workers obtained the employment opportunity again after being laid off, most of them reemployed in the service sector, and their wages were lower than before. From 1987 to 1992, only 25% of the 5.6 million unemployed U.S. workers who had been employed for more than three years in the US had the same wage; 23% could only find jobs with low wages; 36% remained unemployed; and 8% became part-time temporary workers.[34] As Henry S. Farber, an economist in Princeton University pointed out in the survey report in 1997[35]: about 25% unemployed people still cannot be employed after three years and many can only retire early; while 75% of workers who can be employed have to face with a 6% reduction from their previous wages and assume the loss of income because of their unemployment.

(II) The out-sourcing deteriorates the living conditions of white-collar workers

With the relocation of the factories during de-industrialization and the business out-sourcing of enterprises in the industrial transfer, the employment status of laborers in developed countries tended to be worse. Outsourcing has had a particularly significant impact on the conditions of the white-collar employees:

First, the increasingly serious unemployment of white-collar employees who have become the mainstay of the unemployed army. The so-called "wave of white collar unemployment" have emerged in developed countries. As Zhang

---

33   The data quoted from Liu Chongyi and Li Dachang, et.al., *Structural Economic Crisis of Contemporary Capitalism*, Commercial Press, 1997, p. 277.

34   Zhou Suiming, *The Civilized Shock – The "Phenomenon" in the Contemporary West in the Past 30 Years*, Haitian Press, p. 126.

35   Quoted from Chen Baosen *Analysis of US's "New Economy"*, China Financial Economic Publishing House, 2002, p. 325

Haitao has argued: "according to the official statistics, by the beginning of 1993, the number of unemployed white-collar workers nationwide was about 200,000 more than the unemployed "blue-collar" workers which is unfrequented in the unemployment history of the working class in the US."[36]

Forrester survey report issued by the world famous information industry research institute wrote: according to a conservative estimation, 3.3 million jobs will be lost by 2015, due to out-sourcing business. Other studies have argued that 14 million jobs regarding the US service industry will be lost due to outsourcing.[37]

It also indicated that the unemployment rate in the United States has been unusually high during the process of cyclical recovery since 2001. In 2001, the US unemployment rate was 5.8%, compared with 6.0% in 2002 and 6.4% in 2003 which set the highest level in the past nine years. However, the US economy presented the recovery trend. This condition was called as "recovery without employment".[38] Some scholars even made it clear that "the US economy with such macroeconomic indicators is a fact emerged in US history for the first time. The economic recovery is good except for the employment rate".[39] Since the outbreak of international financial crisis in 2008, the US unemployment rate was sharply increased, and kept at over 8%, and even arrived at 10.1% on October 2009 which was a historical level. Even more noteworthy is the long-term sharp increase in the number of unemployed workers: when Obama was sworn into office in January 2009, the number of unemployed people for more than 6 months was 2.6 million. By June 2012, this number increased to 5.3 million by increasing more than 100%.[40]

Secondly, the income level of the white-collar group has declined. The increase in the out-sourcing type of operations directly threatens the status of white-collar laborers in the developed countries, or even the white-collar technicians and managers who earn high incomes. On January 7, 2004, Charles Schumer told a true story on "free trade in the new global economy" held by the Brookings institution, the famous US think tank[41]: In a computer security company in New York has 800 employees engaged in advanced computer software programs, and they integrate and process many large-scale software programs, involving the risk of investing massive capital, and the average annual

36   Zhang Haitao, *Discussion on the US: State Monopoly Capitalism*, Contemporary China Publishing House, 1998, p. 405.

37   Jing Linbo, An Hypothesis for Doubting the Decrease of Out-sourcing Service Cost – Examination of the Information Technology Out-sourcing as an Example, *Journal of Economic Research*, 2005(1).

38   Mishel, Lawrence, Jared Bernstein, and Sylvia Allegretto, *The State of Working America 2004/2005*, An Economic Institute Book, Ithaca, New York: ILR Press, an imprint of Cornell University Press. 2005, p. 9.

39   Gao Bai, Structural Characteristics of Globalization and China's Economic Development Model, *Sociology Research*. 2005(4).

40   Jim Powell, Why the Unemployment Has Doubled during Obama Administration ? *Journal of International Economic Review*. 2012(5).

41   China Daily Net, January 9, 2004, http: //news.xinhuanet.com/world/2004-01/09/content_1268229.htm.

wage is over 150,000 US dollars. However, the boss said all workers will be transferred to India within 3 years, because the wages in India is 1/4 of white Americans. As Robert Reich, the former US Minister of Labor solemnly pointed out: "the economic growth has nothing to do with the well-being of the labor force. Millions of white-collar management personnel and middle-level managers participate in the work undertaken by the blue-collar workers in the past, and become the frayed-collar in the golden age".[42]

Thirdly, the social status of white-collar employees has descended. Edward Luttwak, an US economist, wrote the book the "Endangered American Dream" in 1993 and pointed out:[43] the so-called "American dream" of the 1950s has been an illusion which has become bygone years, since the 1970s. The US's socialist left has evaluated the decline of the living conditions caused by the economic recession as "falling down a hill". The so-called US "middle-class dream" has become a history. The living conditions and social status of the most American laborers are declining, and the two-pole-class society consisting of 20% elite groups and the 80% the new working class is forming.[44]

Table 1. Incomes of the Common US family (1947-1993)

Year	Household Income of common families (dollar)	Year	Decrease and increase (dollar)
1947	18099	1947 - 1967	13480
1967	31599	1967 - 1973	5314
1973	36893	1973 - 1979	1354
1979	38248	1979 - 1989	1448
1989**	39696	1989 - 1992	-2028
1993	36959	1989 - 1993	-2737

**) The income includes all kind of incomes, self-employment income, pension, interest, rent, government cash allowance and other cash type disposable incomes.*

***) The figures were corrected according to the population census data in 1990.*
Data source: Richard C. Longworth, Crisis of Global Economic
Neo-liberalism, translated by Ying Xiaoduan, SDX Joint Publishing, 2003.
Life, Reading and New Knowledge, Sanlian Bookstore, 2002, p. 117.

As for the income level, the original income of the middle class which was increased in the past begun to decrease. From 1947 to 1973, the labor productivity rate of U.S. economy increased by 103.5%; and the income of the middle-class families increased approximately by 103.9%; from 1973 to 2003,

---

42   Richard C. Longworth, *Crisis of Global Economic Liberalism*, translated by Ying Xiaoduan, SDX Joint Publishing. 2002, p. 101.
43   Xu Chongwen, *New Changes in Contemporary Capitalism*, Chongqing Publishing House, 2004, pp. 168-169.
44   Perrucci, Robert and Wysong Earl, *The New Class Society, Good Bye American Dream?*, Lanhamm Maryland: Rowman & Littlefield Publishers, Inc, 1999.

the labor production rate and family income rate were respectively 71.3% and 21.9%, while the growth of the income of the middle-class families was less than 1/3 of the production rate.[45]

As shown in Table 1, the middle-income Americans accounted for half respectively before 1970s. Moreover, the number of people that has left the middle class ranks is much lower than the number of people who have joined middle class coming from the lower classes, therefore the middle class had increasingly expanded. However, this trend has reversed since 1980s. The possibility of degrade the low income class from the middle-class exceeds the possibility to rise to the higher income group, and smaller families with lower incomes are able to rise to the middle-class. "The proportion of the U.S. people in the middle income group was decreased from 71% in 1969 to less than 63% in the early 1990s."[46] In the United States, the number of the rich and the poor are much more than before, while the middle class has decreased.

IV. Conclusion

Evaluating from a Marxist viewpoint the economic globalization launched by the big capital of the developed countries since the 1970s is essentially the reconstruction of the social class relationships by the force of capital, which has particularly aimed to re-construct labor-capital relationships. This re-construction of labor-capital relationships is in tandem with the efforts of recovering the profit rates by using the information technology—the two are inseparable—we can say that capital has launched the class struggle against the labor's class forces.[47]

In this struggle, the wage labor class is seriously hit: "De-industrialization" process has weakened the organization and class forces of the blue-collar labor class; besides "out-and off- sourcing" has mainly deteriorated the living condition of the white-collar employees in the developed countries. The change could not happen so radically without the mild and appeasing attitude of the wage labor class.

Marx has advocated that the working class bears the historical mission of transforming the capitalist society. However, we should dialectically understand the revolutionary nature of the working class and its movement, which encounters both low-ebb and vigorous victorious periods. The social movements such as "Occupy Wall Street" and a series of great strikes in the West indicate that the labor class forces in the developed countries are taking the

45   Mishel, Lawrence, Jared Bernstein and Sylvia Allegretto, *The State of Working America 2004/2005*, An Economic Institute Book, Ithaca, New York: ILR Press, an imprint of Cornell University Press, 2005, p. 46.

46   Jeremy Rifkin, *The End of Work: Decline of the Global Labor Force and the Dawn of the Post-market Era*, translated by Wang Yantong, Shanghai Translation Publishing House, 1998, pp. 198-199.

47   Mei Haibo, Critique of Neoliberal Globalization: Class Perspective, *Journal of Research on Marxism*, 2013(10).

stage since 21ˢᵗ Century, particularly after the outbreak of the financial crisis, after the period of 30 years, when they had assumed the mild and appeasing attitude, we are witnessing once again that we are at the dawn of revival, wherein socialist movement resurges.

References

Chen Baosen, *Analysis of US's "New Economy"*, China Financial Economic Publishing House, 2002.

David Coates, *Models of Capitalism: Growth and Stagnation in the Modern Era*, translated by Geng Xiulin and Zong Zhaochang, Jiangsu People's Publishing House, 2001.

Robert Reich, *The Work of Nations: Preparing Ourselves for 21ˢᵗ Century Capitalism*, translated by Shanghai Municipal CPPCC translation group and oriental compilation, Shanghai Translation Publishing House, 1998.

Edward Luttwak, *Turbo Capitalism – Winners and Losers in the Process of Global Economy*, translated by Chu Lvyuan, Guangming Daily Press, 2000.

Zhang Haitao, *Discussion on the Future of US: State Monopoly Capitalism*, Contemporary China Publishing House, 1998.

Mishel, Lawrence, Jared Bernstein, and Sylvia Allegretto, *The State of Working America 2004/2005*, An Economic Institute Book, Ithaca, New York: ILR Press, an imprint of Cornell University Press, 2005.

Xu Chongwen, *New Changes in Contemporary Capitalism*, Chongqing Publishing House, 2004.

Robert Perrucci and Earl Wysong, *The New Class Society*, Lanham, Maryland: Rowman & Littlefield Publishers, Inc., 1999.

Mei Haibo, Critique of Neoliberal Globalization: A Class Perspective, *Journal of Research on Marxism*, 2013(10).

Originally published in the Journal of Research on Marxism, 2014(8)

Analysis on Institutional Regulation and Corporate Social Responsibility: Different Views from Europe

Zhang Xian and Tan Kecheng

329

Abstract: The theory and practice of corporate social responsibility (CSR) in the USA, which is characterized by the voluntariness principle, are regarded by some scholars as having universal significance and predicted to become a prevalent corporate social responsibility concept. However, this concept ignores decisive effect and role of the institutional regulations on the corporate social responsibility mode which is regarded as the corporate operation background, and cannot explain the objectively existing differences in regard to various CSR modes. Therefore, the introduction of institutional analysis approach into the researches of corporate social responsibility (CSR) by the European scholars in the recent years has become a new trend. This new trend has greatly shaken the dominance of the American mode of CSR which is solely based on voluntariness principle and emphasizes the explicit responsibility, consequently this new trend can provide a useful theoretical reference for the countries that are establishing CSR guidelines and modes which are in line with their own institutional structures.

Key words: Corporate social responsibility (CSR); institutional analysis; explicit social responsibility; implicit social responsibility

Generally, known the US was the first country where the term corporate social responsibility was mentioned and debated.[1] However, due to the US's institutional structural design, the government cannot directly intervene in the enterprise issues. This institutional structure has fundamentally contributed to the American-style corporate social responsibility concept, which takes social contract thought as its basis, promotes companies to undertake voluntary corporate social responsibility as the sole principle and they assume explicit social responsibility as the display form.

Since the 1980s, European countries have begun to relax the controls on enterprises, and corporate social responsibility issues have become high in their agenda. Under this background, the American mode of CSR theory and practices were promoted in the regions outside of the USA, and quickly became the mainstream trend in researches of corporate social responsibility issues. And, almost all researches related to corporate social responsibility have regarded the US's institutional structure as a ready-made environment, they even ignore to consider the unique institutional backgrounds in their empirical researches and undermine that different institutional backgrounds can become important determinant to affect corporate social responsibility, which severely limits the further enrichment of the CSR theory. However, this kind of approach has encountered a significant transformation since 2000s, and this transformation has just occurred among the European academic circles in which American mode of the CSR concepts and practices were vigorously promoted. The major evidence of such transformation is the introduction of institutional approach into the CSR researches, thus numerous brand new important research results have been created. The distinction made between the minimal corporate social responsibility concept and the explicit and implicit corporate social responsibility (CSR) concepts which were proposed and found out on the base of institutional approach analysis has been the most noteworthy contents in these new research results. The proponents of the new trend have proposed impressive ideas which challenge the mainstream American mode of CSR conceptions.

I. Reflections on the American Mode of Corporate Social Responsibility and an Introduction to Institutional Analysis

In the 1980s the neo-liberal wave has swept across Europe and brought American mode of corporate social responsibility concept to Europe. As a result, a wide range of CSR claims, which were based on social contract and emphasized the principle of corporate voluntariness, were popular in Europe. The programmatic document "Promoting CSR Framework in Europe" formed on this basis, clearly stated that "Corporate social responsibility is based on a

---

1 Although the time when the CSR concept was first, mentioned is still controversial, the CSR Theory which is generally accepted by the Western academic circles was probably mentioned in the US in the 1950s. US scholar, Bowen published *Social Responsibilities of the Businessman*, therefore Bowen is known as the father of "Corporate Social Responsibility" concept.

voluntary basis, and enterprises will integrate the concerns to the environment and society into their business operation, as well as will integrate them into the interaction with their interest stakeholders……"[2]

But soon, some scholars questioned the voluntary implementation mechanism of social contractual CSR through a large number of observations. Prof. Geddes from Warwick Business School in the UK, after examining the realization mechanism of CSR (in 2000, 2001), has pointed out: "(corporate and social) partnership (mode) essentially brings the current society into the neo-liberal framework, according to its main contents and concerns, enterprises should not assume fair and just obligations for the community, rather turns the society to one of the stakeholders of business corporations."[3] Prof. Deakin from the Cambridge University Business Research Center (in 2006) strongly questioned whether corporations in the UK had a real willingness to fulfill their social responsibilities in a community partnership mode: "Within the listed company sector, management tends to view CSR as concerned with 'external' issues," ...excludes to make CSR applied to solving internal problems, such as labor relations..... Based on this, we cannot help but ask: "for the British corporate social responsibility movement, although the concept is very attractive, whether it lacks material meaning or not, especially in dealing with the employment relationship?"[4]

In order to demonstrate his viewpoint, Prof. Deakin has examined whether UK's enterprises would consciously comply with the law that limited employees' working time to less than 48 hours per week. "The British government is more generous about working time regulation ... If according to the logic of social partnership mode of stakeholders, the enterprises will voluntarily utilize their initiative to reduce staff's working time, because too long working hours not only damage the happiness of employees (sometimes even health and life safety) but also damage the organization's innovation ability due to the reduced efficiency."[5]

But the research results achieved by Prof. Deakin's observation is as follows: "working time is an area which is only loosely regulated by law in the UK; the 48-hour working week which is contained in UK legislation implementing the EU Working Time Directive, can be modified upwards in the UK according to the needs of individual enterprises, and varies according to either collective or individual agreements by the worker and employer. At the same time, a 'business case' for working time reductions can be made, on the grounds that excessively long working hours are not simply detrimental to the well-being (and in

2 Josep Lozano, Laura Albareda, *Governments and Corporate Social Responsibility*, translated by Li Kai, Intellectual Property Press, 2009, p. 27.
3 Geddes, Benington, *Local Partnerships and Social Exclusion in the European Union*, London, 2001, Routledge, p. 194.
4 S. Deakin, R.Hobbs, "False Dawn for the CSR? Shifts in Regulatory Policy and the Response of the Corporate and Financial Sectors in Britain", *Corporate Governance*, 2006, Vol. 15, p. 1.
5 Ibid., p. 4.

some instances the health and safety) of employees, but may also undermine organizational innovation, with negative repercussions for productivity (see Barnard, Deakin and Hobbs, 2003 for a review of the arguments). On the face of it, then, the issue of working time is an ideal one for uniting the organizational and regulatory dimensions of CSR: within the framework set by law, there is space for voluntary corporate behaviour 'beyond compliance' which would enhance the sustainability of the enterprise while also addressing a significant issue of social policy."[6] In order to facing the serious conflict between the concept and the reality, Prof. Deakin concluded: "It is generally accepted that the concept of corporate social responsibility (CSR) provides a more flexible way of regulating enterprises, and worker-employer relations, that is, by using a kind of regulation by soft laws as in the UK,[7] by the effect of soft laws enterprises can consciously fulfill the responsibilities through the learning process so as to free themselves from either this or that regulatory mode between planned regulation and laissez-faire regulation. ... But the regulation by means of soft law is inefficient, because abundance evidence shows that, in the absence of hard law restrictions, most of the enterprises will feel satisfied once meeting the minimum requirements, and it is unrealistic to expect that enterprises will voluntarily respond to social demands."[8]

The dissatisfaction and critique towards the American mode of the CSR has prompted some scholars to turn their attention to the external institutional arrangements that could have decisive significance in effecting the CSR behaviors corporate enterprises. In this respect, the analysis by J.L. Campbell, professor of political economy at the Copenhagen Business School in Denmark (in 2006) was striking. In his article "Institutional Analysis and the Paradox of Corporate Social Responsibility" he has critically examined the existing defects in the CSR research, he wrote: "So far, almost most of the literature on CSR has ignored to debate on the role of institutional factors."[9] Campbell examined the institutional environment in many countries and proposed the following which could help enterprises behave in socially responsible ways: (1) if there is an effective strong state intervention as the backup force, the enterprises will be more willing to take social responsibilities; (2) If there are independent third-party institutions (such as the NGOs and other independent organizations, social movement organizations, institutional investors and media) which can exercise supervision, enterprises will be more willing to take social responsibility; (3) If enterprises can

---

6 Ibid., p. 5.

7 Soft Law method is a quasi-legal tool, it is not legally binding or binding force is weaker compared to conventional (hard) laws. which have clear binding force and which clearly stipulates rights and obligations. Soft law and hard law terms are often used in international law, meanwhile partly used in domestic law system, the British legislation on working time mentioned in this text is essentially a soft law.

8 S. Deakin, R.Hobbs, "False Dawn for CSR? Shifts in Regulatory Policy and the Response of the Corporate and Financial Sectors in Britain", *Corporate Governance*, 2006, Vol.15, p. 14.

9 John L. Campbell, "Institutional Analysis and the Paradox of Corporate Social Responsibility", *American Behavioral Scientist*, 2006, Vol. 49, pp. 927-928.

maintain a dialogue with trade unions, employees and community organizations, the enterprises will actively take social responsibility; (4) If enterprises belong trade or employer associations and interact on a more systematic and frequent basis with their peers, they are more likely to develop a relatively long-term view of their interests that may supersede their short-term views, thus enterprises will likely undertake take social responsibility. Thus, it can be seen that J.L. Campbell advocates that the institutional factors can play a key role for promoting enterprises to willingly bear social responsibility or not.

On this basis, Prof. A. Midttun from the Norwegian School of Management (in 2006) conducted an empirical study and proposed the concept of "symmetric embeddedness"[10] hypothesis, argued: An emerging model of corporate social responsibility (CSR) or embedded relational governance seems to share the basic market orientation of the liberal model, yet, at the same time, sharing many of the social and collective goals of the welfare state. This combination is apparently achieved by embedding the social dimension into civil society and self-regulatory market processes.

The higher the degree of "embeddedness" in the whole system, the higher the degree of participation by the enterprises in fulfilling social responsibilities. This research displays that Nordic governments have spent large amount of funds on social security and public welfare and that they have maintained intervention and supervision on labor markets, meanwhile strong trade unions have ensured a relatively high level of wage structure. This high-level of sensitive embeddedness in the system have made the social responsibility performance in the enterprises of Nordic countries, become superior in all aspects and rank them at the top (in regard to SRI[11] indicators, annual corporate social responsibility reports, CR[12] indicators, corporate social responsibility standards ISO 14001). "Corporate social responsibility has certain institutional preconditions, to understand the prerequisites and premises of these systems (state intervention systems, welfare systems, trade union systems, etc.) can help shaping better corporate social responsibility performance."[13] Researcher Gjolberg from the Development and Environmental Research Center of University of Oslo has agreed with this view (Gjolberg, 2009) and further pointed out that corporate

333

---

10   This statement has borrowed the concept of "embedded liberalism", which refers to co-ordinating the contradiction between free markets and state intervention by "embedding" the market mechanism into the framework of state intervention, and achieving the co-existence of free market system and state intervention. Under the advocacy of this idea, the Western countries have began to establish public (state) intervention systems and social welfare systems successively in the 1950s and 1960s. This concept was first proposed by the political scientist John Ruggie in 1982.

11   SRI (Socially Responsible Investment) looks for investments that are considered socially conscious because of the nature of the business the company conducts.

12   CR indicator is an indicator system established by BITC, the British Social Responsibility Organization to evaluate the performance of corporate social responsibility. See http://www.bite.org.uk/services/benchmarking/cr-index/about-cr-index.

13   A. Midttun, K. Gautesen, M Gjolberg, "The Political Economy of CSR in Western Europe", *Journal Corporate Governance*, 2006, 6(4), p. 369.

social responsibility was counter-liberalized, in those countries where welfare and government intervention system has been more perfect, wherein socialized attitudes of corporations were more sensitive and wherein social performance of corporations have been better.[14]

In short, the institutional approach in the studies of corporate social responsibility is preferred by the scholars, and the newly achieved research results have changed the prevalent cognition which regarded the American mode of the CSR as the standard and universal mode that has been formed since the 1990s, and the new approaches to CSR "strategy" also emphasize the effect of the "public domain."

II. Re-definition of corporate social responsibility based on institutional perspective: definition of minimum corporate social responsibility to be abided by the enterprises

Currently, in the academia there are two definitions of CSR which are generally accepted and adopted: one definition emphasizes the corporate social responsibility approach from the three-dimensional concept model of corporate social performance proposed by Carroll in 1979.[15] The second definition is based on the "stakeholders theory". Although, these two definitions treat the US's institutional CSR regulation as the default institutional background, they do not leave enough room for the debate on "the role of institutions", so they have following shortcomings: firstly, they ignore the external social and public regulations in promoting corporate social responsibility and argue that the business enterprises should take social responsibility with their own initiatives and behave voluntarily, without any external institutional environment pressure. Secondly, since the institutional arrangements are not considered and not discussed, they lead to the conclusion that "the primary purpose of CSR research should be to promote the profitability of enterprises", rather than enhancing public welfare, resulting in the tactical approach employed by business-led initiatives in their attempts to build and maintain legitimacy in the eyes of societal stakeholders or general customers in the society. This approach contrasts the original intention of corporate social responsibility.[16] Finally, due to the lack of institutional research approach, how to regulate corporate social responsibility has become a difficult issue. Campbell has evaluated the deficiencies of the prevalent corporate social responsibility,

---

14　M. Gjolberg, "The Origin of Corporate Social Responsibility: Global Forces or National Legacies?", *Socio-Economic Review*，2009(7), pp. 605-637.

15　Quoted from *The Origin and Evolution of Corporate Social Responsibility* co-authored by Shen Hongtao and Shen Yifeng, Shanghai People's Publishing House, 2007, p. 89.

16　According to French Scholar Aurelien Acquier's recent re-reading of Bowen's classic work "Social Responsibility of Businessmen," Acquier has evaluated that the early CSR scholars always understood corporate social responsibility from a public welfare perspective rather than from the business enterprise perspective. And currently, the general view of corporate social responsibility inherits this legacy with a strong criticism against elevating business enterprises to a central status in the CSR approach. See Aurelien Acquier's article, "Rediscovering Howard Bowen's Legacy", *Journal of Business & Society,* Nov. 2011 pp. 607-646.

and put forward the concept of "substantive corporate social responsibility"[17] and pointed out: "I view corporations as acting in socially responsible ways if they do two things. First, they must not knowingly do anything that could harm their stakeholders. Second, if they do harm to stakeholders, then they must rectify it whenever it is discovered and brought to their attention. This is a definition that sets a minimum behavioral standard (norm) with respect to the corporation's relationship to its stakeholders below which corporate behavior becomes socially irresponsible."[18] Obviously, according to our understanding, in the definition of Campbell, the substantive corporate social responsibility is based on the principle of "restricting harm" and "accountability and obligation to correct such harms."[19] Campbell thus makes an obvious progress compared with the prevalent definition of corporate social responsibility.

Firstly, different from the traditional concept of corporate social responsibility which rather emphasizes entrepreneurial humanitarian philanthropy and corporate donations (Mc Williams, Siegel 2001), Campbell's definition emphasizes restricting enterprises that they should not intentionally harm the stakeholders' interests, thereby changes the focus of CSR research and clearly puts forward the minimum norm CSR behavior, in regard to enterprises. He wrote: " The issue of doing harm (intentionally or not) largely has been ignored in the literature on corporate social responsibility (but see Bartley, 2003; Grant, 1997; Grant & Downey, 1996). .... This is both surprising and important, given the fact that some firms may score quite high on corporate social responsibility by conventional definitions but very low according to my definition."[20]

Secondly, on the premise that enterprises can have opportunistic tendencies, this definition of Campbell also implies that enterprises are not willing to actively fulfill their social responsibilities, especially minimal social responsibilities, thus emphasizes the role of external institutional regulations to improve corporate social responsibility, which has opened more room for the studies based on institutional approach. This breaks the logic of the prevalent CSR approach which tacitly considers the operation of enterprises as happening in the "vacuum" and ignores the external institutional environment, and argues that they can solely rely on "self-regulation" mode to solve the social responsibility issue. Finally, Campbell's concept of "substantive corporate social responsibility" has changed the "corporate centered" theory of CSR approach and has emphasized public welfare view of CSR analysis as its starting point, which means returning to CSR's original intention.

---

17   John L. Campbell, "Institutional Analysis and the Paradox of Corporate Social Responsibility", *American Behavioral Scientist*, 2006, Vol.49, p. 928.

18   Ibid.

19   We have proposed a two-dimensional view of CSR, that is, compulsory social responsibility and selective social responsibility. Among them, the compulsory social responsibility has the meaning of minimum standards thus its two principles are "Prohibition of damages" and "penalty and compensation for damages." See references [1] and [2].

20   John Campbell, Institutional Analysis and the Paradox of Corporate Social Responsibility, *Journal of American Behavioral Scientist*, 2006, Vol.49, p. 928.

In fact, the "substantive SCR attitudes" of the enterprises as suggested by Campbell should not be a kind of tactical, instrumentalized, consideration for enterprises, also shouldn't take maximizing profit and maximizing shareholder value as best as they can , but the enterprises cannot exchange their own development by harming the social benefit as the cost, and should be accountable and correct their behavior, if they cause a harm. Therefore, the substantive corporate social responsibility should be a kind of compulsory obligation.

In conclusion, Campbell's definition poses a challenge to the definition of corporate social responsibility proposed by the prevalent American model, which suggests that a thorough understanding of corporate social responsibility requires in-depth research on the institutions, and his approach has laid the foundation for subsequent research work in this direction.

III. Demonstration of corporate social responsibility based on institutional perspective: Explicit social responsibility and implicit social responsibility

For a long time, there is only one approach and experience form of corporate social responsibility recognized by people that is the practice of corporate social responsibility rooted in the US's institutional environment. Generally, US's CSR behavior has become the default standard research approach of scholars, without any consideration in regard to institutional conditions and without any consideration if any concept can be directly applied to other countries. What scholars have to do is just to prove and supplement them with more details, which can be fully proved when compared with contents of US scholar's definitions on the CSR as well as their research framework and research methods which are admired and largely quoted.

For a long time after the introduction of the CSR idea to Europe, the European scholars have followed the US-style CSR approaches and focused on handling the micro-management and CSR strategies elevating the enterprises to a central level. This is also evident, as we observe the successful replication of the US's CSR model, in the UK. According to Kinder man's research on the UK's CSR thought (in 2012), he commented that US have played a crucial role in promoting the US-style CSR concept disseminated in the UK: "At the Sunningdale Park Conference (the meeting directly contributed to the birth of BITC, the UK's largest corporate social responsibility organization. Quoter), with 27 delegates attending, 17 of them from the UK business and government sectors, and 10 from the US ... The early development of Corporate Social Responsibility in the UK has directly benefited from the US corporate policy."[21] It can be seen that US has profoundly influenced the spread of corporate social responsibility practices in the other countries not only theoretically but also in practice.

21   Daniel Kinderman, "Free us up so we can be responsible!", "The Co-evolution of Corporate Social Responsibility and neo-liberalism in the UK, 1977-2010", *Socio-Economic Review*, November 2012, Vol. 10, p. 38.

However, the research results of Matten and Moon have posed a challenge to the situation that American mode of corporate social responsibility being viewed as the only universal and universally applicable CSR mode. Matten and Moon have made two judgments based on their observations: 'Firstly, if corporate social responsibility is only recently introduced to other regions and other countries by the US, does this mean that enterprises in other countries have ignored to bear social responsibility till recently? Secondly, what's the reason behind the recent entrance of the CSR practice (referring to American mode) the agenda of business circles of other countries?"[22]

In order to answer the above-mentioned questions, the author has concentrated on the research perspective which focuses to institutional differences, "taking into account that different social-cultural environments develop different market modes, which inevitably reflect their (specific) institutions, ethical customs, and social relations. Therefore, the enterprises in different societies tend to be different in their performances and pursuit of social responsibility."[23] The author compares the differences between European and the US politics, finance, labor management and culture in detail as follows:

Firstly, in regard to political system, the significant difference between Europe and US is that, in the former government enjoys more powers. "European countries' governments are highly involved in economic and social activities, and governments in some countries provide universal health care and endowment insurance, while others (not doing so) will compulsorily require enterprises to undertake a part of these duties or obligations. In the US, the government's role is very limited, which leaves a huge independent decision-making space for the enterprises."[24]

Secondly, in the financial system, "the stock market financing is the main financing platform for US companies, almost all large companies fund their financial needs from this source, and shareholding structure of the companies are relatively dispersed. Therefore, US companies must have high degree of transparency and accountability for their investors. However, in Europe, corporate stocks are often concentrated in the hands of a small number of large investors, and banks play an important role in their financial needs, in this cross-shareholding network, their focus is how to maintain long-term cohesion, effectiveness and power."[25]

Thirdly, in the labor force management, "Europe has a public-oriented training and habits, plus active labor market management policies, and companies are generally restricted, either by customs or by legal regulations, but in US, companies make their decisions according to their own company strategies.

---

22   Dirk Matten, Jeremy Moon, "Implicit and Explicit CSR: A Conceptual Framework For A Comparative Understanding of Corporate Social Responsibility", *Academy of Management Review*, 2008, Vol. 33, p. 405.
23   Ibid., p. 407.
24   Ibid.
25   Ibid., p. 498.

There has always been a higher proportion of union members, which has led that the problems in labor-capital relations are generally resolved through inter-industry and even national-level negotiations, and accordingly, European companies are more inclined to defend their collective interests through National Business Associations or collective action."[26]

Finally, in regard to culture, US is prone to individualism, but skeptic against the state, reflection of such culture in the business circles is that businessmen feel responsibility to contribute to the society, but its reflection in the enterprise level is that the enterprises should bear social responsibility. However, European culture have made people more dependent on representative organizations, such as political parties, trade unions, employer associations, churches and certain local state organizations (e.g. the communes in Germany).

Differences between Europe and the US in regard to politics, finance, labor force management and cultural institution make their national business systems (NBS) entirely different, which is reflected in enterprise nature, market organizations, corporate monitoring & management and so on. Firstly, in regard to enterprise natures, "the ownership structure of the US enterprises is mostly formed through the market in the form of signing contracts; but the ownership of European enterprises displays a kind of direct ownership, or joint ownership which is formed in connection with banks, insurance companies, and even related to state network. European countries, such as France and the United Kingdom, have historically a relatively high proportion of state-owned enterprises and municipal companies which have heavily invested in the private sector."[27] Secondly, in the market organization, the way in which US coordinates and organizes market participants and their relationships is by the spontaneous force of the market, "people pass this mission to self-regulatory role of the market, which is supervised by the governments and state courts through legislation such as anti-trust laws. In Europe, the market is realized through group coalitions, which reflect the consensus and consultation between employers and employees or reflect a strong government leadership."[28] Thirdly, in the terms of governance conditions in the enterprises, employees in US corporations are basically passive and have little impact on corporate governance. On the contrary, in Europe, employee representation rights and participation rights are strictly protected by various labor laws and regulations, which make the behavior of European enterprises largely open to the supervision of employees and the government. However, in US, due to low employee participation and supervision problems are generally resolved through the way of enterprises assuming social responsibility actively.

26   Ibid., p. 408.
27   Dirk Matten, Jeremy Moon, "Implicit and Explicit CSR: A Conceptual Framework For A Comparative Understanding of Corporate Social Responsibility", *Academy of Management Review*, 2008, Vol. 33, p. 408.
28   Ibid., p. 409.

Based on the comparative analysis of the above institutions, the author concludes there are differences in CSR practices and forms in Europe and the US, "the American mode of CSR is embedded in a system where enterprises may have more motivations and opportunities to clearly bear the social responsibilities."[29] Thus, D. Matten presents the definition and characteristics of explicit social responsibility and implicit social responsibility: "explicit social responsibility refers to the responsibility that enterprises actively bear and explicitly claim to promote the social interests, to this end, enterprises set a suite of corporate policies, which are usually made up of corporate voluntary projects or strategies, and are made on the basis of enterprises combining business and social values...... The characteristic of explicit social responsibility is that it must rely on corporations' independent decision rather than relying on governments' compelling force or external institutional regulations ... Implicit social responsibility means that the role of enterprises are positioned in a broader formal and informal systems which are designed to promote social interests. Implicit social responsibility includes the values, norms and rules that need to be abided by enterprises (mandatorily or customarily), and the definition of these responsibilities is often defined in a collective form, rather than in an individual form."[30] There are two main differences between explicit social responsibility and implicit social responsibility in their expression form: firstly, it is the difference in language, the enterprises that bear the explicit social responsibility will use the term " Corporate Social Responsibility " to explain their social behaviors and policies, but the enterprises that bear the implicit social responsibility will not do so, even they don't realize that they are bearing social responsibilities. Secondly, implicit corporate social responsibility is not like explicit corporate social responsibility to be achieved through voluntary, deliberate and strategic decision-making, but to be achieved through passive reaction to external institutional pressures.

---

29   Ibid.

30   Dirk Matten, Jeremy Moon, "Implicit and Explicit CSR: A conceptual Framework For A Comparative Understanding of Corporate Social Responsibility", *Journal of Management Review*, 2008, Vol. 33, p. 404-424.

**Table 1. Comparison between explicit social
responsibility and implicit social responsibility**

Explicit social responsibility	Implicit social responsibility
Corporate self-regulated behavior undertaking responsibilities for the purpose of promoting social interests	The role of enterprises is designed in a broader formal and informal system in order designed to promote social interests
Including voluntary enterprise policies, projects and strategies.	Including (compulsory or legalized written) values, norms and regulations, etc that need to be abided by enterprises
Motivations and opportunities for enterprises to bear responsibility come from the expectation of corporate stakeholders	Enterprises bearing responsibility, is due to the fact that the major groups in the society (including the enterprises themselves) have reached a consensus on their respective contributions and roles.

*Note: See Dirk Matten, Jeremy Moon. "Implicit and Explicit CSR: A Conceptual
Framework For A Comparative Understanding of Corporate Social Responsibility",
Academy of Management Review, 2008, Vol.33, pp. 404-424.*

340   The introduction of explicit social responsibility and implicit social responsibility has affirmed the differences in the CSR modes and forms, and such distinction has further deepened scholars' reflection on the American mode of CSR. Based on this theory, in the recent years scholars including Marens (2010, 2012, 2013), Brammer (2012) and others have developed new concepts of the CSR from different perspectives. Among them, Marens has made a detailed research on the history of the emergence of American mode of CSR perspective: he has asserted that the unique formation process of the American mode of CSR is also the promotion process of corporate hegemonism. In this stage, the entrepreneurs have mastered the CSR discourse hegemony and have commissioned the US business MBA schools that they donated to promote their own social responsibility concept to the whole world: "as donors of US business schools and also as their students' employers, entrepreneurs have carefully determined those teaching courses suitable for teaching ... corporate donations have flowed to those colleges which advocated restricting government intervention and emphasize unlimited freedom."[31] Influenced by this, a large number of unrealistic, abstract, but far-reaching corporate social responsibility concepts were first borne in the US. "Since the 1980s, the field of corporate social responsibility has been occupied by a group of business school professors who profess to be business ethicists; they have received philosophical training and pushed corporate social responsibility into the abstract

---

31   Richard Marens, "Destroying the Village to Save It: Corporate Social Responsibility. Labour Relations, and the Rise and Fall of US Hegemony", *Organization* 2010(10), p. 756.

conception of traditional philosophy, as well as almost deliberately ignored what exactly happened in the US business circles. Although they have used an obscure writing style, they have essentially promoted CSR mode which is essentially centered on corporate interests and corporate governance; which saw strong business management capabilities as the definition and implementation of the CSR, as the only guarantee and justification... Freeman's stakeholder theory and Donaldson's social contract theory are typical ones."[32] Marens quoted Donham's (927) comments to indicate that "all the rhetoric related to voluntary services is simply the self-complacent excuse for those enterprises who don't want to be supervised.[33]

In conclusion, the introduction of explicit social responsibility and implicit social responsibility concepts have enriched the connotation of CSR and has gotten rid of the analysis drawback of solely taking US's CSR structure and practice as its research object.

IV. Revelation

The various new viewpoints by European scholars we have presented above in this paper, emphasize the importance of institutional regulations for a comprehensive understanding of corporate social responsibility, they have highlighted the differences in corporate social responsibility forms, and have challenged the dominant tendency which has discussed corporate social responsibility taking USA as the ready-made universal institutional background and premise, which was created in the 1980s. These new research results provide valuable theoretical references for the anew construction of corporate social responsibility system and its basic concepts which will fit to our own characteristics.

Firstly, introduction of the institutional approach into the CSR analysis expands the theoretical research perspective, and affirms the currently existing objective differences among the CSRs (without discarding commonalities) which can happen under the background of different institutional environments and regulations.

Any enterprise must bear social responsibility, which is determined by a series of contradictions inherent in its long-term development. However, different institutional environments and regulations which are regarded as the external environment of corporate operations determine that there will be obvious differences in CSR principles, expression forms of corporate social responsibility, even CSR dimensions and other core aspects.

The facts demonstrate that there are at least two forms of corporate social responsibility: one is the explicit social responsibility centered on enterprises

---

32 Richard Marens, "What Comes Around: The Early 20th Century Roots of Legitimating Corporate Social Responsibility in the US", *Journal of Management* 2013(20), p. 471.
33 Donham, W. B., "The Emerging Profession of Business", *Harvard Business Review*, 1927 (5), p. 404.

based on the with voluntariness principle, the second is the implicit social responsibility. The former is generated in the US environment suitable to its unique conditions; the latter is generated in the institutional environments which are different from the US's, and its prominent feature is that there is a set of institutional regulations, including government guiding, regulating and intervening into the CSR behaviors of the corporations. Implicit social responsibility is also the form of corporate social responsibility, and there is already a basis for its existence. The American mode, i.e. the explicit social responsibility form cannot be regarded as the only form of corporate social responsibility. I also should mention that, even in the large-scale neo-liberalized European countries, the governments' intervention on the CSR behaviors is not completely abandoned. In the explicit social responsibility aspect of CSR, the governments are the main forces to promote enterprises to fulfill their social responsibility; especially the German government maintains a high degree of intervention on the CSR.[34]

China is a socialist market economy country, which means there is a radical difference in regard to nature of enterprises, market structures and government regulation compared to US and European countries. Therefore, it is natural that the corporate social responsibility system of China should have both explicit and implicit expression forms. When promoting the CSR construction in China, to highlight the necessity and legitimacy of implicit social responsibility will be favorable to reflect the institutional advantages of socialism and can be more in line with China's current economic and social development stage and can meet institutional environment of socialist market economy.

Secondly, the introduction of the distinction between the explicit and implicit social responsibility forms provide a unique perspective for understanding corporate social responsibility and its construction process in China. The dissemination process of the CSR theory in China is a process, in a unique historical context wherein the proportion of non-public enterprises are continuously increasing and the proportion of public-owned enterprises are continuously declining, through restructuring and incremental reform measures, which is in fact a structural transformation of the current economic system. This unique context determines that the implicit corporate social responsibility form will gradually change towards the explicit social responsibility.

With the deepening of the market economy and the relaxation of government control on the enterprises, especially alongside the 1990s and the early 21st Century, the CSR issues have began to concern people and has triggered people's strong demand.

In order to make up for the blank of CSR concept in China, and in order to respond to the increasingly strong voices which demanded that enterprises

---

34 Sun Qinghua, "An Investigation Report on the European Corporate Social Responsibility", see the website of the Policy and Regulation Department of the Ministry of Industry and Information Technology of the PRC, December 26, 2011.

should bear social responsibility, a large number of US literature was studied and scholars, have begun to quote some ideas from them. Thus the explicit CSR theory which takes the US environment as its basis was gradually familiar among the people.

At the same time, in the practices of corporate social responsibility, the form of explicit social responsibility based on voluntary principle was adopted, as the dominant form.

However, it is worth noting that CSR theory has aroused scholars' extensive debate in China at the beginning of its dissemination , especially around the legitimacy of the CSR, its dimensions and realization mechanisms, etc. However, the disputes in the debate were only the repetition of the earlier debates which had occurred among the US scholars, and the debate results had not made much achievement and did not make real an impact or breakthrough, to reveal the hidden contradictions of the American mode, its explicit CSR theoretical system.

On the contrary, due to the profound impact of explicit corporate social responsibility research paradigm—upon the Chinese scholars—with its main theoretical characteristics being as the social contract, the people could not think of a unique CSR suitable to China's unique institutional environment. Some scholars even opposed to all other CSR forms except the American paradigm, and deemed the explicit social responsibility form which was generated in the soil of US system as the undoubted classics. Conceptualizing the CSR on the basis of "market-oriented" and "internationalization" concept will split the history of Chinese CSR construction and deny institutional environment's shaping and choice on CSR. Obviously this conceptualization has not been conducive to the construction of the unique CSR mode in line with China's specific institutional environment.

In addition, if we look into the actual situation of the implementation of explicit social responsibility in China, and if we look into the annual CSR reports published by the enterprises we can say that they demonstrate almost a corporate self-confession and looks like marketing papers, and there is hardly solid evidence to judge whether they are true or not.[35]

Thirdly, the minimum CSR requirements defined by institutional approach analysis are important for improving the scope and dimensions of corporate social responsibility and the principles of corporate social responsibility. This concept will deepen the studies. Whether enterprises should undertake other social responsibilities besides law-regulated duties has been the focus of the CSR debate all the time. Hayek, Friedman and other liberal economists and their followers insist that the only corporate social responsibility is to operate abiding by laws and earn profits for their shareholders, namely economic

343

---

35   For example, in Foxconn's CSR Reports (2010-2011), there are many places mentioning about caring for the staffbut no mention about the numerous events wherein the staff committed suicide

responsibility. Hayek, Friedman and other liberal economists, oppose to bear other social responsibilities except this profit- oriented operation. While undertaking other social responsibilities are considered understood as the behavior that managers of the corporations acting in the name of the enterprises, spending and donating the money which belongs ing to shareholders in contributing to the society, which is considered as the to be in violation of the will of the shareholders and violate the spirit of a free spirit of the society. Friedman has repeatedly stressed that to realize "corporate social responsibility" enterprises should increase their profits[36], and criticizes the viewpoint that enterprises should undertake social responsibility is "a fundamental misunderstanding in regard to characteristics and nature of the free liberal economics. In a free economy, "There is one and only one social responsibility of business–to use it resources and engage in activities designed to increase its profits so long as it stays within the rules of the game, which is to say, engages in open and free competition without deception or fraud."[37]

If the enterprise donates for a social responsibility, it means shareholders' money is not used according to their own interests and wishes, therefore, "such donations should only be provided by the owners of the properties in the society".[38] At the same time, if the enterprises undertake other social responsibilities such as donations for social responsibility, this will increase their operating costs. This is also a threat to the free economic system.[39]

344 Obviously, this kind of controversy is inevitable for the proposition of CSR which is based on the sole voluntariness principle and which had emerged and generated under US's unique institutional environment. The reason why Friedman and others oppose that enterprises bear social responsibilities, other than their economic responsibilities is because they not only firmly believe that "the capitalist enterprises never harm the interests of others when they are fighting in pursuit of profits", but also, such radical neo-liberal economists, more importantly worry that the foundation of free society will be shaken if the enterprises bear other social responsibilities. Freedman asserted: "those corporate managers seeking to please the demands for social responsibility rather than making their best to earn the most money for the corporate shareholders, will completely shake the foundation of our free society."[40] Friedman thus concluded that corporate social responsibility is "fundamentally a subversive doctrine"[41]. Guided by such an ideology, the debate is destined to lead nowhere. In addition, within the discourse field of the American mode of CSR concept based on the

---

36   Milton Friedman, "The Social Responsibility of Business is to Increase its Profits", *The New York Times Magazine*, September 13, 1970.

37   Milton Friedman, *Capitalism and Freedom*, University of Chicago Press, 1962, p. 133

38   Ibid., p. 135.

39   This is G. Manne's point of view, please refer to "The Origin and Evolution of CSR Thought" written by Shen Hongtao and Shen Yifeng, Shanghai People's Publishing House, 2007, pp. 32-35.

40   Milton Friedman, *Capitalism and Freedom*, University of Chicago Press, 1962, p. 133.

41   Ibid.

solely voluntariness principle, the dimensions and boundaries of the CSR can only depend on interests of stakeholders, and will be enumerated according to this conception, consequently its guiding significance will not be great.

At the same time, the introduction of the concept of minimum requirements (Campbell's analysis) for the CSR affirms the fact that there is an opportunistic behavior tendency among enterprises, also denies the CSR concept based on solely voluntariness principle, this new concept provides a new way to reasonably determine the dimension and scope of the CSR, and indicates that CSR should contain compulsory obligations as its contents. In fact, in the USA, corporate social responsibility has fundamentally emerged as a product of managing labor-capital conflicts, rather than being a product of voluntariness emerging in the corporations. In the 1930s and before, the emergence form of the American CSR was mainly manifested as a forced responsibility after intense conflicts between labor and capital, the Homestead Steel Production Town Tragedy and the Ludlow Miners Tragedy which have shocked the USA and world successively. The high degree of confrontations between employers and employees indicate that entrepreneurs are reluctant to accept social responsibility for workers. In other words, the American mode of CSR does not carry the "genes" that enterprises have voluntarily decided to contribute to "social responsibilities" perform at the beginning of their birth, but a kind of compensation by capitalists employers to workers and the town community due to social pressures from the US public. Therefore, looking from this perspective, the emergence history of the CSR in US is also a struggle history. Although the US scholar Bowen has emphasized the voluntariness principle of the CSR in the beginning of his studies, in the later phase he began to question and later abandoned the voluntariness principle, finally Bowen put forward that the concept of (corporate) social responsibility should be established on the basis of the social control upon the companies (enterprises).[42] However, his later ideas was hidden by the mainstream researches.

A theoretical economics analysis shows that enterprises cannot take the initiative to assume social responsibilities, unless they earn higher profits for such an act, which is determined by their inherent nature.[43] China is in the transitional period in regard to its economic system, the capital accumulation behavior regardless of social responsibility is a common phenomenon. It will be a sheer fantasy divorced from practice in China, to give up government intervention and hope that enterprises will voluntarily assume social responsibilities. Theoretical analysis and empirical evidence show that without the intervention of the government on the CSR behaviors, those enterprises that will assume social responsibilities will be expelled as "good money".[44] In our view,

345

---

42   Refer to *The Origin and Evolution of CSR Thought* written by Shen Hongtao and Shen Yifeng, Shanghai People's Publishing House, 2007, pp. 53-54.
43   Zhang Xian, Tan Kecheng, The CSR Problems: A Thinking Based on Marxist Economics", *Journal of Teaching and Research*, 2014(1).
44   Zhang Xian, Zhang Xiuli, "Game Theory Analysis on Government Regulation and Its Relevance for Enterprises to Perform Social Responsibility", Working Paper, 2011.

CSR should have two dimensions: firstly, the compulsory social responsibility dimension on the two dialectical principles of "restricting harm " and "accountability and obligation to correct such harms; secondly is the selective social responsibility or voluntary social responsibility dimension on the principle of "social welfare improvement". Compulsory social responsibility belongs to the minimum responsibility requirement that an enterprise must fulfill; no matter what the corporate size is, industry and nature, they should fulfill such responsibilities. To some extent, compulsory social responsibility should constitute the basic premise and minimum moral requirement for the existence and development of an enterprise. The realization degree of such social responsibility should be independent of the enterprise's own economic performance, that is to say, regardless its business success CSR should be performed. Once the enterprise violates the compulsory social responsibility duties, the enterprise should act to compensate for its misgiving, and should receive the relevant sanctions.

If we start from the actual situations of China's current stage, enterprises will not voluntarily fulfill their compulsory social responsibilities. The fact that China is still suffering from the lack of compulsory CSR is very clear. Under such circumstances, suggesting the voluntariness principle of CSR will be equal to suggest the abandonment of the most basic social responsibilities, suggesting it is infeasible.

Selective social responsibility is basically a kind of social responsibility that can be voluntarily selected by an enterprise on the basis of fulfilling its compulsory social responsibilities. Since, such selective social responsibility is based on the principle of "welfare improvement" as I have suggested above, the enterprises cannot be forced, instead such act can only be chosen by these enterprises according to their social responsibility concepts, according to their cognition, entrepreneurial preferences, corporate ethics and morality as well as the economic capacity of the corporate economic capacity, all in all the enterprises cannot be forced.

The content of corporations' "selective social responsibility" includes various corporate behaviors that can promote social welfare. These behaviors can be summarized as "good deeds or charity by enterprises". Obviously, such selective social responsibility is the high-level realm of the CSR concept.

Dividing the CSR into compulsory social responsibility dimension and selective social responsibility dimension will be helpful to get rid of the concept of American mode of the CSR. Besides such division will enrich the debates on the CSR issue among the academic circles at home and abroad, which is in line with the actual situations of CSR in current stage of China. Moreover, the two-dimensional division of the CSR will provide a solid theoretical basis for the government's intervention on the CSR behaviors of enterprises. According to the division between the compulsory social responsibility and selective social responsibility, it is clear that government's intervention on the CSR behaviors should cover compulsory social responsibility sphere. By strengthening the government's regulation and intervention on compulsory CSR behaviors we can effectively protect "good money" and promote the construction of CSR.

All in all, the new research trend of European scholars on the CSR, from the aspect of institutional approach analysis, provides a new perspective for further enriching the study of the CSR theory. The new research trend has offered a deep questioning and posed a strong challenge to the American mode of the CSR theory, its concepts and practices, also provides a useful theoretical reference for objectively understanding the CSR theory and practices.

References

Zhang Xian, Xiao Bin, Corporate Social Responsibility: Basis and Dimension, *Journal of Sichuan University* 2010(2).

Zhang Xian, Tan Kecheng, A New Exploration on Corporate Social Responsibility, *China Business and Market* 2011(1).

McWilliams. A. Siegel, D., "Corporate Social Responsibility: A Theory of the Firm Perspective", *The Academy of Management* 2001(1).

Aurelien Acquier, "Re-discovering Howard Bowen's Legacy", *Journal of Business & Society* 2011(11).

Richard Marens, "Generous in Victory? US Managerial Autonomy, Labor Relations and the Invention of Corporate Social Responsibility". *Socio-economic Review* 2012(10).

Gregory Jackson, Androniki Apostolakou, Corporate Social Responsibility in Western Europe, An institutional Mirror or Substitute?, *Journal of Business Ethics* 2012, Vol. 94.

H.R. Bowen, Social Responsibility of the Businessman, Harper & Row, 1953.

Stephen Brammer, Corporate Social Responsibility and Institutional Theory, *New Perspectives on Private Governance* 2012(10), pp. 3-28.

Originally published in the journal Studies on Marxism, 2014(2)

On the Slight Recovery and Deeply Hidden
Dangers in the Current World Economy

Ding Bing

349

Between Jan 22-25, 2014, the 44th Davos International Forum was held. There were about 2500 political, business, academic elites from nearly 100 countries and regions, including 1500 businessmen, more than government heads from 40 countries, and 25 leaders from international organizations. They gathered together to discuss those ideas that will reshape the world. Participants have made a general estimation of the current economic situation in the world. It was generally agreed that the current world economy is entering a moderate recovery period, but risks still exist. The author agrees that this estimate basically conforms to the reality.

IMF's revised report Outlook on World Economic on January 7 predicted that: The global economy will further increase its growth to 3.7% and 3.9% in 2014 and 2015 respectively, after the slow pace of 3% growth in 2013. At the same time, IMF also lowered its growth estimations of some economies and regions, which shows that there are also risk factors for the global economy, and the economic differences and gaps between major economies and regions have become very obvious.[1]

---

1   News Report by journalist Gao Weidong, "This Year Global Economy Increases by 3.7%", *Economic Daily*, January 24, 2014(4).

I. The USA

According to the estimations of the above IMF report, on the basis of the growth of 1.7% in 2013, US economy has grown 2.8% and 3.0% in 2014 and 2015 respectively. Main basis of the estimation was as follows: after the crisis in 2008, the US implemented a series of policies and measures such as quantitative easing (QE) and industrialization, which gradually improved the employment situation, and the unemployment rate decreased from a peak of 10% in October 2009 to 7.3%, 7%, 6.7% and 6.6% in each month from October 2013 to January 2014, respectively. Thus, the consumption capacity and the confidence of residents may continue to increase; Secondly, shale oil and gas development makes the oil and gas production of the US constantly increase; in 2013, the domestic oil production exceeded the US's import volume for the first time, which caused the oil price much lower than other countries, this oil price advantage has both enhanced US's international competitiveness and accelerated the development of domestic manufacturing industries; the third factor is the recovery and development of the real estate industry. By September 2013, the US average house prices have recovered to the highest level, since July 2008; the price of various types of old houses set about 200,000 USD in October in the same year, has seen an increase of 12.8%. These all indicate that five years after the outbreak of the 2008 financial crisis, the United States has gradually embarked on a moderate recovery track. However, the hidden dangers of crisis in the United States still remain.

First of all, although US's unemployment rate has declined, it is still in a high level. According to private statistics, the actual unemployment rate of the US is as high as 12.1%.[2] Even we look from the official unemployment statistics which are lower, the unemployment rate is also as high as 6.5%, 4% far higher than the 1950s and 1960s. It is also 4.75% higher than that before the outbreak of the subprime crisis in 2007. Even the Fed's new chairman, Janet Yellen, also said that the unemployment rate was "extraordinarily high". One of the direct consequences of this long-term high unemployment rate is that the gap between rich and poor widens, and even in the process of economic recovery, this process of widening of the gap has not ceased. Data show that since the recession has begun in mid-2009, 95% of the income growth has flowed to the pockets of the 1% of the country's rich. The 1% rich people possessed the 20% of the total income before tax, while they had possessed only 10% in the 1970s.[3]

Secondly, the US governments' serious debt burden has fallen. Although the fiscal deficit of the 2013 budget has dropped by 51%, from 1.42 trillion USD of last year to 680 billion USD in 2013. However, if we analyze this together with the accumulative total state debt of 169 trillion USD (government bonds) over the years, it is a huge amazing astronomical figure. What's more, these figures

2   The journalist of Xinhua News Agency, Fan Yu, Liu Jie; "Employment Data is Difficult to Drive the Clouds of the US Economic Outlook", "Beijing Reference", February 10, 2014/12.
3   See The Christian Science Monitor, US website's report on January 23, 2014, *Reference News*, January 25, 2014/6.

are official figures which are greatly mitigated. Prof. James D. Hamilton from the university of California, San Diego said: if added with the government's short-term debts, the actual "total debt of the government would reach a staggering USD 70 trillion",[4] while the debt ceiling[5] that the United States should issue bonds was only 16.69 trillion USD by the end of 2012; even if combined with the raised 62 billion USD in regard to the debt ceiling which was increased by the two central parliaments of the USA, as an emergency measure in December 2013 in order to avoid the second event of government shutdown, the debt ceiling was only 16.752 trillion USD, which cannot meet the requirements of the government (16.9 trillion USD).

However, the Congress has issued a bill in which the Treasury should take extraordinary measures so as to enable that debt ceiling increase will be delayed, this debt ceiling will be fully used by February 27, the US Treasury Department cannot issue any more Treasury bills to borrow.

Despite the rapidly approaching debt default, the US Congress passed another bill to raise the debt ceiling to 17.2 trillion US dollars on February 12, thus temporarily delaying the debt default crisis. Nevertheless, in the United States, since it will be difficult to avoid the current system to determine its future fiscal year's budget deficit, the outstanding debt obligations to pay will continue to rise, which will certainly break through the debt ceiling and the debt default crisis will still break out like a buried "time bomb".

Thirdly, to maintain its world economic hegemony, the United States guided to conclude and sign TPP and TTIP agreements across two oceans, which is not well received by some other countries. Besides, against the emerging economies, especially for China, US frequently implement the "double reverse" protectionism, thus the US acts against the world trend, aggravates the trade frictions and becomes unpopular. These above clearly indicate that the development of the US economic system is dominated by its inherent periodic cyclical development law. Although its economy will see recovery or even prosperity after the crisis, another crisis era will inevitably occur, and see a worsening trend on the whole, and the times when imperialism could do whatever it desired is bygone times forever.

II. Eurozone

According to the survey report released by European Commission in early 2014, the European Union and the Eurozone's economic sentiment index (ESI) in December 2013 rose to 103.5 and 100 points respectively, with a chain increase of 1.4 points and 1.6 points. Among them, the EU economic index has kept rising for

---

4   The website of Fox News TV in the United States, from August 14, 2013: "The US government's debt reaches $70 trillion dollars", *Reference News*, August 16, 2013(4).

5   The debt ceiling is a limit that Congress imposes on how much debt the federal government can carry at any given time. When the ceiling is reached, the U.S. Treasury Department cannot issue any more Treasury bills, bonds, or notes to borrow cash money.

8 consecutive months by maintaining the momentum.[6] These figures show that the EU's economic recession trend has basically ended. Take UK (not joining in the Eurozone) for example. According to the data released by the Bureau of Statistics of Great Britain and Northern Ireland, Britain's annual economic growth in 2013 was 1.9%, the highest growth rate since the crisis in 2007, and has been gradually accelerating. GDP from the first quarter to the third quarter grew 0.5%, 0.8% and 2.2% respectively. Although this is a slow growth trend, it is still relatively faster than other EU countries. This is mainly because that without joining in the Eurozone, the debt crisis had a relatively low impact. In the mean time, due to the easing of credit conditions by the central bank and increasing market confidence, small and medium-sized enterprises which relocated in the past have moved back in their business in recent years. According to British Prime Minister David Cameron's statement in January 2014, in 2013, more than 10% of the small and medium-sized enterprises which have already relocated some of their production capacity from the emerging economies back to the United Kingdom.

In the Eurozone, overall, the economy has gotten over the most difficult times. Except a few heavily indebted countries which have not yet emerged from the shadow of the crisis, all other countries have embarked on a path of gradual recovery to varying degrees.

First is the Germany, which has an annual economic growth rate increase by 0.4% in 2013, following its 3% growth in 2011 and 0.7% in 2012. Although decreasing over the years, it is still in the state of sustainable growth; the IMF predicts that it will continue to increase 1.7% and 2% in 2014 and 2015 respectively. The reason is that the residents have a strong spending power and the government's financial resources are relatively abundant. Although there were 1.7 billion Euros of fiscal deficit in 2013, it was only equivalent to 0.1% of GDP, which was far below the upper limit of 3% set by the Eurozone. At the same time, the Germany's export power is stronger. Although its exports have dropped in 2013 and its export growth has decreased from 3.6% in 2012 to 0.6% in 2013, but its foreign trade surplus increased instead of decreasing in 2013. The German Economic Research Institute in Munich predicts that Germany's current account balance of payment surplus will reach 260 billion US dollars in 2013, ranking first in the world.[7]

The second is France. According to the data released by the country's National Bureau of Statistics on August 14, 2013, the initial value of GDP in the second quarter was up 0.5% from the previous quarter, being better than the expected, and is emerging from a slight recession, setting a record high since teh rise in the early 2011. In the same period, the entire Eurozone economy also grew by 0.3%, marking the end of the 18-month recession in the Eurozone.[8]

---

6   The source of data: *Economic Daily*, January 13, 2014(4).

7   Refer to Wang Zhiyuan, The German Economic Mode Is Unsustainable, *Economic Daily*, January 30, 2014/5.

8   Refer to AFP, "The Brussels Report on August 14, 2013", *Reference News* from August 16, 2013(4).

Third is Italy, from 2008 to 2013, its total economic power has dropped to nearly 10% in total in the past six years, the debt ratio to GDP was as high as 134%, and the unemployment was 12.1%. The situation has been serious. However, by the end of 2013, the financial situation was slightly improved and no longer continued to deteriorate; the business climate index rose significantly to 98.1, reaching the highest level since August 2011.

The fourth is Spain. After two years of economic recession, it has already shown signs of improvement at the end of 2013. According to the statistics, the economy by 0.1% in the third quarter rose from a year earlier. Government finances also appeared to have certain strength. By being one of the original debt-ridden countries, it has announced that it would withdraw from the EU rescue mechanism in 2014; it was predicted that the economy would increase 0.5% and 1.7% in 2014 and 2015, respectively. There are indications about that the Spanish economy has begun to gradually recover. The deterioration of the economic situation in those countries with heavy debt in the Eurozone has also eased slightly. The OECD has estimated that Portuguese economy would grow 0.4% in 2014, and would determine the best way to leave behind the rescue plan after the first quarter. In the past, after exiting from the international rescue package, Ireland successfully returned to the market.

At present, the countries with the most difficult situation in the Eurozone are Greece and Cyprus. The OECD has predicted that the Greek economy would drop by 0.4% in 2014, and was about to become a country which has suffered a recession for seven consecutive years. In 2010 and 2011, Greece has accepted financial debt aid from the "Troika" countries as 110 billion Euros and 130 billion Euros twice successively. Although the debt crisis has been eased slightly so far, Greece is still in the heavy debt and difficult to extricate itself. The IMF predicted that in 2014, 4 billion of Euros would not be available; besides, in order to repay the debt, Greece would also face the risk of inflation and fiscal austerity. The decline in the welfare of residents and the unemployment rate as high as 27% poses a direct threat to the political stability of this country. As another country with heavy debt to accept bailout, Cyprus's GDP in this year is expected to continue to decline, the government's sovereign debt rate is still rising, and is expected to remain so within one or two years.

In short, in Europe, although the economic recession and sovereign debt crisis now has basically ended in general, the European countries are not out of the shadow of crisis. Not only a few countries with heavy debt are still trapped in deep economic trouble, but also the general unemployment rate stays at a high level. According to the data released by the EU Statistical Bureau on January 8th, 2014, in November 2013, the unemployment rate in the Eurozone is 12.1%, of which the young people is 24.2%; over the same period, the unemployment rate of EU is 10.9%, of which the young people is 23.6%.[9] What is especially not optimistic is that since 2009, the Eurozone has been strictly enforcing austerity policies in order to save the debt crisis. By January 2014, the

___

9 See "The Eurozone's Unemployment Rate Remains at A High Level", *Economic Information Daily*, January 9, 2014(11).

inflation rate has dropped to a dangerous level of 0.7%. This not only caused a drop in prices and investment returns which forced the enterprises to reduce or stop their production, but also caused a debt burden of the heavily indebted countries to rise implicitly. At present, the sovereign debt ratio Greece, Italy and Portugal are 171.8%, 132.9% and 128.7% respectively.[10] This, in turn, will hinder the economic growth. As a result, the austerity measures will likely make it possible for the fragile Eurozone economy to regain its recession.

III. Japan

After the 1990s, Japan has long been in a state of deflation and economic stagnation. In December 2012, when Prime Minister Shinzo Abe took office, he launched the policy of "fighting against the economic issues" with attempted to revive the Japanese economy, which is advertised by the Japanese media as "Abeconomics" Its basic contents have three aspects, known as the "three arrows": first, Japan proposed the largest quantitative easing (QE) monetary policy in its history, and the central bank purchases 7.5 trillion yen of national debt per month (about 75 billion US dollars); second is to break through the former Prime Minister's expansionary fiscal policy with a total budget of 70 trillion yen; third is to study the long-term "economic growth strategy", including its decision to participate in the US-led TPP negotiations despite the domestic opposition. Mr. Abe boasted that the "three arrows" have been successful in Davos Forum: "People are more energetic and optimistic now; Japan is ushering in a new dawn instead of the twilight."[11] We recognize that these "three arrows", especially the first two have achieved some success in the short term. For example, due to the increased liquidity and government investment, the Japanese economy continued to grow in 2013 after plunging from the fourth quarter of 2012, up by 4.3%, 3.8% and 1.9% respectively over the first three quarters and with an annual growth 1.7%. The IMF report estimated that in 2014 and 2015, the Japanese economy would also increase 1.75% and 1% respectively. However, it should be noted that the declining trend of growth rate in sustained growth in 2013 in itself suggested that the Japanese economy still had hidden dangers. In addition, Japan's foreign trade deficit has worsened in recent years and the government debt has only risen to as high as 1008.62 trillion yen by the end of June 2013, all of which the crux of Japan's problems. On February 4, 2014, Tokyo's Nikkei stock index plunged 610 points, which has also poured cold water to "Abeconomics". Since Mr. Abe's quantitative easing (QE) policy has aimed at "realizing the depreciation of yen and the rising of share prices"; now the situation of falling share price appears. It is no wonder that the US media has also commented that "Mr. Abe's economic policies will not work."[12]

---

10 See Yan Hengyuan, Eurozone's Deflation Risk Increases, *Economic Daily*, February 11, 2014(4).

11 See "The Survey Said the Effect of "Abeconomics" is Limited, *Economic Information Daily*, January 28, 2014(5).

12 See article published in the USA, bimonthly website, blog of National Interests; on August 14, 2013: article by Jay Zawahiri, "Tokyo's Time bomb: The Imminent Time Bomb of Japan Tokyo"; quote from *Reference News*, August 16, 2013(4).

IV. Emerging market economies

This mainly refers to the BRICS countries including China and other developing countries. On June 16th, 2009, the leaders of four emerging market economies of China, Russia, India and Brazil met for the first time in Yekaterinburg, Russia and began to form the BRICS Group as the emerging market economies. In December 2010, with the attendance of South Africa, it was called as "5 BRICS countries" (BRICS). Today, the BRICS account for 26% of the world's land area, 43% of the population, 20% of the total economy, 17% of the foreign trade and 50% of the contribution to the global economic growth. From 2011 to 2013, the average annual growth rate of the BRICS was 4.11%, of which China's annual growth rates were 9.3%, 7.7% and 7.7% respectively, compared with only 1.3% in developed countries over the same period. It can be seen that the BRICS countries have clearly played an "engine" role in the slow recovery of the world economy in recent years and have contributed a great share. In order to further strengthen mutual economic cooperation and achieve mutually beneficial and win-win development, in addition to regularly hold consultation and coordination in different forms and at different levels, on September 5, 2013, the heads of the BRICS also held informal meetings in St. Petersburg prior to the opening of the G20 summit, reached the agreement to create billions of dollars of "emergency reserve funds", and continued to promote the establishment of BRICS Development Bank to resist external shocks and prevent financial turmoil. At present, one of its major tasks is to cope with the financial shocks and instability brought by the gradual withdrawal of the United States from QE.

After the outbreak of the international financial crisis in 2008, the developed countries generally adopted quantitative easing (QE) policy to conduct bailout. According to Brazilian media reports, in the 3 years up to 2010, the capital injected by the main developed countries of Europe and US to conduct bailouts has been about 8.8 trillion USD. If we take the United States for example, 900 billion USD of capital was injected in the 2008 alone. After Barack Obama came to power in 2009, he carried out 3 consecutive rounds of QE policy. By the end of 2013, the Fed still had to borrow by bonds a debt of 85 billion USD per month, amounting to more than 4 trillion US dollars. Relying on their economic and monetary hegemony and their huge difference from the emerging economies, the developed countries have forced a considerable portion of the new capital to flow into the emerging market economies through various channels, but have basically not entered the real economy. Instead, they have conducted speculative arbitrage deals in the financial markets or the stock markets, futures, real estate markets etc., thus pushing up the latter's assets and commodity prices, and causing inflation, currency devaluation, and increase in exchange rates. By May 2013, the Fed would gradually withdraw from quantitative easing and tighten monetary signals. Especially on December 18, the US Fed formally announced that after the monthly purchase of debt decreases from 85 billion USD to 75 billion USD from January 2014, it would naturally cause to adverse financial turmoil in the emerging economies. In other words, the emerging market economies would flow out with "hot money" under the background of the United States' withdrawal from the quantitative easing, the foreign exchange reserves decreased, deflation appeared, and the foreign exchange market and stock market fell. According to the statistics from the "International Capital Flow Monitoring and Research Institute's" (EPFR), two or three months after May 2013, the accumulated losses of the emerging market bond funds were 24 billion USD.[13] In the emerging market countries, such as India, Nepal, Thailand, and Brazil, the exchange rates and stock indexes fell sharply, along with the economic slowdown or even decline. By January 2014, the Fed started a reduction in its borrowing, 10 billion USD per every month; this has further stimulated the financial turmoil in the emerging market economies. According to the EPFR statistics, as of February 5, 2014, investors from securities markets in developing countries withdrew 12 billion USD of funds, which forced the devaluation of the currencies in emerging market countries such as Argentine peso, the Turkish lira, Indonesian shield, South African rand and other emerging markets' national currencies, thus leading the global stock market to fall 4.1% in January. Among them, Argentina's turmoil has been the most serious among them.

Of course, Argentina's financial turmoil has a long history. Since 2009, due to the effect of the financial crisis, the economic growth continued to decline and its trade surplus continued to shrink. In order to maintain economic growth, the Argentina's government continued to carry out expansionary fiscal and monetary policies. This monetary policy has led to serious inflation and only in the two years of 2012 and 2013, the annual inflation rate was around 25% or more. This would inevitably lead to an expected decrease in the peso exchange rate. After May 2013, under the stimulation that the Fed's announcement and implementation of gradual withdrawal from the QE policy, "hot money" flows out and the depreciation trend of the peso inevitably erupted. According to official data, the loss of Argentina's foreign exchange reserves has reached 12 billion USD in 2013, and the remaining foreign reserves were only enough to pay the foreign debt of about 9.8 billion USD due in 2014, thus forcing a significant depreciation of peso. In January 2014, it had a cumulative depreciation of 20%, creating the highest record for the monthly depreciation history in 12 years. Among them, on January 23, 2014, it had plummeted 12.4% in one day, making the proportion of peso against dollar fall from 1:1 in 2001 to 8:1 at that year. Some were expected that the decline would continue in 2014 to the level of 12:1. In order to curb the outflow of the foreign reserves and the depreciation of peso, the government firstly strengthened the control on foreign exchange and then conducted deregulation, but to no avail. This was really like a doctor who was in a panicked mood, self-contradictory and overwhelmed. Fortunately, the recent situation has been improved recently.

---

13   Refer to the report by journalist Liao Feiqing, Emerging Market Economies Have Began the Currency "Defending Battles", *Economic Information Daily*, September 2, 2013(5).

The above indicates that after the outbreak of the international financial crisis in 2008, the emerging market economies including the BRICS and other developing countries, have increasingly demonstrated their non-negligible "engine" role in driving the world economic recovery, but they also inevitably affected by the restriction of quantitative easing and withdrawal policy of the developed countries led by the United States. Since May 2013, the promulgation and implementation of the United States' gradual withdrawal from the QE policy has already caused an acute financial and economic shock in several emerging market economies. This is the reality we have to confront. At present, although China's economy can still continue to maintain the high growth of more than 7.5% and the financial turmoil is also relatively smaller, after all, it is still in the period of extensive adjustment, and there are also many problems, complex issues and abundant hidden dangers. Therefore, considering the shock caused by the Fed's withdrawal from QE quantity, we should maintain a high degree of vigilance, respond calmly, and strictly prevent the outflow of "hot money". On the other side, we should take appropriate hedging resolving measures in order to ensure the national financial and economic security and stable development. In the long run, in order to fundamentally guarantee the security and stability of China's national financial and economic development, so as to successfully realize the two-hundred-year "Chinese rejuvenation dream" and eventually realize the lofty ideal of communism, we must firstly and resolutely learn to eliminate the interference of neo-liberalism, firmly implement the spirit of the 18th Congress of the CPC, adhere to the path of socialism with Chinese characteristics, unswervingly and earnestly implement the basic economic system of maintaining the public economy as the mainstay, state-owned economy as the leading sector, and promote the co-development of diverse economic sectors in order to create the optimum conditions for achieving the goal of "common prosperity", and at the same time lay the solid material foundation and institutional foundation for reversing the shock of the international financial and economic fluctuations. Otherwise, if we take the evil way of neo-liberalism and if we ignore the effect of the shock caused by the developed countries ceasing QE policies, we could possibly fall into the "overwhelmed" dilemma which is faced by the Argentina.

Originally published in Academic Review, 2014(3)

Part Four

Comparative Studies on Marxist Economics and Western Economics

The Neo-liberalism in Western Economics

Wu Yifeng

The "neo-liberalism" of Western economics discussed in this article is the neo-liberalism which is also written as neo-liberalism in the English language, this article does not discuss "new liberalism" that is also translated as "neo-liberalism". The liberalism in the field of Western economics is commonly referred to as economic liberalism. Usually, in order to distinguish between contemporary economic liberalism and the economic liberalism in the history, the economic liberalism since the 1930s is usually called as the neo-liberalism.

I. A Historical Review of Western Economic Liberalism

The western economic liberalism has a long history. Before the Great Depression of the 1930s, the development history of economic liberalism can be divided into three stages.

The first stage is the economic liberalism from mid-17th Century to the early 19th Century. Classical economics has maintained a dominant position during this period. The British classical economist Adam Smith accepted predecessors' concept about the laws of nature and freedom, put forward the "natural freedom" thought system, and argued that the capitalism was a system of natural freedom. He advocated giving full play to the "invisible hand" of markets, thus letting capitalist economy adjust by itself and develop forward according to its own inherent laws. Smith's statement has theoretical defects, but in practice it had its historical progressive significance at that time. His theories has served the interests of the emerging bourgeoisie, and demanded that the feudal class (estate) or monarch should not intervene in the economy so as to ensure the development of capitalist economy and so that the bourgeoisie becomes free from restrictions and interference.

The second stage is the economic liberalism from 1830s to 1860s. After the when British and French bourgeoisie seized power in the 1830s, thus the vulgar economics of the late 18th Century has replaced classical economics, and became the mainstream economic theory which justifies the bourgeoisie and the capitalist system. At this stage, "Say's law" was the core of economic liberalism theory. Say said at the beginning of the 19th Century, "Production creates demands for commodities." This statement later evolved into "Supply creates their own demands", known as "Say's law" or "Say's market law".

The third stage is between 1870s-1920s. In this period, the mainstream economics mainly represented by the British scholars A. Marshall, A.C. Pigou, etc. was called the "neo-classical economics" in the West. The "neo-classical economics" has combined "Say's market law" with the hypothesis that wages, prices, interest rates have complete flexibility together, and proposed the general equilibrium theoretical model of free market capitalism economy. According to this theoretical model, due to the spontaneous regulation of the market mechanism, the labor market will have a balanced supply and demand, and thus will realize the full employment; the commodity markets also have balanced supply and demand without causing over-production. The capital markets will also have balanced supply and demand without causing capital surplus. Thus, "neo-classical economics" has asserted that the fully developed competitive free capitalist market economy, could realize the efficient allocation of resources, and achieve equilibrium of full employment on its own. In terms of economic policy, the "neo-classical economics" has advocated laissez-faire and state's non-intervention in the economy. The essence of this kind of economic liberalism was to beautify the capitalist free market economic system, deny the basic contradiction of the capitalist economic system, especially deny the possibility and inevitability of the capitalist overproduction economic crises and deny the existence of unemployment, which obviously had the defensive nature.

During the Great Depression in the 1930s, Pigou was still stubbornly propagating the stereotypical doctrine of the liberal economics, he asserted: "in stable conditions, all the people who are willing to work in fact will have the opportunity for employment." The historically serious unprecedented capitalism crisis gave a devastating blow to the economic liberalism of the "neo-classical economics". The reality of the Great Crisis proved that "Say's market law" established by the liberalism of "neo-classical economics" did not reflect the objective law of the capitalist free market economy but it was subjective conjecture that completely went against the objective reality. During the Great Depression, there were many Western scholars who doubted, blamed, and criticized the economic liberalism of "neo-classical economics".

When British economist John Maynard Keynes with keen eyes criticized that the "neo-classical economics" which denied economic crisis and the possibility of a large number of unemployment, he said, "the postulates of the classical theory are applicable to a special case only and not to the general case, the situation which it assumes being a limiting point of the possible positions of equilibrium. Moreover, the characteristics of the special case assumed by the classical theory happen not to be those of the economic society in which we actually live, with the result that its teaching is misleading and disastrous if we attempt to apply it to the facts of experience".

II. The formation and development of neo-liberalism in the West

Neo-liberalism is the contemporary economic liberalism, which is the resurrection and reproduction of the bankrupt economic liberalism in the Great Depression of the 1930s under the new historical situation.

In the Great Depression of the 1930s, the state interventionism represented by Keynesian has faced the realities of economy, admitted the serious problem of the unemployment in capitalist society, acknowledged the seriousness of the economic crisis, and recognized the possibility of "complete perishment" of capitalist free market economy. The economic liberalism of "neo-classical economics" went bankrupt with the Great Crisis (1929), and numerous economists who had originally in the past who embraced the economic liberalism turned to accept the Keynesian. However, a small number of economists who believed in economic liberalism, such as the Austrian School's Mises, Hayek etc. were still stubbornly insisting on their original positions and perspectives.

361

The masterpiece of Keynes's state interventionism, The General Theory of Employment, Interest and Money, was published in 1936. Only one year later, namely in 1937, Lippmann, heavily influenced by Mises and Hayek, published the book *An Inquiry into the Principles of the Good Society*, which exerted great echo in safeguarding the free market economy and defending the economic liberalism. Then, in 1938, 26 people including Mises, Hayek, and Lippmann, gathered in Paris, and held the seminar with "crisis of liberalism" as its theme. The main idea of the book *The Road to Serfdom* which was called "the symbol of the charter for the establishment of neo-liberalism" was published in 1944 by Hayek as the product of this seminar.

Neo-liberalism is also called the neo-conservatism trend. After the capitalist world hardly achieved survival after the Great Depression in the 1930s, the neo-liberalism gradually recovered in the West, and became increasingly active, and formed many schools. In addition to the new Austrian school headed by Mises, Hayek, etc., there were the London School in England, Freiburg school in Germany, Chicago school, Monetary School, the Supply-Side School and the Rational Expectation School in the US, the Neo-Classical Macroeconomics School, Public Choice School and Modern Property Rights School headed by Coase and so on.

After the formation of the neo-liberalism economics trends, it was once at the status of non-mainstream for a long time. From 1930s to 1970s, Keynesian economics was in a dominant position in the western economical and political circles. The economic policies of Keynesianism mainly had two aspects: expansionary policies and tightening policies. Its basic approach was: during the financial crisis, we should implement expansionary fiscal policies and monetary policies in order to stimulate the economic growth and increase the employment; while at the inflationist, periods we should implement tightening fiscal and monetary policies in order to ease the inflation. In the economic policy practices of capitalist countries, Keynesian expansionary policies and tightening policies have temporarily defused the crises and inflations and achieved certain results. However, these policies were only a temporary palliative. They could only temporarily ease the contradictions, and were unable to overcome the contradictions, could only cure the symptoms and not the root causes. Keynesian expansionary policies and tightening policies had a lot of side effects. Their alternately long-term use could lead to economic stagnation and inflation at the same time, which is called the "stagflation". Stagflation took place in the United States and other western countries in the 1970s. In the face of stagflation, Keynesians were at a loss. If the expansionary policies were adopted, the "stagnation" in "stagflation" would not be cured, and the "inflation" in "stagflation" would be more serious. If a tightening policy was adopted, the "inflation" in "stagflation" was not cured, and the "stagnation" in "stagflation" would be more serious. "Stagflation" put Keynesian theory and policy in serious dilemma.

When Keynesianism was trapped in serious frustration and dilemma, the neo-liberalism seized the opportunity to rapidly rise to become the western mainstream economics. From the 1970s to the 1990s, it was the heyday of Western neo-liberalism and was referred to as the "golden age" of neo-liberalism. The neo-liberalism remained essentially the same.

The "market omnipotence theory" and "free resource allocation of market can achieve the most efficient state" were still the core creeds and doctrine of "neo-liberalism", namely the market fundamentalism.

III. Three Economic Policy Systems of the Western New Liberalism

New liberalism schools are numerous numbers. Although the fundamental aspects of their various economic theories and a number of policy proposals are similar, their differences are not minor. The neo-liberalism policy systems adopted and promoted by the western governments mainly included "Thatcherism" or "Thatcher-economics" in the United Kingdom and "Reagan-economics" in the United States. This policy systems were advocated by the United States and other western countries to all over the world especially to the developing countries as "Washington consensus".

(I) The neo-liberal economic policies of the British Thatcher government

Britain is the hometown of Keynes. The state interventionism advocated and represented by Keynesian had an extensive and profound effect in Britain. From the 1930s to 1970s, British government basically pursued the state intervention economic policy of Keynesianism. After the World War II, the British economy saw a fast recovery and development. However, as mentioned earlier, long-term alternate implementation of expansionary and tightening fiscal and monetary policies have led to the existence of economic stagnation and inflation at the same time, causing the failure of Keynesian economic policies.

Thatcher served as the British Prime Minister in 1979. Thatcher, who believed in the neo-liberalism, fully implemented the neoliberal free-market economic policies in the late 1970s and the whole 1980s. Thatcher government's neoliberal policy system was called as "Thatcherism" or "Thatcher economics", mainly including the following internal and external policies: implementing privatization of the state-owned enterprises (named privatization and denationalization) to energetically push forward the free market economy, removing the government's regulation and oversight of the market including the financial supervision, fighting against and weakening the union power, cutting down the social welfare, reducing the taxes mainly for large companies and the rich, cancelling the exchange control, executing the free float of the exchange, and pursuing policies aiming to weaken and disintegrate the Soviet union. Thatcher strived to promote its neoliberal policies abroad and said with pride, "People are no longer worried about catching the British disease, they are enthusiastically lined up to get the new British prescription."

(II) The US Reagan administration's neoliberal policies

Since the New Deal policy in the United States, successive governments have been implementing Keynesian state intervention policies for a long time. During the economic recession, they implemented expansionary fiscal policy and monetary policy; at inflation, they implemented the tightening fiscal policy and monetary policy. However, Keynesians were at a loss in the face of the stagnation of coexistence of economic stagnation and inflation. At this time, the neo-liberal ideological trend rose from non-mainstream status to the mainstream status, and reached its peak, of which the Monetary School and Supply-side School had a significant impact on the policies of the US government directly.

Ronald Reagan served as the President of the United States in 1981. He believed in the economic theory and policy proposals of the Monetary School and Supply-side School. He had a famous saying: "The government cannot solve problems; the government itself is the problem." The Reagan administration's neoliberal policies mainly included implementing the "big market" and "small government", vigorously reducing the government's intervention in the market, lifting the government's regulation and oversight on the market, reducing the tax rate, especially that of the Rich's income, with the maximum income tax rate decreased from 70% in the early 1980s to 28% in 1982, cutting down the social welfare spending, suppressing the unions led the strikes, promoting the "Star Wars" program, substantially increasing the military spending, with the attempt to drag down the Soviet union through arms race.

(III)   The neoliberal policies of "Washington consensus"

"Washington consensus" included the series of policies put forward by John Williamson in the Institute of International Economics of the United States with the neo-liberalism as the theoretical basis in 1989, which served for the economic reform in Latin America, for the first time , and subsequently for the transitional economies, i.e. the countries of the former Soviet Union and East Europe. The policies were recognized and supported by the U.S. government and the International Monetary Fund and the World Bank in the seminar held in Washington, thus known as the "Washington Consensus".

The neo-liberal economic policy of "Washington consensus" covered a series of policies such as corporate policy, fiscal policy, monetary policy, tax policy, trade policy, interest rate policy and exchange rate policy and foreign investment policy.

The famous US economist Joseph Stiglitz summarized the core content of "Washington Consensus" as "three changes": "the minimization of the government's role", "the rapid privatization" and "the rapid liberalization". "The minimization of the government's role" in Washington consensus was essentially the same with Reagan economics' "big market" and "small government"; "The rapid privatization of speed" was the same with Thatcherism's privatization of state-owned enterprises; "The rapid liberalization" included the liberalization of trade, the interest rate and the exchange rate, which was consistent with the relief of regulation and oversight in Thatcherism and Reagan-economics.

US scholar Robert Wade has argued that the "Washington consensus" aimed at reforming the "economic system", "political system" and "cultural system". That is to say, the "Washington consensus" did not only aim to popularize the western capitalist economic system to the world, but also tried to impose the western political and cultural system of the western capitalism upon the countries around the world. This clearly represented the interests and demands of the international monopoly capitalism.

IV. Failure of Neo-liberalism

When the neo-liberalism has achieved its peak in the 2000s, another great crisis has occurred in the western countries unprecedented since the Great depression of the 1930s. The crisis at the early stage 21th Century (2007) has derived from the US, and rapidly spread to Europe and to the rest of the world. Many western countries were trapped into the serious crisis successively since the summer of 2007. This crisis was not only the financial and economic crisis, or the European "sovereign debt crisis" and US "financial crisis", but also a systematic crisis of the whole capitalist market economy, including the crisis of finance, economy, society, politics, ideology, and the lasting ecological and environmental crisis.

The economic recession which has occurred in the Western countries was caused by this crisis. It is reported that Britain economy was retrograded for 8 years, US for 10 years, Greece for over 12 years, Ireland, Italy, Portugal and Spain for over 7 years, which was measured according to the standard of the journal *Economist*. This systematic crisis caused tens of millions of unemployed workers and highly unemployment rate of the youth in the Western countries, and the people being in hungry exceeded 0.9 billion in the world. All this also strongly proved that the free market did not only fail to effectively allocate the resources, on the contrary, it caused an "invalid market" said by the western economists occurs to, i.e., the invalid market allocation.

The recent capitalist crisis (2007), particularly the great crisis of capitalism crisis, vigorously triggered the critique of "Market Fundamentalism" and "Market Omnipotence". It has rapidly awaken those who blindly believed in "Market Omnipotence" and "Free Market Fundamentalism" and made them re-think about and understand the essence of neo-liberalism. A Japanese scholar wrote a famous book titled "Why Did Capitalism Collapse Itself?: The Confession of Neo-liberalist". Its sub-title is very interesting, This Japanese author's book who once believed in the neo-liberalism in the past, is in fact, is a book which made the public confession of the failure of neo-liberalism.

Just like how the Great Depression of the 1930s gave a devastating blow to the economic liberalism of "Neoclassical Economics", the first world-wide systematic crisis of the capitalist market economy in the 21st Century, has given a devastating blow to neo-liberalism.

The essay written by Leo Panitch, a professor of York University in Canada, which was published in US Foreign Policy Bimonthly on May/June 2009 pointed out that: "the large scope and collapsing force of this crisis have scared the global capitalism and the ideology of the people defending the neo-liberalism. The faith of orthodox neoliberalism has already been collapsed internally." Obviously, "the ideological panic" and "the faith of orthodox neo-liberalism has been collapsed internally" said by Panitch means that the neoliberal ideologies and beliefs are deeply in crisis.

The article entitled "Ideological Crisis of Western Capitalism" written by the US economist Joseph Stiglitz and published on the World Press Syndicate on July 6, 2011 pointed that: "a few years ago, a strong ideology, i.e., unbridled faith in the free market, almost pushed the world economy into an abyss of no return."

After the publications of the essays of Panitch and Joseph Stiglitz, the crisis of neoliberalism has gradually become the common view of many people in the Western countries. There have been many reports, interviews and articles in western newspapers and websites that criticize the neo-liberalism and condemned the neoliberalism and its massive consequences in unison.

Different scholars in many western countries use different terms when criticizing the neo-liberalism. In addition to the above-mentioned "ideological panic", "crisis of ideology" and "the faith crisis of orthodox neoliberalism", there are also "crisis of market fundamentalism", "crisis of free market capitalism", "crisis of neoliberal capitalism", "crisis of laissez faire", "crisis of neoliberal market economy advocated by US" and "the crisis of exaggerating the role of the market role". Although the terms are different, the meanings are identical, i.e. the neo-liberalism crisis.

Some western scholars believed that the crisis of neo-liberalism is the crisis of neoliberal unsustainable social order. When analyzing the crisis Gerard Dumenil, a France economist, wrote: "the current crisis is not a simple financial crisis, but a crisis of the unsustainable social order of neo-liberalism." British scholar Halls Baum said: "over the past few decades, people thought that the market can solve all problems, which in my opinion is more like an unreal religious faith than reality." "Market fundamentalism has failed."

British scholar Michael Johnson said: "The dissatisfaction with capitalism in the West shows that capitalism indeed has many problems ... In the face of all uncertainties under the economic crisis, the only certainty is that the free market capitalism advocated by the United States will inevitably be attacked and abandoned by people." American author Andy Stern said: "The free market fundamentalism which was glorious in 20th Century is being discarded in 21st Century."

Francis Fukuyama, a professor in Stanford University in the United States, was the main preacher of "the end of history" and preached that the history would be end in capitalism. However, the viewpoint of Fukuyama was changed significantly during this crisis. He now believes that US capitalism has been collapsed, the free market or neo-liberalism model will be tried.

The western scholars not only theoretically criticize neoliberalism, but also direct their criticism to the neoliberalism policy of the Thatcher government in the United Kingdom and Reagan government in the United States. It was reported in the English *Financial Times* that when Thatcher died after living in Downing Street for 30 years, many British arrived at such a conclusion after the outbreak of this crisis: the 30-year experiment is failed again.

However, the reason was Thatcherism. Reagan-economics was also criticized. Bruce Bartlett, a former domestic policy adviser to the Reagan government who participated in making the Reagan-economics, is now fighting back against the Reagan's neoliberal economic policy system. He wrote "the failure of Reagan-economics" in the New US Economy with an impressive title: The Failure of Reagan Economics and Future Road.

Not only the Western academic circles but also Western commercial circles criticized the neoliberalism in Britain and the United States and some of them directly blamed the Thatcherism and Reagan-economics.

When the Bloomberg News, interviewed George Soros, the magnate investor, he said: "the most serious crisis is taken place currently since the Great Depression. I have formulated a specific hypothesis for the crash of 2008 which holds that it was the result of a "super-bubble" that started forming in 1980 when Ronald Reagan became President of the United States and Margaret Thatcher was Prime Minister of the United Kingdom. The prevailing trend in the super-bubble was also the ever-increasing use of credit and leverage; but the misconception was different. It was the belief that markets correct their own excesses. Reagan called it the "magic of the marketplace"; I call it market fundamentalism. Since it was a misconception, it gave rise to bubbles. So the super-bubble was composed of a number of smaller bubbles—and punctuated by a series of financial crises. Each time the authorities intervened and saved the system by taking care of the failing institutions and injecting more credit when necessary. So the smaller bubbles served as successful tests of a false belief, helping the super-bubble to grow bigger by reinforcing both credit creation and market fundamentalism."

The neo-liberalism of "Washington Consensus" was also criticized severely. Before the outbreak of this crisis, Stiglitz, the famous US economist has criticized the "Washington Consensus", and pointed that the neo-liberalism policy is unsuitable and harmful for the developing countries. During the crisis, the scholars of western developed countries and developing countries pointed out that "Washington Consensus" had failed in the experiments tried in Latin and East Europe.

V. We Should Attach Great Attention to the Influence of Western Neo-liberalism upon China

Since the 1980s, the western neo-liberalist economists have attempted to influence China's reform by using their economic theories and economic policy ideas. Meanwhile, there has been some Chinese economists who have tried to find solutions for China's reform, from theories and policy measures of western neo-liberalism. Thus, the western neo-liberalism has gradually increased its influence in China.

Some relevant domestic economics works weren't written through a comprehensive analysis of neo-liberalism and its many schools, these works did not use Marxism creatively, consequently economic policy systems of "Thatcherism", "Reagan economics" and "Washington Consensus" were not properly criticized, even some writers have randomly recommended them to on the domestic readers with total affirmation. This kind of works have made extremely negative influence upon many people, particularly the young students, consequently the readers could not gain the capacity to identify and criticize the western neo-liberalism.

Among the various neo-liberalism thoughts, China is mostly influenced by the theories and policies of US scholar Coase, and from his property-rights theory. In the early 1980s, Coase observed the economic system reform in

China and, he considered this transformation in China as the best opportunity to advocate his thoughts on private property rights. His followers in China have carefully pondered on how to advertise Coase's thoughts to promote property rights of private ownership in socialist China.

Their "Sinicized" and "localized" Coase theorem is: once property rights are delimited, all the difficult problems of the market economy can readily be solved. Their basic view and position about property rights reform in state-owned enterprises in socialist countries are: public property rights are not de-limited; only when privatization is practiced and socialist public ownership is transformed into capitalist private ownership and socialist public property rights into private property rights will property rights be delimited and the economy will become efficient.

One of his followers in USA when visiting China said: "I have never har-bored any illusion about the communist system. I have always believed that the system of private ownership is the only reliable way to economic develop-ment...China will gradually evolve something like the system of private owner-ship." He revealed, "Coase completely agrees with my analysis.

Coase has influenced the reform of Chinese property rights by means of sending visitors to China and accepting visitors—famous Chinese econo-mists—to his office in the USA, on his own expense, to participate internation-al academic seminars with the title of "Chinese Economic Reform" organized by him. He said to Chinese visitors in 1997, "the crux of the matter lies with privatization...The Western economists...advise that, 'you'd better practice privatization....' Once you establish the system you won't need to be anxious about privatization."

More noteworthy is that, Coase later not only promoted his private property rights theory in the field of economics, but also went far beyond the field of economics, and further proposed that China needed an "open and free market of ideas", and expressed his hope that China would be "the center of free ideas" in the world. When evaluating Coase's proposal of "open and free market of ideas", some domestic scholars have praised as follows: "Coase's insight-ful expressions, have obvious practical significance for China's Reform and Opening-up." These people have actively promoted Coase's assertion about that China should actively liberalize the market for free thoughts. They have held high the banner of of "deepening the reform".[1]

There has been a report in the domestic media: "When Coase was 100 years old, Chinese economists have organized a celebration activity, and Coase has sent a video address from across the Atlantic to China."

---

1 As we all remember, Coase received his prize at a time when radical changes were taking place in the Soviet Union and Eastern Europe. Coase's disciple Steven Cheung said in his selected writings published mainly in praise of his teacher after Coase won the prize, "The Coase theorem ...opened the eyes of the people of the world to the importance of property rights and has made communism breathe its last."

It was reported in another news that by the domestic media that Coase was invited to visit China in October 2013, but he was unexpectedly dead just one month before visiting China. Some Chinese economists were quite grieved after the death of him and even said: "Coase's theories brighten the rugged reform path of China." "Coase has greatly influenced China under the conditions of economic reform. His theories have won higher recognition and response in China than the US."[2]

In the past, the Chinese economists who advocated privatization were reluctant to use, the term "privatization" but used "de-nationalization" by borrowing French, or used the Japanese term of "private operation" but this is absurd, because people clearly recognize that they have the same meaning with privatization. But, currently, those who advocate further property rights reform, do not act reluctantly when using the term "privatization", but openly argue that the stated-owned enterprise should be vigorously privatized.

The goal of China's economic reform is to establish the socialist market economy. Ignoring this goal , the reform is bound to deviated from the right direction. Deng Xiaoping has not emphasized that the reform should adhere to socialist path, but also stressed that, deviating from the socialist direction in the reform will inevitably lead to serious consequences. He stressed: "the most important question of the reform, is to adhere the socialist path." He insisted: "the publicly owned economic sector should always be in the dominant position', and 'we should follow the path of achieving common prosperity, and avoid polarization, only in this way 'practicing the market economy capitalism will not lead us to capitalism."

369

In regard with the possible consequences that could be caused by deviating from the socialist path, Deng Xiaoping warned: "The aim of socialism is to make all our people prosperous, not to create polarization. If our policies led to polarization, it would mean that we had failed; if a new bourgeoisie emerged, it would mean that we had strayed from the right path."

At the early period of reform, Deng Xiaoping emphasized the importance of "adhering to the Four Cardinal Principles." In his late years, Deng Xiaoping also pointed out: "what is the economic superiority of the socialist market economy? The answer is the Four Cardinal Principles." The domestic "Coase worship trend" can be examined and judged by using Deng Xiaoping theory: "the Coase fever" means to replacing the dominant status of public ownership by private ownership of production means in China, and replacing socialist market economy by the capitalist market economy, which will cause polarization, and the inevitable emergence of new bourgeoisie and the failure of the reform. This is what the entire party and people across the country must attach great importance to and be highly vigilant.

Originally published in the journal Red Flag Manuscript, 2014(5)

---

2   When at the age of 101, Coase published his final book, How China Became Capitalist, co-authored with former student Ning Wang.

Thriving Vitality of Socialism Property Rights System with Chinese Characteristics

— The End of Western Full Privatization Theory

Bai Baoli and Fu Huihuang

Abstract: The property rights system with full privatization may negatively influence the operation of society and economy. The crisis of capitalist world economy that occurred in 1930s has indicated that capitalist system is beyond recovery. The current western developed nations don't adopt the property rights system with full privatization, but have passed to a new property rights system. The socialist property rights system with Chinese characteristics can overcome various negative effects caused by the property rights system with full privatization, and it can be adapted to the historical trend of constant socialization of production as well as adapt to the specific national conditions, consequently can promote the rapid economic development in China. Therefore, we should stick to develop the socialist property rights system with Chinese characteristics, and unswervingly reinforce and develop the public ownership economy, and at the same time promote the various realization forms of public ownership, and unswervingly encourage, support and guide the development of non-public economies.

Key words: socialism with Chinese characteristics; property rights system; historical trend

Socialist property right system with Chinese characteristics is the inevitable result of historical development, the western property rights with full privatization is doomed to perishment. The western property rights privatization theory held that the full privatization is the most effective and reasonable economic system. However, this is not the case. The property rights with full privatization may cause a series of negative effects in the operation of society and economy. The crisis of capitalist world economy which occurred in 1930s has indicated that this system is beyond recovery; the current western developed nations don't adopt the property rights system with full privatization, but have transited to a new property rights system. The socialist property rights system with Chinese characteristics accords with the trend of historical development, and is able to steadily and rapidly develope the economy, and also points to the final perishment of property right privatization theory.

I. Negative effects of economic operation under the full private property rights system

The economic operation under the full private property rights system causes a series of negative effects, including the excessive income distribution gap, insufficient domestic consumer demand, excessive dependence on the domestic economy, economic crisis, resulting in the fierce competition for world markets, or even military wars.

(I) Labor market operation under the full private property rights system

Under the full private property rights system, the business decisions only relies on the ownership of production means. The goal of this decision-making mechanism is just to maximize the profit, characterized with reducing the labor wage level as low as possible in the labor market. The long-standing relative surplus condition of labor supply causes that the actual wage level of labor remain at a low level under this full private property rights system.

Firstly, the labor market equilibrium determines that the labor wage level remains lower than the labor value under the condition of relative surplus (relative excess of labor supply) of the labor supply. This condition is shown in figure 1.

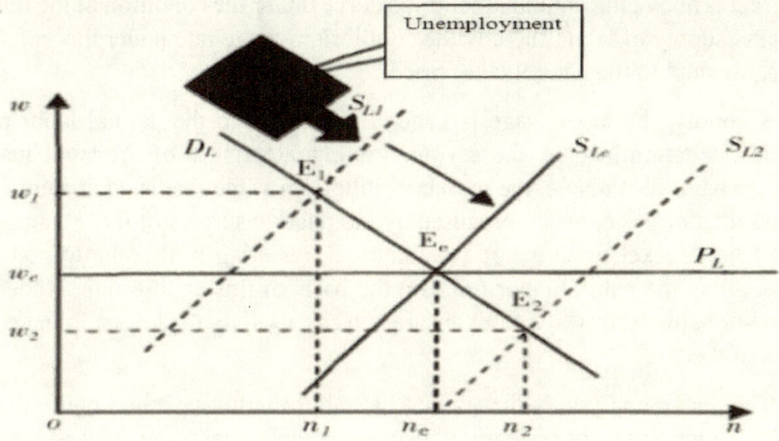

Figure 1: Labor market equilibrium under full private property rights

In figure 1, the horizontal axis n represents the number of laborers; vertical axis ω represents the actual wage rate, wherein S_L represents the labor supply curve, and D_L represents the labor demand curve, and P_L represents the natural labor price curve. The natural labor price is the monetary expression of labor value[1].

Given that the labor supply curve is represented by S_{L1}, and the labor demand curve is represented by D_L in a labor market with perfect competition under the condition of basic equilibrium of labor supply and demand, the equilibrium point of market is E_1, and the market equilibrium wage rate and the equilibrium labor quantity are respectively $ω_1$ and n_1. However, actually the equilibrium point E_1 doesn't exist. The only decision-making goals of enterprises that accords with the full private property rights system is to maximize the profit, therefore the capitalist enterprises can use the unemployment pressure to force the labor supply curve moving from the upper left to the right down under the condition of long-term surplus (excess) of labor supply. When the labor supply curve is S_{Le}, the market equilibrium point is E_e, and the corresponding equilibrium wage rate and quantity of the labor market are respectively ωe and ne. At this time, the equilibrium point Ee is at the natural labor price curve, therefore the wage rate ωe is lower than the natural labor price. If the labor supply curve continues to move towards the right down, i.e. from S_{Le} to S_{L2}, the market equilibrium point will be moved from E_e to E_2; the market equilibrium wage rate corresponding to this point is $ω_2 < ω_e$, i.e. the labor wage is lower than its value. Then, the laborers can't purchase the livelihood means needed for their reproduction, maintenance, development and extension of labor, therefore this state of equilibrium can't remain for a long time.

373

---

1   Marx calls the monetary expression of a commodity's value its "natural price".

The above analysis indicates the following: the equilibrium point of labor market is above the natural labor price curve under the condition of the relative excess supply of labor, thereby the equilibrium wage rate under this condition is equivalent to the natural labor price.

Secondly, the labor wage is generally lower than the natural labor price, which is determined by the asymmetric characteristics of the labor market. As we have seen above, the market equilibrium wage rate is equivalent to the natural labor price, which is caused by the relative surplus of labor supply, but the labor market force is not asymmetrical, resulting in that the wage rate is lower than the natural labor price on the basis of this equilibrium. Under this condition, the labor wage can't ensure and can't satisfy the lowest living condition of them.

The above analysis indicates that the labor market operated under the full private property right system will cause that the actual wage level of labor remains at a low point for a long time.

(II) The economic operation effect under full private property rights system

The features of the economic operation under full private property rights system will cause a series of negative effects which are relevant to each other:

1. Excessive income gap

Under the decision-making mechanism of full private property rights system, the labor market operation causes that the actual labor wage positioned at a natural price for a long time; only serves to maximize the profit and continually and rapidly increases the enterprise profits. On the one hand, the labor wage is positioned at lower point in the market for a long time; on the other hand, the income relevant to profit is at a higher level and continually increases. The income gap in the society is excessively enlarged. This phenomenon is shown in figure 2.

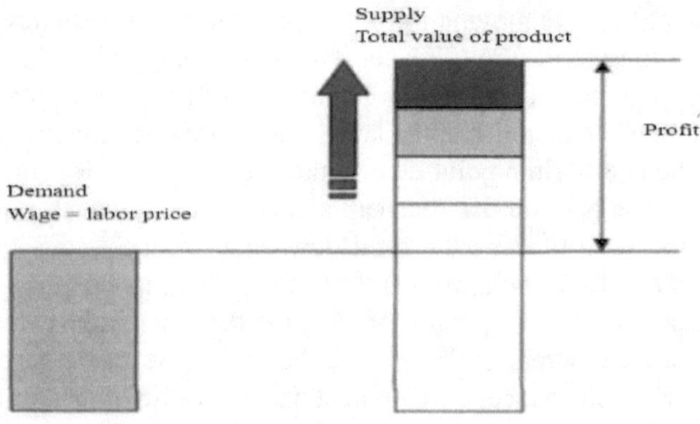

Figure 2

2. Insufficient effective demand

This mechanism for excessively enlarging the income distribution gap can also cause insufficient total social demand. Instead of the absolute(ly) low social purchasing power, the insufficient total social demand refers to the relative low social purchasing power; the total social demand is insufficient in comparison with the total social supply, i.e. the total social demand is less than total social supply. Therefore, the basic factors causing the insufficient total social demand will be characterized as follows : thereby the purchasing power formed is less than the supplied products.

Under full private property rights system, the behavior characteristics of manufacture are the basic factors for insufficient total social demand. In order to obtain more profits, these manufactures may possibly improve the labor productivity so as to increase the sales; on the other hand, the wage is positioned at the natural labor price, or even lower than it. In this way, the gap between the market supply provided by manufacture and the market demand formed by the wage will be larger and larger, and the total social demand is insufficient, resulting in the unbalance of macro economy. This phenomenon is also shown in figure 2.

Moreover, the insufficient total social demand is one of the direct results for enlarging the gap between the labor income and the capital income. On one hand, the total social purchasing power is dependent on the income level of labors mainly constituting the consumers, but most labor demands can't be converted to the effective demand because of the income restriction; on the other hand, the infinite capital pursuit for profit promotes the increasing growth of social supply which is continually greater than total social demand, resulting in the contradiction between the relative surplus of production and effective demand.

3. Economic crisis

As is known to all, the insufficient effective demand will bring about the economic crisis. Just like what said by Marx: "the capital compensation input to the production is dependent on the consumption power of non-production class to a great degree; the consumption power of worker is restricted by the wage laws and the following fact: the labor can be employed by the capitalist class on the condition that they can create the profit. As the basic reasons for the crisis, the poverty of the mass and the limited consumption are neglected by the capitalist class who attempt to develop the productivity; it is seemed that the absolute social consumption power limits the productivity development."[2]

---

2   Karl Marx, *Das Kapital*, Volume 3, People's Publishing House, 1975, p. 548.

4. Export dependence and fierce competition for world markets

The export dependence is formed by the insufficient domestic demand and economic crisis; in order to tap the finite world market, the trade conflict among countries is inevitably.

The relative surplus of production and insufficient demand inevitably bring about negative influences: the manufacturers are faced with the capital chain rupture because of excessive inventory and difficult capital recovery; if the government doesn't intervene, the economic crisis will break out. However, the products consumed through the conventional means such as the fiscal subsidies and government purchase adopted by the government is much less than the surplus products. Therefore, it is inevitable for seeking overseas market to dump the domestic surplus products. However, the world market is finite, and the product surplus is sharpened in countries, and the total products to be dumped are increasing. For the sake of safeguarding the country interests, various countries make efforts to tap the limited world market; the "economic war" such as the trade friction and confliction among countries is continually increased.

5. International and world war

When the above contradiction can't be solved in the economic field, the "economic war" among countries will be evolved and upgraded as the international military war.

376

II. Full private property rights system beyond recovery and evolution of Western property rights system

The economy operated under full private property rights system inevitably causes a series of negative effects, characterized with periodic crisis and wars. The world economic crisis that occurred in 1930s and the following Second World War finally declared that the full private property rights system is beyond recovery, and the western capitalist nations were forced to make profound adjustments in their social and economic systems.

(I) Full private property rights system beyond recovery: the economic crisis that occurred in 1930s

Before 1930s, the western capitalist countries basically carried out the full private property rights system which has caused periodic outbreak of economic crisis. In 1788, the economic crisis that erupted in Britain for the first time and clearly disclosed the production surplus and insufficient demand in history, in 1825, the first periodic outbreak of the production surplus further proved the above-mentioned fact, and the economic crisis almost erupted circa in every 10 years.

The great economic crisis covering the entire capitalist countries from 1929 to 1933 finally indicated the full private property rights system is beyond recovery. In 1929, the income of 5% US rich individuals basically grabbed 1/3 of the total national income, while the number of the poor with the annual income about US 2,000 accounted for 60% of total US families. It is no doubt that the increase of actual social consumption power was limited, which naturally resulted in a relative narrow domestic market.

On the other hand, the output is continually increased because the capitalist pursues the profits endlessly. From 1920 to 1929, the total US industrial output was increased by 53%, wherein the auto quantity was increased from 1.5 million in 1919 to 5.4 million in 1929; the total output of household appliances was increased from US 10.6 million in 1921 to US 0.416 billion in 1929; the gasoline production was surged from 86 million in 1919 to 0.439 billion in 1929,[3] finally resulting in the serious relative surplus of production, and the outbreak of large-scaled economic crisis.

This economic crisis produced negative influences on the US economy: the industrial production decreased by 56.6%, wherein the cast iron production decreased by 79.4%; the steel production decreased by 75.8%, and the auto production had decreased by 74.4%; the unemployment figures arrived at 12 million; at least 130,000 enterprises went bankrupt. With regard to the entire capitalist world, the industrial production had decreased by 44%, 16% lower than 1913, which went backward to 1908-1909 level; the unemployment figure reached to around 50 million, and the unemployment rate of some countries had increased to 30%–50%; the total trade volume in the capitalist world had decreased by 66%, and fell to the level lower than 1913 level.[4]

This crisis indicated that the full private property rights system is beyond recovery, which denies or negates the fundamentality of full private property rights system. Consequently, the western capitalist countries were forced to reform the full private property rights system, and deeply adjust the capitalist social and economic system.

(II) Later evolution of property rights system in the western developed countries

The western developed countries have mainly adjusted the original and classical full private property rights in two aspects:

1. Establish the state-owned economy in a certain scale

With the popularization of Keynesianism and Roosevelt's New Deal, the western countries used the state power to intervene the economy after the Second World War to self-regulate the production relations, and reinforced the national regulation of society and economy through developing the state-owned economy, which reached the peak point in 1970s-1980s.

---

3   *Historical Economic Crisis, North Network*, economy.enorth.com.cn/system/2002/08/24/000404036.shtml.

4   Four Economic Crises of the US in 1980s, Netease Financial, http://money.163.com/08/0918//08/4M424R8F00252G50.html.

In 1993, there were 2750 French enterprises of which 50% or more shares of them were directly controlled by the French state , and 108 enterprises were directly controlled by the state.[5] Today, the proportion of the state-owned enterprises in the economic sectors of France are as follows: electric power industry 90%, gas industry 95%, rail transport 100%, petroleum industry 35%, air transportation 90%, automobile industry 36% and banking industry 55%.[6]

Although the US is called as the fortress of neoliberalism, the assets and employed person of state-owned enterprise accounted for 1% of entire state assets in 1990s, but the economy controlled by the state accounted for 23% of the America wealth.[7]

Although in 1980's the resurgence of neoliberalism has occurred, the general layout has been determined the privatization which occurred due to resurgence of neoliberalism resurgence refers to the selling some shares of state-owned enterprise; but after the wave of privatization, considerable enterprises and certain sectors of the economy are still controlled by the state, therefore all this does not mean that the classical full private property rights system was recovered. Moreover, the western states generally adopts the nationalization policies to save the crisis hit enterprises during the outbreak of economic crises.

During the outbreak of economic crisis in 2008, US bail-out package plans became a typical case of "using nationalization to save the free market": the US treasury department declared to hand over the Fannie Mae and Freddie Mac[8] which were trapped into difficulty on September 2008, and invested in them about 200 billion US dollars through purchasing their relevant preferred stocks.

On November 23, 2008, the US government declared to implement a rescue plan for Citigroup, which included the following: provide US 306 billion for the Citigroup as the debt guarantee, and invest 20 billion dollars in it. At the end of February 2009, the US government agreed to convert US 25 billion preferred stock to the common stock, so as to become the largest shareholder of Citibank by holding 36% of its shares; on December 2008, the treasury department invested 80 billion US dollars into the auto industry thus implemented the "nationalization" rescue policy for GM and Chrysler etc. in order to avoid the great impact caused by the depression of the auto industry.[9]

---

5   Yang Kaifeng, *State-owned Enterprise Path: France*, Lanzhou University Press, 1999, p. 2.

6   Sun Hongwu, *Comparison of Enterprise Development at Home and Abroad*,Tianjin People's Publishing House, 1992, p. 34.

7   Dong Youde, *State-owned Enterprise Path: USA* , Lanzhou University Press, 1999, p. 3.

8   Fannie Mae and Freddie Mac are mortgage giants.

9   State-owned Enterprise of Western Countries and Aspirations for China, *Realistic Theory Network*, http://www.qstheory.cn/jj/hqsy/201204/t20120425_153835.htm.htm; The State-owned Enterprise isn't the Product of Our Country, *Sina Finance and Economics*, http://www.chinareform.org.cn/society/obtain/Experience/201010/t20101029_49038.htm.

Table 1: Socialization degree of main European industrial countries in 1985

	Post and telecommunications	Communication	Electric power	Natural gas	Petroleum	Coal	Aviation	Engine	Steel	Shipbuilding	Railway
Austria	Over 75%	Over 75%	Over 75%	Over 75%	Over 75%	Over 75%	Over 75%	Over 75%	Over 75%	-	Over 75%
France	Over 75%	Over 75%	Over 75%	Over 75%	-	Over 75%	Over 75%	50%	Over 75%	Less than 75%	Over 75%
Federal Germany	Over 75%	Over 75%	75%	50%	25%	50%	Over 75%	25%	Less than 25%.	25%	Over 75%
Holland	Over 75%	Over 75%	75%	75%	-	-	15%	50%	25%	Less than 25%	Over 75%
Italy	Over 75%	Over 75%	75%	Over 75%	-	-	Over 75%	25%	75%	75%	Over 75%
Spain	Over 75%	50%	Less than 25%	Less than 25%	-	50%	Over 75%	Less than 25%	50%	75%	Over 75%
Sweden	Over 75%	Over 75%	50%	Over 75%	-	-	50%	Less than 25%	15%	75%	Over 75%
Britain	Over 75%	Less than 25%	Over 75%	Less than 25%	Less than 25%	Over 75%	75%	50%	75%	Over 75%	Over 75%.

Data source: Federal Germany Economic Weekly on March 27, 1988.

2. Development of modern property rights system in the frame of capitalist system: the power is transited to the labor to a certain degree

With regard to the enterprise inner structure, the western developed countries have abandoned the classical full private property rights system to a certain degree, and have tried to establish the modern property rights system; several economics rights such as the management right, decision-making right and income distribution were gradually and regularly transited from the capitalist to the labor to a certain degree.

In Germany, the company management is obviously characterized as wide participation in the decision-making by the employees, which is also reinforced by the laws.[10] With regard to decision-making participated by the staff, there are two types: first the participation type and secondly the mutual decision-making type, and the former can be considered as the primary initial form of the latter. The participation type and mutual decision-making type differ according to whether the staff can enter into the decision-making body (organ) at a high level. Under the participation type, the staff can only participate in the basic-level decisions of the enterprise, while they can participate in the leadership decision-making under the mutual decision-making type. According to the legal regulation of German Staff Common Decision-making, the number of employees shall account for 1/3 of board of supervisors in the company which have less than 2000 staff, while number of employees shall account for 1/2 in the company over 2000 staff, and the employee must also be represented in the board of directors. The German enterprises have set up the staff committees as one important means for participation in the decision-making. If the staff number exceeds 5, one or more staff committees must be established by the enterprise, and the number of staff committee members depends on the number of employees. The main task of the enterprise staff committee is to safeguard the interests of all staff in the aspects of wage, welfare and work safety.[11] According to the stipulations in Germany Enterprise Staff Committee Participation Management Law, the major decisions of the enterprises must be approved by the staff committee.

In Sweden, the labor unions have been strong. The labor union has the considerable right to speak and air its opinions, which has caused positive results for safeguarding the labor rights. For example, Sweden labor unions have proposed the "collective wage policy" and other two specific policies in the 1950s: orderly wage growth rule and price rises compensation rule.[12] The former specified that the additional wage rise for the laborers will be considered

---

10   Shen Yue, *Analysis of Germany Social Market Economy*, China Labor Social Security Publishing House, 2002, p. 324-325.

11   Not include the "superior officer" holding the post of manager at middle and low level, and these superior officers are the enterprise manager.

12   How does Sweden Handle the Labor Contradiction and Wage Problem, China's Reform BBS, http://www.chinareform.org.cn/society/obtain/Experience/201010/t20101029_49038.htm.

as a standard rule, if the additional wage rise by the collective bargaining — at the end of the year— doesn't arrive at this yearly standard point, at the end of the year, there will be an automatic supplementary increase to make up for the difference. The price rises compensation rule lreferred to the following: if the price rise exceeds a pre-set limit, both of the parties (union and the enterprise) must negotiate with each other again, or specify a compensation term (for example a rate) of agreement in advance so that the employees can get a certain compensation automatically when commodity prices increase substantially.

Among the western countries, the US advertises itself as the fortress of liberalism, and the adjustment of property rights system has been slower and gradual, therefore, it had to use other methods to get solve the problems brought by the full private property rights system. In the US, the main methods include the maintenance of the dollar hegemony and foreign warfare, particularly, the foreign warfare is used for reinforcing the dollar hegemony and the commodity exports . The warfare can consume a large number of munitions and military equipment cost of which is borne and bought by other countries. The US exports considerable amount of arms and munitions to solve the issue of domestic insufficient demand. This is the economic basis for the US led wars, thus The US relies on the dollar hegemony and foreign warfare to support the full private property rights system.

To sum up, the large economic crisis which has occurred in the 1930s indicates that the full private property rights system is beyond recovery, and consequently western countries have deeply adjusted the original property rights system, the current property rights system of the western countries doesn't refer to the classical system.

Certainly, main part of the contemporary western capitalist countries are still established on the basis of private property, therefore economic crises still occur,, and the national economy is constantly plagued by economic crises. If the capitalism had not made constant adjustments in its property rights system in the last 80 years, and sticked to full private property rights system, the western economy would face a collapse and would fall backward towards the "anthropolithic age".

III. Maintain to develop socialist property right system with Chinese characteristics

The socialist property right system with Chinese characteristics can overcome all negative effects caused by overall privatized property right system. It not only adapts to the objective necessity and historical trend of socialized development of production and the specific national conditions of our nation but also boosts speedy development of national economy in practice. Thus, we should maintain socialist property right system with Chinese characteristics.

(I) The core and reflection of socialist property right system with Chinese characteristics

The core of socialist property right system with Chinese characteristics is: common development of various ownerships with public ownership as the mainstay. The mainstay status of public ownership is mainly reflected in two aspects: in terms of quantity, the proportion of state-owned asset holds an advantage in total asset of the society; in terms of quality, state-owned economy controls the destiny of national economy and leads the economic development. On the basis of public ownership's leading status, development of various ownership economies is the objective requirement for socialist market economy system and the requirement for adapting productivity development by various economies at different levels, which accordingly push forward the development of productivity in our nation.

The main reflection of socialist property right system with Chinese characteristics is: regard distribution according to one's performance as the main body and various distribution systems coexist. The dominant state of distribution according to one's performance is mainly reflected in two aspects: on one hand, within the income distribution of whole society, distribution according to one's performance accounts for the largest proportion and plays a critical role; on the other hand, in the laborer's total income within public ownership economy, income from distribution according to one's performance is the major source of income. Apart from distribution according to one's performance, other distribution methods mainly include operation achievement, knowledge, technology, land, capital and distribution of other factors of production.

(II) The advantages of socialist property right system with Chinese characteristics

The development of social productive forces leads the socialization of production to an unprecedented height, resulting in irreversible historical trend of development of public ownership.

Even the western developed countries have to adapt to such historical trend in some degree through various means. As stated above, the economic development of western countries has proven that the fully-privatized property right system cannot maintain the continuous and stable development of economy; western developed countries have abandoned overall privatized property right system during actual economic operation and conducted profound adaption on property right system, which is actually a progressive negation to overall privatized property right system.

The socialist property right system with Chinese characteristics and with public ownership as the mainstay just tallies with the social and historical development trend caused by highly-developed productivity.

The social property right system with Chinese characteristics regards public ownership as the mainstay and distribution according to one's performance as the major distribution method, leading the laborer's income to get rid of restriction on labor force value caused by overall privatized property right system and the laborers to share the achievement of economic growth. In this way, insufficient domestic effective demand will be overcome fundamentally. Accordingly, a series of issues aroused by it such as large income distribution gap and overreliance on export will be resolved fundamentally to ensure that the economic development of our nation may not be fallen into the so-called "middle-income trap".

The rapid development of economy in China also proves the superiority of socialist property right system with Chinese characteristics. Since 1979, except a few years, the increasing rate of China's GDP maintains over 7% and in half of these years the increasing rate has exceeded 10%. It means our nation develops to the second-largest economy in the world from the relatively backward state. What's more important, during the process of development, China's economy keeps high stability and avoids huge attack of global economic crisis. China's domestic economy has not been influenced greatly by Asian economic crisis in 1997 or global financial-economic crisis in 2008. This fully proves the superiority of socialist property right system with Chinese characteristics.

Conclusion

The economic liberalization theory in the west holds that the overall privatized property right system is the most effective and reasonable economic system. However, the overall privatized property right system may lead to a series of negative effects in social and economic operation. In 1930s, the capitalist economic crisis declared the death of the system. At present, western developed countries no longer adopt overall privatized property right system.

The socialist property right system with Chinese characteristics can overcome all kinds of negative effects arising from overall privatized property right system. It not only adapts to the objective necessity and historical trend of socialized development of production and the specific national conditions of our nation but also boosts speedy development of national economy in practice and fully certifies its advantages. Thus, we should maintain to develop socialist property right system with Chinese characteristics, unswervingly consolidate and develop public economy, push forward various means to realize public economy and unswervingly encourage, support and instruct the development of non-public economy.

Originally published in the journal Study on Socialism with Chinese Characteristics, 2014(4)

Das Kapital and Research Methods
of Modern Economics

Feng Jinhua

385

Abstract: Most of domestic scholars studying on political economics favor to realize the innovation and development of research methods of Marxist economics by referring to the research methods on modern economics, but they seldom grasp that certain reasonable and effective research methods in modern economics can be traced back to Marx. Studying and comparing *Das Kapital* and modern economics from the three aspects of micro level and macro level, equilibrium and disequilibrium; empirical and normative, this article discusses the three major analysis methods of Marxism and explains that in *Das Kapital* these methods have emerged in various ways long ago. These three major analysis methods did not only appear but were also fully discussed frequently. And not only fully discussed, but went beyond the understanding of some modern western economists in regard to their approaches and contents, from many aspects.

Key words: *Das Kapital*; modern economics; research methods; comparative study

I. Introduction

Marx's *Das Kapital* is not only a monumental work of economics theory but also a treasure of economics methods. It is particularly noteworthy that this masterpiece written over 100 years ago contains abundant rich thoughts in regard to the analysis methodologies of modern economics—in fact these methodologies have been formed and became prevalent in the modern economics studies long after that.

In the past, in regard to the comparative studies on the methodologies of the Marxist economics and the methodologies of modern western economics, , many domestic scholars mainly emphasized the difference between these two methodologies, for example, some scholars have held that "Marxist economics theory and neo classical economics theory contain different methodologies when analyzing economics, their methods when analyzing object of study (and the aim of their observation and examination) are different, so were their correction methodologies".[1] Although some other scholars have argued that "as to the specific researching methods, Marxist economics has both difference and something in common with the western economics"[2], they have generally focused on discussing the "different aspects" and sufficed to examine and discuss the "common aspects" just superficially. Thirdly, although most scholars approve to "draw on the researching methods of modern economics and learn from them in order to realize constant innovation and development of research methods of Marxist economics"[3], they have hardly noticed that some reasonable and effective researching methods used by western economics was already mentioned and discussed as early as *Das Kapital* and these methods have emerged in various ways long ago, in this monumental work. These three major analysis methods were not only appeared but were also fully discussed frequently. And not only fully discussed, but went beyond the understanding of some modern western economists, in regard to their approaches and contents, from many aspects.

This article discusses the issue from the three aspects, i.e. micro level and macro level; equilibrium and disequilibrium; empirical and normative methodologies.

Through the discussion of these three aspects, we can conclude that many reasonable and effective analysis methods of modern western economics can be traced back to Marx. For example, in the *Das Kapital*, there is not only clear distinction between micro level and macro level, but it also analyzes economy from both aspects which is in line with the methodology or modern western

---

1   Yang Yusheng, Yang Ge, *Value, Capital, Growth—A Debate on the Research of Labor Theory of Value in Western Countries*, China Economics Press, 2005, p. 27.
2   Chief Editor Wu Yifeng, *Comparative Study of Marxist Economics and Western Economics*, Volume 1, China Renmin University Press, 2009, p. 122.
3   He Aiping, Song Yu, et.al., *Comparative Study of Marxist Economics and Western Economics*, Volume 1, China Renmin University Press, 2011, p. 11.

economics; another example is that, in *Das Kapital*, there is not only comprehensive discussion on the connotations of equilibrium, results of equilibrium and adjusting process of equilibrium, but also a unique and profound analysis on the reality, rationality and limitations of the equilibrium and it also demonstrates the ways to overcome this limitation of equilibrium analysis. Another example, in *Das Kapital*, not only "what ought to be" (the normative approach) is emphasized, but also expounded on how to, make empirical analysis free from normative value judgments, and also includes a comprehensive ideas on how to correctly combine the empirical analysis with normative analysis when making an empirical research. All in all, reviewing Marx's point of views on methodology in *Das Kapital* in comparison with modern western economics, we can better realize that the penetration ability into the truth by the former has gone beyond the understanding modern western economists in regard to their approaches and contents, from many aspects.

II. Microeconomic and macroeconomic level methodology

It is an important method in modern economics to conduct microeconomic analysis and macroeconomic analysis according to different "spatial" features of the research object. Microeconomics studies the behaviors of single economic units constituting the entire economic system, studies how these single economic units make their decisions, and examines what factors influence these decisions.

On the other hand, macroeconomics studies the overall operation and movement of the whole economy and reasons behind its behaviors, such as the unemployment, inflation, and decision, determinants of fluctuations and growth in the national income, etc. If we take a "forest" as a metaphor, then the former studies the single "trees" (economic entities) and the latter studies the whole "forest" (Economy as a whole).

Needless to say, in Marx's *Das Kapital* (or in his other writings) we cannot find any terminology of "Microeconomics" or "macroeconomics" view, one of the achievements of western economics after Marx is to specifically classify economics into microeconomics and macroeconomics and expound on the differences (and connections) between these two aspects. In the history of economic thoughts, since the early stages of western economics (including a quite long period before and after Marx), all western economics are nothing more than a general whole, and the boundaries of each component part of this general whole is subtle and ambiguous. In the period beginning with 1930s this ambiguity of boundaries between the microeconomics and macroeconomics has been recognized and the efforts to clear the issue have continued till currently. However, it is unequally undeniable that in Marx's economics, there are abundant rich thoughts regarding microeconomic analysis and macroeconomic analysis.

Marx's *Das Kapital* discusses not only the micro aspects of capitalism but also the macroeconomic aspects of capitalism, but also discusses his study object from microeconomic and macroeconomic aspects, in combination and in a synthetic manner. For example, Marx had once analyzed the connection and difference between "single capitals" and "the total social capital" with a particular emphasis: "it clamors to be considered not only as the general form of the circuit, (refers to circuit of commodity capital—noted by citer), i.e., not only as a social form in which every single industrial capital (except when first invested) can be studied, hence not merely as a form of movement common to all individual industrial capitals, but simultaneously also as a form of movement of the sum of the individual capitals, consequently of the aggregate capital of the capitalist class, a movement in which that of each individual industrial capital appears as only a partial movement which intermingles with the other movements and is necessitated by them."[4]

This movement (refer to circulating motion of commodity capital—noted by citer), as the movement of a single individual capital, may present other phenomena than the same movement does when considered from the point of view of a part of the aggregate movement of social capital, hence in its interconnections with the movements of its other parts...."[5]

This motion (refer to circulating motion of commodity capital—noted by citer), it is particularly noteworthy that the entire theoretical system of Marx is in consistence and tally with modern economics, i.e. which is "from microeconomics to macroeconomics" rather than the other way round.[6]

For example, in the Volume 1 of *Das Kapital*, when discussing "the production process of capital", it states: "The wealth of those societies in which the capitalist mode of production prevails, presents itself as "an immense accumulation of commodities," its unit being a single commodity. Our investigation must therefore begin with the analysis of a commodity."[7]

In fact, in the entire Volume 1 of *Das Kapital*, Marx mainly discussed such "single" commodity, "single" currency, especially "single" capitals. Just as Marx concluded: "In volume I the process of capitalist production was analyzed as an individual transaction as well as a process of reproduction...

---

4   Marx, *Das Kapital*, Volume 2, People's Publishing House, 2004, p. 112.

5   Ibid, p. 113.

6   Although currently most western economists hold that the theoretical system of economics should begin from "microeconomics", but till 1980s, the approach was different and in Samuelson's Economics Textbook (11th edition of English version in 1980) which had become popular in a certain period, the arrangement of the chapters in his book, placed "macroeconomics" before "microeconomics". In addition, today also a few of Marxist economists still maintain the idea of "research methodology beginning from macro towards microeconomics". (Refer to Bai Baoli's *General Theory of Value and Price*, Economic Science Press, 2006, p. 25.)

7   Marx, *Das Kapital*, Volume 1, People's Publishing House, 2004, p. 47.

The changes of form and substance experienced by capital in the sphere of circulation were assumed without lingering over them. It was assumed that, on one hand, the capitalist sells the product at its value, and on the other, that he finds within the sphere of circulation the material means of production required for the renewal or continuation of the process."[8]

Just based on such approach, Marx was able to focus on analyzing the production and re-production of "single capital" in Volume 1 of *Das Kapital* without having to discuss the "connection" between the "single capital" and other capitals, thus he did not need to examine the issue of aggregate "social" capital. In other words, Volume 1 of *Das Kapital* mainly makes the "micro" economic analysis on capital.

Besides, in Volume 2 of *Das Kapital*, "Circuit process of capital", and the first two Parts also conduct microeconomic analysis on capital and later in the third Part it "rises" to conduct macroeconomic analysis. Just as Marx stated: "But in both the first and the second Parts it was always only a question of some individual capital, of the movement of some individualized part of social capital.", "However the circuits of the individual capitals intertwine, presuppose and necessitate one another, and form, precisely in this interlacing, the movement of the total social capital." Therefore, in Part III (Volume II), he began to "discuss the circuit process of each single capital as the component part of aggregate social capital …… that is to say, the process of circulation of this aggregate social capital."[9]

389

Finally, Volume 3 of *Das Kapital*, "General Process of Capitalist Production", conducts "macroeconomic" analysis on capital. Marx stated clearly on this point: "this third book (Volume III) treats, cannot confine itself to general reflection relative to this synthesis (which was made in Volume 2 Part III). On the contrary, Volume III must locate and describe the concrete forms which grow out of the movements of capital as a whole. In their actual movement single capitals confront each other in such concrete shape."[10]

Here, "whole" means the unified analysis embodying both production and circulation process and "the concrete forms" refer to industrial capital, commercial capital, interest-bearing capital, etc. In other words, Volume 3 of *Das Kapital* mainly makes "macro" economic analysis on capital.

Thus, it can be seen that if we classify according to microeconomic and macroeconomic classification method of modern economics, i.e. we can classify all the 3 volumes as "production process", "circulation process" and "unity of production and circulation process", then we can say that *Das Kapital* may be divided into two parts: Part I and II of the Volume 1, belong to microeconomics of *Das Kapital* and Part 3 of Volume 2 and Volume 3 of *Das Kapital* belong to macroeconomics.

---

8   Marx, *Das Kapital*, Volume 2, People's Publishing House, 2004, p. 391.
9   Ibid., p. 392.
10   Marx, *Das Kapital*, Volume 3, People's Publishing House, 2004, p. 29.

I should say that the above "interpretation" on *Das Kapital* from micro-economic and macroeconomic perspectives does not attempt any intention to "re-draw" the meanings of *Das Kapital*. I just intend to express that even evaluated from the framework of modern economics; *Das Kapital* which was written nearly 150-plus years ago still shines with its logic system—if interpreted reasonably.

III. Equilibrium and non-equilibrium

Microscopic and macroscopic methodologies are concerned with the spatial characteristics of the research object. If we look from the point of view of the "state" of the research object, whether it is a micro-phenomenon or macro-phenomenon, it can be divided into 2 "states", i.e. "equilibrium" and "disequilibrium" (or "unbalanced") state.

Many people believe that the term "equilibrium" in economics is originally borrowed from physics or other natural sciences. For example, in Marshall's "Principles of Economics" (neo-classical economics), there is a section entitled "Biology and mechanics on the concept of the opposite force balance" where he wrote "The Mecca of the economist lies in economic biology, not in mechanics."[11]

Some people hold different views on this. Schumpeter once pointed out that "the concept of equilibrium, whether static or dynamic, is never ... from those with similar concepts borrowed from the natural sciences".[12] The rationale is that the concept of equilibrium belongs to the general category of logic, whereas the general category of logic appears both in the natural sciences and also in the social sciences.

Whether or not the concept of equilibrium originates from the natural sciences, its basic meaning is clear: that is equilibrium is a balance between the various forces that determine the system in which all forces that can cause the system to change are exactly offsetting each other, so that it can continue for a period to maintain its state without change.

In Western economics, equilibrium analysis has a long history. According to Robbins, "Quesnay's Economic Table" has essentially tried to use what is now called as equilibrium analysis". Moreover, the most important achievement of Adam Smith's "Wealth of Nations" is that "it demonstrates how the relative price mechanism tends keep the division of labor in an equilibrium state".[13]

In modern times (In 18th-19th centuries), the concept of equilibrium has become the basis and center of the whole western economics. In fact, most theories of the western economics (including the so-called "non-equilibrium" theory) are built around the concept of equilibrium, however the concept of

---

11   Marshall, *Principles of Economics*, Volume II, Commercial Press,1981, p. 17.

12   Schumpeter, *History of Economic Analysis*, Volume III, Commercial Press 1996, p. 322.

13   Robbins, *The Nature and Significance of Economic Science*, Commercial Press, 2001, p. 59.

equilibrium also seems irrelevant to many of the original "united" (integrated) theories. For example, for much of the time throughout the 20th Century, production theory and distribution theory were seen as two separate but inextricably linked parts of economics, but since the development of equilibrium analysis, "... the economists were more inclined to abandon this traditional division methodology". "Instead of dividing our central body of analysis into a theory of production and a theory of distribution, we have a theory of equilibrium, a theory of comparative statics and a theory of dynamic change."[14] Thus, theory of equilibrium that emerged from production theory and theory of distribution (separately) was integrated into the "modern theory" of both the theory of production and the theory of distribution.

As is the case with microanalysis and macroscopic analysis, although as a systematic analytical tool, the emergence and development of equilibrium analysis and disequilibrium analysis is mainly attributed to Western economics, but Marx has also made his own contribution in this respect. For example, Marx, in Chapter 10 of the Volume 3 of *Das Kapital*, once carried out an in-depth analysis of the question of "consistency of supply and demand" (i.e. "equilibrium of the market" in Western economics). In regard to the meaning of market equilibrium, Marx said: "If the supply and demand... Whenever two forces operate equally in opposite directions, they balance one another, exert no outside influence. This means that the market is in equilibrium, which is the most simple and most clear explanation, Marx said, "If supply equals demand, they cease to act, and for this very reason commodities are sold at their market-values."

In modern Western economics textbooks, similar sentences can be seen everywhere, but Western economics has used "equilibrium price" instead of Marx's "market value". When expounding on the equilibrium model, Marx wrote: "Nothing is easier than to realize the inconsistencies of demand and supply; if they are consistent, it is only accidental phenomenon..."

On the rationality of the equilibrium model, Marx said: "But the political economy must assume that supply and demand are consistent. Why? To be able to study phenomena in their fundamental relations, in the form corresponding to their conception, that is, is to study them independent of the appearances caused by the movement of supply and demand. The other reason is to find the actual tendencies of their movements and to some extent to record them.

And, on the limitations of equilibrium analysis, Marx said: "If supply and demand balance one another, they cease to explain anything, do not affect market-values, and therefore leave us so much more in the dark about the reasons why the market-value is expressed in just this sum of money and no other. It is evident that the real inner laws of capitalist production cannot be explained by the interaction of supply and demand...

---

14   Ibid., pp. 58-59.

Objectively speaking, even today, Marx's critique in regard to the limitations of equilibrium analysis is rarely well understood by Western economists. I can also say, the question posed by Marx ("why the market-value is expressed in just this sum of money and no other") has not been correctly answered by the western economists.

On how to overcome the limitations of equilibrium analysis, Marx said: "In this condition (refer to supply and demand – the author) under the various phenomena, it is necessary to use another force, rather than the effect of these two forces". This other force is the law of labor value.[15]

Marx also discussed in detail the adjustment process of equilibrium. For example, he analyzed the distribution of social capital in different sectors (the luxury goods production sector and the basic subsistence goods production sector) in Chapter 17 of Volume 2 of *Das Kapital*, which is the "resource allocation" in the western economics. Marx posed an "interesting" question: What would happen if wages would be generally raised? Some people have replied this question as "a general increase in wages would increase workers' demand for goods, thereby raising the price of goods and eventually offsetting the increase of wage increases." In this regard, Marx criticized: "this is just intimidation of the capitalists and the vulgar economists who flatter them." Marx specifically analyzed: in consequence of a rise in wages, the demand of the laborers for the necessities of life will rise particularly. Their demand for articles of luxury will increase to a lesser degree, or a demand will develop for things which formerly did not come within the scope of their consumption. The sudden and large-scale increase in the demand for the indispensable means of subsistence will doubtless raise their prices immediately. The consequence: a greater part of the social capital will be employed in the production of necessities of life and a smaller in the production of luxuries, since these fall in price on account of the decrease in surplus-value and the consequent decrease in the demand of the capitalists for these articles. On the other hand as the laborers themselves buy articles of luxury, the rise in their wages does not promote an increase in the prices of the necessities of life but simply displaces buyers of luxuries. More luxuries than before are consumed by laborers, and relatively fewer by capitalists." "However, but this change will lead to the transfer of capital from the luxury goods production sector to the sector of basic necessities production." Marx added: "Whenever there is ... this balancing process, under such circumstances, the prices of living materials will raise, then the capital withdrawn from the luxury goods manufacturing sector will be continually added to capital being invested into the basic living materials production sector, until the demand is saturated. At this moment, the equilibrium is restored and the end of the whole process is that the social capital, and therefore also the money-capital, is divided in a different proportion between the production of

---

15 The quotations in this page and above paragraph are quoted from Marx, *Das Kapital*, Volume 3, People's Publishing House, 2004, pp. 211-212.

the necessities of life and that of luxury articles."[16] Equilibrium and non-equilibrium are two states of the economic system. However, in real life, non-equilibrium is even more common. But for a long period of time, Western economists seem to focus only on the former. Their economic treatises are filled with a variety of equilibrium analysis. Equilibrium is seen as "normal", while non-equilibrium or non-equilibrium states are seen as "anomaly" and "deviations". The discussion of non-equilibrium states (if any) is "subordinated" to the equilibrium analysis, lacking the status of "independence". This situation has lasted until the 1930s, when Keynes published the General Theory of Employment, Interest, and Money. In this book, Keynes studied deeply and systematically the phenomenon of "involuntary unemployment" and attributed it to "insufficient effective demand." He concludes that below-full employment is the "normal state" of capitalist society. For this reason, Keynes was praised by many Western economists as the founder of the disequilibrium analysis. In fact, this is a little bit overestimation. Not to mention that Keynes's non-equilibrium analysis has obvious limitations, for example, he attributed the capitalist economic crisis only to lack of effective demand without further analysis of its institutional roots, and, his method of disequilibrium analysis, was far later than Marx. Keynes himself acknowledged that his notion of effective demand and his theory of effective demand, he wrote: "this notion was not mentioned at all" in the works of Marshall et al, but it had long "existed" "in Marx's economic doctrine".[17] In fact, in a sense, even what the whole *Das Kapital* discussed was the capitalist economy in disequilibrium (especially the economic crisis) – which is the cause and consequences the generation of crises.

393

Thus, Marx's economics, not only contains some of the major and meaningful ideas of modern Western economics on equilibrium and non-equilibrium analysis, but also contains many very enlightening equilibrium and non-equilibrium–but for a long time these views—also admitted by Keynes—were ignored by the modern Western economics due to their own limitations.

IV. Empirical and Normative Analysis Aspects in Methodology

When examining economic phenomena (economic variables or economic systems), people often march towards two directions. The first consideration direction is: how are they? The second consideration is: how should they ought to be? The answer to the former constitutes "empirical analysis" or "empirical economics", the answer to the latter constitutes a "normative analysis" or the "normative economics".

To answer the question of "what is the actual situation", it is necessary to describe, explain and even "predict" the facts.

---

16   Marx, *Das Kapital*, Volume 2, People's Publishing House, 2004, p. 377.
17   Keynes, *General Theory of Employment, Interest and Money*, Commercial Press, 1997, p. 31.

In contrast, the question of "what the situation ought to be" cannot be separated from the assessment and judgment of "value" Of the "usefulness" or "consensual" to make judgments.[18] For example, in different economic situations or "states", to determine what is "good", which is "bad"; in those "good" economic states, to further determine which is the "best", which is "good"; and so on. In this way, we can say that empirical economics is independent of value judgments, while normative economics relies on value judgments. The difference between "real/empirical" and "normative" is the difference between "fact" and "value".

There is a view that Marx's *Das Kapital* has been mainly "normative" rather than "empirical" analysis. This is a big mistake. The exact opposite is true. Although the theoretical conclusions of *Das Kapital* are characterized by "party nature" and having "class nature", they are the results of an objective and rigorous empirical analysis.

As is well known, Marx wrote in the preface to the first edition of the first volume of *Das Kapital*: "To prevent possible misunderstanding, a word. I paint the capitalist and the landlord in no sense couleur de rose [i.e., seen through rose-tinted glasses]. But here individuals are dealt with only in so far as they are the personifications of economic categories, embodiments of particular class-relations and class-interests. My standpoint, from which the evolution of the economic formation of society is viewed as a process of natural history, can less than any other make the individual responsible for relations whose creature he socially remains, however much he may subjectively raise himself above them."[19]

In order to better understand the "empirical" nature of *Das Kapital*, we should into three main aspects of empirical research. The first major aspect of empirical research is the "description", i.e. to answer the question of "what it is". Descriptive economics is the main task of arranging and compiling proper data on economic phenomena, and interpret them logically to describe some of the important features of economic phenomena.

For example, the analysis of market behaviors often begins with a description of the market structure: how many firms are in this market? How big are they? Are the products produced exactly the same or slightly different? and many more questions. Such descriptive empirical study in the *Das Kapital* abound. For example, the first volume of *Das Kapital* has devoted much of its length to the history, content, and results of the English factory law. Particularly worth mentioning is that in *Das Kapital*, there is a unique "description" emphasized by Engels, that is, "citations" of the views of other economists, an economic

---

18　"Value judgment" is an English word where the meaning of "value" is mainly refers to "usefulness" or "consensuality." This word translated into Chinese as "value" is easy to misunderstand, because in Chinese, "value" is used for "meaning", "role", or used to describe items of "cheapness and expensiveness" etc.

19　Marx, *Das Kapital*, Volume 1, People's Publishing House, 2004, p. 100

thought was generated in the development process, by considering what, when, who first made it clear.[20] Through this abundant citations, Marx, has actually described briefly the history of the economic theory, while developing his own theory.

The second major aspect of empirical research is "interpretation" which answers the question of "why". The main task of the interpretative economics is to explain the hidden reasons behind the analysis of the available known economic phenomena. For example, an increase in the market price of a commodity is a known economic phenomenon; it may be explained and interpreted by an increase in the demand for this commodity, either by a decrease in the supply of the commodity, or by an increase in demand and a decrease in supply. Undoubtedly, the "interpretation" of the various economic phenomena has constituted the content of *Das Kapital*. For example, Marx's theory of how commodities transform into money, how money transforms into capital, how capital exploits surplus value, and how surplus value transforms into capital, can be defined as the interpretative empirical research.

The third major aspect of empirical research is "forecasting/ prediction", which answers the question of "what will happen". The main task of predictive economics is to discover the unknown economic phenomena based on theories and assumptions. Predictive economics is very similar to interpretative economics. As to its form, prediction is an inference of an unknown phenomenon, and interpretation is a description of a known phenomenon. A theory can be purely predictable and does not contain an explanatory component. A. Kolding once gave an interesting example: we can predict that the sun will rise tomorrow, on the basis of the rising sun every day, but in such a prediction there is no explanation to the question of why.[21]

On the other hand, a theory can also be explained but not predictable. A typical example of this is Darwin's theory of evolution. According to Bragg, "Darwinian Theory can tell us much about the process of evolution, but Darwin's theory can hardly tell us anything where the evolution will head to."[22] As far as *Das Kapital* is concerned, its most important conclusion, that capitalism will inevitably be replaced by socialism, at the time when it was written, this was obviously a prediction. Even according to the viewpoint of Western philosophy of science, a theory is also scientific–because it can be "falsified". Not only that, it has been in fact partially "confirmed" when people can evaluate the currently booming socialist China.

Of course, the best economic analysis is the combination of empirical and normative analysis based on empirical research. In this regard, the economic system analysis in the *Das Kapital* has provided a benign model, of which, the

---

20   Ibid., p. 30.
21   See Kolding's *Empirical Economics*, contained 14th edition of Modern Foreign Economic Papers, the Commercial Press, 1992, pp. 87-88.
22   Mark Bragg, *Economic Methodology*, Peking University Press, 1990, p. 9.

following points are particularly noteworthy. Firstly, Marx has put forward the criterion of productive forces to judge the merits of any economic system, that is, whether an economic system adapts to the development of social productive forces can still have certain progressive character. In his view, any economic system compatible with the development of productive forces is an effective system–it can greatly promote economic and social development, on the other hand, an economic system incompatible with the development of productive forces will fetter and restrict the development of productive forces.

Secondly, Marx argues that institutional design and policy analysis which is linked with normative economics analysis cannot be divorced from empirical economics analysis. This is because the socio-economic development is a natural historical process, in this sense, Marx wrote: "No social order ever perishes before all the productive forces for which there is room in it have developed; and new, higher relations of production never appear before the material conditions of their existence have matured in the womb of the old society itself. Therefore mankind always sets itself only such tasks as it can solve; since, looking at the matter more closely, it will always be found that the tasks itself arises only when the material conditions of its solution already exist or are at least in the process of formation."[23] In other words, you can like or dislike an economic system—but such judgment will be "arbitrary" and subjective desire, but to change it in practice is another question—whether it can be changed will depend on whether the conditions are mature.

Thirdly, although people cannot change the course of social history "at their will freely", it does not mean just completely passively accepting it. As Marx said: "And even when a society has got upon the right track for the discovery of the natural laws of its movement ….. it can neither clear by bold leaps, nor remove by legal enactments, the obstacles offered by the successive phases of its normal development. But it can shorten and lessen the birth-pangs."[24]

Originally published in the journal Jiangxi Social Science, 2014(1)

---

23 *Collected Works of Marx and Engels*, Volume 2, People's Publishing House, 2009, p. 592.
24 Marx, *Das Kapital*, Volume 1, People's Publishing House, 2004, p. 9-10.

The Disadvantages of Modernist Economics Trend and the Value of Pluralistic Orientation in the Study of Economics

Zhang Xu <u>397</u>

Abstract: Neoclassical economics, as part of "mainstream economics", has been gradually changing, but its mathematical deductivist methodology has been its invariant feature, which reflects its modernist orientation and which dominates economic research, currently. Modernist economics trend is the one, which advocates that the only way to do economics is building models. This kind of modernist trend embodies the expansion and exclusion aspects as the basic characteristics of mainstream economics and causes that the study of economics increasingly being detached from the concern of the real issues. As a call to resist against the domination of modernist economics, pluralism is increasingly gains support due to its unique values. The pluralist economics trend can help to deepen the research and bring economics back into the service of society and to real problems and help to promote the innovation of economic theory.

Key words: modernism; expansion and exclusion; pluralism; theoretical innovation

During the British Queen's visit to the London School of Economics in 2008, she asked a question: why did economists fail to predict the financial crisis? While economists were engaged in in-depth thinking and heated discussions on this issue, there were two important events: Firstly, in the fall of 2011, the famous economist N. G. Mankiw suffered embarrassment that is not easy to be encountered for him: Harvard students skipped his class; for the Davos Forum at the end of 2012, "big transformation: shaping the new model" has become the theme of the meeting, reflecting the free market capitalism has become an important topic throughout the meeting.

How do you see the Queen's questions, the embarrassment of N.G. Mankiw and the first 10 years of the 21st Century debate on the free-market capitalist system? Considering that mainstream economics plays an important role in the success of free-market capitalism, we believe that these three issues are closely related to the economic theory, especially the mainstream economic theory. So, what kind of major problems do exist in mainstream economics in the end? Where is the direction to make improvements?

In economics research, there has been ever lack of criticism of mainstream economics, but many criticisms get involved in invalid situations for various reasons. As for general mainstream economic criticism, the reason why the source is not that accurate is that "cannot precisely define the object of its critique, thus, as long as critics' slings and arrows are directed against features of neoclassical economics that the latter can shed strategically, like a threatened lizard 'loses' its tail, they shall miss their target."[1] When reading a large number of critical economic literature on mainstream economics, there is the impression that modern mainstream economics very similar to the economics of 50 years ago and that criticism of what is called neoclassical economics is also very similar to heretics economists critical of mainstream economics in the early 1950s and 1960s, as Crand and other scholars said, the existing criticism is "not reliable", why some critics is "not reliable". The reason is simple, mainstream economics has been changing. If not from the mainstream economics of the changing mainstream of economics to grasp the core features of criticism, similar to a fixed gun to fight mobile targets, the results can be imagined, not only mainstream economics can these criticism ignored, but also further strengthened their belief that heresy of economics "non-scientific" concept. Therefore, in order to accurately identify the typical characteristics of mainstream economics, we need to accurately identify the philosophical basis and negative effects of the mainstream economics, and explore the ways to improve it.

---

1 Christian Arnsperger and Yanis Varoufakis, What is Neoclassical Economics? The Three Axioms Responsible for its Theoretical Oeuvre, Practical Irrelevance, and thus, Discursive Power. *Panoekonomicus* 2006(1), p. 6.

I. The "Modernist" Characteristics of Mainstream Economics

For most mainstream economics, only one way to conduct economic research is required to establish a model, collect the relevant data, and conduct the model test. And the model itself must be consistent with the basic principles of methodological individualism, that is, must be based on the rational behavior of the optimization of the main assumptions. For the defenders of mainstream economics, these simple principles make economics as the foundation of a science.[2]

For the mainstream economics of the above orientation, from various perspectives on criticism of the papers and writings, detailed overview of the relevant criticism has even become a difficult study of the literature. Therefore, many well-known historians of western economic thought and economic methodology have summed up the philosophical foundations of mainstream economics as "modernist trend" and explored the consequences and influences of modernism in economics.

In the study of economic methodology, McCloskey pointed out that modernism is an economic "official wording". McCloskey enumerated 11 principles of modernism[3]: (1) prediction (and control) is the objective of the science; (2) only the observable impact (or prediction) is important to the truth; (3) can be expected to (or control) is the goal of science; (2) Observability implies objectivity, repeatable experimentation; (4) this theory can prove to be wrong when (and only if) the empirical content of a theory proves to be false; (5) should be valued objectivity, The subjective "observation" (introspection) is not scientific knowledge; (6) Kelvin (British physicist, mathematician) saying "when you cannot use digital expression, your knowledge is poor, unsatisfactory (7) Introspection, metaphysical beliefs, aesthetics, and the like may work in the discovery of hypotheses, but should never appear in hypotheses; (8) combine scientific reasoning with non-scientific reasoning, (10) Scientists (e.g. economists) should not say three things about the value issue. (9) A scientific explanation of a fact is to place the fact in a law of covering; (11) Hume's famous quote, said: "When we run over libraries, persuaded of these principles, what havoc must we make? If we take in our hand any volume of divinity or school metaphysics, for instance, let us ask, does it contain any abstract reasoning concerning quantity or number? No. Does it contain any experimental reasoning concerning matter of fact and existence? No. Commit it then to the flames, for it can contain nothing but sophistry and illusion."[4]

---

2   E. Lazear, "Economic Imperialism", *Quarterly Journal of Economics* 2000, 115(1), pp. 96-146.

3   Deirdre McCloskey, *The Rhetoric of Economics*, Economic Science Press, 2000, pp. 177-178

4   Hume, *A Study of Human Understanding*, Commercial Press, 1981, p. 145.

McCloskey's definition of modernism is very close to positivism, although positivism is one of the characteristics of modernism, and positivism on the impact of economics is indeed very large, but the modernism in economics is not the same as positivism. Klamer and Dow gave a broader definition of modernism: (1) A break with the past involving: (a) the search for universal theories, (b) a commitment to the idea of progress; (2) Formalism, with a preference for axiomatic, reductionist, dualistic reasoning, and the use of mathematics; (3) Compartmentalization (e.g. between public and private, positive and normative, and between disciplines) and a turning inwards involving, among other things, the use of jargon and self-referential discourse.[5]

Paul Wendt argues that modernist economics is centered on the metaphor of the machine. He has argued that modernism has three essential characteristics: foundationalism (analysis of an object into its components) objectivism (seeing the object of research as separate from the observer) and control (just as a machine can be controlled) Universalism and rationality, although sometimes proposed as characteristics, are in Wendt's view, they are not essential.[6]

So, when did modernism in the field of economics begin to flourish? According to the above definition, modernism spread to the field of economics in the 1930s. Subsequently, the mathematical formalism closely related to Samuelson began to develop rapidly in the 1940s. In the development of economic modernism, rational, maximizing behavior hypothesis promoted the use of form, mathematical reasoning to derive theory, so that modernism in the development of economics plays an important role in universal significance

II. The Negative Influence of Modernism in Economics

Modernism pushed the replacement of classical economics by neoclassical economics and played an important role in the dispute over the dominance of Marxism and institutionalism.[7] The orientation of modernism studied by mainstream economists created a number of typical characteristics of economic research as follows:

(I) The characteristics of modernism makes economic research detach from the real problems, which is "blackboard economics" or "sand play"

Coase, has been opposed to such kind of economics that "only exists in the minds of economists rather than in the human world", i.e. the so-called "blackboard economics". In Coase's view, the blackboard economics is characterized

<hr>

5   Roger. E. Backhouse, *Explorations in Economic Methodology: From Lakatos to Empirical Philosophy of Science*, London and New York: Routledge, 1998, p. 111.

6   Paul Wendt, "Comment" on Amariglio", in: Warren J. Samuels (ed.), *Discourse*, Boston, Dordrecht and London: Kluwer, 1990, p. 49.

7   It should be said that the establishment of the orthodox status of mainstream economics is not purely a natural selection process. For example, many Western scholars of intellectual history believe that McCarthyism has played a suppressive role against Marxist economics in the United States.

by the fact that when economists find themselves unable to analyze what is happening in the real world, they construct an imaginary world that they can handle. And there is no relationship between this imaginary economy and the real world. McCloskey also pointed out: "a lot of good works, new facts and new ideas are annihilated in economics... the mainstream of conventional science of economics has become the children's sand play, which has become already absurd".[8]

Although the above mentioned judgments have been proposed in various ways by scholars from different schools, they should never be interpreted as an ideological attack on those who are hostile to mathematical methods. In the theoretical reflection after the outbreak of 2008 global financial crisis, many mainstream scholars also recognize that there is a mainstream economics ignoring the real world. For example, the famous economic historian B. Eichengreen said: "The outbreak of crisis in 2008 has cast into doubt much of what we thought we knew about economics. We thought that monetary policies had tamed the business cycle. We thought that because changes in central-bank policies had delivered lower and stable inflation, the economic volatility in the pre-1985 years had been consigned to the dustbin of history; they had given way to the quaintly dubbed "Great Easing". We have thought that financial institutions and markets had come to be self-regulating and that the investors could be left largely, if not wholly to their own devices. Above all we thought that we had learned how to prevent the kind of financial calamity that struck the world in 1929. But we are now aware that a lot of what we used to think as correct, was in fact misleading.[9]

J. Toporowski has argued that the "financial crisis that broke out in 2008 from those countries with the most "advanced" financial systems and which spread to the world has not yet been adequately explained by economic theory. That is, various economic theories have failed to, and could not help policymakers and implementers cope with the crisis, and only few economics theorists could explain the implications of this crisis, in addition to those that we are responding to a crisis in the face of the dazzling failure of the views, they only take out these."[10]

(II) The pursuits of modernist economics is at the expense of a great deal of valuable views, thus and its economics research perspective becomes increasingly narrower

The typical representative of this understanding is D. McCloskey, she has pointed out that the modernist economics "as science and axiomatic and mathematical representation, and separating the scientific field from and the spirit, value, goodness, kindness and all non-measurable fields. As the functionalists,

8   Deirdre N. McCloskey, *The Rhetoric of Economics*, Economic Science Press, 2000, p, 238.

9   Barry Eichengreen, The Last Temptation of Risk, *National Interest* 2009 (May, June). p. 8.

10   Jan Toporowski, "Excess Debt and Asset deflation", in: Steven Kates (ed.) *Macroeconomic Theory and its Failings: Alternative Perspectives on the Global Financial Crisis*, Northampton. MA: Edward Elgar Publishing. 2010, p. 221.

the modernists are anti-historians who do not care about cultural traditions or intellectual traditions".[11]

Hodgson argues that "mainstream economics, especially since Lionel Robbins, focuses on a universalist attempt to establish general economic principles that can be applied to all economic systems, but this attempt fails. This is partly due to the fact that almost all economic history research is conducted through a theoretical perspective derived from a single type of institution – a market society – (which I call market universalism) even when some economists evaluate and analyze those non-market phenomena such as feudalism, modern family or when they analyze entities such as a company or important organizations, they only see 'markets' and 'implicit contract' everywhere, as their intrinsic nature.[12]

In Nelson's view, one of the most important reasons for the "uncritical ideological tendencies" and "narrowing" of the field of economics is that "not only the mathematical model as the only useful constructive theory, it is regarded as the only reasonable method".[13]

We can understand the narrow-mindedness of mainstream economics by analyzing entrepreneurial spirit which lacked in mainstream microeconomics textbooks. Schumpeter gave a metaphorical explanation[14] which compared the situation to "Hamlet without the Danish prince", that is to say, in the theory of the firm of economics, there is no study of the entrepreneur. To this day, Schumpeter's questions still remain unanswered. Dan Johansson has pointed out that in the graduate textbooks of important micro, macro and industrial organization; there is no entrepreneur and entrepreneurial spirit such terms.[15] This is not because entrepreneurial or entrepreneurial spirit is not important in free-market capitalist economic growth or economic activity organization. Anyone knows what entrepreneurship or entrepreneurship means for free-market capitalism. The reason for the situation is very simple and has a methodological dimension: "Each modeling attempt focuses only on one specific feature of entrepreneurship, and the entrepreneurial function broadly perceived eludes analytical tractability."[16]

---

11   Deirdre N. McCloskey, The Rhetoric of Economics, *Economic Science Press*, 2000, p. 176.
12   Hodgson, Geoffrey M., Visions of Mainstream Economics: A Response to Richard Nelson and Jack Vromen, *Review of Social Economy* 2002 (1), p. 126.
13   Nelson, Richard R., Thoughts Stimulated by Reading Geoffrey Hodgson's Economics and Utopia, *Review of Social Economy* 2002, 60 (1): p. 110.
14   Schumpeter, Joseph A., *Capitalism, Socialism and Democracy*, New York: George Allen & Unwin, 1942, p. 86.
15   Johansson, Dan., Economics without Entrepreneurship or Institutions: A Vocabulary Analysis of Graduate Textbooks, *Economic Journal Watch* 2004, 3 (1), pp. 515-538.
16   Milo Bianchi and Magnus Henrekson, Is Neoclassical Economics Still Entrepreneurless?, *KYKLOS*, 58 (3), p. 352.

Alongside with the modernist orientation of mainstream economics, those schools of thought which use less mathematical tools or do not strictly follow logical positivism are dismissed as heresy economics, non-mainstream economics, and are not valued. For example, in addition to Marxist economics school, the Austrian school blames the neo-classical economics school for the view that the economy will eventually be in an equilibrium state, the post-Keynesian school specifically deals with the role of uncertainties in the economy; the complex system theory applies chaos theory to the economics; also there is the evolutionary economics theory which treats the economic system as a biological system.

(III) Modernist economics is becoming more and more homogeneous in its analytical methods, and the tendency of formalism is becoming increasingly prominent.

Roger Backhouse has given a clear account of formalism in economics. Backhouse lists three types of formalism in economics: axiomatization, mathematization and methodological. Axiomatization as a term relatively easy to be understood refers to making a knowledge system simplified as a series of independent axioms, and all propositions are derived from these axioms through the use of well-defined logic rules. Mathematization is more common, that is, to use mathematical techniques (geometry, algebra, set theory, topology, etc.) for economic argument, which is also the meaning of formalism generally called by people in a general sense. Methodological, or methodological formalization refers to using a set of agreed methods to solve specific types of problems. In the 20th Century, economics became more and more formalized in many ways (especially in methodology), the most obvious example is the optimization model of individual behavior. Backhouse argues that the three types of formalism in economics are very different, and they should not be confused. All they have in common is that they can break down a complex chain of reasoning into a series of steps that can be clearly expressed, and each step is simple enough because there is a consensus procedure to analyze this step.[17]

There are many advantages to the formalization or mathematicization of economics, which cannot be denied. After the World War II, due to the influence of the logical positivism trend of thought, the formalization and mathematicization of economics was continuously strengthened. The formalization of the study disciplines is necessary because it has many advantages: (1) Clear. Be able to express the meaning of the concept in a clear way, which contributes to the clarification of a concept and the establishment of a logical basis. (2) Standardization. Contribute to the standardization of study terms and methods. Formalization contributes to the generalization of a theory without regard to the insignificant and unnecessary details. (3) Objectivity. Formalization provides a kind of objectivity with a higher degree that can be achieved under the case of not applicable to this kind of formal method, self-sufficient hypothesis, formalization can provide a

17   Backhouse, Roger E., If Mathematics is Informal, then Perhaps We Should Accept That Economics Must be Informal Too, *The Economic Journal* 1998, 108 (451), pp. 1848-1858.

muddle which can get rid of the implicit assumptions and the associated chaos. (4) The least hypothesis. The formalization of theories contributes to determining the precise conditional assumptions and providing the least assumptions for the analytic statements. Therefore, the mainstream scholars believe that formal method is the only way to meet the rigor and avoid errors.

Many scholars have criticized the formalism problems of mainstream modernist economics. Mark Blaug has explained the reason why formalism is becoming dominant, he pointed out that economics has become more and more mathematically formalized in an accelerating speed since the 1950s, especially in recent years. In other words, almost all focus only on the accuracy of the analysis, but regardless of policy relevance. What economics shows is an unprecedented social mathematics, rather than empirical social science. Economists are sometimes accused of physical envy disease, but this is a completely misleading allegation. Economists are not suffering from physics-envy, as sometimes asserted, for physicists cared about data. Instead, economists are suffering from mathematics-envy, retreating into puzzle solving, and paying lip service to falsification by adopting the position that 'testing' amounted to no more than examining the formal technical properties of a model and adjusting it. Anyone who understands contemporary physics will prove that physics attaches importance to experimental evidence, strives to be consistent between theory and experimental evidence, but does not pay much attention to rigorous theorem structure as a sequence of analytical lemmas. All in all, real problem for economists is mathematics envy disease.[18]

(IV) While the "economics imperialism" trend is rising, simultaneously the academic exclusion by mainstream economics is strengthening

There is an obvious "academic exclusion" trend in the current economics academic field. Articles without models are generally not accepted by the top academic journals, even if the use of certain model doesn't bring any creative insights to the text, this discriminative attitude is applied. The high cost for learning complex mathematics courses makes economic research exclude more descriptive and factual materials from research and teaching, and the disposability of theoretical level is far more important than the analysis on real economic issues.

Although the modernist economics trend has established a variety of models, this kind of different models does not prove that modernist economics trend is not exclusive. D. Schiffman summarized the exclusion effect of modern economics as follows: "modern economics embraces pluralism but in a limited sense. Diversity is allowed in modeling but rhetoric without a model is still derided as unscientific."[19] However, "math does not just make economics look more scientific, at the same time it heightens the barriers for entering into

---

18   Mark Blaug, Not Only an Economist- Autobiographical Reflections of a Historian of Economic Thought, *The American Economist* 38 (2), pp. 12-27.

19   Schiffman, Daniel A., Mainstream Economics, Heterodoxy and Academic Exclusion: A Review Essay, *European Journal of Political Economy*, 2004, 20, p. 1094.

the field of economics, and mathematics also limits the scope of research."[20]

Blaug's view is a good illustration of the exclusion trend in the mainstream economics. Blaug wrote: "Economics in the Western world is dominated by American economics and American economics is dominated by the 400-500 new PhDs in economics that each year seek employment in 3000 institutions of higher education. The way to gain employment and to secure promotion once employed is to publish in one of the 300 or so refereed English-language journals in economics, particularly in the dozen or so leading refereed journals. Whatever we may say against technique-ridden, mathematically expressed modeling of economic phenomena, the fact remains that the papers written in this form are easier to produce once the formula has been learned, and easier to appraise and referee than those written in words and diagrams. With 300 journals publishing semi-yearly or quarterly, something like 4,000-5,000 papers in economics are published every year, which are refereed by perhaps 300 academics at the top American universities, whose students will become the referees of papers in the next generation, papers which will of course look very much like the papers they are now themselves writing and publishing. In other words, we have created a veritable professional locomotive with a built-in momentum that feeds continually on the pressure to publish in prestigious journals in order to gain employment in prestigious institutions whose annual salaries are more or less twice those that are earned in academic "Siberia". To turn this locomotive around is to ask individuals at the beginning of their professional career to ignore the dominant fashion for economics papers and instead to write something unfashionable."[21]

In the article Old Wine in a New Bottle written by Milton Friedman in his article discussing the "Prospects for the 21ˢᵗ Century Economy", published in the *Journal of Economics*(101), he made a detailed analysis in regard to the growing tendency of mathematics and its consequences. Friedman specially pointed out that mathematics and econometrics has made economics more mature and sophisticated, which reflects that the discourse power of economics has been enhanced. Although they can enhance the discourse power of economic analysis, but for their application, "it is most often to impress people rather than to inspire others", Friedman added: "since time and time again, when reading the articles mainly written in mathematics, I find that their core conclusions and reasoning is very easy to be expressed by using words."[22] "In the past century, the substantive content discussed in the field of professional economics has not changed, but at the same time, the language used in economic analysis has undergone dramatic changes... In addition, the scope of the economics literature

---

20 Backhouse, Roger E., Austrian Economics and the Mainstream: View Form the Boundary, *The Quarterly Journal of Austrian Economics*, 2000, 3(2), p. 34.
21 Mark Blaug, "Ugly Currents in Modern Economics", in: Uskali Maki (ed.), *Fact and Fiction in Economics: Models, Realism and Social Construction*, Cambridge: Cambridge University Press, 2003, pp. 44-45.
22 Milton Friedman, Old Wine in New Bottles, https://miltonfriedman.hoover.org/objects/57251/old-wine-in-new-bottles.

has become narrower in some respects."[23]

In short, the adverse effects of mainstream economics are more and more prominent caused by its modernist tendency. It lacks the concern for real economic problems; under the drive of "economics imperialism" motivations, it pushes the formalist analysis model continuously expand on the analysis of most social problems. At the same time, the academic exclusion trend in the mainstream economics is also growing.

III. The Objective Value of Pluralism in Economics

In the past 20 years, in order to resist against various adverse consequences caused by modernism in the economic research, some western economists have begun to strongly advocate promoting the development of pluralism in economics. They emphasized that pluralism in economics could better explain economic realities and solve economic problems, and insist that pluralism in economics could eliminate the adverse exclusion trend that has occurred in the mainstream economics and promote innovation and renovation in economic research.

(I) Pluralism improves investigation into complex economic phenomenon more fully

Economists are a group of people who like to argue. For example, renowned economist Stiglitz, strongly condemned the "imposed and reigning" policy proposals, when some economists were hailing the IMF's "prescriptions" for the Latin American and Russian economies. In addition to the theoretical debate, policymakers despairingly find that economic knowledge is always in an inconclusive state when they desperately need to get some benign economic policy advice.

The debates among economists suggest that a single theory, a set of standard approaches, or a unitary concept should not be used to guide the economic research, which is the most essential reason for the rise of pluralism in economic research. Like other sciences, economics is a system of knowledge, and the different component parts of the system may have some common elements, but the development of this system is driven by different orientations. For example, in today's economic research, most economists belong to "neo-classical paradigm", which emphasizes market efficiency. But there are some economists who look into and care for the socioeconomic system in different ways. For example, Marxists emphasize the priority of the capital accumulation process, not the function of the market; the Keynesians have emphasized the role that the state which might play in ensuring full employment.

In fact, the more important the problem, the more controversial it becomes, what are the causes of unemployment? How to Manage Unemployment? Is the free trade a solution to the problem of poverty in the countries of the South? What role should the state play in the economy? How to solve the problem of

---

23   Ibid.

environmental protection in the course of economic development? For all these important questions, different economists can suggest different solutions, and there is no reason to claim that only single theoretical framework can be able to answer these questions. Therefore, it can be said that pluralism and economics of their own knowledge system corresponds.

Kurz and Salvadori are the two most famous and tenacious proponents of modern "classical" economics, in their views the so-called modern "classical" economics refers to study the law governing the rate of capital accumulation and the way in which outputs are distributed among social classes through rigorous long-term analysis on competitive capitalist economics. Heinz Kurz and Neri Salvadori have also supported the pluralism in economics. They have noted that the economic reality is so complex that the questions that economists ask are therefore inherently difficult, and it is unlikely that they have simple answers. Since no theory can consider all relevant factors in any particular economic context, there is a strong prima facie case for theoretical pluralism. Different theories will often be complementary rather than alternative, so that to seek dominance for one theory over all the others with the possible result that all the rival theories are extinguished amounts to advocating scientific regress. To paraphrase Voltaire: in a subject as difficult as economics a state of doubt may not be very comfortable, but a state of certainty would be ridiculous.[24]

The support by post-Keynesians is equally vigorous, but largely implicit in pluralism. When commenting and analyzing the mathematical model in economics, V. Chick and S. Dow put forward an understanding of pluralism. In their opinion, the formalization of an argument is not like what neo-classic economists think, but an unambiguous advance in economic research. On the contrary, formalization is also a problem of cost and benefit. Formalization trend presents a special view of understanding the world, because it presents a strong event-regularity for analyzing closed systems. Thus, this formalized analysis trend demands that economic terms have a fixed meaning rather than a specific background, and that these terms are separate from each other and not interrelated. In Chick's and Dow's view, economic statements may be correct in certain historical and institutional backgrounds, but may be erroneous in another background. Thus, they have doubted the possibility of "seeking the invariable, fixed laws." From this perspective, The idea that time may be 'right' at a specific time but may be 'wrong' at another time (more precisely, obsolete). Conventions which shape economic actions evolve through time, it is necessary to explore the relationship between results obtained under conditions of closure to this open-system reality. Such an understanding of reality raises the possibility that, as institutions change, theory must also change.

Doubt is cast on the possibility of finding immutable laws applicable to,

24 Kurz. H.D. and N. Salvadori, *On Critics and Protective Belts* (ed.), Understanding "Classical" Economics: Studies in Long-Period Theory, Routledge, 2000, p. 237.

say, feudalism and capitalism alike, or even to capitalism in various stages of its development. From this perspective, a theory can be 'right' at one time and become 'wrong' (more accurately, outdated) at another. The notion of imbuing a closed theoretical system with meaning is thus not an objective procedure; it requires the exercise of judgment."[25]

(II) Pluralism contributes to the innovation of economic thoughts and methods

In the thought field, any demand for a unitary theory is a fundamental obstacle to the birth of new thoughts. The modernist tendency of mainstream economics, has both raised the rigor of economics and caused too much emphasis on modernism at the same time, thus has hindered the innovation and development of economic thoughts and methods.

For example, some economists have harshly criticized the excessive use of formalist methods, and they think that the development of formalism in economics has reached a stage in which has begun to show its harmful effects, and excessive use of formalist methods makes the discipline of economics detach from the research of economic issues and the real world in any meaningful level. Both Bragg and Hodgson are not the "heresy economists" as labelled by mainstream economists, whose roots in dissatisfaction and opposition are against the strengthening role of formalization in the discipline of economics.

Deidre McCloskey, wrote: "the Keynesian revolution in economics would not have happened under the modernist legislation recommended for the method of science."[26] "For better or worse the Keynesian revolution in economics would not have happened under the modernist legislation recommended for the method of science. The Keynesian insights were not formulated as statistical propositions until the early 1950s, well after the bulk of younger economists had become persuaded they were true. By the early 1960s liquidity traps and accelerator models of investment, despite failures in their statistical implementations, were taught to first-year students of economics as matters of scientific routine. Modernist methodology would have stopped all this in 1936: where was the evidence of an objective, statistical, controlled kind? ... "If the modernist methodology was consistently followed, economics will be stalled."[27]

In a widely discussed study of the rhetoric of economics, McCloskey pointed out: "Facts and logic, together with metaphors and stories, can be described as four essentials of economics discourse. Just like other experts and economists aim to make their theories reasonable, none of these four essentials is dispensable."[28] She stressed the rhetoric of economics and put forward "the pluralism principle and each part of the four rhetorical essentials will restrict

25 Chick, V. and S. C. Dow, Formalism, Logic and Reality: A Keynesian Analysis, *Cambridge Journal of Economics*, 2001, 25 (6)9, p. 709.
26 Deidre McCloskey, *The Rhetoric of Economics*, Economic Science Press, 2000, p. 190.
27 Ibid., p. 192.
28 Ibid., p. 137.

the other parts, and make them not excessive. If you are too keen on a simple story or metaphor (or only logic or fact) what would you say in other parts may be foolishness and danger. It is best to be able to properly observe the true fact, follow the true logic, tell the true story, and build the true metaphor, so that they can check each other's abuses, and it can draw valuable scientific truths and realistic public policies only combining the four essentials of rhetoric."[29]

For another example, the institutionalist G.M. Hodgson also supports pluralism. In his view, it will be a dangerous illusion trying to apply a single, generalized theory in regard to human behavior in all societies. "It will encounter a few problems when establishing a general theory. One problem is the difficulty in analysis and calculation. When facing with these calculation constraints, general theorists will simplify their models usually, and thus abandon the generality of theories. Another problem related to general theory is that people are confined to the broad principles which govern all possible structures (in the field of analysis) .In the actual operation, an analytical theory must confine itself to a relatively small subset among all the possible structures. In addition, the cost of over-generalization is to ignore the key features common to the subset of phenomena."[30]

Hodgson has advocated bringing history back to economic analysis, and thus fundamentally, the reconstruction of economic theory that he advocates is the reconstruction of "natural and comprehensive pluralism."[31]

Thus, from the perspective of theoretical innovation, we can fully agree with Dow's view: "the goal of the pluralist research is to ensure that each of the possible approaches is consistent according to its own criteria and to improve the mutual understanding among users of different approaches. this kind of understanding provides a basis for the development of tolerant and creative cross-paradigm research."[32]

IV. Conclusions

The dominant position of modernist trend in economic research, regardless of its specific performance, mainly reflects two basic characteristics: expansion and exclusion. Expansion is mainly reflected in that the dominant mainstream economics tries to make the economic analysis methods of standard mode extended to other research field of social science, the best summarization for expansionism characteristic of mainstream economics is "economics imperialism", in this economics imperialism, although the excellent achievements of interdisciplinary communication can be found occasionally, what is more common is that the formalist economic analysis invades other subjects. However, exclusion is mainly reflected in the field of economic research, namely, the

29   Ibid., p. 151.
30   Hodgson, G. M., *How Economics Forgot History: The Problem of Historical Specificity in Social Science*, London and New York: Routledge, 2001, p. 16.
31   King.J. E., Three Arguments for Pluralism, *Journal of Australian Political Economy*, 2002, 50, p. 84.
32   Dow.S. C., Beyond Dualism, *Cambridge Journal of Economics*, 1990(14), p. 155.

exclusion of non-mainstream economic research results by mainstream economics, which is mainly reflected in the choice of research topics, publishing of different research results, heightening of entry barriers to scientific research institutions, standards and mechanisms of academic evaluation and so on. In brief, since the non-mainstream economic research does not use the formalist analysis methods and procedures that are accepted by mainstream economics, their research is described as "unscientific" which should be excluded from the field of economic research. The consequence of the two above typical characteristics of modernism in economic research is that its economic analysis is becoming more and more detached from the real world, and becoming an academic exercise and intellectual game, rather than a branch of social sciences that grasps and solves the problems of social realities. From the perspective of economics education, modern economics education has become more and more concerned with "technology" rather than "theory", more and more concerned with "training" rather than "education".

After the outbreak of global financial crisis in 2008, the self-reflection of modernist economics tendency has reached a new peak. In a declaration entitled "The Financial Crisis and the Systemic Failure of Academic Economics", 8 European economists have made such a self-criticism: "We believe that economics has been trapped in a sub-optimal equilibrium in which much of its research efforts are not directed towards the most prevalent needs of society. Paradoxically self-reinforcing feedback effects within the profession may have led to the dominance of a paradigm that has no solid methodological basis and whose empirical performance is, to say the least, modest. Defining away the most prevalent economic problems of modern economies and failing to communicate the limitations and assumptions of its popular models, the economics profession bears some responsibility for the current crisis. It has failed in its duty to society to provide as much insight as possible into the workings of the economy and in providing warnings about the tools it created. It has also been reluctant to emphasize the limitations of its analysis. We believe that the failure to even envisage the current problems of the worldwide financial system and the inability of standard macro and finance models to provide any insight into ongoing events make a strong case for a major reorientation in these areas and a reconsideration of their basic premises."[33]

The above statement is a good summary of the fundamental problems of mainstream economics. It is both a confession and a critique. It also implies the direction of economic development–re-emphasizing economic pluralism. Economic pluralism plays an important role in deepening the analysis of complex economic realities and promoting the innovation of economic thought and methodologies. It has been a vigorous resistance to the domination of modernism in economic research. As long as this pluralist approach is achieved

33   David Colander et al., The Financial Crisis and the Systematic Failure of the Academic Economics, in: Jeffrey Friedman (ed.), *What Caused the Financial Crisis*, Philadelphia, PA: University of Pennsylvania Press, 2011, p. 278.

by adhering to the general principles of scientific research and through critical dialogue and tolerant communication of the different theoretical schools, it can avoid falling into the relativism trap when the promoting pluralism.

As far as China's economic research is concerned, in recent years, whether we evaluate from the perspective of academic research or from the perspective of university education, the analytical paradigms of western mainstream economics has occupied the dominant position. However, looking from the perspective of macro aspect, we still emphasize following the guidance of Marxist economics as the basis when teaching Chinese economics education. . As a matter of fact, this situation in its appearance, can be evaluated as a kind of we can think that this is a fait accompli pluralism, i.e. an extremely simple pluralism embodying a binary co-existence. Such binary co-existing pluralism more often leads to mutual accusations and criticisms by both parties which are contending for dominance, and this is indeed a typical characteristic of some important debates in the field of economics, during the past years.

In our opinion, in order to achieve a healthy and benign development in China's economic research, what we should adhere to can be promoting pluralism in an equal footing. This pluralism should take critical dialogue and tolerant communication as its basic characteristic, rather than take the academic, institutional rejection and confrontation. The strength and practical value of Marxist economics which reflects its quality in guiding China's economic construction and practice as well as in solving the macroeconomic aspects of social and economic problems, is obvious and clear for all; scholars who support the research methodologies of western mainstream economics should not simply lean on the reason that Marxist economics lacks mathematical analysis or empirical research, and simply label it as "unscientific". In fact, Marxist economics is also committed to mathematical analysis to enhance its modern characteristics, and Marxist economics more vigorously emphasizes the social and political value of economic analysis, and this is essentially identical with the pluralist orientation. Besides, adhering to the mainstream economic research paradigms should not turn a blind eye to criticism and reflection of mainstream bourgeoisie economics, simultaneously, we should wisely draw on the valuable contents in western economic research.The vigorous analysis power possessed by the western modern economics in the analysis of specific market economy is also very significant we should not paste "vulgar economics" or "bourgeois economics" labels on it just because this research uses the analysis methods and thoughts which are different from ours. In short, the development trend of economic pluralism will help to deepen the research of real problems and promote the innovation of our economic theories.

Originally published in
Journal of Renmin University of China, 2014(1)

Appendix

Growth, Development and Social Justice

*—A Summary of the 9th Forum of
the World Association for Political Economy*

Ding Xiaoqin and Guo Yanqing

The WAPE—The World Association for Political Economy—is an open, non-profit international academic organization founded by world's Marxian economists and related academic institutions around the world. The mission of WAPE is to utilize modern Marxian economics to analyze and study the world economy, reveal its law of development and offer policies to promote economic and social progress on the national and global levels. The last 8 WAPE forums between 2006-2013 were successively held in Shanghai, China; Shimane, Japan; Beijing, China; Paris, France; Suzhou, China; Massachusetts, America; Mexico City, Mexico and Florianopolis, Brazil.

The forums were successful and discussed 8 different themes such as the economic globalization, labor relations, sustainable development, global democratic governance, socialism in the 21st Century, the crisis of capitalism, human development in the 21st Century, inequality and world capitalism, labor relations etc.

Between May 23 to 26, 2014, "The 9th Forum of the World Association for Political Economy—Growth, Development and Social Justice" was ceremoniously held at the Vietnam Academy of Social Sciences (Hanoi). More than

100 scholars from 22 countries including China, Vietnam, Laos, Japan, Korea, India, Sri Lanka, America, Canada, Brazil, Argentina, Mexico, Britain, France, Germany, Ireland, Austria, Ukraine, Portugal, the Netherlands, Australia and South Africa has attended the forum.

On the morning of May 24, Prof. Pham Van Duc, the vice president of the Vietnam Academy of Social Sciences, presided over the opening ceremony; Prof. Hiroshi Onishi of Japan's Keio University, vice president of the World Association for Political Economy, gave an opening speech; and Nguyen Xuan Thang the Dean of the Vietnam Academy of Social Sciences gave a welcoming speech.

At the opening ceremony, the Association issued the 2014 (4th) "Marxian Economics Award", Prof. David Kotz of Economics Department of the University of Massachusetts Amherst, the world famous Marxist economist, vice president of the Association, and Prof. Hong Yuanpeng of Fudan University School of Economics in China, were awarded this honor; it also issued the 6th "Outstanding Achievements Award in World Political Economy of the 21st Century", and 8 professors received the award, including Prof. Nobuharu Yokokawa of Musashi University in Japan, Prof. Michael Lebowitz from Simon Fraser University of Canada, Prof. Dong-Min Rieu of Chungnam University in South Korea, Prof. Patrick Bond from the University of Kwa Zulu-Natal in South Africa, Prof. Venkatesh Athreya of Bharathidasan University in India, Prof. Howard Nicholas of Holland Institute of Social Studies, Prof. V.K.Ramchandran, director of Indian Institute of Statistics and chairman of Indian Agriculture Research Foundation, and Prof. Yan Pengfei of Wuhan University in China. After the opening ceremony, Prof. Cheng Enfu, chairman of the World Political Economics Association and member of Chinese Academy of Social Sciences together with other six famous Marxist economists made the conference theme speech. Subsequently, Chairman Cheng Enfu, Secretary-general Ding Xiaoqin and Prof. Pham Van Duc, the vice president of the Vietnam Academy of Social Sciences together held the opening ceremony for Karl Marx's bronze statue made especially for this forum, and participated in the Association's annual tree-planting commemoration.

During the forum, there were two plenary sessions, 13 symposiums, and two board meetings to be held. The participant scholars carried on a thorough discussion around the theme of "Growth, Development and Social Justice".

I. Economic development and social justice

Prof. Cheng Enfu, chairman of the World Political Economics Association and member of Chinese Academy of Social Sciences, has put forward that development should be "fair development", and argued that every country has paid a big the price in the pursuit of economic growth by mistakenly using the GDP concept as the criterion for their economic development. To sublate this approach he put forward the concept of "Gross Domestic Product of Welfare"

(GDPW) as the index to measure the national welfare level of economic growth. GDPW index refers to the gross welfare which is created by production and operating activities of all the available permanent units in a country (or region) within a given period, and should combine all positive and negative utilities produced by economic, natural, and social systems. It is not a purely economic accounting system, but includes the calculation of natural and social environments, which helps reflect the quantitative relations between production and environmental systems, as well as among social systems. Furthermore, he defined the positive and negative welfare of internal production and negative external welfare. He also put forward the basic framework and accounting principle of GDPW accounting.

Prof. Michael A. Lebowitz from Simon Fraser University of Canada held that capitalism begins from two premises—capital and wage labor. However, in a reproducing system, however, both capital and wage labor are not only premises but also results. Capitalists are subjects seeking the exploitation of workers (past and present) and wage laborers are people who have been produced within capitalist relations of production—that is, they are alienated producers, alienated from their own labor. That is to say, capitalism produces not only one product but two products. We will clearly ignore the results of production if we consider only one product. Since we know that Marx's emphasis upon "the simultaneous changing of circumstances and human activity or self-change" (i.e. "revolutionary practice"), socialist accounting must consider not only the production of things (the change in circumstances) but also the joint product (the progress in human capacities). Socialist cause should support the development of relations which can build a society which, in Marx's words, can "satisfy the worker's own need for development" and helps us to avoid barbarism.

Prof. Yan Pengfei of Wuhan University has stressed that China's development theory and practice has proved that: we should correctly distinguish development from growth, as well as scientific development from non-scientific development. Scientific development strives to achieve innovative development, coordinated development, green development, fair and harmonious development and independent development and strives to provide good answers to the five questions namely, what development is, how to develop, and development for whom, by whom, and for the benefit of whom. Prof. Anton Filipenko from the National Taras Shevchenko University, in Kiev, Ukraine has argued that, the modernization reform in Ukraine will have no prospect if the economic system goes onto practice the current obvious liberal principles which were during the last 20-plus years. As solution: firstly, Ukraine lacks inner, immanent sources, factors, and mechanisms of stable and balanced development. It proves the in efficiency of the current economic system. Secondly, it doesn't put limits on the deepening of social differentiation, growth of inequality, social in justice, and other negative phenomena, which are attributes of the Middle Ages that, as events in the North Africa and Middle East certify, are not supported by wide layers of the population. Thirdly, the national economic system narrows the possibilities of economic interaction with foreign countries and receiving on this basis additional sources to solve economic and social problems. He has argued that Ukraine should build such universal values as development, social justice, economic equality, human dignity, and access to education and social security.

II. Economic development and economic autonomy

Prof. Ana Maria Rita Milani from Federal University of Alagoas in Brazil, has argued that in the last 30 years, in the world economy, there have been great changes that marked a new historical form of dependency, in which developing countries shave specific ways of insertion. The process of asymmetric insertion of developing countries (Latin America and East Asia excluding China) indicates the timeliness of the theory of dependency that is configured in the new historical stage of capitalism. Doctor J.Z. Garrod from Canada's Carleton University has commented: "there has long been a debate over whether Canada should be deemed as a dependent entity or a semi-peripheral imperial power. But more and more evidences indicate that global capitalism has far less a system that penetrates the national economies, it has become a complex system: a globally integrated network of production and distribution. He has argued that the existing Nation-State framework does no longer suit to the geographical distribution of capital accumulation and gave a brilliant specific analysis on Canada's economic structure, ownership structure and economic operation mode and pointed to the monopolistic control by the five most dominant multinationals in Canada. Doctor J.Z. Garrod the existing research models regarding Canada's development are unable to explain Canada's future with in an increasingly global mode of production because they remain stuck within a Nation-State state-centered approach.

Prof. Xu Zhongwei from Chongqing University of Posts and Telecommunications has argued that the very reason for Ukraine going towards national secession instead of toward economic recovery is that an independent national economic system hasn't been established. Ukraine vaciliates between two opinions of joining the European Union or being close to Russia on the economic development and has not established an independent autonomous national economic system as the pinnacle of state governance development is the important reason for its turmoil and the national disintegration. He argued that Ukraine should take economic construction as the central task, choose a benign economic development path suiting the situation of its country, and correctly deal with the relations between developing itself and relying on foreign aid for effective mechanism and the prosperity situation for the independent development of the national economy.

Prof. Shu Zhan from Fuzhou University, evaluating from the aspects of security, crisis, independence, and dependence, has advocated dividing countries into four types: security-independent dominant type; crisis-attachment dependent type, crisis-free (independent) dominant type and security-(attachment) dependent potentially-dependent type. The national economies of security attachment potential dependent countries are only superficially in a safe status. Their autonomy of economic development is weak owing to the low level of industrial structure, the inferiority in scientific and technological innovation, the in adequacy of the market economic system, and due to insufficient supervision of finance. Potentially-dependent countries are less capable of dealing with and resisting crises, and are more likely to relapse into the situation of dependent countries in the process of globalization and in the case an international economic turmoil occurs, therefore, they should focus on enhancing the independence of their economic development. Since their weak ability in facing and resisting crisis, their economic security strategy should attach more importance to strengthening the autonomy in economic development to ensure the long-term security of national economy. From the relationship between national economic security and national economic independence, Prof. Shu Zhan has argued that both of them belong to the relationship of state and capacity, as well as appearance and essence, and she divided the countries into dominant type, dependent type, potentially dependent type and crisis-dominant type countries according to the coupling state of this relationship. The vast majority of developing countries, including China, belong to the potentially dependent countries, that is, although the national economy is in a safe state, the independent economic development is relatively weak. Therefore, China should actively formulate national economic security strategies; focus on strengthening the independence of national economy so as to guarantee the lasting security of the national economy.

Prof. Niemeyer Almeida Filho of the Federal University of Uberlandia, Brazil, has analyzed the current situations of Latin American participating in international division of labor and international economic activities, especially in the case of Brazil. Based on the capital reproduction mode developed from the dependence theory, he has proposed that, although the specialization degree of production of Latin American countries in international markets has increased, however the dependence degree of Latina American countries to primary commodity exports in Latin America has increased. In addition, from the perspective of capital reproduction mode of Brazil reflected by financialization, investment and income distribution in Brazil, the external dependence degree of Brazil's economy is also high. There is a big difference between import and export structure, Brazil's most of the export industries are low-tech industries. And the consumption pattern of Brazil is also not mature.

Professor Jenny Clegg from the University of Central Lancashire, UK, has put forward that "industrial policy should follow the principle of comparative advantage" advocated by Lin Yifu, former chief economist, and vice governor of the World Bank. Ha-Joon Chan, leading scholar of South Korea's development economist, advocated that the IPs should create principles of "comparative advantages" He also provided ideas for the two different development modes: the US implements its market oriented mode through trading partnership agreements (such as the Trans-Pacific Agreement, TPP) and secondly, the government guidance mode represented by China. China is working with other BRICS, and strengthens the co-ordination of industrial policies through promoting cooperation between its strong SOEs thus to develop the model of mixture of state-market. US aims to constrain the pro-active state-led approach exemplified by China, he has argued that differences over the appropriate mix between "state and market" in industrial policy and the role of SOEs indicate that China's Opening-up strategy has opened a new frontier in the terrain of struggle within the world political economy between neoliberalism and multi-polar developmentalism.

III. The economic development and technological innovation

Prof. Luis Sandoval Ramirez from the National Autonomous University of Mexico argues that the technological economic revolution from the end of the 19th Century to the present day is based on the laws and requirements of capital accumulation, mainly on the achievement of the maximum rate of profit of the productive capital. This kind of technological economic revolution (TER) is largely related to the substitution of the primary energy source by a new, qualitatively superior source of energy, the innovation of a suitable engine and the new labor relations are the main contents of the TER. Based on the revolutionary innovations in energy and other related fields, national state emerged in the form of the new global hegemonic country, within which the TER has mainly developed. The USA thus became leader of the system and dominated over most of the globe (1892-2014).

Ryo Kanae, a scholar at Kyoto University in Japan, has constructed a three-sector Marxist optimal growth model, and analyzed the accumulation stages of capital. He divides the capital products into K_1 and K_2 and introduces a production function containing capital. After a careful analysis, the result shows that: the accumulation used for K_1 was zero in the early stage of the industrial revolution. The capital used in accumulation has increased sharply. After the breakout of industrial revolution, the production function changed, and the capital accumulation approached to the equilibrium state. After the second industrial revolution, the accumulation based on the K_2 has greatly increased, at the moment the situations of the distribution of labor forces in three departments (K_1, K_2 and means of consumption goods producing department), showed that K_1 and K_2 has both approached to the optimal path respectively. The adjustment of capital accumulation before and after the two industrial revolutions was abrupt adjustment. When faced with the second industrial revolution, the developed countries' K_1 was larger, capital accumulation based on K_2 was less, and therefore the adjustment process was longer.

Prof. Hiroshi Izumi from Osaka University of Economics in Japan has compared the total labor productivity (TLP) in Marx's economic theory with total factor productivity (TFP) in neoclassical economic development theory. Hiroshi Izumi explained and gave a list of the shortcomings of TFP: First, TFP is based on the theory of perfect competition, and cost minimization however perfect competition is rare in reality and it underestimates the growth of productive forces in developing countries. Secondly, because the input factors of TFP are capital service and labor service, we cannot measure the improvement of fixed capital as a rise of productivity, at the same time TFP does not include the growth of fixed capital, nor includes the progress in labor mode. TLP is a ratio includes ratio of the output to total of both direct labor and indirect labor. The direct labor represents the labor force used for production, (not service labor) labor used in the industry. The indirect labor output represents (not service labor) labor used for Production of intermediate input and (depreciation portion of) fixed capital. TIP can be calculated by using the input-output tables and other data, and TLP shows productivity not for final production process but for all production process including production process of raw material and fixed capital. It also reflects technique progress embodied in fixed capital and labor. Therefore, TLP is better than TFP, it can more fully reflect the technological progress.

IV. The role of government and market in the economy

Roger Seifert from the University of Hampshire in the UK argues that generally, the argument from improving efficiency as a reason for privatizing the public sector and privatizing state services, this is either logically flawed or empirically false. On the contrary only the planned national system can produce higher economic efficiency, which is clear. But the UK Land Registry policy-makers have asserted that privatization can fulfill the task of the land registry and can improve customer service. The political and organizational drivers behind the proposals of the UK government agencies seem to be a combination of a general desire by government to privatize, and they believed that such a move would "free-up" management strategies to improve the Land Registry's operational processes and target achievement and that this would improve services to user customers. But the fact is that this mode and practices does not work better.

Prof. Balwinder Singh Twanwan from the University of Punjab, India, has studied the flaws of marketization of social service marketization and life in India from the perspective of inclusive growth theory. Balwinder Singh also analyzed that due to the defective policy measures India has remained unable to match the welfare measure to their gross domestic product (GDP) performance. He also examined the change in the employment structure and work force-market after neoliberal policies being taken and marketization becoming prominent in India and found that in the capital-intensive sector, the capital-labor ratio increases, the reserve army of labor increases, them is match between wages workers gets larger, and economic growth becomes grave and more difficult.

Prof. Xie Di from Liaoning University, talked about the role of government in the Chinese economy giving examples and has argued that China needs to effectively exert the economic functions of government regulation and control in the process of "steady growth, structural adjustment, growth mode transformation, and in promoting reforms". In this process it's necessary to get the government to play its economic functions such as regulation as well as supervision. At present, Chinese government is confronted with a series of contradictory choices of "economic development-oriented government and public service-oriented government", another choice is the "structural adjustment or total adjustment in macro control, another choice is supply management and demand management", another choice is "macro control and micro regulation or supervision", another choice is "state-owned economy and non-state economy", another choice is between "ecological civilization construction and promoting regional economic growth of backward regions" and so on, which are faced by the current government when it aims to effectively play its functional role in a market economy.

V. The Crisis of Capitalism and the Development of Socialism

Patrick Bond from the University of Kwa Zulu Natal, South Africa, has analyzed the process of how leading "powerful stock market brokers" deliver crises to the Third World through the financial field. The leading "power brokers" reacted to the crisis through "DE valorization" of large parts of the Third World alongside the writing down of selected financially volatile and vulnerable markets in the North. This is obviously shifting the crisis to the Third World through financial tools and means.

Compared to the 1930s, the reason why the crisis has not caused a panic which could overturn the whole system is due to that: this set of partial write-downs of financial capital (kept in check by slap-dash system-wide repairs in late 2008 and 2009) means intensified external economic coercion, extra-economic coercion.

But, the result is a world economy that concentrates wealth and poverty in more extreme ways and brings markets and the non-market spheres of society and nature to get her in a manner adverse to the latter.

Social movements from the bottom may change the relationship among the nation, civil society, and financiers, promoting the reform of the financial system.

German Marxist scholars Richard Corell, Ernst Herzog and Stephan Muller have argued that the underlying cause of European financial instability appears as crisis of the instability of the common currency introduced in some countries of the European Union (EU). The instability prevails because sovereign debt remains far from being under control in the states in question. Underlying the imbalances of European finance is a difference in competitiveness, which results from a difference in production prices per unit. For Germany, if we analysis of the implementation of "Agenda 2010" by Social Democrat Party it shows that German Chancellor Schröder succeeded to pass the austerity measures by streamlining and passivation of his Social Democratic Party, The left-wing of the Social Democrat Party was marginalized and union leaders were appointed to government posts, this further leading to the decrease of unit labor cost in Germany, compared with its main competitors in EU and USA. On the other hand, common currency prevents other countries from devaluating. Thus, based on decreasing relative unit labor cost, Germany exports much more than its imports, increasing trade imbalances, with other countries. They worry that a further increase of austerity measures in Germany, and if this austerity policy is joined by France, may lead to a decline in the level of living conditions and poverty not only in Germany but in many other European economies, where growth, social justice, and eventually the independent development within state's sovereignty will all be put in question.

Prof. Nobuharu Yokokawa from the Musashi University in Japan has used the framework of Marxian institutionalist political economics by integrating the dynamic comparative advantage and financial instability hypothesis into his analysis so as to examine the development of the capitalist world system after the 1980s.

421

Nobuharu Yokokawa has argued that capitalist world system after World War II fell into a structural crisis in the 1970s, the center of capital accumulation shifted to East Asia. However, the USA controlled the world economy by fractionalization and Globalization and strengthened its dynamic comparative advantage in the 1990s. Then, the structural crisis in the 1990s has shifted the center of capital accumulation from Japan and from East Asian Newly Industrialized Economies (small dragons) to China, which has increased international imbalance in the 2000s. The global crisis in advanced economies which erupted since 2007 is a system crisis which destroys the current capitalist world system. Japanese Prof. Hiroshi Setooka from the of University of Komazawa has argued that now, many of the so-called "middle class" members of the society when faced with the current long-term depression seem to favor being the supporters of the conservatives and new liberalism. If they cannot transform themselves to be reformers or revolutionaries in this unendurable great depression, possibly they may soon be unable to live.

Prof. Pritam Singh from the University of Oxford's Oriental School has argued that spatial shift taking place in globalism towards China, India, Indonesia with very large populations has led to the current unbalanced development of capitalism. The rising consumption in these economies is sharpening the global ecological crisis. Different from the past, the previous mode of capitalism cannot be replicated by the BRICS countries and other major developing countries, and the only sustainable way to respond to and overcome the current crisis is ecological socialism. David Kotz, vice president of the WAPE and professor of the University of Massachusetts, has argued that the two reformist capitalist trends modes that attempt to respond to the crisis and which are likely to emerge in coming years—statist form of controlled capitalism and social-democratic capitalism cannot solve capitalism's long-standing problems, and they both pose a potential threat to the long-term progress of human civilization. Prof. Kotz has proposed to solve the current structural crisis of capitalism by shifting to the planned socialism with democratic participation.

The Austrian scholar Hermann Dworczak, discussing the crisis in Greece as an example, has said that that minor reforms in the neoliberal system cannot lead the world to sustainable growth nor realize social equity. Nowadays, capitalism is in a state of stagnation, and the socialist revolution under the guidance of Marxism should be put on the agenda. Xu Jiankang, vice deputy director of Philosophy–Humanities Department of the Journal of Chinese Social Sciences in China , has argued that the fundamental relationship between China and the world capitalist system is the complex correlation between the complex giant system and its high order subsystem together with low order subsystem; the violent shock period of the giant system is the best opportunity for the underdeveloped socialism who participates in the international division of labor in the world market to enhance the self-organizing capability for leaping over the Crafting Gorge.

David S. Pena from American Palm Beach State University held that the most commonly accepted definition of sustainable development—"development that meets the needs of the present without compromising the ability of future generations to meet their own needs" lacks concreteness. If we put the idea of sustainable development under Marxism and specification, capitalist development is necessarily unsustainable, and sustainable development must take the form of socialist development. He thinks that the concrete concept of sustainable socialism depends on coordination of seven elements: (1) a stable, sustainable, and prosperous economic system that develops the productive forces and establishes relations of production that promote common prosperity in a steady, sustainable manner; (2) a political system that upholds a vigorous people's democracy focused on implementing the people's political agenda; (3) strong unified socialist motherland with full sovereign integrity; (4) a progressive socialist culture; (5) rational resource management policy that promote a flourishing natural environment while meeting the people's economic needs; (6) scientific harmonization appropriate to national conditions; (7) to maintain the communist party's leading position. In his opinion, only a strong Communist Party can achieve sustainable development by the people's democratic dictatorship.

In addition, Prof. Pena has argued that only by the leadership of strong communist parties and sustainable development of people's democratic dictatorships the goal of sustainable socialism can be achieved.

In addition, the participant experts also made a thorough discussion around the topics such as including "Economy and Democracy," "Welfare System and Social Justice," "Land Use and Social Justice," "Marx's Theory of Money and Capital," "Marxism and Agrarian Issues," and also "The Climate Change and Sustainable Development" and "Vietnam-China Sea Boundary Demarcation Issues". The discussions have delivered important consensus points. Prof. David Kotz of the University of Massachusetts, the vice president of the Institute of World Political Economics, presided over the closing ceremony of the Forum, Chairman Cheng Enfu delivered the closing speech, Prof. Pham Van Duc, the vice president of the Vietnam Academy of Social Sciences read the Consensus Declaration of the 9th Forum of the World Association for Political Economy. The Declaration stated that economic growth is growth is generally measured by the rate of increase in GDP, at the national or global level, and this criterion is still important for developing countries but this criterion is not equal to economic development. However, the traditional outlook on development is based on expanding material production, which takes for granted that all economic growth is a positive thing but it should not ignore social development, and not take "pure economic growth" as the value goal. The common declaration has argued that GDP is seen as the sole benchmark for evaluating different countries' economic performance. Such an outlook appears as the reflection of over-weighed instrumental rationality and absent human values. On the contrary, a scientific outlook on development, based on Marxist economics, could be taken as a positive response to the shortcomings of the traditional outlook. Besides the declaration has asserted that scientific economic development should serve the people, and as a consequence, economic development should enhance comprehensive human development and elevate the well-being of the people, eventually improving the livelihood of people worldwide and the fairness of economic development and in some distribution. This traditional development concept is generally showed as over-expansion of instrumental rationality and lack of value rationality. However the scientific development concept based on Marxist economics must adhere to caring for the people and serving the people. This means that the purpose of economic development must be closely around the center of overall development of human beings, or improvement of human life and living, which is ultimately reflected on the improvement of quality of materials and spiritual life for people in various countries and the whole world, as well as on the fairness of economic development process and distribution structure. Therefore, all countries should put more emphasis on qualitative not just quantitative changes in the economy and consider the basic purpose of economic growth, strive to achieve what we put out as "fair development". We summarize our advice as follows: Public ownership should be dominant, while the role of other forms of ownership should be decided based on the conditions in each country. Distribution according to work should dominate distribution according to ownership and unjust gaps in wealth and income should be opposed; state regulation should be the major mechanism in addressing environmental issues and marketization as a major mechanism should be opposed.

423

New standards to measure economic welfare should be developed which will sublate the standard which gives excessive attention to GDP.

Finally, Dr. Ding Xiaoqin from the Shanghai University of Finance and Economics, the secretary general of World Political Economy Association and Research Associate in the Asia Center of the Harvard University, announced that the next 10th Forum of the World Association for Political Economy will be held in South Africa in mid-June 2015.

Originally published in the journal
Contemporary Economic Research, 2014(10)